Principles of Business: Finance

Principles of Business: Finance

Edited by
Richard Wilson, Ph.D.
The University of Tennessee at Chattanooga

SALEM PRESS

A Division of EBSCO Information Services, Inc.
Ipswich, Massachusetts

GREY HOUSE PUBLISHING

For information contact Grey House Publishing/Salem Press, 4919 Route 22, PO Box 56, Amenia, NY 12501

Principles of Business: Finance, published by Grey House Publishing, Inc., Amenia, NY, under exclusive license from EBSCO Publishing, Inc.

∞ *The paper used in these volumes conforms to the American National Standard for Permanence of Paper for Printed Library Materials, Z39.48 1992 (R2009).*

Publisher's Cataloging-In-Publication Data
(Prepared by The Donohue Group, Inc.)

Names: Wilson, Richard L., 1944- editor.
Title: Principles of business. Finance / edited by Richard Wilson.
Other Titles: Finance
Description: [First edition]. | Ipswich, Massachusetts : Salem Press, a division of EBSCO Information Services, Inc. ; Amenia, NY : Grey House Publishing, [2017] | Includes bibliographical references and index.
Identifiers: ISBN 978-1-68217-328-2 (hardcover)
Subjects: LCSH: Business enterprises--Finance.
Classification: LCC HG4026 .P75 2017 | DDC 658.15--dc23

PRINTED IN THE UNITED STATES OF AMERICA

CONTENTS

PUBLISHER'S NOTE

PRINCIPLES OF FINANCE

Salem Press is pleased to introduce a new series, *Principles of Business*, to its collection. This volume, *Principles of Business: Finance* is the first of six volumes currently planned. Future volumes include Management, Marketing, Entreprenuership, Accounting, and International Business. This new resource introduces students and researchers to the fundamentals of these business topics using easy-to-understand language. Readers will obtain a solid start and deeper understanding and appreciation of these important and far-reaching business topics.

Entries in this volume range from "Bank Insolvency" to "Warrants & Convertibles" and are arranged in an A to Z order, making it easy to find the topic of interest. Each entry includes the following:

- An Abstract that provides a brief, concrete introduction to the topic and how the entry is organized;
- An Overview that offers clear presentation of the topic;
- Multiple subheads that anchor the reader to the various concepts being discussed;
- Suggested Reading list that relates to the entry;
- Detailed Bibliography.

The book begins with an introduction to business by editor Richard Wilson, PhD. Dr. Wilson offers a brief but concise look at the progression of finance from hunters and gatherers to bankers. He discusses how written language standardized trade, and how money facilitated contracts. Contracts allowed the expansion of immediacy of trade to the promise of paying for goods and services not yet produced. Interest, compound interest, and depositing surplus money followed – and the banking industry was born.

Added features include photographs of significant business leaders and illustrations and diagrams of relevant topics.

The back matter in *Principles of Business: Finance* is another valuable resource and includes:

- Detailed Glossary with 427 terms;
- Subject Index.

Salem Press extends its appreciation to all involved in the development and production of this work. The entries have been written and signed by scholars and experts in business. Without these expert contributions, a project of this nature would not be possible. A full list of contributor's names and affiliations follows this Publisher's Note. *Principles of Business: Finance* is available in print and as an e-book.

INTRODUCTION

Principles of Business: Finance is the first volume in the new *Principles of Business* series by Salem Press. Other volumes will cover management, marketing, entrepreneurship, accounting, international business, and more. *Finance*, as the first volume in the series, provides an important foundation for the rest of the volumes but, indeed, is just as important as a stand-alone topic as it relates to the success and well-being of all businesses and individuals around the world.

Understanding finance is necessary for new businesses, first and foremost to purchase the raw materials, supplies, and equipment needed to get a business up and running. Without the ability to buy things needed to operate, business owners simply could not begin. After initial success, businesses need continued financing to manage their cash flow over the ups and downs of the process. Production of goods and services always precedes sales and consumption, and payment for products may not be immediate.

Indeed, payment for goods and services itself may be subject to financing arrangements, particularly in the long supply chains that are now commonplace. Taxes, insurance, transportation, and other costs of doing business may also need to be financed before payments and profits are possible. Final end users may also need financing in order pay for the products and benefits they receive. The entire economic process depends of the liquidity that lubricates the process, with banks and their equivalents a separate and indispensable industry on its own. This is painfully clear if we look at failed societies in deep depressions due to the failure to keep the process going. Chaos and even violence are the frequent result.

HUNTING/GATHERING TO BANKING

Understanding finance in the twenty-first century may benefit from a brief history lesson. Evidence indicates that human beings have existed for at least 70,000 to 100,000 years. For the first several tens of thousands of years, they struggled as gatherers and hunters with only primitive tools and fire to supplement their natural born intelligence (Diamond, 2005). Their naturally developed power of oral communication made survival possible and gradually led to migration across the globe (Wells, 2003). As remarkable as their survival and migration are, it took human beings thousands of years to settle in small communities and begin farming. With farming supplementing, and then supplanting, hunting and gathering, they gradually produced the meager surplus that led to bartering for better tools. Ultimately, written language was created (Wilson, 2016).

With written language, the pace of progress quickened. Writing made keeping accounts possible so that trade could be managed and tracked. This created standards, trading a cow for a certain number of bushels of grain, for example. Writing eventually propagated the idea that value could be imputed to something called "money," which made trade even easier.

Contracts were the next natural development, extending the trading of immediate goods and services for those not yet produced and services not yet delivered. Such contracts could only be legitimated and valued if some system of government and law—however primitive—enforced the contracts. Government and rule of law began its long and tortuous process. Replacing the rule of power with the rule of law produced a much improved process, one that is still not complete or perfected (Wilson, 2001).

Following the development of money, contracts, and the rule of law, the value of future-oriented transactions led to recognition that a form of payment was needed for this service, leading to interest and compound interest. This was a hard concept to accept initially, indicated by the contempt with which money lenders were initially (and in some quarters still are) held. Usury (lending money at an exorbitant interest) was the charge leveled against such money lenders; borrowers refusing to pay the interest claimed they were only paying "rent" which led to the eventual replacement of "rent" with the more candid "interest."

Another major step forward was taken when interest was broken down into separate loans for discrete time periods, each with a renewable payment of interest on top of the original loan plus the interest paid on it. The miraculous power of compound interest was born. This created an incentive for those with a surplus of money to lend it to the money changers with the promise of compound interest, protected by a contract enforced by a government following the rule of law.

The next giant step occurred when those with surplus money deposited it with the money facilitators (bankers and their equivalents), who lent the money to those who needed it and were willing to pay compound interest to get it. Investment and tremendous economic development were now possible. The banking system was the inevitable—but not immediate—result.

NEED FOR REFERENCE WORKS

From the beginning of time until 2003, humankind collected an estimated 5 exabytes of data (5 exabytes = 1 quintillion bytes). Now, we collect 5 exabytes of data every two days, and it is expected that within two years we will collect that amount every few minutes (Tapscott, 2011).

This explosion of information makes reference books such as this all the more necessary. Unlike textbooks, which are often arranged as a single story, so that missing a bit of knowledge early in the book makes it difficult to understand the connection to a bit of knowledge later in the book, reference books feature stand-alone essays, each providing concise introductions and core facts.

Success of this volume is due to the contributors, listed with each essay and with a short bio in the front matter. Most have graduate degrees in economics and years of experience in business. The diversity of their backgrounds—cultural anthropologists to librarians—is valuable because non-business professionals often offer language that is more accessible than that of business specialists, whose explanations may be narrowly focused.

The essays in this volume are written for a varied audience. Our goals included attention to clarity of wording and avoidance of unnecessary jargon. For those readers who desire more specific information on any one topic, each essay includes a list of further reading.

REFERENCES

Diamond, Jared. (2005) "Out of Eden" segment from National Geographic Society video entitled "Guns, Germs. And Steel" shown. Available on YouTube.

Tapscott. D. (2011). What scientific concept would improve everybody's cognitive toolkit; as cited in Terry Doyle and Todd Zakrajsek, *The New Science of Learning: How to Learn in Harmony with Your Brain*. Sterling, Va.: Stylus Publishing, LLC. 2013, p. 113.

Wells, Spencer. (2003) "Journey of Man," A National Geographic Society video. Available on YouTube.

Wilson, Richard L. (2016) "Educational Portal: Invention of Writing" Available on YouTube.

Wilson, Richard L. (2001). "Rule of Law," in *The Encyclopedia of U. S. Supreme Court: Three Volumes*. Thomas Lewis and Richard L. Wilson (ed.). Pasadena, CA.: Salem: "Outstanding Reference Award" for 2002 by the American Library Association.

CONTRIBUTORS

MICHAEL P. AUERBACH

Michael P. Auerbach holds a Bachelor's degree from Wittenberg University and a Master's degree from Boston College. Mr. Auerbach has extensive private and public sector experience in a wide range of arenas: Political science, business and economic development, tax policy, international development, defense, public administration and tourism.

HEATHER WALL BECKHAM

Heather Wall Beckham is a former vice president of Strategic Planning for the Turner Division of Time Warner. She has also served as a strategic consultant with Bain & Company, a financial analyst with Ford Motor Company, and an adjunct professor in the Economics and Business Department of Agnes Scott College. She holds an undergraduate degree from Duke University and an MBA from Harvard Business School.

NANCY DEVENGER

Nancy Devenger holds a BS degree from the University of New Hampshire and a Masters Degree in Health Policy from Dartmouth College's Center for the Evaluative and Clinical Sciences. Nancy began her career in health care as a registered nurse for many years. Since earning her undergraduate degree in Business, Nancy has worked in private medical practice, home health, consulting, and most currently as Director of Ambulatory Operations for a large Academic Medical Center. Her operational experience as a business manager in private medical practice and for the last decade in a tertiary medical center have allowed Nancy broad insight into both private and academic business endeavors.

JOSEPH DEWEY

Joseph Dewey holds a BA from Villanova University and an MA and PhD from Purdue University. Dr. Dewey is an associate professor at the University of Pittsburgh at Johnstown.

MARLANDA ENGLISH

Dr. Marlanda English is president of ECS Consulting Associates which provides executive coaching and management consulting services. ECS also provides online professional development content. Dr. English was previously employed in various engineering, marketing and management positions with IBM, American Airlines, Borg-Warner Automotive and Johnson & Johnson. Dr. English holds a doctorate in business with a major in organization and management and a specialization in e-business.

MICHAEL ERBSCHLOE

Michael Erbschloe is an information technology consultant, educator, and author. He has taught graduate level courses and developed technology-related curriculum for several universities and speaks at conferences and industry events around the world. Michael holds a Master Degree in Sociology from Kent State University. He has authored hundreds of articles and several books on technology.

SIMONE I. FLYNN

Dr. Simone I. Flynn earned her Doctorate in Cultural Anthropology from Yale University, where she wrote a dissertation on Internet communities. She is a writer, researcher, and teacher in Amherst, Massachusetts.

MARIE GOULD

Marie Gould is an Associate Professor and the Faculty Chair of the Business Administration Department at Peirce College in Philadelphia, Pennsylvania. She teaches in the areas of management, entrepreneurship, and international business. Although Ms. Gould has spent her career in both academia and corporate, she enjoys helping people learn new things — whether it's by teaching, developing or mentoring.

STEVEN R. HOAGLAND

Dr. Hoagland holds bachelor and master degrees in economics, a master of urban studies, and a doctorate in urban services management with a cognate in education all from Old Dominion University. His background includes service as senior-level university administrator responsible for planning, assessment, and research. It also includes winning multi-million dollar grants, both as a sponsored programs officer and as a proposal development team member. With expertise in research design and program evaluation, his recent service includes consulting in the health care, information technology, and education sectors and teaching as an adjunct professor of economics. Recently, he founded a nonprofit organization to addresses failures in the education marketplace by guiding college-bound high school students toward more objective and simplified methods of college selection and by devising risk-sensitive scholarships.

HEATHER NEWTON

Heather Newton earned her J.D., cum laude, from Georgetown University Law Center, where she served as Articles Editor for *The Georgetown Journal of Legal Ethics*. She worked as an attorney at a large, international law firm in Washington, DC, before moving to Atlanta, where she is currently an editor for a legal publishing company. Prior to law school, she was a high school English teacher and freelance writer, and her works have appeared in numerous print and online publications.

CAROLYN SPRAGUE

Carolyn Sprague holds a BA degree from the University of New Hampshire and a Masters Degree in Library Science from Simmons College. Carolyn gained valuable business experience as owner of her own restaurant which she operated for 10 years. Since earning her graduate degree Carolyn has worked in numerous library/information settings within the academic, corporate and consulting worlds. Her operational experience as a manger at a global high tech firm and more recent work as a web content researcher have afforded Carolyn insights into many aspects of today's challenging and fast-changing business climate.

RICHA S. TIWARY

Dr. Richa S. Tiwary holds a Doctorate in Marketing Management with a specialization in Consumer Behavior from Banaras Hindu University, India. She earned her second Masters in Library Sciences with dual concentration in Information Science & Technology, and, Library Information Services, from the Department of Information Studies, University at Albany-SUNY.

WILLIAM J. WARDROPE

Dr. William Wardrope is an Associate Professor of Economics and International Business at the University of Central Oklahoma. He is an author of numerous publications and has made over 200 presentations at professional conferences on topics in business, globalization, communication, and curriculum.

RUTH A. WIENCLAW

Dr. Ruth A. Wienclaw holds a Ph.D. in industrial/organizational psychology with a specialization in organization development from the University of Memphis. She is the owner of a small business that works with organizations in both the public and private sectors, consulting on matters of strategic planning, training, and human/systems integration.

B

Bank Insolvency and Failure

ABSTRACT

Economic historians point out that bank failures have been a part of commercial banking enterprises since the Roman Empire and that a bank failure can be seen as a corrective and thus an element of long-term economic health. Bank insolvency and bank failure not only impact bank employees, executives, shareholders, and depositors but also negatively impact the wider community's confidence in banks as the holders of monies and as the financial center of a region. During the 2008 global economic crisis, more than three hundred banks failed in the United States alone.

OVERVIEW

Although banking is regarded by most customers as primarily a service industry providing a kind of safe-house for keeping significant amounts of personal funds, a bank is actually more an intermediary business engaged in transactions that use depositor account funds to invest in a variety of enterprises. In return for paying interest on monies held in accounts, banks use that money as part of a community (and sometimes global) marketplace, providing critical funding that sustains an economic pipeline for the wider community. Indeed, a bank cannot provide the basic services that customers expect without using the money in its keeping to create a robust business portfolio of its own. Such deposits provide the capital for the bank to pursue investment opportunities for the bank itself.

Each bank location is part of a wider network that usually constitutes a very large banking institution. As banks grew larger, their growing assets both enabled and drove such industry innovations as travelers checks, compound interest, negotiable certificates of deposit, automated teller machines, and online and mobile banking (Thomas, 2015). These big banks that can, of course, fail big but can also be empowered to forward significant projects, using depositors' monies to fund community construction and infrastructure projects; to create and sustain the local housing industry by providing support for mortgage arrangements; to undergird real estate rental networks by acting as intermediary between landlords and renters; to support promising local businesses and/or to provide long-term support for established businesses (and their expansion plans) as a way to maintain community economic stability; and to maintain critical utilities such as electricity and water by acting as agent between consumers and utility providers.

A bank is a business and, like all businesses, operates to make a profit. That profit is determined largely by the soundness of the bank's lending policies, the quality of its loan practices, and the general economic savvy of its management team that oversees that bank's financial stability and growth. Risk Based Capital (RBC) minimum ratios are imposed on banks by regulating agencies, requiring adequate liquid capital to balance risk. In other words, if the bank makes a risky investment that turns into a loss, the bank must have sufficient cash in reserve to continue operating. When a bank cannot meets its risk-adventures, the bank teeters toward insolvency. A bank is said to fail when it cannot service its outstanding debt. Banks that cannot sustain RBC are also considered to have failed (Parnes, 2012).

In response to the Great Depression, a variety of legislation (most of it passed in the decade immediately after the 1929 national economic collapse) put into place a system to protect depositor money held in U.S. banks. For nearly a century, banks have been regulated by the Federal Deposit Insurance Corporation, an independent oversight agency chartered in 1933 to maintain the stability and integrity of the U.S. banking system. The intention of such a national entity, supported by the faith and credit of the federal government, is to prevent banks from floundering by using the financial resources of the

1

federal government to insure individual deposits (up to $250,000) as a way to ensure depositor confidence and prevent "bank runs," that is, large scale withdrawals on short notice in response to fears of an imminent bank failure. The FDIC may also intervene in a bank facing insolvency, with federal banking administrators taking over critical operations. If such intervention succeeds, the bank returns to financial viability (either through realigning its own resources and putting its house in order or by arranging for its acquisition by healthier banks) without impacting bank customers, thus containing the potential for widespread economic disaster. Bank failure impacts not only those with accounts at the bank or those who work at the bank but also those whose businesses are supported by that bank's investments, which is termed a "spillover effect" (Cebula, Koch & Fenili, 2011). In addition, a single bank failure (or far worse the failure of a system of networked banks) can create a much wider environment of panic. Entire communities suddenly restrict normative buying and spending habits, which undermines local businesses (Ramirez & Shively, 2012).

THE GREAT RECESSION

The 2008 financial crisis was triggered in part by a crisis in mortgage dealing. Banks, particularly in California, Texas, and Florida, interested in the potential for long-term lucrative real estate dealings, backed long-shot housing deals significantly below mortgage rates, hoping that long-term real estate market health would cover their financial returns in a big way. In addition, banks invested heavily in construction deals designed to provide housing to cover the demand. It was a high-risk venture. When the global recession upended those assumptions and the demand for housing dried up, banks faced huge losses and in many cases lacked the liquid assets to continue operating (Chennells & Wingfield, 2015).

As the housing market turned stagnant and houses went unsold, creating a large surplus of available housing, many home owners who had taken advantage of the lower introductory mortgage rates suddenly could not meet their obligations. Dozens of banks lost excessive amounts of invested funds and began to face massive revenue shortfalls (Cole & White, 2012). The FDIC protected the integrity of the banking system and individual savings and business investments to ensure that the insolvency of the

banks entangled in the real estate debacle did not, in turn, implode the wider banking system itself.

APPLICATIONS

If a bank can be modeled as a business rather than as a service, causes of the movement toward insolvency—that is the tipping point at which a bank's assets are less than its liabilities—are at once as complicated and as simple as any other business's movement toward bankruptcy. A bank faces insolvency when there has been a significant loss of assets (most often through risky investments and/or loan programs) to the point where the bank can no longer transact the normative operations of a bank: handling and distributing funds for customers, maintaining the integrity of its loan and investment operations, and providing the opportunity for securing loans for potential businesses and entrepreneurs. Those who rely on the bank's financial support for their businesses need the reassurance that such a pipeline is open and secure, and bank depositors need to have timely access to their funds. Without that, a bank faces critical and often urgent questions about its operations and its future.

The reasons why banks can face such a dire predicament are in fact the reasons why any business faces catastrophic financial failure: poor management generally; uninformed network oversight; poor risk management assessments; and a lack of common sense risk diversification. Although economists are quick to point out that banks fail for a variety of reasons well beyond the control of a bank's executive management staff. A bank may be impacted by, for example, political and military events; the poor management of businesses into which the bank has poured its resources; international economic fluctuations and stressors in a global consumer market that is often a most volatile dynamic of supply and demand; the reliability and currency of technology support. Banks, however, usually fall into insolvency for reason that center largely on their own management team.

Banks require tight control of decisions to invest bank funds. Rogue investment managers willing to take grand risks for the potential of large payoffs can determine a bank's often rapid spiral into insolvency. In addition, investing in private and public works is highly competitive. Banks compete against each other to secure the most promising projects, and competitive measures can hamper financial stability (Fungáčová & Weill, 2013). Further, poor management structure can cause investments to accumulate within and around a few massive (and often risky) projects. Lack of diversification can create a domino effect should that centerpiece project fail.

Banks edge toward financial distress when they are directed by ineffective management who often neglect to follow sound (if conservative) protocols for finance management. Bank managers can be inexperienced or promoted too soon; they might lack sound judgment; they might act on ill-advised or inappropriate policy initiatives; they may simply be greedy; they can be poorly advised; they can operate on faulty and/or incomplete information; they may be willing to take inappropriate risks. Without adequate oversight within the bank's organization, management may resort to recordkeeping obfuscation, trying to contain the problem (and potential panic) by denying or minimizing its dimension in the hopes that the market will correct itself or that other investment strategies will pay off.

Such malfeasance runs counter to the foundational premise of banking: Banking succeeds only with complete transparency, critical information about operations available to management, shareholders, investors, and accounts holders. That careful, often choreographed conspiracy of providing minimum information (or even misinformation) only creates significantly more complicated dimensions to the problem.

At the point when the bank has become substantively undercapitalized, the bank's management team notifies the FDIC of its emergency situation in a notarized letter. Timeliness is everything. FDIC intervention is considered a last resort to be called upon only when traditional free-market forces would otherwise dictate bank failure (Adler, 2008). At that point, the FDIC can operate in basically one of two capacities: as conservator or as receiver. If the potential impact of the mismanagement and the financial losses have not seriously impacted the bank's system of operations, it can act as a conservator of the floundering bank, shore up its operations, restructure its management team by offering it to qualified buyers and investors, but essentially maintain that bank's integrity as an independent operating system in an effort to restore it to full health as its own entity under new management. If the bank faces systemic failure, the FDIC can act swiftly to facilitate a receivership and take over the bank, shut down its operations (most often for 60 days or fewer), substantially review all levels of its operations, fire its directing officers, and in that time market the bank's viable operations and investments to healthy banks.

Merging the failing bank to another bank (called a bridge bank) ensures some level of continuity of its still-viable operations. This procedure is termed a "purchase and assumption transaction" and is widely viewed as the most viable remediation for an insolvent bank. The FDIC oversees arrangements for a healthy bank to purchase the failed bank's assets, including giving it the opportunity to perform due diligence by reviewing the books of the distressed bank and thus apprising it of the dimension of the problem and the risk it, in turn, would be taking.

The most efficient and most effective rescue occurs when a single bank, itself healthy and in the market for aggressive expansion, acquires the entire operations of a single failed bank, that is a single bank agrees to assume financial responsibility and provide a significant infusion of capital to an insolvent bank and agrees to underwrite that bank's losses and assume responsibility for continuing its services and for protecting its customers and their savings. Termed "whole bank purchase and acquisition," such a protocol is widely viewed as the least disruptive operation. Often the incoming bank is heralded through marketing and advertising as a way to minimize the potential for panic among shareholders, customers, creditors, and businesses, and to minimize what is termed "contagion," that is, a feeling of anxiety and financial unease among other banks within the system or within the same community.

VIEWPOINTS

Given the volatile nature of the financial industry and the unexpected shocks that regularly impact the local and global money network, bank insolvency and bank failures are an inevitable and even acceptable event. Banks cannot operate under the assumption that 100 percent of their operations will be sound and safe. Banks can anticipate but not foresee shocks. In the United States, for example, the protective net of the FDIC nearly eliminates the potential for the sort of nation-wide catastrophic loss of confidence that signaled the start of the Great Depression. Government collapse and the rapid devaluation of a national currency, however, have caused banking crises in a number of nations in the twenty-first century, most notably Greece, Chile, and Japan. Few economists dispute the critical need for banks to have that sort of holdings guarantee, and, despite conservative anti-government advocates who see such intervention as dead-end bailouts, the quick intervention of the FDIC in the operations of faltering banks have been shown to staunch a problem by rescuing a bank and its position with its immediate economic environment.

Banks are self-directed until they reach the point at which ill-advised policies and high-risk strategies begin to negatively impact operations. Economists argue that only a bank's robust and very hands-on and aware (that is, informed) regulatory superstructure can maintain the sound operations of a bank, whatever its size and whatever its holdings. Risks need to be prudent and thoroughly examined; loan strategies need to be carefully weighed and evaluated by the bank's fullest range of financial experts. Management needs to be directly answerable for all financial enterprises in which it engages, short and long term. But failing that, the best avenue for addressing the reality of a bank's insolvency is prompt remediation to preserve the integrity of that bank and prevent its problems from impacting other banks within that network or, far more catastrophic, all banks in a region.

Bibliography

Adler, J. (2008). Declaring a failure: When should it happen? *American Banker, 173*(152), 1–3. Retrieved December 25, 2015 from EBSCO Online Database Business Source Complete. http://search.ebscohost.com/login.aspx?direct= true&db=bth&AN=33591614&site=ehost-live

Cebula, R., Koch, J., & Fenili, R. (2011). The bank failure rate, economic conditions and banking statutues in the US, 1970–2009. *Atlantic Economic Journal, 39*(1), 39–46. Retrieved December 25, 2015 from EBSCO Online Database Business Source Complete. http:// search.ebscohost.com/login.aspx?direct=true&db=bth&AN=58606849&site=ehost-live

Chennells, L., & Wingfield, V. (2015) Bank failure and bail-in: An introduction. *Bank of England Quarterly Bulletin, 55*(3), 228–241. Retrieved December 25, 2015 from EBSCO Online Database Business Source Complete. http://search.ebscohost.com/login.aspx?direct=true&db= bth&AN=109951698&site=ehost-live

Cole, R., & White, L. (2012). Déjà vu all over again: The causes of U.S. commercial bank failures this time around. *Journal of Financial Services Research, 42*(1/2), 5–29. Retrieved December 25, 2015 from EBSCO Online Database Business Source Complete. http://search.ebscohost.com/login.aspx?direct=true&db=bth&AN=77837086&site=ehost-live

Fungáčová, Z., & Weill, L. (2013) Does competition influence bank failures? Evidence from Russia. *Economics of Transition, 21*(2), 301–322. Retrieved December 25, 2015 from EBSCO Online Database Business Source Complete. http://search.ebscohost.com/login.aspx?direct= true&db=bth&AN=86048254&site=ehost-live

Parnes, D. (2012). Modeling bank failure risk. *Banking & Finance Review, 4*(1), 37–58. Retrieved December 25, 2015 from EBSCO Online Database Business Source Complete. http://search.ebscohost.com/login.aspx?direct= true&db=bth&AN=82899590&site=ehost-live

Ramirez, C., & Shively, P. (2012) The effect of bank failures on economic activity: Evidence from U.S. states in the early 20th century. *Journal of Money, Credit & Banking, 44*(2/3): 433–455. Retrieved December 25, 2015 from EBSCO Online Database Business Source Complete. http://search.ebscohost.com/login.aspx?direct=true&db= bth&AN=73930145&site=ehost-live

Thomas, K. (2015).The U.S. needs "too big to fail" banks. *American Banker, 180*(F327). Retrieved December 25, 2015 from EBSCO Online Database Business Source Complete. http://search.ebscohost.com/login.aspx?direct= true&db=bth&AN=108386802&site=ehost-live

Suggested Reading

Bovenzi, J. (2015). *Inside the FDIC: Thirty years of bank failures, bailouts, and regulatory battles.* Hoboken, NJ: Wiley.

Farrell, G. (2011). *Crash of the titans: Greed, hubris, and the fall of Merrill Lynch, and the near collapse of Bank of America.* New York, NY: Crown Business.

Grind, K. (2013). *The lost bank: The story of Washington-Mutual—the biggest bank failure in American history.* New York, NY: Simon and Schuster.

–Joseph Dewey

BUSINESS FINANCE

ABSTRACT

This article concerns finance, that is, the study of how resources are valued, allocated and invested over time. Having knowledge of the basic concepts of finance is important not only for business owners, corporate executives and financial planners; ultimately, financial planning is each individual's responsibility. Three of the most fundamental concepts in finance are the time value of money, asset valuation, that is, how the value of stocks, bonds, real estate, and other investments is determined, and finally, risk management. While the time value of money is the basis for the other concepts, financial planning and investing ultimately require an understanding of risk management. This article will approach the basic concepts of finance for the individual and provide an overview of financial and investment products.

OVERVIEW

It is becoming increasingly important for individuals to assume responsibility for planning a financial future. Successful financial planning, in turn, requires one to understand the basic concepts of finance since this understanding will afford one the ability to save and invest wisely. This means that the individual needs to have knowledge of a variety of financial products and investments and comprehend how these vehicles work. Moreover, for many people, the largest investment they will make is purchasing a home. Having knowledge of the basic concepts of finance will enable them to understand mortgages and consumer debt in general. Saving, other investments and managing debt are all based upon the foundation of the first financial concept — the time value of money. Further, this concept is a building block to asset valuation and risk management. Asset valuation requires one to understand how the value of assets such as stocks, bonds and real estate are determined. Finally, understanding such concepts as compound interest and inflation can empower an individual to manage the risk of their investments over time.

DECREASED SAVINGS & INCREASED DEBT

However, recent research indicates that many people are financially illiterate — they do not have an understanding of the basic concepts of finance. People cannot differentiate between individual stocks and stock mutual funds, nor do they comprehend that investing in individual stocks is riskier than investing in mutual funds. Further, there is a general lack of knowledge about compound interest and inflation. This lack of knowledge reflects the fact that many people do not understand how money works, and this in turn is manifested in the way people invest or fail to invest their money. For many, their primary investment vehicle is their company provided defined benefit plan or a defined contribution plan. A defined benefit plan is commonly referred to as a fully funded pension. However, pension plans are becoming less common as employers are shifting this benefit to a defined contribution plan such as a 401(k). Unfortunately, many people are not aware of the differences between these two types of plans and some are not certain which type of plan their employer provides. The result of this lack of knowledge is that the overall savings rate declined dramatically during the late twentieth and early twenty-first centuries (Carlson, 2005), and only started to rise in the wake of the 2007 recession (Samavati, Adilov, & Dilts, 2013). More importantly, the amount of consumer debt dramatically increased as the twentieth century came to a close. This is reflected by the fact that more people carried higher amounts of unsecured consumer debt such as credit cards. This trend, as is the case with the overall savings rate, has slightly reversed since the 2007 recession (Brown, Haughwout, Donghoon, & van der Klaauw, 2013). In addition to an expansion of unsecured debt, the rise in home ownership over the last 20 years combined with the rising value of real property has resulted in a surge of mortgage debt. In order for the individual to be able to adequately finance this debt requires an understanding of the basic concepts of finance.

APPLICATIONS

SUCCESSFUL SAVING

While having an understanding of the basic concepts of finance is important to understanding the value of savings and investing, saving is really a matter of common sense money management. In this regard, there are four ways to simply start saving.

- First, large amounts of cash should not be kept on hand, but rather deposited into a savings account.
- Second, although paying outstanding bills on time is important, there is no benefit derived from paying bills early and this money can continue to earn interest.
- Further, some people intentionally have more taxes withheld in order to obtain a refund. However, that excess money could also be put to better use by earning interest.
- Finally, once the amount of money a person is saving begins to accumulate, it can then be invested in other ways to earn even more interest such as by opening an interest bearing checking account (Miller, 2003).

INSTRUMENTS FOR SAVING

CERTIFICATES OF DEPOSIT
Another vehicle available for savings investment is a Certificate of Deposit or a CD. Investing in a CD is essentially a time-deposit savings device that requires an investor to keep the money in the account for a specified period of time. That period can be for as little as 3-6 months or as long as 5 years. In return for this, the interest rate paid by the bank is higher than the interest rates based on savings accounts or interest bearing checking accounts. The longer the term of the CD, the higher the interest rate that will be paid. In addition, there is usually a penalty for withdrawing the money early.

MONEY-MARKET DEPOSIT ACCOUNT
Another type of savings account available for basic investing is a Money-Market Deposit Account (MMDA). This is basically a means of saving that is a cross between a savings account and a Certificate of Deposit. An MMDA requires an investor to maintain a minimum balance ($1,000) while allowing for a maximum number of three checks to be drawn each month (but automated deposit machine withdrawals are not limited).

MONEY MARKET MUTUAL FUND
In addition to the MMDA, an individual can also invest in a Money Market Mutual Fund. Opening

this type of fund requires a minimum initial deposit, usually $1,000, $5,000 or more depending on the financial institution. The institution uses the money invested in these funds to borrow and lend money on a short-term basis. This includes such investment vehicles as commercial paper (short-term debt obligations issued by a corporation), Treasury bills (short term debt issued by the Federal government), federal government securities such as "Ginnie Maes" (GNMAs) and "Fannie Maes (FNMAs) as well as others short term debt instruments (Miller, 2003).

BENEFITS OF SAVINGS INSTRUMENTS
The main benefit of the foregoing savings instruments is that they allow an investor to earn interest on their money without a great deal of risk. The general rule of thumb regarding saving money is that one should have six months of living expenses set aside. This is not money to spend or to be used for making large purchases and should only be used in case of an emergency or loss of income. Having this money set aside will also enable an individual to minimize their debts. As mentioned earlier, not saving enough money is one of the biggest financial mistakes that people make. Another way to save money is to open an Individual Retirement Account (IRA) or contribute to an employer sponsored plan such as a 401(k). Investing in these instruments enables an individual to invest in stocks, bonds, mutual funds, certificates of deposit, money-market funds, and the like (Chatzky, 2004).

INTEREST ACCRUAL
In addition to understanding financial concepts that are at the root of all these investments, it is also helpful to comprehend the goal of investing, and the benefits of investing in stocks, bonds, mutual funds, and even real estate. An investment is basically the use of money for the purpose of creating more money. This can be accomplished by putting money in income-producing vehicles, such as the various savings vehicles that earn interest mentioned above. Interest is essentially the cost of using money, usually over a one-year period and an interest rate is the rate charged for using that money. For example, if a bank was offering an interest rate of 2% per year on a basic savings account, and an initial deposit of $1,000 is made, after one year, that account would have $1,020 On the other hand, interest rates are charged on

bonds, credit cards, and other types of consumer and business loans. If a bank charges $600 per year on a loan of $100,000, the interest rate would be 6% per year (Downes, 2006).

REAL ESTATE

Interest rates on consumer loans are important to understand if a person is buying a home. Financing an investment in real estate usually requires obtaining a mortgage from a financial institution. A mortgage is a debt instrument a lender uses to place a lien on real property purchased by the borrower. A lien is a creditor's claim, in this case the lender, against property (Downes, 2006). By understanding the time value of money, a person will be better able to understand how much a mortgage will actually cost over 30 years. By understanding asset valuation, a person can determine the value of the house, or the asset. An asset, moreover, is anything with financial value that is owned by a business or person.

STOCKS, BONDS & MUTUAL FUNDS

In addition to an asset such as real estate, an individual can also invest in stocks, bonds, and mutual funds. Investing in stock essentially means to have an ownership interest in a corporation. Shares issued by the corporation represent stock ownership, and these are claims against a company's earnings and assets. The value of stock is determined by a number of factors over time. On the other hand, an individual can also invest in bonds. Basically, a bond is an interest-bearing government or corporate instrument that requires the issuer to pay specific amounts of money at certain time intervals until the debt is paid in full by a set date (also referred to as the maturity date). Another way to invest in stocks and bonds is to invest in a mutual fund. A mutual fund is an investment vehicle that is operated by an investment company. Money is raised from shareholders, and that money is used to invest in stocks, bonds, and other investments (Downes, 2006). The benefit of investing in mutual funds is that the investment company manages the risk.

For many people, one convenient way to invest in stocks, bonds and mutual funds is to participate in an employer-sponsored savings and retirement plan like a 401(k) or 403(b) plan. These plans are also called defined contribution plans. In a 401(k), the plan is managed by an investment company and requires the employee to contribute a percentage of their income. In some cases, the employer also contributes to the plan, and this is referred to as a company match. The company match usually equates to 50% of the employee's contribution. For example, an employee that contributes 6% of their income to a 401(k) will see the company make a matching contribution of 3%. In short, this means that a person will be saving and investing 9% of their annual income by participating in such a plan (Carlson, 2005).

For those that do not have access to a 401(k), another way to invest in mutual funds is to invest in an individual retirement account, also known as an IRA (Fryar, Warther, Thibodeau, & Drucker, 2012). There are different types of individual retirement accounts. A traditional IRA is one where an individual makes tax deferred payments. A Roth IRA, on the other hand, enables an investor to contribute money that has already been taxed. Of course, there are many other factors and considerations in regard to IRAs, but investing in these retirement vehicles require an individual to take responsibility for their financial planning. Regardless of the types of investment a person makes, having an understanding of the basic concepts of finance can be helpful. While the fundamental concepts of finance might be considered basic, they can also be complicated. This is so because understanding these concepts requires determining the time value of money, asset valuation and risk management.

TIME VALUE OF MONEY

The first and foremost principle in finance is the time value of money because financial decisions are spread out over time. This concept essentially is a means of calculating the value of a sum of money in the present or in the future. While the outcome of financial decisions cannot be known with certainty, being able to calculate the value of money at some time in the future affords one the ability to manage risk. Understanding the time value of money allows one to calculate present and future values. In the parlance of financial planning present value or "PV" means the present value of an amount that will be received in the future. On the other hand, future value or "FV" is the future worth of a present amount. For example, understanding PV will enable a bond investor to determine the value now of a $1,000 bond that will mature in ten years. On the other hand, FV will enable an individual to determine how much a $1,000 savings account will have at the end of the year if it pays 2% interest compounded annually (Clare, 2002).

INTEREST CALCULATIONS

With respect to interest, there are fundamentally two ways to calculate it — simple interest and compound interest.

- Simple Interest is a calculation based only on the original principal amount of the asset or debt. For instance, in the example mentioned above, a $1,000 deposit in a savings account at 2% simple interest would earn $20 per year (2% of $1,000 = $20). At the end of the first year, the amount of the principal and interest in the account would equate to $1,020.
- On the other hand, compound interest is interest earned on the principal plus any interest that was previously earned. For example, a $1,000 deposit at 5% compound interest at the end of the first year would earn $50 in the first year (5% of $1,000 = $50). If no additional deposits are made in the second year the balance in the account would be $1,102.50 or 5% of $1,050 = $52.50; $1,050 + $52.50 = $1,102.50 (Downes, 2006).

ASSET VALUATION

In addition to understanding the basics of time value, and being able to calculate interest, it is also necessary to understand how assets are valued. The value of an asset, in turn, is partially determined by the market where the asset is bought and sold. With respect to stocks, asset value is determined by the net value of a company's assets on a per share basis as opposed to the shares' market value (Downes, 2006). One of the key ingredients in determining this value is how profitable the company is in a given period of time. In a real estate transaction, the value of real property is determined by an appraisal of the property and there are numerous factors to consider such as the type of property, the number of units in the dwelling, the location and condition of the real property and the value of other properties in the vicinity. The importance of understanding asset valuation as it relates to the property is also an important consideration in determining the loan amount of the mortgage that a financial institution will offer to a purchaser.

RISK ASSESSMENT

The last concept that an investor needs to consider is risk or the potential for the loss of value of an asset. One such way to manage risks is to value assets by using comparative scenarios that consider a range of assumptions (Clare, 2002). Some of the specific considerations in this regard are inflation risk, interest rate risk, credit risk and risk of principal. Inflation risk is the potential that the value of an asset or income will erode as increased prices adversely affect the value of money. Interest rate risk is the possibility that a fixed rate debt instrument will decline in value as interest rates rise. Credit risk is the possibility that a debtor will not repay an obligation. Finally, risk of principal is the chance that money that was initially invested will lose its value. In short, risk management requires one to have knowledge of the asset in which they are investing as well as knowledge of various market and economic conditions affecting that market.

VIEWPOINTS

In the final analysis, financial planning or business planning require an understanding of the basic concepts of finance. For a small business owner, understanding these concepts will enable him or her to consider how to determine the value of the good, product or service being provided to their customers while also being able to ascertain the cost to operate the business. A corporate executive needs to understand a number of financial concepts including the valuation of a company's stock and the products being provided to consumers as well as the cost of operating the business entity. While this has always been the case for chief executive officers and chief financial officers of publicly traded corporations, it is even more crucial in today's regulatory environment by virtue of the requirements of the Sarbanes-Oxley Act of 2002 (SOX). This Federal regulation requires senior management of publicly traded corporations to attest to the accuracy of the financial statements that these companies are required to file on an annual basis. Not having an understanding of the basic concepts of finance can result in serious consequences for these individuals since there have been felony convictions associated with deficiencies in financial reporting requirements. One can look to the recent history of such companies as Enron and Tyco to realize this.

In the end, small business owners, corporate executives and financial planners are not the only ones who need to understand the basic concepts of finance. In fact, every individual should have some knowledge in this regard since this will enable them to be better equipped to save and invest with confidence, and more importantly avoid acquiring excessive debt. Further, if a person plans on buying a home it can to be helpful to understand how the value of the property is determined, and how much a mortgage to finance the purchase of the dwelling will actually cost. Many people mistakenly believe that owning a home will not cost more than renting an apartment, but this is an incorrect notion at best. There are many costs to consider in addition to the actual payment of the mortgage such as the costs to insure the dwelling, the property taxes, costs of furnishing, payment of utilities and maintenance costs. Not having some basic knowledge regarding finance can result in an individual in not being able to afford the cost of a home. These situations often lead people to acquire excessive consumer debt to cover some of these costs, and paying those debts will hinder their ability to save money — and not saving enough money is the costliest mistake a person can make. By having an understanding of the basic concepts of finance, it is possible to avoid these mistakes and plan for an adequate financial future by saving and investing wisely. At the same time, it is a good idea to consult a professional about financial planning and in that regard, this paper is intended for informational purposes only and should not be considered financial advice.

BIBLIOGRAPHY

Brown, M., Haughwout, A., Donghoon, L., & van der Klaauw, W. (2013). The financial crisis at the kitchen table: Trends in household debt and credit. *Current Issues in Economics & Finance, 19*(2), 1-10. Retrieved on November 12, 2013, from EBSCO Online Database Business Source Complete. http://search.ebscohost.com/login.aspx?direct=t rue&db=bth&AN=88300342&site=ehost-live

Carlson, L. (2005, Oct). Lack of basic financial knowledge impairs retirement. *Employee Benefit News, 19*(13) 18-24. Retrieved on January 18, 2007, from EBSCO Online Database Business Source Premier. http://search.ebscohost.com/login.aspx?direct=t rue&db=buh&AN=18501264 &site=ehost-live

Chatzky, J. Bigda, C. & Jervey, G. (2004, Dec). The six biggest money mistakes and how to avoid them. *Money, 33*(12) 92-101. Retrieved on January 18, 2007, from EBSCO Online Database Business Source Premier. http:// search.ebscohost.com/login.aspx?direct=true&db=buh&A N=15060434&site=ehost-live

Clare, M. (2002). Solving the knowledge — value equation (part one). *KM Review, 5*(2) 14-18. Retrieved on January 18, 2007, from EBSCO Online Database Business Source Premier. http:// search.ebscohost.com/login.aspx?direct=tru e&db=buh&AN=6798862&site=ehost-live

Downes, J. & Goodman, J.E. (2006). *Dictionary of financial and investment terms.* Barons Educational Services, Inc. Hauppauge, NY. (Print Content)

Fryar Jr., J., Warther, J., Thibodeau, T., & Drucker, M. (2012). Retirement and estate planning with an emphasis on individual retirement accounts. *Journal of Business & Economics Research, 10*(7), 397-405. Retrieved on November 12, 2013, from EBSCO Online Database Business Source Complete. http://search.ebscohost.com/ login.asp x?direct=true&db=bth&AN=80160731&site=eh ost-live

Gallo, J.J. (2005). Estate planning conundrums worth repeating. *Journal of Financial Planning, 18*(9) 30-31. Retrieved on January 18, 2007, from EBSCO Online Database Business Source Premier. http:// search.ebscohost.com/ login.aspx?direct=true&d b=buh&AN=17857441&site=eh ost-live

Miller, T. (2003). Chapter 2: How to boost your savings. *Kiplinger's Practical Guide to Your Money,* 19-28. Retrieved on January 18, 2007, from EBSCO Online Database Business Source Premier. http:// search.ebscohost.com/login.aspx?direct=true&db =buh&AN=9442231 &site=ehost-live

Miller, T. (2003). Chapter 3: First, maximize your savings. *Kiplinger's Practical Guide to Your Money,* 31-46. Retrieved on January 18, 2007, from EBSCO Online Database Business Source Premier. http:// search.ebscohost.com/login.aspx?direct=true&db =buh&AN=9395859 &site=ehost-live

Samavati, H., Adilov, N., & Dilts, D. A. (2013). Empirical analysis of the saving rate in the United States. *Journal of Management Policy & Practice, 14*(2), 46-53. Retrieved on November 12, 2013, from EBSCO Online Database Business Source Complete.

http://search.ebscohost.com/ login.aspx?direct= true&db=bth&AN=89922139&site=eh ost-live

SUGGESTED READING
Brown, G. & Cliff, M. (2005). Investor sentiment and asset valuation. *Journal of Business, 78*(2) 405-440. Retrieved on January 18, 2007, from EBSCO Online Database Business Source Premier. http:// search.ebscohost.com/ login.aspx?direct=true&d b=buh&AN=17002456&site=eh ost-live

Braunstein, S. & Welch, C. (2002, Nov). Financial literacy: An overview of practice, research and policy. *Federal Reserve Bulletin, 88*(11) 445-458.

Retrieved on January 18, 2007, from EBSCO Online Database Business Source Premier. http:// search.ebscohost.com/login.aspx?direct=tru e&db=buh&AN=8584843&site=ehost-live

Flaig, J.J. (2005). Improving project selection using expected net present value analysis. *Quality Engineering, 17*(4), 535-538. Retrieved on January 18, 2007, from EBSCO Business Source Premier. http://search.ebscohost.com/ login.aspx?direct= true&db=buh&AN=18518221&site=eh ost-live

–*Richa S. Tiwary*

BEHAVIORAL FINANCE

ABSTRACT

This article focuses on behavioral finance. It provides an overview of the history of behavioral finance. The relationship and debate between behavioral finance and neoclassical economic theory is addressed. The topics of investor bias, efficient markets, rational investors, risk attitudes, mental accounting, and investor overconfidence are explored. The issues associated with using behavioral finance to identify investor bias are discussed.

OVERVIEW

Behavioral finance, also referred to as behavioral economics, combines economics and psychology to analyze how and why investors make their financial decisions. The field of behavioral finance, which has much in common with the field of cognitive psychology, offers a theoretical explanation for the sometimes irrational or emotional choices and actions of investors (Salsbury, 2004). Despite the supposition of neoclassical economics that the market is efficient and that investors are rational, investing behavior and market behavior can be wildly irrational and inconsistent. As a result of the psychology of individual investors, stocks may be mispriced and markets may be inefficient. Behavioral economics offers an explanation for economic irrationality and economic anomalies in the market as well as a strategy for capitalizing on the unique psychology and decision-making processes of individual investors. Behavioral

finance, which originated in the 1970s, gained prominence and legitimacy in 2002 when psychologist Daniel Kahneman won the Nobel Prize in economics for his work in the field of behavioral economics.

Behavioral economics incorporates data and theories about investors' cognitive ability, social interaction, moral motivation, and emotional responses into economic modeling to better understand economic outcomes. Behavioral finance recognizes that individuals, including professional investors, use heuristics to make investment decisions. Heuristics, which refer to the use of experience and practical efforts to answer questions or to improve performance, are a form of selective interpretation of information. The use of heuristics, by definition, leads to incomplete information in the decision-making process (Fromlet, 2001). Behavioral finance finds that the following variables affect economic decision-making: Biases, self-control, mental accounting, savings, fairness, altruism, public good, learning, incentives, memory, attention and categorization.

Behavioral finance is an academic field and a portfolio management approach (Stewart, 2006). Financial analysts use behavioral finance to augment or supplement classical and neoclassical financial theory and approaches. The psychological factors that have long been excluded from conventional financial analysis do affect market outcomes (Fromlet, 2001). While behavioral-finance guided investing, also referred to as behavioral investing, has not eclipsed traditional modern portfolio theory, behavioral investing has established itself as a legitimate investment technique or strategy. In particular, behavioral-finance guided investing has grown in favor following the drop in technology stocks in 2000. Behavioral investors use their understanding of human psychology to find underpriced or over-priced stocks to purchase or sell. Mispriced securities have the potential to be lucrative for savvy investors (Singh, 2005). Ultimately, behavioral finance argues that financial decision-making is influenced by in-dividual and market psychology. Behavioral finance addresses the following issues and questions (Taffler, 2002):

- What causes stock market bubbles?
- Why is the stock market so volatile?
- Why are under and overvalued stocks difficult to identify?
- Why do stock prices appear to under react to bad news?
- Why do most boards of directors often believe their companies are undervalued by the stock market?

The field of behavioral finance characterizes inves-tors in the following ways: Investors are often biased in their economic decision-making; investors are known to be overly-optimistic of investment decisions; inves-tors are known to overestimate the chances of their success; and investors are known to overestimate their financial knowledge (Litner, 1998). Behavioral finance operates to create theoretical insight about investor behavior and create a system for more accu-rate predictions of investors' behavior.

The following sections provide an overview of the history of behavioral finance. This overview will serve as a foundation for later discussion of behavioral fi-nance and the challenge to neoclassical economic theory. The issues associated with using behavioral finance to identify investor bias are addressed.

THE HISTORY OF BEHAVIORAL FINANCE
The academic field of behavioral finance began in 1979 when psychologists Daniel Kahneman and Amos Tversky introduced prospect theory. Prospect theory introduced a rubric for understanding how the framing of risk influences economic decision-making. Amos Tversky and Daniel Kahneman devel-oped the field of behavioral finance through their work on the psychology of risk. Their work, and be-havioral economics in general, challenges the basic assumptions of rationality inherent in the classical

Daniel Kahneman. *Via Wikipedia.org*

economic model of decision-making. Tversky and Kahneman studied three main areas: Risk attitudes, mental accounting, and overconfidence (Litner, 1998).

- **Risk attitudes:** While classical economic theory argues that investors are averse to risk, behavioral finance holds that investors exhibit inconsistent and often conflicting attitudes toward and about financial risk. Tversky and Kahneman found that investors have an individualized reference point for risk and will be most sensitive to risk when that reference point is reached.

- **Mental accounting:** While classical economic theory argues that money is fungible and inter-changeable, behavioral finance holds that money is not completely fungible for most people. Tversky & Kahneman developed the idea of individual-ized mental accounts to explain why money is not wholly fungible for most people. Mental accounts, a wholly intangible form of accounting, contain financial resources that for personal and often ir-rational reasons are not easily transferred.

- **Overconfidence:** While classical economic theory argues that investors are rational decision makers who use the financial information that is available to them, behavioral finance holds that investors are prone to overconfidence and bi-ased decisions. Tversky & Kahneman found that investors were often overly optimistic about in-vestment decisions, overestimated the chances of financial success, and overestimated their finan-cial knowledge.

In 2002, Daniel Kahneman received the Nobel Prize in economics. Richard Thaler was another important early contributor to the field of behavioral finance. Richard Thaler, in the 1980s, extended the scope of behavioral finance by making stronger connections between psychological and economics principles (Lambert, 2006). The field of behavioral finance has grown over the last three decades in large part as a result of the support that the field received from universities and research institutions.

THE RUSSELL SAGE FOUNDATION

One of the largest non-profit supporters of the behavioral finance, or behavioral economics, field is the Russell Sage Foundation. The Russell Sage Foundation provides academics and finance professionals interested in the behavioral finance field with significant research and development support. The Russell Sage Foundation began its Behavioral Economics Program in 1986 with the stated goal of "strengthening the accuracy and empirical reach of economic theory by incorporating information from related social science disciplines such as psychology and sociology." The Russell Sage Foundation's Behavioral Economics Program established itself at the intersection between economics and cognitive psychology and dedicated the program's

Headquarters of the Russell Sage Foundation in New York.
Via Wikipedia.org

resources to understanding how the real-world economic decisions of investors often contradict the rational standards in economic theory. The Behavioral Economics Program promotes two major activities in the field of behavioral economics: The Behavioral Economics Roundtable, a forum for discussing new ideas, and a series of National Bureau of Economic Research (NBER) workshops("Behavioral economics," 2007).

Priorities of the Russell Sage Foundation's Behavioral Economics Program have included improving the effectiveness of social programs by establishing connections between behavioral economists and non-profit organizations and understanding consumer decision making regarding their own finances in order to help shape effective and appropriate regulation to promote consumer welfare. Examples of proposed projects include the following: "Programs to increase the use of checking accounts by the poor; programs encouraging taxpayers to save a portion of their federal tax rebates; pre-release programs to decrease recidivism among ex-prisoners; programs to improve portfolio decisions in retirement pension accounts; and programs to increase participation in the Medicare prescription drug benefit" (Russell Sage Foundation—Behavioral Economics, 2007, 2013).

SOCIETY FOR THE ADVANCEMENT OF BEHAVIORAL ECONOMICS

In addition to the efforts of the Russell Sage Foundation to further the field of behavioral economics, the Society for the Advancement of Behavioral Economics (SABE), established in 1982, is an network of scholars committed to intensive economic analysis and interested in learning how other disciplines, such as psychology, sociology, anthropology, history, political science, and biology, promote the understanding of economic behavior. The Society for the Advancement of Behavioral Economics has a stated objective to facilitate communication between economists and scholars from related disciplines. The Society for the Advancement of Behavioral Economics serves as a forum for interdisciplinary research, such as behavioral financing, which may not have been accepted or recognized in traditional economics fields of inquiry (www.sabeonline.org/About.html).

APPLICATIONS

BEHAVIORAL FINANCE & THE CHALLENGE TO NEOCLASSICAL ECONOMIC THEORY

The behavioral finance field challenges the predominant neoclassical economic theory of twentieth century. Economic theory of the twentieth century, characterized by the neoclassical economics and the modern portfolio theory, argues that investors behave in a rational and unbiased manner. Neoclassical economic theory focuses on productivity growth, supply and demand, rational investors, and efficient markets. The field of neoclassical economics emphasizes the belief that the market system will ensure a fair allocation of resources and income distribution. In addition, the market is believed to regulate demand and supply, allocation of production, and the optimization of social organization (Brinkman, 2001). Modern portfolio theory and the efficient market hypothesis (EMH) are tools for analyzing and understanding how securities are valued in the marketplace. Neoclassical economic theory holds that investors are rational, predictable, and unbiased agents and that the market is an efficient system. Modern portfolio theory argues that risk-averse investors construct their portfolios to optimize the expected return on a known and accepted level of market risk. The optimal portfolio will include security valuation, asset allocation, portfolio optimization, and performance measurement. The efficient market hypothesis argues that the market is efficient because stock prices reflect everything that investors know about stocks at any given moment (Singh, 2005).

Traditional economic theories, such as modern portfolio theory and the efficient market hypothesis, do not explain investor bias and anomalies in the marketplace. For example, there are at least five major areas where neoclassical economic theory does not explain the behavior of real investors and market outcomes. These five areas, including volume, volatility, dividends, equity premium puzzle, and predictability will be described below (Thaler, 1999):

- **Volume:** The volume of trade in asset markets is consistently higher than neoclassical economic theory assumes. If investors and traders were rational, as neoclassical economics supposed, than the investors and traders would hold onto investments over the long term rather than buy and sell

with frequency. In practice, investors and traders have liquidity and balancing needs and, as a result, trading volume tends to be high.
- **Volatility:** The volatility of asset markets is consistently higher than neoclassical economic theory assumes. Neoclassical economic theory argues that prices will change only when news arrives. In practice, stock and bond prices are much more volatile than believed possible in a rational and efficient market.
- **Dividends:** Dividends, which refer to payments made by a corporation to its stock holders, have a stronger effect on the stock market than neoclassical economic theory assumes. Neoclassical economic theory cannot explain why stock prices increase when dividends are increased or why companies pay cash dividends.
- **Equity premium puzzle:** The equity premium puzzle, which refers to the observations that returns on individual stocks over the past century are higher than returns on government bonds, cannot be explained by neoclassical economic theory. The equity premium differential between government and non-government stocks and bonds is large and cannot be explained as a product of reward for greater risk.
- **Predictability:** The observed predictability of asset markets cannot be explained by neoclassical economic theory. In a rational and efficient market, future returns cannot be predicted on the basis of known information. In practice, there are predictable patterns in price-to-earnings ratios, company announcements of earnings, dividend changes, share repurchases, and seasoned equity offerings.

The field of behavioral finance developed in the 1970s to account for the unpredictability and seeming irrationality that economists observed in investor behavior that went unexplained in neoclassical economic theory. Behavioral finance offers tools to understand how investors interpret and act on information to make informed economic investment decisions. Neoclassical economics does not explain individual difference and anomalies. In the late 1970s, when psychologists Amos Tversky and Daniel Kahneman introduced behavioral finance, and prospect theory, as a subset of cognitive science, they were engaging and expanding the range of possible economic theory and explanations. Since the late

1970s, academics and investment professionals have been studying, both for intellectual curiosity and profit motive, how emotion, cognitive biases, and psychology of investors affects economic decisions. Despite the refusal of neoclassical economic theory to engage the psychology of investors and markets, behavioral finance theory asserts that cognitive biases have significant affects on financial decisions. The cognitive biases that affect investor decision making, and ultimately market outcome, include the following: Anchoring, availability bias, confirmation bias, disposition effect, framing and reference dependence, illusion of control, optimism bias, overconfidence bias, overreaction, representativeness, and underreaction.

- **Anchoring:** The tendency to anchor expectations based on reference points that may not have any relevance to the value that is being projected.
- **Availability bias:** The propensity to form judgments about the probability of an event based primarily on the availability of information that favors a certain outcome.
- **Confirmation bias:** The seeking of information that supports an investor's belief while disregarding evidence that may be inconsistent or contradictory.
- **Disposition effect:** The tendency to hold losing securities too long and to sell winners too quickly because of an aversion to loss.
- **Framing and reference dependence:** The tendency to take into account irrelevant information when determining return expectations for an asset.
- **Illusion of control:** Individuals' tendency to overestimate the control they have over outcomes.
- **Optimism bias:** The tendency of people to believe that they are better than average and that misfortune are more likely to befall people other than themselves.
- **Overconfidence bias:** The tendency to be overconfident in the ability to predict the behavior of the markets, particularly as it relates to the selection of winning stocks.
- **Overreaction:** Seeing patterns in random events, such as projecting current trends into the future forever.
- **Representativeness:** The tendency to find similarities among prospects whose resemblances are only superficial, thereby taking the sample to be representative of the whole population.

- **Underreaction:** A reluctance to adjust one's expectations to new information.

Investment companies increasingly form behavioral finance teams to evaluate qualitative factors and issues affecting the market and investment decisions. Behavioral finance funds have become common and successful investment vehicles. Investment professionals use the perspective and tools of behavioral finance to study the anomalies in the marketplace and exploit the anomalies to their advantage. The principles of behavioral finance can be used in any asset class including equities, fixed income, convertible securities and real estate investment trusts. Behavioral finance connects investor decision-making and market movements. Behavioral finance investing can be applied across investing styles, industry sectors, and stock domains (Stewart, 2006). Despite the legitimacy and prominence of behavioral finance in academic and corporate sectors, the debate between traditional finance and behavioral finance remains strong (Shiller, 2006).

ISSUES

USING BEHAVIORAL FINANCE TO IDENTIFY INVESTOR BIAS
Financial advisers working to incorporate behavioral finance into their practices face numerous challenges. There is currently no accepted finance industry approved methodology for identifying an individual investor's psychological biases. In addition, even once an investor's behavioral biases have been identified, financial advisers may lack the experience needed to incorporate these biases during the process of determining asset allocation. Most importantly, financial advisers will be challenged by the task of deciding how much individualized behavioral finance research is appropriate for each client. Financial advisers must decide whether to attempt to change their clients' biased behavior or adapt to it. Pompian and Longo (2005) suggest the use of two behavioral finance guidelines or principles:
- First, financial advisers should adapt to biases at high wealth levels and attempt to modify behavior at lower wealth levels.
- Second, financial advisers should adapt to emotional biases and moderate cognitive biases.

Guidelines for incorporating biases in asset allocation decisions will help financial advisers accomplish the following objectives: Moderate the way clients naturally behave to counteract the affects of "behavioral biases so that they can fit a pre-determined asset allocation; adapt to clients' biases, so that clients can comfortably abide by their asset allocation decisions; and establish the quantitative parameters" (p. 2) that will allow the financial adviser to successfully moderate or adapt the client biases. Ultimately, the application of behavioral finance to individual clients is a sensitive process that would benefit from the adoption of finance industry guidelines and direction (Pompian & Longo, 2005).

CONCLUSION

Neoclassical economic theory considers investors and markets to be rational and efficient entities. In practice, investors may be emotional, biased, and overconfident. The market reacts and responds to the individual biases and behaviors of investors and market anomalies occur. The field of behavioral finance, also referred to as behavioral economics, was established in the 1970s to explain how and why the psychology of investors effect financial decision making and market behavior. Behavioral economics combines economics and psychology to analyze how and why investors make their financial decisions. Behavioral finance, which has much in common with the field of cognitive psychology, offers a theoretical explanation for investors' sometimes seemingly irrational or emotional choices and actions. The field of behavioral finance will likely continue to grow in strength and scope; it will likely remain a strong investment tool or approach. Due to the volatility of markets, behavioral finance guided investing is considered to be one of many key investment strategies in a diversified portfolio (Stewart, 2006). The field of behavioral finance is expanding to include the field of neuroeconomics. Neuroeconomics is an area of study that combines neurology, economics, and psychology to analyze how people make economic choices. Neuroeconomics expands behavioral finance by adding in the variable of the nervous system as a factor in economic decision-making. In the final analysis, the growth of the behavioral finance field allows for greater understanding of the ways in which psychological variables affect investment outcomes and market behavior (Shiller, 2006).

BIBLIOGRAPHY

Behavioral economics. (2007). *Research Programs.* Retrieved September 3, 2007, from The Russell Sage Foundation. http://www.russellsage.org/programs/other/behavioral/

Brinkman, R. (2001). The new growth theories: A cultural and social addendum. *The International Journal of Social Economics, 28*(5), 506-526.

Burr, B. (1997). More light shining on the whys of investing. *Pensions & Investments, 25*(11), 32-34. Retrieved September 3, 2007, from EBSCO Online Database Business Source Premier. http://search.ebscohost.com/login.aspx?direct=true&db=buh&AN=9706161328&site= ehost-live

Curtis, G. (2004). Modern portfolio theory and behavioral finance. *Journal of Wealth Management, 7*(2), 16-22. Retrieved September 3, 2007, from EBSCO Online Database Business Source Premier. http://search.ebscohost.com/login.aspx?direct=true&db=buh&AN=14361411 &site=ehost-live

Fromlet, H. (2001). Behavioral finance-theory and practical application. *Business Economics, 36*(3), 63. Retrieved September 3, 2007, from EBSCO Online Database Business Source Premier. http://search.ebscohost.com/ login.aspx?direct=true&db=buh&AN=5057707&site= ehost-live

Herciu, M., & Ogrean, C. (2014). Corporate Governance and Behavioral Finance: From Managerial Biases to Irrational Investors. *Studies In Business & Economics, 9*(1), 66-72. Retrieved November 5, 2014, from EBSCO Online Database Business Source Complete. http:// search.ebscohost.com/login.aspx?direct=true&db= bth&AN=98353325

Hyoyoun, P., & Wook, S. (2013). Behavioral finance: A survey of the literature and recent development. *Seoul Journal of Business, 19*(1), 3-42. Retrieved November 15, 2013, from EBSCO Online Database Business Source Complete. http://search.ebscohost.com/login.aspx?direct=true&db=bth&AN=90591091&site=ehost-live

Lambert, C. (2006, March-April). The marketplace of perceptions. *Harvard Magazine.* Retrieved September 3, 2007, from http://www.harvardmagazine.com/on-line/030640. html

Lintner, A. (1998). Behavioral finance: Why investors make bad decisions. *The Planner, 13*(1), 7-9.

Matsumoto, A. S., Fernandes, J. B., de M. Cunha, G., & de Abreu Araújo, E. (2013). Behavioral finance: A psychophysiological study of decision making. *Journal of International Business & Economics, 13*(4), 189-194. Retrieved November 15, 2013, from EBSCO Online Database Business Source Complete. http://search.ebscohost.com/login.aspx?direct=true&db=bth&AN=91834253&site=ehost-live

Peteros, R., & Maleyeff, J. (2013). Application of behavioural finance concepts to investment decision-making: Suggestions for improving investment education courses. *International Journal of Management, 30*(1 Part 2), 249- 261. Retrieved November 15, 2013, from EBSCO Online Database Business Source Complete. http://search.ebscohost.com/login.aspx?direct=true&db=bth&AN=85634555&site=ehost-live

Pompian, M., & Longo, J. (2005). Incorporating behavioral finance into your practice. *Journal of Financial Planning, 18*(3), 58-63. Retrieved September 3, 2007, from EBSCO Online Database Business Source Premier. http://search. ebscohost.com/login.aspx?direct=true&db=buh&AN=16401771&site=ehost-live

Riepe, M. W. (2013). Musings on Behavioral Finance. *Journal Of Financial Planning, 26*(5), 34-35. Retrieved November 5, 2014, from EBSCO Online Database Business Source Complete. http://search.ebscohost.com/login.aspx?direct=true&db=bth&AN=87563903

Shiller, R. (2006). Tools for financial innovation: Neoclassical versus behavioral finance. *Financial Review, 41*(1), 1-8. Retrieved September 3, 2007, from EBSCO Online Database Business Source Premier. http://search.ebscohost. com/login.aspx?direct=true&db=buh&AN=19398002&site=ehost-live

Salsbury, G. (2004). Psychoanalysis has met investing. What does it mean for advisors? *National Underwriter: Life & Health, 108*(38), 20-22.

Stewart, P. (2006). Behavioral finance-not to be ignored. *Trusts & Estates, 145*(6), 46-51.

Taffler, R. (2002). What can we learn from behavioral finance? *Credit Control, 23*(2), 14-17.

Thaler, R. (1999). The end of behavioral finance. *Financial Analysts Journal, 55*(6), 12-17. Retrieved September 3, 2007, from EBSCO Online Database Business Source Premier. http://search.ebscohost.com/login.aspx?direct=true&db=buh&AN=2762863&site=ehost-live

SUGGESTED READING

Brav, A., Heaton, J., & Rosenberg, A. (2004). The rational-behavioral debate in financial economics. *Journal of Economic Methodology, 11*(4), 393-409. Retrieved September 3, 2007, from EBSCO Online Database Business Source Premier. http://search.ebscohost.com/login.aspx?direct=true&db=buh&AN=15491212&site= ehost-live

Nevins, D. (2004). Goals-based investing: Integrated traditional and behavioral finance. *Journal of Wealth Management, 6*(4), 8-23. Retrieved September 3, 2007, from EBSCO Online Database Business Source Premier. http://search. ebscohost.com/login.aspx?direct=true&db=buh&AN=12415661&site=ehost-live

Statman, M. (1999). Behavioral finance: Past battles and future engagements. *Financial Analysts Journal, 55*(6), 18-27. Retrieved September 3, 2007, from EBSCO Online Database Business Source Premier. http://search.ebscohost.com/login.aspx?direct=true&db=buh&AN=2762864 &site=ehost-live

Wasik, J. F. (2014). Bet Against Human Nature. *Forbes, 193*(9), 120. Retrieved November 5, 2014, from EBSCO Online Database Business Source Complete. http://search.ebscohost.com/login.aspx?direct=true&db=bth&AN=96734055

—Simone I. Flynn

BUSINESS FINANCE

ABSTRACT

This article focuses on business finance and how it relates to the corporate and non-profit sectors. In order for organizations to be successful, they must create a strategic plan that will position the firm for growth and competitiveness. The senior management team will need to analyze all data, including the financial records, to ensure that the organization can make a profit, remain competitive and be in position for continued growth. There is an introduction to the concept of capital budgeting and how it applies to businesses as well as to multinational corporations. Capital budgeting could be the result of purchasing assets that are new for the organization or getting rid of some of the current assets in order to be more efficient. Capital budgeting for the multinational corporation presents many problems that are rarely fund in domestic capital budgeting.

OVERVIEW

In order for organizations to be successful, they must create a strategic plan that will position the firm for growth and competitiveness. The senior management team will need to analyze all data, including the financial records, to ensure that the organization can make a profit, remain competitive and be in position for continued growth. "In discussing corporate financial strategy, the question can well be asked as to how strategy differs from more modest decision making" (Bierman, 1980, p. 1).

ELEMENTS & APPROACHES TO FINANCIAL STRATEGY

Bierman (1980) provided five elements and four approaches that he believed should be considered by corporate financial managers as they planned their strategies for the organizations in which they worked. The five elements were to:

- Identify the problems and opportunities that exist;
- Set goals and objectives;
- Develop a procedure for providing potential solutions or "paths" that the organization could follow in order to find a solution;
- Choose the best solution given the possible solutions and the organization's objectives; Implement a review process where the best solution can be evaluated on its performance.

These elements are very broad so that the corporate finance manager has an opportunity to consider a wide range of financial decisions. For example, the organization's main goal may be to pursue substantial growth with minimum risk. Therefore, the financial management team has to take these factors into consideration when developing the strategic financial plan for the organization. One type of strategy that financial professionals may use is the capital budgeting process.

CAPITAL BUDGETING

Many organizations charge the finance department with overseeing the financial stability of the organization. The chief financial officer (CFO) may lead a team of financial analysts in determining which projects deserve investment. This process is referred to as capital budgeting and is an example of how an organization may conduct a cost-benefit analysis. The process entails a comparison between the cash inflows (benefits) and outflows (costs) in order to determine which is greater. Capital budgeting could be the result of purchasing assets that are new for the organization or getting rid of some of the current assets in order to be more efficient. The finance team is charged with evaluating: Which projects would be good investments; which assets would add value to the current portfolio, and; how much is the organization willing to invest into each asset.

In order to answer the questions about the potential assets, there are a set of components to be considered in the capital budgeting process. The four components are initial investment outlay, net cash benefits (or savings) from the operations, terminal cash flow, and net present value (NPV) technique. Most of the literature discusses how the capital budgeting process operates in the traditional, domestic environment. However, as the world moves to a more global economic environment, consideration needs to be made as to how multinational corporations will conduct the capital budgeting process when operating in countries outside of their home base.

INTERNATIONAL CAPITAL BUDGETING

International capital budgeting refers to when projects are located in host countries other than the home country of the multinational corporation. Some of the techniques (i.e. calculation of net present value) are the same as traditional finance. However, "capital budgeting for a multinational is complicated because of the complexity of cash flows and financing options available to the multinational corporation" (Booth, 1982, p. 113). Capital budgeting for the multinational corporation presents many problems that are rarely found in domestic capital budgeting (Shapiro, 1978; Ang & Lai, 1989). Financial analysts may find that foreign projects are more complex to analyze than domestic projects due to the need to:

- Distinguish between parent cash flow and projects cash flow.

Multinationals will have the opportunity to evaluate the cash flow associated with projects from two approaches. They may look at the net impact of the project on their consolidated cash flow or they may treat the cash flow on a stand alone or unconsolidated basis. The theoretical perspective asserts that the project should be evaluated from the parent company's viewpoint since dividends and repayment of debt is handled by the parent company. This action supports the notion that the evaluation is actually based on the contributions that the project can make to the multinationals bottom line.

Some organizations may want to evaluate the project from the subsidiary's (local point of view) point of view. However, the parent company's viewpoint should supersede the subsidiary's point of view. Multinational corporations tend to compare their projects with the subsidiary's projects in order to determine where their investments should go. The rule of thumb is to only invest in those projects that can earn a risk-adjusted return greater than the local competitors performing the same type of project. If the earnings are not greater than the local competitors, the multinational corporation can invest in the host country's bonds since they will pay the risk free rate adjusted for inflation.

Although the theoretical approach is a sound process, many multinationals tend to evaluate their projects from both the parent and project point of view because of the combined advantages. When looking from the parent company's viewpoint, one could obtain results that are closer to the traditional net present value technique. However, the project's point of view allows one to obtain a closer approximation of the effect on consolidated earnings per share. The way the project is analyzed is dependent on the type of technique utilized to report the consolidated net earnings per share.

Recognize money reimbursed to parent company when there are differences in the tax system.

The way in which the cash flows are returned to the parent company has an effect on the project. Cash flow can be returned in the following ways:

- Dividends — It can only be returned in this form if the project has a positive income. Some countries may impose limits on the amounts of funds that subsidiaries can pay to their foreign parent company in this form.
- Intrafirm Debt — Interest on debt is tax deductible and it helps to reduce foreign tax liability.
- Intrafirm Sales — This form is the operating cost of the project and it helps lower the foreign tax liability.
- Royalties and License Fees — This form covers the expenses of the project and lowers the tax liability.
- Transfer Pricing — This form refers to the internally established prices where different units of a single enterprise buy goods and services from each other.
- Anticipate the differences in the inflation rate between countries given that it will affect the cash flow over time.
- Analyze the use of subsidized loans from the host country since the practice may complicate the capital structure and discounted rate.
- The host country may target specific subsidiaries in order to attract specific types of investment (i.e. technology). Subsidized loans can be given in the form of tax relief and preferential financing, and the practice will increase the net present value of the project. Some of the advantages of this practice include: Adding the subsidiary to project cash inflows and discount; discounting the subsidiary at some other rate, risk free, and; lowering the risk adjusted discount rate for the project in order to show the lower cost of debt.
- Determine if the political risk will reduce the value of the investment. Expropriation is the ultimate level of political risk, and the effects of it depends on: When the expropriation takes place;

the amount of money the host government will pay for the expropriation; how much debt is still outstanding; the tax consequences of expropriation and the future cash flow.

- Assess the different perspectives when assessing the terminal value of the project. Estimating the salvage value or terminal value depends on the value of the project if retained, the value of the project if purchased by outside investors and the value of the project if it were liquidated. The corporation would use the assessment that yields the highest value.

- Review whether or not the parent company had problems transferring cash flows due to the funds being blocked. An example would be when a host country limits the amounts of dividends that can be paid. If this were to occur, the multinational corporation would have to reexamine its reinvestment return and other methods in which the funds could be transferred out of the country. The blocked funds can be used to repay bank debt in the host country and allow the organization to have open lines of credit to other countries.

- Make sure that there is no confusion as to how the discount rate is going to be applied to the project.

- Adjust the project cash flow to account for potential risks. One must assume that every project has some level of risk. The risk is usually seen as part of the cost of capital. International projects tend to have more risk than domestic projects. Therefore, it is advantageous to review the risk based on the parent's and project's perspective. Each perspective has a different way of adjusting risk. For example, the parent company may propose to: Treat all foreign risk as a single problem by increasing the discount rate applicable to the foreign projects, or; incorporate all foreign risk in adjustments to forecasted cash flows of the project. The first option is usually not recommended because it may penalize the cash flows that are not really affected by any sort of risk and it may ignore events that are favorable to the organization. The four components are initial investment outlay, net cash benefits (or savings) from the operations, terminal cash flow, and net present value (NPV) technique.

- "Capital budgeting is a financial analysis tool that applies quantitative analysis to support strong management decisions" (Bearing Point, n.d.). Capital budgeting seeks to provide a simple way for the fi-

nance department to see the "big picture" of the benefits, costs and risks for a corporation planning to make short term and/or long term investments. Unfortunately, many of the leading methods have experienced problems, especially when an organization is using a standardized template. Examples of potential problems include: The benefits, costs, and risks associated with an investment tend to be different based on the type of industry (i.e. technology versus agricultural).

A corporation may highlight the end results of the return on investment model and the assumptions that support the results versus a balanced analysis of benefits, costs, and risks.

DATA ERROR PREVENTION

If an organization does not account for the abovementioned scenarios, there is a possibility for skewed results, which would make the data unusable. This type of error could hinder a project from receiving approval. Therefore, it is critical for financial analysts to have a more effective and efficient technique to use. Bearing Point (n.d.) identified several leading practices that organizations are using in order to avoid reporting faulty information. The theme in all of the techniques is that capital budgeting is not the only factor considered. Other quantifiable factors are utilized in order to see the big picture.

Consider the nature of the request: The type of benefit obtained by the investment will determine the nature of the request. Therefore, it may be beneficial to classify the benefit types into categories such as strategic, quantifiable and intangible.

All benefits are not created equal: Benefits should be classified correctly in order to properly analyze. There are two types of benefits — hard and soft. Hard benefits affect the profit and loss statement directly, but soft benefits do not have the same affect.

Quantify risk: Make sure that the risks are properly evaluated. In most cases, risks are neglected. Also, it would be a good idea to build a risk factor into whatever model is utilized.

Be realistic about benefit periods: Make sure that the expectations are realistic. In the past, corporations have created unrealistic goals for the benefits period by anticipating benefits to come too early and reusing models that reflect the depreciation period for the capital asset.

APPLICATION

BUSINESS FINANCE IN NON-PROFITS

Strategic financial planning is important in all sectors. Having a sound financial planning process is essential to a healthy organization. This section will discuss how a non-profit organization can evaluate its financial position and implement processes to keep them on track.

A social service organization (Strategic financial planning, n.d.) identified four important stages in the financial planning process. These stages are reviewing the past, forecasting the future, setting strategies and plans, and setting annual budgets. Each of these phases is of equal importance and some of the tasks at each phase include:

REVIEWING THE PAST
- Monitor recent trends in demand and expenditure.
- Monitor trends in funding streams.
- Monitor and report on actual performance and outcomes, including end-of-year position and performance against specific performance indicators for social services.
- Collect comparative information about actual costs and cost drivers.
- Review the results and evaluate the recommendations from any external inspection reports and management letters from external auditors (Strategic financial planning, n.d., "Stages of financial planning").

FORECASTING THE FUTURE
- Evaluate the impact of national policies and strategies.
- Identify and estimate levels of the various funding streams.
- Review the impact of local policy initiatives and priorities.
- Determine the future impact of known trends in demand and expenditure.
- Identify the financial implications of demographic trends and other "drivers" of demand which are outside of the control of the council (Strategic financial planning, n.d., "Stages of financial planning").

SETTING STRATEGIES & PLANS
- Take into account the corporate context for strategic planning.
- Link financial planning with service, human resource and asset management planning.
- Collect information on the knowledge and skill base required for effective budget management at all organizational levels.
- Engage all key stakeholders in the strategic financial planning.

SET ANNUAL BUDGETS
- Come to consensus on what the budget process should be.
- Ensure budgets are informed by financial plans.
- Involve budget managers in budget setting.
- Match commitments and expected changes in demand with resources available.
- Respond to unexpected changes.
- Review budget structures.
- Engage with key stakeholders.
- Ensure short term decisions in budget setting do not undermine longer-term priorities and strategies (Strategic financial planning, n.d., "Stages of financial planning").

As the organization goes through the process, key decision makers should determine the types of policies that need to be in effect in order to be successful at each of the individual phases. Although these steps apply to a non-profit organization, the steps are valuable for any type of organization. Therefore, the corporate sector may benefit by comparing and contrasting how each of the sectors operate and discussing what works for both.

VIEWPOINT

STATE CORPORATE TAX DISCLOSURE

One aspect of a business attempting to plan its finances involves the tax structures that are imposed upon it. Some tax professionals and policymakers have been reviewing the state corporate income tax and believe there is a problem with it. "The share of corporate profits in the U.S. collected by state governments via the corporate income tax has fallen sharply in the past quarter century" (Wilson, 2006, p.1). Mazerov (2007) reported that there is data that suggests: "The share of tax revenue supplied by this tax in the 45 states that levy it fell from more than 10 percent in the late 1970s, to less than 9 percent in the late 1980s, to less than 7 percent at the present time; the effective rate at which states tax corporate profits fell from 6.9 percent in the 1981-85 period, to 5.4 percent in 1991-95, to 4.8 percent in 2001-05, and; many state-specific studies have found that most corporations filing income tax returns paid the minimum corporate tax even in years in which the economy was growing strongly" (Mazerov, 2007, p. 1).

- Although there is continuous debate surrounding this information, many in the business community believe that there are organizations that are exploiting the provisions of company income tax mandates that have been enacted (i.e. tax incentives for corporations that make significant financial contributions to the state). However, the policymakers and advocates disagree. This group of individuals believes that corporate tax incentives are not financially efficient and cannot effectively stimulate a positive economic growth. Mazerov (2007) believes that this debate will not be able to reach closure until the states monitor public advertisement of the amount of company income tax that specified businesses pay to certain states. He believes that this type of change would: Help show policymakers and the public whether the corporate income tax is structured in a way that ensures all corporations doing business in the state are paying their fair share of tax. Because of the large number of variables that affect a corporation's tax liability, it is difficult for non-experts to understand the impact of states' tax policy choices. Examples of how these policies actually affect the tax liability of identifiable corporations could be an asset in assisting policymakers and advocates to comprehend the effectiveness and fairness of a state's corporate tax policies.
- Shed light on the effectiveness of tax policies designed to promote economic development. A number of states have enacted corporate tax incentives and/or tax cuts with the aim of creating jobs or encouraging investment in the state. Without the information provided by company-specific tax disclosure, it is difficult to analyze the effectiveness of such policies.
- Stimulate any needed reform of the state's corporate income tax system. Despite the significant

drop in state corporate income taxes in recent decades, very few states have enacted meaningful reforms to address this problem Efforts against this tax shelter have been successful in a number of states, primarily because the public has learned the names of specific well-known corporations that have exploited this shelter. Similarly, corporate tax disclosure could inspire tax reform efforts by encouraging public and policymaker interest in these issues (Mazerov, 2007, p. 1-2).

Essentially, corporate tax disclosure would aid in clarifying the actual results of a state's corporate tax laws and procedures and helps to reform when necessary.

CONCLUSION

In order for organization's to be successful, they must create a strategic plan that will position the firm for growth and competitiveness. The senior management team will need to analyze all data, including the financial records, to ensure that the organization can make a profit, remain competitive and be in a position for continued growth.

Capital budgeting could be the result of purchasing assets that are new for the organization or getting rid of some of the current assets in order to be more efficient. The finance team will be charged with evaluating: Which projects would be good investments; which assets would add value to the current portfolio, and; how much the organization willing to invest into each asset. International capital budgeting refers to when projects are located in host countries other than the home country of the multinational corporation.

Strategic financial planning is important in other sectors. Having a sound financial planning process is essential to a healthy organization. The viewpoint section discussed how a non-profit organization can evaluate its financial position and implement processes in order to keep them on track. A social service organization (Strategic financial planning, n.d.) identified four important stages in the financial planning process. These stages are reviewing the past, forecasting the future, setting strategies and plans, and setting annual budgets.

Some tax professionals and policymakers have been reviewing the state corporate income tax and believe there is a problem with it. "The share of corporate profits in the U.S. collected by state governments via the corporate income tax has fallen sharply in the past quarter century" (Wilson, 2006, p.1). Although there is continuous debate surrounding this information, many in the business community believe that there are organizations that are exploiting the provisions of company income tax laws that have been implemented (i.e. tax incentives for corporations that make large contributions to the state). However, the policymakers and advocates disagree. This group of individuals believes that company tax incentives are not as cost-efficient and do not adequately stimulate economic growth.

BIBLIOGRAPHY

Ang, J., & Lai, T. (1989). A simple rule for multinational capital budgeting. *Global Finance Journal, 1*(1), 71-76. Retrieved July 5, 2007, from EBSCO Online Database Business Source Premier. http://search.ebscohost.com/login.aspx?dir ect=true&d b=buh&AN=6338721&site=bsi-live

Bearing Point (n.d.). Improve your capital budget techniques. Retrieved July 9, 2007, from http://office.microsoft.com/ en-us/help/ HA011553851033.aspx

Bierman, Jr., H. (1980). *Strategic financial planning.* New York, NY: The Free Press.

Booth, L. (1982). Capital budgeting frameworks for the multinational corporation. *Journal of International Business Studies, 13*(2), 113-123.

Brunnermeier, M.K., & Oehmke, M. (2013). The maturity rat race. *Journal of Finance, 68*(2), 483-521. Retrieved November 15, 2013, from EBSCO Online Database Business Source Complete. http://search.ebscohost.com/ login.aspx?direct=true&d b=bth&AN=85938185&site=eh ost-live

Hong, S. (2013). Wheeling and dealing. *Entrepreneur, 41*(5), 76. Retrieved November 15, 2013, from EBSCO Online Database Business Source Complete. http://search.ebscohost.com/ login.aspx?direct=true&db=bth&AN=87079968 &site=ehost-live

Mazerov, M. (2007) State corporate tax disclosure: The next step in corporate tax reform. Retrieved August 10, 2007, from http://www.cbpp.org/2-13-07sfp.pdf

Mina, A., Lahr, H., & Hughes, A. (2013). The demand and supply of external finance for innovative firms. *Industrial & Corporate Change, 22*(4), 869-901. Retrieved November 15, 2013, from EBSCO Online Database Business Source Complete. http://search.ebscohost.com/ login.aspx?direct= true&db=bth&AN=89520165&site=eh ost-live

Shapiro, A. (1978). Capital budgeting for the multinational corporation. *Financial Management (1972), 7*(1), 7-16. Retrieved July 5, 2007, from EBSCO Online Database Business Source Premier. http://search.ebscohost.com/login.aspx?di rect=true&db=buh&AN=5029365&site= bsi-live

Strategic financial planning. (n.d.). *Making Ends Meet.* Retrieved September 3, 2007, from http://www. joint-reviews.gov.uk/money/Financialmgt/1-22. html

Wilson, D. (2006). The mystery of falling state corporate income taxes. *FRBSF Economic Letter, 2006*(35), 1-3. Retrieved August 19, 2007, from EBSCO Online Database Business Source Premier. http:// search.ebscohost.com/login.aspx?direct=true&d b=buh&AN=23637606&site= bsi-live

SUGGESTED READING

Bernhart, M. (2006). Finance and HR: How business gets done. *Employee Benefit News, 20*(15), 18. Retrieved January 4, 2008, from EBSCO Online Database Business Source Premier. http://search. ebscohost.com/login.aspx?di rect=true&db=buh &AN=23201644&site=bsi-live

Financial services used by small businesses: Evidence from the 2003 survey of small business finances. (2006, October 24). *Federal Reserve Bulletin*, A167-A195. Retrieved January 4, 2008, from EBSCO Online Database Business Source Premier. http:// search.ebscohost.com/ login.aspx?direct=true&d b=buh&AN=24429387&site= bsi-live

Put finance at heart of business to succeed. (2006). *Accountancy Ireland, 38*(3), 94. Retrieved January 4, 2008, from EBSCO Online Database Business Source Premier. http:// search.ebscohost.com/login.aspx?direct=tru e&db=buh&AN=21160485&site=bsi-live

—*Marie Gould*

C

CAPITAL MARKETS

ABSTRACT

This article focuses on capital markets and introduces the concepts of stocks and bond markets. Capital markets consist of primary and secondary markets, and are considered a critical factor in American capitalism. There is an exploration of the Capital Asset Pricing Model which compares individual assets and market returns based upon their respective risk and return trade-offs. In closing, there is a discussion of the impact of global capital markets.

OVERVIEW

The success of the financial market is important to citizens worldwide. "We live in a world that is shaped by financial markets and we are profoundly affected by their operation. Our employment prospects, our financial security, our pensions, the stability of the political systems and nature of the society we live in are all greatly influenced by the operations of these markets" (Fenton- O'Creevy, Nicholson, Soane, & Willman, 2005, p. 1–2). If the market is not healthy, there is potential for crises.

Financial markets can be defined in two ways. The term can refer to organizations that facilitate the trade of financial products, or it can refer to the interaction between buyers and sellers to trade financial products. Many who study the field of finance will use both definitions, but economics scholars tend to use the second meaning. Financial markets can be both domestic and international.

"Financial market" can be seen as an economic term because it highlights how individuals buy and sell financial securities, commodities, and other items at low transaction costs and prices that reflect efficient markets. The overall objective of the process is to gather all of the sellers and put them in one place so that they can meet and interact with potential buyers. The goal is to create a process that will make it easy for the two groups to conduct business.

When looking at the concept of "financial markets" from a finance perspective, one could view financial markets as a way to facilitate the process of raising capital, transferring risk, and conducting international trade. The overall objective is to provide an opportunity for those who desire capital to interact with those who have capital. In most cases, a borrower will issue a receipt to the lender as a promise of repayment. These receipts are called securities and can be bought or sold. Lenders expect to be compensated for lending the money. Their compensation tends to be in the form of interest or dividends.

TYPES OF FINANCIAL MARKETS

There are different categories of financial markets, and some of them are:

- **Capital markets** — Capital markets consist of primary and secondary markets and are considered a critical factor in American capitalism. New securities are bought and sold in the primary market, and investors sell their securities in the secondary markets. Companies rely on these markets to raise the funds needed to purchase the equipment required to run the business, conduct research and development, and assist in securing other items needed for the operations of the company.

- **Stock markets** — In order to raise a large amount of cash at one time, public corporations will sell shares of ownership to investors. Investors gain profits when the corporations increase their earnings. Many view the Dow Jones Industrial Average as the stock market, but it is only one of many components. Two other components are the Dow Jones Transportation Average and the Dow Jones Utilities Average. Stocks are traded on world exchanges such as the New York Stock Exchange and NASDAQ.

- **Bond markets** — Bonds are the opposite of stocks. Usually, when stocks go up, bonds go down. The different types of bonds include Treasury Bonds, corporate bonds, and municipal bonds. Mortgage interest rates are affected by bonds.

FINANCIAL MARKET ANALYSIS

When one is analyzing the financial market, he or she has the option of using one of two approaches. Fundamental and technical analyses are two types of analysis, but they have different approaches in terms of whether or not to trade or invest in financial markets. Overall, the process focuses on how to select markets and tools in order to trade or invest and time when it is appropriate to open and close trades or investments in order to maximize returns.

TECHNICAL ANALYSIS

According to Investorwords.com (2009), technical analysis is defined as:

A method in which to evaluate securities by relying on the assumption that market data (i.e. charts of price, volume, and open interest) may assist in predicting future (usually short-term) market trends. Unlike fundamental analysis, the intrinsic value of the security is not considered. Technical analysts believe that they can accurately predict the future price of a stock by looking at its historical prices and other trading variables. Technical analysis makes the assumption that market psychology influences trading in a manner that allows an analyst to predict when a stock will rise or fall. For that reason, many technical analysts are also market timers. Market timers believe that technical analysis can be applied just as easily to the market as a whole as to an individual stock.

FUNDAMENTAL ANALYSIS

According to Investopedia.com (2009), fundamental analysis is defined as:

A method in which to evaluate a security by attempting to measure its intrinsic value by examining related economic, financial, and other qualitative and quantitative factors. Fundamental analysts study those things that may affect the security's value, including macroeconomic factors (i.e. the overall economy and industry conditions) and individually specific factors (i.e. financial condition and management of companies). For example, the goal of fundamental analysis is to identify a value that an investor can compare with the security's current price with

the expectation of determining what position to take with that specific security.

SPECIFIC USES OF EACH APPROACH

Which is better? Both types of analysts have been successful in the designated fields. The "right" answer depends on what the investor is interested in. For example a long-term investor looking for strong companies, growth, and income potential may be interested in the fundamental approach. However, long-term investors who diversify, or spread their investments across multiple organizations in order to minimize risk, or short-term investors waiting for a change in sentiment, may not be overly concerned about a company's current status. These types of investors would probably support the technical approach. Given the strengths of both approaches, many investors tend to find benefits from each type of analysis. Technical analysts can provide information on the broad market and its trends (macro level), whereas, fundamental analysts can assist an investor in determining whether or not an issue has the basics in order to meet the investor's needs (micro level). In order to get a glimpse of the "big picture," it may be beneficial to take the best from both approaches.

APPLICATION

CAPITAL ASSET PRICING MODEL (CAPM)

In order to select investments for a portfolio, modern portfolio theory will use the capital asset pricing model. The capital asset pricing model (CAPM) is utilized to calculate a theoretical price for a potential investment, and illustrates a direct relationship between the returns of the shares and the stock market returns over time. The model compares individual assets and market returns based upon their respective risk and return trade-offs. It can be used to:
- Establish the worth of a company's shares;
- Determine the worth of a company's equity, which accounts for the risk inherent in the company's investments.

There will always be some type of risk associated with an investment portfolio. The degree of risk can fluctuate between industries as well as between companies. A portfolio's risk is divided into two categories — systematic and unsystematic risk. Systematic risk refers to investments that are naturally riskier than others, and unsystematic risk refers to when the amount of risk can be minimized through diversification of the investments.

The table below provides some characteristics of the fundamental and technical approaches to financial analysis.

The CAPM model operates on a set of assumptions such as:

- Due to the risk adverse nature of investors, the model illustrates one period, at the end of which the investor desires to maximize their return (wealth).
- Investors perceive a level playing field in terms of opportunities available to them through investment and returns.

APPROACHES TO FINANCIAL ANALYSIS

Fundamental Approach	Technical Approach
Concerned with why prices will move	Concerned with when prices will move
Rational, cause and effect	Challenging, less risk adverse
Long term	Short and long term
Grains and meats are common markets	Currencies and financials are common markets.
Power of Compounding is helpful. Time is seen as the greatest influence on one's investment portfolio. The power of compounding asserts that an investor can take a small amount of money and watch it grow into a substantial amount over time. Investments have the ability to increase in value over time. As time goes by, the value becomes greater. However, this can only occur if the investors continues reinvest the returns.	Stock Market Volatility is helpful. Volatility can be described "in terms of points and percentages. Percentage volatility reflects percent-age changes in the value of the amount invested. It is therefore useful to talk about percentage changes to discuss the change in a given inves-tor's wealth or in the change in wealth invested in the market, or in the economy as a whole. As a market's base level increases, the point volatility could increase while the percentage volatility could decrease" (Mullins, 2000).
Longer term investing with mutual fund managers like Peter Lynch or John Bogle.	Day Trading is buying and selling stock, options or other trading positions in the same trading day.
Make money out of your stake in companies and how their products or services sell	Make money out of movement from the market, with each movement often measured in pennies.
How traders see investors – mature nurturer.	How investors see traders - risk taker.
Many take this path when the investor has a desire to grow rich slowly. However, depending on how the portfolio is set up; growth can actually be achieved quicker than expected. The approach often involves the "buy and hold" and longer term investing strategies.	The investor relies heavily on market timing rules. This type of investor may participate in a get rich quickly scheme; work on his/her own terms and tends to make quick deci-sions that may not be well thought out. Unfortunately, this type of investor may lose everything if they do not know what they are doing.

- Asset returns can be assumed to distribute along a normal distribution curve.
- Risk free assets are available at a risk free rate and can be borrowed or lent out by investors in unlimited amounts.
- Assets are available in a defined amount; the quantities of assets remain a part of the one period model.
- Pricing of assets occurs in a perfectly competitive market where they are perfectly divisible.
- Information within asset markets is free and readily available to all investors.
- Taxes, regulations, and restrictions do not exist on short selling ("CAPM," 2008).

In addition, the CAPM model includes the following propositions:
- "Investors in shares require a return in excess of the risk free rate, to compensate for the systematic risk;
- Investors should not require a premium for unsystematic risk because it can be diversified away by holding a wide portfolio of investments;
- Since systematic risk varies between companies, investors will require a higher return from shares in those companies where the systematic risk is greater" ("Session 9," n.d.).

The same propositions can be applied to capital investment by companies:
- "Companies expect a return on a project to exceed the risk free rate so that they can be compensated for the systematic risk;
- Unsystematic risk can be diversified away, which implies that a premium for unsystematic risk is not required;
- Companies should strive for a bigger return on projects when the systematic risk is greater" ("Session 9," n.d.).

VIEWPOINT

GLOBAL CAPITAL MARKETS

Litvack (2006) has been quoted as saying that "emerging market companies still lag behind in corporate governance. However, their success in developing businesses outside their home countries and their need to tap global capital markets is forcing them to devote more attention to their rules" (p.

158). Given the growth of the emerging markets, many investors will be attracted to worldwide opportunities. Venture capitalists are particularly attracted to this type of investment. Some venture capitalists specialize in assisting companies when they have reached a point where financing is necessary to expand the business into emerging markets.

VENTURE CAPITAL

Venture capital is usually available for a product or idea that may be risky but has a high potential of yielding above-average profits. Funds are invested in ventures that have not been discovered. The money may come fro individuals, government sponsored Small Business Investment Corporations (SBICs), insurance companies, and corporations. It is more difficult to obtain financing from venture capitalists. A company must provide a formal proposal such as a business plan so that the venture capitalist may conduct a thorough evaluation of the company's records. Venture capitalists only approve a small percentage of the proposals that they receive.

Funding may be invested throughout the company's life cycle, with funding being provided at both the beginning and later stages of growth. Venture capitalists may invest at different stages. Some firms may invest before the idea has been fully developed while others may provide funding during the early stages of the company's life. At other times, as mentioned above, venture capitalists aid an existing business in expanding into emerging markets.

VENTURE CAPITALISTS & COMPANY INPUT

As a result of the high stakes involved with the amount of money being invested and the risk factor, emerging market companies are being challenged to respond to the concerns and questions from their stakeholders, such as venture capitalists. There have been requests to respond to issues such as "weak and unaccountable board of directors, inadequate internal controls, widespread corruption, and opaque ownership structures and transactions" (Litvack, 2006, p. 158). According to Litvack (2006), companies can address these issues by dealing with the following issues:
- The Role of the Board

Many boards are selected based on their ability to champion the position of the current leadership of an organization. Therefore, boards tend not to be a separate entity of the organization. In order to resolve this issue, it may be in the organization's best interest to hold annual elections for board members.

- The Audit Committee

Many emerging market corporations have complex ownership structures, which results in many intertwined transactions. These types of activities must be closely monitored in order to avoid the perception of inappropriate and unethical transactions taking place. There needs to be a check and balance process in place. Therefore, it is crucial that each board of directors entity has an audit committee to validate that the organization is operating ethically.

- Corruption

It is believed that corruption is rampant in emerging market corporations. Therefore, there has to be an attempt to clean up this image. In order to combat corruption, corporations have (1) enacted stricter anti-bribery laws, (2) become tougher when enforcing national and international anti-bribery laws, and (3) required sound corporate governance and business ethics.

- The Laws of the Market

Shareholders become concerned when the local laws and enforcement do not move quickly in order to eliminate corruption. However, laws such as the Foreign Corrupt Practices Act and the Sarbanes-Oxley Act force organizations to be in compliance and allow them to secure funding.

- Corporate Political Influence

It has been suggested that corporate influence and shareholder money has been used to shape public policy, especially in the United States. However, the F&C Asset Management has published a standard of good practice that is designed to keep emerging market companies in compliance. One of the recommendations is that donations to individual political candidates and parties should be avoided. Even when this cannot be validated, following these practices encourages organizations to disclose the information and seek shareholder approval before making a donation.

CONCLUSION

Financial markets can be defined in two ways. The term can refer to organizations that facilitate the trade of financial products, or it can refer to the interaction between buyers and sellers to trade financial products. Many who study the field of finance will use both definitions, but economics scholars tend to use the second meaning. Financial markets can be both domestic and international.

Capital markets consist of primary and secondary markets and are considered a critical factor in American capitalism. The primary market consists of newly created securities, while the secondary market consists of securities that are being sold by investors. Companies rely on these markets to raise the funds needed to purchase the equipment required to run the business, conduct research and development, and assist in securing other items needed for the operations of the company.

The capital asset pricing model (CAPM) is utilized to calculate a theoretical price for a potential investment, and illustrates a direct relationship between the returns of the shares and the stock market returns over time. The model compares individual assets and market returns based upon their respective risk and return trade-offs. It can be used to (1) establish the worth of a company's shares and (2) determine the worth of a company's equity, which accounts for the risk inherent in the company's investments.

Litvack (2006) has been quoted as saying that "emerging market companies still lag behind in corporate governance. However, their success in developing businesses outside their home countries and their need to tap global capital markets is forcing them to devote more attention to their rules" (p. 158). Given the growth of the emerging markets, many investors will be attracted to worldwide opportunities.

BIBLIOGRAPHY

Capital asset pricing model. (2009). Retrieved February 25, 2009, from http://www.investorwords. com/1953/ financial%5fmarket.html

CAPM — Capital asset pricing model. (2008). Retrieved February 25, 2009, from Value Based Management.net. http://www.valuebasedmanagement.net/methods%5fcapm. html

Clark, C. E., & Newell, S. (2013). Institutional work and complicit decoupling across the U.S. capital markets: The work of rating agencies. *Business Ethics Quarterly, 23*(1), 7–36. Retrieved December 2, 2013, from EBSCO Online Database Business Source Complete. http://search.ebscohost.com/login.aspx?direct=true&db=bth&AN=85891629

Fenton-O'Creevy, M., Nicholson, N., Soane, E., & Willman, P. (2005). *Traders: Risks, decisions, and management in financial markets.* Oxford: Oxford University Press.

Financial markets. (2009). Retrieved February 25, 2009, from http://www.investorwords.com/1953/financial%5fmarket. html

Fundamental analysis. (2009). Retrieved February 25, 2009, from http://www.investopedia.com/terms/f/fundamentalanalysis.asp

Glaser, M., Lopez-de-Silanes, F., & Sautner, Z. (2013). Opening the black box: Internal capital markets and managerial power. *Journal of Finance, 68*(4), 1577–1631. Retrieved December 2, 2013, from EBSCO Online Database Business Source Complete. http://search.ebscohost.com/login.aspx?direct=true&db=bth&AN=89079590

Litvack, K. (2006). Emerging markets clean up their act. *Euromoney, 37*(442), 158–160. Retrieved February 25, 2009, from EBSCO Online Database Business Source Complete. http://search.ebscohost.com/login.aspx?direct=true&db=bth&AN=20004075&site=ehost-live

Liu, J. (2013). Fixed investment, liquidity, and access to capital markets: New evidence. *International Review of Financial Analysis, 29* 189–201. Retrieved December 2, 2013, from EBSCO Online Database Business Source Complete. http://search.ebscohost.com/login.aspx?direct=true&db=bth&AN=89898255

Market capitalization. (2009). Retrieved February 25, 2009, from http://www.investorwords.com/2969/market%5fcapitalization.html

Mullins, G.E. (2000). Stock market volatility: Measures and results. *Central Wisconsin Economic Research Bureau.* Retrieved March 25, 2009, from http://www.uwsp.edu/business/cwerb/3rdQtr00/SpecialReportQtr3%5f00.htm

Session 9: Capital asset pricing model (CAPM). (n.d.) Transport financial analysis. Retrieved February 26, 2009, from NetTOM. http://cbdd.wsu.edu/kewlcontent/cdoutput/tom505/page42.htm

Talati, J. (2002, January). Fundamental vs. technical analysis. Retrieved February 25, 2009, from http://www.allbusiness.com/sales/sales-forecasting-market-demand/105511-1. html

Technical analysis (2009). Retrieved February 25, 2009, from http://www.investorwords.com/4925/technical%5fanalysis. html

Venture capitalist (2009). Retrieved February 25, 2009, from http://www.investorwords.com/6722/venture%5fcapitalist. html

SUGGESTED READING

Brown, C. & Davis, K. (2009). Capital management in mutual financial institutions. *Journal of Banking and Finance, 33*(3), 443-455. Retrieved February 26, 2009, from EBSCO Online Database Business Source Complete. http://search.ebscohost.com/login.aspx?direct=true&db=bth&AN=36016189&site=ehost-live

Curtis, C.E. (2009). The new risk management tool kit. *Securities Industry News, 21*(3), 7–11. Retrieved February 26, 2009, from EBSCO Online Database Business Source Complete. http://search.ebscohost.com/login.aspx?direct=true&db=bth&AN=36459819&site=ehost-live

Dorr, D. (2007). Longevity trading: Bridging the gap between the insurance markets and the capital markets. *Journal of Structured Finance, 13*(2), 50–53. Retrieved February 26, 2009, from EBSCO Online Database Business Source Premier. http://search.ebscohost.com/login.aspx?direct=true&db=bth&AN=26133667&site=ehost-live

Hodnett, K., & Heng-Hsing, H. (2012). Capital market theories: Market efficiency versus investor prospects. *International Business & Economics Research Journal, 11*(8), 849–862. Retrieved December 2, 2013, from EBSCO Online Database Business Source Complete. http://search.ebscohost.com/login.aspx?direct=true&db=bth&AN=79567434

Kumar, P. & Langberg, N. (2009). Corporate fraud and investment distortions in efficient capital markets. *RAND Journal of Economics, 40*(1), 144–172. Retrieved February 26, 2009, from EBSCO Online Database Business Source Complete. http://search.ebscohost.com/login.aspx?direct=true&db=bth&AN=36141828&site=ehost-live

Parlour, C. A., Stanton, R., & Walden, J. (2012). Financial flexibility, bank capital flows, and asset prices. *Journal of Finance, 67*(5), 1685–1722. Retrieved December 2, 2013, from EBSCO Online Database Business Source Complete. http://search.ebscohost.com/login.aspx?direct=true&db=bth&AN=79958366

—Marie Gould

CASH & MARKETABLE SECURITIES

ABSTRACT

This article will explain cash and marketable securities and will describe how these assets function in corporate finance analysis. The article will identify the common types of cash accounts and will explain how corporations control the flow of cash to regulate their financial needs. It will also describe the various types of marketable securities, including treasury bills, commercial paper, bankers' acceptances and other forms of money market securities. In addition, discussions of the common reasons why corporations hold marketable securities are provided, such as to earn higher rates of interest than cash accounts, to take advantage of the liquidity in the short-term investment market and because marketable securities require minimal ongoing managerial oversight. Finally, the article will describe how corporations and financial analysts report and use cash and marketable securities in common business activities, such as in creating accurate balance sheets, meeting accounting and financial reporting requirements and building liquid reserves in anticipation of a significant financial transaction.

OVERVIEW

Cash and marketable securities are current, liquid assets that companies may use for a variety of reasons, such as to pay its business obligations, to support its viability during a period of reduced sales or an economic downturn or to earn interest for a short period of time before being used for a significant acquisition. Like most people, many companies prefer to keep a reserve of cash and marketable securities on hand that can easily be sold for cash to cover unanticipated expenses or losses. While cash is readily available legal tender, marketable securities are short-term investments that are routinely sold on exchanges, have a readily determined fair market value and can be converted into cash at any time. The most common types of marketable securities are commercial paper, banker's acceptances, Treasury bills and other money market instruments.

Cash and marketable securities are considered current assets on a firm's balance sheet. The balance sheet is a type of financial statement that shows a company's overall financial position at a given moment in time. Companies typically create a balance sheet at the end of their fiscal year to get an accurate depiction of their financial standing. A balance sheet always lists a company's assets and liabilities, and these are usually displayed side by side in two separate columns: assets in one column and liabilities and shareholders' equity in the other. Under the assets column, the balance sheet lists the firm's current assets in order of their liquidity, beginning with those that are most easily converted into cash within the accounting cycle, which is typically one year. Current assets include cash and marketable securities as well as other types of assets. Thus, using balance sheet entries, companies routinely account for their cash and marketable securities holdings in order to keep an accurate depiction of their monetary position at any point in time. The following sections provide a more in-depth explanation of cash and marketable securities and the role that they play in corporate finance and accounting.

UNDERSTANDING CASH

CASH ACCOUNTS

The most common types of cash accounts are general cash accounts and other corporate accounts, such as payroll accounts, petty cash accounts and bank branch accounts. Corporations hold cash in these accounts for several reasons. The most common reason is to meet payment obligations that arise in the ordinary course of business. Another reason is so that a company has readily available assets that it can use to take advantage of temporary opportunities for investment or the purchase of a significant acquisition. A third reason companies keep cash is to maintain a cushion or buffer to meet any unexpected financial needs that may arise in the event of periodic losses or an economic downturn.

While cash accounts are relatively simple for a company to maintain, companies must also effectively manage the flow of cash that moves into and out of its accounts. For instance, when a company has received payments or experiences an inflow of cash, it must select the best investment or savings account to hold the cash, balancing its short-term and long-term need for readily available cash against the higher returns that are often available from investment options the cash could purchase. In addition, companies must also regulate the collection and distribution of cash payments using procedures that are in its best interest while being ethical and building rapport with its vendors so that it can maximize its financial position at any given point in time. To do so, a company may emphasize prompt collection of cash receipts so to ensure a steady inflow of finances while adopting disbursement methods that slow down its cash payouts to minimize the outflow of company resources. The procedures are described in more detail below.

EXPEDITING CASH RECEIPTS

No matter what its strategy for managing its assets and liabilities, a company must still regulate and report its cash accounts to conform with accounting and financial reporting requirements that are set by generally accepted accounting principles and government regulations. However, there are several techniques that companies can use to enhance the rate at which they send invoices and collect receipts so that their inflow of cash is enhanced. These techniques include expediting the preparation and mailing of company invoices, automating the billing and payment cycle, sending invoices with shipments or faxing invoices with prompt payment due dates and establishing a system of preauthorized debits so that a payor's funds are transferred to the company electronically.

A preauthorized debit is a transfer of funds from a payor's bank account on a specified date to the payee's bank account whereby the payor provides advance authorization for the payee to initiate the transfer when payment is due. This system can be set up so that a payor provides a payee with advance authorization for routine transfers of funds, generally for a specified amount on a specified date, and for a finite period of time or until the payor's financial obligation is fulfilled. Automated payments are a particularly advantageous means by which companies may expedite cash receipts because they minimize the time and expense that is required when an employee would otherwise have to create invoices, mail the invoices (perhaps at the company's expense), credit payments received to individual customer accounts and monitor delinquent accounts for collection efforts.

The reason companies seek to implement policies that will expedite the collection of their cash receipts is to enhance the inflow of corporate cash, which affords a company the possibility of greater returns if it invests its increased cash reserves in interest-bearing accounts or securities. By expediting and automating the process of receiving cash receipts while minimizing company expenses involved in collecting payments, a company may maximize its inflow of cash receipts so that it can use these resources for purposes that are most advantageous to its stability and growth.

HARNESSING CASH PAYOUTS

Another way that a company can enhance its cash resources is to slow down the rate at which it pays its outstanding debts. This process is sometimes referred to as "playing the float," which means that a company will attempt to extend the float, or the time period between the date it makes a payment and the date the payment is debited from its account, so that it is able to draw interest on its funds as long as possible. One way a company may harness its cash payouts is by minimizing its accounts payable into a fewer number of accounts so as to reduce the number of its disbursements. Another method is to use forms of payment that delay the time in which the payee's account is credited with funds from the company's account. For instance, a company may use payable through draft instruments, which are drawn against the payor and not against a bank, as are checks. After the payee presents a payable through draft instrument to a bank for deposit, the payor may still determine whether to honor or refuse the payment, which slows down the time it takes for a payee to receive the funds and increases the time in which the company has control of the funds. In addition, a company may use a remote disbursement method, in which the firm directs checks to be drawn on a bank that is geographically remote from its customer so as to maximize the time it will take for its check to clear. For instance, a California business may pay an Illinois supplier with a check drawn on a bank in Delaware. The supplier must wait until the Delaware bank clears the check in order for the funds to be credited to its account. Finally, a company may also use controlled disbursements, in which the company directs checks to be drawn on a bank that can provide it with notification each morning of the total dollar amount of checks that will be presented against its account later that day so that the company may more accurately predict its total disbursements on a day-to-day basis.

CASH ACCOUNTING PROCEDURES

While companies may use different methodologies to control the inflow and outflow of corporate cash, companies must still comply with proper accounting procedures and governmental regulations regarding corporate finance reporting. Companies must set up proper cash management procedures to ensure that all cash receipts and payments have been promptly and accurately deposited and recorded so that their financial statements remain correct and current. In addition, companies must consider how best to hold and invest cash reserves so that their financial well-being and growth objectives are considered along with the interests of their shareholders, if they are publicly owned. Most companies maintain cash balances that are adequate to meet their financial needs but not excessive, as extra cash can be used to invest in securities and other investments that typically pay higher interest rates than most savings accounts, where cash is typically held.

UNDERSTANDING MARKETABLE SECURITIES

Marketable securities are highly liquid, short-term securities that tend to have maturity dates of less than one year. Companies invest in marketable securities to recoup relatively higher interest rates while retaining the convenience of being able to easily convert these securities into cash should the need arise. Marketable securities are listed as a current asset on a balance sheet. Examples of marketable securities include commercial paper, banker's acceptances and Treasury bills. In addition, marketable securities can include money market instruments such as repurchase agreements, which are agreements to buy securities and resell them at a higher price at a later date; federal agency securities, which are debt securities issued by federal agencies and government-sponsored enterprises and money market preferred stock, or preferred stock that has a dividend rate that is reset at auction every 49 days.

The following sections describe the most common forms of marketable securities in more detail.

TREASURY BILLS

Treasury bills, often referred to as "T-bills," are short-term debt obligations that are backed by the U.S. government and have a maturity date of less than one year. T-bills are sold in denominations of $1,000 and usually have maturities of four weeks, 13 weeks (about three months) or 26 weeks (about six months). T-bills are issued through a competitive bidding process and are sold at a discount and redeemed at maturity for full face value. This means that investors who purchase T-bills do not receive fixed interest payments while holding the bills, but instead receive the appreciation of the T-bill when the U.S. government pays back its IOU on the T-bills' maturity date. For example, if an investor buys a 13-week Treasury bill priced at a discount at $980, the U.S. government essentially writes an IOU promising to pay back the investor $1,000 in three months. The investor does not receive any dividend payments during the time the T-bill is held. Instead, the investor receives the T-bill's appreciation ($20), or the difference between the discounted value she originally paid for the bill ($980) and the amount she receives back at its maturity ($1,000). The interest rate of a T-bill can be determined by dividing its appreciation by its discounted purchase price. For instance, if a T-bill appreciates by $20 during the three months it is held by an investor, who purchased the bill at a discounted rate of $980, the interest rate of the T-bill is 2% over three months ($20/$980 = 2%).

Treasury bills differ from Treasury notes and Treasury bonds. The differences among these three forms of government securities lie in the length of their maturity, the types of returns holders receive and the purposes for which these securities are held. Treasury notes are medium-term debt securities of the U.S. Treasury that have a fixed interest rate, a maturity period of one to ten years and pay interest every six months until maturity. Treasury bonds are long-term obligations of the U.S. Treasury that also have a fixed interest rate, but have a maturity period of more than 10 years and pay interest semiannually until maturity. Treasury notes and bonds are also issued with a minimum denomination of $1,000, and are considered some of the safest mid- to long-term investment options. Thus, unlike Treasury bills, which pay no direct interest but are bought at a discount and sold at full value, Treasury notes and Treasury bonds do pay interest at a fixed interest rate until their maturity date.

Every week, the Treasury Department auctions off new Treasury bills of varying maturities, ranging from one month to one year, with three-month and six-month T-bills being the most common. T-bills are considered very safe investments because they are backed by the full faith and credit of the U.S. Treasury. Because Treasury bills are short-term, low risk investments that are highly liquid, they are one of the most common forms of marketable securities. Companies invest in T-bills as a safe way to invest cash reserves for short periods of time.

Commercial Paper

Commercial paper is an unsecured, short-term promissory note that is issued by a corporation, typically for the purpose of meeting short-term liabilities. Commercial paper is an unsecured IOU that is not supported by any tangible collateral. Instead, it is a promise issued by a corporation that it will pay the holder a sum of money within a relatively short period of time. The maturity date on commercial paper rarely exceeds nine months, or 270 days, and is commonly set at 30 to 90 days. These debt securities are usually issued at a discount that typically tracks current market interest rates rather than paying a fixed interest rate. Hence, instead of the issuing corporation paying interest on the instrument while it is held, the holder receives the face value of the paper upon redemption, which is greater than its purchase price. Commercial paper is most commonly purchased by large corporations with temporary surpluses of cash and issued by other commercial entities. By purchasing commercial paper, corporations are able to use their cash reserves to lend money to other commercial firms in return for IOUs that will mature with a higher return than the corporation might have received by depositing its funds into a bank savings account. However, because commercial paper is not usually backed by any collateral, only large corporations with high credit ratings are considered sufficiently safe entities to attract buyers to purchase their unsecured promissory notes at a discount rate.

Bankers' Acceptances

Bankers' acceptances are short-term investments that are promissory notes created by a company and guaranteed by a bank. When a bank "accepts" these instruments, the company promises to pay the bank the value of the bill and the bank promises to pay the holder the face amount at maturity. Bankers' acceptances are typically used when a company that is in

need of short-term financing signs an order, or instruction to pay a set amount of money at a set date in the future to the bank. The order functions much like a postdated check. If a bank accepts the order, it agrees to pay the amount of the order to its holder, and thus the bank becomes liable for the acceptance and its creditworthiness, not the original company's, determines the risk of the acceptance. The bank can then simply hold the acceptance or sell it in the money markets. While a bank does not have to sell a bankers' acceptance, if it does do so, the acceptances are sold at a discount from their face value. This means that the bank sells the acceptances for less than their face value, and when the maturity date is reached, the company pays the issuing bank the value of the acceptance and the bank pays the ultimate holder of the acceptance its face value.

Bankers' acceptances can be a way for new companies with a good relationship with a bank, but with minimal credit established with its vendors, to purchase goods using the bank's credit rating instead its own. Because there is some risk, banks usually only accept orders from companies with which they have a satisfactory track record and banks charge a fee for their acceptance of the liability.

Money Market Instruments

The money market is the securities market that deals in short-term borrowing and lending of monetary instruments. Securities traded in the money market mature in 13 months or less. The money market should be contrasted with the capital market, where medium-term and long-term instruments and credits are traded. Trading in money markets takes place between banks in such money centers as New York, London, Chicago, Frankfurt, Hong Kong, Sydney and Mumbai.

Money market instruments are forms of debt that are traded in the money markets and that are highly liquid and mature in less than one year. Money market instruments include bankers' acceptances, commercial paper and Treasury bills, which are described above. However, other common money market instruments include the following:

- Certificates of Deposit: A time deposit with a specific maturity date shown on the certificate.
- Eurodollar Deposit: A deposit made in U.S. dollars at a bank or bank branch located outside the United States.

- Federal Agency Short-Term Securities: Short-term securities issued by government-sponsored agencies or enterprises such as the Farm Credit System, the Federal Home Loan Banks and the Federal National Mortgage Association.
- Municipal Notes: Short-term notes issued by municipalities in anticipation of tax receipts or other revenues.
- Repurchase Agreements: Short-term loans — normally for less than two weeks and frequently for one day — arranged by selling securities to an investor with an agreement to repurchase them at a fixed price on a fixed date.
- Money Market Mutual Funds: Pooled funds consisting of short-term, high quality investments that are used to buy money market securities on behalf of retail or institutional investors.

Although money markets trade both in the U.S. and around the world, the basic function of this market is to connect companies with surplus short-term funds that are is willing to lend their funds at an interest with companies that need to borrow short-term credit at an interest. Buyers and sellers are connected through middlemen, who facilitate the transaction for a profit. Thus, money markets allow for the rapid transfer of cash and marketable securities between buyers and sellers, who purchase and sell securities according to their individual needs and objectives.

COLLATERAL MARKETS

Collateral markets came under scrutiny after the crash of AIG in 2008. These markets allow investors in the assets markets to finance short positions, that is, hedging. In a collateral market transaction, cash from a securities-backed transaction is used as collateral and reinvested rather than held. Aggresive investment of cash collateral may give rise to high-risk activity, especially where agent compensation is tied to returns but not losses. Nevertheless, collateral markets are an essential component of the asset markets, in particular the trading of Treasury bills and mortgage-backed securities.

REASONS CORPORATIONS HOLD MARKETABLE SECURITIES

There are several reasons why corporations hold marketable securities. One reason is so that they can put a short-term surplus of cash to use and earn a higher interest rate than possible through collecting interest on a savings account. Another reason is that marketable securities are highly liquid, so companies can invest in these securities while retaining the confidence that they can be quickly converted back to cash if companies face a sudden need for funds. Also, marketable securities are an attractive investment option for companies because they require minimal management. These factors are discussed in more detail below.

INCREASED INTEREST EARNINGS

When marketable securities appear on a company's financial statement such as a balance sheet, they are listed as a current asset and they generally indicate that the company has made a short-term investment of its excess cash. Marketable securities typically earn a higher rate of return than banks pay for savings accounts, where companies generally hold cash reserves. This is because marketable securities may receive interest and dividend payments before their maturity date and may appreciate in value so that they may be sold for more than their purchase price. These benefits, coupled with the fact that marketable securities tend to be safe, low risk investments means that companies can use their cash reserves to invest in marketable securities and create even greater returns on their surplus with minimal risk of loss.

LIQUIDITY OF SECURITIES MARKET

The securities market is usually quite liquid, meaning marketable securities can quickly and easily be converted, or sold for cash. Marketable securities, such as Treasury bills, bonds or stocks, are routinely and actively traded and thus have a reliable market value. When a company lists securities on its balance sheet, the securities are properly classified as marketable securities when the company can readily convert them into cash and it intends to do so when it needs additional cash resources. If either of these two tests for marketable securities does not apply, then the securities are considered to be investment in securities. Investment in securities differ from marketable securities in that investment in securities are securities held for long-term goals and are classified as long-term assets by a company, while marketable securities are held as a temporary investment are classified as current assets. The long-term nature of investment in securities results in these securities being generally less liquid. Thus, companies are less likely to hold investment in securities because they cannot be readily converted into cash, and more likely to hold marketable securities because of their liquidity.

EASE OF MANAGEMENT OF INVESTMENTS

Management of marketable securities does not require ongoing operational decisions. Generally, a company simply holds marketable securities as a short-term investment, and thus the only decision that must be made regarding their administration is whether and when to buy or sell these securities. Once the decision is made to convert marketable securities into cash, this can be readily accomplished because of their liquidity, and the company can then use the cash as it sees fit.

APPLICATIONS

HOW CORPORATIONS REPORT AND USE CASH AND MARKETABLE SECURITIES

CREATING ACCURATE BALANCE SHEETS

A balance sheet is the financial statement that reports the assets, liabilities and net worth of a company at a specific point in time. Assets represent the total resources of a company, which may shrink or increase depending on the results of operations. Assets are listed in the order of their liquidity, or the ease with which they may be converted into cash. Not only do companies distinguish between assets and liabilities, they further divide these two classifications into two categories: current and noncurrent.

Current assets, which are assets that can be convertible to cash within a year, include cash, accounts receivable, notes receivable, inventory, fixed assets and other miscellaneous assets. Cash refers to cash on hand or in banks, checking account balances, and other instruments such as checks or money orders. Marketable securities include Treasury bills, commercial paper, bankers' acceptances and other types of money market securities. Accounts receivable indicate sales made and billed to customers on credit terms, such as when a retailer lists its customer charge accounts that have been billed but are unpaid. Notes receivable represent a variety of obligations with terms coming due within a year, such as a

retailer with an entry for merchandise sold on installment terms. Inventory is a list of goods and materials, or those goods and materials themselves, held available in stock by a business. Fixed assets are materials, goods, services and land used in the production of a company's goods, such as real estate, buildings, plant equipment, tools and machinery. Noncurrent assets are items a corporation cannot easily turn into cash and does not consume within a year, such as investments or advances to and receivable from a subsidiary company.

Liabilities represent what a company owes. Current liabilities are obligations that a business must pay within a year on a set of dates for recurring liabilities or on a specific date for one-time obligations, usually within 30 to 90 days of the purpose for which they arose. In order to meet their current liabilities, most companies keep sufficient cash reserves readily available to pay these obligations on time for a period of several months. The most common current liabilities listed on a company's balance sheet are accounts and notes payable, bank loans and other miscellaneous debts. Accounts payable represent merchandise and other materials that a company has purchased on credit but has not paid in full by the date of the balance sheet. Notes payable represent amounts that a company has borrowed from other companies or individuals. Other current liabilities may include wages and salaries that are due employees for time between the last payday and the date of the balance sheet, as well as taxes and other expense that are unpaid at the time the balance sheet is prepared. Noncurrent liabilities, also called long-term liabilities, are items that mature in excess of one year from the balance sheet date. Maturity dates, or the date that the payment is due, on these liabilities may run up to 20 or more years, as with a real estate mortgage.

The reason that companies create balance sheets is to get a clear indication of their financial standing at a particular point in time. Balance sheets are often created at the end of the year to establish the total inflow and outflow of resources within a company as well as to determine the net worth of a company's owners or founders. Each item on the balance sheet plays an important role in determining the true financial state of a company, and this is why even short-term assets, such as cash and marketable securities, are always included on a company's balance sheet.

MEETING ACCOUNTING REQUIREMENTS

Companies must record any cash and marketable securities they hold, both for internal audit purposes and to comply with governmental financial reporting requirements, according to generally accepted accounting principles. Marketable securities are initially recorded by a company in its financial records at their acquisition cost, which includes the purchase price plus any commissions, taxes or other costs related to the acquisition of the security. However, the market value of these securities may rise or fall while they are held by a company. This results in a holding gain or loss that is not due to the normal operations of a firm. These gains or losses must be indicated on a company's financial records, as the purpose of balance sheets and other financial statements is to reflect an accurate estimation of the company's economic worth.

Accounting procedures regarding marketable securities can be complicated in that a company must decide whether to report these instruments at their acquisition cost or at market value, and if at market value, whether to report the changes as part of any period's income or to record the gain or loss in income in the period in which the company sells the securities. If a company decides to determine the valuation of marketable securities after their acquisition, these securities will fall into three different classifications. Debt held to maturity are debt securities that a company intends to hold for their full term, or until the securities mature. Trading securities are debt or equity securities a company intends to use in generating trading profits, and it is assumed these securities are held for short-term profit. Securities available for sale are debt or equity securities that are neither "trading" nor "held-to-maturity." They are securities that companies typically hold for a specific cash need, such as when a manufacturing firm builds a large fund of securities to pay for a renovation to its plant or to retire bonds that will come due.

Companies want to report their assets in a way that places their financial standing at that particular point in time in the best possible light, and this desire must be counterbalanced by the need of investors and corporate oversight bodies to have a true and fair indication of a company's financial assets and liabilities. Thus, companies must consider how to report the holdings of their assets, including cash and marketable securities, in a way that is most advantageous to them while being ethical and in compliance with the relevant accounting principles and governmental requirements.

HOLDING RESERVES FOR FINANCIAL TRANSACTIONS

Companies may hold cash and marketable securities in reserve to pay for significant transactions, such as a major purchase. For instance, a company may decide to build its reserves of liquid assets in anticipation of the purchase of land or a building. The company may decide to shift some long-term assets to more liquid assets, and thus may convert some of its assets to marketable securities. Marketable securities are attractive to companies that anticipate a significant outflow of cash because these securities generally pay a higher interest rate than cash savings accounts and yet are highly liquid so that they can be sold for cash in a very short period of time. Marketable securities allow a company to continue to earn interest on its pool of reserves without the entanglement of a long-term investment. In addition, most marketable securities, such as Treasury bills, are considered to be very safe, low-risk investments, which further enhances their viability as a top option for companies that are holding reserves of cash and liquid assets in anticipation of a significant financial transaction.

During the financial crisis following the crash of 2008, companies slowed or froze cash investments in development and expansion and "stockpiled" their cash reserves. New technologies and the Internet, however, allowed for real-time supply chain transactions. This more efficient approach cut banks out of the process, in many cases, and companies were able to use their own idle cash reserves to purchase their own receivables.

CONCLUSION

Cash and marketable securities represent the most common forms of a company's current assets. Companies keep cash reserves to pay for sudden expenses or to keep them viable during periods of financial losses. Businesses control their cash flow to regulate their financial needs by expediting their cash receipts and slowing down their disbursements. Companies hold marketable securities to receive a higher rate of return on these investments while taking advantage of the liquidity in the securities market and the fact that marketable securities require minimal ongoing management oversight. The most common forms of marketable securities held by companies include treasury bills, commercial paper, bankers' acceptances and other types of money market securities. Companies and financial analysts deal with marketable securities in many common business activities, such as creating accurate balance sheets, meeting accounting and financial reporting requirements and pooling reserves of cash and marketable securities to pay for a major financial transaction.

BIBLIOGRAPHY

Anselmo, J. (2005). All that dough. *Aviation Week & Space Technology, 162*(13), 44-45. Retrieved April 23, 2007, from EBSCO Online Database Business Source Complete. http://search.ebscohost.com/login.aspx?direct=t rue&db=bth&AN=16619782&site=ehost-live

Banerjee, S., & Graveline, J.J. (2013). The cost of short-selling liquid securities. *Journal of Finance, 68*(2), 637- 664. Retrieved October 31, 2013, from EBSCO Online Database Business Source Complete. http://search.ebscohost.com/login.aspx?direct=true&db=bth&AN=85938182&site=ehost-live

Billett, M. & Garfinkel, J. (2004). Financial flexibility and the cost of external finance for U.S. bank holding companies. *Journal of Money, Credit & Banking, 36*(5), 827-958. Retrieved April 23, 2007, from EBSCO Business Source Complete. http://search.ebscohost.com/login.aspx?direct=t rue&db=bth&AN=14427956&site=ehost-live

Brace, R. (2012). The stars align. *Global Finance, 26*(11), 56. Retrieved October 31, 2013, from EBSCO Online Database Business Source Complete. http://search.ebscohost.com/login.aspx?direct=true&db=bth&AN=83388223&site=ehost-live

Fink, R. (2004). Too much cash. *CFO, 20*(10), 34-40. Retrieved April 23, 2007, from EBSCO Online Database Business Source Complete. http://search.ebscohost.com/ login.aspx?direct=true&db=bth&AN=14023028&site=ch ost-live

Garbade, K. & Ingber, J. (2005). The treasury auction process: Objectives, structure, and recent adaptations. *Current Issues in Economics & Finance, 11*(2), 1-11. Retrieved April 23, 2007, from EBSCO Online Database Business Source Complete. http://

search.ebscohost.com/login.aspx? direct=true&db=bth&AN=16302944&site=ehost-live

Holliday, K. (2005). Low rates = tough challenge. *Financial Executive, 21*(2), 52-54. Retrieved April 23, 2007, from EBSCO Online Database Business Source Complete. http://search.ebscohost.com/login.aspx?direct=true&db=bth&AN=16284827&site=ehost-live

Keane, F.M. (2013). Securities loans collateralized by cash: Reinvestment risk, run risk, and incentive issues. *Current Issues in Economics & Finance, 19*(3), 1-8. Retrieved October 31, 2013, from EBSCO Online Database Business Source Complete. http://search.ebscohost.com/login.aspx? direct=true&db=bth&AN=88300302&site=ehost-live

Miller, G. (2005). Accounting for marketable securities and the "recycling" of income. In *Harvard Business School Cases.* (pp. 1-5). Retrieved April 23, 2007, from EBSCO Online Database Business Source Complete. http://search. ebscohost.com/login.aspx?direct=true&db=bth&AN=24090137&site=ehost-live

O'Connell, J. (2005). Liquid assets. In *Blackwell Encyclopedic Dictionary of International Management.* (p. 1). Retrieved April 23, 2007, from EBSCO Online Database Business Source Complete. http://search.ebscohost.com/login.aspx? direct=true&db=bth&AN=20987313&site=ehost-live

Pinkowitz, L., Williamson, R. & Stulz, R. (2007). Cash holdings, dividend policy, and corporate governance: A cross-country analysis. *Journal of Applied Corporate Finance, 19*(1), 81-87. Retrieved April 23, 2007, from EBSCO Online Database Business Source Complete. http://search. ebscohost.com/login.aspx?direct=true&db=bth&AN=9003848&site=ehost-live

Weiss, J. (2004). Analysis and implementation. *Miller GAAP Update Service.* 4(1)2-8. Retrieved April 23, 2007, from EBSCO Online Database Business Source Complete. http://search.ebscohost.com/login.aspx?direct=true&db=bth&AN=12029052&site=ehost-live

SUGGESTED READING

Berg, A. (2006). Money's sordid tale of dirty floats, debasement and doom. *Futures: News, Analysis & Strategies for Futures, Options & Derivatives Traders, 35*(11), 72-74. Retrieved April 23, 2007, from EBSCO Online Database Business Source

Complete. http://search.ebscohost.com/ login.aspx?direct=true&db=bth&AN=22191681&site=ehost-live

O'Brien, E. (2005). Audit details N.Y. health corp. losses. *Bond Buyer, 353*(32210), 1- 40. Retrieved April 23, 2007, from EBSCO Online Database Business Source Complete. http://search.ebscohost.com/login.aspx?direct=true&db=bth&AN=18154574&site=ehost-live

Schadewald, M. (2006). Apportionment issues: Redemptions of short-term marketable securities: The Microsoft case. *Journal of State Taxation, 25*(1), 9-51. Retrieved April 23, 2007, from EBSCO Online Database Business Source Complete. http://search.ebscohost.com/login.aspx?direct=t rue&db=bth&AN=23858882&site=ehost-live

–Heather Newton

CASH FLOW

ABSTRACT

This essay covers important topics related to the management of cash flow within companies. Cash is defined as currency in corporate accounts, short term investments or commercial paper that's easily convertible to cash. A steady cash flow enables a business to pay its employees and vendors and to invest in new projects and opportunities. Companies face many risks associated with running out of cash; without a ready supply of cash, businesses cannot replay loans, provide goods and services to customers or invest in future growth opportunities. Businesses are required to file a statement of cash flow as outlined by the Financial Accounting Standard's Board Statement of Cash Flow (FASB statement 95). Trends in cash management are evolving to meet the opportunities offered by global markets and to mitigate risks associated with cash shortfalls. Emerging topics in cash management include more active methods of forecasting company cash flow. Other factors that will impact cash management forecasting include: Improved technology, centralization of corporate forecasting, tighter regulatory controls, and new statistical techniques for cash flow analysis.

OVERVIEW

Without the proper accounting of cash flow intake and outflow over time, businesses would be operating at great risk of coming up short on liquid capital. Having a tally of cash on-hand, what's coming in (accounts receivable) and what's going out (accounts payable), allows a business to meet expenses and plan future operations. Depending upon the size and complexity of the business operation, a firm is likely to want to project future cash flow in the short-term (12 months) or long-term (5-10 years). Small business with limited access to credit may find that they must forecast cash flow needs for a number of weeks or months. In all cases, cash flow management requires planning and projections into the future and should take into account reasonable risks that might cause a company to fall short of cash.

HISTORY OF BUSINESS CASH FLOW REPORTING

Originally, businesses were required to file a statement of changes in financial position, or a funds statement. In 1961, Accounting Research Study No. 2, sponsored by the American Institute of Certified Public Accountants (AICPA), recommended that a funds statement be included with the income statement and balance sheet in annual reports to shareholders.

By 1963, the Accounting Principles Board (APB) had issued its Opinion No. 3 as a guideline to help with preparation of the funds statement. While the funds statement was not mandatory for many, businesses saw its value and began to use it regularly. In 1971, Opinion No. 19 (Reporting Changes in Financial Position), also issued by the APB designated the funds statement as one of the three primary financial documents required in annual reports to shareholders. The APB also said a funds statement must be covered by the auditor's report, but did not specify a particular format for the funds statement. That flexibility came to an end in late 1987, with the Financial Accounting Standards Board's (FASB) issuance of Statement No. 95, which called for a statement of cash flows to replace the more general funds statement. Additionally, the FASB, in an effort to help investors and creditors better predict future cash flow, specified a universal statement format that highlighted cash flow from operating, investing, and financing activities. This format is still used today (Managing Your Cash Flow, 2005).

Cash flow statements provide essential information to company owners, shareholders and investors and provide an overview of the status of cash flow at a given point in time. Cash flow management is an ongoing process that ties the forecasting of cash flow to strategic goals and objectives of an organization.

This article outlines some of the most common strategies, challenges and issues related to managing cash flow. Issues and challenges include: Maintaining good customer and vendor relations while managing accounts payable and receivable, and paying close attention to the time lag between cash inflows and outflows.

The newest trends in cash management forecasting are also covered in detail. Current methods of forecasting cash flow typically involve the use of regression techniques which don't take into account many business operational variables. This essay details some of the current trends in cash flow forecasting that involve improved computer applications, new statistical methods, the centralization of the forecasting function and other significant developments.

APPLICATIONS

FASB STATEMENT 95

FASB Statement 95 *Statement of Cash Flows* governs the format of a business's reporting of cash flow. Statement 95 encourages enterprises to report cash flows from operating activities directly by showing major classes of operating cash receipts and payments (the direct method). Enterprises that choose not to show operating cash receipts and payments are required to report the same amount of net cash flow from operating activities indirectly by adjusting net income to reconcile it to net cash flow from operating activities (the indirect or reconciliation method) (FASB, 2007).

The following are cash flow measurements required by the FASB:

- Cash Flow Statements: The cash flow statement acts as a kind of corporate checkbook that reconciles the other two statements. Simply put, the cash flow statement records the company's cash transactions (the inflows and outflows) during the given period.
- Cash Flow from Operating Expenses: Measures the cash used or provided by a company's normal operations. It shows the company's ability to generate consistently positive cash flow from operations. Think of "normal operations" as the core business of the company.
- Cash Flows from Investing Activities: Lists all the cash used or provided by the purchase and sales of income-producing assets.
- Cash Flows from Financing Activities: Measures the flow of cash between a firm and its owners and creditors. Negative numbers can mean the company is servicing debt but can also mean the company is making dividend payments and stock repurchases (Essentials of Cash Flow, 2005).

Cash flow from investment and financing activities are fairly straightforward as outlined by Statement 95. However, Statement 95 allows businesses to report using one of two different methods when it comes to reporting cash flows generated or consumed by operations: The direct method and the indirect method.

- The direct method reports inflows of cash (e.g., from sales) and cash outflows for payment of expenses (e.g., purchases of inventory).
- The indirect method which begins with the net income number, a mixture of cash (e.g., cash proceeds from sales) and non-cash components (e.g., depreciation) and removes non-cash or accrual items, then adjusts for the cash effects of transactions not yet reflected in the income statement (e.g., cash payments for inventory not yet sold).

However, only the direct method reports actual sources and amounts of cash inflows and outflows; the information investors need to understand to evaluate the liquidity, solvency, and long-term viability of a company.

Although the standards generally allow managers to select either method for reporting cash flows, the overwhelming majority have chosen to use the indirect method; the approach that provides the least useful information for investment decisions (Direct-versus Indirect-Method Reporting for Cash Flows, 2007).

CURRENT CHALLENGES TO COMPANIES MANAGING CASH FLOW

According to Brian Hamilton, CEO of Sageworks, "Businesses don't fail because they are unprofitable; they fail because they get crushed on the accounts receivable side" (Feldman, 2005).Companies that run short on cash have to use credit cards or lines of credit to fund operations and pay bills. Lack of cash can cause damage to relationships with vendors and banks result in missed market opportunities, and an overall hit to a company's reputation. Running short of cash can result from poor forecasting, unforeseen risks and poor internal management of cash flow. One of the biggest reasons that businesses run short on cash has to do with unrealistic expectations about how quickly cash will come in the door.

Companies need to be realistic about the length of time it will take to get paid — if one assumes payment in 30 days and it takes 60 days to get the cash, then adjustments to "cash in hand" figures need to be made. Corporations are becoming slower to pay vendors; companies want to make more of their cash which means that they are holding on to it longer. Many businesses are also revising their payables to 45-60 days instead of the previous standard of 30 days (Feldman, 2005).

The lag between the time you have to pay suppliers and employees and the time you collect from customers is the problem. The solution is cash flow management and the idea is to delay outlays of cash as long as possible, while encouraging those who owe you to pay quickly.

Creating a cash flow projection is a preemptive action that is meant to alert a business owner or management to the possibility of a cash crunch before it strikes. Projecting cash flow is not a difficult undertaking, but it does require that accurate and timely information regarding payables and receivables be documented. The following information needs to be considered:

- Customer payment history;
- Assessment of upcoming expenditures;
- Patience of vendors (terms of payment);
- Assume that receivables will arrive at a non-constant rate.

Once the above points have been considered, as accurate a figure for cash inflow and outflow as possible should be calculated.

Gather cash inflow information from salespeople, service representatives, collections, credit workers and your finance department. In all cases, you'll be asking the same question: How much cash in the form of customer payments, interest earnings, service fees, partial collections of bad debts, and other sources are we going to get in, and when? (How to Better Manage Your Cash Flow, 2003).

Gather cash outflow information. Have a line item on your projection for every significant outlay, including rent, inventory (when purchased for cash), salaries and wages, sales and other taxes withheld or payable, benefits paid, equipment purchased for cash, professional fees, utilities, office supplies, debt payments, advertising, vehicle and equipment maintenance and fuel, and cash dividends (How to Better Manage Your Cash Flow, 2003).

STRATEGIES

There's no question that in today's business environment, cash flow management must be a required company activity. Cash flow management means more than tracking where your dollars are, it also requires working with vendors, partners and bankers to insure that cash is always on hand.

- Set up a line of credit before you need it. Banks are not the only source of credit. Sometimes a company's suppliers are more vested in a company's viability than the bank and may extend payment terms to mitigate a cash shortfall.
- Ask your best customers to accelerate payments and offer a discount if they pay quickly.
- Ask your worst customers to pay and ask them often; offer steep discounts if they are willing to pay up.
- In many cases, negotiated agreements can be worked out with vendors; vendors are managing their cash flow too.
- Consolidate vendors and negotiate more favorable terms — this strategy will allow a company to hold on to working capital longer.

ISSUES

This article has reviewed some of the challenges that face businesses in managing cash flow. Organizations, both large and small, are becoming adept in cash management practices through better accounting of cash and improved customer and vendor management tactics. The global business landscape demands even greater levels of diligence in tracking company cash flow through cash flow management forecasting. The benefits of deliberate and well planned cash management forecasting cannot be overstated.

BENEFITS OF FORECASTING

Precise forecasting can help companies guarantee payments to suppliers on specific dates, allowing a company to secure better credit terms. Another benefit from cash flow forecasting is a firm's ability to optimize working capital. By tightening up payment plans and investment activities, many companies are actually able to minimize the amount of cash they need on hand. Good forecasters are adept at "extracting" cash from operations and improving cash flow. Cash management is about knowing where cash is and when it will be needed. If cash is not going to be needed right away, a savvy forecaster may be able to move cash from one investment area to another and thus create value through higher returns-while still maintaining access to the liquid funds. Another benefit to cash management involves debt. Covenants or restrictions on debt financing often require that a minimum cash balance be maintained. Violations of the covenant could lead to higher interest rates, penalties and loan terminations. Overall, good cash management can help to improve or maintain a company's financial reputation.

NEW TECHNOLOGY

Spreadsheets have been the predominant cash flow management tool for many years. Analysis of data accuracy on spreadsheets and the analysis reveals that financial data on spreadsheets is highly prone to error. Errors in reporting of company financial information sound alarm bells and makes those who are responsible for corporate compliance very nervous. Large organizations (typically early adopters of new technology) are moving to integrated financial databases such as Treasury Information Systems (TIS). Though the cost of implementation can be significant, improved efficiency and data sharing is a big benefit. Information systems can be shared across networks with multiple users accessing secure information which also makes them a superior choice to spreadsheets. Another option is a web-based treasury module that is incorporated within an ERP

(Enterprise Resource Planning) system. Properly integrated treasury functions within an enterprise system can track: Account balances and transactions, cash positions, fund transfers, short-term investments and cash flow forecasts.

CENTRALIZED FORECASTING

Most cash flow management to-date has been handled at a local business unit level, with each division handling cash management in their own way. The past few years have seen a significant rise in the trend toward centralized cash flow forecasting. The benefits are numerous; from a staffing stand point, it is possible to consolidate cash management personnel from across an enterprise to one central area which cuts down on personnel costs. Increased uniformity and standardization of methodologies is another benefit to centralizing cash management analysis and management. Decentralized reporting of cash flow and forecasting was often completed orally within departments. There has also been a lack of incentive for local divisions to report into a central unit, with many operating in silos. As forecasting becomes a more centralized function, companies will initiate benchmarks to monitor locally provided data and eventually will be used across units to provide incentive to managers to provide accurate and timely data for central forecasting.

COMPLIANCE

The requirements of Sarbanes-Oxley (SOX) compliance have generated more and better financial data for forecasting. The generation of more detailed and timely cash flow information was a somewhat unexpected benefit of increased compliance and regulatory laws. Compliance added significantly to the cost of tracking corporate financial data, but the careful monitoring and greater visibility of cash flow for treasury personnel has also been a windfall for increasing the accuracy of forecasting. Treasury Information Systems are becoming an essential tool for storing the growing volume of financial data. Cash flow management data can be extracted out of overall financial data, and be shared more easily. Information systems for tracking company financial data have allowed access by senior managers to data that was formerly hard to access. Integrated financial information systems allow easy access to company financial data for strategic planning purposes.

NEW STATISTICAL & ECONOMIC ANALYSES

Most firms, to date, have used basic regression techniques to model cash flow forecasting. Regression is a useful model, but makes the assumption that the firm's business won't change over time (Germaise, 2007).

A more flexible and accurate approach to cash flow forecasting is the project-level forecast. This method forecasts cash flow patterns by project which are modeled separately rather than lumped together and reported as a firm-wide forecast. This method has the following advantages:

- Good method for modeling a small number of large projects.
- Good for modeling a changing mix of projects.
- Reveals the impact that larger projects might have on cash flow-this impact can be significant and varies by project.

Once all projects have been modeled, start dates can be estimated and project totals generated to provide a firm-wide forecast as well as the individual-by project.

Driver-based cash flow modeling is acknowledged to be the best forecasting strategy available. Driver-based models model are designed to link central business decisions and risks to financial forecasts. Business drivers are being widely used across organizations to link operational strategy with functional areas such as performance management, sales and finance. Driver-based forecasting for cash flow moved away from a purely financial model and incorporates variables that drive business.

The three main types of drivers that affect cash flow forecasting are:

- Internal: New products, new marketing strategies, expansion. Senior managers can use this information to assess if firm has financial resources to undertake internal initiatives.
- External: Factors outside firm's control such as regulatory changes or competitor price cut.
- External Macroeconomic: Also outside of firm's control such as recession, inflation, increased transportation costs.

CASH FLOW AT RISK (CFaR)

Cash Flow at Risk (CFaR) is defined as the likelihood that a firm will run out of cash. CFaR is just one of the modeling scenarios that define an entire universe of corporate risk and predict the chance of severe shock in an organization. The CFaR model is focused on the likelihood of risk of a disastrous event that could specifically impact cash flow. CFaR is modeled after the Value at Risk tool that is often used by financial firms to assess risk to their overall portfolios. This model can be used successfully by non-financial firms to predict the likelihood of a liquidity crisis.

PRIVATE EQUITY & FIRM DEBT

Firms financed by private equity (PE) deals as leveraged buy-outs (LBOs) typically carry a very heavy debt burden, with as much as 60%-80% debt financing. These firms are required to make substantial interest payments and even a small liquidity crunch can spell disaster for a company holding this much debt. Cash flow forecasts keep buyers informed of cash flow risk scenarios. The accuracy of cash flow models in this case is absolutely imperative for buyers to make informed decisions about risk. Multiple cash flow outcome methods should be run to insure that none is overly optimistic or pessimistic; both potentially to making financial decisions. PE managers state that accurate forecasting; along with openness to investors, are the most critical factors in managing cash flow in an LBO. It is a good idea to run cash flow models in times of economic expansion and not wait until an economic downturn; the term "forecast" implies that these models are most useful in predicting future events.

PAYMENT SYSTEMS

Several of the trends in cash flow forecasting favor the use of electronic payments and payment cards over checks. Many companies manage cash flow on very tight schedules by holding onto cash as long as possible and encouraging customers to pay quickly. This method helps to keep a maximum of cash on hand. Being able to move funds electronically in and out of cash accounts helps firms stay on top of cash flow.

Some of the benefits are obvious and listed below:

- More timely and predictable schedule;
- More secure transactions;
- Allow for more precise forecasting;
- Can strengthen relationships between vendors/customer by allowing them to manage their own cash flows better.

CONCLUSION

This paper has discussed many issues related to tracking, managing and reporting business cash flow. All companies are required to submit a statement of cash flow as part of their required financial statement. FASB Statement 95 provides guidelines for reporting cash flow. A Business's *Statement of Cash Flow* reports cash flow in three areas: Business operations, financial activities and investing. Businesses are managing their cash flow very carefully these days. Careful management of accounts receivable and payables is essential in keeping cash on hand. Companies are negotiating better terms with vendors while creating incentives to get customers to pay up.

Businesses operate in global markets and are often open for business 24/7. Cash management forecasting is an essential function within large multinational organizations. Some best practices for cash management forecasting include:

- Technological innovation. Systems move toward an integrated TIS (treasury information system) or ERP.
- Employ driver-based forecasting; simulations or regressions.
- Payment methods. Integrate electronic payment system with customer and supplier accounts.
- Focus treasury staff's attention on analysis of cash flow variability not just data collection.
- Incorporate forecasting into operational planning. Larger firms are doing a better job and a gap is widening between large and S/M enterprises.

GENERAL FORMAT FOR A STATEMENT OF CASH FLOW

Cash provided (or used) by:	
Operating activities	$XXX
Investing activities	$XXX
Financing activities	$XXX
Net increase (decrease) in cash and cash equivalents	$XXX
Cash and cash equivalents at beginning of year	$XXX
Cash and cash equivalents at end of year	$XXX

Cash shortfalls can be very costly to an organization. Firms that are debt-laden can easily become financially constrained and default on debt payments. Projects may be delayed and new business opportunities can be missed because there's no cash to fund them. Securing emergency lines of credit are expensive; a line of credit should be set in a time when there is no cash crunch. Lastly, having a steady, adequate and predictable cash flow is the best protection against business insolvency and failure.

BIBLIOGRAPHY

Call, A. C., Chen, S., & Tong, Y. H. (2013). Are analysts' cash flow forecasts naïve extensions of their own earnings forecasts? *Contemporary Accounting Research, 30*(2), 438-465. Retrieved November 15, 2013, from EBSCO Online Database Business Source Complete. http://search. ebscohost. com/login.aspx?direct=true&db=bth&AN=8815 5561&site=ehost-live

CFA Institute. (2007). Direct- versus indirect-method reporting for cash flows. Retrieved September 27, 2007, from http://www.aimrpubs.org/centre/positions/reporting/ direct%5fvs%5findirect.html

Dasgupta, S., Noe, T. H., & Wang, Z. (2011). Where did all the dollars go? the effect of cash flows on capital and asset structure. *Journal of Financial & Quantitative Analysis, 46*(5), 1259-1294. Retrieved November 15, 2013, from EBSCO Online Database Business Source Complete. http://search. ebscohost.com/login.aspx?direct=true&db=bt h&AN=67547639&site=ehost-live

The essentials of cash flow. (2005, July 15). Investopedia. Retrieved September 24, 2007, from http:// www.investopedia.com/articles/01/110701.asp

Feldman, A. (2005, December). Cash flow crunch. *Inc.com.* Retrieved September 24, 2007, from http://www.inc.com/ magazine/20051201/handson-finance.html

Garmaise, M. (2007, September). Optimize business performance through cash flow management. *Visa Commercial.* Retrieved September 24, 2007, from http://www.corporate.visa.com/md/dl/documents/downloads/ CashFlowForecasting.pdf?src=sym

Hales, J., & Orpurt, S. F. (2013). A review of academic research on the reporting of cash flows from operations. *Accounting Horizons, 27*(3), 539-578. Retrieved November 15, 2013, from EBSCO Online Database Business Source Complete. http://

search.ebscohost.com/login.aspx?direct=t rue&d
b=bth&AN=90327375&site=ehost-live

How to better manage your cash flow. (2003, December 11). *Entrepreneur.com*. Retrieved September
24, 2007, from http://www.entrepreneur.com/
money/moneymanagement/ managingcashflow/
article66008.html

Managing your cash flow. (2005). *Virtual Advisor*. Retrieved September 24, 2007, from http://www.va-
interactive.com/ inbusiness/editorial/finance/
ibt/cash%5fflow.htmlWengroff, J. (2001, June 1).
Cash management: Forecasting the flow. *CFO.com*.
Retrieved September 27, 2007, from http://www.
cfo.com/article.cfm/2996251

SUGGESTED READING

Kagan, P. (2006). Cable kings of cash flow. *Cable-
FAX's CableWORLD, 18*(25), 14-14. Retrieved
September 24, 2007, from EBSCO Online
Database Business Source Premier. http://

search.ebscohost.com/login.aspx?direct=tru
e&db=buh&AN=23327569&site=ehost-live

Kintzele, P. (1990, February). Implementing SFAS
95, statement of cash flows. *The CPA Journal*. Retrieved September 27, 2007, from http://www.nys-
scpa.org/cpajournal/old/08209170.htm

Krell, E. (2003). BPM accelerates as short-
term forecasting slows. *Business Finance*. Retrieved September 27, 2007, from http://
www.bfmag.com/magazine/archives/article.
html?articleID=13962&pg=1

Weiss, N., & Yang, J. (2007). The cash flow statement: Problems with the current rules. *CPA
Journal, 77*(3), 26-31. Retrieved September
24, 2007, from EBSCO Online Database Business Source Premier. http://search. ebscohost.
com/login.aspx?direct=true&db=buh&AN=243
10856&site=ehost-live

—Carolyn Sprague

COMMON STOCK

ABSTRACT

This article will explain the financial security of
common stock. The overview provides an introduction
to the characteristics of common stock. These characteristics include the rights of common stockholders,
dividend priority of a common stock shares, the role
of common stockholders in corporate governance and
the liability of common stockholder. In addition, other
concepts that relate to factors that can affect the growth
in value of common stock are explained, including
supply and demand, earnings and market volatility.
Explanations of corporate financial dealings in which
the issuance or dividend payment of common stock
shares is an important consideration, such as long-term
financing, capital appreciation and liquidation, are included to help illustrate the ways that a corporation's
board of directors, investors and shareholders make financial decisions about their common stock holdings.

OVERVIEW

Corporations are a form of business ownership in
which the legal entity is created under state law so
that it exists as a distinct enterprise from its owners.
Once formed, corporations are generally managed
by a board of directors, which elects officers to perform the day-to-day duties necessary to run the company. The articles of incorporation that are filed with
the formation of the corporation typically set out the
business purpose of the corporation. This statement
of the business purpose may be specific, or it may
simply allow the corporation to perform any lawful
business. However, once the corporation is operative,
it is ready to do business and grow successfully.

While some corporations may be financially
self-sustaining, most companies need an influx of
working capital at some point in order to grow in
profitability. Some companies may need initial start-
up funds to begin their operations. Other companies
may be financially solvent for a period, only to arrive
at a point where additional financing will be necessary to survive a time of reduced profits or to underwrite the purchase of major equipment to expand its
operations.

Whatever the reason, a steady flow of profits and
capital is the lifeblood of corporations. When a corporation faces the prospect of acquiring additional

capital, the board of directors must decide what type of financing will be necessary to enable the corporation to profit and thrive. Most companies must choose between short-term financing and long-term financing options when weighing their cash flow needs against their corporate growth objectives. Short-term financing and long-term financing serve different purposes. Corporations typically choose short-term financing options to cover a periodic loss of funds or a sudden surge in expenses, such as when companies borrow funds to purchase a large quantity of goods in anticipation of a seasonal demand for the item. Short-term financing, then, is the best option for a corporation that needs to borrow funds to cover sudden expenses when an inflow of cash is anticipated at some future date that will enable the company to repay the funds in a relatively short amount of time. Most short-term borrowing is done with the help of financial intermediaries, such as banks, finance companies and money market funds. Sometimes, however, corporations need a more substantial inflow of cash to finance the company's significant costs or future growth objectives. In this situation, most companies must look to long-term financing options to meet their fiscal needs. Long-term financing may be necessary to subsidize marketing and other supportive functions in order to generate more substantial future sales or to purchase more efficient equipment or finance ongoing research and development projects. Long-term financing is generated either from internal cash flow or from external sources of funds. As the company grows, it will generate income and it can spend, save or invest this income to generate internal cash flow. However, these internal sources of funds generally are insufficient to cover all of the long-term investments required by a company. Thus, corporations must look to external sources of funds to subsidize its more significant growth objectives.

Most long-term external financing is generated when a company issues stocks or bonds. If a firm decides to issue stocks to finance its long-term financing needs, it must then decide which types of stock it will issue. The most typical types of stocks are common stock and preferred stock. When a corporation is considering issuing stocks to generate long-term financing, the central question that the corporation must address is the likelihood of its ability to generate future earnings, which will be translated into dividends to common stockholders and capital appreciation. The greater the company's ability to assure potential investors of its growth opportunities, the better its chances of selling its stock to investors.

The following sections provide a more in-depth explanation of these concepts.

BASIC FINANCIAL CONCEPTS

Every corporation must finance its operations. Corporations typically generate long-term financing through external sources of funds, including stocks and bonds. The most common types of stock are common stock and preferred stock. Common stock carries certain rights and limitations that investors must understand before becoming shareholders in a corporation. This section provides an overview of the basic characteristics, privileges and limitations of common stock.

CHARACTERISTICS OF COMMON STOCK

Common stock shares are traditionally conceived as ownership or equity interests in the corporation, so that the body of common shareholders is the corporation's owners. Stock is sometimes referred to as shares, securities or equity. The more shares you own, the larger the portion of the company (and profits) you own. The majority of stock is issued by corporations is common stock. The other type of shares that the public can hold in a corporation are known as preferred stock.

BASIC RIGHTS OF COMMON STOCKHOLDERS

When investors purchase shares of common stock, they are purchasing a security that represents ownership in a company. This ownership gives common stockholders some basic rights. The following sections will explain the fundamental rights of shareholders, including holders of common stock.

CORPORATE OWNERSHIP

Shareholders, also called stockholders, are essentially part owners of any company in which they have invested by purchasing shares, or stock. A stock, represented by a stock certificate, is a share in the ownership of a company, and thus in the ownership of the company's assets and earnings. An investor's ownership in a company depends on the percentage of the company's total stock she owns. An investor who purchases 10 shares out of the 1,000 shares that a corporation issues would probably be a minor owner and thus would have a relatively small say in company policy. However, an investor who purchased 300 shares would own a much larger share of the company and thus would likely be a more influential decision maker on the future of the company's growth. Corporate ownership is beneficial because it allows investors to participate in steering the direction of a company and it allows investors to profit as the company grows through the increase in the value of their shares and through the distribution of any corporate dividends. Dividend distribution will be discussed in more detail in the next section.

PARTICIPATION IN DIVIDEND DISTRIBUTION
When a company grows and makes money, the management of the company can do one of two things with the profit: they can reinvest the profit back into the firm to give the company extra cash for use on new equipment or some other type of venture, or the money can be paid out to the corporation's shareholders in the form of a dividend. Thus, as a company grows and builds its earnings, stockholders are entitled to participate in the distribution of corporate earnings, called dividends. However, corporations do not have to pay dividends, and thus common stockholders are not guaranteed an annual distribution. While many corporations do pay dividends, they are distributed only upon the approval of the corporation's board of directors, which also sets the amount of dividends. In addition, common stock has a lower priority than the claims of a corporation's creditors and other forms of stock. Thus, even if a distribution is approved, there may not be sufficient corporate funds for distribution to all common stockholders. However, when a corporation is growing and profitable and its board of directors approves the distribution of dividends, common stockholders can receive a return on their investment in the company stock in the form of dividends.

VOTING POWER
While at first glance, common stock may seem to be a less than ideal investment, common stockholders may protect their investment and exercise some control over the direction of a company's growth through their voting power. The voting rights of investors are typically determined by one vote per share. Shareholders may exercise their voting power

by electing a board of directors. The board of directors sets corporate policy and hires managers to run the firm. In addition, common stockholders may vote on important corporate matters, including any proposals that would effect fundamental changes on the company, such as mergers or liquidation. Shareholders vote on these issues at the company's annual meeting. If shareholders are unable to attend the annual meeting in person, they may choose to vote by proxies, which allow someone else to vote at the meeting, or by mailing in their vote.

LIMITED PRIORITY
The principle of absolute priority of a security establishes rules that dictate each place in line that a company's creditors or investors have for the distribution of dividends or the collection of assets in the event of a corporate default and liquidation. While common shareholders are considered owners of a company, the priority of common stock is beneath the claims of a company's creditors and the holders of other forms of corporate securities. This means that if a company liquidates, the creditors get the first chance to settle their debts from a company's assets during the insolvency proceedings. After the creditors, the holders of other types of corporate securities, including bondholders and preferred shareholders, are next in line. Only once these debts are settled may common shareholders look to recover their investment from what remains of a company's liquidated assets.

In addition to the rules of absolute priority, there are other rights that govern the distribution of dividends for each class of shareholder. For example, usually a company's charter states that preferred stockholders must receive dividends before common stockholders. Thus, while common stock generally yields higher returns over the long term than almost every other investment by means of capital growth, this higher return comes at a cost because common stocks entail the most risk. If a company goes bankrupt and liquidates, the common shareholders will not receive money until the creditors, bondholders and preferred shareholders are paid.

LIMITED LIABILITY
While common stockholders do face limited priority in dividend distribution and in insolvency proceedings, their liability is limited in that owners of stock are not personally liable if the company becomes insolvent.

While some business entities, such as partnerships, allow for creditors to look to the personal assets of partners to recover the partnership's expenses, an important characteristic of corporate ownership as a stockholder is that the most a shareholder could lose is the value of his original investment in a company. Thus, even if a stockholder owns a significant percentage of shares in a corporation, a company creditor could never seek to pursue a stockholder's personal assets to settle a corporate debt. And, if a company ultimately goes bankrupt, shareholders never face losing their personal assets along with their business assets. Limited liability, therefore, means that stockholders are not responsible for the corporate debts and their maximum loss would be their original investment.

PREEMPTIVE RIGHTS

Some corporate investors choose to buy a significant percentage of a company's shares so that they posses a stronger voting power. However, their power could be undermined if the corporation simply issued more stock as it grew and profited, thus diluting the ownership percentage of current shareholders. To prevent this from happening, shareholders generally possess the right to buy new shares of stock before others so that they can maintain the same proportion of ownership they originally had. This is known as their preemptive right. Today, the preemptive rights of shareholders, if they exist, are typically expressed in the articles of incorporation that are filed when a corporation is formed.

TRANSFER AUTHORITY

In addition to preemptive rights, stockholders also possess the ability to transfer ownership of their shares to another investor. Basically, this allows investors to trade stocks on an exchange. The right to transfer ownership may not seem to be an important feature of stock, but the ease with which securities such as common stock can be bought and sold, also known as their liquidity, is one of the primary reasons for their popularity. Liquidity means that investors can buy and sell investments within minutes rather than having their money tied up in investments such as equipment or land that may take weeks or months to sell.

Originally, when a shareholder bought or sold a share, the shareholder had to physically transfer the stock certificates, which represent the number of shares the stockholder owned, to a broker. But with the advent of online trading, stocks are traded over the Internet without any actual transfer of documents. Thus, since most stockholders do not actually retain stock certificates, the certificates are held in an electronic format by brokerage firms. This is known as holding shares "in street name." This allows shares to be bought and sold on exchanges without the physical presence of either the seller or the buyer.

SHAREHOLDER LAWSUITS

Shareholders may not only assert power over a corporation through their election of the board of directors and voting rights, shareholders may also enforce a corporation's lawful cause of action through a derivative action. In a derivative action, a shareholder is essentially enforcing the rights of the corporation where the directors have not done so, and any recovery gained from such an action goes back to the corporation, not the shareholder. However, before a shareholder may commence a derivative action, the shareholder must first make a written demand that the corporation or its directors take suitable action. This action may arise where the interests of the board of directors and shareholders diverge, although such an action may only proceed if doing so would be in the best interest of the corporation.

ISSUANCE OF CORPORATE SECURITIES

CORPORATE FINANCING

While purchasing shares of common stock is a popular investment vehicle for many investors who are looking to expand their financial portfolios, the question may arise as to why a company would even sell stock in the first place. By doing so, the company's original owners must share profits and decision-making authority with many different people.

The primary reason why companies issue stock is to create equity. To raise money for future expansion, a company must either finance its growth objectives through debt financing or equity financing. A company can generate debt financing by borrowing a loan from a commercial bank or by issuing bonds, in which the issuer of the debt is obligated to repay both the debt principal plus any interest when the bond matures. Bonds are considered a safer investment than stocks because investors are guaranteed repayment of their original investment plus interest. On the other hand, a company may seek to create equity financing by issuing shares of stock. A corporation must surrender some of its control to shareholders, who become owners in the company by purchasing shares, but companies are often willing to make this concession because the dividends on stocks are not required and, when paid, come only out of the company's earnings. Thus, corporations may choose to issue common stocks to generate funds for their growth objectives while minimizing their repayment obligations.

Initial Public Offerings

Once a company decides to issue stock, the first sale of a stock, which is issued by the private company itself, is called the initial public offering ("IPO"). At this point, a determination must be made as to the price that the new stock can be sold. Corporate boards of directors and investors can look to organized exchanges for the quoted price of shares of similarly situated companies, or even of competitors. For an IPO to be most profitable, the shares should be issued in favorable market conditions. The ideal condition for the issuance of new shares is a rising market. This is because in an expanding market, investors are optimistic and thus more likely to invest in new offerings whose value has not been tested over time.

Once a company has decided on the timing of the issuance, the number of shares that a firm will issue must be settled. The number of shares in any issuance is generally a function of the amount of money that the company wants to finance and the price per share of each new stock. In addition, the company may issue enough additional shares to cover the floatation costs that will be owed to the investment bank that issues the new shares. When trying to determine the pricing of new common stock, there are often competing interests at work. For instance, the issuing company will try to set the price as high as possible to maximize its profits, while the investment firm that is underwriting the IPO will want to offer more moderately priced shares to attract more investors. Thus, in many IPOs, the initial shares that the corporation issues are sold quickly and rise in value as demand for further shares increases. This creates an influx of capital for the corporation, both in the form of equity from the sale of shares and from the overall increase in value of the corporation's outstanding shares.

Classes of Stock

The elements of common stock, and other forms of corporate securities such as preferred stock and debt, are sometimes disassembled and re-combined to design other, newer types of corporate securities. For example, preferred stock is often issued in several classes, such as cumulative, non-cumulative, convertible or participating preferred stock. Similarly, common stock may be issued in classes as well, such as when corporations issue classified common stock in Class A and Class B designations. When there is more than one class of stock, the classes are traditionally designated as Class A and Class B.

Corporations issue classes of stock to control the voting, dividend or liquidation rights of each class of stock. A corporation may issue a class of shares with the fewest number of votes attached to it to the public, while reserving the class with the largest number of votes per share for the owners. This allows the corporation's management to retain a stronger hold over the governance of the company. For instance, a corporation may issue one share of Class A stock to each owner, with each share providing the owner with 10 votes per share, while issuing one share of Class B stock for sale to the public that offers only one vote per share. By doing so, the corporation can provide its owners with an equivalent, or even a greater, voting power than shareholders from the general public. This system can be advantageous for some classes of stockholder and disadvantageous for other classes. Thus, investors must carefully investigate the terms of any stock purchase so that they are fully informed regarding the rights, or lack thereof, that their shares will provide.

Factors Affecting the Price of Stock

Stock prices change every day as a result of market forces. This means that share prices may change because of supply and demand. If more people want to buy a stock than want to sell it, there is a demand for the stock in the market and the price of the stock moves up. Conversely, if more people want to sell a stock than buy it, there is an excessive supply of the stock in the market, and the price of the stock moves down. In addition, the price of a stock may fluctuate according to the release of earnings reports, and by extension, according to the risk that investors attach to stocks based on these reports. Thus, the price of common stock is affected by factors such as market volatility, earnings and risk. The following sections explain these factors in more detail.

EARNINGS

The most important factor that affects the value of a company is its earnings. Earnings are the profit a company makes. Earnings are central to the existence and growth of a company because if it does not make money, it will not stay in business. Public companies are required to report their earnings four times a year; once each quarter. Investors and analysts watch these earnings reports very carefully because they base their future value of a company on the company's earnings projection. If a company's results are better than expected, the price of the company's shares increases. By contrast, if a company's earnings are lower than expected, the price of its shares will fall. Thus, earnings reports can have a significant impact on the value of a company's stock.

MARKET VOLATILITY

While earnings reports are the basic factor that investors and analysts use to determine a valuation of a company, there are other indicators that investors use to predict stock price, such as investors' sentiments, attitudes and expectations regarding a stock's value. When investors anticipate that a company or industry will perform well, the stock prices of the company or companies within the industry will likely rise. This increase may not be specifically attributable to a rise in corporate earnings or other readily identifiable factors. Instead, the volatility may simply mirror the collective sentiment of what investors feel a company's stock is worth. In addition, the price of a stock may fluctuate to reflect the change in value, either up or down, that investors expect for the stock in the future.

Thus, market volatility can result from factors that may not be measured or explained with precision. As a result, many investors only look at long-term data to evaluate a company's worth or a stock's value. Other investors prefer to examine extensive amounts of data to make an educated assessment of the valuation of a stock's or company's performance. Because of the elusive nature of the market's sentiment of a particular stock, company or industry, the value of stocks can be greatly affected by market volatility and can face rapid changes in price.

Occassional crashes in stock markets are profoundly disruptive to an economy. The collapse of the esteemed investment banks Bear Stearns and Lehman Brothers in 2008 was almost immediately followed by the bankruptcy of American International Group (AIG), and soon after by the meltdown of General Motors. U.S. stocks lost approximately 55% of their value between 2007 and 2009. Dire economic conditions globally led companies to hold onto their cash reserves and streamline operations, resulting in widescale and prolonged unemployment. Stock values, however, recovered ahead of the economy, many surpassing their pre-recession highwater mark by 2013.

RISK

When an investor purchases common stock, he becomes an owner in the company. By becoming an owner, he assumes the risk that the company may lose money or may even face insolvency. This means that if a company goes bankrupt and liquidates, a common stockholder will not be able to recoup her investment until the company's creditors and preferred shareholders have been paid, and then, only if the company has any remaining assets. When General Motors, long a Blue Chip icon of U.S. industry and proverbially sound investment, melted down in 2009, the federal government stepped in with a controversial bailout, which saved the company and allowed it to radically reorganize. As part of the reorganization, G.M. was purchased by a liquidation company and all stock was deemed completely worthless. What remained of G.M. issued an initial public offering. One of the more contentious provisions of the rescue was government acquisition of a controlling interest in new G.M. stock. By 2013, the Treasury still owned more than 100 million shares of the now thriving automaker, which it was gradually selling off. The U.S. Treasury recovered much of taxpayers' extraordinary investment; however, G.M.'s original shareholders lost their entire investment.

Ordinarily, however, common stockholders are rewarded for their risk through a stock's capital appreciation and dividend distributions. Capital appreciation occurs when a stock's value increases over time so that when an investor sells it, it is worth more than he paid for it and the investor receives a profit. Dividend distributions are payments that are made to a company's shareholders, typically on a quarterly basis, out of a company's profits. Common shareholders are not guaranteed a dividend distribution however. Dividends are paid only if the company has accrued earnings and only if the board of directors authorizes a dividend payout.

Thus, shareholders of common stock may see potentially significant rewards for their investment, or they may lose their entire investment if the company goes bankrupt and there are not sufficient corporate assets to repay the shareholders for their original investment. While every investor assumes this risk in purchasing shares of common stock, history has shown that common stock remains a solid investment. Common stocks average returns of 11 to 12% per year, which is better than the typical returns for shares of preferred stock or other forms of corporate securities. In addition, the risks associated with common stock are generally a function of the company's solidity. Companies that are profitable and well managed generally have shares of common stock that perform consistently well. On the other hand, shares of start-up or poorly managed companies can be extremely volatile. Thus, investors must investigate the performance history and management of companies before making an investment, although investing in common stock of reputable companies remains an ideal investment vehicle.

APPLICATIONS

COMMON STOCK IN CORPORATE RESTRUCTURING CONSIDERATIONS

Corporations may issue an initial public offering of new common stock or simply more shares of common stock to create an influx of equity to fund new projects, product offerings or to invest in other growth objectives. In addition, a corporation may choose to repurchase shares of common stock that have already been issued for a number of reasons, such as to raise its earnings per share, to accumulate shares to acquire another company or to fund employee or management incentives. Common stock that has been re-purchased by the corporation is known as treasury stock and is available for a variety of corporate uses. In still other instances, a corporation may undergo a stock split by dividing the number of shares currently held by shareholders into an even larger amount of shares. There are a number of reasons why a company would split its stock, such as the belief that a split would create a lower market value for its stock shares in hopes that its stock will become more attractive to

investors. The following sections will explain the role that common stock plays in various corporate financial considerations.

EQUITY CREATION

Corporations sell common stock to finance expansion. Corporate managers prefer selling common stock for a number of reasons. It is a form of equity and does not have to be repaid. Investors purchase shares of common stock to participate in the appreciation of the shares over time and in dividend distributions. However, dividends must be approved by the board of directors and are not mandatory. In addition, dividends are paid to a company's shareholders from its retained or current earnings. In other words, dividends are paid out of profits and if a corporation has had a bad year, dividend payments may be reduced or omitted. Since payment of dividends hinges on a company's capacity to grow or at least maintain its current or retained earnings, the ongoing payment of dividends cannot be guaranteed. Thus, corporations issue stock as a form of equity financing in which the company benefits from the addition of equity without the obligations of debt from borrowed lines of credit or the sale of bonds.

However, stock issuance is not a form of free money for corporations. In return for the financing, a corporation's management must yield to stockholders, who become the corporation's owners, and may encounter considerations in which the management's interests diverge from the interests of shareholders. Since corporations are required to have an annual meeting at which stockholders may vote, either in person or by proxy, to elect the board of directors or approve major changes in corporate policies, the rights of shareholders to express their voting power are protected. Issuance of stock to create equity, then, has pros and cons that corporations must carefully weigh when determining how to finance their expansion objectives.

STOCK REPURCHASE PROGRAMS

Companies may choose to repurchase their stock for several reasons. One reason is that buying back some of the shares will boost the company's earnings per share. When fewer shares are outstanding, earnings per share will rise because there are a smaller number of shares over which to distribute the earnings, or profits.

A stock-repurchase plan can also signal that a company has excess cash available. When a company chooses to use its excess cash to repurchase shares of its own stock, it may be because the company may think the shares are selling below a level that they're actually worth. This sends a signal to investors that the company thinks its own stock is the best investment it could make. When the company buys back its own stock, it forgoes investing in other securities or making additional capital investments.

A stock-repurchase program also can be implemented to acquire shares for management and employee incentive plans, including stock options and stock-purchase plans, or for employer contributions to a 401(k) or other qualified retirement plan. Many businesses that are expanding do so through mergers and acquisitions. Companies initiate stock-repurchase plans to build currency for acquisitions. After the company purchases its stock, the shares are then held as treasury stock. Since a company would increase its amount of treasury stock so that it could use those shares to acquire another company, a stock-repurchase program could be considered a sign of growth.

However, even though a stock-repurchase program is authorized, the company is not required to then repurchase the shares. Just like any investor, the company will buy shares when the price is right.

STOCK SPLITS

A stock split is a procedure in which the shares of stock owned by existing stockholders are divided into a larger number of shares. Corporations split their stock for a number of reasons. One reason why a company splits its stock is because the current price of the company's shares has grown prohibitively expensive and beyond the reach of the average investor. When a company declares a stock split, the number of shares investors hold increases by the multiple of the split and the price of each share drops accordingly. For instance, if an investor owns 500 shares of a company that are trading at $100 a share and the company declares a two-for-one stock split, the investor will own a total of 1,000 shares at $50 a share after the split. While a stock split does not directly affect the value of the shares that investors own, the media attention incurred by the split, coupled with the affordability of the new shares often draws new investors to purchase

shares of the stock. This can have the effect of driving up the value of the shares of the stock, and by extension, the net worth of the corporation.

CONCLUSION

Common stock represents partial ownership in a company and with this ownership comes certain rights. Common shareholders are entitled to the right to vote on certain corporate matters such as stock splits and company objectives. Typically, common stock shareholders receive one vote per share, unless the corporation's articles of incorporation provide otherwise. Common shareholders also vote to elect the company's board of directors. A company's board of directors oversees major decisions for the company but appoints officers to fulfill the day-to-day operations.

In addition to voting rights, common stock shareholders generally have "preemptive rights," which allow common shareholders to purchase sufficient shares of stock to maintain their proportional ownership in the company any time the company approves an issuance of a new stock offering. Common shareholders also have the right to freely transfer ownership of their shares on exchanges.

Thus, although common stock entitles its holders to a number of different rights and privileges, common stock does come with a degree of risk in that common stock has limited priority. This means that common shareholders are among the last to have access to a company's assets. When a company is profitable, common stock shareholders receive dividend payments only after all preferred shareholders have received their dividend payments. And if a company goes bankrupt or faces liquidation, common stock shareholders receive only those assets left after all creditors, bondholders and preferred shareholders have been paid in full. However, because common stock shareholders have a chance to participate in dividend distribution and share price appreciation, common stock ownership remains a popular form of investment for many modern investors.

BIBLIOGRAPHY

AMD to offer $500M in common stock. (2006). *Electronic News,* 52(5), 28. Retrieved April 16, 2007, from EBSCO Online Database Business

Source Complete. http://search. ebscohost. com/login.aspx?direct=true&db=bth&AN=1979 7915&site=ehost-live

Bae, G., Jeong, Jinho J., Sun, H., & Tang, A. (2002). Stock returns and operating performance of securities issuers. *Journal of Financial Research, 25*(3), 337-352. Retrieved April 16, 2007, from EBSCO Online Database Business Source Complete. http://search.ebscohost.com/login.aspx? direct= true&db=bth&AN=7311204&site=ehost-live

Browdie, B. (2013). Tarp to cost less than previously estimated: CBO. *American Banker, 178*(83), 4. Retrieved October 31, 2013, from EBSCO Online Database Business Source Complete. http://search. ebscohost.com/login.aspx? direct=true&db=bth& AN=87863503&site=ehost-live

The equity-income menu. (2006). *Morningstar DividendInvestor,2*(6), 13-18. Retrieved April 16, 2007, from EBSCO Online Database Business Source Complete. http://search.ebscohost.com/login. aspx?direct=t rue&db=bth&AN=21294092&site=e host-live

Euronet offers common stock to raise funds for acquisition. (2007). *CardLine,7*(11), 11. Retrieved April 16, 2007, from EBSCO Online Database Business Source Complete. http://search.ebscohost.com/login.aspx?direct=true&db=bt h&AN=24405417&site=ehost-live

Folkinshteyn, D., & Meric, G. (2014). The financial characteristics of large and small firms before and after the 2008 stock market crash. *International Journal of Business & Finance Research (IJBFR), 8*(1), 1-16. Retrieved October 31, 2013, from EBSCO Online Database Business Source Complete. http://search.ebscohost.com/login.aspx?direct=t rue&db=bth&AN=90154794&site=ehost-live

Hill, K. (2007). Clearwire nets $600M in IPO. *RCR Wireless News,26*(10), 9. Retrieved April 16, 2007, from EBSCO Online Database Business Source Complete. http://search. ebscohost. com/login.aspx?direct=true&db=bth&AN=2451 4307&site=ehost-live

Koehn, N. (2013). The brain-and soul-of capitalism. *Harvard Business Review, 91*(11), 44. Retrieved October 31, 2013, from EBSCO Online Database Business Source Complete. http://search. ebscohost.com/login.aspx?direct=t rue&db=bth& AN=91571371&site=ehost-live

Lockyer, S. (2005). IPOs. *Nation's Restaurant News, 39*(51), 66. Retrieved April 16, 2007, from EBSCO Online Database Business Source Complete. http://search.ebscohost.com/login.aspx?direct=t rue&db=bth&AN=19296733 &site=ehost-live

Ultra Clean offers common stock. (2006). *Electronic News,52*(12), 4. Retrieved April 16, 2007, from EBSCO Online Database Business Source Complete. http://search. ebscohost.com/ login.aspx?direct=true&db=bth&AN=2035 9165&site=ehost-live

Williams, D. & Young, C. (2006). Trends in biopharmaceutical IPOs: 1996 –2005. *Journal of Health Care Finance,33*(2), 39-54. Retrieved April 16, 2007, from EBSCO Online Database Business Source Complete. http://search.ebscohost.com/ login.aspx?direct=true&db=bth&AN=23606134 &site=ehost-live

SUGGESTED READING

Daniel, K. & Titman, S. (1997). Evidence on the characteristics of cross sectional variation in stock returns. *Journal of Finance, 52*(1), 1-33. Retrieved April 16, 2007, from EBSCO Online Database Business Source Complete. http://search. ebscohost.com/login.aspx?direct=true&db=bt h&AN=9707012808&site=ehost-live

Hegde, S. & Miller, R. (1989). Market-making in initial public offerings of common stocks: an empirical analysis. *Journal of Financial & Quantitative Analysis, 24*(1), 75. Retrieved April 16, 2007, from EBSCO Online Database Business Source Complete. http://search.ebscohost.com/ login.aspx?d irect=true&db=bth&AN=5722870&site=eh ost-live

Panton, D. (1989). The relevance of the distributional form of common stock returns to the construction of optimal portfolios: Comment. *Journal of Financial & Quantitative Analysis, 24*(1), 129. Retrieved April 16, 2007, from EBSCO Online Database Business Source Complete. http://search. ebscohost.com/login.aspx?direct=true&db=bt h&AN=5722909&site= ehost-live

–Heather Newton

Corporate Finance

ABSTRACT

This paper provides an illustration of the field of corporate finance as it relates to business. It looks at some of the decision-making processes involved in maintaining the delicate balance between profitability and cost. The reader gleans an in-depth understanding of the situations and issues that can mean the difference between a path toward success and the road to bankruptcy.

OVERVIEW

At the turn of the 20th century, industrialist John D. Rockefeller found himself the target of the ire of his competitors and the scrutinizing eye of the media. In order to circumvent laws that prevented businesses from owning property out of state, Rockefeller decided to incorporate his oil business and create for it a holding company (or trust) known as Standard Oil. His move paid off — Standard Oil would in short time dominate the entire industry; from production to refining to shipping and barrel-making.

For his decimated competitors, who lay prostrate at the feet of Standard Oil, Rockefeller had gone too far by single-handedly destroying his competition. Journalist Ida Tarbell joined the fight against Standard, writing articles designed to inflame simmering public opinion against Rockefeller's business practices. The public backlash was powerful, as was the nation's political response. Rockefeller countered that the price of oil was decreasing due to Standard's presence in the industry, but his claims fell on deaf ears. Anti-trust suits were lodged against Standard Oil, and by 1911, the corporation was broken down into dozens of smaller companies.

However, Rockefeller got the last laugh. Ironically, the dissolution of his company meant that his holdings in each of these "splinter" groups would increase in value. With Rockefeller's presence in every one of these offshoot oil providers, his personal wealth increased exponentially. Already retired from business, Rockefeller could now breathe much easier — as America's first billionaire (Anecdotage.com, 2008).

In the latter 20th century, as well as the early years of the 21st century, corporations are arguably the most powerful entities in commerce. They are as myriad in size and configuration as the business environment in which they operate. From the smallest, non-profit association to the largest multinational entity, corporations are the preferred vehicle for those who seek to maximize profit-generation while minimizing costs and liability.

It is this latter point that suggests a difficult balancing act. Although risk is always a factor to consider in the development of a business, it is considered sage advice for those who invest in a business to protect his or her investment at all costs. By ensuring that profits are flowing consistently, systems and operations are streamlined and obstacles to long-term growth are addressed or circumvented, companies engaged in the practice of corporate finance are galvanizing the foundations on which the organization is built.

This paper provides an illustration of the field of corporate finance as it relates to business. It looks at some of the decisionmaking processes involved in maintaining the delicate balance between profitability and cost. The reader gleans an in-depth understanding of the situations and issues that can mean the difference between a path toward success and the road to bankruptcy.

The Crux of Corporate Management

Business owners and entrepreneurs must tread a delicate path. In their quest for commercial success, they must be wary of the pratfalls and obstacles that await them in business. Managers and owners must make a series of critical decisions that weigh the costs and investments as well as real and potential profits to be generated through the business process. This decision-making process is known as "corporate finance."

A relatively new practice (the notion was introduced in the 1950s), the traditional model of corporate finance encompasses three major concerns by which the entrepreneur or business manager makes financial decisions. These three arenas are:

- Optimal investment;
- Financing;
- Dividends.

Of course, how each of these three elements impacts the others has long been the source of debate

John D. Rockefeller. *Via Wikipedia.org*

— without a thorough understanding of this interaction (as well as the equilibrium that must be established in light of this triumvirate of areas), the traditional view of corporate finance must be updated (Jensen & Smith, 1984).

An interesting and as-yet underanalyzed aspect of corporate finance is the rationale of corporate managers in their pursuit of effective long-term financial policy. Weighing the best options at the disposal of chief financial officers and CEOs is a difficult and yet extremely important undertaking. Many experts, although not averse to attempting to understand the mindset of these managers (like corporate finance as a whole, the field of "behavioral finance" is still in its fledgling stages), look to the actual activities themselves as the basis for corporate financial behavior. For example, the benefits of a corporate acquisition, which may disproportionately favor the target rather than the corporation itself (such a move may therefore prove suboptimal for the CFO as an extension of corporate financial policy) (Subrahmanyam, 2008).

The decision-making process of corporate financial managers such as chief financial officers may be better understood by paying attention to the three basic concerns facing a corporation's fiscal strategy. Before one can analyze the relationship between these three critical elements of corporate finance, it is important to provide a clear definition of each individual issue. This paper next turns to each of these arenas, beginning with one of the most salient (and preferable) courses of action: Optimal investment strategy.

Optimal Investment

By its very nature, investment is a risk. Of course, some investments are more risky than others, and some potentially reap greater returns and therefore appear worth the risks. In any business setting, investments are critical even if the potential exists for negative returns in the short-run. It is therefore incumbent upon corporate financial officers and CEOs to weigh the myriad of investment options that exist and pursue the strategy that best meets corporate goals.

Effective corporate financial policy is dependent on infusions of funds into key endeavors. From an internal point of view, some of these areas include research and development, staff development and training, mergers and acquisitions and marketing activities. For some companies, the endeavor may not be to continue development of key products or expand operations — it may be to ensure that a new company grows to the status it needs to in order to succeed, or it may even be to revitalize a corporation that is struggling to regain its former stature in the face of a troubled market or previous internal mismanagement. Regardless of the rationale behind the pursuit of optimal investment, the goal of the investment strategy is not always to simply meet established performance goals and benchmarks. In fact, in most cases, investment is offered in order to exceed expectations.

Investment strategy often comes in two varieties. The first is based largely on reactive, so-called "naïve" strategies in which the trader acts on his or her experience and interpretations of the market or target area. The second, and more preferable according to empirical study, stems from careful, scientific analysis of not only the target area, but the conduciveness of the environment in which the investment will transpire (Salter, 2006).

Regardless of the approach to investment policymaking, it is clear that, of the three components of corporate finance, investment is considered by business leaders to be pivotal. In a recent survey of 140 chief financial officers from five different countries, an overwhelming majority cited investment as their top priorities (Cohen & Yagil, 2007).

Of course, a corporation's investment in its own endeavors (whether research and development, marketing initiatives, sales territory expansions or even mergers and acquisitions) is central to business growth. While this fact remains strong on the minds of corporate leaders, and is likely the first matter that comes to fore in the development of corporate financial policy, investment is not the sole factor worthy of attention. In fact, as suggested earlier, to focus on but one of the three primary factors in corporate finance is to discount the other two and therefore create a disruption to the equilibrium that should exist. It is to these two elements that I now turn attention.

FINANCING

In 2002, French telecommunications giant France Telecom (FT) was on life support. It was in debt by over 68 billion Euros and was in desperate need of government intervention. Investor confidence in FT was waning, and there seemed to be little hope for the company to reemerge from its debt load. FT seemed to be on its last legs. In the last month of 2002, however, the company's chief financial officer, Michel Combes, spearheaded an aggressive effort to refinance the debt load. Using funds from the French government, and employing a comprehensive effort to streamline internal operations as well, FT embarked on a 180-degree turnaround. To catalyze the transformation, the company took out nearly several billion Euros in bonds in early 2003 to help refinance the balance of its debt. The market's positive status helped Combes' endeavor, enabling the company to make the necessary changes to pay down debt, revitalize operations and entice investors to return to the fold (Neville, 2004).

Borrowing to bolster a company's long-term financial health is not always as successful as France Telecom's example illustrates. In fact, the second element of corporate financial decision-making involves arguably a greater risk than the investment side. This statement holds water due to the very nature of financing. In this arena, a company borrows against its estimated worth or future anticipated revenues. In other words, a company utilizing financing is beholden not just to reaching its speculative fiscal performance — it is relying on the conduciveness of the markets from which the external financing comes.

In one study, attention was paid to institutional investors' rates of credit supply uncertainty (CSU). The authors use CSU as a sort of "investment horizon," in that the degree to which credit supply is plentiful or lacking has an impact on the size, length and terms of any bond issuance or refinancing authorization. High CSU, according to the study's revelations, leads to lower leverage and a lower probability of issuing bonds in the next quarter or financial period. However, high CSU also tends to prod borrowers toward banking institutions instead of bonding firms. There is, therefore, an unexpected benefit for borrowers that results from supply uncertainty and the segmented credit market, which gives corporate financial decision-makers a wide range of choices from which to borrow (Massa, Yasuda & Lei, 2007).

Bonding and other forms of borrowing are indeed important arenas for finance managers to include in their efforts to maximize available revenues for long-term growth. As suggested in the above example of France Telecom, however, the role of investors in the success of a corporation cannot be understated. This paper next looks at an invaluable tool designed to draw and retain that critical group.

DIVIDENDS

Publicly traded corporations understand the value of the investor. Without investor-based revenues and, more importantly, investor confidence, a corporation whose stock is traded on the open market may suffer. It is for this reason that a great many corporations offer dividend payments to their shareholders. Put simply, dividends are incentives. Shareholders of stable companies (that is, corporations that are already fully developed) are often offered a portion of those companies' profits, as the business does not see the need to reinvest this surplus. With little need to use extra profits for infrastructure improvements, flagship product development or other arenas, these established corporations may see great potential returns by offering quarterly dividends to shareholders.

The rationale behind dividend packages is obvious — if shareholders are given a larger return on their investments (especially since, in light of the company's stability and modest growth, they will likely not see much profit in selling their blue chip stocks), they could use it to purchase more shares or otherwise use the dividend income to bolster their standings.

As one might expect, dividends represent a sizable percentage of corporate finance practice. In 1999, US multinational corporations listed in Standard and Poors' Compustat database reported after-tax earnings of $516 billion, but paid nearly $200 billion back to common shareholders. Those same companies reported generating $182 billion overseas, but returned to US-based shareholders $97 billion in dividend packages (Desai, Foley & Hines, 2007).

In a recent study, it was revealed that dividends do more to increase consumption among shareholders than other forms of financial returns on investment (such as capital gains). In fact, while sales of stocks may prove useful for forward-thinking investors, it appears that dividend income is more likely to be used and reinvested by shareholders than capital gains (Baker, Nagel & Wurgler, 2007). With the perception in mind of stockholders that dividends are considerably more desirable and consistent than are capital gains, it comes as no surprise that corporations are often all too happy to offer such programs in order to retain shareholders. In fact, corporate managers are likely to determine dividend payout levels before they make decisions on investment strategies. Only when corporate earnings are lagging do financial officers cool on the size of dividend distributions, but they still tend to divest in assets and defer on projects that would potentially generate positive returns before they forgo freezing dividends (Bray, 2006).

As an incentive, dividends are an invaluable tool for retaining shareholders and investors. It is perhaps due to the sheer clarity of the benefits of dividend programs that, ironically, financial officers pay more attention to optimal investments than dividends (a point raised earlier in this essay), as investment policies are more complex in nature and demand a greater degree of scrutiny in order to realize the potential returns. The benefits of dividends in terms of retaining the faith of investors are far easier to gauge.

CORPORATE FINANCE & ITS AGGREGATE COMPONENTS

Corporate finance entails, as demonstrated in this paper, the use of investment, financing and dividends as means to bolster profits and retain long-term growth. However, each of these individual components is not an island unto itself. They are part of an aggregate set of procedures. As such, an interesting point to discuss is how this collective group interacts as Chief Financial Officers work them into a larger overall business plan. As was the case with France Telecom, office machine giant Xerox was,

until recently, suffering major stagnation. Financial mismanagement had given rise to a case with the Securities and Exchange Commission. Additionally, in a market that had become saturated with competitors, a lack of 21st century vision left the once iconic manufacturer of printers, copiers and other office machines in search of a path back to its previous stature. In addition to revising its accounting practices to reach a settlement with the SEC, as well as streamlining operations, Xerox invested its funds into a new joint venture with GE Capital and the development of a fast, high-priced commercial printer (Deutsch, 2002).

In its efforts to right the ship, Xerox also took out a series of bonds to help enable its turnaround. The combination of investment and financing seem to have paid off. The company is now reporting profits, and its bond rating has been upgraded in light of the company's improved financial health. Finally, with the corporation finally turning a profit, Xerox is reaching out in appreciation to its shareholders — in late 2007, the company announced that is about to resume its quarterly dividend payments (Bulkeley, 2007).

Examples such as France Telecom and Xerox provide interesting illustrations of how the three major elements of corporate finance work in conjunction in order to enhance the strength of a business. As discussed earlier in this paper, it is clear that, in the future study of corporate finance, greater attention should be paid to the dynamics by which these concepts, which are often viewed separately, work in concert.

CONCLUSION

Corporate business is a fickle endeavor in the 21st century commercial world. Success in this field depends not only on smart, innovative management practices — it depends on external factors as well. Corporations that take this fact to heart tend to find long-term success.

Chief financial officers know that such success is contingent upon sharp corporate finance strategies. These strategies encompass three major areas: optimal investment, financing and dividends.

The former of these three arenas entails, as its name suggests, making the right choices on investments. Some corporate managers rely on "gut decisions" to drive their investment pursuits. It is the manager who initiates a careful analysis of the environment in which investments will be made to ensure that driving corporate dollars into one or more program will both bring returns and ensure the company's long-term growth. It comes as no surprise, therefore, that CFOs overwhelmingly embrace investment as the more critical of the three major elements of corporate finance.

Of course, one cannot view investment as the sole issue on the minds of financial officers. Especially for those companies attempting an upgrade or revitalization, corporate financial planners must look outside of their environs for assistance. Such policies are often integral to a company's revival, as the case of France Telecom clearly demonstrates. Furthermore, a corporation's turnaround can also improve its standing in the eyes of lending and credit institutions, which means an improvement in status for companies and in turn, an influx of additional investors. While corporate finance experts believe this second area is not as high a priority as optimal investment, it is clear that financing can help make the difference between a successful company and one that has fallen flat.

Third among the chief issues for which a corporate financial officer must account is that of rewarding investors for their loyalty and contributions to the corporation. As investors believe that a flat quarterly payment is more stable than capital gains and other forms of shareholder appreciation payouts, dividends are the preferred vehicle. This practice keeps investors loyal to the company and, at the same time, continues to increase consumer consumption.

The study of corporate finance is a relatively new discipline, with roots back only as far as the 1950s (when corporations became more prevalent in the modern economy). Although the three basic components of this critical practice are worthy of in-depth study, corporate finance as an academic topic is somewhat limited in its information in one vital area. While each individual component is critical to corporate finance, success is achieved based upon how each of these three practices work in concert with (or in conflict with) one another. This paper has presented two cases of major corporations that had previously experienced downturns and, utilizing all three elements of corporate finance, experienced revivals that appear to be long-term. There are likely more examples to be found as the discipline of corporate finance continues its evolution.

BIBLIOGRAPHY

Baker, M., Nagel, S. & Wurgler, J. (2007). The effects of dividends on consumption. *Brookings Papers on Economic Activity,* (1), 231-276. Retrieved January 20, 2008, from EBSCO Online Database Business Source Premier. http:// search.ebscohost.com/login.aspx?direct=true&db=buh&AN=26650521&site=bsi-live

Billion dollar question. (2008). Anecdotage.com. Retrieved January 16, 2008, from http://anecdotage.com/index. php?aid=4090.

Bradley, C., Dawson, A., & Smit, S. (2013). The strategic yardstick you can't afford to ignore. *Mckinsey Quarterly, (4),* 24-35. Retrieved November 15, 2013, from EBSCO Online Database Business Source Complete. http://search. ebscohost.com/login.aspx?direct=true&db=bth&AN=91665806&site=ehost-live

Brav, A., Graham, J.R., Harvey, C.R. & Michaely, R. (2006). Payout policy in the 21st century. *CFA Digest, 36(1),* 18-19.

Bulkeley, W.M. (2007). Xerox will declare first dividend since 2001. *Wall Street Journal Eastern Edition, 250*(119), A14.

Cohen, G. & Yagil, J. (2007). A multinational survey of corporate financial policies. *Journal of Applied Science, 17(1),* 57-69. Retrieved January 19, 2008, from EBSCO Online Database Business Source Premier. http://search.ebscohost.com/login.aspx?direct=true&db=buh&AN=28066263&site=bsi-live

Dambra, M., Wasley, C.E., & Wu, J. (2013). Soft-talk management cash flow forecasts: Bias, quality, and stock price effects. *Contemporary Accounting Research, 30*(2), 607- 644. Retrieved November 15, 2013, from EBSCO Online Database Business Source Complete. http://search.ebscohost.com/login.aspx?direct=true&db=bth&AN=88155569&site=ehost-live

Desai, M.A., Foley, C.F. & Hines, Jr., J.R. (2007). Dividend policy inside the multinational firm. *Financial Management (2000), 36*(1), 5-26. Retrieved January 20, 2008 from EBSCO Online Database Business Source Premier. http:// search.ebscohost.com/login.aspx?direct=true&db=buh&AN=26087817&site=bsi-live

Deutsch, C.H. (2002, June 2). At Xerox, the chief earns (grudging) respect. *New York Times Online Edition.* Retrieved January 20, 2008, from http://

query.nytimes. com/gst/fullpage.html?res=9B05E
EDE143AF931A35755C 0A9649C8B63&sec=&spo
n=&pagewanted=3.

Fulghieri, P., & Suominen, M. (2012). Corporate governance, finance, and the real sector. *Journal of Financial & Quantitative Analysis, 47*(6), 1187-1214.
Retrieved November 15, 2013, from EBSCO Online Database Business Source Complete. http://
search.ebscohost.com/ login.aspx?direct=&d
b=bth&AN=87363442&site=eh ost-live

Jensen, M.C. & Smith, Jr., C.W. (1984). The theory
of corporate finance: A historical overview. In *The
modern theory of corporate finance* (pp. 2-20). New
York: McGraw-Hill Inc. Retrieved January 19,
2008, from http://papers.ssrn. com/sol3/papers.
cfm?abstract%5fid=244161.

Massa, M. , Yasuda, A. & Lei, Z. (2007). The effects
of bond supply uncertainty on the leverage of
the firm. *INSEAD Working Papers Collection, 57*,
1-61. Retrieved January 19, 2008, from EBSCO
Online Database Business Source Complete.
http://search.ebscohost.com/login.aspx?direct=t
rue&db=bth&AN=27952794&site=bsi-live

Neville, T. (2004, March). Financing E 68 billion debt
was the easy bit. *Corporate Finance*, (229), 18-20. Retrieved January 19, 2008, from EBSCO Online Database Business Source Complete. http://search.
ebscohost.com/login.aspx? direct=true&db=bth&
AN=12699448&site=bsi-live

Salter, S.P. (2006). NASDAQ REITs and optimal
investment policy. *Journal of Real Estate Portfolio
Management, 12(3)*, 201-207. Retrieved January
19, 2008 from EBSCO Online Database Business Source Premier. http://search. ebscohost.
com/login.aspx?direct=true&db=buh&AN=235
03158&site=bsi-live

Subrahmanyam, A. (2008). Behavior finance. *European Financial Management, 14(1)*, 12-29.

SUGGESTED READING

The age of anxiety. (2007). *CFO, 23*(10), 77. Retrieved January 20, 2008, from EBSCO Online
Database Business Source Premier. http://
search.ebscohost.com/login.aspx?direct=tru
e&db=buh&AN=27149332&site=bsi-live

Baeyens, K. & Manigart, S. (2003). Dynamic financing
strategies. *Journal of Private Equity, 7(1)*, 50-58. Retrieved January 20, 2008, from EBSCO Online
Database Business Source Premier. http://search.
ebscohost.com/login.aspx?direct=true&db=buh&
AN=11583800&site= bsi-live

Lintner, J. (1963). The cost of capital and optimal
financing of corporate growth. *Journal of Finance,
18*(2), 292- 311. Retrieved January 20, 2008, from
EBSCO Online Database Business Source Premier.
http://search.ebscohost.com/login.aspx?direct=t
rue&db=buh&AN=6643481 &site=bsi-live

—Michael P. Auerbach

CORPORATE FINANCIAL MANAGEMENT

ABSTRACT

The article focuses on the strategic planning process
of financial management. In order for an organization to be successful, they must create a strategic plan
that will position the firm for growth and competitiveness. The senior management team will need to
analyze all data, including the financial records, to
ensure that the organization can make a profit, remain competitive and be in position for continued
growth. The use of the strategic financial process in
other sectors is discussed. In addition, there is an exploration of how different types of financial risk are
key components in the enterprise risk management
process.

OVERVIEW

In order for an organization to be successful, it must
create a strategic plan that will position the firm for
growth and competitiveness. The senior management team will need to analyze all data, including the
financial records, to ensure that the organization can
make a profit, remain competitive and be in position
for continued growth. "In discussing corporate financial strategy, the question can well be asked as to how

strategy differs from more modest decision making" (Bierman, 1980, p. 1).

Bierman (1980) provided five elements and four approaches that he believed should be considered by corporate financial managers as they planned their strategies for the organizations in which they worked. The five elements were to:

- Identify the problems and opportunities that existed.
- Set goals and objectives.
- Develop a procedure for providing potential solutions or "paths" that the organization could follow in order to find a solution.
- Choose the best solution given the possible solutions and the organization's objectives.
- Implement a review process where the best solution can be evaluated on its performance.

These elements are very broad so that the corporate finance manager has an opportunity to consider a wide range of financial decisions. For example, the organization's main goal may be to pursue substantial growth with minimum risk. Therefore, the financial management team has to take these factors into consideration when developing the strategic financial plan for the organization.

APPLICATION

Financial Planning in Other Sectors
Although the focus of this article is on corporate finance, strategic financial planning is important in other sectors as well. Having a sound financial planning process is essential to a healthy organization. This section discusses how a non-profit organization evaluated its financial position and implemented processes in order to keep them on track.

A social service organization (Making Ends Meet, n.d.) identified four important stages in the financial planning process. These stages are: Reviewing the past, forecasting the future, setting strategies and plans, and setting annual budgets. Each of these phases is of equal importance and some of the tasks at each phase include:

Reviewing the past:
- Audit current and recent trends in demand and consumption.
- Watch the trends in funding streams.

- Follow and research the true performance and results, such as end-of-year position and conduct against certain signs for social services.
- Collect similar research regarding the real costs incurred and the cost drivers.
- Review the results and evaluate the recommendations from any additional research reports and administration letters from outside auditors.

Forecasting the future:
- Evaluate the force behind countries' policies and plans of action.
- Find and approximate levels of the differing funding streams.
- Review the force of nearby policy initiatives and prerogatives.
- Decide what the future results of known trends may be in relation to supply and demand.
- Recognize the economic significance of demographic tends and similar drivers of demand that the council does not control.

Setting strategies and plans:
- Include the recognition of institutional context for strategic planning.
- Include the linking of economic planning with service, human resources and asset management initiatives.
- Include the collection of research on the knowledge and abilities needed in order to effectively budget all levels of organizational management.
- Include the engagement of every key stakeholder in the planning of strategic finances.

Setting annual budgets:
- Come to consensus on what the budget process should be.
- Make sure that budgets include the recognition of financial plans.
- Integrate budget managers into budget setting initiatives.
- Connect every commitment and foreseen change in demand with the nearby and usable resources.
- React to unintended and unforeseen differences.
- Review budget structures.
- Engage with key stakeholders.
- Make sure that short term choices regarding budget setting don't weaken the priorities of long-term strategizing.

As the organization goes through the process, key decision makers should determine the types of policies that need to be in effect in order to be successful at each of the individual phases. Although these steps apply to a non-profit organization, the steps are valuable for any type of organization. Therefore, the corporate sector may benefit by comparing and contrasting how each of the sectors operate and discussing what works for both.

VIEWPOINT

RISK MANAGEMENT

With scandals such as Enron, one would think that corporations would adhere to ethical standards. Unfortunately, many view companies like Enron as the "ones that got caught," and changes have not occurred in the operations of some businesses because the issue has not been taken seriously. However, the trend is changing. According to a survey conducted in January, 2007 by the Risk Management Association (RMA), many organizations "are moving toward a fully integrated enterprise risk management approach where a myriad of risk types are measured and many of the processes automated and standardized" (p. 14).

CATEGORIES OF ORGANIZATIONAL OBJECTIVES

- There are many situations that can affect the future of a business. These situations can be positive or negative. Situations with negative impact may be viewed as risks, whereas, situations with a positive impact can be seen as opportunities. The overall objective of most businesses is to minimize risk and seize opportunities. Enterprise risk management (ERM) addresses the risks and opportunities facing an organization by classifying objectives into four categories:
- **Strategic** — "big picture" goals focused on supporting an organization's mission.
- **Operations** — effective and efficient use of the company's resources.
- **Reporting** — reliability of reporting.
- **Compliance** — compliance with laws and regulations.

By placing an organization's objectives into categories, one can focus on different aspects of enterprise risk management. Although the categories are different, they can overlap in terms of objectives.

COMPONENTS OF ERM

ERM is made up of eight interrelated components which define the manner in which a management team runs an organization and how the practices are processed (CSO, 2004). The components are:

- **Internal Environment.** The internal environment is the tone and culture of an organization. It sets the bar for how risk is viewed by the organization and the employees. Organizations develop their philosophy, integrity standards and ethical values on risk management.
- **Objective Setting.** Although an organization may have objectives in place prior to the implementation of a risk management plan, the ERM process ensures that the established objectives are in alignment with the organization's mission and position on risk.
- **Event Identification.** An organization must identify the internal and external events that may affect its ability to achieve goals, and the events have to be classified as risks or opportunities. Opportunities are shared with the management team to determine if they should be incorporated into the organization's goals and objectives.
- **Risk Assessment.** Risks are assessed and evaluated on a regular basis so that the organization can analyze what type of impact each has on the entity.
- **Risk Response.** The management team is responsible for selecting the appropriate action to risk events. Responses are based on an organization's risk tolerance and risk appetite.
- **Control Activities.** Policies and procedures are put in place to ensure that risk responses are effectively implemented.
- **Information and Communication.** Relevant information is identified and communicated in a timeframe that will allow employees to perform their responsibilities. The communication process should flow up, down, and across the organizational structure.
- **Monitoring.** The ERM system is monitored and modified when appropriate. Monitoring is achieved through management interventions, separate evaluations, or a combination of both.

ENSURING THE SUCCESS OF ERM

If one wanted to determine the effectiveness of an organization's ERM, he or she would have to assess whether or not the eight components are working effectively. In order for the components to be work effectively, material weaknesses must be eliminated and the risk level has to be within the organization's risk appetite. In addition, the management team and board of directors must have an understanding of how the four categories of objectives are being achieved and know that the reporting process is reliable and addresses compliance with laws and regulations.

The senior management team could also implement a corporate risk policy in order to ensure that the ERM process is successful. Brown (n.d.) suggested a four step process for this type of policy. The first step

would be to identify the major risks faced by the organization. Once they have been identified, the next step would be to formulate an organizational method to evaluate, monitor and govern the risks.

During the measuring phase, a value is assigned to each risk level, and it could be quantitative or qualitative. The next phase, monitoring, requires the organization to track changes in risk over a period of time. The final step, controlling, requires the risk level to be modified in other to be in compliance with the risky appetite and procedures put in place by the shareholders and the board of directors. This foundation is enforced and adapted to every risk category.

RISK TYPES

Category	Identification	Measurement	Monitoring	Control
Financial: Market Risk	Adverse movements in price or rates	Notional measures such as position values; sensitivity measures such as duration, and optionality measures.	Position reports, value at risk, scenario simulations and stress testing.	Establish and closely monitor a limit structure appropriate for the organization's level of risk.
Financial: Credit Risk	Counterparty fails to perform as agreed under contract due to unwillingness or inability to pay on time.	Credit risk is measured with a relative value score. Assessment factors include financial capacity such as current levels of earnings, cash flow and capital, and historical payment patterns.	An annual review of the person's credit file.	Limits on exposure to individuals, netting agreements across subsidiaries and products, third party guarantors.
Financial: Liquidity Risk Financial: Liquidity Risk	Liquidity risk involves funding and market liquidity.	Cash on hand, working capital, lines of credit	Provide credible advanced warning of a pending liquidity crisis. Cash flow forecasting can measure short-term liquidity positions.	The contingency liquidity plan.
Operational: Systems Risk	The risk that an information technology system will fail to perform.	Mean time between failures, average down time per period and processing error rates.	Capacity utilization and other monitoring software should be installed.	W ell-developed business continuity and disaster recovery plan's response to major systems failures.

Operational: Human Error Risk	The risk that an employee, agent or contractor will fail to perform.	Processing error rates can measure mistakes that have occurred. Academic and professional qualifications assess the potential for human errors.	Regular organizational testing of employee knowledge, specific audits programs, and quality control programs.	A set of critical procedures covering all aspects of operations as well as an ongoing objective testing and training function.
Strategic: Legal and Regulatory Risk	Civil and criminal lawsuits, regulatory sanction, costs of compliance and other restrictions imposed by an external authority.	Settlement costs, penalties and fines paid, and the operating budgets of the legal and compliance departments.	Compliance testing	Corporate policies, internal audits, new product reviews, legal reviews and company training programs.
Strategic: Business Strategy Risk	The risk of loss associated with bad decision making by senior management.	Earnings, capital and stock price. Others include economic value added and risk adjusted return on capital.	Annual or quarterly benchmarking analysis of performance against peer group's results.	An independent, informed and active board of directors providing oversight of management decision making.
Hazard: D&O Risk	The exposure of corporate managers to claims from shareholders, government agencies, employees and other alleged mismanagement.	Litigation settlements, claims paid and the cost of insurance.	Claims tracking and analysis, time spent by directors on corporate matters and performance evaluations.	Sophisticated corporate governance and related compliance programs.

THE TYPES OF RISK BY CATEGORY

Brown (n.d.) provided a summary of eight types of risk that are placed into four different categories (i.e. financial risk, operational risk, strategic risk, and hazard risk).

Every business realizes that it will need to take some level of risk.management should include competitive advantages. When reviewing the competitive advantage, it may be best to create a grid such as the one listed above in order to compare and contrast the different categories. Three of the categories focus on the financial aspect of the organization. Therefore, this model can be considered a valuable tool in the strategic planning phase of financial management.

CONCLUSION

In order for organization's to be successful, they must create a strategic plan that will position the firm for growth and competitiveness. The senior management team will need to analysis all data, including the financial records, to ensure that the organization can make a profit, remain competitive and be position for continued growth.

Although the focus of this article is on corporate finance, strategic financial planning is important in other sectors as well. Having a sound financial planning process is essential to a healthy organization. The application section discussed how a non-profit organization evaluated its financial position and implemented processes in order to keep them on track. A social service organization (Making Ends Meet, n.d.) identified four important stages in the financial planning process. These stages are: Reviewing the past, forecasting the future, setting strategies and plans, and setting annual budgets.

With scandals such as Enron, one would think that corporations would adhere to ethical standards. Unfortunately, many view companies such as Enron as the "ones that got caught," and changes have not occurred in the operations of some businesses because the issue has not been taken seriously. However, the trend is changing. According to a survey conducted in January, 2007 by the Risk Management Association (RMA), many organizations "are moving toward a fully integrated enterprise risk management approach where a myriad of risk types are measured and many of the processes automated and standardized" (p. 14).

The senior management team could also implement a corporate risk policy in order to ensure that the ERM process is successful. Brown (n.d.) suggested a four step process for this type of policy. The first step would be to recognize the crucial and most important risks that the organization faces. Once they have been identified, the next step would be to form an organizational method to evaluate, watch and govern the risks.

During the measuring phase, a value is assigned to each risk level, and it could be quantitative or qualitative. The next phase, monitoring, requires the organization to track changes in risk over a period of time. The final step, controlling, requires the risk level to be modified in other to be in compliance with the risky appetite and procedures put in place by the shareholders and the board of directors. This foundation is enforced and adapted to every risk category. Brown (n.d.) provided a summary of eight types of risk that fall into four different categories (i.e. financial risk, operational risk, strategic risk and hazard risk).

BIBLIOGRAPHY

Andreou, P., et al. (2014). Corporate governance, financial management decisions and firm performance: Evidence from the maritime industry. *Transportation Research, 63,* 59–78. Retrieved November 14, 2014, from EBSCO Online Database Business Source Complete. http:// search.ebscohost.com/login.aspx?direct=true&db=bth&AN=94578935

Bierman, H., Jr. (1980). *Strategic financial planning.* New York, NY: The Free Press.

Brown, B. (2007). Step-by-step enterprise risk management. *Risk Management Magazine.* Retrieved May 14, 2007, from http://www. rmmag.com/MGTemplate.cfm?Section=RMMagazine&template=Magazine/DisplayMagazines. cfm&AID=1142&ShowArticle=1

Campello, M., Giambona, E., Graham, J. R., & Harvey, C. R. (2011). Liquidity management and corporate investment during a financial crisis. *Review of Financial Studies, 24*(6), 1944-1979. Retrieved November 15, 2013, from EBSCO Online Database Business Source Complete. http://search.ebscohost.com/login.aspx?direct=true&db=bth&AN=61047578&site=ehost-live

Enterprise risk management – Integrated framework: Executive summary. (2004, September). *Committee of Sponsoring Organizations.* Retrieved May 14, 2007, from http://www.coso.org/Publications/ERM/COSO%5FERM%5FExecutiveSummary.pdf

FEI's 12 recommendations for improving financial management, financial reporting and corporate governance. (2012). *Financial Executive, 28*(6), 43-44. Retrieved November 15, 2013, from EBSCO Online Database Business Source Complete. http://search.ebscohost.com/ login.aspx?direct=true&db=bth&AN=77603897&site= ehost-live

Hung-Gay F., Jr-Ya W., & Jot Y. (2011). Toward a new paradigm for corporate financial management in the wake of the global financial crisis. *International Review of Accounting, Banking and Finance, 3*(3), 27–47. Retrieved November 14, 2014, from EBSCO Online Database Business Source Complete. http://search.ebscohost.com/ login.aspx?direct=true&db=bth&AN=93980897

Strategic financial planning. (n.d.). *Making Ends Meet.* Retrieved September 3, 2007, from http://www.jomtreviews.gov.uk/money/Financialmgt/1-22.html

RMA announces results of enterprise risk management survey. (2007). *Secured Lender, 63*(1), 14. Retrieved May 14, 2007, from EBSCO Online Database Business Source Complete. http://search.ebscohost.com/login.aspx?direct=true&db=bth&AN=23789434&site=bsi-live

Zavorotniy, R. (2012). Place of value management in a system of corporate management and its financial methods. *Journal of Knowledge Management, Economics & Information Technology, 2*(5), 179-187. Retrieved November 15, 2013, from EBSCO Online Database Business Source Complete. http://search.ebscohost.com/ login.aspx?direct=true&db=bth&AN=88272948&site= ehost-live

SUGGESTED READING

Dhaouadi, K. (2014). The influence of top management team traits on corporate financial performance in the US. *Canadian Journal of Administrative Sciences, 31*(3), 200– 213. Retrieved November 14, 2014, from EBSCO Online Database Business Source Complete. http://search.ebscohost.com/login.aspx?direct=true&db=bth&AN=97851187Guillen, G., Badell, M., & Puigjaner, L. (2007). A holistic framework for short-term supply chain management integrating production and corporate financial planning. *International Journal of Production Economics, 106*(1), 288-306.

Holder-Webb, L. & Cohen, J. (2007). The association between disclosure, distress, and failure. *Journal of Business Ethics, 75*(3), 301-314. Retrieved September 28, 2007, from EBSCO Online Database Business Source Complete. http://search.ebscohost.com/login.aspx?direct=true&db=bth&AN=26618798&site=bsi-live

Newman, K. (2007). Treasury benchmarking – what's getting in the way? *Financial Executive, 23*(7), 21. Retrieved September 28, 2007, from EBSCO Online Database Business Source Complete. http://search.ebscohost.com/ login.aspx?direct=true&db=bth&AN=26472692&site= bsi-live

Ryan, E., & Trahan, E. (2007). Corporate financial control mechanisms and firm performance: The case of value-based management systems. *Journal of Business Finance & Accounting, 34*(1/2), 111-138. Retrieved September 26, 2007, from EBSCO Online Database Business Source Complete. http://search.ebscohost.com/loginaspx?direct=true&db=bth&AN=24181262&site=bsi-live

Stewart, J. (2005, September). Fiscal incentives, corporate structure and financial aspects of treasury management operations. *Accounting Forum (Elsevier), 29*(3), 271-288. Retrieved September 26, 2007, from EBSCO Online Database Business Source Complete. http://search.ebscohost.com/login.aspx?direct=true&db=bth&AN=17830034 &site=bsi-live

–Marie Gould

CORPORATE FINANCIAL STRATEGY

ABSTRACT

This article focuses on corporate financial strategy. It provides an overview of the history, strengths, and weaknesses of the corporate financial strategy field. The main components of corporate financial strategy, including value-based management, strategic planning, mergers and acquisitions, cost analysis, and capital budgets, are addressed. The relationship between corporate financial strategy and investor relations are described.

OVERVIEW

Corporate financial strategy is a business approach in which financial tools and instruments are used to assess and evaluate the likely success and outcomes of proposed business strategies and projects. In the twenty-first century, corporate leaders and decision makers use corporate financial strategy to:

■ Actively enhance shareholder value
■ Fundraise
■ Attain venture capital
■ Promote corporate growth.

Corporations promote growth through organic or inorganic business activities. Corporate growth refers to economic expansion as measured by any of a number of indicators such as: Increased revenue, staffing, and market share. Issues that effect corporate value and growth include human capital, intellectual property, change management, and investment funding. Growth corporations tend to have an operating business plan that guides the company toward growth choices and activities. An operating business plan refers to a dynamic document that highlights the strengths and weakness of the company and guides the company toward learning and increased efficiency. A corporation's operating business plan is informed and driven by its corporate financial strategy.

THE COMBINATION OF FINANCE & STRATEGY
The field of corporate financial strategy brings together the forces of corporate finance and corporate strategy to compliment and balance one

another. In successful corporate finance strategy, corporate finance and strategy functions work together to create shareholder value. Corporate financial strategy is a multi-faceted and multi-field approach to business operations and management. The history of finance and strategy in corporate settings has been one of divisiveness and territoriality. Finance and strategy, and financial and strategic decision making in general, have long been considered separate intellectual and decision-making forces. Chief financial officers have been known to favor either finance or strategy as their main decision making influence. For example, chief financial officers and managers that favor economic or finance-based decision-making may rely on managerial economics or applied economics to make business decisions. Ultimately, there is no substantial conflict between corporate finance and corporate strategy tools and instruments. Finance and strategy, which have a history of being separate endeavors in the corporate sector, are complimentary functions that have the potential to reinforce and balance one another. Corporations that integrate finance and strategy functions have the greatest opportunities for growth and value added endeavors (Thackray, 1995). Corporations, in the twenty-first century, share many of the same characteristics. For example, the modern corporation is usually organized into business units. Each business unit within the modern corporation is accountable for its' own profits or losses. Business planning is generally decentralized. Business unit product line managers focus on profits for single products over the shorter term. Rapid development and innovation in information technology continues to change production functions and the nature of the products and services sold and delivered to customers (Egan, 1995). Despite the similarities that characterize modern corporations, corporations do differ in their ability to combine finance and strategy factors. In the increasingly competitive global market, successful integration between finance and strategy dimensions may mean the difference between corporate success and corporate failure. Chief financial officers, managers, and planning teams that use financial strategy as their decision-making compass may create more wealth and growth for their companies and shareholders than those corporations that base their business decisions on either finance or strategy.

STEPS FOR DEVELOPING SUCCESSFUL CORPORATE FINANCIAL STRATEGY

Corporate financial strategy is most successful when the strategy is maintained internally and aligned with the operations of the corporation. Fully integrated corporate financial strategies can be developed using the following steps (Mallette, 2005):

- Build a sufficient capital structure: Capital structure refers to the means through which a company finances itself. Financing may come from long term-debt, common stock, and retained earnings. Corporations can determine the best capital structure for its purposes through the use of three forms of analyses: Downside cash flow scenario modeling, peer group analysis, and bond rating analysis. Downside cash flow scenario modeling is a process in which a capital structure is taken from a set of downside cash flow scenarios. Peer group analysis is a process in which common capital structures and fads of peer businesses, are evaluated for insight into operating features. Bond rating analysis is a process in a review of the debt capacity within certain debt ratings.
- Determine the correct market valuation: Correct market valuation evaluates whether the corporation is undervalued or overvalued in the marketplace. Market valuation refers to a measure of how much the business is worth in the marketplace. Review financial measures such as investor expectations for growth, margins, and investments. Compare investors' expectations and managements' expectations to check for disparity.
- Establish the optimum corporate financial strategy: Develop an optimum strategy for value creation that provides sufficient funding, financial balance, and a growing cash reserve.

Ultimately, corporate financial strategy is a firm-specific enterprise. Corporations design their individual corporate financial strategies based on their available tools, resources, insights, goals, and objectives. Common components of corporate financial strategies include: Value-based management, strategic planning, mergers and acquisitions, cost analysis, and capital budgets. The following section describes and analyzes the main components of corporate financial strategies used today in the private sector. This section serves as the foundation for later discussion of the relationship between corporate financial strategy and investor relations.

APPLICATIONS

Chief financial officers, managers, and planning teams develop their corporate financial strategies to maximize and optimize growth and shareholder value. Corporate financial strategies are characterized as return driven strategies. A return driven corporate strategy refers to a set of corporation specific guidelines for creating, maintaining, and analyzing corporate strategy focused on utmost, long-range wealth development. In the twenty-first century, managers have an increased responsibility to create shareholder value, watch the performance of a business, and safeguard long-term business success. Return driven corporate financial strategy prioritizes value added outcomes and directs the business with a critical eye toward return, value, and growth (Frigo, 2003). The following components of corporate financial strategies, including value-based management, strategic planning, mergers and acquisitions, cost analysis, and capital budgets, are used by chief financial officers, managers, and planning teams to create shareholder value.

VALUE-BASED MANAGEMENT

Chief financial officers, managers, and planning teams may choose to base their corporate financial strategy on the principles of value-based management. Value-based management refers to a management approach focused on maximizing shareholder value. Value-based management includes strategies for creating, measuring, and managing value. Value-based management is an integrated and holistic approach to business that encompasses and informs the corporate culture, corporate communications, corporate mission, corporate strategy, corporate organization, corporate decision making, and corporate awards and compensation packages. The economic value added (EVA) strategy is one of the most common tools used in value-based management. Economic value added refers to the net operating profit minus a charge for the opportunity cost of all the capital invested in the project. Economic value added analysis is considered a beneficial lens for looking at varying company unit performances on a cost-of-capital basis where risks are adjusted. Value

added managers may receive compensation based on the outcome of economic value added analysis. Ultimately, the economic value added approach is a measure of economic performance and a strategy for creating shareholder wealth (Bhalla, 2004). Critics of economic value added approaches have two main complaints. First, critics argue that economic value added approaches are too costly to apply. Second, critics argue that economic value added approaches are too intellectually rigorous and demanding for many managers to use successfully and effectively (Thackray, 1995).

STRATEGIC PLANNING

Chief financial officers, managers, and planning teams may choose to base their corporate financial strategy on strategic planning. Growth companies tend to engage in active organizational and strategic planning. The leaders and managers of growth companies tend to excel at understanding, assessing, and forecasting potential problems. This long-range vision allows managers to address problems and plan solutions before situations become destructive to the organization and inhibit growth. Strategic planning refers to the process of establishing a business's long-term corporate goals and deciding on the most effective way to achieving those aims. There are five key elements vital to strategic planning (Bhalla, 2004):

- Identification of the problems and opportunities that exist
- Formation of goals and objectives
- Procedures for providing solutions or paths that the firm can follow
- Choosing the best solution based on possible solutions and firm objectives
- Instituting a review procedure to evaluate how the best solution has performed.

Corporations' strategic plans and corporate financial strategies are usually integrated intro a general business strategy. The corporate business strategy refers to the context for specific business decisions and operating strategies. Examples include a strategy for growth, business focus, product cannibalization, partnerships, and global focus. All successful corporations engage in corporate development and strategic planning.

MERGERS & ACQUISITIONS

Chief financial officers, managers, and planning teams may choose to base their corporate financial strategy on corporate mergers and acquisitions as the vehicle for creating growth and shareholder value. The convergence of the financial industry that began in the 1970s started a process of ongoing and frequent mergers and acquisitions. Corporations that choose merger and acquisition as their path or engine for increased value and growth must make decisions regarding what mode of merger or acquisition to choose based on their resources, industry, and goals. There are three main types of mergers and acquisitions: Horizontal merger, vertical merger, and conglomerate merger.

- Horizontal merger refers to the business act in which one company obtains the rights to another company that whose products are similar and whose consumers are in the same area. Thus, competition is greatly reduced and, in many cases, eliminated.
- Vertical merger refers to the business act in which one company acquires customers or suppliers, thereby lowering the cost of production and distribution.
- Conglomerate mergers refer to all non-vertical and non-horizontal mergers and acquisitions. Examples of common conglomerate mergers and acquisitions include pure conglomerate transactions, geographic extension mergers, and product-extension mergers.

DETERMINING MERGER TYPE

Corporations decide what type of merger or acquisition to pursue based on their overall financial strategies, objectives, and resources. Corporations with significant capital resources may choose to pursue the purchase of assets. In the purchase of assets scenario, the buyer purchases another company's assets and, in some instances, its debts. Corporations may choose to pursue the purchase of stock. In the purchase of stock scenario, the buyer purchases some of the seller's stockholdings and inherits the seller's obligations and rights, including debt, in proportion to the purchased share. Corporations may choose to pursue a statutory merger. In the statutory merger scenario, the merger allows the merging companies to continue existing as a single legal entity. Ultimately, there

are numerous different types of mergers and acquisitions that correspond to varying business needs and business models (Lu, 2006). Common management problems and issues experienced during and after mergers and acquisitions include strategic, moral, organizational, legal, financial issues, and human resource issues.

MERGER & ACQUISITION MANAGEMENT

Mergers and acquisitions, throughout their lifecycle from first proposing the idea to post-merger, require careful oversight and management. Corporations are increasingly implementing ongoing merger and acquisition management policies to guide merger and acquisition activities. Corporate merger and acquisition management policy ranges from very simple to very complex. Simple corporate merger and acquisition policy generally includes the mandate that any merger and acquisition transaction over a certain dollar amount must go to the board of directors for approval. Complex merger and acquisition management policy may include, for example, rules and strategies for strategic plan approval, sale of company assets, reporting of inquiries, and formulating a takeover defense. Corporate development officers are generally in charge of developing merger and acquisition management policy as well as overseeing all merger and acquisition proposals (Liebs, 1999).

Cost Analysis

Chief financial officers, managers, and planning teams may choose to base their corporate financial strategy on the data gathered from ongoing cost analysis. Cost analysis refers to the microeconomic techniques used to assess the effectiveness of production, the best factor allocation, the economies of scale, and cost function. Cost analysis incorporates the expenses associated with raw materials, components, subassemblies, communications, transportation, and customer support services (Egan, 1995). Corporations use multiple cost analysis tools to aid financial and strategic decision-making. There are four main kinds of cost analysis: Cost-benefit, cost-effectiveness, cost-minimization, and cost-utility. Each of the four types is used by corporations for decision-making share the same the same framework or guiding principles. For example, the type of cost analysis:

- Specifies the analytic perspective that provided

the framework for determining who pays the costs for and who benefits from a particular service or intervention.
- Defines and specifies the anticipated benefits and outcomes of a service or intervention.
- Identifies all of the actual and potential costs using the specified analytic perspective to determine the costs.
- Accounts for how time may affect projected costs.
- Evaluates the results and considers alternative explanations for the conclusions.
- Calculates a cost-benefit or cost-effectiveness ratio as a summary measure (Beyea, 1999).

While there are four related types of cost analysis, cost benefit analysis is the most popular and widely used analytical tool for economic decision-making in the private sector. Cost benefit analysis (CBA), a type of investment appraisal also referred to as benefit-cost analysis, is one of the most prominent and widely used analytical and quantitative tools for decision making in the corporations. Cost benefit analysis produces data about the cost and benefit of a product, service, production method, or investment. This data can be presented in three main ways to aid the evaluation stage of analysis:
- First, data can be presented in a cost-benefit ratio.
- Second, data can be presented through a calculation of the present total project value.
- Third, data can be presented by evaluating the internal rate of return of the investment. The third method, the internal rate of return, or rate-of-return analysis, is the most common cost benefit analysis tool used to evaluate investments and make decisions (Hough, 1994).

CAPITAL BUDGETS
Chief financial officers, managers, and planning teams may choose to base their corporate financial strategy on their capital budgets. Capital budgets, determined in the capital budgeting process, refer to a financial plan to finance long-term capital expenses such as fixed assets, facilities, and equipment. Capital budgeting is the analytical process of determining the optimal investment of scarce capital so as to realize the greatest profit from that investment. Capital budgeting ranks proposed investments in order of their potential profitability. There are two main criteria for selecting potential business investments:

- First, business managers, engaged in capital budgeting, generally have a minimum desired rate of return specified as the cut-off point to determine whether or not a project should be accepted of rejected.
- Second, business managers, engaged in capital budgeting, generally experience constraint from top management regarding the total amount of potential investment.

Corporate managers, engaged in capital budgeting, take hold of stockholders' funds and work to maximize their earning potential through four main strategies: The postponability method, the payback method, financial statement method, and discounted cash flow technique. Corporate managers engaged in capital budgeting also develop an economic forecast for each proposed project. The corporate manager generally chooses the project that has the highest future earnings and the lowest associated costs. This approach is complicated by the different risks associated with each potential project. Thus, competing investment projects have different levels of associated risk (Parkinson, 1971).

Ultimately, the components of corporate financial strategies, including value-based management, strategic planning, mergers and acquisitions, cost analysis, and capital budgets, can lead organic and inorganic corporate growth efforts. Investors and economists debate the relative strengths and weaknesses of organic and inorganic business growth. Inorganic and organic business growth each move in and out of favor depending on the strength of the economy, political environment, and government regulations. Organic growth is created by expanding existing business resources rather than through mergers and acquisitions. Inorganic growth is created by corporate development practices. Corporate development refers to the activities that companies undertake to grow through inorganic means such as mergers and acquisitions, strategic alliances, and joint ventures.

ISSUES

INVESTOR RELATIONS AS CORPORATE FINANCIAL STRATEGY
Corporate financial strategy is a holistic endeavor that involves every level and aspect of corporate life.

Corporate financial strategy, which endeavors to create shareholder value, is dependent on successful and harmonious investor relations. Investor relations refer to the communication of company information to the financial community, analysts, investors and potential investors. An investor relation is a strategic tool in a corporation's overall financial strategy. Corporations rely on investors to provide capital. Corporations turn to investors for fundraising and raising capital. To facilitate this relationship and promote trust, corporations engage in investor relations. Investor relations offer present and future investors with the precise portrayal of a corporation's accomplishments and potential and influences the corporation's overall image and financial reputation. Financial reputation refers to the general assessment of a business's economic prospects made by the financial rating industry. Investor relations, also referred to as customer relationship management (CRM) or investor communication, is overseen by corporate communication executives; financial directors; company secretaries; or external consultants. "Investor relations involves continuous, planned, deliberate, sustained marketing activities that identify, establish, maintain and enhance both long and short term relationships between a company and not only its prospective and present investors, but also other financial analysts and stakeholders. Corporate communication strategy attempts to win the approval of financial stakeholders" (Dolphin, 2004, p. 25). Investor relations help corporations gain support of important financial opinion formers. Ultimately, strategic corporate marketing combines the disciplines of finance and communication for the purpose of creating shareholder trust and value (Dolphin, 2004).

CONCLUSION

In the final analysis, corporate leaders and managers, including the chief executive officers of large firms and the business managers of small family businesses, need to have an understanding of how market forces affect business practices in order to be competitive in their industry. Corporate decision makers use and rely on the tools, methods, and approaches of corporate financial strategy to make informed business decisions that maximize profit and secure market share.

BIBLIOGRAPHY

Acs, Z., & Gerlowski, D. (1999). Teaching managerial economics. *Financial Practice & Education, 9*(2), 125-131. Retrieved September 7, 2007, from EBSCO Online Database Business Source Complete. http://search.ebscohost.com/login.aspx?direct=true&db=bth&AN=4398648 &site=ehost-live

Beyea, S & Nicoll, H. (1999). Finding answers to questions using cost analysis. *AORN Journal, 70*(1), 128-131.

Bhalla, V. (2004). Creating wealth corporate financial strategy and decision making. *Journal of Management Research, 4*(1), 13-34. Retrieved September 8, 2007, from EBSCO Online Database Business Source Premier. http://search. ebscohost. com/login.aspx?direct=true&db=buh&AN=134 91200&site=ehost-live

Castañer, X., & Kavadis, N. (2013). Does good governance prevent bad strategy? A study of corporate governance, financial diversification, and value creation by French corporations, 2000-2006. *Strategic Management Journal, 34*(7), 863-876. Retrieved November 15, 2013, from EBSCO Online Database Business Source Complete. http://search. ebscohost.com/login.aspx?direct=true&db=bt h&AN=87783809&site=ehost-live

Costa, J., Godinho, P., & Clímaco, J. (2005). Exploring financial strategies: A multiobjective visual reference point approach. *International Transactions in Operational Research, 12*(4), 455-472. Retrieved September 9, 2007, from EBSCO Online Database Business Source Premier. http://search. ebscohost.com/login.aspx?direct=true&db=b uh&AN=17519123&site=ehost-live

Dolphin, R. (2004). The strategic role of investor relations. *Corporate Communications, 9*(1), 25.

Egan, T. (1995). Updating managerial economics. *Business Economics, 30*(3), 51. Retrieved September 7, 2007, from EBSCO Online Database Business Source Complete. http://search.eb-scohost.com/login.aspx?direct=true&db=bt h&AN=9508070977&site=ehost-live

Frigo, M. (2003). Strategy and the board of directors. *Strategic Finance, 84*(12), 8.

Hough, J. (1994). Educational cost-benefit analysis. *Education Economics, 2*(2), 93. Retrieved Sunday, September 7, 2007, from EBSCO Online Database Business Source Complete. http://search.

ebscohost.com/login.aspx?direct=t rue&db=bth& AN=9707160475&site=ehost-live

Ingley, C., Mueller, J., & Cocks, G. (2011). The financial crisis, investor activists and corporate strategy: will this mean shareholders in the boardroom?. *Journal of Management & Governance, 15*(4), 557-587. Retrieved November 15, 2013, from EBSCO Online Database Business Source Complete. http://search.ebscohost.com/login.aspx?direct=t rue&db=bth&AN=66643866&site=ehost-live

Kennedy, M. (2004). Using customer relationship management to increase profits. *Strategic Finance, 85*(9), 37-42. Retrieved September 8, 2007, from EBSCO Online Database Business Source Premier. http://search.ebscohost.com/login.aspx?direct=t rue&db=buh&AN=12298685 &site=ehost-live

Liebs, A. (1999). More U.S. companies have corporate development on their minds. *Mergers & Acquisitions Report, 12*(24), 3. Retrieved September 8, 2007, from EBSCO Online Database Business Source Complete. http://search. ebscohost. com/login.aspx?direct=true&db=bth&AN=1971 973&site=ehost-live

Lu, C. (2006). Growth strategies and merger patterns among small and medium-sized enterprises: An empirical study. *International Journal of Management, 23*(3), 529-547. Retrieved September 8, 2007, from EBSCO Online Database Business Source Complete. http://search.ebscohost.com/ login.aspx?direct=true&db=bth&AN=22433919 &site=ehost-live

Mallette, F. (2005). A financial plan with options to create maximum value. *Mergers & Acquisitions: The Dealermaker's Journal, 40*(4), 26-33. Retrieved September 9, 2007, from EBSCO Online Database Business Source Premier. http:// search.ebscohost.com/login.aspx?direct=tru e&db=buh&AN=16756475&site=ehost-live

Parkinson, P. (1971). Investment decision-making: Conventional methods vs. game theory. *Management Accounting, 53*(3), 13-17.

Sandberg, C. M., Lewellen, W. G., & Stanley, K. L. (1987). Financial strategy: planning and managing the corporate leverage position. *Strategic Management Journal, 8*(1), 15-24. Retrieved November 15, 2013, from EBSCO Online Database Business Source Complete. http://search. ebscohost. com/login.aspx?direct=true&db=bth&AN=5343

357&site=ehost-live

Slater, S., & Zwirlein, T. (1996). The structure of financial strategy: Patterns in financial decision making. *Managerial & Decision Economics, 17*(3), 253-266. Retrieved September 9, 2007, from EBSCO Online Database Business Source Premier. http://search.ebscohost.com/login.aspx?direct=t rue&db=buh&AN=6136935 &site=ehost-live

Thackray, J. (1995). What's new in financial strategy? *Planning Review, 23*(3), 14-19.

Van Auken, H., & Holman, T. (1995). Financial strategies of small, public firms: A comparative analysis with small, private firms and large, public firms. *Entrepreneurship: Theory & Practice, 20*(1), 29-41. Retrieved September 9, 2007, from EBSCO Online Database Business Source Premier. http:// search.ebscohost.com/login.aspx?direct=tru e&d b=buh&AN=9608222288&site=ehost-live

Walker, J., & Price, K. (2000). Perspectives: why do mergers go right? *Human Resource Planning, 23*(2), 6-9.

SUGGESTED READING

Breen, W., & Lerner, E. (1973). Corporate financial strategies and market measures of risk and return. *Journal of Finance, 28*(2), 339. Retrieved September 9, 2007, from EBSCO Online Database Business Source Premier. http:// search.ebscohost.com/login.aspx?direct=true&db=buh&A N=4656712&site=ehost-live

Hamilton, C. (1978). Corporate financial strategies under uncertainty: Valuation and policies in dynamic disequilibrium. *Journal of Financial & Quantitative Analysis, 13*(4). Retrieved September 9, 2007, from EBSCO Online Database Business Source Premier. http://search.ebscohost.com/ login.aspx?direct=true&db=buh&AN=4760177 &site=ehost-live

Shilling, A. (1998). The cleanup crew has arrived. *Forbes, 162*(13), 287-287. Retrieved September 9, 2007, from EBSCO Online Database Business Source Premier. http:// search. ebscohost.com/login.aspx?direct=true&db=buh&A N=1333652&site=ehost-live

—Simone I. Flynn, Ph.D.

D

DEBT VALUATION

ABSTRACT

Debt valuation can be defined as the appraisal of the amount of debt that has been incurred by a company. Companies incur debt or secure credit for a number of reasons that may include the financing of organizational growth, financing a merger or acquisition or to keep an organization solvent during a financial downturn. Some organizations wish to avoid debt at any cost and use the pay-as-you-go strategy to finance growth and operations. Other organizations see debt (or securing credit) as a way to finance growth and opportunities that might otherwise be beyond reach. This essay discusses the implications of business debt from the opportunity standpoint and explores the ways in which debt has been used to fund an era of recent and unprecedented corporate growth and mergers and acquisitions. The rise in the levels of corporate debt will be discussed in terms of its historical significance and the current challenges that organizations face in securing and managing their debt. No current review of this topic would be complete without discussing the role of private equity firms (PE) and the phenomenon of leveraged buyouts (LBO) and their role in the explosion of corporate debt.

OVERVIEW

The rise of the issuance of corporate debt from 2003-2007 has been astounding by almost any measure. Low interest rates, rising corporate profits and lots of global credit are cited as helping to fuel an era of rising corporate debt. The early years of the new millennium are somewhat reminiscent of the credit markets that were the norm in the 1990s. In the 1990s, corporate bond issuance or selling of corporate debt was very high. Rapid economic growth was occurring, but the corporate debt load was also bigger than it had ever been. Many felt that even a slight slowing of the economy combined with a rise in interest rates could change manageable debt into debt that would put corporations and individuals under strain. In the 1990s, big debt payments caused companies to cut back on capital expenditures and the potential downturn in the economy was seen as a sure sign that defaults would rise, liquidity would dry up and an overall credit crunch would arise. In the late 1990s, companies were borrowing at rates that had never previously been experienced. Corporate debt was being used for:

- Corporate stock buy-backs (re-purchases)
- Financing for acquisitions and mergers
- Funding of high tech prospects for exponential growth
- Telecom industry growth

RISING CORPORATE DEBT

The following examples show the trend toward rising corporate debt in the late 1990s. Computer Associates (a high tech darling) had just $50 million in long term debt in 1995, but by 1999, its debt service was $5 billion. Telecom growth was spurred by de-regulation, new technology and competition and debt was incurred by many companies to make a move in the market. During the first half of 1999 alone, $20 billion in corporate defaults had occurred worldwide with 85% being in the USA.

The following warning was being sounded in late 1999. "The most alarming sign of trouble ahead may be what's happening to corporate balance sheets. Despite the huge gains in the stock market, there is a pronounced tilt in corporate financing toward debt and away from equity. Even at today's prices, companies are buying back far more stock than they are issuing. Over the past 12 months, an eye-popping 3.6% of gross domestic product went into stock buybacks, and even with the IPO boom, nearly $500 billion in equities have been taken off the market since 1997" (Mandel, 1999).

NEGATIVE IMPACTS OF DEBT

The dotcom bust of early 2000 was a wakeup call to many investors and financial institutions. Stock prices fell 40%. The Federal Reserve lowered interest rates to help stimulate the economy as threats of recession loomed. Stock prices remained stagnant, but corporate profits kept rising. Many saw the rise of private equity (PE) firms as an natural outcome to economic conditions shortly after the tech/telecom bust. Those conditions were: Depressed stock prices, low interest rates and rising corporate profits. With a "dollop" of cash and loads of debt, PE firms began to snap up companies on the cheap. The average buyout in 2002 was 4 times the price of the company's cash flow (aka EBITA). It was not uncommon for PE firms to borrow 70% of the purchase price for these acquisitions. The loans were then put on the acquired company's balance sheet which doubled or even tripled the company's debt load (Tully & Hajim, 2007).

By 2003, the Federal Reserve had slashed interest rates in an effort to get the economy growing after the tech/telecom bust. Corporate profits continued to remain strong, and with the opening of global markets and associated global credit, the era of corporate mergers was ushered in. Lots of cheap and readily available credit and a higher tolerance for risk helped bolster many private equity firms and their LBO deals.

A brief discussion of differing attitudes about the value of debt will follow as well as an overview of corporate credit ratings as they pertain to today's trends in corporate debt. Finally, this essay will outline some of the current trends and outlooks related to

tightening credit markets, investor risk tolerance and the potential for market corrections in relation to potential corporate failure.

APPLICATIONS

RISK ASSESSMENT OF DEBT

Corporate credit ratings help investors determine the amount of risk associated with acquiring debt. Credit ratings are independent objective assessments of credit worthiness. Ratings "measure the ability or willingness of an entity (person or company) to keep its financial commitment to repay debt obligations (Heakal, 2003). Three of the most widely respected raters of corporate credit are: Moody's, Standard & Poor's, and Fitch IBCA. Each of these rating agencies provides a rating system that helps to determine the credit risk when acquiring a corporation's debt. Ratings can be assigned to long term or short term debt. For example, Standard and Poor's AAA rating is given to companies with the highest investment grade and very low credit risk. This credit-worthiness indicated a company's high ability and willingness to repay its debt. "Investment grade" is the level of quality that is generally thought to be required for an investor considering overseas investments. It is interesting to note that in the 1990s, investment grade was more of a requisite for incurring debt than it has been in recent years. PE firms have not paid as much

AN OVERVIEW OF MOODY'S AND STANDARD & POOR'S RATINGS

Bond Ratings			
Moody's	Standard & Poor's	Grade	Risk
Aaa	AAA	Investment	Lowest Risk
Aa	AA	Investment	Low Risk
A	A	Investment	Low Risk
Baa	BBB	Investment	Medium Risk
Ba, B	BB, B	Junk	High Risk
Caa/Ca/C	CCC/CC/C	Junk	Highest Risk
C	D	Junk	In Default

attention to the ratings (since 2003) and have basically been much more tolerant of risk as many PE firms have bought and sold lower grade or "junk" investments.

THE VALUE OF DEBT

Many companies are opposed to borrowing funds or leveraging debt to fund operations and growth. Many privately-held companies are debt-free by choice, while many other companies (ex: service companies) don't have the means to support long-term borrowing and are debt-free by necessity. Many business owners and corporate management teams feel a great deal of security in knowing that their organizations are not mired in debt, and may even have a sense that a lack of debt makes their business more attractive in the marketplace. However, in the age of global markets and virtual customers in a "flat world" economy, many see debt as a strategic tool to be leveraged to support growth

GROSS VALUE

Having some debt on the books may be a selling point when it comes to the overall "gross value" of an organization. Gross value, to many, includes what a company earns, but also may reflect its value or brand in the marketplace. Intangible assets can be leveraged by companies who expand their market reach and presence in global markets. Sophisticated buyers or investors will look at overall capital structure. Debt is necessary for many organizations to invest in growth and gain increased market share. Lack of debt may indicate a non-aggressive stance in the marketplace; global brands can't afford to shy away from opportunity that might hinder growth. From a growth and expansion view, corporate debt can be seen a very positive thing. However, investors would be well advised to avoid debt that is not necessary, overly costly or of high risk (Fraser, 2000).

GROWTH OF DEBT

The amount of debt that is on many company's balance sheets went from reasonable to outrageous between 2003 and 2007. Debt, once thought of as a necessary evil to help companies finance growth and expansion, became the hottest investment opportunity of the early 21st century.

"Like every mania, this one carried the seeds of its own destruction. The lure of easy riches drew new players, and the pace of deal making picked up. In 2005 there was a string of splendid deals at reasonable prices. As the good times rolled, the buyout binge took on a life of its own. The real craziness started in 2006. Dazzled by rich returns, investors threw more and more money at private equity firms. Flush with cash, the PE shops started pushing prices to unsustainable heights" (Tully & Hajim, 2007, 10).

DEBT MANAGEMENT

In 2007, the economy slid into recession and bad debt began to have serious repercussions worldwide. Shudders in financial markets surrounding subprime mortgage troubles shouldn't have affected most holders of corporate debt, but many saw the tightening of global credit as inevitable. The cycle headed down from its heady high, and there was renewed pressure on management teams at public companies to manage debt; private equity was not be able to "bail out" troubled companies, notably General Motors, and the federal government stepped in with taxpayer money to prevent the collapse of institutions considered "too big to fail." Credit became scarce, even after the federal reserve lowered interest rates to near zero to stimulate lending. Lenders are not likely to return to the liberal lending policies of the early 2000s (Shearer, 2007).

The media is full of sound bites that warn investors that much of what happens in the stock market is cyclical ("Spreading caution," 2007).

ISSUES

PROPPING UP COMPANIES

"Low interest rates and a flood of cash have helped many troubled companies skirt certain demise in recent years, which has led to an era of record low defaults and put a strain on the entire sector" (Kirby, 2007, 4). According to Alex Jurshevski, CEO of Recovery Partners in Toronto, "'The whole industry has been depressed because of the default rate,' says Jurshevski. who, despite having $500 million at his disposal, has yet to put any of it to work. Now, as the sub-prime mortgage collapse sends ripples beyond the housing sector, some foresee a credit crunch spreading to other sectors. 'I hope so,' he says. 'All the bad loans have already been made. They're just waiting to turn bad, like fruit left out on the counter'" (Kirby, 2007, 4).

The Federal Reserve System's headquarters in Washington, DC. *Via Wikipedia.org*

During the global financial crisis of 2008, central banks around the world pumped hundreds of billions of dollars in cash into financial markets to stave off a crisis. Yet failure is an integral part of the business cycle. "If you don't have a cleansing process where certain firms go under, the pain is delayed. Generally that means the pain will be that much greater later on" (Kirby, 2007).

"Defaults, which are triggered when companies fail to make debt repayments or break the terms of their loan contracts, have hovered around zero for the last three years. In a typical year, default rates on corporate loans and bonds can be anywhere from 3% to 10% or even higher. Even the riskiest of loans have handily dodged insolvency until now. That's because companies struggling with their debt have found a steady stream of investment funds willing to give them ever more money. 'On the one hand nobody is going bankrupt and nobody's getting thrown out of work,' says Jurshevski. 'But it also means there may be a lot of people lending money on non-economic terms and that means firms that shouldn't be surviving are being kept afloat by cheap credit.' Investors are worried buyers won't be able to handle their debt loads if interest rates rise further" (Kirby, 2007, 7).

PRIVATE EQUITY

Between 2006 and 2008, there was huge activity in the high yield and leverage loan market. Sub investment grade ratings loans raised $146 trillion in 257 deals and $950 billion in 2219 leveraged loan deals. The increase in transactions is attributed to an increase in debt-raising by private equity firms which are used to fund buyouts. Blackstone Group, a private equity firm, financed 75-80% of its deal through debt. Blackstone has acted as a buyer, a broker w/other firms that it owns and as a lender. Blackstone has had huge success in its deals — many attribute Blackstone's success to a core of talented partners with industry and financial expertise. Because Blackstone partners have vertical and sector depth of knowledge, "they have the wherewithal to dig deep when doing transactions and figure out the most flexible and cost-efficient capital structures to match the investment needs of the businesses they are buying. This has paid off regarding their ability to handle complex transactions" ("Blackstone group," 2007; Segal, 2013).

Some think the level of debt of private equity firms is too high and that the same firms may not be informing investors of the true level of risk when they buy debt. Some high profile LBO deals have happened in industries that investors would normally shy away from. However, firms like Blackstone have gained a huge amount of trust in the debt business. There's an underlying fear that liquidity will dry up and private equity firms will get left holding debt that they won't easily be able to dispose of. Many LBOs are actually completed with unfavorable credit terms and then are renegotiated with financial institutions at a better rate. A firm like Blackstone has capitalized on the debt business and has gained the confidence of investment bankers who trust firms like Blackstone that are experts in debt ("Blackstone group," 2007).

PRICING RISK

Firm failure is a natural part of the business cycle. However, it has been a rare part of the cycle since 2003 and is likely due to a couple of factors. After the collapse of the tech bubble around 2000, the Federal Reserve slashed interest rates. Low interest rates and increased global liquidity that was raised by hedge funds and private equity firms produced tons of cash in global markets. Businesses took advantage of the cheap cash by borrowing heavily to fund acquisitions and expansions. The rate of defaults on loans and business failures has been very low to almost nonexistent during this period. Defaults result from a failure of a company to repay its debt, or when a company fails to honor the terms of a loan contract.

Many contend that money was so cheap and easy to come by that even firms that should have gone under found a steady flow of cash to keep them solvent. Banks ceased operating on a "slash and burn" or "close-the-door liquidations" policy as they once did. Lenders are looking for alternatives to foreclosures and defaults and usually reserve those scenarios for firms that are responsible for fraudulent business practices or gross mismanagement. In mid 2007, there were a few high profile examples where private equity firms had trouble selling corporate debt. While these examples are still relatively rare, concern lingered that some small and medium firms could have also fall into debt trouble.

Risk for some firms means opportunity for others — there are companies that will benefit from a rise in the corporate default on loans. Miscalculations on

the risk/reward equation will cost some companies their very existence and many investors acknowledge that this is a necessary part of the business cycle. Central banks have been accused of pumping billions into financial markets to stave off corporate collapse (some of which should be allowed to happen). Recovery Partners, a Toronto based company, is in just that market. Recovery Partners has cash in hand for the sole purpose of buying portfolios of underperforming corporations. According to Alex Jurshevski, "By snatching up the debt of struggling companies, he aims to take over the businesses, turn their fortunes around, and resell them. It's a precarious strategy, akin, he says, to safely catching a falling knife, but it's one that promises huge returns" (Kirby, 2007).

CONCLUSION

Private equity firms were blamed for creating a "market that is completely out of touch with economic reality." Private equity has been called the perfect Wall Street bubble for its part in making fortunes from increasingly risky investments and strategies. Predictions of tightening of credit markets came true, while optimism that robust global markets would provide investors with corporate debt as well as investment capital fell far short, at least for a time. The financial crisis of 2008 was accompanied by a credit drought and worldwide contraction and was followed by a glacial recovery.

Putting corporate debt on a company's balance sheet can provide necessary capital from investors to fund expansion or acquisition. Reasonable amounts of investment grade debt are the safest bet for companies to incur. In 2002 the average buy-out of a company was four times its cash flow; in 2007 buyout prices were closing at 15 times cash flow-or 4 times the rate of 2002 (Tully & Hajim, 2007). By 2012, as the economy began to show signs of recovery from the worst downturn since the Great Depression, private equity firms were once again able to borrow the lion's share of funds toward a leveraged buyout — at a very low interest rate — if the target companies were stable, had tangible assets, and maintained a healthy cash flow (Sheahan, 2012).

BIBLIOGRAPHY

Beware of the debt bomb. (1999, November 1). *Business Week*, (3653), 220. Retrieved September

17, 2007, from EBSCO Online Database Academic Search Premier. http://search. ebscohost. com/login.aspx?direct=true&db=aph&AN=241 0703&site=ehost-live

Blackstone group. (2007). *Euromoney, 38*(458), 100. Retrieved September 14, 2007, from EBSCO Online Database Business Source Premier. http://search.ebscohost.com/ login.aspx?direct=true&d b=buh&AN=25585141&site=eh ost-live

Corporate finance. (2007). *QuickMBA.com.* Retrieved September 14, 2007, from http://www.quickmba. com/finance/cf/

Frasier, J. (2000) Giving credit to debt. *Inc.com: The Daily Resource for Entrepreneurs..* Retrieved September 15, 2007, from http://www.inc.com/magazine/20001101/20913. html

Kirby, J. (2007). Let the feasting begin. *Maclean's, 120*(33), 30-31. Retrieved September 14, 2007, from EBSCO Online Database Academic Search Premier. http://search. ebscohost. com/login.aspx?direct=true&db=aph&AN=262 95581&site=ehost-live

Heakal, R. (2003). What is a corporate credit rating? *Investopedia.* Retrieved September 14, 2007, from http:// www.investopedia.com/articles/03/102203.asp

Mandel, M. (1999, November 1). Is the U.S. building a debt bomb? *Business Week,* (3653), 40-42. Retrieved September 17, 2007, from EBSCO Online Database Academic Search Premier. http:// search.ebscohost.com/ login.aspx?direct=true&d b=aph&AN=2409107&site=eh ost-live

Rosenbush, S. (2007, July 30). Corporate debt: Dressed up, nowhere to go. *Business Week Online,* 11. Retrieved September 14, 2007, from EBSCO Online Database Academic Search Premier. http://search.ebscohost.com/ login.aspx?direct= true&db=aph&AN=26003795&site=eh ost-live

Segal, J. (2013). Blackstone Group's GSO Capital: lenders of last resort. *Institutional Investor, 47*(6), 12. Retrieved November 15, 2013, from EBSCO Online Database Business Source Complete. http://search.ebscohost.com/ login.aspx?direct= true&db=bth&AN=90371235&site=eh ost-live

Sheahan, M. (2012). Private equity firms writing smaller checks. *High Yield Report, 23*(21), 23. Retrieved November 15, 2013, from EBSCO Online Database Business Source Complete. http:// Database Business Source Complete. http://

search.ebscohost.com/ login.aspx?direct=true&d b=bth&AN=75649108&site=eh ost-live

Shearer, B. (2007). Deal market braces for credit crunch. *Mergers & Acquisitions: The Dealermaker's Journal, 42*(9), 74-91. Retrieved September 14, 2007, from EBSCO Online Database Business Source Premier. http://search. ebscohost. com/login.aspx?direct=true&db=buh&AN=264 84343&site=ehost-live

Spreading caution. (2007). *Economist, 384*(8539), 76. Retrieved September 14, 2007, from EBSCO Online Database Academic Search Premier. http:// search.ebscohost.com/login.aspx?direct=true &db=aph&AN=25952117 &site=ehost-liveTully, S., & Hajim, C. (2007). Why the private equity bubble is bursting. *Fortune, 156*(4), 30-34. Retrieved September 14, 2007, from EBSCO Online Database Academic Search Premier. http:// search.ebscohost.com/login.aspx?direct=tru e&db=aph&AN=26199030&site=ehost-live

SUGGESTED READING

Clouse, C. (2007). Mounting debt may spell opportunity for some investment banks. *Private Placement Letter, 25*(31), 1-6. Retrieved September 14, 2007, from EBSCO Online Database Business Source Premier. http://search.ebscohost.com/ login.aspx?direct=true&db=buh&AN=2609649 2&site=ehost-live

Karp, A. (2006). Cash crunch. *Air Cargo World, 96*(2), 10-11. Retrieved September 14, 2007, from EBSCO Online Database Business Source Premier. http:// search.ebscohost.com/login.aspx?direct=true&db =buh&AN=19819894 &site=ehost-live

S., M. (2007). Distressed debt outlook: Make room for a little doom and gloom. *Bank Loan Report, 22*(2), 5. Retrieved September 14, 2007, from EBSCO Online Database Business Source Premier. http:// search.ebscohost.com/ login.aspx?direct=true&d b=buh&AN=23768870&site=eh ost-live

Woyke, E., & Henry, D. (2007, August 13). The buyout boom's dark side. *Business Week,* (4046), 40-42. Retrieved September 14, 2007, from EBSCO Online Database Academic Search Premier. http:// search.ebscohost.com/ login.aspx?direct=true&d b=aph&AN=26057452&site=eh ost-live

—Carolyn Sprague

DERIVATIVES & MANAGEMENT OF RISK

ABSTRACT

Derivatives are investments that depend on an underlying security based on some future date. Since it is difficult to predict when something will occur, derivatives are seen as something of a gamble. As a result, many liken derivatives to a lesson in how to manage risk. Risk is the uncertainty an investor experiences regarding the outcome of an investment. Risks abound and can be due to many unforeseen and uncontrollable factors. Investors typically balance risk by making sound financial goals and objectives, managing the allocation of the investment portfolio and by selecting investments based on individual appetite for risk.

OVERVIEW

Risk and uncertainty are an inescapable part of investing. Fredman & Wiles (1998) called risk "the possibility of loss, damage, or harm" where risk depends on the individual and the individual's appetite or tolerance for risk. Managing risk is very important for successful long term investing. Investors can use various strategies such as diversification and asset allocation to reduce risk. Ultimately, the investor must compare financial objectives to the risk and return rates of investments.

DERIVATIVES

A derivative is a financial asset that gets its value from an ordinary security like a stock or bond (Morgenson & Harvey, 2007). Faerber (2006) defined derivatives as "securities that derive their value from other securities and involve transactions that are completed at a future date." Derivatives are used to hedge against changes in interest rates and currency exchange rates. Numa (n.d.) stated that derivatives are typically used to provide the investor with several investment strategy options including "speculation, hedging, arbitrage" and a combination of these. Speculation is when the investor buys financial products with the hope of profiting from the fluctuation in the products. Hedging is a financial strategy where the investor chooses assets based on the attempt to reduce the possibility of negative portfolio impact

by balancing or canceling out the risk. Arbitrage is buying a financial asset at one price and selling it at a different one, hopefully higher, in a different market such as a different country.

STRENGTHS

Molvar & Green (1995) noted that derivatives are the results of wizardry by financial engineers on Wall Street. These engineers have taken ordinary financial instruments and combined them in new ways to exploit various risk and reward scenarios. The impact of 'derivatives' have made them a case study in how to manage risk. A Federal Reserve board member is quoted as saying that derivatives are not the problem but the reaction to the risk caused by them is the issue. Derivatives are found to be popular with many types of entities because of the flexibility in choosing risk and reward scenarios. Derivatives are a multi-trillion dollar market and are popular with insurance companies, manufacturers, banks, not-for-profit organizations and government.

WEAKNESSES

Some focus on the historical negatives of derivatives while others caution against generalizing derivatives as bad. Liu (2002) traced the "beginning of finance globalization" to the oil crisis of the 1970s that required multinational banks to find borrowers in other countries. These developing countries became embroiled in debt. The International Monetary Fund created bailouts for developing countries that decreased spending and currency devaluation in the 1980s. In the 1990s, derivatives became a new form of finance flowing to developing countries which were termed "newly industrialized economies" (NIEs). Some feel that derivatives were a critical factor in the 1997 Asian financial crisis. Derivatives in this case were used to creatively reallocate risk and help financial institutions gain tax advantages, avoid accounting rules and receive advantages over the exchange rates. Liu believes that investors become interested in derivatives because of high returns but want higher profits than risk which causes financial institutions to have some unfunded risk.

Tyson (2003) considered derivatives such as futures and options no better than gambling and advised against investors (especially novices) getting involved with them. "Options on futures and futures do walk hand in hand; most traders are trading these two interchangeably and simultaneously" says Ira Krulik, C.O.O. of New York Portfolio Clearing (Timberlake, 2011). One reason futures and options can be risky is because the investor is trying to predict activity in the short-term movement of a specific security and can result in large losses. Short term market movements tend to be rapid and unpredictable in any direction. The short term changes are catalysts that make investors jump in and out of markets quickly (Alvares, 2007). Tyson noted that some professional investors use options and futures to provide a hedge against some risk but found the value limited for the average investor.

INVESTOR ATTRACTION TO DERIVATIVES

Fredman & Wiles (1998) indicated that derivatives rose on the investor radar screen in 1994 because of high profile failures of bond and money market funds. Some feel that the 1994 crisis put a permanent blemish on the derivatives market. Because of action by the Securities and Exchange Commission (SEC), today there is less risk from derivatives today as some of the more dangerous ones have been outlawed. Although derivatives can be used in a generic sense to include futures and options, they can also be seen in several customized versions such as collateralized mortgage obligations and structured notes. Derivatives have inherent leverage and can move in the same or in a different direction than the underlying security and are more volatile than the underlying security. Derivatives have a "gearing" feature with attracts attention from investors because the derivative could experience a large return of say 100% in a very short period such as days while the underlying security only rises 10%. Gearing is the ratio of what you put in and your return. Fredman & Wiles (1998) stated that bond managers would use derivatives for the following reasons:

- To reduce or hedge an unwanted risk.
- To make speculative bets on a market or security.
- To increase returns in an effort to offset lofty expenses, especially 12b-1 fees.

The pressure to deliver high returns in a competitive market can make the benefits of derivatives attractive. The increased volatility that derivatives offer can be exciting to the speculative investor but often beyond the individual investor's educational understanding. Fredman & Wiles agreed that derivatives aren't necessarily bad but felt that it was more of a question of how and when derivatives are used, for what purpose and in what quantities. The preferred method is to use derivatives in moderation. Fredman & Wiles suggested avoiding any mutual fund with extra high returns as compared to others and any portfolio with higher than average performance and expenses.

TYPES OF DERIVATIVES

In 1994, the derivatives market was divided into exchange-traded and over-the-counter (OTC) derivatives. Exchange traded derivatives are futures and options contracts, while OTC derivatives are less liquid swaps, options and forward contracts. OTC trading, which tends to be less strictly regulated and thus can be more flexibly applied, is positively associated with abnormal return (AR) and return on asset (ROA), while exchange trading is not. After the US financial crisis, exchange trading, which is more heavily regulated and thus has lower credit risks, is positively associated with AR and ROA (Jin-Yong, 2013). *Economic Trends* (1994) noted the 1992 year-end dollar value of exchange traded derivatives as $5 trillion and the over-the-counter derivatives as $7.5 trillion. Economic Trends pointed to financial institutions using derivatives as a hedge against interest rate changes as the reason for the rapid growth in derivatives. Davenport (2003) positioned the amount of derivatives in U.S. banks in mid-2003 as nearly $62 trillion. This value is 10 times the national debt. The ten year growth in derivatives is stunning but derivatives still remain a mystery to most investors. Davenport (2003) listed seven companies as primary participants in dealing in derivatives. These companies are:

- J.P. Morgan Chase & Co.
- Bank of America Corp.
- Citigroup. Inc.
- Wachovia Corp.
- Bank One Corp.
- HSBC Holdings PLC
- Wells Fargo & Co.

Davenport suggested that instead of hedging against risk, these banks were assuming more risk because they saw a marked increase in the risk exposure from derivatives.

Numa (n.d.) found that the most common derivatives the average investor would see would be "futures, options, warrants and convertible bonds." However, the other types are limitless based on how investment banks choose to combine investments. Because a derivative is based on a contract and not an asset, they tend not to be standardized. According to Numa, if an investor has any money in a pension fund or insurance policy, the investor's funds are probably invested in derivatives with or without the investor's knowledge.

WHAT IS RISK?

INVESTING
Investors have many reasons for investing. Preparing for a variety of future events is a major thrust. Planning for retirement, a child's education, future medical costs or simply ensuring that the investor can manage rising costs and live comfortably. Faerber (2006) suggested five steps to decide how to invest. These include:
- Determine your financial objectives.
- Allocate your assets.
- Prepare your investment strategy.
- Select your investments.
- Evaluate your portfolio.

While this may seem like a straightforward plan, many investors may not have the patience to be thorough in executing it.

FINANCIAL OBJECTIVES
Financial objectives are as varied as the number and type of investors in the myriad of investments possible. Some objectives may be fairly short term such as saving for a car or long term such as planning for retirement. When considering the alternatives, the investor must evaluate the timeline for the investment, when the return may be needed and the risk involved. When thinking about time, the investor must also consider what time or stage of life he or she is in. Young investors are likely to have different objectives than middle aged or older investors. (2006). Once the investor is clear on their financial objectives, the next step in the process is to figure out where to invest among the alternatives available.

TYPES OF INVESTMENTS
Faerber divides the types of investment available into financial investments and non-financial investments. Non-financial investments include real estate, collectibles and precious metals. Financial investments can be grouped into four major categories:
- Money market securities: Short term with maturities of one year or less.
- Debt securities: Fixed income with maturities greater than one year.
- Equity securities: Long term securities that do not mature.
- Derivative securities: Securities deriving value from other securities involving transactions completed at a future date.

TYPES OF INVESTMENT RISK
Faerber defined risk as "the variability of returns from an investment or the uncertainty related to the outcome of an investment." There are many different types of risk. Risk is the "degree of uncertainty of return on an asset" (Morgenson & Harvey, 2002, p. 284). There have been three types of investment risk identified: Business risk, valuation risk and force of sale risk.
- Business risk means losing value due to "competition, mismanagement financial insolvency." There can also be a high level of risk based on industry.
- Valuation risk is when a stock may be valued too high for its future performance.
- Force of sale risk is being forced to potentially unload a stock that due to market circumstance. This risk can be incurred by attempting to predict when the appreciation of the stock will occur.

Faerber (2006) mentioned additional types of investment risk including: Business risk, financial risk, market risk, operating risk, interest-rate risk, purchasing power (inflation) risk, event risk, exchange rate risk, liquidity risk.
- Business risk is uncertainty related to a company's sales and earnings.
- Financial risk is when a company cannot meet financial obligations. If a company has little or no debt then it has little or no risk.
- Market, interest-rate, exchange-rate, inflation and event risk all fall under the category of systematic or non-diversifiable risk. This risk type is external to an entity and affects all securities.

- Unsystematic risk such as operating risk is specific to a company or industry.
- Groz (1999) called investment risk the chance that you will not achieve the goals you set for investment in the time you wanted to achieve them. If that were to happen, the investor might have to forego various financial plans or look for other sources to address financial obligations. Market risk is when an investment is volatile or goes up or down rapidly and possibly unexpectedly. Many investors have little appetite for volatility. In these cases, the investor should only invest what he or she can accept losing and invest only in investments with limited risk.

How to Manage Risk
Diversifiable risk can be described as risk that can be managed or averted by "pooling risks." Investors who wish to avoid risk will pay for insurance against that risk's occurrence. Insurers increasingly manage asset risk with options, futures, and other derivatives (Fodor, Duran, Carson, & Kirch, 2013). Choudhury advises using derivatives or hedging (correlating stocks) to mitigate risk. Systematic risk can be accomplished by diversification but would require a portfolio of an incredible size to completely allow for this type of risk.

Mutual Funds
Lim (2005) recommends mutual funds as having the advantage of providing the investor with "instant" diversification. Lim noted that stock funds could own about 170 stocks at a time while bond funds could own 300 — 400. Avoiding stock specific risk requires the investor to have at least 50 stocks in a portfolio and mutual funds are an easy answer to this dilemma. Another benefit Lim pointed out is the professional management of mutual funds which allows the investor to have less of an educational burden when trying to manage risk. Mutual funds can also be obtained at reasonable minimum investments of $1000 — $3000 putting them within reach of the average investor.

Asset Allocation
Other ways to reduce risk include diversification through different types of assets (not just a large, balanced quantity) and by investing for the long term instead of getting in and out or expecting instant riches. Investors will lose less money in the long run by holding investments longer. The odds of losing money in a one year period are 27% as compared to holding an investment for 10 years when the odds of losing money are 4%. This practice is called this asset allocation or spreading the risk around. Asset allocation requires looking at financial goals and the additional step of weighing the advantages and disadvantages of a particular investment. Tyson (2003) advised students of investing to engage in "focusing on the risks you can control." The investor has to accept some volatility with stocks and growth oriented investments. Diversification is also recommended as a strategy to mitigate risk. He felt there were two big benefits of diversification including reduced volatility and higher returns for the risk involved.

Risk/Reward Relationships
Managing risk means understanding what risk means to the investor's personal portfolio. Alvares (2007) noted that investors may shy away from a certain percentage of loss on the investment portfolio but may be more tolerant of the risk when the percentage is translated into a real sum of money. Risk isn't easy to calculate because of an inability to predict market volatility. The investor should note the level of risk and reward for specific investments. Alvares (2007) showed the lowest risk-return scenario as having cash invested but has a risk of being susceptible to inflation. Next highest in risk but still low in return are government savings instruments and bonds. Debt mutual funds have higher risk but better returns than guaranteed instruments. Real estate and precious metals are riskier but have returns that usually beat inflation. Equity mutual funds have high risks and returns while direct equity investments have the highest returns and the highest risks. It is also recommended that investors take a long term, 10 year view of investments to reduce risk and spreading the risk around among stocks. A disciplined investor will also regularly buy when the market is down to increase portfolio returns. Alvares (2007) found that real estate investors were most vulnerable to risk because the risk is too concentrated in one type of asset.

Alvares (2007) suggested six ways investors can mitigate risk including:
- Obtaining life insurance.
- Don't invest based on the highest return because the risk may be equally high or higher.

- Diversify your portfolio.
- Avoid over-leveraging because it can multiply your losses.
- Invest for the long term.
- Mix your portfolio with different kinds of assets to beat inflation.

VIEWPOINT

IMPLICATIONS OF UNMANAGED RISK

Quantifying risk can be difficult because a number of factors seen and not seen have to be taken into account and ultimately the investor can only control his or her own actions. Investing in the stock market can be compared to investing money through a savings account, as the stock market may exhibit volatility but outperform the savings account in terms of inflation. Investors may make mistakes in managing risk because of emotion or may simply choose not to manage risk because of a lack of information and education about investments. Sometimes investors end up in riskier situations than needed because of an over-reliance on professional investment advisors. Bad experiences in investing may also create an environment where the investor refuses to take any risk at all.

Risk can be created and unmanaged by habits the investor has such as unbridled, excessive spending and consumer credit card debt. It is suggested that those serious about investing eliminate personal addictions that cost money such as smoking, drinking, drugs or gambling. These habits create risk because they cost money unnecessarily, jeopardize the investor's financial clarity and position and reduce the amount of money available to invest. These may seem like small issues but can result in long term ramifications to the investor's health and financial status. A reduction in general spending can be used to fund retirement accounts. In addition, when unmanaged risk is incurred through heavy speculation in derivatives and the investor wins, it adds to the "aura" of the fund manager as a genius and fuels more investment in derivatives. This occurs even though neither the fund manager nor the investor knows why the investment won (Davenport, 2003).

ORANGE COUNTY & DERIVATIVES DECLINE

Orange County, California (National Review, 1994) was one of the entities that suffered from the derivatives decline in 1994. The treasurer had to rebuild the County's image and struggle to meet payroll for more than 70,000 employees (Banham, 1998). The County was positioned to profit if interest rates fell because the derivatives in the County's investment portfolio were destined to fall if the interest rates rose. The risk was high because the investments were funded through borrowing and cash-on-hand would have to be used to cover margin calls. Other organizations that were adversely affected included Proctor and Gamble and Sears. The National Review (1994) blamed the money managers and those in charge of financial affairs for the governments and companies affected. Their actions did not protect stockholders and stakeholders and ignored risk. Although derivatives were heavily regulated in 1994, these events still occurred, prompting additional action by the SEC. Another result of unmanaged risk — wherever blame is placed — is additional government and regulatory intervention to protect investors against poor decision-makers and advisors.

Banham (1998) looked at the aftermath of the Orange County derivatives scandal and noted that over $600 million in settlements was negotiated by the Orange County treasurer from Merrill Lynch, Morgan Stanley, Dean Witter and Nomura Securities for "bad advice on derivatives." Davenport (2003) noted that Orange County lost $2 billion through derivatives. Tsiantar & Schneider (1994) reported that Proctor & Gamble lost $102 million, PaineWebber bond fund — $33 million and a BankAmerica fund lost $17.4 million all from derivatives.

Orange County ended up with a large settlement but also had to increase taxes and suffer bankruptcy. A partner at a local accounting firm ran against the Orange County treasurer and won in part by revealing the danger of the County's portfolio of derivatives. Another result of unmanaged risk even though the former Orange County treasurer bears some blame is market regulation or correction to investment companies that provide advice. Molvar & Green (1995) noted the fear of systematic risks that could collapse financial markets as the thrust for greater derivative regulation. Investors may hope that this makes financial advisors more wary and twice as careful, but the investor has to take responsibility for risk acceptance and financial understanding of investments.

Bibliography

Alvares, C. (2007). Balancing the risks. *Business Today, 16(15), 134-138*. Retrieved September 16, 2007, from EBSCO Online Database Business Source Complete. http://search.ebscohost.com/login.aspx?direct=true&db=bth&AN=25829723&site=ehost-live

Banham, R. (1998). Local hero. *Treasury & Risk Management, 8(8), 26*. Retrieved September 16, 2007, from EBSCO Online Database Business Source Complete. http://search.ebscohost.com/login.aspx?direct=true&db=bth&AN=1246341&site=ehost-live

Choudhury, G. (n.d.). What is financial risk? [Working Paper]. Retrieved September 16, 2007, from http://www.theshortrun.com/finance/Chou's%20SR%20article.doc.

Davenport, T. (2003). Assessing risk: Peeling apart data on derivs. *American Banker, 168(125), 1*. Retrieved September 16, 2007, from EBSCO Online Database Business Source Complete. http://search.ebscohost.com/login.aspx?direct=true&db=bth&AN=10170344&site=ehost-live

Derivatives. (1994). *Economic Trends (07482922), 17*. Retrieved September 16, 2007, from EBSCO Online Database Business Source Complete. http://search.ebscohost.com/login.aspx?direct=true&db=bth&AN=94092175 61&site=ehost-live

Faerber, E. (2006). *All about investing: the easy way to get started*. New York: McGraw-Hill.

Fodor, A., Doran, J. S., Carson, J. M., & Kirch, D. P. (2013). On the demand for portfolio insurance. *Risk Management & Insurance Review, 16*(2), 167-193. Retrieved November 21, 2013, from EBSCO Online Database Business Source Complete. http://search.ebscohost.com/login.aspx?direct=true&db=bth&AN=91957828&site=ehost-live

Fredman, A.J. & Wiles, R. (1998). *How mutual funds work : Second Edition (New York Institute of Finance*. New York: Prentice Hall Press.

Groz, M. M. (1999). *Forbes guide to the markets: becoming a savvy investor*. New York: John Wiley and Sons.

Jin-Yong, Y. (2013). Volume of derivative trading, enterprise value, and the return on assets. *Modern Economy, 4*(8), 513-519. Retrieved November 26, 2013, from EBSCO Online Database Business Source Complete. http://search.ebscohost.com/login.aspx?direct=true&db=bth&AN=91690771&site=ehost-live

Kennon, J. (2007). The 3 types of investment risk. About.com investing for beginners. Retrieved September 22, 2007, from http://beginnersinvest.about.com/cs/valueinvesting1/a/080103a.htm

Lim, P.J. (2005). *Investing demystified: a self-teaching guide*. New York: McGraw-Hill.

Liu, H.C.K. (2002). The dangers of derivatives. *Asia Times Online*, Retrieved September 22, 2007, from http://www.atimes.com/global-econ/DE23Dj01.html

Molvar, H.D. & Green, J.F. (1995). The question of derivatives. *Journal of Accountancy, 179(3) 55-61*. Retrieved September 16, 2007, from EBSCO Online Database Business Source Complete. http://search.ebscohost.com/login.aspx?direct=true&db=bth&AN=9503214684&site=ehost-live

Morgenson, G. & Harvey, C. R. (2002). *The New York Times Dictionary of Money Investing*. New York: Times Books.

Numa.com. (n.d.). The derivatives FAQ. Retrieved September 16, 2007, from http://www.numa.com/ref/faq.htm

Squeezing Orange County. (1994). *National Review, 46(25), 17*. Retrieved September 16, 2007, from EBSCO Online Database Business Source Complete. http://search.ebscohost.com/login.aspx?direct=true&db=aph&AN=9501077508&site=ehost-live

Timberlake, J. (2011). NYPC eyes options for growth. *Wall Street Letter, 01-02*. Retrieved November 21, 2013, from EBSCO Online Database Business Source Complete. http://search.ebscohost.com/login.aspx?direct=true&db=bth&AN=65205732&site=ehost-live

Tsiantar, D. & Schneider, M. (1994). Looking out for derivative dangers. *Newsweek, 124(1), 64*. Retrieved September 16, 2007, from EBSCO Online Database Business Source Complete. http://search.ebscohost.com/login.aspx?direct=true&db=bth&AN=9406287539&site=ehost-live

Tyson, E. (2003). *Personal finance for dummies*. Indianapolis: Wiley Publishing.

Suggested Reading

Dempsey. M. (2002). The nature of market growth, risk, and return. *Financial Analysts Journal, 58*(3), 45-59. Retrieved September 16, 2007, from EBSCO Online Database Business Source Complete. http://search.ebscohost.com/login.aspx?direct=

true&db=bth&AN=7026952&site=eh ost-live

Financial Pipeline (n.d.). Derivatives related termi-nology glossary. Retrieved September 22, 2007, from http://www. finpipe.com/derivglossary.htm

Fitzgerald, J. (2007). Don't put all your risk in one bucket. *Money Management, 21*(27), 24-25. Re-trieved September 16, 2007, from EBSCO On-line Database Business Source Complete. http://search.ebscohost.com/login.aspx?direct=t rue&d b=bth&AN=26235188&site=ehost-live

Methanex, Nova blossom on methanol price runup. (1995). *Chemical Marketing Reporter, 247*(6), 8. Re-trieved September 16, 2007, from EBSCO On-line Database Business Source Complete. http://search.ebscohost.com/ login.aspx?direct=true&d

b=bth&AN=9503035098&site= ehost-live

Robertson, K. (2007). The other side of generally ac-cepted financial theories. *401K Advisor, 14*(8), 3. Retrieved September 16, 2007, from EBSCO On-line Database Business Source Complete. http://search.ebscohost.com/ login.aspx?direct=true&d b=bth&AN=26225650&site=eh ost-live

Webb, J.A. (2001). Hedging your bet. *LP/Gas,* 61(9), 38-40. Retrieved September 16, 2007, from EBSCO Online Database Business Source Com-plete. http://search.ebscohost.com/login.aspx?d irect=true&db=bth&AN=5331294& site=ehost-live

–Marlanda English

DIVIDEND POLICY

ABSTRACT

This article examines the payment of stockholder dividends and how policies are set or how practices evolve that govern the payment of dividends. The scope of stockholder rights is explained along with methods that stockholders utilize to assure that their rights are properly manifested when investing in a company. Conflicts of interest between stock-holders and corporate executives that may result in stockholders not receiving dividends are explained. Financial scandals of the last decade are reviewed as well as new laws, regulations, and management prac-tices that have been implemented to help prevent companies from releasing false or misleading finan-cial reports.

OVERVIEW

A company's dividend policy provides guidance on when to pay stockholders dividends or when not to pay the dividends and use profits for other purposes. When profits are held and not paid out as dividends, funds can be used for new product development, market expansion, or acquisition of other compa-nies (Sheppard, 2008). Other factors that impact dividend policy in some companies include corpo-rate tax situations as well as the impact on the tax conditions of the shareholders receiving dividends (Cohen & Yagil, 2008). The type of stockholder that has invested in the company may also impact divi-dend policy. When a company is publicly traded and there is institutional ownership stock by investment funds or retirement funds, there may be more pres-sure to pay dividends (Guo & Ni, 2008) (Aivazian, Booth, & Cleary, 2006).

WHY PAY DIVIDENDS?

Dividends can be paid for several reasons. In some cases, dividends are paid to satisfy existing stock-holders (Azhagaiah & Priya, 2008) (Ben Naceur, Goaied & Belanes, 2006). When high-level executives hold large quantities of stock, paying dividends can be viewed as a form of a bonus for the executives.

In other cases, dividends may be paid as a signal that the company is successful. This may influence the opinions of stock analysts or future investors in the company (Li & Zhao, 2008) (Dickens, Casey & Newman, 2002). Companies have attempted to use dividend payouts as a way to favorably influence their stock price. Many have found that announcing a large dividend pay out, or making a larger than normal pay out of dividends, may result in improved stock prices for a short time — there is little supporting evidence that the strategy is always effective (Wann, Long, Pearson, & Wann, 2008).

ALTERNATIVE INVESTOR INCENTIVES

Although dividends are the primary mechanism by which an investor increases their wealth through company investment, there are other means by which companies can reward their investors. Stockholder wealth can also be increased through stock buy-back programs where, instead of paying a direct dividend, a company buys stock back from investors at a preferred and attractive price (Wiemer & Diel, 2008). Another approach aside from dividend payments or payouts to shareholders is the distribution of additional shares of stock in proportion to the number of shares already owned. This can result in concentrating power in the hands of very few shareholders (Denis, 1990).

COMPANY VALUE & DIVIDEND PAYOUT

The value that a company achieves by paying dividends varies with economic conditions. As the mood of investors shifts, so do their investments. At times, they prefer dividend-paying stocks; at others, they prefer growth stocks such as many of those in the high-tech sectors. Under the Bush administration there was a short-lived effort to promote dividend payout as a practice to lower taxes on dividends for recipients. This had very little impact on the number of companies paying dividends (Bank, 2006) (Henry, 2003). However, the managers of NASDAQ firms generally concur that a consistent history of dividend payouts helps to sustain company value, at least in the perception of investors (Baker, Powell & Veit, 2002).

The big question about whether to pay or not to pay stock dividends concerns who benefits from firm wealth. Stockholders are obviously seeking a return or they would not have invested in the company. Managers, on the other hand, may be both stockholders as well as employees that receive bonuses such as revenue growth or increased market share. Thus stockholders seek ways of assuring their rights.

APPLICATIONS

METHODS OF ASSURING STOCKHOLDER RIGHTS

Some form of shareholder rights is a part of corporate law in most countries throughout Europe and North America. These rights may include the right to hold periodic shareholders' meetings and be provided annual or other reports from management. In addition, in most situations stockholders will usually have the right to receive dividends paid out of corporate profits. In the event that new stock is issued, existing stockholders may have the right to purchase shares prior to public sale ("Shareholder rights," 2008). The more established the shareholder group in age, organization, and tradition, the more likely it is that there will be dividends paid. This rewards the shareholder for investing their money and supporting the company over a long term. It is also seen as a method of keeping control of wealth and preventing managers from using the funds solely for their desired purposes (Jiraporn & Ning, 2006).

CORPORATE GOVERNANCE

Boards of directors control a corporation through a governance process. Laws relating to corporate governance have been evolving around the world. The Organization of Economic Cooperation and Development (OECD) has provided a framework for countries to structure their laws and to help guide boards of directors to develop their own governance approaches. The OECD framework promotes both stockholder rights and board responsibilities. The scope of shareholder rights ranges from timely access to accurate information, accurate financial statements, voting power, and redress when their rights are violated. The framework also charges the board of directors with a range of responsibilities including monitoring the management of the company, reviewing and approving corporate strategy, assuring the accuracy of financial statements, and deciding the compensation and tenure of high-level executives ("OECD principles," 2004)

SHAREHOLDER ACTIVISM

Shareholders have become more organized and more active over the last two decades. This activism has taken many shapes and forms. In some cases, shareholder activism can be motivated by desires for social change or protection of the environment achieved through changing corporate policy or managerial practices. Most often, such activism surfaces in the form of a resolution to be considered at an annual meeting. Few such resolutions pass and when they do they are generally considered to be only advisory in nature. These resolutions do help raise concerns and may actually be acted upon, but in informal manners (Hendry, Sanderson, Barker & Roberts, 2007). There are, however, many criticisms of shareholder activism including the fact that it is expensive, time consuming and, many argue, not very effective (Thomas, 2008).

The intensity level of activism and the direction of the activism of stockholder groups are changing considerably. Some of the more high-intensity groups now practicing shareholder activism include religious organizations and institutional investors holding large amounts of stock (Van Buren, 2007). Among the most active institutional investors are public pension funds, union pension funds, mutual funds and hedge funds that hold large blocks of stock (Minow & Hodgson, 2007). Religious organizations have well-tuned capabilities when it comes to putting pressure on corporations and at this time, they do seem to focus on socially oriented agendas. Institutional investors tend to focus on the financial stability of the held company and for the last several years have spent considerable time and effort on reducing high managerial salaries.

The activism of the institutional investors, especially those that have considerably high levels of funding from retirement funds of labor unions or public employees, has been fueled by relatively recent events. When Enron and WorldCom collapsed, several investment funds and retirement funds belonging to thousands of individuals lost value. Individual members of retirement funds were outraged and angry with the people managing their retirement funds. The fund managers in turn had little choice but to pass this anger on and to do so in a manner that better helped to protect the value of the retirement funds for which they are responsible (Minow & Hodgson, 2007).

SARBANES-OXLEY ACT
As a result of numerous corporate failures, the Sarbanes-Oxley Act was passed in 2002 by the United States Congress. This act was a very significant step in the regulation of publicly traded companies and was intended to help protect investors by requiring more stringent controls on corporate financial reporting and disclosures. As one of many control mechanisms, the act established the Public Company Accounting Oversight Board (PCAOB). "The PCAOB is a private-sector non-profit organization that is charged with overseeing the audits of public traded companies" (Walther, 2009). These companies are regulated by numerous securities laws and must submit regular reports to the Securities and Exchange Commission (SEC).

One of many issues surrounding the massive financial collapses of Enron and WorldCom was the accuracy and reliability of internal audits. These audits are provided to the board of directors and the stockholders as accurate depictions of the financial health and condition of a publicly traded company. Reports are also filed with the SEC as a matter of public record. The Sarbanes-Oxley Act addressed the reliability and independence of audits and requires that any and all documentation regarding financial statements be persevered. (The urban legend surrounding the Enron collapse is that managers in the company and those in the independent auditor's office were shredding documents that showed the fabricated annual financial statement. This is like Richard Nixon erasing tapes.) The act also holds executive officers and boards of directors more accountable for the accuracy of financial reports and prescribes rather severe criminal penalties for false or misleading reports ("Sarbanes-Oxley Act," 2006).

ISSUE

CONFLICT OF INTEREST IN DIVIDEND POLICY

CORPORATE SCANDAL
In the first decade of the twenty-first century there occurred numerous business scandals that make television soap operas look dull in comparison. Some very large or long-standing companies in the United States went bankrupt or got into very complex a deep financial problems. A partial list includes Enron, WorldCom, Xerox, Global Crossing and Halliburton Oil Services. It was one thing to be in the news as a poorly managed company. Citizens for the most part would find that laughable. But these scandals not only rocked financial markets with losses, they also resulted in job loss and drew the attention of the public as well as the United States Congress. Eventually, some chief executives were even convicted of fraud (Bhamornsiri, Guinn & Schroeder, 2009).

The big question on the minds of many ordinary citizens and thus eventually the minds of regulators as well as lawmakers was about the competence of the highly paid executives of these failing companies. The news of the large salaries and bonuses being paid to executives as workers lost their jobs led to considerable public outrage about how private corporations are managed, and especially about executive compensation (Thomas, 2008). Shareholder activism on executive compensation accelerated and has resulted in the ouster of several CEOs or the reduction and restructuring of compensation packages (Nicholas, 2007) (Melican & Westcott, 2008).

MANAGER CONDUCT & DIVIDEND POLICY

As investigation after investigation unfolded, questions about executive competence evolved into questions about honesty. Among the key questions about executive honesty was to what extent can executives manipulate financial results of a company in order to influence their own personal salaries? Such dishonesty can directly relate to dividend in its development and execution. Thus executive actions can be potentially riddled with conflicts of interest (Ghosh & Sirmans, 2006). If executives manipulate financial statements or redirect corporate assets in a self-serving manner, stockholders not only loose their dividends, but the value of their stock can radically decline.

Many investors prefer long term but steady dividends as part of their personal wealth building strategies. Conservative investors often fear over spending by managers. An organization's performance goals have an effect on how trustworthy a manager is. When revenue growth, for example, is a performance goal, then managers may be overzealous when it comes to expanding manufacturing or distribution channels. In other cases, managers may push to acquire competitors or smaller companies in the hope that this will improve their performance and result in greater compensation (Belden, Fister & Knapp, 2005).

LENDERS & DIVIDENDS

Lenders (such as an investment bank) can also hold significant equity in a company and may attempt to exert control over dividends or to even liquidate a failing company as a means to recover part of their investment in a short period of time (Kanatas & Qi, 2004). Institutional investors such as retirement funds can also hold considerable equity positions in private corporations which put the funds at risk, but also provides opportunities for involvement and oversight (Xu, 2007). These positions may very well help a company as well as all of the shareholders but can also lead to conflicts.

OVERSIGHT

There are several ways that shareholders, through the board of directors of a corporation, can attempt to control how the company is managed. These include performance-based salary systems, long-term compensation plans tied to long-term performance, or compensation plans tied to specific performance goals such as revenue increases or size of dividend payments (Thomas, 2008). "Since the adoption of the Sarbanes-Oxley Act in 2002, most public companies have established a compensation committee to aid in setting and evaluating executive compensation. Compensation committees are an important corporate governance tool to ensure that executives are fairly compensated" (Wilson, 2009). This also provides the shareholders with oversight opportunities to potentially control executive corruption.

AUDITING

The relationship between executives and financial audit firms also came into question during the course of the scandals of the last decade. In the Enron case for example, Arthur Andersen LLP was the independent auditor. Upon the collapse of Enron, conflict of interest questions were raised about the relationship between the auditors and the corporate executives. Although there are still unanswered questions about what happened, Arthur Andersen LLP pretty much closed up shop in the United States.

Sarbanes-Oxley limits the scope of services that an auditing firm can provide a publicly traded company. Registered accounting firms cannot provide non-audit services if they serve as the auditor of the financial statements for the public company. Such services may include bookkeeping, appraisal services, internal audit services, or management functions (Sarbanes-Oxley Act, 2006). In addition, those firms that provide financial audit services are required to be rotated over time so that one audit firm cannot have control over the financial audit for long periods of time. It is difficult to predict the effect of the required rotation of auditing firms. But most analysts contend that there will additional costs incurred as new firms take over the financial audit function and spend time and resources becoming familiar with the company ("Public accounting firms," 2003).

INVESTMENT BANKS

In addition to potential conflicts of interest when auditors and executives are allowed extensive freedom, there are also other conflicts that can arise when investment banks are involved. There were some investment banks that helped to facilitate and participated in several financial transactions with Enron which helped to obscure Enron's true financial condition. Since Enron, and other financial scandals occurred, research analysts at investment banks or brokerage houses have come under considerable public scrutiny for giving existing or potential investors deceptive investment advice so as to gain favor with the companies whose stock is being extolled.

PREVENTATIVE ACTION

Such financial scandals led to several court cases, investigation, and prosecutions. In June 2001, the New York Attorney General started investigating the practices of one large brokerage firm. In 2002 the New York AG reached a settlement with the firm which resulted in $100 million worth of fines and regulatory reform which limits the ties between analysts and the investment banking industry.

To help control or reduce losses the stock exchanges also took several actions. In 2002, the NYSE and NASDQ attempted to prevent conflicts of interest by placing guidelines on analysts who may have investment banking interests in the firms they analyze. The rules necessitated a distinct division between the investment banking and research branches of large multi-service brokerage firms. One regulation requires that investment banking personnel be kept from viewing research reports before they are published. In addition, dialogue between research teams and the company being researched is controlled. The rules are very strict with regard to investment or brokerage companies receiving preferred pricing on stock issues as compensation for business services. Rules also extend to the family members of investment bankers and investment analysts.

United States Government regulators also took several actions. In 2003 the SEC adopted regulations that require research reports distributed by a broker, dealer, or certain associated persons to be certified by the research analyst as an accurate reflection of the analyst's personal views. The rules also required disclosure as to whether the analyst received compensation or other payments in connection with his or her specific recommendations or views ("Investment banks," 2003).

CONCLUSION

The financial scandals of the last have decade have raised many questions about the honesty of corporate managers and the adequacy of the laws that govern how publicly traded companies should be managed. Corporate failures cost the United States thousands of jobs and cost many citizens a considerable portion, if not all of their retirement savings that was invested in 401k plans or other retirement funds.

There were public hearings and criminal investigations. Many corporate executives were found to be out and out criminals. New laws were passed. Executives were convicted. Independent financial audit firms were found to be not so independent and their reputations have been severely tarnished; at least one of the largest auditing firms ceased to exist. New laws and regulations govern the behavior of financial audit firms along with the relationships they have with the companies they audit.

Stockbrokers were found to be misrepresenting the financial condition of companies. Some of these brokerages had a severe conflict interest as they released analyst reports with buy recommendations for companies that the brokerage had other financial relationships with. New requirements of the stock exchanges were implemented to reduce conflict of interest between brokers and publicly traded companies.

BIBLIOGRAPHY

Al-Shubiri, F., Al Taleb, G., & Al-Zoued, A. (2012). The relationship between ownership structure and dividend policy: an empirical investigation. *Review of International Comparative Management / Revista De Management Comparat International, 13*(4), 644-657. Retrieved November 15, 2013, from EBSCO Online Database Business Source Complete. http://search.ebscohost.com/ login.aspx?direct=true&db=bth&AN=85294717&site=eh ost-live

Azhagaiah, R., & Priya .N, S. (2008). The impact of dividend policy on shareholders' wealth. *International Research Journal of Finance & Economics,* (20), 181-187. Retrieved February 18, 2009, from EBSCO Online Database Business Source Complete. http://search.ebscohost.com/ login.asp

x?direct=true&db=bth&AN=35893465&site=eh
ost-live

Baker, H., Powell, G., & Veit, E. (2002). Revisiting
managerial perspectives on dividend policy. *Journal
of Economics & Finance, 26*(3), 267. Retrieved
February 19, 2009, from EBSCO Online Database Business Source Complete. http://search.
ebscohost.com/login.aspx?direct=true&db=bt
h&AN=7388066&site=ehost-live

Bank, S. (2006). Dividends and tax policy in the long
run. *American Law & Economics Association Papers,*
(39), 1-57. Retrieved February 19, 2009, from
EBSCO Online Database Business Source Complete. http://search.ebscohost.com/login.aspx?di
rect=true&db=bth&AN=20846968&site=ehost-live

Belden, S., Fister, T., & Knapp, B. (2005). Dividends
and directors: Do outsiders reduce agency costs?
Business & Society Review (00453609), 110(2), 171-
180. Retrieved February 19, 2009, from EBSCO
Online Database Business Source Complete.
http://search.ebscohost.com/ login.aspx?direct=
true&db=bth&AN=16878177&site=eh ost-live

Bhamornsiri, S., Guinn, R., & Schroeder, R. (2009).
International implications of the cost of compliance with the external audit requirements of
section 404 of Sarbanes-Oxley. *International Advances in Economic Research, 15*(1), 17-29. Retrieved
February 25, 2009, from EBSCO Online Database Business Source Complete. http://search.
ebscohost.com/login.aspx?direct=true&db=
bth&AN=36296388&site=ehost-live

Caskey, J., & Hanlon, M. (2013). Dividend policy at
firms accused of accounting fraud dividend policy
at firms accused of accounting fraud. *Contemporary
Accounting Research, 30*(2), 818-850. Retrieved November 15, 2013, from EBSCO Online Database
Business Source Complete. http://search.ebsco-
host.com/login.aspx?direct=t rue&db=bth&AN=8
8155563&site=ehost-live

Cohen, G., & Yagil, J. (2008). On the catering theory
of dividends and the linkage between investment,
financing and dividend policies. *International Research Journal of Finance & Economics,* (17), 33-39.
Retrieved February 16, 2009, from EBSCO Online Database Business Source Complete. http://
search.ebscohost.com/login.aspx?direct=t rue&d
b=bth&AN=34389568&site=ehost-live

Denis, D. (1990). Defensive changes in corporate
payout policy: Share repurchases and special

dividends. *Journal of Finance, 45*(5), 1433-1456.
Retrieved February 18, 2009, from EBSCO Online Database Business Source Complete. http://
search.ebscohost.com/login.aspx?direct=t
rue&db=bth&AN=4652220&site=ehost-live

Dickens, R., Casey, K., & Newman, J. (2002). Bank dividend policy: Explanatory factors. *Quarterly Journal
of Business & Economics, 41*(½), 3-12. Retrieved
February 19, 2009, from EBSCO Online Database
Business Source Complete. http://search.ebsco-
host.com/login.aspx?direct=t rue&db=bth&AN=1
1587116&site=ehost-live

Ghosh, C., & Sirmans, C. (2006). Do managerial mo-
tives impact dividend decisions in REITs? *Journal
of Real Estate Finance & Economics, 32*(3), 327-355.
Retrieved February 18, 2009, from EBSCO Online Database Business Source Complete. http://
search.ebscohost.com/login.aspx?direct=true&db
=bth&AN=20253396&site=eh ost-live

Guo, W., & Ni, J. (2008). Institutional ownership
and firm's dividend policy. *Corporate Ownership
& Control, 5*(2), 128-136. Retrieved February
16, 2009, from EBSCO Online Database Business Source Complete. http://search. ebscohost.
com/login.aspx?direct=true&db=bth&AN=3137
5316&site=ehost-live

Hendry, J., Sanderson, P., Barker, R., & Roberts, J.
(2007). Responsible ownership, shareholder value
and the new shareholder activism. *Competition &
Change, 11*(3), 223- 240. Retrieved February 20,
2009, from EBSCO Online Database Business
Source Complete. http://search.ebscohost.com/
login.aspx?direct=true&db=bth&AN=25944910
&site=ehost-live

Henry, D. (2003, September 15). Dividends just
aren't dazzling enough. *BusinessWeek,* (3849), 48.
Retrieved February 19, 2009, from EBSCO Online Database Academic Search Complete. http://
search.ebscohost.com/login.aspx?direct=t rue&d
b=a9h&AN=10754889&site=ehost-live

Jiraporn, P., & Ning, Y. (2006). Dividend policy,
shareholder rights, and corporate governance.
Journal of Applied Finance, 16(2), 24-36. Retrieved
February 19, 2009, from EBSCO Online Database Business Source Complete. http://search.
ebscohost.com/login.aspx?direct=true&db=bt
h&AN=25301695&site=ehost-live

Investment banks: The role of firms and their analysts
with Enron and Global Crossing. (2003, March

17). United States General Accounting Office. Retrieved February 19, 2009, from http://www.gao.gov/products/GAO-03-511

Kanatas, G., & Qi, J. (2004). Dividends and debt with managerial agency and lender holdup. *Management Science, 50*(9), 1249-1260. Retrieved February 19, 2009, from EBSCO Online Database Business Source Complete. http://search.ebscohost.com/login.aspx?direct=true&db=bth&AN=14536665&site=ehost-live

Li, K., & Zhao, X. (2008). Asymmetric information and dividend policy. *Financial Management (Blackwell Publishing Limited), 37*(4), 673-694. Retrieved February 18, 2009, from EBSCO Online Database Business Source Complete. http://search.ebscohost.com/login.aspx?direct=true&db=bth&AN=35859327&site=ehost-live

Melican, J., & Westcott, S. (2008). What the proxies tally: A rising tide of activism. *Directors & Boards, 32*(4), 8-53. Retrieved February 20, 2009, from EBSCO Online Database Business Source Complete. http://search.ebscohost.com/login.aspx?direct=true&db=bth&AN=32897214&site=ehost-live

Minow, N., & Hodgson, P. (2007). Shareholder activism and the eclipse of the public corporation. *Corporate Board, 28*(164), 1-5. Retrieved February 20, 2009, from EBSCO Online Database Business Source Complete. http://search.ebscohost.com/login.aspx?direct=true&db=bth&AN=24876959&site=ehost-live

Nicholas, A. (2007). Salary clampdown. *Inside-Counsel, 17*(186), 16-18. Retrieved February 20, 2009, from EBSCO Online Database Business Source Complete. http://search.ebscohost.com/login.aspx?direct=true&db=bth&AN=25079130&site=ehost-live

Public accounting firms: Required study on the potential effects of mandatory audit firm rotation. (2004, February). United States General Accounting Office. Retrieved February 19, 2009, from http://www.gao.gov/new.items/d04217.pdf

Ramalingegowda, S., Chuan-San, W., & Yong, Y. (2013). The role of financial reporting quality in mitigating the constraining effect of dividend policy on investment decisions. *Accounting Review, 88*(3), 1007-1039. Retrieved November 15, 2013,

from EBSCO Online Database Business Source Complete. http://search.ebscohost.com/login.aspx?direct=true&db=bth&AN=87541650&site=ehost-live

Sarbanes-Oxley Act: Consideration of key principles needed in addressing implementation for smaller public companies. (2006, April 13). United States Government Accountability Office. Retrieved February 19, 2006, from http://www.gao.gov/products/GAO-06-361

Shareholder rights. (2008, July). *International Financial Law Review, 27*(7), 75. Retrieved February 20, 2009, from EBSCO Online Database Business Source Complete. http://search.ebscohost.com/login.aspx?direct=true&db=bth&AN=33767692&site=ehost-live

Sheppard, B. (2008). Corporate governance: To distribute or not distribute? That is the question. *New Zealand Management, 55*(8), 66-67. Retrieved February 16, 2009, from EBSCO Online Database Business Source Complete. http://search.ebscohost.com/login.aspx?direct=true&db=bth&AN=34620237&site=ehost-live

Thomas, R. (2008). The evolving role of institutional investors in corporate governance and corporate litigation. *Vanderbilt Law Review, 61*(2), 299-313. Retrieved February 20, 2009, from EBSCO Online Database Academic Search Complete. http://search.ebscohost.com/login.aspx?direct=true&db=a9h&AN=32194060&site=ehost-liveVan Buren, H. (2007). Speaking truth to power: Religious institutions as both dissident organizational stakeholders and organizational partners. *Business & Society Review (00453609), 112*(1), 55-72. Retrieved February 20, 2009, from EBSCO Online Database Business Source Complete. http://search.ebscohost.com/login.aspx?direct=true&db=bth&AN=24367603&site=ehost-live

Walther, L.M. (2009). Chapter 15: Financial reporting and concepts. In *Principles of accounting*. Retrieved March 24, 2009, from http://www.principlesofaccounting.com/chapter%2015.htm

Wann, C., Long, D., Pearson, D., & Wann, G. (2008). Liquidity shock induced dividend change: market reaction by firm quality. *Journal of the Academy of Business & Economics, 8*(4), 137-151. Retrieved February 19, 2009, from EBSCO Online Database

Business Source Complete. http://search.ebsco-host.com/login.aspx?direct=t rue&db=bth&AN=3 5618402&site=ehost-live

Wiemer, J., & Diel, S. (2008). Strategies for share buybacks. *Journal of Corporate Treasury Management, 1*(4), 297- 304. Retrieved February 19, 2009, from EBSCO Online Database Business Source Complete. http://search.ebscohost.com/login.aspx?di rect=true&db=bth&AN=34391741 &site=ehost-live

Practices at publicly traded southeastern banks reflect compensation and governance trends. *Community Banker, 19*(1), 10-11. Retrieved February 25, 2009, from EBSCO Online Database Business Source Complete. http://search. ebscohost. com/login.aspx?direct=true&db=bth&AN=360 48556&site=ehost-live

Xu, X. (2007). Institutional investor activism revisited: Investment determination and evidence of control. *Proceedings of the Northeast Business & Economics Association,* 385-386. Retrieved February 20, 2009, from EBSCO Online Database Business Source Complete. http://search.eb-scohost.com/login.aspx?direct=true&db=bt h&AN=27535465&site=ehost-live

SUGGESTED READING

Aivazian, V., Booth, L., & Cleary, S. (2006). Dividend smoothing and debt ratings. *Journal of Financial & Quantitative Analysis, 41*(2), 439-453. Retrieved February 19, 2009, from EBSCO Online Database Business Source Complete. http://search.ebsco-host.com/login.aspx?direct=t rue&db=bth&AN=2 1066565&site=ehost-live

Banerjee, S., Gatchev, V., & Spindt, P. (2007). Stock market liquidity and firm dividend policy. *Journal of Financial & Quantitative Analysis, 42*(2), 369-397. Retrieved February 19, 2009, from EBSCO Online Database Business Source Complete. http://search.ebscohost.com/login.aspx?direct=t rue&d b=bth&AN=25331843&site=ehost-live

Ben Naceur, S., Goaied, M., & Belanes, A. (2006). On the determinants and dynamics of dividend policy. *International Review of Finance, 6*(½), 1-23. Retrieved February 19, 2009, from EBSCO Online Database Business Source Complete. http:// search.ebscohost.com/ login.aspx?direct=true&d b=bth&AN=24732702&site=eh ost-live

Brav, A., Graham, J., Harvey, C., & Michaely, R. (2008). The effect of the May 2003 dividend tax cut on corporate dividend policy: Empirical and survey evidence. *National Tax Journal, 61*(3), 381-396. Retrieved February 19, 2009, from EBSCO Online Database Business Source Complete. http://search.ebscohost.com/login.aspx?direct=t rue&db=bth&AN=34991370&site=ehost-live

Cadenillas, A., Sarkar, S., & Zapatero, F. (2007). Optimal dividend policy with mean-reverting cash reservoir. *Mathematical Finance, 17*(1), 81-109. Retrieved February 16, 2009, from EBSCO Online Database Business Source Complete. http:// search.ebscohost.com/login.aspx?direct=t rue&d b=bth&AN=23415871&site=ehost-live

Cole, J. (2006). Dividend policies seen helping banking stocks. *American Banker, 171*(134), 2-2. Retrieved February 16, 2009, from EBSCO Online Database Business Source Complete. http:// search.ebscohost.com/login.aspx?direct=t rue&d b=bth&AN=21579941&site=ehost-live

Desai, M., Foley, C., & Hines, J. (2007). Dividend policy inside the multinational firm. *Financial Management (Blackwell Publishing Limited), 36*(1), 5-26. Retrieved February 16, 2009, from EBSCO Online Database Business Source Complete. http://search.ebscohost.com/ login.aspx?direct=true&db=bth&AN=26087817&site=eh ost-live

Dhanani, A. (2005). Corporate dividend policy: The views of British financial managers. *Journal of Business Finance & Accounting, 32*(7/8), 1625-1672. Retrieved February 16, 2009, from EBSCO Online Database Business Source Complete. http:// search.ebscohost.com/login.aspx?direct=t rue&d b=bth&AN=18155845&site=ehost-live

Eriotis, N., Vasilou, D., & Zisis, V. (2007). A bird's eye view of the dividend policy of the banking industry in Greece. *International Research Journal of Finance & Economics,* (11), 21-29. Retrieved February 16, 2009, from EBSCO Online Database Business Source Complete. http://search. ebscohost. com/login.aspx?direct=true&db=bth&AN=265 60320&site=ehost-live

Gilson, G., & Torline, M. (2008). Control for the taking: Activist shareholder election contests. *Boardroom Briefing, 5*(2), 33-34. Retrieved February 20, 2009, from EBSCO Online Database

Business Source Complete. http://search.ebscohost.com/login.aspx?direct=true&db=bth&AN=32023414&site=ehost-live

Hardjopranoto, W. (2006). Interdependent analysis of leverage, dividend, and managerial ownership policies. *Gadjah Mada International Journal of Business, 8*(2), 179-199. Retrieved February 16, 2009, from EBSCO Online Database Business Source Complete. http://search.ebscohost.com/login.aspx?direct=true&db=bth&AN=23140776&site=ehost-live

Hazak, A. (2007). Dividend decision under distributed profit taxation: Investor's perspective. *International Research Journal of Finance & Economics,* (9), 201-219. Retrieved February 19, 2009, from EBSCO Online Database Business Source Complete. http://search.ebscohost.com/ login.aspx?direct=true&db=bth&AN=25170171&site=eh ost-live

Khang, K., & King, T. (2006). Does dividend policy relate to cross-sectional variation in information asymmetry? Evidence from returns to insider trades. *Financial Management (Blackwell Publishing Limited), 35*(4), 71-94. Retrieved February 16, 2009, from EBSCO Online Database Business Source Complete. http://search.ebscohost.com/login.aspx?direct=true&db=bth&AN=23337047 &site=ehost-live

Kim, Y., Rhim, L., & Friesner, D. (2007). Interrelationships among capital structure, dividends, and ownership: Evidence from South Korea. *Multinational Business Review, 15*(3), 25-42. Retrieved February 16, 2009, from EBSCO Online Database Business Source Complete. http://search.ebscohost.com/login.aspx?direct=true&db=bth&AN=33062135&site=ehost-live

Mancinelli, L., & Ozkan, A. (2006). Ownership structure and dividend policy: Evidence from Italian firms. *European Journal of Finance, 12*(3), 265-282. Retrieved February 16, 2009, from EBSCO Online Database Business Source Complete. http://search.ebscohost.com/login.aspx?direct=t rue&db=bth&AN=20482561&site=ehost-live

McGowan Jr., C. (2005). A simplified approach to demonstrating the irrelevance of dividend policy

to the value of the firm. *Applied Financial Economics Letters, 1*(2), 121- 124. Retrieved February 16, 2009, from EBSCO Online Database Business Source Complete. http://search.ebscohost.com/login.aspx?direct=true&db=bth&AN=16999888&site=ehost-live

Michaelson, J. (1962, December). Determinants of corporate dividend policies. *Academy of Management Proceedings,* 156-163. Retrieved February 18, 2009, from EBSCO Online Database Business Source Complete. http://search. ebscohost.com/login.aspx?direct=true&db=bth&AN=506 8298&site=ehost-live

Pinkowitz, L., Williamson, R., & Stulz, R. (2007). Cash holdings, dividend policy, and corporate governance: A cross-country analysis. *Journal of Applied Corporate Finance, 19*(1), 81-87. Retrieved February 19, 2009, from EBSCO Online Database Business Source Complete. http://search. ebscohost. com/login.aspx?direct=true&db=bth&AN=2431 2434&site=ehost-live

Raymond, D. (2009). Invitation to mischief by minority shareholders. *Directors & Boards, 33*(2), 12-12. Retrieved February 20, 2009, from EBSCO Online Database Business Source Complete. http://search.ebscohost.com/ login.aspx?direct=true&d b=bth&AN=36498836&site=eh ost-live

Singhania, M. (2005). Trends in dividend payout. *Journal of Management Research (09725814), 5*(3), 129-142. Retrieved February 19, 2009, from EBSCO Online Database Business Source Complete. http://search.ebscohost.com/login.aspx?direct=t rue&db=bth&AN=21388369 &site=ehost-live

Yilmaz, M., & Gulay, G. (2006). Dividend policies and price-volume reactions to cash dividends on the stock market. *Emerging Markets Finance & Trade, 42*(4), 19-49. Retrieved February 19, 2009, from EBSCO Online Database Business Source Complete. http://search.ebscohost.com/login.aspx?direct=true&db=bth&AN=22173094&site=ehost-live

—Michael Erbschloe

THE FINANCE OF FIXED INCOME SECURITIES

ABSTRACT

This article focuses on the relative advantages and disadvantages of fixed income securities, which are investments that provide a predictable rate of return over a specified period. As is discussed, fixed income securities include various types of government and corporate bonds, savings accounts, certificates of deposit, and preferred stocks. Fixed income securities are usually evaluated in terms of factors such as level of risk, rate of return, and the special features different types of securities offer. In general, fixed income securities are considered an important part of investment portfolios.

OVERVIEW

The money you earn comes from essentially two sources: salary from your job, and income from your investments. While a salary is almost always the same amount from month to month, how much money you earn from investments can vary, or, like a salary, it can be the same amount. In the latter scenario, your income is fixed-that is, the amount you earn doesn't change; you know what to expect each month. Investment earnings that stays the same on a regular basis are referred to as fixed income, and often come from investment securities-tradable instruments such as stocks and bonds that reflect an investor's ownership in, or debt obligations from, a company or government agency ("Definitions," 2007). Many investors prefer at least a part of their investment portfolios to be fixed because they can count on a certain amount of their income to be predictable and steady.

Fixed income securities-those investments which produce the same amount of money on a regular basis-have several advantages besides producing steady income. They often give conservative investors piece of mind, because, unlike stocks, their performance is characterized by low volatility. They also help diversify a portfolio by offering a steady, stable stream of revenue. Finally, many forms of fixed income securities provide tax advantages; in the case of many bonds, income from some sources may be exempt from Federal, state, and local taxes. There are also disadvantages to holding fixed income securities (Fidelity Investments, 2007). For example, they may react negatively to an increase of interest rates, represent a credit risk if the company or agency has financial problems, or lose their value because of inflation over a long period of time. They may also be "called in" or redeemed early, if the issuer pays off its debt early, in which case the investor would not receive the expected amount of earnings. Finally, especially in the case of long-term investments in which money is obligated for many years, other more advantageous investment opportunities may be by-passed, which is referred to as reinvestment risk. Astute investors therefore must balance the pros and cons of fixed income securities as they clarify their investment goals and build their portfolios.

APPLICATIONS

TYPES OF FIXED-INCOME SECURITIES
One of the most common types of fixed-income securities is a bond, or loan one entity makes to another. Bonds commonly offer fixed income in the form of Treasury Securities, Agency Securities, Corporate Bonds, and Municipal Bonds (U.S. Department of the Treasury, 2007).

TREASURY SECURITIES
Treasury securities are debt obligations issued by the U.S. Government. They are backed in "full faith" by the government, which means they are virtually risk-free (Fidelity Investments, 2007). A treasury security is a type of bond, or loan, made to the government, and earns interest over its period of ownership, which is usually several years. At the end of the specified period, the bond reaches maturity-the

date at which the principal (the amount invested) is returned to the buyer. Treasury securities are known for their safety, tax advantages, and liquidity. Their downside is that they generally have lower rates of return than other types of more assertive investments. Savings bonds are also forms of treasury securities, as are T-Bills which are short-term government obligations.

AGENCY SECURITIES

Agency securities are also relatively low-risk obligations that are issued by "agencies" or enterprises that the U.S. government supports. They are not fully backed by the government and are taxed differently. Because they are technically considered a greater risk than treasury securities, they typically earn higher interest. Examples of agency securities include mortgage-based investments sponsored by the Government National Mortgage Association (Ginnie Mae), the Federal National Mortgage Association (Fannie Mae), and the Federal Home Loan Mortgage Corporation (Freddie Mac).

MUNICIPAL BONDS

Municipal Bonds (called "munis") are securities issued by local governments such as states or cities. Munis are typically exempt from Federal, state, and local taxes and are issued in denominations of $5,000. They are usually created to help fund public projects, such as new highways, school facilities, or hospitals (Securities and Exchange Commission, 2007). Depending on their purpose, the terms of these bonds can vary from several months to as long as 30 years. Munis are generally low-risk and low-yield but contribute an important aspect to an investor's portfolio.

CORPORATE BONDS

Corporate bonds work like municipal bonds, but the issuer is a private company rather than an agency of government. Unlike munis, which are usually offered over-the-counter in denominations of $5,000, corporate bonds are sold through exchanges and are sold in denominations of $1,000. Because they are not backed by the government like municipal bonds and treasury bonds, they are considered riskier and therefore produce a higher rate of return. They are also not backed by any agency of the U.S. government.

OTHER TYPES OF FIXED-INCOME SECURITIES

Although bonds, in their various forms, represent a major type of fixed-income security, there are other instruments that provide a steady, predictable stream of revenue. These include savings accounts, certificates of deposit, and preferred stocks.

SAVINGS ACCOUNTS

The most basic type of investment, a savings account is essentially a loan a depositor makes to a financial institution. If the institution is insured by the Federal Deposit Insurance Commission (FDIC), the deposit is guaranteed safe by the government up to $100,000. Therefore, it is a considered a safe type of investment. However, while savings accounts provide regular income-usually credited to a depositor's account once a month based on an annual percentage rate, or APR-that yield is usually very low, usually below one percent. Thus, a savings account with $1,000 in it would earn less than $10 of interest a year. Savings accounts are also very liquid, i.e., the depositor can take all of the money out at any given time without a penalty or loss.

CERTIFICATES OF DEPOSIT

A certificate of deposit (CD) works in a way very similar to a savings account, with the primary difference being a specified term or period in which the institution may use the money. CDs can be issued for varying periods, including one month, three months, six months, one year, five years, or any other denomination of time in between. Because the commitment period of a CD is specified, unlike that of a regular savings account, the interest rates are higher; usually the longer the period, the higher the rate. Also protected by the government if issued by an FDIC-insured institution, CDs can pay simple interest or compounded interest. Simple interest is merely a promised rate of return based on an annual percentage rate: If you deposit $5,000 and the interest rate is 5%, you will earn $250 a year for the use of your money. Compounded interest uses each bit of interest earned as the basis for the next interest payment. In other words, that same $5,000 at a 5% compounded rate would produce approximately $256.36. However, holders of CDs who withdraw their funds before the date of the maturity will have to pay a penalty, which is usually a portion of the interest that becomes forfeited.

PREFERRED STOCKS

Revenue from preferred stocks is also considered a form of fixed security income. Unlike bonds, stocks represent a portion of ownership in a company and provide dividends for the holders. However, obligations on preferred stocks must be met before holders of common stock can be paid. Also, should a company file bankruptcy, preferred stock holders are considered creditors and may be entitled to relief, whereas holders of common stock may have no such recourse. Like interest earned from savings accounts and CDs, dividends from preferred stocks are fully taxable.

ISSUES

RISK

Like any investments, fixed securities come with some level of risk (except for treasury securities, which are considered virtually risk-free). Corporate bonds, in particular, may be risky if the financial management of the company is weak. Bonds are rated by Moody's and by Standard and Poor's to give investors an idea of how safe an investment might be; both of these resources can be accessed online (See "Suggested Reading" below). Debenture bonds, which may have relatively high rates of return, can be particularly risky because they are "secured" only on the name and credibility of the issuing company-i.e., there is no collateral put forth to ensure investors of a safe return (Kapoor, Dlabay, & Hughes, 2007). However, companies with well-established names and histories may be good risks; conducting ample research in a company or fund is always recommended before making any type of investment.

Risk also comes in the form of inflation. If a security is held for a long period of time (some bonds are issued for 30 years), the profit from the interest can be "eroded" because the money will have less value when the bond matures than when it was issued. Such a loss can be offset to a certain degree if the bond produces tax-free interest and is less of a risk with short-term notes such as T-Bills.

Another form of risk exists among bonds that are "callable." Callable bond issuers may withdraw, or "call" the bonds before their maturity, especially if interest rates increase. When interest rates go up, the issuers can re-assign the bonds to commercial lending institutions and receive a greater return for their money (morgankeegan.com). Mortgage-based bonds are also susceptible to calls, if the mortgage holders re-finance their loans or pay them off early. While bond holders would not lose their principal, they would not receive the amount of interest they expected when they purchased the bond. This can also cause a "reinvestment risk," which occurs when the principal and interest may have to be re-invested at a potentially lower rate of return.

SPECIAL FEATURES OF BONDS

We have already discussed the basic types of fixed-income securities and their comparative advantages and disadvantages. Additionally, there are special types of securities that offer unique features that may be attractive to investors. These include zero coupon bonds, bond laddering, bond funds, and Treasury Inflation-Protected Securities (TIPS).

ZERO COUPON BONDS

Zero coupon bonds are securities that are purchased at a fraction of their face value, or par value, and pay no interest until they mature (remember that most bonds pay interest while being held). When the bonds reach their maturity, the bond owner receives the full value of the bond, which has been earned through the interest accrued during the time of holding. Zero-coupon bonds tend to be more volatile than other forms of bonds and have a higher risk factor; the advantage is that they call for a small initial investment.

BOND LADDERING

Bond laddering is a strategy involving the purchase of several bonds, each with different maturity dates. Bond laddering is used to diversify portfolios and to reduce risks related to inflation. For example, an investor buys a series of bonds, and as each matures, the principal and interest from that bond can be re-invested in other, more profitable securities. The advantages to bond laddering are liquidity and low call risk; the disadvantage is that the shorter-termed intervals will typically produce lower rates of return.

BOND FUNDS

Bond funds are groups of funds, managed by a professional financial manager, who takes investors' money collectively and buys a variety of different bonds, spreading the combined principal across different types of investments. Thus, the individual investor does not have to make specific investment decisions, can make a greater return because a larger amount of money is "pooled," and enjoy a wider diversification of their portfolio. Fees may be charged for the management of bond funds.

TREASURY INFLATION-PROTECTED SECURITIES

Treasury Inflation-Protected Securities (TIPS) were first issued by the U. S. Treasury Department in 1997. Their purpose was to attract investors whose goal was to avoid erosion of principal and interest because of inflation. TIPS are adjusted (with a three-month lag) for inflation-if inflation goes up, the investor's principal is increased; if deflation occurs, the amount of interest is reduced-but the principal can never be less than its original value (Smith-Barney, 2007). TIPS are based on the activities of the Consumer Price Index (CPI) and pay interest semi-annually (Smith Barney, 2007).

CONCLUSION

Fixed-income securities represent one type of investment that can play an important role in a portfolio. Compared to stocks, the advantages are safety, diversification, and, in the case of government securities, tax benefits. Their rates of return tend to be lower than riskier forms of investments, but they have the ultimate benefit of predictability-an investor knows how much money he or she will have at the end of a certain period. Various types of bonds, as well as savings accounts, certificates of deposit, and preferred stock can also produce fixed incomes. These investment venues are regarded by many financial planners as a critical component of investment portfolios. They should also, however, be balanced with other forms of long-term planning, in accordance with the investor's goals, available resources, and level of risk aversion.

BIBLIOGRAPHY

Costandinides, C., & Sinclair, L. (2013). Considerations when investing in and pricing emerging market fixed income securities. *Journal of Securities Operations & Custody, 6*(1), 31-41. Retrieved November 15, 2013, from EBSCO Online Database Business Source Complete. http://search. ebscohost. com/login.aspx?direct=true&db=bth&AN=905 89272&site=ehost-liveDefinitions. (2007). Traders' log. Retrieved October 4, 2007, from http://www.traderslog.com.html

Dubil, R. (2013). Make callable bonds part of your fixed income allocation. *Journal of Financial Planning, 26*(3), 54-60. Retrieved November 15, 2013, from EBSCO Online Database Business Source Complete. http://search. ebscohost. com/login.aspx?direct=true&db=bth&AN=864 45559&site=ehost-live

Fidelity Investments. (2007). Why fixed income? Retrieved October 4, 2007, from Personalfidelity. com. http://personal.fidelity.com/products/ fixedincome/fiwhyfixed.shtml

Fisher, D. (2013). Dodging disaster. *Forbes, 191*(11), 64. Retrieved November 15, 2013, from EBSCO Online Database Business Source Complete. http://search.ebscohost.com/login.aspx?direct=t rue&db=bth&AN=89457923 &site=ehost-live

Kapoor, J. R., Dlabay, L. R., & Hughes, R. J. (2007). *Personal finance* (8th ed.). New York: McGraw-Hill Irwin.

Morgan Keegan & Co., Inc. (2007). Bonds. Retrieved October 5, 2007, from MorganKeegan.com. http://www.morgankeegan.com/MK/investing/ IProducts/fixedincome/default. htm.

Smith-Barney. (2007). U.S. treasury inflation indexed securities (TIPS). Retrieved October 5, 2007, from SmithBarney.com. http://www.smithbarney.com/ pdf/tipsbrochure

U. S. Department of the Treasury. (n.d.). FAQ: Fixed income. Retrieved October 5, 2007, from http://www.treas.gov/ education/faq/markets/ fixedincomefaq.shtml.

U. S. Securities and Exchange Commission. (2005). Bonds, corporate. Retrieved October 4, 2007, from http://www. sec.gov/answers/bondcrp.htm.

SUGGESTED READING

Fabozzi, F. (2001). *The handbook of fixed income securities* (6th ed.). New York: McGraw Hill.

Lewis, J. (2007). GEAM shifts fixed-income focus. *Investment Management Weekly, 20*(27), 1-7. Retrieved October 10, 2007, from EBSCO Online Database Business Source Complete. http://search.ebsco-host.com/login.aspx?direct=t rue&db=bth&AN=2 5776986&site=ehost-live

Martellini, L., Priaulet, P., & Priaulet, S. (2003). *Fixed income securities: Valuation, risk management, and portfolio strategies.* Hoboken, NJ: Wiley & Sons.

Sorondo, M. (2007). WSIB seeks two investment pros. *Investment Management Weekly, 20*(27), 4-5. Retrieved October 10, 2007, from EBSCO Online Database Business Source Complete. http://search.ebscohost.com/login.aspx? direct=true&db=bth&AN=25776994&site=ehost-live

White, J. & Meigs, R. (2007). Know when to hold 'em. *Employee Benefit News, 21*(9), 37. Retrieved October 10, 2007, from EBSCO Online Database Business Source Complete. http://search.ebscohost.com/login.aspx?direct=t rue&db=bth&AN=25813625&site=ehost-live

—William J. Wardrope

FINANCIAL DERIVATIVES

ABSTRACT

Financial derivatives are risk management instruments that derive their value from an underlying asset such as interest rates, government bonds or currencies. Financial derivatives are relatively new financial instruments; having come about in the early 1970s. There were a number of factors that helped financial derivatives to gain popularity, including: The reinstitution of variable monetary rates, the rise of computer technology and the globalization of markets and economies. Financial derivatives allow investors to hedge risk when investing in asset classes that are subject to unexpected and unpredictable price fluctuations. Some derivatives gain their value from commodities that are not considered financial derivatives such as oil, natural gas or corn. Financial derivatives are increasingly tracked through broader indexes that emulate securities indexes. There are several categories of financial derivatives that are widely used in today's market; these include: Futures and forwards; options, and; swaps. Financial markets are very innovative; the rise in popularity of derivatives instruments exemplifies how creatively markets are able to package and manage risk. There is seemingly no end to the ways that assets can be sliced and bundled to mitigate risk. Derivatives are instruments that help investors manage risk particularly where there is volatility. Tightening credit markets and fluctuating interest rates have spawned a number of credit derivatives that include credit/debt swaps and collateralized debt obligations. Likewise, the volatility of real estate markets has increased the popularity of real estate derivatives.

OVERVIEW

"Derivatives are financial instruments that have no intrinsic value, but derive their value from something else. They hedge the risk of owning things that are subject to unexpected price fluctuations, e.g. foreign currencies, bushels of wheat, stocks and government bonds" (Davies, 2007, 2). There are three main types of financial derivatives: Futures and forwards; options, and; swaps. Derivatives are a risk management tools used by investors to mitigate risk in any market or with any "underlier" or underlying asset class that has risk associated with its particular market. The scope of this essay concentrates on financial derivatives and discusses some of the more common asset classes on which financial derivates are based. Some of the more common assets that financial derivatives are based upon are: Bonds, currencies and interest rates. In essence, any underlying asset that is subject to market volatility and price fluctuations is a good candidate for being the basis for a financial derivative. Financial derivatives have really only been around since the late twentieth century. Prior to creating futures trading that is tied to financial instruments; futures were exclusively tied to commodities (most of which were agricultural). In the late 1960s and early 1970s, there was already talk amongst some of the more innovative leaders and economists in the U.S. about creating a new class derivative based on underlying financial instruments. There were several watershed events that took place in the early 1970s that ushered in the era of futures trading based on financial instruments.

THE COMMODITIES FUTURE TRADING COMMISSION

One of the pivotal events that brought about the inception of financial derivatives was the establishment of the Commodities Future Trading Commission (CFTC) in 1974. Several years prior to the establishment of the CFTC, there was talk of establishing interest rate futures, but since interest rates were clearly "securities," this proposal did not fall under the "then current" definition of a commodity. It was the CTFC Act of 1974 that "redefined what a commodity was and it also granted exclusive jurisdiction by the CFTC to retain that [jurisdiction]. The Act is credited with defining futures stock indexes and interest rates" (Collins, 2007). On September 11, 1975, the CTFC approved the first futures contract based on a financial instrument; it was known as the Government National Mortgage Association Certificates (Ginnie Mae).

MERC & LEO MALMED

Leo Malmed became head of the Chicago Mercantile Exchange (Merc) in 1969. At the time, the exchange traded futures based exclusively on meats and other agricultural products. At the time Leo Malmed became head of the Merc, the exchange was just in meats; according to Malmed, even butter and eggs weren't trading. Still he didn't give up and by his own admission tried trading futures on many different commodities including: Apples, turkeys, shrimp, potatoes and oranges. All these products had one thing in common; they were all agricultural commodities and they had limited market appeal. In his own words, Malmed stated his concern; "I was deathly afraid that I'd be chairman of a single product exchange. Anything happened to that product, you're out of business." Mr. Malmed started asking himself if currency futures could be traded like pork bellies and beef. Malmed understood that if currency futures were possible, then it was conceivable that any

financial instrument could be used to trade futures (Ryan, 2006). It was at this time that the fixed rate monetary exchange system (as had been established in the Bretton Woods Agreement of 1944) was being abandoned. Malmed's idea was to establish a way to trade foreign exchange futures that would be based on the floating exchange rates. As Malmed pointed out, agricultural commodities were limited and had limited appeal, but with financial instruments it was "anything you want" (Ryan, 2006).

RISK

Because financial derivatives are based on assets that are inherently risky themselves (for example interest rates), financial derivatives can also be risky financial instruments. Like many financial market instruments, the higher the risk, the greater the chance for high financial rewards. Derivatives allow for investors to look at industries and sectors that face risk and use a mechanism (derivative) to price and transfer that risk. Understanding where current risks are and where future risks will be is crucial to the success of effectively using derivatives as an investment tools (Collins, 2007).

Warren Buffet is famous for making the following statement about derivatives in 2002. "We view them as time bombs both for the parties that deal in them and the economic system ... In our view ... derivatives are financial weapons of mass destruction, carrying dangers that, while now latent, are potentially lethal" ("At the risky end of finance," 2007). Financial derivatives have been described by many proponents as financial instruments that threaten the status quo; they are also credited for making opaque markets more transparent. The love/hate relationship with financial derivatives will continue in the future and new derivative products are introduced to investors. As with most change, there will be reluctance, speculation and fear regarding new derivative products. As

Futures	Forwards
Publicly traded contracts	Private contract between buyer and seller
Traded on exchanges	Traded privately (aka: Over the Counter)
Transactions handled by brokers	Transactions handled by contract holders
Exchange assumes risk	Parties assume risk

investor confidence in derivatives rises, however, markets and investors will embrace instruments that will help them manage the risk/return paradigm. This essay discusses both sides of the risk/return spectrum of financial derivatives: Do derivatives disperse risk or boost it?

APPLICATIONS

There are three main types of derivatives that fall under the broader heading of financial derivatives. These derivative types are: Futures and forwards; options, and; swaps.

FORWARDS & FUTURES

Forward and futures contracts are one category of financial derivatives. Forward and futures contracts are similar in that they are contracts that allow for the purchase or sale of an underlying security or asset with the actual delivery date to occur in the future. A future or forward contract allows for the buyer to "lock in a price today for a transaction that will take place in the future" ("Forward and futures contracts," 2007).

Over the Counter (OTC) derivatives are the fast growing financial instruments in modern capital markets. OTC derivatives are hitting the mainstream and allowing fund managers to add long and short term strategies to retail investor's portfolios. OTC derivatives are both novel and complex instruments and their growing popularity is straining the operational infrastructure that supports the markets. OTC derivatives were initially traded by the brokerage arms of investment banks to structure hedge fund investments (Stillabower, 2007). Today, OTC derivatives are straining the operational platforms of firms that don't have the capacity and systems that have been built into exchanges. The risk of OTC financial derivatives has been outlined in the table, above, but that is not stopping institutional and retail investors from pursing OTC financial derivatives in droves. "There's a "need to improve the processing, servicing and valuation of OTC derivative instruments" as they become more widely accepted as financial instruments that mitigate risk and diversify investor portfolios (Stillabower, 2007).

OPTIONS

Options are defined as the right, but not the obligation, to buy or sell a specific amount of X (currency, index, debt) at a specific price during a specific period of time. Another way of stating what an options contract is, is to say that two parties have the right to engage in a future transaction of some underlying security. The buyer of the option is known as the option holder. The seller of the option is known as the writer of the option. The option holder and option writer are the two parties that must uphold the terms of the contract. The option holder has a couple of choices in exercising the option. Exercising an option can occur in the following ways:

- The option holder can buy a call option which gives him the right to buy a specified quantity of security at a set price at some point on or before the contract expiration date.
- The option holder can buy a put option that allows him to sell (the same as above).

In either case, the terms of the contract must be fulfilled by the two parties that have entered into the contract (Options/option contracts," 2006).

SWAPS

Swaps are the third common category of financial derivatives. In a swap, an agreement is made between two parties (counterparties) in which the parties involved swap cash flow streams, liabilities or debt. For purposes of illustration, we will assume that a contract involves a cash flow swap. Cash flows can be defined in various ways, but what matters most is that the two cash flows that are being swapped have equal value. The present value of the swapped assets must be equal at the time of the swap. Swaps can be used to hedge risk or to speculate in markets, but their fundamental purpose is to change the character of an asset or liability without liquidating the asset or liability. Parties use swaps to change the nature of a cash flow stream to one that is less risky. Instead of renegotiation with the original counterparty, you enter into a swap with another party. Swaps allow investors to change existing contracts to ones that better meet their needs. When a swap occurs, the original counter party from the originating contract doesn't even need to know about the swap ("Swap," n.d.). Today, credit default swaps are a derivative tool that is commonly used to transfer risk and is part of a larger class of credit derivatives. Credit derivatives are gaining popularity and finding their ways into many investment portfolios. The topic of credit derivatives is timely because of the role that they play in financing risk for commercial and residential mortgages in the United States. This essay discusses the trends in credit derivatives as related to the sub-prime credit troubles of 2007 and the emerging trend of derivatives that track real estate markets.

ISSUES

CREDIT DERIVATIVES
Credit markets experienced extraordinary turmoil as 2007 drew to a close. In just a few years, credit derivatives moved from "being a highly technical byway for financial markets used primarily by insiders to a mainstream path traveled by nearly every investor on Wall Street" (O'Leary, 2006). The freewheeling credit markets of the early 2000s drew attention to the inevitability of a credit crunch. Banks that had diversified their investments into credit derivatives in 2001-2002 weathered the worst of that market downturn much better than some other lenders (O'Leary, 2006). Not surprisingly then, the market looked for ways to hedge against a credit downturn. Credit derivatives were perceived as the Holy Grail for hedging credit risk. The credit derivatives market grew 109% from 2005 to 2006 — accounting for $26 trillion in outstanding derivatives. Unfortunately, in all the enthusiasm, a fatal flaw developed in the quality of derivatives, especially those backed with mortgage securities. Reckless lending practices and a real estate bubble contributed to a catastropic collapse of financial institutions around the world. Tien, Tri, & Min-Ming (2013), after studying the performance of giant U.S. banks J.P. Morgan and Citigroup, reported that significant returns were generated before the crisis, but the negative effect of credit derivatives during the crisis was clear.

Credit derivatives have gained an important foothold in financial markets. There's no question that the inception of a number of index-related derivatives has created more widespread appeal amongst more traditional investors. Index-related derivatives offer a broader balance of products than the more traditional single name derivatives that are pegged to a specific issuer. Tying credit derivatives to indexes more closely emulates equity market risk exposure. Investors are more confident in credit derivatives if the risk is spread across wider indexes. Nearly every

product with a credit exposure has a number of derivative products tied to its performance and include a spectrum from high grade corporate bonds to leveraged bank loans (O'Leary, 2006).

THE UNDERLYING BOND MARKET
Credit derivatives have yielded benefits to all levels of investors. In today's market that boasts low interest rates and narrow credit spreads, it is not difficult for investors at all risk levels to make gains. As mortgage borrowers with poor credit ratings begin to default on their mortgages (aks sub prime mortgages), the true test of credit derivatives may lie in the offing. Credit derivatives derive their value from the bond markets (remember a derivative is defined as "deriving" its value from an underlying asset). In this case, the underlier is a bond. Collateralized debt obligations (CDOs) are the bundling of bonds, loans and swaps; each component carries different levels of risk.

Some investors, such as banks and insurers prefer to own less risky slices of the risk pie — these slices are known as tranches. The tranches that have less risk associated with them are called senior securities. Investors that own these slices of risk in the CDO will get paid first from the interest on the bonds. The middle tranches are held by junior investors and this level holds more risk because these investors won't get paid unless primary obligations have been met. If defaults happen that affect any area of the CDO, the junior tranches will take the first hit. The very lowest level tranches carry the most risk and are referred to as "toxic waste." Even at this high risk and potential high return investment level, returns have flowed to investors over the past few years. Low interest rates, low instances of default and plenty of liquidity may have lulled even these investors into thinking that they are safe from risk.

RESIDENTIAL MORTGAGE BACKED SECURITIES & RISING DEFAULTS
There's no question that some CDOs are linked to subprime mortgages through the purchase of other bundled investments known as residential mortgage backed securities (RMBS). CDOs bought RMBS bundles, and with the number of subprime borrowers defaulting, "the pain is trickling through the system" ("At the risky end of finance," 2007). According to Moody's credit rating agency, slightly less than 50%

of CDO were invested in RMBS in 2007. However, in some extreme cases, some CDOs may have had as much as 90% exposure to risky mortgages and as defaults rose, many of these tranches headed toward junk bond status. Perhaps one of the biggest questions is just how complex some of these credit derivative structures are. "The ever inventive financial sector has taken the ingredients and cooked up a bewildering alphabet soup of risk debt" now know as a portfolio ("At the risky end of finance," 2007). One analyst described credit derivatives with the following characteristics: "Credit derivatives are currently the fastest growing, most heavily traded and most complex securities" (O'Leary, 2006) of all derivative instruments.

EFFECTS ON THE GLOBAL CREDIT SUPPLY

"A second serious problem was the effect of derivatives on the global supply of credit. David Roche, of Independent Strategy, argued that derivatives had created a form of liquidity outside the control of central bankers. 'It is pretty obvious that if one can buy a security that represents an asset for 3-5% of its value, an awful lot of liquidity has been freed up,' he says. 'Derivatives have led to many more assets and liabilities being created. By reducing the cost of buying assets, you increase the demand'"("At the risky end of finance," 2007, 31).

THE REAL ESTATE MARKET

Financial derivatives are a way for investors to manage risk, and for a decade or so the U.S. real estate market had been seemingly "risk free." Neal Elkin, president of Real Estate Analytics LLC, makes the following point, "In a market that's going up 10% a year, nobody's thinking about hedging their portfolio, but we really are at a tipping point where the hedging of assets starts to make sense" (Hudgins, 2007).

Commercial real estate remains a strong investment option for many but the credit crisis and softening market of summer/fall of 2007 have spooked some investors about future prospects of real estate values. As the growth rate currently experienced may not be attainable in coming years, some are considering putting hedges in place in the form of derivatives ("Credit crunch in U.S. good news for derivatives," 2007).

CME HOUSING FUTURES & OPTIONS

In the spring of 2006, the Merc announced the launch of the S&P CME Housing Futures and Options. This derivative enables investors to invest in the futures market for nationwide home prices or in 10 major U.S. cities, including: New York, Los Angeles and Chicago. Yale Economist Rober Shiller points out that this development is long overdue. "Of the 3 major asset classes, the bond, the stock and the housing markets, only the housing market, with $20 trillion in assets cannot be speculated on easily. How can it be that we have no way of trading it [housing]?" (Christie, 2006).

"In the U.S., derivatives have yet to catch on, sources say, largely because the real estate industry here has been accustomed to thinking in terms of assets that are concrete, not derived. 'It's still a relatively new concept in the U.S. real estate industry, a new way to manage risk,' said Kiva Patten, a director at Merrill Lynch who specializes in real estate derivatives. 'Like any new concept, it's taking time for traditional players to get up to speed, but we're beginning to see that now.' Moreover, in recent years, real estate investors have perceived no need for the kind of sophisticated risk management that derivatives offer because, on the whole, commercial real estate values have been going up, sources say" ("Credit crunch in U.S. good news for derivatives," 2007, 2).

THE INDEX OF REAL ESTATE MARKET PERFORMANCE

Derivatives are tracked using an index of real estate market performance. The derivative gains or loses value in tandem with the ups and downs of the index. The idea that investors will be able to invest in a market such as real estate without having to acquire and hold a hard asset is a very radical concept for many investors. In the U.S., investment in real estate markets

has always been thought of in terms of acquisition of tangible assets, so real estate derivatives will take some getting used to. Investors can participate in the investment of property by going to the futures market without actually having to go through all the legal hurdles of actually buying the hard asset. Trading in real estate derivatives makes "it easier to get in, it's easier to get out" (Hudgins, 2007).

Both Standard & Poor's and Moody's investor services have introduced commercial property indices in 2007. Several of the indices have been developed collaboratively between real estate analytics and research firms and the major investor services firms. The indices include the following historical data: Construction records, real estate sales transactions, property values and appraisals (Hudgins, 2007).

The Merc began hosting futures trading based on S&P/GRA indices in October 2007. The concept of a derivative to manage and trade real estate futures won't be an overnight hit, but as the credit crunch worsens, risk increases, and property values fall, derivatives are going to become more and more attractive. Real Estate transactions amounted to $330 billion in 2006 leaving the potential for 10s of billions of dollars in domestic derivatives trading. Those most familiar with derivatives point out that the biggest obstacle to the wholesale adoption of derivatives in most markets is the lack of familiarity of investors with the necessary tools (Hudgins, 2007).

RISK MANAGEMENT & REDUCTION

Derivatives will appeal to large institutional investors for the most part as a risk management and reduction tool. "Mortgage bankers for example, could hedge against falling real estate markets that would increase exposure to delinquencies and foreclosures" (Christie, 2006, 7). Ordinary investors could also buy futures in housing prices and profit if prices continue to increase. Economist David Stiff believes that the individual homeowner will be able to buy home equity insurance to protect against the loss of falling home prices. If homeowners can purchase insurance against the risk of fire or theft, then why not protection against losses from home price decreases? Many unfamiliar with derivatives ask if trading housing price futures might make the markets volatile. "According to Stiff, 'Real Estate is already volatile and risky — like the stock market. The risk is increasing daily — there's an erroneous assumption that the real estate market only goes up. [Stiff continues:] 'We need hedging on both sides (Christie, 2006).'"

CONCLUSION

Fears remain that some investors don't understand this complex instrument and may well be exposed to risk that they don't understand. Individuals will lose money in the market, but that is nothing new. Systemic risk is a valid worry. For now, risk seems to be well diversified, with many more investors involved than at any previous time (for derivatives). Holders of risk tranches should act like the concerned parent watching the toddler at the swimming pool; never letting their eyes stray from their charge. The real challenge for some investors is that they may be two or three moves away from the borrower; this is the best illustration of a recipe with too many ingredients. Many questions remain, regarding credit derivatives and derivatives in general, but one is the following: "Will credit derivatives encourage investors to take on more risk? In the sub prime mortgage arena, underwriting standards fell sharply leading to defaults. What will happen if corporate defaults increase and senior tranches are hurt? What will investors be able to recover and how much risk will derivatives actually mitigate? ("At the risky end of finance." 2007).

BIBLIOGRAPHY

At the risky end of finance. (2007, April 19). *Economist.com*. Retrieved December 21, 2007, from http://www.economist.com/business/display-story.cfm?story%5fid=9033348

Christie, L. (2006, March 22). New way to bet on real estate. *CNNmoney.com*. Retrieved December 20, 2007, from http://money.cnn.com/2006/03/22/real%5festate/playing%5fthe%5fhome%5fprice%5fmarket/

Collins, D. (2007). Richard Sandor: Inventing markets out of thick air. *Futures: News, Analysis & Strategies for Futures, Options & Derivatives Traders, 36,* 12-43. Retrieved December 13, 2007, from EBSCO Online Database Business Source Premier. http://search.ebscohost.com/login.aspx?direct=true&db=buh&AN=27392717 &site=ehost-live

Credit crunch in U.S. good news for derivatives. (2007). *SCTWeek, 12*(44), 3. Retrieved December 18, 2007, from EBSCO Online Database Business Source Complete. http://search.ebscohost.com/login.aspx?direct=true&db=bth&AN=27390759&site=ehost-live

Davies, R. (2007). Gambling on derivatives. University of Exeter. Retrieved December 21, 2007, from http://www. projects.ex.ac.uk/RDavies/arian/scandals/derivatives.html

Fischer, D. (2013). The hidden effects of derivatives on bank balance sheets. *CPA Journal, 83*(9), 67-69. Retrieved November 15, 2013, from EBSCO Online Database Business Source Complete. http://

search.ebscohost.com/ login.aspx?direct=true&d
b=bth&AN=90499228&site=eh ost-live

Forward and futures contracts. (2007). *Financial Web.*
Retrieved December 20, 2007, from http://www.
finweb. com/investing/forward-and-futures-con-
tracts.html

Hudgins, M. (2007). Derivatives debut in commercial
real estate. *National Real Estate Investor, 49*(11), 12-
13. Retrieved December 18, 2007, from EBSCO
Online Database Business Source Premier. http://
search.ebscohost.com/login.aspx?direct=true&db
=buh&AN=27478833 &site=ehost-live

Jin-Yong, Y. (2013). Volume of derivative trading, enterprise value, and the return on assets. *Modern
Economy, 4*(8), 513-519. Retrieved November
15, 2013, from EBSCO Online Database Business Source Complete. http://search. ebscohost.
com/login.aspx?direct=true&db=bth&AN=9169
0771&site=ehost-live

McMahon, C. (2007). William Brodsky: Writing the
rules, shaping the future. *Futures: News, Analysis &
Strategies for Futures, Options & Derivatives Traders,
36*, 14-15. Retrieved December 13, 2007, from
EBSCO Online Database Business Source Premier.
http://search.ebscohost.com/login.aspx?direct=t
rue&db=buh&AN=27392718 &site=ehost-live

Nour, A., AbuSabha, S., Al Kubeise, A., & Nour, M.
(2013). The fundamental issues with financial
derivatives within the framework of International Accounting Standard No. (39) and their
relative responsibility for the current global financial crisis. *Journal of Business Studies Quarterly, 4*(3), 173-222. Retrieved November 15,
2013, from EBSCO Online Database Business
Source Complete. http://search. ebscohost.
com/login.aspx?direct=true&db=bth&AN=8687
4030&site=ehost-live

Options/option contracts. (2006). *Reference for business.* Retrieved December 19, 2007, from http://
www.referenceforbusiness.com/encyclopedia/
Oli-Per/Options-Options- Contracts.html

Ryan, O. (2006). The man who saw the futures.
Fortune, 154(12), 114-116. Retrieved December
18, 2007, from EBSCO Online Database Business Source Premier. http:// search.ebsco-
host.com/login.aspx?direct=true&db=buh&A
N=23452144&site=ehost-live

Swap. (n.d.) Risk glossary. Retrieved December 26,
2007, from http://www.riskglossary.com/link/
swap.htm

Stillabower, P. (2007, February 17). The economics
of OTC derivatives processing. *The Trade News.* Retrieved December 26, 2007, from http://www.thet-
radenews.com/ expert-opinion/530

Tien, M., Tri, T., & Min-Ming, W. (2013). Bank's
performance, the use of credit derivatives and financial crisis: Cases of Citigroup and J.P. MOrgan
Chase & Co. *Journal of International Finance &
Economics, 13*(4), 87-92. Retrieved November 15,
2013, from EBSCO Online Database Business
Source Complete. http://search.ebscohost.com/
login.aspx?direct=true&db=bth&AN=91830972
&site=ehost-live

Van den Berg, B. (2007). Derivatives — futures. In
B. van den Berg (Ed.), *Understanding financial instruments* (ch. 6). EagleTraders.com. Retrieved December 18, 2007, from http://www.eagletraders.
com/books/afm/afm6.htm Van den Berg, B.
(2007). Derivatives — options. In B. van den Berg
(Ed.), *Understanding financial instruments* (ch. 7).
EagleTraders.com. Retrieved December 18, 2007,
from http://www.eagletraders.com/books/afm/
afm7.htm

SUGGESTED READING

Clary, I. (2007). CME launches S&P futures contracts
as Russell exits. *Pensions & Investments, 35*(16), 14-
14. Retrieved December 13, 2007, from EBSCO
Online Database Business Source Premier. http://
search.ebscohost.com/login.aspx?direct=true&db
=buh&AN=26247590 &site=ehost-live

Hintze, J. (2007). OTC vendors see fertile ground
in U.S. *Securities Industry News, 19*(38), 16-22. Retrieved December 18, 2007, from EBSCO Online
Database Business Source Premier. http://search.
ebscohost.com/ login.aspx?direct=true&db=bth&
AN=27390759&site=eh ost-live

Kaza, G. (2006). Derivatives regulation of financial derivatives in the US code. *Derivatives Use,
Trading & Regulation, 11*(4), 381-386. Retrieved
December 13, 2007, from EBSCO Online Database Business Source Premier. http://search.
ebscohost.com/login.aspx?direct=true&db=b
uh&AN=20798442&site=ehost-live

—Carolyn Sprague

FINANCIAL HEDGING

ABSTRACT

Calculating the presence of risks is but one part of investment strategy. Another important part is weighing the extent of those risks against the potential returns. For many market participants, such an analysis helps to gauge which investments are worth the risk and which ones should be avoided. For others, however, this calculation helps determine how much risk may be worth the potential returns, as well as what might be done to minimize the negative effects while experiencing a positive effect. At the core of this latter practice is the practice of financial hedging. As its name suggests, this term refers to placing investments within a framework that keeps losses to a minimum. This paper presents a careful analysis of the idea of financial hedging, how it is conducted and the positive and negative aspects to such a practice. The reader gleans a better understanding of how this concept is utilized to protect the interests of the investor.

OVERVIEW

Winston Churchill once commented on what he saw as the benefits to a life of uncertainties. "Without a measureless and perpetual uncertainty," he said, "the drama of human life would be destroyed" ("Winston Churchill quotes," 2006). In terms of investment practices, Churchill's statement certainly has validity. Indeed, much of market investment depends heavily on calculating risk and uncertainty in order to maximize returns and avoid loss.

Then again, calculating the presence of risks is but one part of investment strategy. Another important part is weighing the extent of those risks against the potential returns. For many market participants, such an analysis helps to gauge which investments are worth the risk and which ones should be avoided. For others, however, this calculation helps determine how much risk may be worth the potential returns, as well as what might be done to minimize the negative effects while experiencing a positive effect

At the core of this latter practice is the practice of financial hedging. As its name suggests, this term refers to placing investments within a framework that keeps losses to a minimum. This paper presents a careful analysis of the idea of financial hedging, how it is conducted and the positive and negative aspects to such a practice. The reader gleans a better understanding of how this concept is employed to protect the interests of the investor.

A BRIEF OVERVIEW OF HEDGING

There are countless factors within the vast series of networks which make up the capitalist market system that can impact, positively or negatively, a financial investment. For example, an American company that purchases a factory in China might see positive returns because of the strength of the US dollar against the Chinese yuan, but if that currency exchange rate falters, the return might be less than anticipated. Similarly, lending practices may be greatly enhanced by a federally-imposed reduction in interest rates, and conversely, leveled or increased interest rates may negatively impact the maturity of long-term investments.

Indeed, the financial world is affected by a myriad of influences, from inflation to war to weather. When a hurricane moves its way into the Gulf of Mexico, for example, its potential destructive force often causes oil companies to halt operations on off-shore oil drilling rigs. The lack of production in turn causes an increase in the average cost of fuel, which in turn impacts manufacturing facilities, transportation companies and the airline industry. Put simply, a storm located in one geographic region of the United States can send ripples across every sector of the American economy.

Because of these potential "flies in the ointment," investments always occur with risks. Of course, no investment can be perfectly sheltered from the elements. Still, some of the most critical but vulnerable corporate investments may be at least partially covered from such issues. In this regard, many investors, therefore, will seek to minimize these risks by entering into other investments or trade relationships that will properly frame the size of the return the investment will generate. In many cases, this is done by hedging the investment.

In 1949, Alfred Winslow Jones, who was a reporter for *Fortune* magazine, was researching an article about the latest in investment trends and market forecasting. During his study, he developed his own theories about how an investor might wisely direct his or her pursuits as well as how he or she might protect those investments from great risk. Jones raised $100,000, including $40,000 of his own money, to conduct a number of long-term market investments. However, this investment strategy included a set of short-term stock purchases and leveraged funds (borrowed money), which he added to his portfolio in order to offset risks to the long-term securities. Less than 20 years later, Jones's "hedge fund" was the top five-year mutual fund with an 85 percent return (Gabelli, 2000).

DERIVATIVES

The practice of financial hedging varies in substance. In general, however, hedging in financial terms entails the use of derivatives that will offset the volatility of the investment. Derivatives are arrangements or contracts between two parties that are based on fluctuations and fluid conditions. The two most common types of derivatives are options and futures. An option is essentially a contract between an investment purchaser and seller whereby a security is bought based on the presumption that the value of the shares involved will either rise or fall compared to the agreed-upon price. The buyer will seek to purchase the share at a low point but believes that the shares will increase in value, while the seller will proceed from the idea that the stock price will fall compared to the agreed-upon price ("A beginner's guide to hedging," 2009). Under an option, the buyer is not under an obligation to buy or sell at a given price, but does reserve the right to do so.

The second type of derivative is a futures arrangement. Futures are contracts that arrange for the delivery of securities at a future date in exchange for a cash payment. Futures transactions occur within the framework of futures exchange markets, wherein the contracts are standardized (and not established by the parties themselves), performances are guaranteed by the market and gains and losses are carefully computed and managed by the exchange (Arditti, 1996). Because futures contracts create potential gains for the buyer but are carefully managed by a third party, they represent an effective tool by which financial hedging may occur.

HEDGE FUNDS

Hedging may occur via hedge funds, which have since evolved from Alfred Jones's brainchild, or through other mechanisms. In many cases, an investor may imitate the classic hedge fund by investing 50 percent of his or her securities in a traditional long-term mutual fund (or more than one), and 50 percent in short-term mutual funds. Such 50-50 investment strategies have yielded an average return little more than 12 percent. Even during the bear market of 2002, an investment strategy along these lines might have included Prudent Bear, which saw a return rate of nearly 63 percent in 2000, and Meridean Growth Fund, which was experiencing the adverse impacts of a stagnant economy ("How to build your own hedge fund," 2005).

Financial hedging is an investment strategy designed to offset risks. While this financial pursuit would by its very definition suggest a positive return for the investor, there are positive and negative aspects to hedging. This paper will next turn to a study of the benefits and drawbacks of financial hedging.

THE BENEFITS OF HEDGING

The list of financial hedging benefits begins with a point already discussed in this paper — the practice of hedging mitigates the risks of long-term investments. Hedge funds involve small investments that are less risky and provide significant returns — the aggregate of hedge fund securities therefore creates a cushion for investors whose larger interests rest in more volatile markets.

This lack of risk and promise of positive returns underscores another important benefit of hedging. In the stock market, investors must take into account the myriad of factors that may play a role in increasing or decreasing returns. During the course of investment strategy development, investors must also calculate the timing of entry into and exit from the market. Hedging, however, provides the potential for fewer risks and higher returns — as such, investors are fortunate to see a broader window of entry or exit from the markets ("Magnum funds," 2009).

Derivative markets became extremely popular among investors and, in particular, institutional investors in the late 20th and early 21st century. Over a 15-year period, hedge fund investment increased dramatically, from less than $30 billion in 1990 to $1.2 trillion in 2005 (Center for International Securities and Derivatives Markets, 2006). Corporations, public pensions and bank trusts are among those who have increasingly sought the security of hedge fund trading. In addition to the reasons just described, observers offer a number of advantages to derivatives trading over cash market investments. According to a 2002 study, investors saw lower transaction costs, lower market impact costs and reasonably priced access to leverage. Hedge fund markets, the study added, offer greater security and government oversight, thereby preventing wild fluctuations that can adversely impact fund performance (Schneeweis, 2002). Still, the diversity of the types of investments involved in hedge funds are flexible enough to entice a tremendous volume of financial players. For example, the world's largest hedge fund, JP Morgan Asset Management, has $33 billion in assets. That fund has securities located worldwide, including China and India. It is heavily invested in infrastructure, including roadway construction and toll highways. The third-largest hedge fund, Bridgewater Associates, caters largely to foreign governments, banks, educational institutions and non-profit groups, and therefore spreads its ventures across a broad spectrum of non-aligned markets and instruments ("The list," 2007).

Like any investment strategy, financial hedging has its benefits and at the same time, poses risks for the investor. It is to the negative aspects of hedging that this paper next turns focus.

THE DOWNSIDE OF FINANCIAL HEDGING

As demonstrated in this paper, the diversity of hedge fund investing practices has proven beneficial for investors; giving them wide degrees of flexibility and, in most cases, reliable returns. Hedge markets are to a large degree well-protected, by both the nature of the investments and the fact that many of the investments are protected by government oversight. However, as the popularity of hedging and hedge funds increased over recent years, markets and investment practices have diversified to the point where oversight and security became stretched thin. Still, given the returns, both real and potential, expected through hedge fund investments, consumers showed willingness to put their monies into such funds, even if it meant higher fees, a lack of access to those monies and secretive investments.

In late 2008, Bernard Madoff, a Wall Street icon, appeared in front of his employees (including his sons, who had worked for him throughout their

careers) and said that he had had enough. "It's all one big lie," he said, a statement his sons and other employees knew would have devastating implications. Madoff was admitting to the fact that his hedge fund, which involved at least $50 billion, was a fraud (Securities and Exchange Commission, 2008).

Madoff was considered a pioneer of the New York Stock Exchange. An investment innovator, he established deep roots in the Jewish philanthropic community and in networks around the globe. Madoff made sure to include such friends in his investments and, in light of his reputation and experience on Wall Street, made participation in his business opportunities unquestioned among clients. The fact that such investments consistently brought supposed returns of 15 percent annually regardless of market conditions made the attraction even stronger.

However, Madoff's hedge fund in fact had no substance. Instead, Madoff had concocted what is known as "Ponzi scheme" — Madoff would take client funds and invest them in what they thought was a vast network of opportunities but instead, when other clients would seek redemptions, he would simply transfer the money invested by others. With over 4,000 investors (the number of which was consistently growing, thanks to the aforementioned reputation Madoff held), Madoff was able to continue his pyramid scheme for many years without fear of the bubble bursting. In fact, although Madoff was under suspicion by a number of whistle-blowers nearly a decade earlier, they could not trace the monies.

When the market began turning for the negative in 2008, however, Madoff's clients increasingly sought redemptions (while new investor numbers shrank). With Madoff's hedge fund consistently losing money to transfer, he was backed into a corner and forced to confess to his crime (Lendman, 2008).

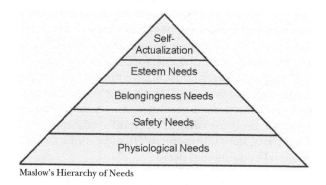

Maslow's Hierarchy of Needs

The Madoff case underscores a number of issues about the nature of hedging. Designed to create security for investors, hedge investing also presents risks. As demonstrated in the 2002 study discussed earlier in this paper, there is a measure of government oversight over hedging, but Madoff demonstrated that there are ways to avoid such oversight. Additionally, Madoff employed third-party agents to administer many of his transactions, adding a large degree of secrecy to the hedge fund. While the $50 billion (or more) Madoff mismanaged represented a fantastic crime, the fact is that many hedge funds employ a similar degree of secrecy and lack of access to investor monies. The recession which helped bring Madoff's crimes to light has generated increased interest in more government oversight and safeguards regarding financial hedging and the returns such practices promise.

EFFORTS TO REGULATE HEDGING PRACTICES

Although hedging is not an option readily available to every citizen (certainly, millions of people simply cannot afford to pay the high fees associated with hedging), the fact that so many pension funds and personal retirement accounts have contact with hedge fund investors means that it is a financial sector whose influence is significant. When an incident like Madoff's arrest occurred, therefore, it cast a spotlight on hedging. The recession that began in 2008 added to the concern. In 2007, a presidential working group looking into regulatory measures governing financial hedging concluded that no further oversight was necessary. Foreshadowing the events that would occur a year later, however, the then-Chairman of that commission called hedge funds a "dark corner" of the market and said that hedging was a central figure in a significant number of market trading abuse cases. A number of regulatory measures were introduced to govern who invested in hedge funds (based on their personal incomes) and to discourage risk-taking investments, but neither the commission nor Congress took any steps to make any major changes in this arena (Labaton, 2007). Two years later, a weak economy and more instances of hedge fund abuse powered calls for hedge fund licensure and direct regulations. The Obama administration pledged to implement such measures as long as they have a direct and "meaningful" effect (Reuters, 2009). The problem that exists is the fact that hedging occurs in such great volume that over time, it has become difficult to regulate or even quantify. Hedging consists of more than $1.4 trillion in assets, handled by a large number of managers, only a few of whom were registered and licensed before the 2008 financial crisis. Efforts to update the current regulatory system have fallen short of comprehensive changes (Younglai, 2009; VanDenburgh, 2013).

CONCLUSION

Although a large population is unable to afford the high prices for investing in hedge funds, financial hedging has become an increasingly popular venture for those whose incomes and investment capabilities can support such activities. While hedging has been in practice since the end of the Second World War, the practice has truly taken flight over the last 20 years, coinciding with market fluctuations.

As discussed in this paper, the reasons for increased interest in financial hedging are clear. Hedging offers the investor an opportunity to protect his or her assets in other markets. Long-term stock market investments, as shown in this essay, are easily impacted by a whole range of factors that may cause losses for the investor. Hedging presents reliable, short-term returns that can be used to offset such losses.

Of course, there are risks inherent in the practice of hedging. Much of these negative aspects have to do with the fact that hedging has grown exponentially over the last two decades, to the point where there are countless types of investments placed into hedge fund markets. It is this growth that has made oversight and security a challenge and created openings for illegal management of such investments.

The Bernard Madoff scandal caused the losses of tens of billions of dollars to investors around the world, although the true extent of the damages caused by one of the largest frauds in US history has yet to be determined. This extraordinary incident, coupled with an anemic economic condition, has led to an increased call among political leaders and industry experts for an overhaul of the way hedging is conducted. However, such efforts have yielded little in terms of meaningful reforms, due in no small part to the fact that the industry's exponential growth has made full understanding of the breadth of financial hedging a challenge; one that cannot be easily mitigated even when the stakes are at their highest.

BIBLIOGRAPHY

A beginner's guide to hedging. (2009). Retrieved February 20, 2009, from Investopedia.com. http://www.investopedia. com/articles/basics/03/080103.asp

Autor, F. (1996). Derivatives: A comprehensive resource for options futures. Boston, MA: Harvard Business School Press. Retrieved February 20, 2009, from http://books.google.com/books?id=uXDYmMJRA-sC&printsec=frontcover

Bollen, N.B., & Pool, V.K. (2012). Suspicious patterns in hedge fund returns and the risk of fraud. *Review of Financial Studies, 25*(9), 2673-2702. Retrieved November 15, 2013, from EBSCO Online Database Business Source Complete. http://search.ebscohost.com/login.aspx?direct=t rue&db=bth&AN=79306484&site=ehost-live

Center for International Securities and Derivatives Markets. (2006, May). The benefits of hedge funds. Retrieved February 22, 2009, from http://airtdatabase.com/research/ pdffiles/benefitsof-hedgefunds.pdf

Gabelli, M.J. (2000, October 25). The history of hedge funds. GAMCO Investors, Inc. Retrieved February 21, 2009, from http://www.gabelli.com/news/articles/mario-hedge%5f102500.html

How to build your own hedge fund. (2005, December 26). Business Week. Retrieved February 22, 2009, from http:// www.businessweek.com/magazine/content/05%5f52/ b3965453.htm

Kolhatkar, S. (2013). Hedge funds are for suckers. *Bloomberg Businessweek, (4338)*, 8-10. Retrieved November 15, 2013, from EBSCO Online Database Business Source Complete. http://search.ebscohost.com/login. aspx?direct=t rue&db=bth&AN=89024642&site=e host-live

LaBaton, S. (2007, February 23). Officials reject more oversight of hedge funds. New York Times. Retrieved February 28, 2009, from http://www. nytimes.com/2007/02/23/business/23hedge. html?pagewanted=1&%5fr=1

Lendman, S. (2008, December 27). Early suspicions about Bernard Madoff Ponzi Scheme fraud. The Market Oracle. Retrieved February 28, 2009, from http://www.marketoracle.co.uk/Article7973. html

The list: the world's largest hedge funds. (2007, September). Foreign Policy. Retrieved February 24, 2009, from http:// www.foreignpolicy.com/story/cms.php?story%5fid=3967

Magnum funds. (2009). Retrieved February 22, 2009, from Magnum Global Investments Ltd. http://www.magnum. com/About. aspx?RowID=14&GroupName=AHF

Schneeweis, T. & Georgiev, G. (2002, June 19). The benefits of hedge funds. University of Massachusetts. Retrieved February 22, 2009, from http://www.nymex.com/media/ bhf.pdf

US Securities and Exchange Commission. (2008, December 12). SEC charges Bernard L. Madoff for multi-billion dollar Ponzi Scheme. Retrieved February 27, 2009, from http://www.sec.gov/news/press/2008/2008-293.htm

VanDenburgh, W.M. (2013). Advising individuals on hedge fund investments. *CPA Journal, 83*(9), 36-43. Retrieved November 15, 2013, from EBSCO Online Database Business Source Complete. http://search.ebscohost.com/ login.aspx?direct=true&d b=bth&AN=90499223&site=eh ost-live

Winston Churchill quotes. (2006). Retrieved February 20, 2009, from Thinkexist.com. http://thinkexist.com/quotation/without%5fa%5f measureless%5fand%5fperpetual%5f uncertainty/187840.html

Younglai, R. (2009, February 4). Top US regulator backs hedge fund oversight. Retrieved February 28, 2009, from Reuters. http://www.reuters.com/article/americasHedgeFundsNews/idUSLNE51304A20090204

SUGGESTED READING

Jacobius, A. (2009). Funds pour big money into realm of real assets. *Pensions and Investments, 37*(2), 30-33. Retrieved February 28, 2009, from EBSCO Online Database Business Source Complete. http://search.ebscohost.com/ login.aspx?direct=true&d b=bth&AN=36590313&site=eh ost-live

Landis, D. (2009). Hedges that didn't get hosed. *Kiplinger's Personal Finance, 63*(3), 42-43. Retrieved February 28, 2009, from EBSCO Online Database Academic Search Complete. http://search.ebscohost.com/login.aspx?direct=t rue&db=bth&AN=3 6414784&site=ehost-live

New hedge funds smaller in '08. (2009). *American Banker, 174*(26), 6. Retrieved February 28, 2009, from EBSCO Online Database Business Source Complete. http://search. ebscohost.

com/login.aspx?direct=true&db=bth&AN=3662
9000&site=ehost-live

Temple-West, P. (2009, February 2). Proposed legislation to expand SEC role in hedge fund oversight. *Bond Buyer, 367*(33053), 4. Retrieved February 28, 2009, from EBSCO Online Database Business Source Complete. http://search. ebscohost. com/login.aspx?direct=true&db=bth&AN=364 06709&site=ehost-live

Terzo, G. (2009). Re-starting a hedge fund? *Investment Dealers' Digest, 75*(2), 10-22. Retrieved February 28, 2009, from EBSCO Online Database Business Source Complete. http://search.ebscohost.com/login.aspx?direct=t rue&db=bth&AN=36094404&site=ehost-live

–Michael P. Auerbach

FINANCIAL INCENTIVES

ABSTRACT

Most organizations use financial incentives to motivate their employees to exude higher performance in support of organizational goals and objectives. On an individual basis, financial incentives include piecework programs, bonuses, promotions, and merit pay raises to encourage consistent above average performance. On a broader level, financial incentives can be given to all employees according to the profitability of the organization; an act which encourages employees to harbor a vested interest in the organization's success. No matter the type of financial incentive used, it must be tied to performance in order to ensure that the employee is fairly compensated and that the organization reaches the high performance it needs and desires.

OVERVIEW

WHY WORK?

Many of us have a love/hate relationship with our jobs. While on some days we can barely drag ourselves out of bed to go to work, on other days the thought of the tasks to be done is so invigorating that we cannot wait to get started. One is truly fortunate if the latter type of mornings outnumber the former. However, all too often this does not seem to be the case. Yet, we still continue to go to work if for no other reason than that we need the paycheck.

MASLOW'S HIERARCHY OF NEEDS

A number of observers have posited various motivations to explain why people work. Although some theorists have tried to reduce motivation to an equation that connects the probability of increased performance with such things as the employee's perceived expectancy of obtaining a reward for doing so, other theorists have posited that different people are motivated by different things such as having one's physical needs met (e.g., food on the table and a roof over one's head), a need for the esteem of others, or some other internal incentive. Abraham Maslow, for example, described a hierarchy of needs ranging from meeting basic physiological needs (e.g., food, clothing, shelter) to safety, belongingness, and esteem needs and eventually self-actualization. According to this theory, people are motivated by different things depending on where there are on the hierarchy at any given point. For example, a person who has earned a high level position in his/her career and has adequate income for whatever s/he wants to do may be able to focus on self-actualization. However, if that same person loses his/her job or investments, s/he may once again be concerned about meeting basic physiological needs.

IMPORTANCE OF FINANCIAL INCENTIVES

Although virtually every organization tries to motivate its employees through financial incentives, these are not seen as motivators in the scientifically used meaning of the word. Rather, at various places on the hierarchy of needs (or other motivation theory), financial incentives give people the means by which they can meet their needs. For example, in Maslow's hierarchy of needs, a person who is out of work and fears losing his/her house could probably be easily motivated to work for a financial reward that would help him/her put food on the table or pay the mortgage.

Once such immediate needs have been met, however, money or other financial incentives allow the person to meet his/ her safety needs through such things as obtaining a steady job that brings in a sufficient and reliable paycheck, one's belongingness needs by providing a high enough income to allow the person to be identified with other successful people (either at the work place or through other fee-based institutions like country clubs). Money can also be used to help meet one's esteem needs as people look at the situation that money has allowed the person to attain.

No matter the theory, however, most motivation theorists recognize the fact that most people working in organizations both need and expect remuneration. Sometimes financial incentives are required to meet basic physical needs or to have the security of knowing that those needs will continue to be met for the foreseeable future. In other cases, financial incentives in the form of bonuses, raises, or promotions fill a need for recognition from others. However, no matter what motivators an employee has, from the employee's point-of-view, pay is always a consideration. Although job titles and other perquisites can be important motivators, in most cases employees need more from the organization than to know that they are helping it succeed. To motivate employees to perform at a consistently high level, the organization must give them what they want or need. In most cases, this is some kind of financial incentive that, in turn, allows the employee to obtain or work towards the reward that s/he really wants. One of the things that successful organizations do to motivate employees to contribute to the company's high performance is to link the desired performance to rewards.

The truth is that money and other financial incentives are one of the reasons why people in Western culture work. Although many of us could keep ourselves mentally and physically engaged through other activities, if one does not have the financial status to meet one's needs, a job is the most typical solution. Although other perquisites (e.g., a corner office, a more important title) can be used to reward an employee in the workplace, because of the flexibility of financial incentives to meet one's needs, they are one of the most frequently used rewards. However, to be effective in motivating the kind on the job behavior that will most effectively support the business, the financial incentives need to be linked to

Abraham Maslow. *Via Wikipedia.org*

job performance. Otherwise, rather than reinforcing the type of behavior that supports the organization, the financial incentives can actually reinforce behavior that is contrary to the good of the organization. For example, one of the reasons that the piecework approach to paying assembly line workers has historically been so widely used is because it ties the financial remuneration that the worker receives to the number of widgets that the worker produces. The more widgets (that are within specification) that the worker produces, the more the worker gets paid under this method. However, if workers were only paid for the number of widgets that they completed — whether or not they were within the standards for an acceptable widget — the financial incentive might actually encourage the workers to produce more widgets that were unacceptable, thereby rewarding them for shoddy work and costing the organization money rather than saving it.

TYPES OF FINANCIAL INCENTIVE PLANS

There are a number of common approaches to financial incentives in business.

VARIABLE PAY PLANS

Variable pay incentive plans tie the employee's pay to a predetermined measure of overall profitability for the organization in general or for the specific facility in which the employee works. In profit sharing plans, most of the employees of the organization receive a share of the annual profits of the organization, typically on a one-time, lump sum basis. In profit sharing plans, all employees share in the profitability of the company. Therefore, the more profitable the company is during a given time period, the greater the reward the employee will receive. In theory, therefore, the employee is motivated to do his/her best in order to increase the profitability of the company and, thereby, also increase his/her financial reward. There are several general types of profit sharing plans.

- Under cash plans, a percentage of the profits of the organization (usually 15 to 20 percent) are distributed to workers at regular intervals.
- Under the Lincoln incentive system, employees work in a guaranteed piecework basis and receive a percentage of the total annual profits of the organization based on their merit rating
- Under deferred profit sharing plans, a predetermined portion of the organization's profits are placed in an account for each employee. These accounts are supervised by a trustee and payment is often deferred until retirement, thereby offering a tax advantage.

However, although profit sharing plans are currently a popular way to provide financial incentives to employees, research on the effectiveness of profit sharing plans — particularly from the point of view of increased profits for the organization — tend to be ambivalent (Dessler, 2005).

PIECEWORK PAY PLANS

In addition, there are number of financial incentive programs that are used to motivate employees on an individual basis. Piecework plans are pay systems that are based on the number of items processed by an individual employee during a specified unit of time. This is one of the oldest individual incentive plans, and is still widely used.

- An example of a straight piecework plan would be to pay a worker based on how many widgets the worker produces during an eight hour shift. The more widgets that the worker produces during

that time, the more pay the worker receives; a specified amount for each unit s/he completes (e.g., widgets made; sales calls completed).

- Another type of piecework plan is the standard hour plan. Under this type of financial incentive plan, the employee receives a premium that corresponds to the percent by which the employee's performance exceeds the standard. So, for example, if the standard for making widgets is 100 widgets per day and Harvey produces 120 widgets that day, he would receive a 20 percent bonus on top of his standard pay for that day. Although still widely used today, piecework incentive plans have earned a poor reputation in some industries. For example, in the garment industry, workers may be paid based on how many garments they complete. However, in some cases, a worker may not complete sufficient garments during a day in order to meet the minimum-wage standards.

BONUSES, STOCK OPTIONS & PROFIT SHARING

Piecework systems, of course, are difficult to implement for professional or creative employees. It would be unreasonable in most situations, for example, to pay a computer programmer based on the number of lines of code s/he produces per day. A few lines of good code are worth much more to the organization than many lines of poor code. Therefore, many organizations offer professional employees financial incentives in the form of such things as bonuses, stock options, and profit sharing.

MERIT PAY

Another financial incentive that is widely used is merit pay. This is an increase in salary that is given to an employee based on the employee's individual performance. Merit pay can be given to an employee on a one time, lump sum basis in the form of a bonus for outstanding work. Merit pay raises for outstanding work, on the other hand, become part of the employee's salary and are given on a continuing basis. For example, at his annual review, Harvey's supervisor might determine that Harvey's work was consistently outstanding enough to warrant a pay raise. This merit raise would be added to Harvey's current base salary to become his new base salary from that point on.

PAY FOR PERFORMANCE

Another popular approach for motivating desired

behavior in high performing organizations is an approach frequently referred to as "pay for performance." In these plans, employees are rewarded financially for high performance and contributing to the organization's goals. This is true not only for workers at the bottom of the organizational structure as is done in piecework plans, but also all the way up to the chief executive officer. Research performed by the government's General Accounting Office (GAO) has found that there a number of factors that make pay for performance incentive plans successful (U.S. General Accounting Office, 2004).

- First, the GAO found that it is important to use objective competencies to assess the quality of the employee's performance. These should be based on empirical research and directly related to the goals of the organization.

- Second, the GAO found that employee performance ratings should be translated into pay increases or awards so that employees can see a direct, positive consequence for their actions.

- Third, the GAO found that both the employee's current salary and contribution to the organization should be considered when making decisions about compensation, so that rewards for similar contributions are equitable.

- Finally, to be successful and to prevent possible abuse, the GAO found that pay for performance systems should be clear and well-published so that employees know the basis on which decisions are made and what kind of awards are made across the organization.

APPLICATIONS

FINANCIAL INCENTIVES WITHIN THE SALES INDUSTRY

Although financial incentives are used across industries and at all organizational levels, one of the first groups for which financial incentives often springs to mind is sales personnel. Typically, sales personnel are paid a regular salary, on the basis of commission, or some combination of the two plans. In the straight salary approach, the sales person is paid a salary (with occasional incentives) just as is done with most employees. This approach to remunerating sales personnel is particularly appropriate when the salesperson is required to generate leads in addition to making a sale or when the sales job involves customer

service in addition to straight sales. Although salary plans are simple to administrate, they have the disadvantage of not

linking pay to performance. As a result, members of the sales staff have no particular incentive to become high performing employees. Commission plans, on the other hand, pay sales persons only for results. Under this plan, the salesperson does not receive a regular salary, but is paid only on commission, a set fee or percentage of the sale. However, although commission plans have the advantage of motivating high performance, not every salesperson has the skills and abilities necessary to excel at sales. This can not only lead to dissatisfaction with the plan (and, by extension, the job), but also lead to burnout. Because of the drawbacks of both the straight salary and straight commission approach to remunerating sales employees, most organizations use a plan that is a combination of the two approaches, giving salespersons both a steady salary as well as a commission on any sales made. Most organizations use an 80/20 split between percent of pay coming from base salary and from commissions, although other combinations are also possible.

DEFINING CRITERIA FOR SUCCESS

However, although tying the performance of a salesperson to his/ her performance makes sense, defining the criteria of success to which financial incentives are attached for a sales job can be a challenging exercise. Two general approaches to linking pay to sales performance have been widely implemented.

OUTCOME-BASED STANDARDS

The first of these is the outcome-based system that focuses on the final outcomes of the sales process (e.g., whether or not a sale was made, total revenues earned by a salesperson in a given period of time). Outcome-based standards tend to be both objective and clear: Either a sales quota was met or it was not. Outcome-based systems tend to be easy to implement because of the relative availability of criteria against which performance can be measured (e.g., number of sales made or dollar volume earned within a given performance assessment period). However, because sales jobs tend to be performed in isolation, it is easy for sales personnel to actually harm the organization while still making a sale (e.g., a salesperson might skimp on customer service and follow-up in order to make another sale or focus on selling more items with a smaller price tag or on items or services that have been proven easier to sell). Outcome-based control systems do not take into account a number of factors that affect the success of a salesperson. Sales often occur over a period of time, particularly when the decision to purchase is a complicated or major one. Further, for many sales personnel, making the sale is only part of the job; the salesperson is also often required to perform customer service not only to make the sale but also after the sale has been made. As a result, it can be difficult to tell whether a salesperson is not doing his/her job well or if s/he is immersed in associated activities that will bear fruit later.

BEHAVIOR-BASED STANDARDS

Because of the problems with outcome-based control systems arising from the nature of the sales job, many experts argue in favor of a behavior-based rather than an outcome-based control system for sales personnel. Behavior-based systems focus more on the behavior of the sales person rather than his/her final sales. Although these systems better link pay to performance, they also require significantly more monitoring of both the activities and the results of the sales force's efforts. Behavior-based control systems are also more dependent than outcome-based control systems on the knowledge, skills, and abilities that the salesperson brings to the job (e.g., aptitudes, personality traits, general or specific product knowledge), the activities of the sales force (e.g., number of calls made), and the sales strategies employed in trying to make a sale (Anderson & Oliver, 1987). However, although behavior-based control systems overcome a number of the disadvantages associated with outcome-based control systems, they also tend to be complex to develop and implement and more subjective than outcome-based systems. This can lead to employee dissatisfaction and work against the very motivation that it was meant to establish.

CONCLUSION

Virtually every organization uses some sort of financial incentive to motivate high performance from its employees in support of the organization's goals and objectives. Financial incentives can be as simple as paying the employee for each unit of work performed or as complicated as a package that pays the

employee on a combination of salary and reward for either individual or team performance. However, to be effective, financial incentives need to be linked with performance in order to ensure not only that the employee is fairly compensated, but also that the organization is paying for high performance in support of its goals and objectives.

BIBLIOGRAPHY

Anderson, E. & Oliver, R. L. (1987). Perspectives on behavior-based versus outcome-based salesforce control systems. *Journal of Marketing, 51*(4), 76-88. Retrieved February 17, 2009, from EBSCO Online Database Business Source Complete. http://search.ebscohost.com/login.aspx?direct=true&db=bth&AN=4996249&site=ehost-live

Dessler, G. (2005). *Human resource management* (10th ed.). Upper Saddle River, NJ: Pearson/Prentice Hall.

U.S. General Accounting Office. (2004). *Human capital: Implementing pay for performance at selected personnel demonstration projects* (GAO-04-83). Retrieved March 27, 2007, from EBSCO Online Database Business Source Complete. http://search.ebscohost.com/login.aspx?direct=true&db=bth&AN=18173828&site=ehost-live

SUGGESTED READING

Atul, M., Gupta, N., & Jenkins, G. D. Jr. (2007). A drop in the bucket: When is a pay raise a pay raise? *Journal of Organizational Behavior, 18*(2), 117-137. Retrieved March 2, 2009, from EBSCO Online Database Business Source Complete. http://search.ebscohost.com/login.aspx?direct=true&db=bth&AN=12493230&site=ehost-live

Darmon, R. Y. (1987). The impact of incentive compensation on the salesperson's work habits: An economic model. *Journal of Personal Selling and Sales Management, 7*(1), 21-32. Retrieved March 2, 2009, from EBSCO Online Database Business Source Complete. http://search.ebscohost.com/login.aspx?direct=true&db=bth&AN=6652095&site=ehost-live

Kahn, L. M. & Sherer, P. D. (1990). Contingent pay and managerial performance. *Industrial and Labor Relations Review, 43*(3), 107S-120S. Retrieved March 2, 2009, from EBSCO Online Database Business Source Complete. http://search.ebscohost.com/login.aspx?direct=true&db=bt

h&AN=9603275758&site=ehost-live

Palia, D., Abraham, R. S., & Wang, C.-J. (2008). Founders versus no-founders in large companies: Financial incentives and the call for regulation. *Journal of Regulatory Economics, 33*(1), 55-86. Retrieved March 2, 2009, from EBSCO Online Database Business Source Complete. http://search.ebscohost.com/login.aspx?direct=true&db=bth&AN=27978131&site=ehost-live

Peterson, S. J. & Luthans, F. (2006). The impact of financial and nonfinancial on business-unit outcomes over time. *Journal of Applied Psychology, 91*(1), 156-165. Retrieved March 2, 2009, from EBSCO Online Database Business Source Complete. http://search.ebscohost.com/login.aspx? direct=true&db=bth&AN=19504997&site=ehost-live

—Ruth A. Wienclaw

FINANCIAL INFORMATION SYSTEMS

ABSTRACT

This article focuses on the financial accounting process and the benefits of automating the process. The financial accounting process is defined and each step of the financial accounting cycle is explained. The accounting department is a key player in an organization's ability to be successful. This department is responsible for providing information to internal and external entities so that they can make effective financial decisions that will benefit the organization. These decisions will have a profound effect on the organization so it is imperative that the data collected is accurate.

OVERVIEW

The accounting department is a key player in an organization's ability to succeed. This department is responsible for providing information to internal and external entities so that they can make effective financial decisions that will benefit the organization. These decisions will have a profound effect on the organization so it is imperative that the data collected is accurate. One way to ensure that the data is accurate is to install an accounting information system (AIS).

An accounting information system (AIS) is a system that records an organization's financial data and transactions. This information consists of the organization's revenues and expenditures as well as other financial transactions. A business will implement an AIS in order to accumulate data so that those responsible for making decisions have a supply of information over a period of time.

COMPONENTS OF ACCOUNTING INFORMATION SYSTEMS

Most accounting information systems have two components — financial and managerial accounting. The objective of financial accounting is to provide information to external decision makers, whereas, the objective of managerial accounting is to provide information to internal decision makers. Although both areas need to use an organization's accounting records, there are differences between the two areas of accounting.

TYPES OF ACCOUNTING

	Managerial Accounting	Financial Accounting
Primary User	Internal decision makers	External decision makers
Time Focus	Present and future	Historical
Organizational Focus	Segmented	Aggregate
Time Span of Reports	As needed	Quarterly and annually
Rules and Regulations	Does not need to follow GAAP	Mandatory to follow GAAP
Record-keeping	Formal or informal	Formal

CHOOSING THE APPROPRIATE SYSTEM

An organization's management team has the ability to create any type of internal accounting system. However, cost may be a key factor in deciding what type of system will be selected. The type and amount of information that needs to be stored is another factor in selecting the most appropriate information system.

THE FOREIGN CORRUPT PRACTICES ACT

Both financial and managerial accounting is bound by the Foreign Corrupt Practices Act. This act is a "U.S. law forbidding bribery and other corrupt practices, and requiring that accounting records be maintained in reasonable detail and accuracy, and that an appropriate system of internal accounting be maintained" (Horngreen, Stratton, & Sundem, 2002, p. 7). In summary, Drury (1996) stated that managerial accounting focuses on the provision of information to people within the organization so that they can make better decisions, whereas, financial accounting emphasizes the need of an organization having the ability to provide financial information to stakeholders outside of the organization.

One of the main objectives of financial accounting is to be able to process an organization's financial transactions in an effective manner in order to produce accurate financial statements, such as income statements and balance sheets (Moscove & Simkin, 1981). Managerial accounting has three main areas of operation: Cost accounting, budgeting and systems study.

FINANCIAL ACCOUNTING

Financial accounting focuses on preparing financial statements for external decision-makers such as banks and government agencies. The primary purpose of the field is to review and monitor an organization's financial performance and report the results of the evaluation to potential stakeholders. Financial accountants are expected to create financial statements based on Generally Accepted Accounting Principles (GAAP). Financial accounting exists in order to: Produce general purpose financial statements, provide information to decision makers in the accounting field, and meet regulatory requirements.

THE FINANCIAL ACCOUNTING AUDIT TRAIL

The basic inputs of the financial accounting structure are transactions that measure money. Organizations should be able to conduct an audit trail of their accounting transactions. This audit trail will show the flow of data that moves through the accounting information system. The financial accounting audit trail consists of inputs, processing and outputs. Inputs consist of documents such as sales invoices and payroll time cards, whereas, the outputs are final documents such as financial statements and other external reports. Processing will go from the input phase to the output phase. Steps taken in between these two points include: Recording journal entries, posting the entries to a general ledger, and preparing a trial balance from the general ledger account balances. Processing these transactions is considered to be a part of an organization's accounting cycle, which has nine steps.

THE NINE STEPS OF THE ACCOUNTING CYCLE

According to Moscove & Simkins (1985), the nine steps in the accounting cycle are:

- Prepare transaction source documents. Any type of transaction that causes a change in assets, liability, or owners' equity must be accounted for through documentation. Business transactions are the result of source documents being created. For example, the sales invoice represents a transaction source document (also referred to as an original record). Source documents are visual representation that a transaction exists. Many corporations will have a policy indicating that a financial transaction cannot be entered into its accounting information system until the proper source documents are prepared and approved. Other common forms of source documents include purchase invoices, receiving reports, bills of lading, employee time cards, and voucher checks.

- Sourcing documents allow an organization to collect its transaction data for subsequent entry into the accounting information system. In addition, transaction source documents act as the starting point in an organization's audit trail flow of data through its information system's accounting cycle.

- Recording business transactions in a journal. Once the accounting data has been collected, it is recorded in the organization's journal. Many organizations will maintain a journal within an accounting information system in order to keep a chronological record of the activities that have occurred throughout its lifecycle. There are large amounts of transactions that need to be processed. Therefore, many organizations will switch from a manual system to a computerized financial information system. The computerized system can provide a more efficient approach to tracking the various categories that will occur when the company is performing business transactions. Some of the most common categories are: Assets, operating expenses, the sale of products and/or services, and the receipt and payment of cash.

- Posting business transactions from the journal to the general ledger and determining individual account balances. The general ledger contains detailed information about the organization's assets, liabilities, owners' equity, revenue and expenses. A "T" account is created for each type of monetary item in the organization. In order for an organization's management team to have the appropriate information, the individual debits and credits from journal entries must be transferred from their proper accounts within the general ledger. This process is called posting. Once the posting process has been completed, managers can determine the balance of each general ledger.

- Preparing a trial balance. Each organization determines when it wants to prepare financial statements. Common timeframes include annually, quarterly and monthly. Based on the established timeframe, all of the posting work must be completed by the designated time so that the value of each general ledger can be determined. Once the information is computed, the trial balance is prepared. The trial balance highlights all of the general ledger accounts together with their end of period balances. In addition, the trial balance (1) determines whether the total debit and total credit account balances equal one another and (2) prepares the financial statements for the organization.

- Recording adjusting entries in a journal. Before one can prepare the organization's financial statements, adjustments (adjusting journal entries) may need to be made. The need to adjust is based on the periodicity principle and the matching principle. In addition, there are four major types of adjusting entries at the end of the organiza-

tion's accounting period. The major types are unrecorded expenses, unrecorded revenues, deferred expenses or prepaid expenses and deferred revenues.

- Posting adjusting journal entries to the general ledger, determining updated general ledger account balances and preparing an adjusted trial balance. An adjusted trial balance must be prepared before the organization can prepare its income statement and balance sheet. The purpose of preparing the second trial balance is to determine if the debit and credit account balances are still equal once the adjusting entry process has been completed.

- Preparing financial statements from adjusted trial balance. The organization will use the adjusted trial balance to prepare its financial statements.

- Recording closing entries in a journal, posting them to the general ledger and determining new balances of those accounts affected by closing entries.

- An organization will record and post closing entries in order to eliminate its individual revenue and expense account balances and transfer the net income into the owner's equity account. Organizations should prepare financial statements immediately after the close of its accounting period so that the information is available to its decision makers.

- Preparing a post-closing trial balance. Once the closing entries are journalized and posted, all of the revenue and expense accounts will have zero balances and the owners' equity capital accounts will have the current period's net income or loss. Once this information has been confirmed, a post-closing trial balance will be conducted in order to verify that the accounts with debit balances equal the accounts with credit balances. This is the final step.

APPLICATION

FINANCIAL MANAGEMENT INFORMATION SYSTEMS

CHARACTERISTICS OF FINANCIAL MANAGEMENT INFORMATION SYSTEMS
A financial management information system (FMIS) is a system that computerizes the public expenditure

management process. According to Diamond and Khemani (2006), some of the characteristics of this type of system are:

- **It is a management tool.** A FMIS should cater to the needs of the management team, and be a tool that supports change.
- **It should provide a wide range of nonfinancial and financial information.** It should provide information that will assist the managers in making decisions. Also, the system should be imbedded in the government accounting system as well as be able to collect data on nonfinancial areas such as employee information, performance based budgets and types of goods and services produced.
- **It is a system.** The system should be able to connect, collect, process and provide data to all essential personnel in the budget system on a regular basis. Thus, all key personnel should have access to the system so that they can perform their designated duties.

The core components of a FMIS are general ledger, budgetary accounting, accounts payable, and accounts receivable. The non-core components are payroll system, budget development, procurement, project ledger, and asset module.

CHARACTERISTICS OF A WELL DESIGNED FINANCIAL MANAGEMENT INFORMATION SYSTEM

According to Diamond and Khemani (2006), a well designed FMIS should:

- "Be modular, and capable of progressive upgrading to cater to future needs."
- "Offer a common platform and user interface to the stakeholders in different agencies responsible for financial management, for adding to and accessing the information database."
- "Maintain a historical database of budget and expenditure plans; transaction data at the highest level of detail; cash flows and bank account operations including checks issued, cancelled, and paid; cash balances, and; floats."
- "Have dedicated modules to handle monthly, rolling, short-term and long-term forward estimates of revenues, expenditures prepared by agencies, and corresponding estimates of the resulting cash flows."
- "Compile formal government accounts from the database of authorization and cash allocations, pri-

mary revenue and expenditure transactions of the agencies; and treasury operations, avoiding the need to duplicate data entry for accounting purposes."
- "Enable real-time reconciliation of parallel and related streams of transaction data."
- "Be flexible enough to provide user defined management information, aggregated at the desired level of detail from the database" (Diamond & Khemani, 2006).

VIEWPOINT

FMIS IN DEVELOPING COUNTRIES

In most developing countries in the early 21st century, the budget and accounting process was either completed manually or with outdated software applications. As a result, their output was often unreliable and untimely. This created a concern when they needed to conduct budget planning, monitoring, expenditure control and reporting.

"Further, governments have found it difficult to provide an accurate, complete, and transparent account of their financial position to Parliament or to other interested parties, including donors and the general public. This lack of information has hindered transparency and the enforcement of accountability in government, and has only contributed to the perceived governance problems in many of these countries" (Diamond & Khemani, 2006, p. 98).

In order to overcome these problems, many developing countries have adopted financial management information systems in order to be more effective and efficient in the accounting reporting process. Additionally, as global markets became both more open and more competitve, by 2011 more than 120 countries moved to adopt the International Financial Reporting Standards (IFRS). High-quality financial reporting was seen as necessary to attract foreign investment and increase domestic surpluses and economic growth rates (Lasmin, 2012).

THE FOUR-STEP FMIS CREATION PROCESS FOR DEVELOPING COUNTRIES

Diamond and Khemani (2006) devised a four step process for developing countries to introduce a FMIS.

Step 1: Preparatory
- "Preliminary concept design including an institutional and organizational assessment.
- Analysis of the key problem areas and ongoing reform programs.
- Feasibility study.
- Design project and draft project proposal.
- Formal approval of the project — securing government approval and donors' funding" (Diamond & Khemani, 2006).

Step 2: Design
- "Develop functional specification.
- Outline information technology (IT) strategy, including hardware and organizational issues.
- Prepare tender documents" (Diamond & Khemani, 2006).

Step 3: Procurement
- "Issue tenders for hardware and software and associated requirements.
- Evaluation of bids and award contract" (Diamond & Khemani, 2006).

Step 4: Implementation
- "Configuration analysis and specification of any additional IT, infrastructure, and communication requirements.
- Detailed business process and gap analysis mapping required functionality to package and identifying and specifying detailed parameterization, customization, procedural changes.
- Agreed customization and configuration of the system.
- Determine training needs and conduct training of personnel.
- Pilot run — parallel run of the system; resolve initial problems and evaluate system performance for roll-out.
- Roll out system to other ministries and agencies.
- Phased implementation of additional modules.
- Strengthening of internal system support and phasing out of consultant/contractor support" ((Diamond & Khemani, 2006, p 104).

CONCLUSION

The accounting department is a key player in an organization's ability to be successful. This department is responsible for providing information to internal and external entities so that they can make effective financial decisions that will benefit the organization. These decisions will have a profound effect on the organization so it is imperative that the data collected is accurate. One way to ensure that the data is accurate is to install an accounting information system (AIS).

Most accounting information systems have two components — financial and managerial accounting. The objective of financial accounting is to provide information to external decision makers, whereas, the objective of managerial accounting is to provide information to internal decision makers. Another objective of financial accounting is to process an organization's financial transactions in an effective manner in order to produce accurate financial statements, such as income statements and balance sheets (Moscove & Simkin, 1981).

A financial management information system (FMIS) is a system that computerizes the public expenditure management process. According to Khemani & Diamond (2006), the core components of a FMIS are general ledger, budgetary accounting, accounts payable, and accounts receivable. The noncore components are payroll system, budget development, procurement, project ledger, and asset module.

In most developing countries, the budget and accounting process is either completed manually or with outdated software applications. As a result, their output has been unreliable and not timely. Therefore, many have sought to implement a FMIS. This type of project should be viewed as a long term endeavor, and there should be a strong commitment to the project's successful completion.

BIBLIOGRAPHY

Al-Laith, A. (2012). Adaptation of the internal control systems with the use of information technology and its effects on the financial statements reliability: an applied study on commercial banks. *International Management Review, 8*(1), 12-20. Retrieved October 31, 2013, from EBSCO Online Database Business Source Complete. http://search. ebscohost. com/login.aspx?direct=true&db=bth&AN=7550 0334&site=ehost-live

Drury, C. (1996). *Management and cost accounting* (4th ed.). London: International Thompson Business Press.

Diamond, J., & Khemani, P. (2006). Introducing financial management information systems in developing countries. *OECD Journal on Budgeting, 5*(3), 98-132. Retrieved July 25, 2007, from EBSCO Online Database Business Source Complete. http://search.ebscohost.com/login.aspx?direct=t rue&db=bth&AN=21777790&site=ehost-live

Eccles, R.G., & Armbrester, K. (2011). Integrated reporting in the cloud. *IESE Insight,* (8), 13-20. Retrieved October 31, 2013, from EBSCO Online Database Business Source Complete. http://search.ebscohost.com/login.aspx?direct=t rue&db=bth&AN=60227579&site=ehost-live

Horngreen, C. T., Stratton, W. O., & Sundem, G. L. (2002). *Introduction to management accounting* (12th ed.). New Jersey: Prentice Hall.

Lasmin. (2012). Culture and the globalization of the international financial reporting standards (IFRS) in developing countries. *Journal of International Business Research,* 1131-44. Retrieved October 31, 2013, from EBSCO Online Database Business Source Complete. http://search.ebscohost.com/login.aspx?direct=true&db=bth&AN=85227515&site=ehost-live

Moscove, S., & Simkin, M. (1981). *Accounting information systems: Concepts and practice for effective decision making.* New York: John Wiley & Sons.

SUGGESTED READING

Burrowes, A. (2005). Core concepts of accounting information systems. *Issues in Accounting Education, 20*(2), 216-217. Retrieved July 25, 2007, from EBSCO Online Database Business Source Premier. http://search.ebscohost.com/ login.aspx?direct=true&db=bth&AN=17022718&site=eh ost-live

Bushman, R., Chen, Q., Engel, E., & Smith, A. (2004, June). Financial accounting information, organizational complexity and corporate governance systems. Journal of Accounting & Economics, 37(2), 167-201. Retrieved July 25, 2007, from Business Source Premier database. http:// search.ebscohost.com/login.aspx?direct=true&db=bth&A N=13576670&site=ehost-live

Gowland, D., & Aiken, M. (2005, September). Changes to financial management performance measures, accountability factors and accounting information systems of privatized companies in Australia. *Australian Journal of Public Administration, 64*(3), 88-99. Retrieved July 25, 2007, from Business Source Premier database. http:// search.ebscohost.com/login.aspx?direct=true&db=bth&A N=18102619&site=ehost-live

–Marie Gould

FINANCIAL MARKETS & INSTITUTIONS

ABSTRACT

Financial markets are an important contributor to the economy and provide an environment for investors to make decisions and act on investment opportunities. Various financial institutions are a part of financial markets and offer not only opportunity for buyers and sellers but play a role as major employers of finance professionals. Success in investing requires having an understanding of the financial markets and the products that are available for investing. These products can include stocks, bonds, mutual funds and international securities. Investors must weigh the risk and reward of these products and compare them to investing in other items or choosing to do nothing. Participation in financial markets and working with financial institutions requires understanding how they work and the process of investing. While this knowledge doesn't guarantee success, it can prevent investors from making avoidable mistakes.

OVERVIEW

Successful investors become educated about the environment in which they operate. Part of that success is in understanding financial markets and institutions, to understand what investments are available, and to understand how and where to invest and the basic rules of investing. According to the Bureau of Labor Statistics (www.bls.gov) the financial services industry includes banking, insurance and securities and commodities trading. The industry also includes the real estate and rental and leasing sector. The finance and insurance institutions engage in financial transactions that create financial instruments, dispose of them or change ownership. The Bureau of Labor Statistics has identified three activities related to financial transactions including:

- "Raising funds by taking deposits and/or issuing securities and, in the process, incurring liabilities.
- Pooling of risk by underwriting insurance and annuities.
- Providing specialized services, facilitating or supporting financial intermediation, insurance, and employee benefit programs."

Real estate, rental and leasing transactions have to do with the "use, sale or rental" of "tangible or intangible assets." Simply put, financial markets are a place where the buying and selling of financial instruments is facilitated and where access to market demand is provided.

KNOWLEDGE NECESSARY FOR SAVVY INVESTING

Groz (1999) suggested ten categories of knowledge one needs to become a "savvy" investor. These categories are:

- The Products
- The Players
- The Procedures
- The Rules
- The Regulators
- Risk And Performance
- Resources
- Costs
- Scams
- Jargon

This list is an overwhelming one and it could take an investor a lifetime to master many of these subjects. Groz's last point, *jargon*, is an important concept. Every industry has its own language and shorthand. The financial industry is no different, other than its jargon can be very complex and difficult to understand. Some financial terms come from very old concepts and have survived over time and may not have a meaning similar to a current situation or item. The complexity of the language of finance frightens many would-be investors and may cause novice investors to rely heavily on advisors to assist in understanding and navigating the financial system.

FINANCIAL STOCK MARKETS

There are two major financial markets for stocks in the United States. The New York Stock Exchange and the Nasdaq Stock Market are the places where public companies list their stock. The oldest is the New York Stock Exchange which began in 1792 (Kansas, 2005). At this point in history, brokers who served as mediators between buyers and sellers, offered to trade securities and stock for a commission. The New York Stock Exchange started with only five securities but now lists stocks that value over $20 trillion (Kansas, 2005). There are many famous companies, old and new, that have stock listed on the New York Stock Exchange. Large corporations like Exxon Mobil, General Electric and IBM are listed and have long, established histories as companies. Others like Verizon Communications are more recent entries that resulted from mergers in their industries. The NASDAQ has been home to companies that are in technology or newer companies. While the New York Stock Exchange (NYSE) relies on specialists who trade stocks, the NASDAQ uses market traders who specialize in a grouping of similar stocks (Kansas, 2005). An individual investor deals with a broker to invest in stocks on the NYSE who interact with floor brokers and post specialists or "referees" (Kansas, 2005).

INTERNATIONAL EXCHANGES

There are international markets for stocks and bonds and there are exchanges that govern those financial markets. Some large international exchanges include the London Stock Exchange, the Deutsche Borse Exchange in Franfurt, the Tokyo Stock Exchange and the Hong Kong Stock Exchange (Kansas, 2005). Globalization is increasing the connection of economies that were previously separated. As a result, the financial markets in one part of the world can have a powerful effect on markets in another part of the world.

ELECTRONIC COMMUNICATIONS NETWORKS

A new trend in financial markets trading stocks are ECNs or electronic communications networks which allow large buyers and sellers a convenient way to find each other (Kansas, 2005). Investors like to know the general direction of financial markets. Certain types of information can provide an average of how major stocks in major industries are faring. One such index is the Dow Jones Industrial Average. The Dow Jones Industrial Average (DJIA) gives investors an idea of how things are going in a market and can be used in concert with other information. Other indexes include the Standard & Poor's 500 stock index of blue chip companies (Kansas, 2005).

Bull & Bear Markets

Investors realize that things change with financial instruments and are always looking for growth stocks. These are stocks that tend to perform well or grow, even when the economy is not very good (Kansas, 2005). Two symbols of the rising and falling fortunes of financial markets are the bear and the bull. The bull symbolizes a time when the market is going higher while the bear signifies a "downward trend" in stocks (Kansas, 2005). The common anecdotal reason for these symbols is that bulls move their horns in an upward motion when going for the kill and bearskin traders would sell the skins before they were caught hoping that they would be able to deliver them later. When the DJIA declines 20% or more it is considered to be a bear market. Similarly, if the market were to increase 20% or more it would be considered a bull market.

Kansas (2005) notes several characteristics of bull and bear markets. A bull market is characterized by rising stock prices, an increase in earnings, low inflation and interest rates. Meanwhile, a bear market is characterized by falling stock prices and earning, rising inflation and high or rising interest rates. Rapid changes in the financial markets make the action dynamic and exciting for those involved. However, at the same time, financial markets can be difficult to follow and even scary. In one moment, an investor can make a fortune and lose it in the next moment. Many say that is why there are brokers and traders. These professionals may enjoy gambling with someone else's money but can't take a chance on their own.

How Financial Markets Work

Groz (1999) defines the basic products in financial markets to be stocks, mutual funds, bonds, options, and futures. These products are typically managed and affected by a number of players including the investor as well as brokers, money managers, financial planners and information providers. All players can be adversely impacted on returns except information providers who are likely to disclaim or explain away any results that aren't entirely favorable. Some players assume multiple roles. Investors have to look

carefully for conflicts of interest when taking the advice of an entity that plays multiple roles. In fact, there is a sales opportunity for entities that play multiple roles. Most financial services products require gathering personal information from the consumer and that information may be shared amongst all of the entities that a company owns regardless of what they sell. Investors should read privacy statements from companies and act decisively to ensure that information is not shared without their consent and to minimize additional sales prospecting that is unwanted.

Part of being a smart investor is to be an educated investor. Groz (1999) feels that it is difficult for the average investor to get good information about financial markets and investing. However, Groz recommended what he called "financial information supermarkets" such as Yahoo or InvestTools.com. Free information is also available from the companies themselves, which are listed on the stock exchanges, from actual stock exchanges such as the NYSE and from investor associations. Much of this information is free. There are also magazines and other publications that strictly cover financial issues. The interested investor may want to become an avid reader of these to become familiar with the language and to follow the activity. The use of "intelligent agents" or technological robots that search endlessly for specific information on search engines and through databases can also be valuable software tools for investors (Groz, 1999) Small investors may choose to join investment clubs to share the burden of learning about financial markets and institutions and to increase the pool of money to invest (Kansas, 2005).

Stocks

Stock is ownership in a corporation and is represented by shares which are a percentage of the company's assets and earnings (Morgenson & Harvey, 2002). Corporations issue stock in order to finance large expenditures with a lower risk than assuming the total responsibility for the expenditure. Investors buy stock for long term investment potential and short term income from dividends (Groz, 1999). For some investors, the idea of owning a piece of a company — especially an important, large and established one with a good reputation is also an investment that feels good. Investors looking for opportunities may wish for stock splits or look into stock options. But as with much of the financial investing landscape neither are sure things. A stock split occurs when a company decides to issue a 2 for 1 offer for their shares giving investors twice as many shares as when they started. However, the shares are now worth half the price. The idea for making money in financial markets with stock splits is to drive up the price of the newly split stock to increase the value. Stock options are the "chance to buy a … stock at a future date at a certain price" (Kansas, 2005). If the option is worth more at the end of a "vesting" period than the investor is better off.

BONDS

Another investment opportunity that is even larger than the stock market is the bond market. Bonds are a form of debt issued for more than a year and allow companies and governments to raise money (Morgenson & Harvey, 2002). The bond yields a return on investment called interest that is paid to the holder once it is redeemed. The United States government is a big seller of bonds and was often able to use the idea of investing in yourself and patriotism as a reason for buying bonds. Not only would the investor get a good return but could feel good about helping the country. Treasury bonds help the U.S. government function because not enough is raised in taxes (Kansas, 2005). Bonds are considered to be less interesting than stocks but are considered safe because Treasury bonds are backed by the U.S. Government. The U.S. Government sells bonds at auction to foreign and domestic financial institutions. Individuals can also purchase bonds directly from the government. (Kansas, 2005).

Municipal Bonds are bonds that are issued by city, county and state governments. These bonds pay higher yields than treasury bonds and have tax advantages for investors. Because of the focus on the stock market, many may forget the bond market and not consider the many players that operate including companies, government, individuals and financial institutions. Bond markets have ratings agencies that determine the credit worthiness of the entities that issue bonds. Two major ratings agencies are Moody's Investors Service and Standard and Poor's (Kansas, 2005). These agencies study the bond issuers in terms of how they repay and what their financial status is in order to rate them as credit risks and ultimately use their issued bonds as investments.

MARKET REGULATIONS

There are rules and procedures that govern how financial markets work. In addition, there are regulators who maintain control so that markets can operate fairly. Important rules for investors include knowing how various players are regulated and what their rights are as investors (Groz, 1999). Hood & Taylor (1992) discussed the many changes that force restructuring of the financial services industry and explained what regulation control banks offer as services and how those services are offered. There are a number of regulations that banks have to adhere to including "Equal Credit Opportunity Act, the Home Mortgage Disclosure Act, the Truth-in-Lending Act, the Funds Availability Act, the Real Estate Settlement Procedures Act, the Fair Housing Act, the Bank Secrecy Act, the Community Reinvestment Act, and various IRS and federal insurance regulations" (Hood & Taylor, 1992). These regulations are usually complex and filled with legal, government and financial jargon. Although regulations are supposed to protect consumers, the increased cost of implementing them is usually passed on to the consumer by the financial institution. Consumers may also face a reduction in service based on the institutions decision making regarding how to balance regulatory cost.

The American Banking Association (ABA) estimated a cost of $19 million a year in 1991 to comply with regulations. Much of the administrative paperwork can be alleviated by technology but the cost of investing in and upgrading technology is expensive as well. Smaller institutions usually find the administrative burden overwhelming and affiliation with or takeover by larger institutions may look favorable (Hood & Taylor, 1992).

Insider trading is a constant attraction within financial markets as the 'insiders' have information that if shared in a particular and unethical way could cause the 'insiders,' and those they choose to partner with, to prosper. Kansas (2005) felt illegal insider trading thrives because of difficulties in enforcing it. Legal insider trading involves executives and managers in companies who trade their own stocks and securities based on how they feel about their company, industry and the market in general. This type of trading is not illegal if the investor did not use what Kansas (2005) calls "nonpublic" information. However, some watch the trading habits of large investors with large chunks of specific stocks to adjust their own actions.

THE STRATEGY OF INVESTING

Investors have many ways to get involved in investing and to interact with financial markets and institutions. The sheer number of alternatives presents yet another way that investors can be paralyzed and overwhelmed by too much information and too many choices. If an investor decides to invest in stocks, some preparation and study must be done to decide how and what to buy. The goals of the investor and the resources available to the investor are important considerations when developing an investment strategy.

Kansas (2005) noted that stock investments require investors to consider: Valuation, strategy, diversification and appetite for risk.

- Valuation is looking at the value of a stock based on the underlying company's assets, earnings, history and projected market value.
- Strategy is the approach that the investor takes to achieve investment objectives.
- Diversification is dividing investments among securities with different risk and reward to minimize extensive and untenable risk.
- Finally, the investor's appetite for risk is a measure of how much risk the investor can sustain short and long term (Morgenson & Harvey, 2002).

BANK INVESTMENTS

Investors can choose to align themselves with specific players in the financial markets and pool all of their investments with a player they trust. Some investors will place the bulk of their investment funds with their local bank and only invest in investments that are offered by the bank. These investments can include savings and checking accounts, certificates of deposit, and bonds. Often, if real estate is the selected investment, an investor may decide to obtain mortgage loans through banks where relationships exist.

FIRM INVESTING

Other trusted players are often the investor's employer who may issue stock, offer employee stock purchase programs or recommend investment advisors. These options make it easy and non-intimidating to participate in the financial markets. Mutual funds offer a way to participate in the stock market without much of the risk and are popular with individual investors. The use of financial planners by securities firms can help make these institutions more accessible to individual investors. Financial planners will often put a personal face on a big company and give the individual investor a feeling of security and continuity. According to Kansas (2005) securities firms are also called brokerage firms or investment banks and deal in stocks and bonds, primarily. They include Merrill Lynch, Goldman Sachs and Morgan Stanley. These firms may also make the reports of research analysts available to investors as part of the educational process.

HELPFUL INFORMATION FOR INVESTORS

Regular information and data is released for public consumption regarding the economy and information about government activity, jobs and employment data, as well as inflation and spending indexes that can influence the strategy of the investor. A big part of strategy that isn't easily measured is gut-feel. Investors must react to activity in the markets and make decisions based on how they feel the market will trend. The Department of Commerce (DOC) issues an inflation gauge called the Consumer Price Index (CPI) which measures consumer buying activity for items that are purchased on a regular basis. The DOC also measures the Producers Price Index (PPI) which is a measure of wholesale, business to business buying and selling. Changes in the buying habits of consumers up or down can influence where the economy is trending just as changes for businesses influence what consumers are able to buy and at what price. The Treasury Department issues the Gross Domestic Product (GDP) index which tells the investor whether the economy is getting healthier, is staying the same or is becoming less robust. The Federal Reserve oversees that banking system and manages the economy by taking action based on what the indexes indicate about the economy (Kansas, 2005).

Since most investors do not have direct contact with these governmental entities, their investment strategy will be driven by the personal spin they put on what this information means. That can be influenced by media coverage, information that the investor tracks on a regular basis, conversations with others and advice of financial advisors. In the end, the investor must enter the financial markets and deal with financial institutions based on an investment strategy that maximizes growth and minimizes risk. A sound strategy will also provide for changes that are likely to occur.

VIEWPOINTS

THE IMPACT OF THE FINANCIAL SERVICES INDUSTRY

The financial services industry has significant impact on the life and health of the general economy. In Illinois, a state court judge ordered the state government to stop using money in funds to finance financial institutions for general government expenses (Credit Union Journal, 2005). The stability of banks, credit unions and savings and loans could be damaged if state legislatures attempt to fill holes in their budgets by accessing safety net funds. If these institutions were to fail, panic could ensue and jeopardize depositor savings.

Because the flow of money is so important to the stability and growth of a nation, the financial services industry has been a prime target of terrorists. To disrupt the flow and exchange of money would disturb the entire economy on a temporary and possibly a long term basis. The U.S. Treasury has developed procedures by which financial institutions can exchange information about financial transactions and possible money laundering by terrorists (Kite, 2002). The new procedures mean a greater reporting burden for financial managers. Additions to these regulations prescribe how information about transactions and money laundering should be shared with law enforcement.

Financial institutions engage in measurement of a customer's profitability to the institution. The profitability from customers is invested in capital and equipment projects and used to cover risks of investments. Institutions also look at the profitability of customers to see how well portfolio managers perform (Weiner, 2000/2001).

OPPORTUNITIES IN THE FINANCIAL SERVICES INDUSTRY

The opportunities for employment in the financial services industry are great. People involved in financial services include commercial and personal bankers, mortgage counselors, financial advisors and investment bankers, economists, actuaries and securities traders. According to the Bureau of Labor Statistics (ww.bls.gov) the banking industry shows a slight decline in pay and employment as consumers move their investments to higher yielding products with investment firms and others. The BLS noted "The banking industry employed about 1.8 million wage and salary workers in 2004. About 7 out of 10 jobs were in commercial banks; the remainder ... concentrated in savings institutions and credit unions." In 2004, there were 355,000 financial analysts and personal financial advisors. This group is expected to have better than average growth through 2014. Many financial services industry jobs require advanced education and some even require certification if the individual is engaging in certain types of securities or other sales. The securities industry employed 767,000 people in 2004 and is expected to see a 16% increase in growth by 2014.

While many of the jobs in financial services 'sound' financial, there are also opportunities in compliance and regulatory enforcement for government entities and others. Some have titles such as financial examiners and investigators or less obvious ones. The impact of financial institutions on other industries brings others into the financial services arena of opportunity. Governments are also looking for people with advanced financial skills because many governments are facing unprecedented financial issues and need higher quality solutions to address them. Investors are also looking for more information and control making information technology companies natural partners for financial ones and indicating a continued convergence of the two.

BIBLIOGRAPHY

Bureau of Labor Statistics. (2006). *Industry at a glance: financial services supersector.* Retrieved September 16, 2007, from http://www.bls.gov/iag/financial.htm.

Groz, M. M. (1999). *Forbes guide to the markets: becoming a savvy investor.* New York: John Wiley and Sons.

Hood, J. & Taylor, J.A. (1992). Consumers bear costs of banking regs. *Consumers' Research Magazine, 75*(10), 21-24. Retrieved May 19, 2007, from EBSCO Online Database Business Source Complete. http://search.ebscohost.com/ login.aspx?direct=true&db=bth&AN=9212211909&site=ehost-live

Kansas, D. (2005). *The Wall Street Journal: complete money & investing guidebook.* New York: Three Rivers Press.

Kite, S. (2002). Treasury adds secure network to battle terrorism. *Securities Industry News, 14*(6), 23. Retrieved September 16, 2007, from EBSCO Online Database Business Source Complete. http://search.ebscohost.com/ login.aspx?direct=true&db=bth&AN=9 612824&site=bsi-live

Morgenson, G. & Harvey, C. R. (2002). *The New York Times Dictionary of Money Investing.* New York: Times Books.

The Credit Union Journal daily. (2005). *Credit Union Journal, 9*(11), 17. Retrieved September 16, 2007, from EBSCO Online Database Business Source Complete. http://search. ebscohost.com/login.aspx?direct=true&db=bth&AN=1649 2306&site=bsi-live

Weiner, J. (2000/2001). Return on capital: The primary measure of customer value. *Bank Accounting & Finance, 14*(2), 15-20. Retrieved September 16, 2007, from EBSCO Online Database Business Source Complete. http://search. ebscohost.

com/login.aspx?direct=true&db=bth&AN=409 5646&site=bsi-live

SUGGESTED READING

Kirchhoff, S., Waggoner, J. and Hagenbaugh, B. (2007). Spirits, markets get a lift. *USA Today.*

Long-term market views unchanged by credit crisis. (2007). *Emerging Europe Monitor: Russia & CIS, 11*(10), 3. Retrieved September 21, 2007, from EBSCO Online Database Business Source Complete. http://search.ebscohost.com/login.aspx?direct=true&db=bth&AN=26551309 &site=bsi-live

Socorro, M. P. (2007). Mergers under certainty; the effects of debt financing. *Manchester School, 75*(5), 580-597. Retrieved September 21, 2007, from EBSCO Online Database Business Source Complete. http://search.ebscohost.com/login.aspx?di rect=true&db=bth&AN=26225119 &site=ehost-live

–Marlanda English

FINANCIAL PLANNING & POLICY FOR LARGE CORPORATIONS

ABSTRACT

Financial planning and policy is essential for large corporations to manage financial decisions and to report accurate results internally and externally. Financial planning and policy is conducted by a firm's financial leaders often led by the CFO (chief financial officer). The financial arm of a corporation understands reporting requirements and establishes plans and policies to guide financial decisions regarding dividends, financing, investment and capital management.

OVERVIEW

Large corporations have a need to establish guidelines for financial planning and policy. The guidelines are needed because corporations are typically managing large amounts of money and have obligations to employees and stockholders to carefully manage the money that is generated within the company. These obligations require corporations to employ internal and external financial experts to develop and implement financial decisions such as financing, investment, dividends and maximizing the use of funds created. Experts have postulated a relationship between financial policy and the ability to create wealth for stockholders (Bah & Dumontier, 2001). There is a verified relationship between certain types of financial decisions such as research and development, debt financing, investment and dividends.

PROPER FINANCIAL PLANNING FOR THE CORPORATION

Financial managers are central to corporate governance, and in addition to expertise in financial areas, these individuals must also possess a high-level sense of ethics to ensure that the decisions they make will be honest and straightforward. Financial planning is necessary because without it companies may lose money and jeopardize the survival of the organization. Poor financial planning can cause companies to lose value, which has ramifications for stockholders, potential investors, customers and creditors.

Financial Analysis, Planning & Reporting (2002, p. 6 — 7) listed ten financial planning mistakes corporations should seek to avoid. These included:

- Having a vague business plan.
- Ambiguous financial reports.
- Unmanaged earnings expectations.
- Bad mergers and acquisitions.
- Overvalued stock repurchases.
- Misaligned executive pay levels.
- Faulty measurement systems.
- Too much detail.
- Playing it too close to the vest.
- Lack of automation.

BUSINESS PLANS

Business plans are important to detail how a business is run and how it plans to make and use its finances. Financial Analysis, Planning & Reporting (2002) reminded investors that Enron was a company where investors did not understand how Enron was making its money and advised investors to be wary of things they don't understand in business plans. If the plan is too complex, lacks detail or seems impossible it may not be a good plan.

A comprehensive formal business plan should contain the following elements: cover page, table of contents and table of appendices, executive summary, body of the business plan (Niemand, 2013). The business plan in itself does not, and cannot, guarantee success, but "coupled with a rather large dose of discipline" can be valuable in enhancing the chances of success, Niemand writes.

REPORTS

Reports, like business plans, should be clear and easy to understand. Anything that is not standard should be called out in the financial reporting notes and explained. Many corporations may be anxious to report good news to prevent fluctuations in stock price. However, once it is discovered that reports are inflated, stock prices may still react. Similarly, corporations should be straightforward in earnings projections as well. However, many companies often underestimate earnings so that a number is reported that is known to be achievable. Investors will need to monitor these actions to determine if a company is a good investment or simply good at managing the reporting of its earnings achievements.

MERGERS & ACQUISITIONS

Mergers and acquisitions are dangerous for corporations because they usually involve the merging of different cultures and management/reporting practices. A merger or acquisition may be seen as a positive for a company and a way to make money and improve earnings. However, many mergers and acquisitions cost money in terms of figuring out how to merge cultures, staffing, equipment and real estate. As a result, the path to greater earnings and benefits may be longer than anticipated by management and stockholders. This area is another one requiring companies to manage and set expectations appropriately internally and externally. Corporations may often engage in stock buy-back programs but investors must be clear on the true value of a company's stock to avoid loss of value. Most corporate financials managers hold a belief that their corporation is worth more than stock price and analyst projections suggest.

Rehm, Uhlaner, and West looked at what kind of merger strategy is most apt to generate excess returns for shareholders (2012). The authors looked at more than 15,000 non-bank mergers that occurred over a 10-year period. Companies that made frequent acquisitions of smaller firms recorded higher returns than did those who focused on making "the occasional large deal." Among those pursuing the latter strategy, companies in "slow-growing, mature industries" were more likely to be successful than those in fast-growing segments such as high technology (Rehm, Uhlaner & West 2012).

STOCK OPTIONS

Stock options are usually a way to provide incentives in the compensation of corporate executives. However, when stock prices fall, so does the value of the executive compensation package. In some cases, companies will make adjustments to alleviate the pain felt by executives. These adjustments may make the executives feel better but doesn't hold them to endure the same risk and reward structure as stockholders. It also seems unfair to allow top CEOs and other executives to prosper while stockholders feel pain.

MEASUREMENT SYSTEMS

Corporations must engage in strategic performance measurement to keep track of how the company is performing against its internal targets and against the industry. Corporations must ensure that they are measuring the right things, measuring these things accurately, and have in place accountabilities and early warning systems to indicate when the company is off-course.

DETAIL

If corporations reduce the amount of detail in planning processes they will be able to concentrate on the things that are most important, measure accurate performance and take steps to improve performance. Too much detail is confusing internally and externally and creates a planning infrastructure that is difficult to manage and that does not suit the purposes of the company.

ACCOUNTABILITY

When Financial Analysis, Planning & Reporting (2002, p. 7) discussed companies "playing it too close to the vest" in financial planning, it meant that involvement by all facets of the business is necessary to ensure that accurate, relevant information is used in the planning process.

Following the financial scandals of Worldcom, Tyco, and Enron in the very early 2000s, popular opinion pointed to a failure of corporate accountability. Karim and Taqi (2013) wrote that research does suggest that "a number of interdependent variables defining overall corporate performance are positively influenced by accountability effects, including performance, satisfaction, conformity, and goals and attentiveness." When planning is done by a few and others are not consulted, only a few are accountable and much of the needed information is not available. Greater involvement by various business units can also improve the performance of those units as they have greater understanding, involvement and accountability for company performance. Financial Analysis, Planning & Reporting (2002) also recommends the use of electronic software for financial planning. Software can reduce the amount of time spent collecting financial information and can improve the accuracy of reporting. Some systems also have the capability to allow financial managers to do high level analysis and modeling of complex 'what-if' scenarios.

IMPLICATIONS OF FINANCIAL POLICY

Corporate financial policy can have a variety of implications for firms, industries, investors and the economy in general. In the retail industry, companies have to be concerned about the fact that consumers don't have as much money available to spend on typical retail items. This shortage is due to consumers being saddled with heavy debt and small pay increases being given to workers. Retailers are also looking at the fact that the global consumer is becoming wealthier and has more disposable income to spend. So, companies may be looking more closely at global markets to increase opportunities. Technology has also allowed retailers to reach out to customers across the globe.

WAL-MART

Home Textiles Today (2007) reported on Wal-Mart's explanation of its financial policy that encompasses a very long range view of 10 — 15 years in the future. This policy includes:

- Stock buybacks.
- Increasing dividends.
- Reducing domestic capital expenditures.
- International expansion.

Some of Wal-Mart's international expansion includes investment in a joint venture with a Japanese company. Wal-Mart may be easily able to increase the dividends it offers because of a high cash flow. Home Textiles Today (2007) reported that Wal-Mart paid $2.8 billion in dividends and $1.4 billion in repurchasing shares of stock. In fiscal year 2008, Wal-Mart is planning to offer $3.6 billion in dividends and has already made $5 billion in share buybacks. Wal-Mart has a vested interest in remaining atop the retail industry and financial policy must reflect knowledge of consumer behavior while predicting where that behavior is headed. Additionally, Wal-Mart plans to reduce capital expenditures and expects its return on investment to remain constant. Industry analysts and ratings agencies may have some concerns about the risk of Wal-Mart's international investments. Wal-Mart must be able to show clear financial policy that mitigates that risk. Such evidence might include the identification of criteria that prove the decisions are in line with sound financial policy. Home Textiles Today (2007) noted Wal-Mart's successful international expansion in Canada and Mexico that was criticized by industry analysts and less successful expansions in Germany and South Korea that fuel criticism of Wal-Mart's plans.

Cable & Telecommunications

Siderman (2007) discussed the cable and telecommunications industry by describing the competitive landscape. For example, phone companies find themselves losing land line customers due to the proliferation of cellular phones and competitors with lower packaged rates. However, these same companies have seen increases in the demand for digital subscriber lines (DSL). Cable and phone companies are competing for video customers and telecommunications company mergers have resulted in companies attempting to mitigate the risk by acquiring a growing market.

Companies in the telecommunications industry may continue to be a part of a growing market but only if they determine how to best position themselves in a time when there are no dividing lines between what a company is, does and what it can offer. Siderman (2007) predicts that cable companies will be the winners by peeling off phone customers interested in voice over IP (VoIP). Cable companies may also be able to benefit from dissatisfied phone company customers.

Siderman (2007, para. 6) noted that "financial policy must reflect maturing markets" when referring to traditional land line phone companies. In addition to offering a wide variety of products, Siderman (2007) recommended that land line phone companies adjust their financial policies in order to allow their credit ratings to remain high. Some companies have experienced difficulties in credit ratings because they are in the middle of negotiating mergers and acquisitions or buyout agreements. Company financial policy may indicate how a company will use the available cash in the business. Mature industry companies may choose to use that cash to invest in new technology or to buy other companies in growing telecommunications sectors. These companies are essentially betting their business and creating policy based on what they believe will happen in their mature sector while investing in what may happen in a newer or growing sector.

Another example of the implications of financial policy according to Siderman (2007) are the decisions that cable companies, which are performing well now, will need to make as the industry matures. Cable companies are flush with cash and will have to make decisions such as how to use the cash available. Should they invest in newer technology? Will

they have to make significant capital outlays to improve or upgrade existing equipment? Could they possibly improve the technology used by technicians? Companies like this will also have to consider what should be done to face off competition and solidify industry position.

Cable companies, though reaching saturation of the video product market, are choosing to offer other kinds of services such as digital video recording and high speed Internet. Cable companies must consider how to manage competition from satellite and DirecTV. Product differentiation may be needed along with company differentiation. Siderman (2007) noted that companies are also rated on their liquidity which continues to be a challenge for companies as they acquire other businesses. Even companies with high credit ratings have to consider the cost of credit acquisition and how to avoid becoming overly laden with debt.

Boyer (2007) reported on the airline industry accepting more credit and debit purchases from passengers. This has resulted in an increase in purchases on board. Credit and debit cards are used to pay for food, beverages, phone calls and entertainment on board airplanes. Airline financial policies that support bringing this technology to passengers on all planes require capital investments in infrastructure for processing payments. An airline's financial decisions also depend on the available cash and debt load of the company.

The Role of Financial Policy

Federal monetary financial policy and the corporate financial policy of various growing industries are viewed as influencers of the broader economy. The Economist (2007) pointed to successful financial policy as responsible for the benefits to the economy in the last twenty years. Some of these benefits include low inflation, few fluctuations in unemployment figures and expanding economies for rich nations. However, the 2007 subprime mortgage crisis is seen by some as the result of progress in policy now taking a turn for the worse. Industries that are improving, growing and experiencing good results can mean that there is a willingness to take on more debt and risk. As inflation increases, companies are forced to raise their prices and the workers will want to share in the company's profits. Federal and corporate financial policies are tied together. The Economist

(2007) indicated that as companies take on more risk and debt they will seek lower interest rates to manage the cost of debt.

Riccio (2007) reported that U.S. companies are at the lowest point in history in terms of the credit profile of these firms. Weakening of corporate credit ratings could indicate a trend toward increasing defaults among companies. Riccio (2007, para. 2) identified two possible causes of lowering of credit ratings as "investors accepting higher risk" and "more aggressive corporate financial policies aimed at appeasing shareholders." Industrial firms that are in the Standard and Poor's 'B' rating category make up about half of the corporate credit ratings today and were only 7% of corporate ratings in 1980. Middle market companies have become involved in bond and loan markets and the number of leveraged buyouts has increased. Riccio also observed drops in A-rated companies and investment grade (BBB-rated) companies. The financial risk taking by industrial companies can't always be mitigated by federal intervention but there is federal responsibility to monitor and adjust interest rates to influence the economy and avoid problems.

VIEWPOINT

FINANCIAL PLANNING & POLICY DECISIONS
Leary & Roberts (2005, p. 2575) described a traditional corporate finance viewpoint which states that corporations will gravitate to an "optimal capital structure that balances the costs and benefits associated with varying degrees of financial leverage." These benefits can include tax benefits, profitability, the ability to obtain cash and the favorability of interest rates.

Financial policy decisions have to evolve with the changing economic times and what is best for a company based on its size, financial position, industry and growth opportunities. Although corporate budgets help companies grow by placing an emphasis on improving company profitability, the traditional focus on earnings is not suitable for changing corporate needs. Companies must incorporate performance measurements in budgeting, control and other financial planning and policy decisions. Many companies use benchmarking, the practice of matching their financial practices against best practices in an industry, for example. Other companies are using activity based costing making it easy to allocate costs to the

cost center responsible for the cost. Corporate financial planning and policy are increasingly tied more closely to company strategic plans and benchmarks are set to achieve specific financial goals.

Financial pressures can cause some companies to resort to changing balance sheets based on company financial policies (Benito & Young, 2007). The decisions made by financial managers are tied to the corporate budget, the availability of funds and how those funds may be used. Balance sheet changes can help a company exhibit a higher level of profit than may actually be present. Companies may also take on greater debt to avoid becoming insolvent (Benito & Young, 2007).

Corporations can make financial policy decisions such as how to allocate cash between corporate accounts and pension accounts (Kim, 2004). The decisions related to pension management are found to be important financial policy decisions that affect the benefits to stockholders. Pension fund financial policy was also directly related to company value prior to the enactment of ERISA (Employee Retirement Income Security Act). Kim (2004) noted that a company's financial policy can affect consumers through stock value, dividends and labor cost.

Corporate taxation affects corporate financial policy because taxes impact profit (Contos, 2005). Gordon and Lee (2007) noted the relationship between taxes and the corresponding effect on corporate decisions regarding the use of debt financing or equity financing. Companies may have tax based incentives to use debt depending on the short versus long term cost of debt tied to overall interest rates. The effect of reducing the corporate tax rate is to reduce the amount of debt financed capital (Gordon & Lee, 2007). Contos (2005) also found that corporations have incentives to borrow because interest paid on financing is tax deductible. The dividends that are paid to stockholders are not

tax deductible thus influencing financial decisions related to dividends and borrowing. These findings were confirmed regardless of the size of company, although large companies feel the impact of taxes greatest on their decision to use debt.

THREE CATEGORIES OF CORPORATE FINANCIAL POLICY
There are three categories of theories on corporate financial policy. These include taxes, contracting costs and information costs (Barclay & Smith, 2005).

- The taxes category notes that companies can deduct interest rates but not dividends so companies can add debt to improve tax liability and improve cash flow after taxes. The disadvantage of this approach is that it only takes into account the affect of taxes.
- Contracting costs begin to include other financial considerations of higher debt and not just looking at the tax advantages. If a company ends up bankrupt there are financial costs associated with what Barclay and Smith (2005) call financial distress costs. If there is too much debt, a corporation may miss out on investments and without enough debt, a corporation can over-invest.
- Information costs are based on the fact that financial managers within a firm know more about the firm's finances and decisions than investors (Barclay & Smith, 2005). Barclay and Smith (2005) noted three important theories of financing decisions related to information costs, including market timing, signaling, and the pecking order.

Market timing describes an asset allocation where investment increases if the investor believes that the equity market will outperform T-bills and decreases if the equity market doesn't outperform treasury bills (Morgenson & Harvey, 2002). Leary and Roberts (2005) explain market timing as a corporation's timing its decisions about issuing securities and participating in the equity market. It also becomes important for corporations to consider the cost of adjusting to these decisions. Acquiring debt or taking on equity financing does not occur without cost (Leary & Roberts, 2005).

Signaling is when corporate managers want to communicate confidence to investors. Debt may indicate that a company is confident because it knows it must make debt payments. Pecking order indicates that there are varying costs associated with external financing so companies have a pecking order or preference in the sources considered for financing (Morgenson & Harvey, 2002).

The investor must believe the financial information received from corporate financial managers. But, the information is likely to be biased because internal managers may be more optimistic than reality reflects and may naturally feel that the valuation of their company is lower than reality. Unfortunately, the cost of bad financial planning and policy may not be easily or readily seen and the ramifications of these decisions may only be felt later at the expense of stockholders.

BIBLIOGRAPHY

10 corporate financial planning mistakes to avoid in 2003. (2002). *Financial Analysis, Planning & Reporting, 2*(5), 6. Retrieved November 17, 2007, from EBSCO Online Database Business Source Premier. http://search.ebscohost.com/login.aspx?direct=true&db=buh&AN=6760098&site=ehost-live

Bah, R. & Dumontier, P. (2001). R&D intensity and corporate financial policy: Some international evidence. *Journal of Business Finance & Accounting, 28*(5/6). Retrieved October 1, 2007, from EBSCO Online Database Business Source Complete. http://search.ebscohost.com/login.aspx?direct=true&db=buh&AN=4889788&site=ehost-live

Barclay, M. & Smith, C. (2005). The capital structure puzzle: The evidence revisited. *Journal of Applied Corporate Finance, 17*(1), 8-17. Retrieved October 1, 2007, from EBSCO Online Database Business Source Complete. http://search.ebscohost.com/login.aspx?direct=true&db=bth&AN=16672067&site=ehost-live

Benito, A. & Young, G. (2007). Financial pressure and balance sheet adjustment by firms. *Oxford Bulletin of Economics & Statistics, 69*(5), 581-602. Retrieved November 17, 2007, from EBSCO Online Database Business Source Complete. http://search.ebscohost.com/login.aspx?direct=true&db=bth&AN=26771862&site=ehost-live

Boyer, M. (2007). Airlines moving toward cashless in-flight buying. American Banker, *172*(152), 10. Retrieved November 17, 2007, from EBSCO Online Database Business Source Complete. http://search.ebscohost.com/login.aspx?direct=true&db=bth&AN=26161164&site=ehost-live

Contos, G. (2005). An essay on the effects of taxation on the corporate financial policy. *Proceedings of the Annual Conference on Taxation*, 415-423. Retrieved October 1, 2007, from EBSCO Online Database Business Source Complete. http://search.ebscohost.com/login.aspx?direct=true&db=bth&AN=23548667&site=ehost-live

Gordon, R. & Lee, Y. (2007). Interest rates, taxes and corporate financial policies. *National Tax Journal, 60*(1), 65-84. Retrieved October 1, 2007, from

EBSCO Online Database Business Source Complete. http://search.ebscohost.com/ login.aspx?direct=true&db=bth&AN=24699957&site=ehost-live

Karim, N., & Taqi, S. (2013). The importance of corporate management accountability. *Journal of Managerial Sciences, 7*(1), 59-73. Retrieved November 19, 2013, from EBSCO Online Database Business Source Complete. http://search.ebscohost.com/login.aspx?direct=true&db=bth&AN=87064137&site=ehost-live

Kim,C. (2004). Corporate financial policy with pension accounts: An extension of the Modigliani — Miller Theorem. *International Economic Journal, 18*(2), 215-236. Retrieved October 1, 2007, from EBSCO Online Database Business Source Complete. http://search.ebscohost.com/ login.aspx?direct=true&db=bth&AN=14333847&site=ehost-live

Leary, M. & Roberts, M.R. (2005). Do firms rebalance their capital structures? *Journal of Finance, 60*(6), 2575-2619. Retrieved October 1, 2007, from EBSCO Online Database Business Source Complete. http://search.ebscohost.com/ login.aspx?direct=true&db=bth&AN=18795361&site=ehost-live

Morgenson, G. & Harvey, C. R. (2002). The New York Times Dictionary of Money Investing. New York, NY: Times Books.

Niemand, T. (2013). Do all business plans provide a recipe for success? *Finweek*, 50-52. Retrieved November 19, 2013, from EBSCO Online Database Business Source Complete. http://search.ebscohost.com/login.aspx?direct=true&db=bth&AN=91608861&site=ehost-live

R. K. (2007). Landry's up on legal remedy, AMO down on more debt. *Bank Loan Report, 22*(34), 6. Retrieved November 17, 2007, from EBSCO Online Database Business Source Complete. http://search.ebscohost.com/login.aspx?direct=true&db=bth&AN=26543871&site=ehost-live

Rehm, W., Uhlaner, R., & West, A. (2012). A clearer-eyed view of M&A. *McKinsey Quarterly*, (2), 10-12. Retrieved November 19, 2013, from EBSCO Online Database Business Source Complete. http://search.ebscohost.com/ login.aspx?direct=true&db=bth&AN=74755472&site=ehost-live

Riccio, N. (2007, September 27). Corporate credit ratings hit a low point. *Business Week Online*, 19.

Retrieved November 17, 2007, from EBSCO Online Database Business Source Complete. http://search.ebscohost.com/login.aspx?direct=true&db=bth&AN=26844385&site=ehost-live

Siderman, R. (2007, October 11). Cable vs. Telco: The battle heats up. *Business Week Online*, 9. Retrieved November 17, 2007, from EBSCO Online Database Business Source Complete. http://search.ebscohost.com/login.aspx?direct=true&db=bth&AN=27032322&site=ehost-live

The turning point. (2007). *Economist, 384*(8547), 35-37. Retrieved November 17, 2007, from EBSCO Online Database Business Source Complete. http://search.ebscohost.com/login.aspx?direct=true&db=bth&AN=26710269&site=ehost-live

SUGGESTED READING

Baker, M. & Wurgler, J. (2002). Market timing and capital structure. *Journal of Finance, 57*(1), 1. Retrieved October 1, 2007, from EBSCO Online Database Business Source Complete. http://search.ebscohost.com/login.aspx?direct=true&db=bth&AN=5889290&site=ehost-live

Bris, A., Koskinen, Y. & Pons, V. (2004). Corporate financial policies and performance around currency crises. *Journal of Business, 77*(4), 749-795. Retrieved October 1, 2007, from EBSCO Online Database Business Source Complete. http://search.ebscohost.com/login.aspx?direct=true&db=bth&AN=15648481&site=ehost-live

Brummer, A. (2007). No one can yet say how bad it is. *New Statesman, 137*(4868), 21. Retrieved November 17, 2007, from EBSCO Online Database Business Source Complete. http://search.ebscohost.com/login.aspx?direct=true&db=bth&AN=27397303&site=ehost-live

Faulkender, M. & Wang, R. (2006). Corporate financial policy and the value of cash. *Journal of Finance, 61*(4), 1957- 1990. Retrieved October 1, 2007, from EBSCO Online Database Business Source Complete. http://search.ebscohost.com/login.aspx?direct=true&db=bth&AN=21796398&site=ehost-live

Finance: Think long, think global. (2007). *Home Textiles Today, 28*(27), 8. Retrieved November 17, 2007, from EBSCO Online Database Business Source Complete. http://search.ebscohost.com/login.aspx?direct=true&db=bth&AN=27325827&site=ehost-live

Food and Agriculture Organization of the United Nations. (2007). *Financial and budgetary control.* FAO Corporate Document Repository. Retrieved November 17, 2007, from http://www.thetimes100. co.uk/theory/theory — financial-budgetary-control — 120.php

Potter, A. (2007). So we fool God with financial loopholes. What of it? *Maclean's, 120*(40), 16. Retrieved November 17, 2007, from EBSCO Online Database Business Source Complete. http://search. ebscohost.com/login.aspx?direct=t rue&db=bth&

AN=27074964&site=ehost-live

Rossett, J. (2003). Labour leverage, equity risk and corporate policy choice. *European Accounting Review, 12*(4), 699- 732. Retrieved October 1, 2007, from EBSCO Online Database Business Source Complete. http://search.ebscohost.com/ login.aspx?direct=true&db=bth&AN=11762979 &site=ehost-live

—Marlanda English

FINANCIAL SECURITY ANALYSIS

ABSTRACT

This article examines the process of financial securities analysis as well as the work conducted my financial securities analysts. Various specialties with which financial securities analysts are concerned are illuminated. In addition, the regulation of the financial services industry is reviewed along with how the regulations impact financial securities analysts and their clients. The organizations that lead or participate in these government and self-regulatory efforts are reviewed. The impact of globalization on the complexity of financial markets and thus the work of the financial securities analysts are also examined. Finally, the studies called for by the Emergency Economic Stabilization Act of 2008 (EES Act) are reviewed.

OVERVIEW

Financial securities are economic investment instruments that provide a means for individuals, investment banks, mutual funds, or retirement funds to invest money in a company, an industry sector, or even a region of the country or the world. These securities have several purposes.

- First, they facilitate the process of attracting investors by providing an investment mechanism that is openly and publicly scrutinized by securities analyst and other investors.
- Second, they provide a means for investors or securities buyers to invest their funds and track their wealth and eventually receive dividends. There is a

wide range of financial securities including stocks, bonds, and notes.

These securities are brought to the market in a variety of ways. Companies can issue and sell stock publicly or to private investment groups. Mutual funds can sell shares to individuals or retirement funds. Government entities such as municipalities, school districts, or libraries, can issue bonds for building projects. Governments can also establish programs like the United States Savings Bond which allows investors to gain a low yield in a highly secure investment instrument.

FINANCIAL SECURITIES ANALYSTS

The financial securities market is complex and detailed. The role of the financial securities analyst is to understand and research a specific aspect of the marketplace and provide analysis to investors or others interested in the market. Financial securities analysts are versed in the many forms of written material about their area of expertise. This could include corporate financial statements, annual reports, industry news, or government indices that may show trends that impact companies or sectors reviewed by the analyst. Market activity is monitored by the securities analyst which includes stock prices, product or service pricing offered by companies in their area of expertise, and global trends and events that could impact either stock prices or corporate revenues.

USE & IMPORTANCE

Financial securities analysts are employed by a variety

of organizations. Investment management firms, or those companies that help individuals or institutional investors mange their portfolio, employ financial securities analysts to help determine if a company or even an industry sector will provide a good return. Brokerage firms, those companies that sell financial securities to investors on behalf of the organizations seeking investors, employ financial securities analysts to help advise or attract potential buyers of the securities. Mutual funds, as another example, may employ their own financial securities analysts to help guide the investment strategy of the fund ("Financial analysts," 2009).

Large financial services firms that sell stock or invest large sums in a company are most likely to employ securities analysts to focus on the specific company. The analyst responsible for that research watches the activities of the company on a daily basis. This includes monitoring stock prices, reading reports issued by the company, as well as reports from other analysts about the company. The securities analyst may also attend meetings or conferences sponsored by the company or events where the company or industry may be a topic. The 2008 economic downturn resulted in many financial securities analysts being laid off from large brokerage and investment firms (Pressman, 2009).

INDUSTRY-SPECIFIC ANALYSTS

Securities analysts that focus on an industry, such as the automotive, telecommunications, or computer industries, watch the activities of the large or otherwise significant companies in that industry sector. The analyst also reviews reports issued by or about the companies that have an impact in or on the industry. Most of the analyst's attention is focused on the larger companies as they draw the largest amount of outside investment. However, newcomers or start-up companies to the industry are also of interest if they have a new or innovative product offering that may impact the industry or make them an acquisition target. Industry analysts must also monitor business trends or government actions that could significantly change business practices in an industry (Ennis, 2009).

REGION-SPECIFIC ANALYSIS

When financial securities analysts focus on a specific region of the United States or of the world, their research is far broader but generally has less depth. These analysts are often fluent in one or more of the languages of the region in which they specialize. The regional analyst is also likely to spend considerable time in the region in which they specialize and will attend major business or trade events that examine or showcase the companies in the region. The activities of the larger companies in the region are monitored by the analyst along with the policies of local governments toward business, globalization, and world trade.

KEY CONCEPTS

Regardless of their specialization, a financial securities analyst needs an in-depth understanding of business financial practices; especially those that impact stock prices or draw investors. Analysts must constantly research their areas; most observers agree that research is the most important aspect of analysis (Birkner, 2009). Financial securities analysts also need to understand how political, economic, and social conditions impact business. An understanding of investors focusing on what investors desire to know about individual businesses and trends is also necessary (O'Dowd, 2009).

Globalization has made the work of financial securities analysts far more complicated. There are now numerous well-established financial markets in the world. The interconnectedness of these national economies means that when there is a downturn in one country, most markets will feel some sort of shock wave ("A three-year global recession," 2009). The globalized economy also means that government policies around the world, especially monetary policies can have far more than a local impact. This potential impact is often complicated to understand and sometimes impossible to predict (Mishkin, 2009).

The globalization of the economy and the accompanying widespread global trading of commodities, technology, and consumer products has also increased the speed of change. The benefit of this proliferation to national societies is that people have faster access to a wider variety of products and services. The downside of this interconnectedness is that when things go wrong, the damage is more widely spread. Polluting products or technologies, for example, are being sent all over the world with little if any effort to minimize their negative impact. Ecosystems, cultures, and communities can change and grow but they can also collapse. This adds more pieces to the puzzle that the financial securities analyst is trying to piece together (Halal, 2009).

APPLICATIONS

INVESTMENT PORTFOLIO MANAGEMENT

PERSONAL & PROFESSIONAL PORTFOLIO MANAGEMENT

Financial securities analysis is an essential and on-going activity for individuals who manage their own investment portfolio and for the managers of mutual funds or retirement pension funds.

There is considerable public concern for the management of pension funds. This is especially true for multi-employer pension plans that typically cover workers in trucking, building and construction, and retail food sales. Many of these plans were established by labor unions and the companies that employ the union workers. These plans allow a union worker to maintain their pension fund even though they may work for several different employers over a period of years (Private Pensions: Multiemployer Plans Face Short- and Long-Term Challenges, 2004). The decline in value for pension funds can be very troublesome because the funds can end up being under funded, or in practical terms: Lacking enough assets to pay the promised pensions to members when they retire.

Individuals who manage their own funds have numerous sources of information that they can access and take into consideration. Opinions are mixed as to whether or not individuals should go it alone in managing their own investment portfolio. However, the dynamics of the 2008 economic crisis clearly show that many managers of large organized funds did not fair very well in protecting the wealth of their investors.

Fund managers also have access to many sources of information and expertise but they also have a fiduciary responsibility for the decisions that they make which impact the value of the fund that they manage on behalf of fund investors. This responsibility requires that the board properly directs fund activities and establishes a process by which investment decisions are appropriate and adequately documented (Moynihan, 2009).

Many mutual funds or pension funds have a board of directors that oversee the policies and investment decision making process utilized by the fund. The board is also responsible for regulatory compliance. Under the direction of the board, there is often one or more managers responsible for the investment process and operational activity of the fund. The fund manager may have considerable financial securities experience that can help guide the investment decisions. Most funds also rely on outside financial securities analysts to advise in investment strategies and decisions.

INVESTMENT ADVISERS

Financial securities analysts provide support to individual investors, managers of mutual funds, and managers of pension funds. Investors turn to analysts for knowledge and advice about the potential promise of an investment opportunity. Fund managers as well as individuals use the information from financial securities analysts to help them decide what risks are inherent in a specific security and thus in their investment strategy. When investors are uncertain of their own risk analysis, they often turn to investment advisers.

BENEFITS

The use of investment advisers, especially for pension fund managers, has several benefits.

- First, the adviser supposedly provides a level of expertise or insight that the fund managers or in-house financial securities analysts do not have.
- Secondly, when an adviser charges a retirement fund for advice, the adviser then has fiduciary responsibility for the impact that such advice has on solvency of the fund.

THE 2008 DOWNTURN

The economic downturn of 2008 was considered to be a very severe situation by most analysts. Blame for the downturn abounds with many pointing the accusing finger at Wall Street, while still others criticize government regulation or lack there of as major reason why financial services firms turned to ashes (Reinganum, 2009). The boards of directors and the managers of many pensions and mutual funds also came under public scrutiny because so many funds lost value; combined, over $100 billion was lost in value in 2008 (Morgado, 2009).

The 2008 economic downturn has also led to many lawsuits against investment advisers (Morgado, 2009). The outcome of those lawsuits is yet to be determined. The legitimacy of many of the lawsuits will eventually come into question and the judicial system will have a difficult time sorting things out. Many of the tried and true investment strategies that advisers relied on including diversification of risk seemed to all fail at one time. The value of a wide range of assets including real estate, stocks, bonds, and commodities all fell dramatically in a short period of time (Steverman, 2009).

ISSUE

MAINTAINING INTEGRITY WITH FINANCIAL SECURITIES ANALYSIS

The financial securities analysis field is complicated and imperfect (Duan, Hu & McLean, 2009). As economic conditions tumbled into chaos in 2008, many people wondered why the financial analysts on Wall Street got paid so much money to be so wrong. Newspapers and weekly magazines were full of articles depicting various scandals, lies, or deceptions. By the end of 2008, it looked like the rapid economic downturn consisted of a series of events in which most securities analysts had trouble keeping their bearings or drawing rational conclusions (Morse, 2009).

Two questions plague the contemporary financial securities analyst profession.

- First, are financial securities analysts honest? Honesty in this case requires a lack of bias in pursuing their work as well as real due diligence and fiduciary responsibility.
- Second, are financial securities analysts competent and using proven research and forecasting methods as opposed to fabricated formulas aimed at guessing what the future will bring?

GOVERNMENTAL REGULATION EFFORTS

Numerous laws govern the behavior of people working in the financial securities industry including the Securities Act of 1933, Securities Exchange Act of 1934, Investment Company Act of 1940, and Investment Advisers Act of 1940. The industry and the workers in the industry also operate under the administrative rules that were developed by the major enforcing agency, the Securities and Exchange

Commission (SEC). There is also The Securities Enforcement Remedies and Penny Stock Reform Act of 1990 (Remedies Act) which imposes penalties for a range of securities trading violations. The SEC has indeed enforced these and other laws and fined investment firms and individual advisers in those firms hundred of millions of dollars ("Mutual fund trading abuses," 2005).

The New York Stock Exchange (NYSE) and the National Association of Securities Dealers Automated Quotations (NASDAQ) are also active in regulatory efforts. Both exchanges have established a division to enforce marketplace rules and federal securities laws. They have also developed Rulebooks that contain principles of trade and business practices that the members of the exchange are required to follow. The rules were developed to prevent fraudulent or manipulative acts and practices and support appropriate disciplinary actions against members when violations occur. The SEC is the government agency that oversees the exchange activities and all rules and rule amendments must be submitted to the SEC for approval.

The Financial Industry Regulatory Authority (FINRA), performs market regulation under contract for the NASDAQ, the American Stock Exchange, the International Securities Exchange, the Chicago Climate Exchange. In its regulatory efforts, FINRA oversees nearly 5,000 brokerage firms, about 173,000 branch offices and approximately 659,000 registered securities representatives.

NON-GOVERNMENTAL REGULATION EFFORTS

In addition to the stock exchanges which many brokerages are members, there are also several other non-government organizations that set standards and codes of conduct for investment and financial advising firms. Many of these organizations were established as the securities laws were going into effect in the 1930s and 1940s.

THE INVESTMENT ADVISER ASSOCIATION

One of the oldest organizations is the Investment Adviser Association (IAA) which has established principles of conduct for investment advisers. The IAA contends that its principles continue to be used by Congress and the Securities and Exchange Commission in the development of legislation and regulations concerning the practices and conduct of investment advisers. The IAA principles also influenced the definition of fiduciary conduct, established by the United States Supreme Court, which applies to all investment advisers.

IAA contends that investment advisers have a special relationship of trust with their clients. To live up to this trust, an investment adviser must always place the interests of clients first and utilize a reasonable basis for its investment advice. In addition, to meet standards of conduct, advisers are required to fully disclose to clients all material facts about the advisory relationship and especially those that relate to potential conflicts of interest.

THE SECURITIES INDUSTRY AND FINANCIAL MARKETS ASSOCIATION

The Securities Industry and Financial Markets Association (SIFMA), as another example, has members that include international securities firms, U.S.-registered broker-dealers, and asset managers. The association supports the securities industry in regulatory and legislative issues, and assists in outreach, training, education and community involvement.

THE EMERGENCY ECONOMIC STABILIZATION ACT

Even though these regulatory efforts are in place and there a rules and codes of conduct, 2008 seemed to be a year ripped with scandals and disappointment. The downturn basically turned many earnings forecasts into worthless speculation (Clark & Karr, 2009). Many investment funds and millions of people lost value in their investments during the year.

Commonly called the bailout bill, on October 3, 2008, the Emergency Economic Stabilization Act of 2008 (EES Act) was signed into law. The bill provided for several types of emergency funding for financial institutions but also required steps be taken to remedy some of the problems in the financial sector. The EES Act, in addition to establishing an oversight process also called for several studies to be conducted that will examine problems in the financial sector. One of the studies focuses on regulatory modernization and examines the financial regulatory system and its effectiveness. Other studies focus on trading practices and investment instruments.

The EES Act established an oversight board composed of the Chairman of the Federal Reserve Board, the Treasury Secretary, the Chairman of the SEC, and the Secretary of the U.S. Department of Housing and Urban Development. One of the many tasks that the board is charged with is reporting suspected fraud, misrepresentation, or malfeasance regarding any actions relating to the economic crisis or use of emergency recovery funds to appropriate authorities.

To the satisfaction of many people who lost money in the 2008 meltdown, the EES Act also called for limitations on the salaries of top executives of firms that are receiving assistance under the bailout program. The yearly limit was set at $500,000 and also addresses incentive payments that may require unnecessary and excessive investment risks. The compensation limits applied to both publicly traded and privately held companies (Foley & Lardner, 2008).

At the heart of the global financial crisis that began in 2008 were mortgage backed securities (MBS). Reckless lending practices allowed uncreditworthy persons to make real estate purchases, which drove rising real estate values, which in turn drove a thriving market in lucrative securities backed by loans that closer scrutiny would have concluded were doomed to default. Billions of dollars in MBSs were bundled and sold into secondary markets where individual mortgages became thoroughly entangled in instruments too complex to effectively sort out when the avalanche of defaults began. The Dodd–Frank Wall Street Reform and Consumer Protection Act was signed into law in 2010. This law required securitizers to bear 5% of losses suffered by MBS investors, thus incentivizing more prudent behavior by lenders. A limited exception was made for loans meeting very high standards. In 2013, Bair & Frank warned that capitulating to industry efforts to amend the 5% rule to apply only to loans that do not meet the basic lending standards set by the Consumer Financial Protection Bureau (CFPB) would reintroduce large numbers of questionable loans back into the MBS market. CFPB standards are aimed at eliminating the worst pre-crisis lending practices without eliminating all but buyers with stellar credit and a large downpayment from the home buying mix. Mortgages continue to carry a higher risk for banks than in the more conservative past, and analysts must be wary as well as savvy in weighing the value of MBSs.

CONCLUSION

Modern economies depend largely on the ability to manage financial investments and the financial securities markets which enable the investment process. These markets allow large as well as small investors to participate in the economic process by providing funds for companies, governments, and entire nations to utilize capital that they would otherwise not have available.

The role of the financial securities analyst is to research investment opportunities and advise their clients or potential investors as to the benefits and risks associated with an investment. It is critical that the work of the financial securities analyst proceed and is diligently executed without bias or self-interest on the part of the adviser.

BIBLIOGRAPHY

A three-year global recession. (2009). *Asia Monitor: South East Asia Monitor Volume 1, 20*(2), 8. Retrieved March 11, 2009, from EBSCO Online Database Business Source Complete. http://search.ebscohost.com/login.aspx?direct=t rue&db=bth&AN=3 6170540&site=ehost-live

Bair, S., & Frank, B. (2013). Watch out. the mortgage securities market is at it again. *Fortune, 167*(8), 69. Retrieved November 15, 2013, from EBSCO Online Database Business Source Complete. http://search.ebscohost.com/ login.aspx?direct=true&d b=bth&AN=87863611&site=eh ost-live

Bartolini, L., Hilton, S., Sundaresan, S., & Tonetti, C. (2011). Collateral values by asset class: Evidence from primary securities dealers. *Review of Financial Studies, 24*(1), 248- 278. Retrieved November 15, 2013, from EBSCO Online Database Business Source Complete. http://search.ebscohost.com/ login.aspx?direct=true&db=bth&AN=56517010 &site=ehost-live

Birkner, C. (2009). Getting started in trading. *Futures: News, Analysis & Strategies for Futures, Options & Derivatives Traders, 38*(2), 46-48. Retrieved March 4, 2009, from EBSCO Online Database Business Source Complete. http://search.ebscohost.com/login.aspx?direct=true&db=bt h&AN=36665067&site=ehost-live

Clark, E., & Karr, A. (2009). Warnings weigh on retail stocks. *WWD: Women's Wear Daily, 197*(9), 20-1NULL. Retrieved March 5, 2009, from EBSCO Online Database Business Source Complete. http://search.ebscohost.com/ login.aspx?direct=true&db=bth&AN=36281437&site=eh ost-live

Duan, Y., Hu, G., & McLean, R. (2009). When is stock picking likely to be successful? Evidence from mutual funds. *Financial Analysts Journal, 65*(2), 1-12. Retrieved March 5, 2009, from EBSCO Online Database Business Source Complete. http://search.ebscohost.com/login.aspx?direct=t rue&db=bth&AN=36797901&site=ehost-live

Ennis, R. (2009). End of an era. *Financial Analysts Journal, 65*(1), 6-8. Retrieved March 5, 2009, from EBSCO Online Database Business Source Complete. http://search.ebscohost.com/login.aspx?di rect=true&db=bth&AN=36179348 &site=ehost-live

Financial analysts and personal financial advisers, nature of the work. (2009). United States Department of Labor, Bureau of Labor Statistics. Retrieved March 4, 2009, from United States Department of Labor, Bureau of Labor Statistics. http:// www.bls.gov/oco/ocos259.htm

Foley, F., & Lardner, L. (2008). A comprehensive summary and analysis of the Emergency Economic Stabilization Act of 2008. *Blue Chip Financial Forecasts, 27*(11), 1-8. Retrieved March 4, 2009, from EBSCO Online Database Business Source Complete. http://search.ebscohost.com/ login.aspx?direct= true&db=bth&AN=35647894&site=eh ost-live

Freund, S., Prasad, D., & Andrews, F. (2013). Security selection factors: novice versus experienced investors. *International Journal of Business & Finance Research (IJBFR), 7*(4), 115-126. Retrieved November 15, 2013, from EBSCO Online Database Business Source Complete. http://search.ebscohost.com/ login.aspx?direct=t rue&db=bth&AN=86260859& site=ehost-live

Halal, W. (2009). Emerging technologies and the global crisis of maturity. *Futurist, 43*(2), 39-46. Retrieved March 11, 2009, from EBSCO Online Database Academic Search Complete. http://search.ebscohost.com/login.aspx?direct=t rue&db=a9h& AN=36400461&site=ehost-live

Mishkin, F. (2009). Globalization, macroeconomic performance, and monetary policy. *Journal of Money, Credit & Banking (Blackwell), 41*, 187-196. Retrieved March 11, 2009, from EBSCO Online Database Business Source Complete. http:// search.ebscohost.com/login.aspx?direct=t rue&d b=bth&AN=36190638&site=ehost-live

Morgado, D. (2009). Economic consequences to companies, states, and municipalities sponsoring pension plans from recent market losses and potential ERISA fiduciary liability to investment advisers.

Employee Benefit Plan Review, 63(9), 7-8. Retrieved March 12, 2009, from EBSCO Online Database Business Source Complete. http://search. ebscohost. com/login.aspx?direct=true&db=bth&AN=3667 4585&site=ehost-live

Morse, N. (2009). Who's to blame? Many answers, few certainties. *Mortgage Banking, 69*(4), 98-101. Retrieved March 4, 2009, from EBSCO Online Database Business Source Complete. http://search. ebscohost.com/login.aspx? direct=true&db=bth& AN=36112289&site=ehost-live

Moynihan, M. (2009). Key issues for mutual fund boards in the midst of the financial crisis. *Investment Lawyer, 16*(3), 1-11. Retrieved March 12, 2009, from EBSCO Online Database Business Source Complete. http://search.ebscohost.com/ login.aspx?direct=true&db=bth&AN=36674567 &site=ehost-live

Muller, F.L. (1994). Equity securities analysis in the U.S. *Financial Analysts Journal, 50*(1), 6-9. Retrieved November 15, 2013, from EBSCO Online Database Business Source Complete. http:// search.ebscohost.com/login.aspx?direct=tru e&d b=bth&AN=9405244150&site=ehost-live

Mutual fund trading abuses: SEC consistently applied procedures in setting penalties, but could strengthen certain internal controls. (2005). United States Government Accountability Office. Retrieved March 12, 2009, from the Government Accountability Office. http://www.gao. gov/new. items/d05385.pdf

O'Dowd, S. (2009). Ten predictions for financial services in 2009. *Securities Industry News, 21*(2), 6-6. Retrieved March 6, 2009, from EBSCO Online Database Business Source Complete. http://search. ebscohost.com/login.aspx? direct=true&db=bth& AN=36334826&site=ehost-live

Pressman, A. (2009, January 19). In search of stock research. *BusinessWeek,* (4116), 56-57. Retrieved March 5, 2009, from EBSCO Online Database Academic Search Complete. http://search.ebscohost. com/login.aspx?direct=t rue&db=a9h&AN=3608 7720&site=ehost-live

Private pensions: Multiemployer plans face short- and long-term challenges. (2004). United States General Accounting Office. Retrieved March 12, 2009, from the Government Accountability Office. http://www.gao.gov/ new.items/d04423.pdf

Reinganum, M. (2009). Setting national priorities:

Financial challenges facing the Obama Administration. *Financial Analysts Journal, 65*(2), 1-4. Retrieved March 6, 2009, from EBSCO Online Database Business Source Complete. http://search. ebscohost.com/login.aspx?direct=t rue&db=bth& AN=36798026&site=ehost-live

Steverman, B. (2009, February 12). A changed world for financial advisers. *Business Week Online,* 29. Retrieved March 12, 2009, from EBSCO Online Database Academic Search Complete. http://search. ebscohost.com/login.aspx? direct=true&db=a9h &AN=36540813&site=ehost-live

SUGGESTED READING

Bogoslaw, D. (2009, February 11). Should you manage your own portfolio? *Business Week Online,* 14. Retrieved March 5, 2009, from EBSCO Online Database Business Source Complete. http:// search.ebscohost.com/login.aspx? direct=true&d b=bth&AN=36564490&site=ehost-live

Carlson, G. (2009). The focused 10 funds hold their own in a trying year. *Morningstar FundInvestor, 17*(5), 16-17. Retrieved March 4, 2009, from EBSCO Online Database Business Source Complete. http:// search.ebscohost.com/ login.aspx?direct=true&db =bth&AN=36065881&site=eh ost-live

Foley, F., & Lardner, L. (2008). A comprehensive summary and analysis of the Emergency Economic Stabilization Act of 2008. *Blue Chip Financial Forecasts, 27*(11), 1-8. Retrieved March 4, 2009, from EBSCO Online Database Business Source Complete. http://search.ebscohost.com/ login.aspx?direct= true&db=bth&AN=35647894&site=eh ost-live

Garmhausen, S. (2009). In turmoil, bankers see a chance to woo advisers. *American Banker, 174*(31), 8-9. Retrieved March 12, 2009, from EBSCO Online Database Business Source Complete. http:// search.ebscohost.com/login.aspx? direct=true&d b=bth&AN=36586711&site=ehost-live

Hanna, S., & Lindamood, S. (2008). The decrease in stock ownership by minority households. *Financial Counseling & Planning, 19*(2), 46-58. Retrieved March 4, 2009, from EBSCO Online Database Academic Search Complete. http://search. ebscohost.com/login.aspx?direct=true&db=a 9h&AN=36318531&site=ehost-live

How the crash will reshape America. (2009, March). *Atlantic Monthly* (10727825), 303(2), 44-56. Retrieved March 11, 2009, from EBSCO Online

Database Academic Search Complete. http://search.ebscohost.com/login.aspx?direct=t rue&db=a9h&AN=36539332&site=ehost-live

Larson, M. (2009). Fiduciary prudence in uncertain economic times. *Employee Benefit Plan Review, 63*(9), 13-14. Retrieved March 12, 2009, from EBSCO Online Database Business Source Complete. http://search.ebscohost.com/ login.aspx?direct=true&db=bth&AN=36674587&site=eh ost-live

–Michael Erbschloe

FINANCIAL STATEMENT ANALYSIS

ABSTRACT

Financial statements are records that can provide indications of the financial health of a company. Accurate financial records are necessary to keep track of financial warning signals such as inordinately high expenses, high levels of debt or a poor record of collecting bills. Public companies often have specific procedures for gathering, verifying and reporting financial information. Recent corporate scandals have placed greater scrutiny on the managers and corporate officers of publicly held firms. Privately held firms are not held to the same standard but often adhere to strict guidelines in order to increase the value of the firm and viability in case of sale.

OVERVIEW

Financial statements are reports that show the financial position of a company. Recordkeeping is important in order to understand a company's value and to comply with various regulations and tax requirements. Accurate records allow companies to account for how money was spent and handled, what assets are owned and what debts are owed.

Businesses differ in how they are valued depending on whether they are public or private firms. Information about public companies is available, especially to shareholders, while it is difficult to get audited and financially sound information about the financial workings of a private company (Antia, 2006). Antia (para. 2) calls the value of a business the "free cash flow" that has various adjusted risk elements deducted from it. Private companies don't provide information on their cash flow and have greater opportunities to engage in financial benefits not available to public companies, such as:

- Above-market salaries for family members.
- Mixing of personal and business funds.
- Exaggeration of business expenses to reduce taxes.

Other concerns regarding a business' value can depend on what a buyer sees in the business. If the business represents a strategic purchase, a higher price might be garnered even for an over-valued private business. If a buyer is a minority buyer, they may want to pay less due to the minimal amount of control they can exert on the business (Antia, para. 3).

TYPES OF FINANCIAL STATEMENTS

Basic financial statements include the balance sheet, the income statement, cash flow statement and notes to account. There are different types of reports because different types of information are needed to effectively manage a company and plan for the future. Sometimes companies use financial reporting information internally, and in some cases they are required to release this information externally. Tracy (1999) called cash the "lubricant" of business. Without cash it is difficult for a business to function and it increases the likelihood that a business may fail. But, Tracy warned that cash flows only show part of the picture and give no information about the business' profit or financial condition. Since cash flows only show part of the picture, other types of financial reports are needed.

The most common financial reports are the balance sheet and the income statement.

- The balance sheet (also called the statement of financial position) provides information about the financial condition of a company.
- The income statement (also called the earnings or profit and loss statement) shows the profitability of the business.

BALANCE SHEETS

The general categories on balance sheets are assets and liabilities. A publicly traded firm also includes shareholder equity. A typical balance sheet shows assets a company owns. Assets include cash, accounts receivable, inventory and any prepaid expenses. Balance sheets also record property the company owns and any depreciation on assets. The balance sheet is a two-sided report because it records assets on one side and liabilities on the other. Liabilities include accounts payable and accrued expenses, income tax owed, loans and stockholders' equity. Stockholders' or shareholders' equity is any claim that owners of company stock have against the assets that a company has. Stockholders' or shareholders' equity is also called net worth. Stockholders' equity is found by deducting liabilities and debt from assets (Morgenson & Harvey, 2002).

INCOME STATEMENTS

Income statements show the profitability of a business. The income statement is for a period of one year and shows the total sales revenue for the year. Subtracted from sales revenue is the cost of goods sold or the expenses a company incurs in producing finished goods to sell. Also deducted from the revenue are expenses for operating costs and depreciation. If a company is publicly owned, its income statement must also report earnings per share (Tracy, 1999). Earnings per share is a measure of company profitability (Godin, 2001). It is calculated by dividing net income by the total shares of stock. When looking at the income statement of a company, the profitability isn't just the gross profit, it is also important to look at the ratio of expenses as a percentage of profit. If a company has high profits but also has high expenses, the company could be mismanaged.

Balance sheets are not only important to companies but also to investors (Godin, p. 52). Balance sheets can tell investors whether or not a company is a good investment based on its financial condition. Financial statements are often prepared by accountants and reviewed by auditors to ensure that the records are accurate and to avoid the temptation not to report factual information or to hide financial flaws. A reason business owners may use financial professionals is to reduce the chance of error and to stay out of an area where they may not have expertise. O'Bannon (2005) cautioned business owners against being lulled to sleep by the power of current accounting software products, which cannot replace the knowledge gained by using professional financial advice. O'Bannon felt that one of the primary benefits of the newer software is that it allows owners and financial advisors to speak the same language and lets business owners provide easy to use documentation to their accountant. Accountants and other financial advisors can use software to quickly perform somewhat complex analysis and generate reports for their clients.

Arar (2012) wrote that small businesses operating in the 2010s have "more accounting software options than ever, including Web-based subscriptions." For those businesses with large inventories or client databases, however, or those that choose not to entrust data to the cloud, such desktop tools as Acclivity AccountEdge Pro 2012, Intuit QuickBooks 2013, and Sage 50 Complete Accounting 2013 are good options (Arar 2012).

ANALYZING BALANCE SHEET & INCOME STATEMENTS

Analyzing balance sheets and income statements requires more than simply reading the categories of figures. The numbers have to be read with an eye towards what they mean and what they might mean in combination. Scott (2005, p. 108) stated that financial statement analysis means interpreting the data "in a meaningful way" instead of looking at "past results." This can mean looking at the company's management strategy, the way the business is operated and the plans the business has for the future. Scott suggested asking the following questions to get close to figuring out how internal factors, especially management, influence financial statement content:

- How is the company distinguishing itself from the competition?
- How does it compete? E.g., on price, quality, responsiveness, availability?
- Is the company's strategy viable given the marketplace economy?
- Is management adapting its strategy to a changing environment?

These questions and others can provide qualitative information in addition to the quantitative numbers provided in financial statements. Using the information in aggregate can give a broader picture of the company's financial health.

Ratio Analysis

Ratios are one method of analyzing what financial statements may mean. There are several types of ratios including liquidity and profitability ratios. Ratio analysis shows the relationship between financial information, the way it behaves over time and what risks are implied by the behavior (Morgenson & Harvey, 2002).

Liquidity ratios are a measure of how 'liquid' a company is or how well it can come up with cash or quickly converted assets that can help the company meet its financial obligations. If the ratio is high, that is a good number. An example of a liquidity ratio is to divide current assets by current liabilities. The result shows how much cash is available for the company to manage current financial requirements. A quick ratio is a liquidity ratio that eliminates slow moving inventory from current assets to give a more accurate picture of a company's liquidity. Companies can compare their liquidity to others in their industry to see how they fare among similar companies. A debt to equity ratio is a measure of the ability of a company to use debt to finance its operations. Profitability ratios measure the company's profit performance by comparing profits to sales. Companies that last are able to remain profitable even under unfavorable conditions.

Help in Financial Analysis

Many business owners and managers, especially in small businesses, may need help in using financial information to analyze company position. Managing credit (2005) directed readers to a website where they could download a free financial statement analysis worksheet that not only helps the user prepare financial statements but has preconfigured formulas for calculating ratios and ratio analysis. Technology has made it easier to find tools that will help demystify managing and using financial data. Some of these tools can help non-financial managers understand what the financial information means and make a connection between the financial information reported and the day-to-day operations they know and understand.

Bankruptcy Prediction

Hol (2007) discussed the analysis of financial statements as a predictor of business bankruptcy for firms in Norway; over 19,000 firms were studied. Most studies have shown that healthy companies are compared to financially distressed ones based on how they differ financially. However, a stronger predictor of bankruptcy is to consider industry factors and business cycle movements and not just financial statement information to determine how likely a company is to fail. The industry and external factors include the "gross domestic product gap, industrial production index and the money supply" (Hol, p. 88). There are complex bankruptcy prediction models that are used by banks but they tend to only consider the internal financial information and usually do not rely much on external factors over which a company may not have any control. Hol recognized that many of bankruptcy prediction models were developed in the 1960's and 1970's and did not take into account market factors. When looking at internal financial statement information, Hol noted that four financial ratios need to be high to indicate a lower likelihood of bankruptcy:

- Cash flow to debt.
- Financial coverage to financial costs.
- Liquidity to current debt.
- Solidity to total capital.

If company managers are aware of what factors are important, they can put management strategies in place to maximize the positive factors and reduce the negative factors. A comprehensive strategy adds to internal factors an allowance for external ones.

VIEWPOINT

Who Analyzes Financial Statements & Why

Microsoft (2007) notes that many different types of people may want to read and analyze financial statements for different reasons. One group that is interested in and that uses financial statements includes credit lenders to small business. Scott (2005) noted that, at the time of his writing, there were over 24 million small businesses, which accounted for over 50% of U.S. private gross domestic product. A market this large seems as if it would be very attractive to lenders and could offer many opportunities. However, Scott (p. 105) warns that the market is large but hardly uniform and can be plagued with a number of problems. These companies may have undependable financials with "volatile earnings swing[s]" and are more likely to present a risk of fraud. The small business market is also difficult to categorize by industry because descriptive factors and trends may not be consistent across industry lines. Scott recommends using stringent, consistent and traditional underwriting practices that treat each case as a unique one and take into account the unique factors that affect the business. This means careful examination of financial documents within the context of the business.

Scott (2006) describes a context model for analyzing small business financials that uses a cause and effect relationship to determine what information should be available and what that information should look like when examined. The primary measures Scott recommends using are "profitability, cash flow, liquidity and solvency."

- Profit is a company's revenue less its costs.
- Cash flow is a measure of how much cash is coming into a company and flowing out of a company. The company may also be interested in tracking the rate of cash inflow and outflow.
- Tracy (p 75) calls liquidity "having too little ready cash" and described solvency as "not being able to pay liabilities on time."

Company managers should have ready knowledge of these factors in order to plan and manage the business. If any of these factors reaches a dangerous point, the health of the company could be in serious jeopardy.

There are various parties beyond the business owner with an interest in reading financial statements. These entities can include investors, creditors, customers, suppliers, auditors, and industry analysts and fund managers.

- Investors that currently invest in a company or have an interest in investing in a company want to know if the company is a good investment. If a company's financials and performance indicate that the company is a good investment, the investor can expect a good rate of return by sharing in the profits of the company. Investors want to monitor financial performance because it is important to know when to pull out of a losing investment and investors could be limiting themselves by tying up capital that could be invested in a better prospect.
- Creditors want to know if a company is a good risk to loan money to and if the company will be able or likely to pay a loan back. If a company defaults on a loan, that is a bad risk for the creditor; if the

company pays back the loan plus the fees associated with the loan, the creditor receives a profit.

- Customers are concerned about a company's financial health because they want to be sure the company will be around if they plan to continue to purchase products. In addition, those who have already purchased products want to do business with a company that will be around to service the products purchased. If a company cannot stand behind its products, the customer may decide to go elsewhere. Some customers considering engaging in a long term relationship with a company and planning to purchase high volumes may ask for financials to determine whether of not such a relationship is advisable.
- Suppliers want a relationship with their customers and want to align themselves with financially sound companies that they can grow with and that can afford and value the products they sell. Inconsistency in a company's financial health means it won't be a consistent buyer of the supplier's products which jeopardizes the financial health of the supplier. Suppliers can often attract investors or impress creditors by their customer list.
- Auditors have to provide an objective viewpoint on the financial health of the audited company. Auditors are expected to be accurate and impartial and additional business is based on the credibility of the auditor. Recent corporate scandals have also charged auditors with irresponsibly overlooking financial warning signals. Aligning an auditor with such activity could ruin the auditor's reputation. Auditors might look at the financial information of a company to find errors and inaccuracies such as "duplicate or missing items and unauthorized transactions" (Lanza & Brooks, 2006, p.29). Auditors can be more accurate in analyzing the financial picture of a company if they go beyond the financial statements, competitive factors and risk analysis. The Securities and Exchange Commission (SEC) has online information that helps auditors to identify disclosure requirements and issues to look for in an audit.
- Industry analysts and fund managers advise others as to whether or not to invest in a company. The information that they provide, if accurate, can give them satisfied customers and greater credibility as industry analysts. These examples show that many people may be interested in the financial health

and financial reporting of a company. The examples also indicate the importance of carefully and accurately prepared financial statements as they affect the ability of a company to do business, receive credit and attract investors and customers.

ETHICS IN FINANCIAL REPORTING

The recent corporate financial scandals and crises have caused government intervention in the regulation of corporate financial reporting. These changes have increased the penalties corporate officers face if found to engage in fraud or providing misleading financial information. Without government regulation, many believe that it is impossible to ensure adequate protection for the investors and employees of companies when companies are driven by profit.

The United States Sarbanes-Oxley act of 2002 is federal legislation that was enacted in response to many of the corporate scandals such as Enron. The act governs accounting and financial reporting and provides for holding corporate officers and even accounting and auditing personnel responsible for giving accurate information about the financial health of corporations.

Another piece of legislation, the Dodd-Frank Wall Street Reform and Protection Act, was enacted in 2010. One of its main goals was to consolidate and strengthen consumer financial protection by granting the newly created Consumer Financial Protection Bureau (CFPB or Bureau) the power to enforce existing financial protection laws and to promulgate additional rules (Administrative law - agency design - Dodd-Frank Act creates the consumer financial protection bureau - Dodd-Frank Act, Pub. L. No. 111- 203, 124 Stat. 1376 (2010), 2011).

ETHICS TRAINING

The increased temptation to fudge the numbers to present a more appealing picture has not just affected government regulation of corporations. An emphasis on ethics in business and accounting classes is being made to have a positive affect on the future business leaders and managers (Smith, Smith, & Mulig, 2005). Smith et al (2005) found that exposure to ethics training "influenced student ethical development" as well as how students perceive ethics in terms of importance and how they view unethical behavior as acceptable or not.

TRUST

Trust is noted as the underpinning of ethical business transactions. Without trust, there can be a breakdown in communication and lack of trust can ultimately affect buyer and seller willingness to engage in open market transactions. When trust is

missing, energy is taken out of the economic systems and unfavorable ethical conditions could cause the collapse of the entire economic system. Smith et al (2005) list ten universal ethical values including "honesty, integrity, promise-keeping, fidelity, fairness, caring, respect for others, responsible citizenship, pursuit of excellence and accountability." Some of these values may come from a person's background, upbringing, religious beliefs, or from things a person has learned from reading or observation.

ETHICS GUIDELINES

Smith et al suggested that management use ethical guidelines for decision-making and noted that most corporations have ethics guidelines for employee behavior. The employee business conduct guidelines often include topics like ethics, safety, harassment, operations, alcohol and drug use as well as conflicts of interest. Company guidelines cannot stop unethical behavior by employees nor can it stop fraud and abuse by employees who handle and manage financial information. However, the company can identify behaviors and suggest consequences for those who violate the rules.

Dubbink and Smith (2011) in fact argued that in liberal, democratic societies, there is an "underlying political need" to attribute greater levels of moral responsibility to corporations. "Corporate moral responsibility is essential to the maintenance of social coordination that both advances social welfare and protects citizens' moral entitlements," they wrote. When making decisions, there are certain questions to ask when considering whether or not a decision is ethical. These questions include (Smith et al, 2005):

- Are there legal concerns?
- Is it right?
- Does it comply with company values?
- Does it comply with principles of your profession (accountants, etc.)?
- Would you be embarrassed by your decision if others knew about it?
- Who else is affected by this (co-workers, customers, etc.)?

- Are you willing to take sole responsibility for this decision?
- Is there another course of action that does not create an ethical dilemma?
- How will it look in the newspaper?
- Do you think a reasonable person would agree with your decision? (Ask an appropriate person).

These questions are good guidelines for individuals facing an ethical dilemma. It is likely that someone might realize there is an ethical dilemma just by the fact that they have questions about it. While educating students and employees on ethical behavior is no guarantee to stopping financial fraud, it is a way to ensure that people who might be tempted are at least presented with information to avoid problems.

BIBLIOGRAPHY

Administrative law - agency design - Dodd-Frank Act creates the consumer financial protection bureau - Dodd-Frank Act, Pub. L. No. 111-203, 124 Stat. 1376 (2010) (to be codified in scattered sections of the U.S. Code). (2011). *Harvard Law Review, 124*(8), 2123-2130. Retrieved November 20, 2013, from EBSCO Online Database Business Source Complete. http://search.ebscohost.com/ login.aspx?direct=true&db=a9h&AN=61294566&site=ehost-live

Antia, M. (2006). Principles of private firm valuation. *Financial Analysts Journal, 62*(3), 77-78. Retrieved October 1, 2007, from EBSCO Online Database Business Source Complete. http://search.ebscohost.com/login.aspx? direct=true&db=bth&AN=21054271&site=ehost-live

Arar, Y. (2012). Reviews & rankings: accounting software saves time and money. *PC World*, 46-48. Retrieved November 20, 2013, from EBSCO Online Database Business Source Complete. http://search.ebscohost.com/ login.aspx?direct=true&db=a9h&AN=82535589&site= ehost-live

Dubbink, W., & Smith, J. (2011). A political account of corporate moral responsibility. *Ethical Theory & Moral Practice, 14* (2), 223-246. Retrieved November 20, 2013, from EBSCO Online Database Business Source Complete. http://search.ebscohost.com/login.aspx?direct= true&db=a9h&AN=59928596&site=ehost-live

Godin, S. (2001). *If you're clueless about the stock market and want to know more.* Chicago: Dearborn Trade Books.

Hol, S. (2007). The influence of the business cycle on bankruptcy probability. *International Transactions in Operational Research,14*(1), 75-90. Retrieved October 1, 2007, from EBSCO Online Database Business Source Complete. http://search.ebscohost. com/login.aspx?direct= true&db=bth&AN=23408 631&site=ehost-live

Konchitchki, Y. (2013). Accounting and the macroeconomy: the case of aggregate price-level effects on individual stocks. *Financial Analysts Journal, 69*(6), 40–54. Retrieved November 24, 2014, from EBSCO Online Database Business Source Complete. http://search.ebscohost.com/ login.aspx?direct=true&db=bth&AN=92504364 &site=ehost-live

Kumaraswamy, M. R. (2012). Ethic-based management vs. corporate misgovernance—new approach to financial statement analysis. *Journal of Financial Management & Analysis, 25*(2), 29–38. Retrieved November 24, 2014, from EBSCO Online Database Business Source Complete. http:// search.ebscohost.com/login.aspx?direct= true&d b=bth&AN=86710877&site=ehost-live

Lanza, R.B. & Brooks, D. (2006). Are you looking outside enough? *Internal Auditor, 63*(4), 29-33. Retrieved October 1, 2007, from EBSCO Online Database Business Source Complete. http://search. ebscohost.com/login.aspx?direct= true&db=bth& AN=21904239&site=ehost-live

Morgenson, G. & Harvey, C. R. (2002). *The New York Times dictionary of money investing.* New York: Times Books.

Need help understanding financial statements? (2005). *Managing Credit, Receivables & Collections, 5*(9) 8. Retrieved October 1, 2007, from EBSCO Online Database Business Source Complete. http://search.ebscohost.com/ login.aspx?direct= true&db=bth&AN=18002299&site= ehost-live

O'Bannon, I. M. (2005). Lost in translation. *CPA Technology Advisor, 15*(7), 44-50. Retrieved October 1, 2007, from EBSCO Online Database Business Source Complete. http://search. ebscohost.com/login.aspx?direct=true&db= bth&AN=18883435&site=ehost-live

Prepare financial statements. (2007). *Microsoft Help and How-to.* Retrieved October 1, 2007, from http://office. microsoft.com/en-us/help/HA011622271033.aspx

Scott, S. (2005). A systematic approach to contextual financial analysis in small business asset-based lending. *Secured Lender, 61*(6), 104-113. Retrieved October 1, 2007, from EBSCO Online Database Business Source Complete. http://search.ebscohost.com/login.aspx?direct=true&db=buh&AN=19176308&site=ehost-live

Smith, L.M., Smith, K. & Mulig, E. V. (2005). Application and assessment of an ethics presentation for accounting and business classes. *Journal of Business Ethics, 61*(2), 153-164. Retrieved October 1, 2007, from EBSCO Online Database Business Source Complete. http://search.ebscohost.com/login.aspx?direct=true&db=buh&AN=18506364 &site=ehost-live

Tracy, J.A. (1999). *How to read a financial report: For managers, entrepreneurs, lenders, lawyers, and investors.* New York: John Wiley & Sons.

SUGGESTED READING

Biddle, I. (2007). Watching for warning signs (analysing financial records). *Businessdate, 15*(5), 4-7. Retrieved October 1, 2007, from EBSCO Online Database Business Source Complete. http://search.ebscohost.com/login.aspx? direct=true&db=bth&AN=26597069&site=bsi-live

Financial fraud study shows patterns. (2007). *Financial Executive, 23*(7), 15. Retrieved October 1, 2007, from EBSCO Online Database Business Source Complete. http://search.ebscohost.com/login.aspx?direct=true&db=bth&AN=26472673&site=bsi-live

Junker, L. (2007). Meet your new (audit) standards. *Associations Now, 3*(10), 55-57. Retrieved November 12, 2007, from EBSCO Online Database Business Source Complete. http://search.ebscohost.com/login.aspx?direct=true&db=bth&AN=26635012&site=bsi-live

Konchitchki, Y., & Patatoukas, P. N. (2014). Taking the pulse of the real economy using financial statement analysis: implications for macro forecasting and stock valuation. *Accounting Review, 89*(2), 669–694. Retrieved November 24, 2014, from EBSCO Online Database Business Source Complete. http://search.ebscohost.com/login.aspx?direct=true&db=bth&AN=95293399&site=bsi-live

NACM offers attendees a boost with financial statement analysis. (2007). *Business Credit, 109*(10), 63. Retrieved October 1, 2007, from EBSCO Online Database Business Source Complete. http://search.ebscohost.com/login.aspx? direct=true&db=bth&AN=27392577&site=bsi-live

–Marlanda English

FINANCIAL STATEMENTS

ABSTRACT

This essay highlights current issues that are relevant to the discussion of financial statements and financial reporting. In particular, this article will review the current state of GAAP (US accounting standards) and the current trend toward adoption of IFRS (International Financial Reporting Standards). Mandatory auditing and reporting of company financials has been a major focus of public companies since adoption of Sarbanes-Oxley in 2002. Five years after it became law, Sarbanes-Oxley requirements continue to challenge companies in terms of meeting internal reporting and accountability standards. Federal mandates have impacted companies in terms of costs, IT requirements and added responsibilities for CFOs (Chief Financial Officers). Companies must continuously adapt to changing auditing and reporting requirements in terms of globalization and the need to raise the capital to compete in global marketplaces.

OVERVIEW

Financial statements document the status of a company's assets, expenses, revenues, and liabilities. The overall financial health of a company can be ascertained from the quantitative analysis of financial statements—which serve as the complete record for an organization's financial records. A financial statement is an internal business tool that tracks the intake and outflow of money and illustrates changes in financial status over time. Financial statements are used for both short-term and long-term planning, for business forecasting, and for raising capital.

TYPES OF FINANCIAL STATEMENTS

There are four main types of financial statements that document the financial aspects of a company (SEC, 2007).

- Balance sheets, which portray how much a company owns and the amount of money it owes at a certain point in time.
- Income statements, which demonstrate the amount of money a company earned and spent during a certain period of time.
- Cash flow statements, which display the amount of money flowing into a company and the money flowing out of the company during a certain period of time.
- Statements of shareholder equity, which present all the changes in the interests of the company's shareholders that have taken place over time.

USERS OF FINANCIAL STATEMENTS

Depending upon the size and nature of a company there may be different users of the information on a financial statement. Internal users of financial information include

- Owners or managers, who use financials to determine future operations and planning.
- Individual employees, who may be negotiating compensation or groups of employees (unions) who are involved in collective bargaining.
- Stockholders, who review annual report figures.

External users of financial statements include

- Prospective investors, who may want to invest personal money.
- Banks or financial institutions, who may lend capital (money).
- Government bodies, which ensure compliance and accurate reporting.

The audience of an organization's financial statement will differ, often depending upon the size and complexity of an organization. In small companies, financial statements are used primarily for the benefit of the business owner in documenting the cash flow (revenue and expenses) of the company. The basic information on the financial statement allows owners or managers to see financial trends over time and to plan accordingly. For large organizations or corporations, financial statements can be complex documents and often include footnotes that provide additional information about each item on the balance sheet, income statement, and cash flow statement. Larger organizations will likely have more external users accessing their financial information and will therefore have much more complexity in their statements.

TRENDS IN FINANCIAL REPORTING

Two trends have profoundly shaped how companies are required to compile and report on their financial status.

- The rise of global organizations and markets has highlighted the need for the adoption of worldwide accounting standards—Americans use GAAP, and much of the rest of the world uses IFRS.
- Corporate scandals involving financial mismanagement and accounting fraud led to the adoption of the Sarbanes- Oxley Act of 2002.

The changing role of the CFO (chief financial officer) in organizations is also a topic that is closely related to the topic of financial reporting and disclosure. Regulatory burdens have added much to the plate of finance departments and CFOs. Changes in accounting standards and stringent compliance mandates are only two of the many tasks facing CFOs, even as they are taking on a greater strategic role within organizations.

The affects of compliance and reporting are also discussed in terms of the implications for investors who have become increasingly wary of risky capital investments. Organizations are balancing the need to loosen compliance and auditing standards with the desire for potential investors to have confidence in the organizations that they are seeking to invest in.

APPLICATIONS

ACCOUNTING STANDARDS

GAAP

Accounting standards or principals have been put into place as guidelines for helping companies to prepare, present, and report financial statements. American companies use GAAP or US-GAAP standards for this purpose; GAAP standards are applied to financial reporting for all publicly traded companies in the United States and many privately held companies too. The SEC (Securities and Exchange Commission) requires that US-GAAP principals be followed for publicly traded companies. The GAAP standards are not directly set by the U.S. government but are overseen by the FASB (Financial Accounting Standards Board). The FASB is a nonprofit organization that has been designated by the SEC as the entity responsible for setting accounting principals in the public interest.

GASB & FASAB

Local and state governments adhere to a set of GAAP standards that is different from those that govern private-sector organizations. The policy board for state and local GAAP standards is the Government Accounting Standards Board (GASB). Financial reporting for federal government entities is regulated by the Federal Accounting Standards Advisory Board (FASAB).

IFRS

The International Financial Reporting Standards (IFRS) is a third set of common accounting standards that have been adopted by more than one hundred countries in the world, including the European Union and many emerging markets. The United States is the only major economy in the world to operate outside IFRS standards, but there is a general agreement that US-GAAP and IFRS standards should be reconciled to move toward a global standard.

EFFECTS OF GLOBALIZATION ON FINANCIAL STANDARDS

The rise of globalization of markets around the world has increased the interaction among companies in many markets and across supply chains. Many American companies maintain offices outside U.S. borders and still other U.S.-based companies have been acquired by non-American owners. The rise of cross-border and multinational organizations has only highlighted the differences in practices kept by different divisions of multinationals. In the area of financial reporting and accounting, this is illustrated by the differing accounting standards of GAAP versus IFRS.

GAAP vs. IFRS

The United States continues to feel pressure to adopt

international accounting standards and to reconcile those standards within GAAP. With emerging markets (such as China) having adopted IFRS, many U.S.-based CFOs are likely to continue to feel intense pressure to adopt too.

Edward E. Nusbaum, CEO of Grant Thornton, LLP, in Chicago, said "I would recommend that U.S. CFOs become acquainted with International Financial Reporting Standards and convergence related issues." He continued: "The impact will be significant, as U.S. companies will see U.S. GAAP written in a revised way. These changes could dramatically affect U.S. companies' financial statements." And "U.S. CFOs may also sense a shift in standards style toward an ever more principles-based approach. For global U.S. companies, foreign statutory reports may be due in IFRS. Overseas controllers will have a better understanding of IFRS than U.S. GAAP, and U.S. CFOs may want to know IFRS to speak the language" (Hansen, 2007).

INTEGRATION OF INTERNATIONAL STANDARDS

Japan announced in 2011, and again in 2013, that it was working on converging its accounting standards with international standards (IASPlus, 2013). Capital markets are expected to grow for countries that integrate international standards. The end goal of creating a single high-quality global-accounting standard is only part of the process. Some are already seeing inconsistencies with the way the standards are applied—there will likely be many divergent views about how to apply the new standards. The IASB (International Accounting Standards Board) has been aiming for application consistency.

All European Union countries along with U.S. subsidiaries of EU-owned companies converted to IFRS in 2005. Lessons learned from the EU conversions should help American companies make the conversion with fewer problems. US GAAP rules are considered to be much more detailed than IFRS rules. The reason given is that the chance of litigation is much higher in the United States.

RECONCILIATION OF IFRS & GAAP

The United States realizes how critical it is to remove impediments to non-American companies and the free flow of capital. The use of IFRS on a stand-alone basis is possible for foreign private issuers and American issuers (D.A., 2007).

One important point about reconciliation is that

both GAAP and IFRS standards need significant improvement, and the resources being used to try and eliminate the difference could be better applied to developing a new common set of standards.

"Although the transition to global accounting and audit standards creates difficulties for CFOs who must still work with multiple standards, FRS/US GAAP convergence will streamline the capital raising process for U.S.-based companies, reduce costs and risks in the market, and bring greater transparency and comparability to all companies engaged in international business. Investing in the process today will yield high returns in the not-so-distant future" (Hansen, 2007).

AUDITING

Internal auditing of company financials has changed radically since 2002, when Sarbanes-Oxley (also referred to as SOA or SarbOx) became law. The infamous corporate accounting scandals including WorldCom and Enron drove lawmakers to implement sweeping changes in the accountability and reporting of corporate finances. The decline in public trust resulting from the well-publicized scandals was the true impetus for the legislation.

The following posting from the Karl Nagel & Company website provides a good layperson's overview of the SarbOx objective.
[SarbOx was made law]

> "To improve quality and transparency in financial reporting and independent audits and accounting services for public companies, to create a Public Company Accounting Oversight Board, to enhance the standard setting process for accounting practices, to strengthen the independence of firms that audit public companies, to increase corporate responsibility and the usefulness of corporate financial disclosure, to protect the objectivity and independence of securities analysts, to improve Securities and Exchange Commission resources and oversight, and for other purposes" (Nagel, 2002).

Section 302 and 404 of SarbOx are discussed here; these two sections cover the establishment of internal controls and the auditing of the same. Section 302 specifically requires that the "signing" officers of the company have established mandates that ensure the establishment and maintenance of internal controls (and internal control certifications). Section 404 requires that company management produce an internal audit report. Without question, section 404 of SarbOx is the most costly and labor intensive aspect of the legislation for companies to enact. Section 404 requires that companies test all manual and automated controls having to do with financial reporting. A report, issued by company management and external auditors, must be compiled to show due diligence in meeting the auditing requirements.

COMPANY ISSUES WITH SARBOX & REMEDIATION

With the passage of SarbOx legislation in 2002, many companies were acknowledged to have "over-reacted" by putting excessive processes in place to avert any potential accounting issues or any semblance of impropriety by the organization in its financial

disclosure. Both external auditors and CEOs are blamed for a "cover your behind" approach to SarbOx implementation and the high costs associated with this strategy.

Remediation of issues has provided significant feedback and self-accountability for companies. Remediation allows companies to identify internal deficiencies in the design or operation of the internal controls. Many organizations have had trouble distinguishing between operational and design weaknesses, but the identification and rectification of issues is valuable. Some of the processes cited as deficient included insufficient staffing, inefficient division of work, problems in the financial closing process and, application of accounting principals. Key trouble areas included revenue recognition, management of contracts, and application of complex financial transactions (Fargher & Gramling, 2005).

"SOA represents an opportunity to restore investor confidence. Some companies have previously operated with less than satisfactory internal controls. Implementing SOA sections 302 and 404 can provide benefits through the identification of control deficiencies and, more importantly, through the improvement of internal controls which often result in improved corporate governance" (Fargher & Gramling, 2005).

The pendulum has swung back toward the center in terms of reactions to SarbOx legislation. Calls for less stringent oversight cite the following (Woellert, 2006):

- Compliance costs are too high.
- Testing of internal controls should be based on risk (focus on the assessment for most critical risk areas)
- Audit requirements for small companies should be scaled back.
- Loosen the yearly requirement for some tests that are not high risk.
- Clarification of terminology and rules need to be assessed regularly.
- SEC and PCAOB feedback has helped to streamline the process.
- Increased confidence, judgment, and experience of auditors and management is growing as scandals recede into history and memory.

Surveys indicate that the cost of compliance is falling for companies, but will remain a significant cost. Regulators will need to work within existing statues for the time being; changes in auditing standards will require a change in law. It is widely acknowledged that changing the regulation will not help cut compliance costs.

"The real benefit of change could be a legal one—a shield from exposure to shareholder lawsuits. Without specific direction from regulators, companies fret that anything intimating even the slightest hint of a shortcut could leave them vulnerable to expensive shareholder litigation. It's that fear, probably as much or more than actual compliance costs, that's driving the call for change" (Woellert, 2006).

ISSUES

ROLE OF CFO

"Few people have been more profoundly affected by the wave of regulation that followed America's post bubble corporate scandals than chief financial officers. Beginning with the landmark Sarbanes-Oxley Act of 2002, which was designed to prevent fraud in the wake of debacles at Enron, WorldCom and other companies, new rules and laws have rained down on CFOs, requiring them to pay more attention to even the smallest details of financial reporting and accounting. Most daunting of these: Sarbanes-Oxley's Section 404, which requires public companies to document and have audited all internal financial controls" (Taub, 2007).

CFOs are frustrated in many organizations. While many can manage both the big picture (strategic planning) and the minutiae (spreadsheets and regulatory issues), many CFOs dislike the continuing regulatory weight of SarbOx. CFOs are being tasked with playing a more strategic role within organizations, but their attention is divided. CFO expertise is needed to help organizations gain efficiencies, integrate supply chains, and approve acquisition of technology and additional staff. CFOs also figure prominently in succession planning, and many are considered to be CEOs "in waiting."

Job churn has been high at Fortune 500 companies in the years since SarbOx was made into law. The lasting burdens are blamed for high turnover of CFOs, many of whom admit that they are "too consumed with regulatory compliance and without enough time for corporate strategy" (Leone, 2006). Many organizations are hesitant to promote trusted CFOs in a time when capital markets are volatile and compliance risks are still looming. The Catch-22 for companies is that without being able to focus CFOs on overall financial strategy and management and away from compliance issues, corporate finance departments may be at risk.

Post Enron and Worldcom, CFOs are sometimes being referred to as the chief police officers of their respective organizations. There is zero tolerance in the accounting world for financial mismanagement, and a company's financial statement is the record. A CFO is responsible for more than management of a company's financial statement; a CFO is also responsible for a company's reputation. "A CFO sets the integrity bar in an organization" and, as such, can make or break a company's ability to raise and maintain the capital needed for expansion (Taub, 2007). Investors are one of the many "customers" of an organization's financial statement and are particularly concerned with transparency in compliance reporting.

IMPLICATIONS FOR INVESTORS

"Information regarding a company's earnings is one of the most important factors that many investors consider in making an investment decision, and it is essential that the information companies provide be clear and accurate," said Linda Chatman Thomsen, former director of the SEC's division of enforcement (Taylor, 2007).

An ongoing tug of war exists between businesses and investors regarding the amendment of rules on internal controls and procedures for financial reporting. In the wake of corporate accounting scandals, investor confidence was shaken in light of improprieties in financial reporting.

Investors may be one of the few groups that are actually fans of increased regulatory scrutiny for auditing and compliance. The more transparency available in financial reporting, the more likely investors are to loosen the purse strings.

Companies also realize that investors have raised the bar in terms of reporting on financial statements. Investors are holding companies liable for the accuracy of their reporting.

CFOs and other executives understand their role in regaining and maintaining investor confidence. Without access to (worldwide) capital, companies are at a strategic disadvantage. In dealing with investors, one CFO stated, "We get very high marks for our disclosure. We try to be a transparent company" (Taub, 2007).

It may not be necessary for executives to tie every action to the bottom line. "Most investor rating services include an assessment of the control environment as a part of their overall evaluation of the company. Scores from these services can have a significant impact—either positive or negative—on investor sentiment and the company's cost of capital" (Wagner & Dittmer, 2006).

CONCLUSION

Financial statements document the overall financial status of an organization and include information about assets, liabilities, revenue, and expenses. This essay focused on the trends in accounting and auditing standards that are influenced by globalization. Customers, collaborators, and capital sources are increasingly "borderless" in the global economy. American companies need to adapt to international standards in accounting practices to manage non-American subsidiaries, and to gain access to foreign capital. Good compliance practices, financial disclosure, and transparency are also required to partake in global business and attract much needed investment money.

The role of the CFO is multifaceted and is one of the most strategic roles within an organization. CFOs are responsible for setting the vision of an organization, for gaining investor confidence, and for overseeing regulatory policies. A company's financial statements can be equated to an annual physical, which shows how well the company has functioned as a holistic entity and how likely it is to grow and thrive in the future.

BIBLIOGRAPHY

D. A. (2007). US moves to accept IFRS accounting. *International Financial Law Review, 26*(6), 11-11. Retrieved August 16, 2007, from EBSCO Online Database

Business Source Premier. http://search.ebscohost. com/ login.aspx?direct=true&db=buh&AN=2555 6711&site=eh ost-live

Fargher, N., & Gramling, A. (2005). Toward improved internal controls. *CPA Journal, 75*(6), 26-29. Retrieved August 16, 2007, from EBSCO Online Database Business Source Premier. http:// search.ebscohost.com/login.aspx?direct=tru e&db=buh&AN=17869833&site=ehost-live

Hansen, F. (2007). Convergence come together. *Business Finance, 13*(3), 16-19. Retrieved August 16, 2007, from EBSCO Online Database Business Source Complete. http://search.ebscohost.com/login.aspx?direct=true&db=bt h&AN=24519956&site=ehost-live

Harper, D. (n.d.) Financial statements introduction. *Investopedia* .Retrieved August 16, 2007, from http:// www.investopedia.com/university/financialstatements/ default.asp

IASPlus. (2013). Japan. *IASPlus.com*. Retrieved November 24, 2013, from http://www.iasplus.com/ en/jurisdictions/asia/ japan

Johnson, S. (2007). What if IFRS replaced GAAP? *CFO.com*. Retrieved August 16, 2007, from http://www.cfo.com/ article. cfm/9634508/c%5f2984368?f=singlepage

Leone, M. (2006). SarbOx Burdens Prompt CFO Job Churn. *CFO.com*. Retrieved August 20, 2007, from http://www. cfo.com/article. cfm/7051704/c%5f2984409

Libby, R., & Brown, T. (2013). Financial statement disaggregation decisions and auditors' tolerance for misstatement. *Accounting Review, 88*(2), 641-665. Retrieved November 15, 2013, from EBSCO

Online Database Business Source Complete. http://search.ebscohost.com/login.aspx?direct=true&db=bth&AN=86040372&site=ehost-live

Nagel, K. (2002). Sarbanes-Oxley financial and accounting disclosure information. Retrieved August 20, 2007, from http://www.sarbanes-oxley.com/section.php

SEC establishes advisory committee. (2007, June). *ComplyNet*, 21. Retrieved August 16, 2007, from EBSCO Online Database Business Source Complete. http://search.ebscohost.com/login.aspx?direct=true&db=bth&AN=25900730&site=ehost-live

SEC. (2007). Beginner's guide to Financial Statements. *US Securities and Exchange Comission.*. Retrieved August 15, 2007, from http://www.sec.gov/investor/pubs/begfinstmtguide.htm

Taub, S. (2007). The toughest job in corporate America. *Institutional Investor, 41*(2), 37-44. Retrieved August 16, 2007, from EBSCO Online Database Business Source Premier. http://search.ebscohost.com/login.aspx?direct=true&db=buh&AN=24202687&site=ehost-live

Taylor, C. (2007). SEC: IBM withheld earnings info, misled investors. *Electronic News, 53*(24), 21-21. Retrieved August 16, 2007, from EBSCO Online Database Academic Search Premier. http://search.ebscohost.com/login.aspx?direct=true&db=aph&AN=25487252&site=ehost-live

Wagner, S., & Dittmar, L. (2006). The unexpected benefits of Sarbanes-Oxley. *Harvard Business Review, 84*(4), 133-140. Retrieved August 16, 2007, from EBSCO Online Database Business Source Premier. http://search.ebscohost.com/login.aspx?direct=true&db=buh&AN=19998923&site=ehost-live

Ward, S.P., & Ward, D.R. (2013). A proposed new vision for financial statements: A primer for non-financial executives. *Business Studies Journal, 5*(1), 77-94. Retrieved November 15, 2013, from EBSCO Online Database Business Source Complete. http://search.ebscohost.com/login.aspx?direct=true&db=bth&AN=87717982&site=ehost-live

Woellert, L. (2006, December 5). The SEC opens up SarbOx. *Business Week Online*, 1. Retrieved August 16, 2007, from EBSCO Online Database Academic Search Premier. http://search.ebscohost.com/login.aspx?direct=true&db=aph&AN=23365473&site=ehost-live

SUGGESTED READING

Accounting & auditing. (2007). *Practical Accountant, 40*(8), 21-22. Retrieved August 15, 2007, from EBSCO Online Database Business Source Premier. http://search.ebscohost.com/login.aspx?direct=true&db=buh&AN=26011587&site=ehost-live

Brodkin, J. (2007). SOX: Five years of headaches. *Network World, 24*(29), 1-16. Retrieved August 16, 2007, from EBSCO Online Database Business Source Premier. http://search.ebscohost.com/login.aspx?direct=true&db=buh&AN=25985000&site=ehost-live

Carlino, B. (2007). Who needs GAAP? *Accounting Today, 21*(13), 1-30. Retrieved August 15, 2007, from EBSCO Online Database Business Source Premier. http://search.ebscohost.com/login.aspx?direct=true&db=buh&AN=25898455&site=ehost-live

Government Accounting Standards Board. (2006; rev. 2013). Why governmental accounting and financial reporting is-and should be-different. Retrieved November 24, 2013, from http://www.gasb.org/cs/ContentServer?c=Document %5FC&pagename=GASB%2FDocument%5FC%2FGASBDocumentPage&cid=1176162354189

Miller, R. (2007). Implementing the new internal control audit standards the time is now. Are you ready? *Sum News, 18*(3), 18-21. Retrieved August 16, 2007, from EBSCO Online Database Business Source Complete. http://search.ebscohost.com/login.aspx?direct=true&db=bth&AN=25753382&site=ehost-live

Tysiac, K. (2013). New mechanisms eyed by FASB, IASB in long march toward global comparability. *Journal of Accountancy* (November, 2013). Retrieved November 24, 2013, from http://www.journalofaccountancy.com/News/20137119.htm

—Carolyn Sprague

FINANCING THE CORPORATION

ABSTRACT

This article focuses on how to finance a corporation. One of the greatest challenges for new ventures is the ability to secure capital that will allow the corporation to grow. There is no magic formula, and the management team will need to evaluate and assess which options are beneficial for the company. Each business will need to weigh the pros and cons of each option in order to determine what would be best. There are two options that these businesses may consider. The two types of financing - debt financing and equity capital - are explored. The role of commercial banks, the Small Business Administration, angel investors, and venture capitalists is introduced and discussed.

OVERVIEW

Corporations believe in the success of their dream, and they expect their ventures to take off and expand. One of the greatest challenges for new ventures is the ability to secure capital for investments that will allow the company to grow. All projects will reach a crossroad where sufficient cash flow is necessary in order to go to the next level. It could be after a period of time or it could be because the venture was so popular and the company is growing at a rapid rate due to demand. Regardless of the situation, the company's management team will need to determine when and how they will invest in the future through, for example, purchasing new equipment, hiring new staff or putting more money into marketing initiatives. Raising money can be a difficult task if the company has not established a reputation or is still new.

When determining the amount of capital needed, the decision makers must analyze the situation and decide how much and what type of capital is required. Since the situation is not the same for all businesses, there is no magical formula. Some businesses may only need short term financing for items such as salaries and inventory; whereas, other businesses may need long term financing for major items such as office space and equipment. Each business must develop a customized plan that will meet its unique needs.

Securing capital is a choice made after weighing the pros and cons of various options. There are three popular sources for obtaining funding for new ventures: borrowing from financial institutions, partnering with venture capitalists, and selling equity and possession in order to obtain a share of the revenue (Goel & Hasan, 2004). All financing options can be classified into two categories: debt financing and equity capital.

- Debt financing may include bank loans, personal and family contributions and financing from agencies such as the Small Business Administration. Loans are often secured by some type of collateral in the company and are paid off over a period of time with interest.
- On the other hand, venture capitalists and angel investors provide funding in the form of equity capital.

Pierce (2005) offers some advice which may be of assistance when assessing which option may be best for the company. Some of the tips include:

- A Small Business Administration program may not be the best option if the company needs less than $50,000.
- Debt financing is often less expensive and easier to obtain than equity capital. Financing the venture via debt entails the responsibility of making monthly payments regardless of whether the business has an affirmative cash flow.
- Equity investors assume that there will be very little return during the beginning stages of the profession, but need additional research about the business' development. In addition, they assume that the company will definitely succeed in achieving the aforementioned aims and objectives.
- Debt financing is often offered to all forms of corporations. However, equity capital tends to be reserved for companies with quick and significant growth potential.
- Angel investors tend to invest money in companies that are within a 50-mile radius, and the amounts of funding tend to be in the range of $25,000 and $250,000. Angel investors may be companions, relatives, customers, suppliers, financial experts or even competitors.
- It is difficult to secure venture capital funding, even in a good economy.

TWO OPTIONS OF FINANCING

Debt financing and equity capital options both require the financial professionals of an organization to complete detailed documentation prior to the award of financing. The finance team should be prepared to produce quarterly balance sheets, background information on the company and projections.

DEBT FINANCING

COMMERCIAL BANKS

If the company cannot finance the expansion through personal investments, the management team will need to develop a business plan that meets the criteria for potential lenders. Commercial banks may be the first choice, especially if the owner has a relationship with a specific lender. Since traditional lenders tend to be conservative, good rapport and an established relationship will be beneficial when applying for a loan. According to the University of Maine's Cooperative Extension, a 1980 Wisconsin study of smaller corporations discovered that 25% of the companies that underwent the interview process were denied at first, but 75% of them were approved when they submitted their proposal to another group. It is important for potential borrowers to understand the mindset of potential lenders. Most lenders tend to focus on five important factors when deciding whether or not to extend credit, and business owners need to be prepared to address them. The five factors are:

- **Character** — what are your personal characteristics? Are you ethical and have a good reputation? Will you do everything possible to pay the loan back?
- **Capacity** — will your business be able to generate sufficient cash flow to pay the loan back? Do you have access to other income?
- **Collateral** — do you have collateral to cover the loan in the event the venture does not perform well? Is there a qualified individual willing to co-sign on the loan?
- **Conditions** — have you researched the environment to see if there are any circumstances that could negatively impact your business (i.e. nature of product, competition)? How will you deal with these situations if they arise?
- **Capital** — what are you personally willing to invest in the venture? Most lenders are not willing to invest in ventures if you have not made a major investment in the future of the project. Why should they invest in the venture if you are not willing or able to?

DEBT FINANCING: TO DIVERSIFY OR NOT?

Colla, Ippolito, and Li (2013), looking at debt structure using a newer, comprehensive database of types of debt employed by public U.S. firms, found that 85% of the sample firms borrow "predominantly with one type of debt, and the degree of debt specialization varies widely across different subsamples." Large, rated firms tend to diversify across multiple debt types, while small, unrated firms specialize in fewer types. The authors showed that firms employing few types of debt "have higher bankruptcy costs, are more opaque, and lack access to some segments of the debt markets" (Colla, Ippolito, & Li, 2013).

EQUITY CAPITAL

VENTURE CAPITALISTS

Venture capital is usually available for start-up companies with a product or idea that may be risky, but has a high potential of yielding above average profits. Funds are invested in ventures that have not been discovered. The money may come from wealthy individuals, government sponsored Small Business Investment Corporations (SBICs), insurance companies, and corporations. It is more difficult to obtain financing from venture capitalists. A company must provide a formal proposal such as a business plan so that the venture capitalist may conduct a thorough evaluation of the company's records. Venture capitalists only approve a small percentage of the proposals that they receive, and they tend to favor innovative technical ventures.

Funding may be invested throughout the company's life cycle with funding being provided at both the beginning and later stages of growth. Venture capitalists may invest at different stages. Some firms may invest before the idea has been fully developed while others may provide funding during the early stages of the company's life. However, there is a group of venture capitalists who specialize in assisting companies when they have reached the point when the company needs financing in order to expand the business.

ANGEL INVESTORS

Many firms receive some type of funding prior to seeking capital from venture capitalists. Angel

Investors have been identified as one source that entrepreneurs may reach out to for assistance (Gompers, 1995). "In a nationwide survey of more than 3,000 individual angel investors conducted by the Angel Capital Association, more than 96 percent predict they'll invest in at least one new company in 2007. Also, 77 percent expect to invest in three to nine startups, and five percent think they'll fund 10 or more new companies" (Edelhauser, 2007). This is good news for entrepreneurs with a dream.

Including angel investors in the early stages of financing could improve the changes of receiving venture capital financing. Madill, Haines and Rlding (2005) conducted a study with small businesses and found that "57% of the firms that had received angel investor financing had also received financing from venture capitalists. Firms that did not receive angel" investing in the early stages (approximately 10% of the firms in the study) did not obtain venture capital funding (Madill, et. al., 2005, "Abstract"). It appears that angel investor financing is a significant factor in obtaining venture capital funding. Since obtaining venture capital tends to be difficult, businesses can benefit from the contacts and experience of angel investors in order to prepare for a venture capital application and evaluation. The intervention of an angel investor may make the company appear more attractive to the venture capitalists.

Regardless of how a company decides to finance the venture, it will have to make an agreement that is beneficial to the investor since they are the ones providing the money. Therefore, it is important to select a choice that benefits the business in the long run. Initial decisions may set the tone for future deals. Advani (2006) has provided some recommendations to consider when determining what will work best. These suggestions include:

- **Don't give pro-rata rights to your first investors.** If your first investor is given pro-rata rights, chances are your future investors will want the same agreement. It would be wise to balance the needs of your early investors to protect their stake in the company with how attractive the company will be to future investors.
- **Avoid giving too many people the right to be overly involved.** If too many people are involved, it could create a bureaucracy and make it difficult for decisions to be made in a timely manner. In addition, the daily tasks of a business may be prolonged due

to the need for multiple authorization signatures.
- **Beware of any limits placed on management compensation.** Some investors may place a cap on the earning potential of senior management personnel. This type of action could create a problem with human resource needs such as attracting and hiring quality talent to run and grow the business.
- **Request a cure period.** Many investors will request representation for every legal agreement to protect themselves if the management of a company is not in compliance with laws, licenses, and regulations that govern the operation of the business. Although all parties may have good intentions, errors do occur. If a "cure period" is added to the financing agreement, the entrepreneur will have the opportunity to find a solution to the problem within a given period of time (i.e. two to four weeks).
- **Restrict your share restrictions.** Having unrestricted shares is often a good negotiating factor with future investors. Therefore, it would be wise to evaluate any requests to restrict the sale of shares owned by the founders and/or management team.

APPLICATION

TYPES OF CORPORATE VENTURING
The first corporate venture funds appeared in the mid-1960s, which was approximately 20 years following the first formation of the institutional venture capital funds (Gompers, 2002). "Since that time, corporate venturing has undergone three boom-or-bust cycles that closely track the independent venture capital sector" (Gompers, 2002, p. 2). It has been found that many corporations will consider entering the business venture market when the independent sector starts to show hints of achievement and prosperity (Gompers & Lerner, 1998).

Large corporations have shown an interest in venture capital investing over the years, and they tend to use many different means to achieve their clever and budgeting aims for venture capital investments. Gomper (2002) described three of these models, which are internal corporate venture group, dedicated external fund, and passive limited partner in a venture. What is involved with these three models? Some organizations will create an internal corporate venture group to assess venture capital options and invest successfully. Other corporations will put investment capital in a loyal fund that exists as a separate entity external to the organization. Finally, there are real venture funds that offer businesses the chance to be acquiescent, limited partners and perform diverse investments in ambitious corporations.

VIEWPOINT

FUNDING

In order to avoid a "backlash of no cash," a business may determine that selling shares of equity would be the best way to secure working capital. This alternative could alleviate some of

the stress associated with starting a new venture and provides the company an opportunity to grow at a quicker rate. However, the business will be required to give the investors some control and profits. Angel investors may want to take a role in the company, but the venture capitalists will probably want to remain in the background as a silent partner. If the venture is not successful, the investor loses. Therefore, angel investors and venture capitalists will probably require a higher return on investment than a conventional lender since the risks are greater.

TRENDS IN FINANCING

New ventures will continue to grow, and corporate management teams will need to look to the trends when determining how to finance. From about 2006 to 2008, the availability of financing and the cost of options changed. Advani (2006) provided a list of trends that might assist corporations in getting funding for new ventures at the time of his writing. The trends for start-up financing in 2007 were:

- Angel investing continued to grow. "There were about 250,000 angel investors in the United States investing in approximately 50,000 small companies each year," and this number was expected to continue to grow as angel investing became more popular (Advani, 2006, 2). One reason for the growth may have been the proposed tax incentives at the time that were to be provided to high-net-worth investors who privately invest.
- Valuations and investment terms were good. "The yield rate on angel investments (the rate at which investments presented to angels result in funding)

increased from 10 percent in 2003 to 23 percent in 2005. Pre-launch startup valuations involving first-time corporations escalated to more than $5 million. However, they were expected to stabilize at $2 million to $3 million in the future" (Advani, 2006, 4).

- Business credit scores supplemented personal credit scores. As of the mid-2000s, credit cards remained the most used form of capital for companies wanting to finance their debt. In the past, credit card companies made decisions based on the owner's personal credit history, but more recently many companies are using credit data on the business to make decisions. Business credit information may be collected from data banks such as the Small Business Financial Exchange (SBFE). Banks and other lenders utilize the information on the companies in conjunction with their supported instructions for businesses. Nearly every one of the top 20 banks in the United States was using this method as of about 2007.

- Getting $50,000 in funding continued to be difficult. According to the Global Corporationship Monitor, the average amount of start-up capital used by small businesses in industrialized countries was $53,000 as of the mid-2000s (Advani, 2006, 6). Unfortunately, most corporations could not secure $50,000 in credit card financing, and angel investors were usually not interested in companies where they were the only investor in businesses with insufficient working capital. In addition, programs, such as the Small Business Administration's Micro Loan Program, were facing cuts and so weren't being marketed by SBA lenders. However, nonprofit micro lenders were sometimes able to fill the gap. In the past, these lenders were not able to compete with banks, but as of the mid-2000s they were considering forming an alliance to more effectively convert credit bureau protocol to include performance of micro loans in credit scores. This action may make this option more attractive to corporations and small business owners.

In fact, Paul Quintero, CEO of microlender Accion East in New York, said in 2013 that although he lends to mom-and-pop business owners who typically do not qualify for bank loans, his hope is that banks will someday view microlending as a "viable line of business" (Kline, 2013). Accion's loan rates are attractive to potential borrowers at around 12% as of 2013, but "depository institutions, with their built-in funding advantages, could offer even lower rates, and Quintero would have no problem ceding business to them if it reduced customers' borrowing costs" (Kline, 2013).

- Low credit scores were no longer considered harmful to financing, but patient capital remained a significant obstruction to potential success. In the past, if a potential corporation did not have a high credit score, credit options were limited. Many used the equity in their homes in order to get a good rate. But Internet lenders and non-traditional one-on-one lenders have developed alternatives for businesses without high credit scores. Although the cost of the capital may be higher for those without a good credit score, options exist. Unfortunately, the lack of patient capital and long-term financing choices for companies with sub-prime credit presents problems. The interest rates that these companies charge can be very high and businesses may not be able to generate earnings while paying these rates.

As for venture-capital trends, venture capitalists invested $8.1 billion into 981 U.S.-based companies in the final quarter of 2012, according to Fortune.com and PitchBook Data (Primack, 2013). Those numbers show little change from the previous quarter and suggest that year-end 2013 totals will be a bit lower than in 2012. Furthermore, venture capitalists are "acquiring smaller and smaller stakes of portfolio companies upon investment, particularly on Series A deals. Back in 2004, VCs acquired 40% of a company on Series A rounds and 24% of a company on Series D rounds." For the first three quarters of 2013, those figures have fallen to 29% and 13%, respectively (Primack, 2013). Additionally, there have been more VC-backed IPOs in 2013 than in any other year since 2000 (Primack, 2013).

CONCLUSION

Corporations believe in the success of their dream, and they expect their ventures to take off and expand. One of the greatest challenges for new ventures is the ability to secure capital for investments that will allow the company to grow. All projects will reach a cross-road where sufficient cash flow is necessary in order

to go to the next level. It could be after a period of time or it could be because the venture was so popular and the company is growing at a rapid rate due to demand. Regardless of the situation, the company's management team will need to determine when and how they will invest in items such as purchasing new equipment, hiring new staff and putting more money into marketing initiatives. Raising money can be a difficult task if the company has not established a reputation or is still new.

Securing capital is a choice made after weighing the pros and cons of various options. There are three popular sources for obtaining funding for new ventures: Borrowing from financial institutions, partnering with venture capitalists, and selling equity/ownership in exchange for a share of the revenue (Goel & Hasan, 2004). All financing options can be classified into two categories — debt financing and equity capital.

Debt financing and equity capital options both require the financial professionals of an organization to complete detailed documentation prior to the award of financing. The finance team should be prepared to produce quarterly balance sheets, background information on the company and projections.

The first business venture funds were developed in the mid- 1960s, approximately 20 years following the formation of the first institutional venture capital funds (Gompers, 2002). "Since that time, corporate venturing has undergone three boom-or-bust cycles that closely track the independent venture capital sector" (Gompers, 2002, p. 2). It has been found that many corporations will consider entering the corporate venture market when the independent sector starts to show hints of capability and achievement (Gompers & Lerner, 1998).

In order to avoid a "backlash of no cash," a business may determine that selling shares of equity would be the best way to secure working capital. This alternative could alleviate some of the stress associated with starting a new venture as well as provide the company an opportunity to grow at a quicker rate. However, the business will be required to give the investors some control and profits. Angel investors may want to take a role in the company, but the venture capitalists will probably want to remain in the background as a silent partner. If the venture is not successful, the investor loses. Therefore, angel investors and venture capitalists will probably require a higher return on investment than a conventional lender since the risks are greater.

BIBLIOGRAPHY

Advani, A. (2006, November 10). Start-up financing trends for 2007. *Entrepreneur.com*. Retrieved April 9, 2007, from http://www.entrepreneur.com/money/financing/startupfinancingcolumnistasheeshadvani/article170218.html

Advani, A. (2006, October 12). Raising money from informal investors. *Entrepreneur.com*. Retrieved April 9, 2007, from http://www.entrepreneur.com/money/financing/ startupfinancingcolumnistasheeshadvani/article168860. html

Capital sources for your business. (2006). *University of Maine Cooperative Extension, Bulletin # 3008*. Retrieved April 9, 2007, from http://www.umext.maine.edu/onlinepubs/ htmpubs/3008.htm

Colla, P., Ippolito, F., & Li, K. (2013). Debt specialization. *Journal of Finance, 68*(5), 2117-2141. Retrieved November 24, 2013, from EBSCO Online Database Business Source Complete. http://search.ebscohost.com/login.aspx?direct=t rue&db=bth&AN=90167647&site=ehost-live

Edelhauser, K. (2007, April 11). Angel investing to grow in '07. *Entrepreneur.com*. Retrieved April 11, 2007, from http://www.entrepreneur.com/blog/entry/176926.html

Goel, R. K., & Hasan, I. (2004). Funding new ventures: Some strategies for raising early finance. *Applied Financial Economics, 14*(11), 773-778. Retrieved on April 9, 2007, from EBSCO Online Database Business Source Complete. http://search.ebscohost.com/login.aspx?direct=t rue&db=bth&AN=13867653&site=ehost-live

Gompers, P. A. (1995). Optimal investment, monitoring, and the staging of venture capital. *Journal of Finance, 50*(5), 1461-1490. Retrieved on April 9, 2007, from EBSCO Online Database Business Source Complete. http://search. ebscohost.com/login.aspx?direct=true&db=bth&AN=9601 031352&site=ehost-live

Gompers, P. (2002). Corporations and the financing of innovation: The corporate venturing experience. *Economic Review, 87*(4), 1. Retrieved October 24, 2007, from EBSCO Online Database Business Source Complete. http://search.ebscohost.com/login.aspx?direct=true&db=bt h&AN=8969400&site=ehost-live

Gompers, P., & Lerner, J. (1996). The use of covenants: An empirical analysis of venture partnership agreements. *Journal of Law & Economics, 39*(2), 463-498. Retrieved October 16, 2007, from EBSCO Online Database Business Source Complete. http://search.ebscohost.com/login.aspx? direct= true&db=bth&AN=11511897&site=ehost-live

Kline, A. (2013). Banks urged to team up with micro-lenders. *American Banker, 178*(165), 13. Retrieved November 24, 2013, from EBSCO Online Database Business Source Complete. http://search. ebscohost.com/login.aspx?direct=t rue&db=bth& AN=91684938&site=ehost-live

Madill, J., Haines Jr., G., & Rlding, A. (2005). The role of angels in technology SMEs: A link to venture capital. *Venture Capital, 7*(2), 107-129. Retrieved April 14, 2007, from EBSCO Online Database Business Source Complete. http://search. ebscohost.com/login.aspx?direct=t rue&db=bth& AN=16968283&site=ehost-live

Pierce, C. (2005). How to prepare and present a successful business funding request. Retrieved April 10, 2007, from http://www.businessfinance.com/books/workbook.pdf

Primack, D. (2013). Behind the VC numbers: higher prices, less control. *Fortune.com*, 1. Retrieved November 24, 2013, from EBSCO Online Database Business Source Complete. http://search.ebscohost.com/login.aspx?direct=t rue&db=bth&AN=9 1541840&site=ehost-live

SUGGESTED READING

Atanasova, C. (2007). Access to institutional finance and the use of trade credit. *Financial Management (2000), 36*(1), 49-67. Retrieved October 25, 2007, from EBSCO Online Database Business Source Complete.

Claessens, S., & Tzioumis, K. (2006). Ownership and financing structures of listed and large non-listed corporations. *Corporate Governance: An International Review, 14*(4), 266-276. Retrieved October 16, 2007, from EBSCO Online Database Business Source Complete. http://search. ebscohost. com/login.aspx?direct=true&db=bth&AN=2143 7470&site=ehost-live

O'Leary, C. (2004). Corporate financing thrives amid modest rate hikes. *Bank Loan Report, 19*(38), 1-11. Retrieved October 16, 2007, from EBSCO Online Database Business Source Complete. http://

search.ebscohost.com/login.aspx? direct=true&db=bth&AN=14613650&site=ehost-live

Platt, G. (2006). Corporate financing focus: Fed's shift from automatic to neutral leaves next move up in the air, analysts say. *Global Finance, 20*(6), 65-67. Retrieved October 25, 2007, from EBSCO

Online Database Business Source Complete. http://search.ebscohost.com/login.aspx?direct=true&db=bth&AN=21276386&site=ehost-live

–Marie Gould

FIXED INCOME SECURITIES & ECONOMICS

ABSTRACT

A main purpose of this essay is to convey information relevant to the exchange of a specific type of debt instrument. Factors under consideration herein center on gains that may accrue whether a holder buys, sells, or keeps the instrument. With respect to exchanges of debt, timing may be everything and certainly some times are better for some actions than are other times. One feature is the relationships between security price and other financial market variables including interest rates. This essay focuses its attention mostly on risk-free bonds, which the federal government buys and sells on a daily basis and in cycles. Open market operations, as a monetary policy tool, are used on a daily basis often influencing domestic and global economies. The essay approaches the topic from a broad perspective, but it may yield benefits for those readers who want consider adding fixed income securities to their investment portfolio.

OVERVIEW

This essay condenses the basic concepts regarding fixed income securities and applies them in a manner that is relevant to the reader. The essay targets undergraduate college students as readers who may benefit from an initial condensed summary on a specific type of a fixed income security; namely those securities issued by the federal government of the United States. Persons around the globe hold a significant portion of those securities. While the essay ultimately approaches the topic from a broad domestic macroeconomic perspective, its contents may be instrumental in helping readers reap some financial gain from their own investment activities.

As a concise introduction to the topic, the government securities referred to herein are virtually default free and they pay holders a fixed amount of income in the form of interest payments. Readers should note, however, several varieties of securities are available through the financial market, which consist of individuals who exchange quantities of debt instruments at given interest rates. The interest rate and some other key requirements regarding the exchange of funds are expressed in a variety of ways. A private borrowing agreement governs loans whereas a public agreement governs bonds. Loan transactions usually involve a few individuals such as the lender, the borrower, and perhaps a co-signer.

BONDS

Bond transactions however usually involve the public at large. Moreover, almost any bond sold is one from a set of bonds called a bond issue. The total amount of a bond issue may range in value from tens to hundreds of millions of dollars. An objective of a bond issuer is to borrow funds in large bundles from individual members of larger society. Bond issues may originate from corporations or local, state, or federal government agencies. A sequential process begins as bond issuers receive cash from each bond sold. Those who purchase a bond will receive interest payments on a regular basis until the date arrives at which the issuer returns cash to the buyer.

A security is a specialized form of bond. Nonetheless, readers will find them used interchangeably in the remainder of this essay. A house mortgage is one example of a bond secured through market value of the property and income of the borrower. While maintaining a clear distinction between loans and bonds, readers may find it convenient to think of a security as resembling a loan that has enough collateral to satisfy all the terms in an agreement. In brief, collateral effectively lessens the potential negative financial exposure faced by lenders or bond holders. Securities or bonds issued by the federal government are virtually a default-free and a risk-free loan given the expectation that the issuer will be fiscally solvent and perpetually functional beyond the foreseeable future and across a countless number of generations.

STOCKS VS. BONDS

Another important distinction is appropriate at this point. It arises because references to stocks and bonds often give the appearance that they are interchangeable terms. Substantive distinctions exist between them though they share at least one common feature relevant to this essay. A stock involves taking equity or partial ownership in a company, which is exchanged on a daily basis in the stock market through sales and purchases. In contrast, as mentioned before, a bond resembles a loan. Typically, the bond holder owns only the debt it represents. On occasion, the issuer of corporate bonds will allow for their conversion into stocks, which means trading organization debt for organization equity or ownership. A far more common feature between stocks and bonds resides with the practice of purchasing them at the lowest price possible and then selling them at the highest price possible.

Generally, the expectation is that bonds act "primarily as a stabilizer" for portfolios; their role is to protect principal, "offer reasonable income with modest volatility, and serve as a diversifier of the more volatile equity allocation" (Co-published chapter: A different future for fixed income, 2013). Interestingly, between 2001 and 2011, a time during which "equities lost ground while bonds soared 9% a year" (Lim, 2011), "fear and greed worked together to send money pouring into bonds." Two-thirds of a trillion dollars flowed into bond mutual funds from the start of 2009 to the time of Lim's writing, in 2011, which represented more money than all stock funds attracted during the Internet bubble of 1998 to 2000 (Lim, 2011).

FIXED INCOME SECURITIES

BASIC COMPONENTS

With the aforementioned distinctions and clarifications, we are now ready to examine fixed income securities in more detail. Fixed income securities contain three basic components according to Strumeyer (2005). This section describes those components and

it provides a foundation for their application in a larger economic context.

- First is the coupon rate which specifies the security's interest payment.
- Second is maturity which specifies the security's term of investment.
- Last is the price or yield which specifies the security's market value.

BOND PRICING & EXCHANGES

The price of a bond generally reflects the time value of money, which means that a dollar today is worth more than a dollar tomorrow; conversely, a dollar received later is worth less than one in hand today. Furthermore, the present value of that dollar is likely to be less than its future value unless the loan period and the interest rate provide adequate compensation to the lender. Let us consider some additional terminology and basic mathematical calculations regarding bond pricing and exchanges.

Bonds are available in various denominations. An amount common to public issues of bonds is the $10,000 denomination. It represents the bond's face value, which by definition is the amount borrowed or the principal amount. In essence, individual members of the public can purchase the bond by providing $10,000 in cash to the bond issuer. By doing so, the issuer promises to return that sum of cash at a later point in time and to pay interest on that cash between now and then. Repayment of the $10,000 will occur on a specific date in the future, which by definition is the bond's maturity date. More precisely, payments of the principal amount and the last interest payment occur at maturity, but the bond holder receives interest payments every six months during that investment period. The amount of interest paid on an annual basis to the bond holder is by definition a form of fixed income.

ISSUANCE & PURCHASE OF BONDS

Consider now what happens over time with the issuance and purchase of bonds. Let us begin by examining the hypothetical case of a bond bought on this date last year for $10,000. It promises to pay the purchaser or holder $1,000 per year in interest until maturity. By definition, the income payment on a bond is a coupon and the interest rate for a bond is its coupon rate. Exactly one year later, the issuance of another $10,000 bond contains an $800 coupon.

In a basic sense, interest rates declined over the year from 10 percent ($1,000/$10,000) to 8 percent ($800/$10,000).

Next readers face the question: If the holder wants to sell the bond bought last year, what price is it likely to receive today? Armed with the general knowledge that an inverse relationship exists between bond prices and interest rates, we will find the bond fetching a price higher than the original amount. Now, let's do the math. The annual promise is $1,000 and the current interest rate is 8 percent. We expect the price of the older bond to be around $12,500, which is the result from dividing the promise amount by the current interest rate ($1,000/0.08). Publication of the price at which a bond sells at maturity is in the form of a ratio per $1,000 of the denomination or face value; by definition this is its par value. The aforementioned bond sold with a par value of 1.250 ($12,500/$10,000).

RATE OF RETURN

Bond market conditions change and sometimes traders pay higher prices for bonds. In general, this affects the yield, which by definition is a rate of return measure, because the par and coupon rates are fixed. Yields change over time with market conditions and investors can use them to estimate the expected rate of return. Specifically, an increase in a bond's price, which is determined within the financial market, reduces a bond's yield. Note that the calculation of yield involves estimating the present values of benefits and of costs and setting the net present value to zero.

A few commitments of terms and relationships to memory may help investors know when to sell and/or to buy bonds, fixed income securities, and the like. Perhaps more important is gauging what happens, or what one expects to occur, between the instrument purchase point and its sale point. In essence, the rate of return for the holding period is the result of two opposing influences. On the one hand, a decrease (increase) in financial market interest rates affects the rate of return and it increases (decreases) price. On the other hand, an increase in price also affects the rate of return but it generates capital gains. Readers may begin to appreciate the complexities associated with decisions of whether to buy or sell debt instruments and whether to opt for holding onto their cash. All told, considering the opportunity cost

for a bond requires taking into account various factors including risk comparability. The terms from above provide a foundation for examining possible decisions that bond holders face and for applying them in a variety of ways.

APPLICATIONS

Some financial gain may accrue to the holder whether the bond is sold or it is kept. First, the holder is likely to receive a greater amount of interest than possible if the funds were to remain in a savings account. Second, the return is likely to be greater than the expected annual rate of inflation, which usually hovers around three percent. Third, the holder is currently in a position to sell the bond at a price higher than its purchase. In brief, a decline in interest rates since the bond's purchase signifies an increase in its price. Much like most other commercial exchanges, a key objective is to buy when the price is as low as one would expect and to contemplate its sale when the price is as high as one would expect.

A KEY RELATIONSHIP: RISK & RETURN

As a minor point of departure considering this essay's treatment of risk-free bonds, let's enter risk into the calculus for a brief moment before directing attention toward additional aspects of those bonds. A general positive or direct relationship is common in matters of economics and finance: A low (high) risk translates into a low (high) return and/or a low (high) interest rate; in the banking industry, for example, lenders charge low-risk borrowers a low rate of interest. Readers should be aware that bonds or securities omitted from this essay may vary in the amount of actual or potential risk and in the sources of risk. More precisely, risk is an expression of the likelihood that the issuer will abandon the agreement and/or cease to make timely payments.

ASSESSING RISK

The issue of risk seems to beg the question: How does one assess the degree of risk? On the conceptual side of this assessment matter, one valid, reliable, and simple method is to compare a default-free minimal-risk bond such as a government security to another type of fixed income security on their interest or coupon rates. The difference between the rates is a good rough estimate of the amount of risk attached to the investment. If the coupon rate on a government bond is 10 percent and it is 20 percent on a corporate bond, then one may conclude that the risk approximates 10 percent. Certainly, risk and uncertainty are items for consideration in contemplating what markets may present for corporate operations and the quality of the corporation's credit; they are beyond the scope of this essay, but they are topics that a prospective buyer needs to examine and understand. On the practical side of the matter, most issuers obtain ratings for their bonds from independent sources. Various rating schemes are expressed and found in books and other publications.

With a basic knowledge of fundamentals regarding bonds and especially fixed income securities, it is time to shift reader attention to the larger context of security exchanges and their possible effects on the state of a domestic economy. Those exchanges are also relevant to the global economy because individuals who reside in other countries own a significant portion of debt issued by the government of the United States. For instance, foreign entities hold more than one-third of that debt in terms of their total dollar value (Guell, 2007). This fact alone highlights the public context and global nature of security exchanges. As topics beyond this essay's immediate scope and depth, readers again receive encouragement to consult various publications on international trade, macroeconomics, and money and banking; they are rich sources of information about the complex interrelationships among interest rates, foreign exchange rates, and a host of other factors.

Authors of introductory textbooks in economics (Arnold, 200n; Guell, 2007; McConnell & Brue) point out that, in the broadest sense possible, the federal government occasionally borrows internally from a few of its affiliated agencies. Beginning with the next section, the remainder of this essay elaborates on some mechanics of those actions. As a preface to those elaborations, readers need to keep in mind that the benefits of most actions usually accrue long after the initial expenditures. In any given year, the expenditures of the federal government will likely exceed its tax revenues thereby generating a need to find ways to finance its budgetary deficits; infrequently, there is a budgetary surplus. By the way, the US national debt is an accumulation over time of federal government budget deficits and surpluses.

GOVERNMENTAL BUDGETS & DEBT EXCHANGE METHODS

The federal government buys and sells fixed income securities in a series of ongoing cycles. In the first cycle, the government collects cash as a result from their sales of securities to the public and deposits it with the U.S. Department of Treasury. Those members of the public who purchase them in effect become debt owners or bond holders. In a subsequent cycle, these holders will present them for cash as the securities mature. The federal government becomes the owner of those securities as it provides cash in return for them. The primary source of that cash is the U.S. Treasury because it buys them at maturity. In short, the federal government sells the debt it owns to the public via transfers to the treasury.

These transfer and exchanges are part of an even larger chain of daily events as dollars trade hands and cycle through the economy in the form of bank deposits and withdrawals. The Federal Reserve Bank conducts operations on a daily basis in which it coordinates publicly the sales and the purchases of securities. As the reader will discover in the forthcoming subsections of this essay, those operations partially determine and alter the nation's supply of money and the financial market's rate of interest. Before we enter those discussions, readers will receive an introduction of how the federal government borrows from itself.

The federal government can avoid direct engagement in the financial market by accessing the revenue collections of some of its agencies. The revenues of those agencies usually exceed their expenditures. Their net revenues originate through payroll taxes such as Social Security and Medicare and through the operations of the Postal Service. In brief, they hold funds that other agencies within the federal government can borrow; a major ongoing debate surrounds the issue of what will happen when the Social Security Administration's surpluses begin to disappear around 2010 as a large segment of the nation's population retires and begins to collect retirement benefits. From a historical perspective, casting the current debate aside, those funds allowed the government to borrow fewer dollars directly from the public via bond issuances.

OPEN MARKET OPERATIONS: MONEY SUPPLY & INTEREST RATE DYNAMICS

Open market operations entails the buying and selling of government securities. Conducted on a daily basis, it is one of the tools of federal monetary policy and it often influences market interest rates. As we move toward closure of this essay, here's a brief synopsis of how that entire process unfolds. On the one hand, a security sale means that buyers pay cash by withdrawing funds from their own bank accounts. Cash withdrawals act to reduce bank balances and the amount of money that banks can loan to businesses and to households. Consequently, there is a reduction in the amount of cash in circulation and the supply of money within the economy. In effect, that supply reduction drives interest rates upward. On the other hand, a security purchase means that debt instrument holders sell them and receive cash. The effects are in reverse of those mentioned above. Cash receipts act to increase bank balances and the money supply, driving interest rates downward.

CONCLUSION

This essay condenses the basic concepts regarding fixed income securities and applies them in a manner that is appealing to varied audiences. It targets undergraduate college students as readers who can gain some ground by examining a specific type of a fixed income security. The focal point is those securities issued by the federal government of the United States. It is interesting that persons residing in other countries all around the globe choose to hold these securities. In conclusion, the essay approaches the topic from a broad perspective and it may prove useful in helping some readers reap more financial gain from their own investments. Indeed, the few years leading up to 2013 saw dramatic shifts in investment flows from equity into fixed income, with fixed income viewed as a safe bet (Dubil, 2013). Ken Taubes, head of investment management U.S. at Pioneer Global Asset Management SpA as of 2013, agrees, stating, "Tepid economic growth over the past few years coupled with volatile equity markets has driven many investors to the perceived safe haven of fixed income" (Co-published chapter: A different future for fixed income, 2013).

BIBLIOGRAPHY

Arnold, R.A. (2005). *Economics* (7th ed.) Mason, OH: Thomson South-Western.

Choudhury, M. (2005). *Fixed-income securities and derivatives.* Princeton: NJ: Bloomberg Press.

Co-published chapter: A different future for fixed income. (2013). *Asian Investor*, 1. Retrieved November 22, 2013, from EBSCO Online Database Business Source Complete. http://search.ebscohost.com/login.aspx?direct=t rue&db=bth&AN=9 0616665&site=ehost-live

Dubil, R. (2013). Make callable bonds part of your fixed income allocation. *Journal of Financial Planning*, *26*(3), 54-60. Retrieved November 22, 2013, from EBSCO Online Database Business Source Complete. http://search. ebscohost. com/login.aspx?direct=true&db=bth&AN=864 45559&site=ehost-live

Guell, R. C. (2007). *Issues in economics today* (3rd ed.). Boston, MA: McGraw-Hill Irwin.

Lim, P.J. (2011). Stop gobbling up bonds. *Money*, *40*(1), 118?128. Retrieved November 22, 2013, from EBSCO Online Database Business Source Complete. http://search. ebscohost.com/ login.aspx?direct=true&db=bth&AN=572 26845&site=ehost-live

McConnell, C. R. & Brue, S. L. (2008). *Economics* (17th ed.). Boston, MA: McGraw-Hill Irwin.

Strumeyer, G. (2005). *Investing in fixed income securities.* Hoboken: NJ: John Wiley & Sons, Inc.

SUGGESTED READING

Clarke, R., de Silva, H., & Murdock, R. (2005). A factor approach to asset allocation. *Journal of Portfolio Management*, *32*(1), 10-21. Retrieved October 12, 2007, from EBSCO Online Database Business Source Premier. http://search. ebscohost.com/login.aspx?direct=true&db=b uh&AN=21880057&site=ehost-live

Fabozzi, F. J. (2007). *Fixed income analysis.* Hoboken: NJ: John Wiley & Sons, Inc.

Herold, U., Maurer, R., & Purschaker, N. (2005). Total return fixed-income portfolio management. *Journal of Portfolio Management, 31*(3), 32-43. Retrieved October 12, 2007, from EBSCO Online Database Business Source Premier. http://search.ebscohost.com/login.aspx?direct=true&db=buh&AN=16975630&site=ehost-live

Johnson, R., Zuber, R., & Gandar, J. (2006). Binomial pricing of fixed-income securities for increasing and decreasing interest rate cases. *Applied Financial Economics, 16*(14), 1029-1046. Retrieved October 12, 2007, from EBSCO Online Database Business Source Premier. http://search. ebscohost. com/login.aspx?direct=true&db=buh&AN=22483109&site=ehost-live

Schellhorn, C., & Lushbough, S. (2005). Managing the maturity of fixed-income investments in rising interest-rate environments. *Journal of Financial Planning, 18*(9), 62-68. Retrieved October 12, 2007, from EBSCO Online Database Business Source Premier. http://search.ebscohost.com/login.aspx?direct=true&db=buh&AN=17857447&site=ehost-live

–Steven R. Hoagland

Interest Rates

ABSTRACT

This paper will take an in-depth look at interest rates. Interest rates remain an integral part of the modern economic institution. As the global economy continues to develop and integrate, leaders and analysts consistently look to interest rates as both a vital indicator of that system's health and a useful vehicle by which it may remain healthy. The paper provides a summary of interest's historical development, current characteristics and impact on economic systems; the reader will glean a better understanding of the significance interest rates have as part of the fiscal and economic commercial field of the 21st century.

OVERVIEW

Lending and borrowing is a formalized, complex, and often daunting process. Still, the practices of lending and credit have been part of human commerce for millennia, although they have evolved considerably during that historical course. In the modern world, lending and borrowing entail such concepts as credit ratings, collateral, assets, and debts.

Two factors to consider when lending and borrowing are time and return. On one hand, the lender seeks to have his or her loan returned as soon as possible (the borrower also hopes to pay off the loan as quickly as he or she can). On the other, the lender's return on that loan must be of value to the lender, reimbursing him or her for the loan as well as the time it took to repay the debt. The primary vehicle used to address these two aspects is interest. The health of an economy's credit and lending systems is vital to short-term and long-term productivity and growth. For this reason, the rate at which interest is applied is integral to both understanding economic trends and, where necessary, correcting negative economic conditions.

This paper will take an in-depth look at interest rates. By providing a summary of interest's historical development, its current characteristics, and its impact on economic systems, the reader will gain a better understanding of the significance interest rates have as part of the fiscal and economic systems of the twenty-first century.

LENDING & INTEREST: AN INTRODUCTION

Lending and borrowing date back as far as prehistoric times, before formalized systems of trade and barter were established. One individual, for example, might lend some seed to his or her neighbor or family member, with the promise that the borrower would return the debt once the fall harvest took place. Of course, a considerable amount of time would transpire between the day the loan was given and the day the loan was repaid, and in light of that fact, some sort of agreement needed to be established whereby the lender was compensated for both the original sum and the time it took for him to receive repayment. This agreement more often than not involved the borrower repaying the debt and adding to that repayment more of his or her harvest than he or she had borrowed (Homer & Sylla, 1964).

Such "contracts" represent the earliest forms of interest payments. Interest is, in essence, the price a person pays for borrowing. Because it entails a repayment that is more than the original sum lent, the money involved is also considered a form of equity for the lender. Typically, the interest rate is determined during the establishment of the loan. Interest rates are expressed as a percentage of the money that is owed over the course of the loan, so that the longer a borrower does not pay his or her debt in full, the more s/he will have to pay over the course of the loan.

SIMPLE & COMPOUND INTEREST

Interest is usually divided into two categories: simple and compound. Simple interest adds the interest to the principal (the amount of money originally lent) at the end of the year. For example, a bank that loans $10,000 to a customer might apply a 5 percent simple interest rate. At the end of the year, if the individual has not paid against the principal, he or she would owe $10,000 plus $500 (or 5 percent of the principal), and every year subsequent, $500 would be applied. Compound interest is a more common type of interest, applying the interest to the principal over the course of the loan. For example, the same $10,000 loan would, at the end of the year, have $500 in compounded interest added to it; however, in the subsequent year, the principal would total $10,500 and the interest would be $525, which is 5 percent of $10,500 ("Flexo," 2009).

INTEREST RATE

Central to the calculation of interest is the interest rate, which is normally seen as an annual percentage of the principal involved. Interest rates are determined by dividing the amount of interest by the amount of principal. Of course, there are a number of external elements that can affect the rate at which interest is accrued. Chief among them is the government, which determines the parameters by which interest rates may be applied. The US federal government, for example, assesses the US economy for signs of inflation, deflation, stagnation, recession, and other issues, and raises or lowers interest rates in response to those conditions.

The application of interest rates depends on conditions in the economic system in which the lending occurs. It is therefore important to present a brief history of interest rates and the conditions that can affect such rates over the short and long periods of time.

FURTHER INSIGHTS

INTEREST RATES & THE GREAT DEPRESSION

In the 1920s, the US stock market was skyrocketing. Prices were rapidly increasing as investors took part in the countless opportunities Wall Street had to offer. In 1928 and 1929, however, the federal government became concerned that these astronomical prices were overinflating the market and, as a result, ran the risk of creating a financial bubble. The newly established Federal Reserve's response was to attempt to cool off the market's growth by discouraging stock speculation and lending by making it more expensive to borrow funds through an increase in interest rates.

The theory seemed sound at the time; working to keep legitimate investors involved in the market while discouraging those who did not appreciate the risks of investment. However, in practice, the policy proved overly obstructive, as far more investors stayed out of the market, causing a precipitous drop in prices that began before the chaos that ensued on Black Tuesday, the day in 1929 when the entire market collapsed.

The Federal Reserve again did little to lower interest rates, which further contributed to the ongoing disaster that was the Great Depression. Monetary value decreased significantly and banks became aware that any loan issued would see a high risk of default because of a loss of principal. The Depression lasted even longer than originally anticipated as a recession, due in no small part to the fact that the federal government sought to use it to clear away what it saw as toxic elements of the economy. Even as credit and lending froze, high interest rates were the primary mechanism toward this end (DeLong, 1997).

When Franklin D. Roosevelt assumed the presidency in 1933, interest rates had come down to nearly zero, as the value of the dollar was at negligible levels and lending was at a virtual standstill. The low interest rates caused an increase in interest-sensitive spending on durable goods, such as car sales, while consumer spending on services remained stagnant (Romer, 2009), a rare bright spot in an otherwise bleak economic environment.

The example of the Great Depression points to two interesting points pertaining to interest rates. First, they may be set (or reset) by the government in order to offset negative fiscal conditions. The failure of President Herbert Hoover's administration to do so was seen by many as part of the myriad of influences that perpetuated and exacerbated the Great Depression. Second, interest rates may adjust themselves naturally in parallel to economic conditions—the crash of prices during that period sent interest rates downward as well.

The Great Depression is considered an extreme case of economic collapse in the international economy, but it is still viewed as one of the most significant economic periods in modern world history. Throughout the twentieth century and in the early twenty-first century, there have been smaller (though not insignificant) contractions in the economy.

Interest rates once again played a role in the causes of and solutions to these periods.

RECESSIONS

As suggested earlier, the Great Depression has long stood as the standard example of the most feared economic condition into which a system might fall. However, the wounds of the Depression were so deep that, in the years that followed, affixing the term "depression" to an economic downturn (prior to the 1930s, the term was used commonly in this context) amounted to rekindling fears of a return to that dark period. The alternative term for such economic downturns, recession, has helped foster an image of a condition whose duration and scope can be quantified, as opposed to the near fiscal chaos of the 1930s. The difference between a depression and a recession, many argue, is a matter of perception. In the late 1970s, for example, when President Jimmy Carter's economic adviser Alfred Kahn spoke of a fear of an impending "depression," he was immediately rebuked by the president, who did not want to scare the public by warning of an impending depression. During Kahn's next speech, he cautioned instead, "We're in danger of having the worst banana in forty-five years" ("Diagnosing depression," 2008).

Since the Great Depression, the United States has experienced a number of economic recessions. In the twentieth century, the longest of these recessions occurred from 1973 to 1975 and from 1981 until 1982 (both lasted sixteen months each). The recession that began in December 2007 lasted eighteen months until June 2009. During that time, 86 percent of industries in the United States reduced their production, every state reported an increase in unemployment rates, and the average household wealth dropped considerably. The gross domestic product, the most extensive measuring tool for economic performance, slipped approximately 3.4 percent, its worst fall since World War II, but this decline nevertheless pales in comparison to the 26.5 percent drop in GDP that occurred between 1929 and 1933 during the Great Depression (Isidore, 2009).

The 2007 recession paints an important illustration of the impact of interest rates on the economy. One of the bright spots of the recession in 2009 was the fact that gasoline prices declined after a year in which gas prices topped out at a national average of $4.11 per gallon. High interest rates coincided with that rise in oil prices—when the price of fuel fell, so too did interest rates, helping to breathe new life into the housing market and other lending areas. Ironically, the coinciding drops in gasoline prices and interest rates in late 2008 and early 2009 led many consumers to believe that the recession was coming to an end. The result was increased consumer confidence and, due to the resulting increase in consumer demand, a return to higher gas prices and interest rates.

One of the largest contributors to the ongoing recession was the inability of consumers to pay back credit card and mortgage debt. This issue sent shockwaves through the financial sector, causing many banks to fold and others to look to the government in 2009 for assistance. In response, the Bush and Obama administrations and the US Congress implemented two major recovery spending packages, adding nearly $1.5 trillion to the federal deficit. In fact, the administration's ambitious spending requests, coupled with long-standing costs of military operations in Iraq and Afghanistan, caused the deficit (spending versus tax collections) to bloat well beyond historic levels (Montgomery, 2009). As the deficit soared to record levels, the Federal Reserve lowered the short-term interest to 0 percent in December 2008 for the first time in history.

The recession of 2007 and similar recessions throughout the twentieth and twenty-first centuries provide examples of how economic conditions can drive interest rates up and down based on consumer confidence, federal deficits, and other factors. They also provide examples of how leaders may use interest rates to address key issues that may create or continue recessions.

As the US economy slowly recovered from the recession, unemployment and stagnant production were kept wages low. Meanwhile, fears of inflation caused by the monumental influx of money into the economy by the government were downplayed. In order to facilitate economic recovery, the US Federal Reserve argued against increasing interest rates (Cooper, 2009), citing the Great Depression and the 1990s Japanese recession as examples. In those cases, increasing interest rates and tightening fiscal policies before recovery was established helped to maintain economic stagnation. By reducing the short-term interest rates to historically low levels, the Federal Reserve eased the cost of borrowing to encourage easy access to credit in order to increase consumption.

CONCLUSIONS

The rate at which interest is applied is a critical factor in a given economic system. As this paper has demonstrated, interest rates play a central role in the short and long term health (or lack thereof) of an economy. The significance of interest rates is twofold. First, they are effective tools of economic policy. As seen in the examples of the Great Depression, government-sanctioned higher interest rates contributed to the reluctance of consumers to invest both before and at the tail end of that period. The failure of the Hoover administration to lower those rates is widely considered to have heightened the Depression's longevity and severity. At the outset of the recession that began in December 2007, the Bush and Obama administrations calculated the government's response to one of the worst recessions since the Depression; it took into consideration the mistakes of the Hoover administration and deliberately kept interest rates low in order to help foster investment and debt repayment.

Second, while the government may intervene to raise or lower interest rates, this economic component has behind it natural forces. The rate of inflation, consumer confidence levels, the rate production, and other macroeconomic factors may affect a change in interest rates, driving them upward or downward. This effect may in turn exacerbate or benefit an economy.

Interest rates remain an integral part of the modern economic system. As the global economy continues to develop and integrate, leaders and analysts consistently look to interest rates as both a vital indicator of that system's health and a useful vehicle by which it may remain healthy.

BIBLIOGRAPHY

Anecdotage.com. (2009). Morgan loan. Retrieved June 18, 2009 from http://anecdotage.com/index.php?aid=11829.

Chernenko, S., & Faulkender, M. (2011). The two sides of derivatives usage: hedging and speculating with interest rate swaps. *Journal of Financial and Quantitative Analysis, 46*(6), 1727–1754. Retrieved November 21, 2013 from EBSCO online database Business Source Premier. http://search.ebscohost.com/login.aspx?direct=true&db=buh&AN=71818599

Cooper, J. (2009, June 1). The Fed will be in no rush to raise rates. *Business Week,* (4133), 10. Retrieved June 23, 2009 from EBSCO Online Database Business Source Complete. http://search.ebscohost.com/login.aspx?direct=true&db=bth&AN=40416896&site=ehost-live

Davidson, P. (2009, June 4). Bernanke: U.S. deficit poses risk to financial stability. *USA Today.* 1B.

DeLong, J. B. (1997). The Great Depression in outline. In, Slouching *Towards Utopia? The Economic History of the 20th Century.* Retrieved June 22, 2009 from University of California at Berkeley. http://econ161.berkeley.edu/TCEH/Slouch%5fCrash14.html.

Diagnosing depression. (2009). *The Economist, 390*(8612), 57. Retrieved June 23, 2009 from EBSCO Online Database Business Source Complete. http://search.ebscohost.com/login.aspx?direct=true&db=bth&AN=35884015&site=ehost-live

Economic ups and downs. (2009, June 17). *USA Today.* 8A.

"Flexo." (2009, April 22). What is interest? *Money basics: Simple interest, compound interest, APR and APY.* Retrieved June 22, 2009 from ConsumerismCommentary. com. http://www.consumerismcommentary.com/2009/04/22/money-basics-simple-interest-compound-interest-apr-and-apy/.

Isidore, C. (2009, March 25). The great recession. *Special Report: Road to Rescue.* Retrieved June 23, 2009 from CNNMoney.com. http://money.cnn.com/2009/03/25/news/economy/depression%5fcomparisons/index.htm.

Lehmann, R. (2013, September 23). Cushioning the blow of rising rates. *Forbes, 192*(4), 1. Retrieved November 21, 2013 from EBSCO online database Business Source Premier. http://search.ebscohost.com/login.aspx?direct=true&db=buh&AN=90151467

Love, T., & Miller, W. C. (2013). Repercussions of a sustained low-interest-rate environment on life insurance products. *Journal of Financial Service Professionals, 67*(2), 44–52. Retrieved November 21, 2013 from EBSCO online database Business Source Premier. http://search.ebscohost.com/login.aspx?direct=true&db=buh&AN=85802247

Montgomery, L. (2009, March 21). Deficit projected to swell beyond earlier estimates. *The Washington Post,*

A1. Retrieved June 23, 2009 from website http://www. washingtonpost.com/wp-dyn/content/article/2009/03/20/ AR2009032001820.html.

Romer, C. (2009, March 9). Lessons from the Great Depression for economic recovery in 2009. Unpublished paper presented at the Brookings Institution. Retrieved June 22, 2009 from the Brookings Institution http://www.brookings.edu/~/media/Files/ events/2009/0309%5fClessons/0309_lessonsromer.pdf.

Sidney, H. & Sylla, R. (1996). *A history of interest rates,* 3d Edition. New Brunswick: Rutgers University Press.

SUGGESTED READING

Barro, R. (2006). Rare disasters and asset markets in the twentieth century. *Quarterly Journal of Economics, 121*(3), 823-866. Retrieved June 24, 2009 from EBSCO Online Database Business Source Complete. http://search.ebscohost.com/login.aspx?direct=true&db=bth&AN=21722271 &site=ehost-live

Landon-Lane, J. & Rockoff, H. (2007). The origin and diffusion of shocks to regional interest rates in the United States, 1880-2002. *Explorations in Economic History, 44*(3), 487-500. Retrieved June 24, 2009 from EBSCO Online Database Business Source Complete. http://search.ebscohost.

com/login.aspx?direct=true&db=bth&AN=25746000&site=ehost-live.

Laubach, T. (2009). New evidence on the interest rate effects of budget deficits and debt. *Journal of the European Economic Association, 7*(4), 858-885.

Little, S. & Mirfin, D. (2005, September 19). Are there any benefits to interest rates being compounded monthly for lifetime mortgages? *Mortgage Strategy,* 26. Retrieved June 24, 2009 from EBSCO Online Database Business Source Complete. http://search.ebscohost.com/login.aspx? direct=true&db=bth&AN=18397407&site=ehost-live

McNulty, L. (2013). Bank of England: the risk of zero interest rates. *International Financial Law Review, 32*(5), 42. Retrieved November 21, 2013 from EBSCO online database Business Source Premier. http://search.ebscohost. com/login.aspx?direct=true&db=buh&AN=89074228

Samuelson, R. (2003, December 15). Greenspan's finest hour? *Newsweek, 142*(24), 39. Retrieved June 24, 2009 from EBSCO Online Database Business Source Complete. http://search.ebscohost.com/login.aspx?direct=true&db=bth&AN=11614078&site=ehost-live

—*Michael P. Auerbach*

INVESTMENT CONCEPTS

ABSTRACT

This article focuses on investment concepts such as modern portfolio theory and post modern portfolio theory. Modern Portfolio Theory (MPT) provides an opportunity for investors to utilize diversification in order to maximize the potential of their portfolio, and assumes that the investor is adverse to risk. Post modern portfolio theory points the way to an improved science of investing that incorporates not only DRO but also behavioral finance and any other innovation that leads to better outcomes. There is a discussion of why people should invest as well as an introduction of the capital asset pricing model.

OVERVIEW

It has been suggested that most Americans do not know how to save or prepare for their future. As a result, many financial investment companies have approached employers as well as individuals in an attempt to educate the masses on the benefits of investing. Some of the tips that have been provided by organizations, such as the American Association of Individual Investors, include:

- Build and advance a cash reserve that can cover short-term dangers and liquidity requirements.
- Develop an overall investment strategy even if it cannot be implemented immediately.
- Select mutual funds that fit into the overall investment strategy, then consider what the minimum initial investments are.

- Choose a balanced fund for those who invest less aggressively and choose a wider-based index fund for those who invest more aggressively. Build the portfolio after this initial investment has been completed.
- Review the rate and level of commitment in relation to each of the stock market segments as a means to decide whether or not to increase the amount of funds given to the initial investment.
- Do not agonize over small deviations from the original allocation plan. Stay the course! (p. 1-2).

MODERN PORTFOLIO THEORY

Financial counselors may inquire about whether or not an organization has some type of retirement plan, such as a 401 (k) plan, in place for their employees or they may go directly to the employee for supplemental retirement opportunities. One popular approach that has emerged is the modern portfolio theory. Modern Portfolio Theory sounds like it is an academic and analytical concept; however, "it is the accepted approach to investment and portfolio management today" (American Association of Individual Investors, n.d.). The relationship between risk and return tend to form the foundation for investment theory. However, a third dimension, modern portfolio theory, can be added to the equation in order to create a framework that can assess investment opportunities that exist for the sole purpose of making money (Dunn, 2006).

Modern Portfolio Theory (MPT) provides an opportunity for investors to utilize diversification in order to maximize the potential of their portfolio, and assumes that the investor is adverse to risk. Therefore, the investor will only take a risk if he/ she has determined that the risk will provide them with a higher expected return. In essence, the investor has to be willing to take on more risk in order to be compensated with higher returns.

PARTS OF THE MODERN PORTFOLIO THEORY APPROACH

The concept can be used by both individuals and corporations, and can be used in determining how one can optimize his/her portfolio as well as what the price should be for a risky asset. According to the Association of Individual Investors, there are two parts of this approach and they are:

- First part — focus on the concept that the best combination of assets should be developed by focusing on how the various components perform relative to each other.
- Second part — focus on the belief that the natural outcome of many people searching for under priced securities in the markets should be an "efficient market" in which it is difficult to add value by finding under priced securities, especially since it is expensive to do so (par. 4 and 5).

HARRY MARKOWITZ

MPT was introduced by Harry Markowitz, an economist and college professor, when he wrote an article entitled "Portfolio Selection" in 1952. He eventually became a Nobel Prize recipient for his work in the field. Prior to his work, most investors only focused on the best way to assess risks and receive rewards on individual securities when determining what to include in the portfolio. Investors were advised to develop a portfolio based on the selection of those securities that would offer them the best opportunity to gain. Markowitz took this practice and formulized it by creating a mathematical formula of diversification. "The process for establishing optimal (or efficient) portfolio generally uses historical measures for returns, risk (standard deviation) and correlation coefficients" (Money Online, n.d., para. 6). He suggested that investors focus on selecting portfolios that fit their risk-reward characteristics (Markowitz, 1959).

APPLICATION

CAPITAL ASSET PRICING MODEL (CAPM)

In order to select investments for a portfolio, modern portfolio theory will use the capital asset pricing model (Wise Geek, n.d.). The capital asset pricing model (CAPM) is utilized to calculate a theoretical price for a potential investment, and has a linear correlation between the returns of the shares and what the stock market earnings as time passes. The model analyzes the risk and return rates that can be expected for individual capital to market returns. It can be used to:

- Institute the preferred equilibrium market price of a company's assets.

- Institute the price that a company's equity is expected to cost, taking into consideration the risk components involved in a business's investments.

There will always be some type of risk associated with an investment portfolio. The degree of risk can fluctuate between industries as well as between companies. A portfolio's risk is divided into two categories — systematic and unsystematic risk. Systematic risk refers to investments that are naturally riskier than others, and unsystematic risk refers to when the amount of risk can be minimized through diversification of the investments.

CAPM ASSUMPTIONS
The CAPM operates on a set of assumptions such as:
- Investors are risk adverse individuals who maximize the expected utility of their end of period wealth, which implies that the model is a one period model.
- Investors have homogenous expectations about asset returns, which indicate that all of the investors perceive themselves to have the same opportunity sets.
- Asset returns are distributed by the normal distribution.
- A risk free asset exists and investors may borrow or lend unlimited amounts of this asset at a constant rate, which is the risk free rate.
- There are definite numbers of assets and their quantities are fixed within the one period model.
- All assets are perfectly divisible and priced in a perfectly competitive market.
- Asset markets are frictionless and information is costless and simultaneously available to all investors.
- There are no market imperfections such as taxes, regulations, or restrictions on short selling (Value Based Management.net, n.d., p. 7).

In addition, the CAPM model includes the following propositions:
- Investors in shares require a return in excess of the risk free rate, to compensate for the systematic risk.
- Investors should not require a premium for unsystematic risk because it can be diversified away by holding a wide portfolio of investments.
- Since systematic risk varies between companies,

investors will require a higher return from shares in those companies where the systematic risk is greater.

The same propositions can be applied to capital investment by companies:
- Companies expect a return on a project to exceed the risk free rate so that they can be compensated for the systematic risk.
- Unsystematic risk can be diversified away, which implies that a premium for unsystematic risk is not required.
- Companies should strive for a bigger return on projects when the systematic risk is greater (Value Based Management.net, n.d., p. 7).

DISADVANTAGES OF CAPM
However, there are some disadvantages to the CAPM, which include:
- The model assumes that asset returns are normally distributed random variables. However, it has been observed that returns in equity and other markets are not normally distributed, which results in large swings in the market.
- The model assumes that the variance of returns is an adequate measurement of risk.
- The model does not appear to adequately explain the variation in stock returns.
- The model assumes that given a certain expected return, investors will prefer lower risk to higher risk.
- The model assumes that all investors have access to the same information and agree about the risk and expected return of all assets.
- The model assumes that there are no taxes or transaction costs. However, this assumption may be relaxed with more complicated versions of the model.
- The market portfolio consists of all assets in all markets where each asset is weighted by its market capitalization.
- The market portfolio should in theory include all types of assets that are held by anyone as an investment and people usually substitute a stock index as a proxy for the true market portfolio.
- Since CAPM prices a stock in terms of all stocks and bonds, it is really an arbitrage pricing model which throws no light on how a firm's beta is determined (Value Based Management.net, n.d., p. 7).

VIEWPOINT

POST-MODERN PORTFOLIO THEORY

Although modern portfolio theory has been instrumental and valuable in the investment world, there are limitations. "MPT is limited by measures of risk and return that do not always represent the realities of the investment markets" (Rom & Ferguson, n.d., p. 349). As a result, there has been a paradigm shift that expands on the risk-return formula. The new model is referred to as the post-modern portfolio theory.

According to Swisher and Kasten (2005), some of the highlights of the post-modern portfolio theory are:

- The theory presents a new method of asset allocation that optimizes a portfolio based on returns versus downside risk instead of mean-variance optimization.
- The core innovation of post modern portfolio theory is its recognition that standard deviation is a poor proxy for how people experience risk.
- Downside risk is a definition of risk derived from three sub-measures, which are downside frequency, mean downside deviation, and downside magnitude. Each of these measures is defined with reference to an investor-specific minimal acceptable return (MAR).
- Portfolios created using a mean-variance optimization model and downside risk optimization are often similar and the differences in absolute risk and return values are small, which means that diversification works regardless of how it is measured.
- Post modern portfolio theory points the way to an improved science of investing that incorporates not only DRO but also behavioral finance and any other innovation that leads to better outcomes (Swisher & Kasten, 2005, p. 1).

CONCLUSION

It has been suggested that most Americans do not know how to save or prepare for their future. Financial counselors may inquire about whether or not an organization has a some type of retirement plan (i.e. 401 (k) plan) in place for their employees or they may go directly to the employee for supplemental retirement opportunities. Some of the most common myths about retirement planning include:

- **Myth 1 — You will not need as much money during retirement as you do now.** The general rule of thumb is that you will need at least 70% of the income that you earned prior to retiring in order to maintain the type of lifestyle that you have become accustomed.
- **Myth 2 — Retirement years will not last long.** Today, people are living longer, and the life expectancy is approximately 21 years after the age of 65. Therefore, it is important to plan knowing that there is a strong possibility that one will have time to enjoy the retirement years.
- **Myth 3 — It's possible to start planning for retirement a few years before it is time to actually retire.** It's never too early. The sooner you start, the better. You will have the opportunity to accumulate and earn more money.
- **Myth 4 — Social Security will provide enough income for the retirement years.** Social Security only provides approximately 38% of the retirement income.
- **Myth 5 — Pension Plan will provide enough income for the retirement years and there is no need to save more.** If one does not plan ahead of time, there is no way to determine whether or not the pension plan plus social security is enough for the retirement years. In addition, many employers have replaced defined benefit plans with 401 (k) plans.
- **Myth 6 — Medicare will take care of health insurance.** Medicare pays less than half of a person's healthcare expenses and a person has to be 65 years old in order to be considered eligible for Medicare.
- **Myth 7 — All of a person's assets are in safe vehicles for long-term accumulation and do not need to be watched closely.** All investment should be watched in order to determine if changes need to be made. The market can be volatile and people should make sure that they are not positioned to experience devastating risk.
- **Myth 8 — A person can use the equity in home to add to retirement income.** It is unlikely that the equity will add much to a person's retirement income. The price of homes fluctuates. However, if the home is not used to supplement retirement income, a person should take advantage of all the tax breaks that are available, especially when downsizing.

- **Myth 9 — If need be, my family can always help me out.** It is not wise to be expecting others to come to your rescue, especially for financial issues. Also, most people do not want to rely on their family members, but use this excuse as a way of delaying retirement planning.
- **Myth 10 — Money is everything when it comes to retirement planning.** Although money is important, it's actually the lifestyle decisions that a person should be concerned with when planning for retirement.

Modern Portfolio Theory (MPT) provides an opportunity for investors to utilize diversification in order to maximize the potential of their portfolio, and assumes that the investor is adverse to risk. Therefore, the investor will only take a risk if he/ she has determined that the risk will provide them with a higher expected return. In essence, the investor has to be willing to take on more risk in order to be compensated with higher returns.

In order to select investments for a portfolio, modern portfolio theory will use the capital asset pricing model (Wise Geek, n.d.). The capital asset pricing model (CAPM) is utilized to calculate a theoretical price for a potential investment, and has a linear correlation between the returns of the shares and what the stock market earnings as time passes. The model analyzes the risk and return rates that can be expected for individual capital to market returns. It can be used to:

- Institute the preferred equilibrium market price of a company's assets.
- Institute the price that a company's equity is expected to cost, taking into consideration the risk components involved in a business's investments.

HIGHLIGHTS OF POST MODERN PORTFOLIO THEORY
According to Swisher and Kasten (2005), some of the highlights of the post-modern portfolio theory are:
- The theory presents a new method of asset allocation that optimizes a portfolio based on returns versus downside risk instead o mean-variance optimization.
- The core innovation of post modern portfolio theory is its recognition that standard deviation is a poor proxy for how people experience risk.
- Downside risk is a definition of risk derived from three sub-measures, which are downside frequency, mean downside deviation, and downside

magnitude. Each of these measures is defined with reference to an investor-specific minimal acceptable return (MAR).
- Portfolios created using a mean-variance optimization model and downside risk optimization are often similar and the differences in absolute risk and return values are small, which means that diversification works regardless of how it is measured.
- Post modern portfolio theory points the way to an improved science of investing that incorporates not only DRO but also behavioral finance and any other innovation that leads to better outcomes (p. 1).

BIBLIOGRAPHY
American Association of Individual Investors (n.d.). From theory to practice: How to apply MPT concepts to your 401(k) plan. Retrieved September 27, 2007, from http://www.aaii.com/includes/DisplayArticle. cfm?Article%5fId=2974&ro=2245

American Association of Individual Investors (n.d.). Investing basics: Investing questions that every successful investor should know how to answer. Retrieved September 27, 2007, from http://www.aaii.com/faqs/investingbasics.cfm

American Association of Individual Investors (n.d.). The ten myths of retirement planning. Retrieved September 27, 2007, from http://www.aaii.com/includes/DisplayArticle. cfm?Article%5fId=2977&digit=256

Bigda, C. (2012). The end of investing. *Money*, 41(10), 84-90. Retrieved November 15, 2013, from EBSCO Online Database Business Source Complete. http://search.ebscohost.com/login.aspx?direct=true&db=bth&AN=82564126 &site=ehost-live

Dunn, B. (2006, August). Modern portfolio theory — with a twist: The new efficient frontier. *Aquillian Investments, Inc.* Retrieved on September 27, 2007, from http://www. aquillian.com/docs/AquillianEfficientFrontier.pdf

Geambasu, C., Sova, R., Jianu, I., & Geambasu, L. (2013). Risk measurement in post-modern portfolio theory: differences from modern portfolio theory. *Economic Computation & Economic Cybernetics Studies & Research*, 47(1), 113-132. Retrieved November 15, 2013, from EBSCO Online Database Business Source Complete. http://search.ebscohost.com/login.aspx?direct=true&db=bth&AN=86991912&site=ehost-live

Markowitz, H. (1959). *Portfolio selection: Efficient diversification of investments.* New York, NY: John Wiley.

Modern portfolio theory. (2007). *Money Online.* Retrieved September 27, 2007, from http://www.moneyonline.co.nz/ calculator/theory.htm

Rom, B., & Ferguson, K. (n.d.). Post-modern portfolio theory comes age. *Sponsor-Software Systems, Inc.* Retrieved September 27, 2007, from http://www.actuaries.org/AFIR/ colloquia/Orlando/Ferguson%5fRom.pdf

Smart investing: It's really as easy as one, two, three. (cover story). (2012). *Kiplinger's Personal Finance, 66*(11), 30-34. Retrieved November 15, 2013, from EBSCO Online Database Business Source Complete. http://search.ebscohost.com/login.aspx?direct=true&db=bth&AN=82153660 &site=ehost-live

Swisher, P., & Kasten, G. (2005, September). Post-modern portfolio theory. *Journal of Financial Planning,* 7. Retrieved September 27, 2007, from http://www.fpanet. org/journal/articles/2005%5fIssues/jfp0905-art7.cfm

Value Based Management.net (n.d.). CAPM — Capital asset pricing model. Retrieved September 27, 2007, from http:// www.valuebasedmanagement.net/methods%5fcapm.html

Wise Geek (2007). What is modern portfolio theory? Retrieved September 27, 2007, from http://www.wisegeek. com/what-is-modern-portfolio-theory.htm

SUGGESTED READING

Bland, L. (2005). A modern take on an old portfolio theory. *Money Management, 19*(16), 26-26. Retrieved September 27, 2007, from EBSCO Online Database Business Source Complete. http://search.ebscohost.com/login.aspx?direct=true&db=bth&AN=17176205&site=bsi-live

Curtis, G. (2002). Modern portfolio theory and quantum mechanics. *Journal of Wealth Management, 5*(3), 7. Retrieved October 5, 2007, from EBSCO Online Database Business Source Complete. http://search.ebscohost.com/ login.aspx?direct=true&db=bth&AN=8594085&site= bsi-live

Simon, W. (2005). Illuminating the broad range requirement of ERISA section 404(c) with the language of modern portfolio theory found in the Uniform Prudent Investor Act and the Restatement 3rd of Trusts (Prudent Investor Rule). *Journal of Pension Benefits: Issues in Administration, 13*(1), 87-90. Retrieved September 27, 2007, from EBSCO Online Database Business Source Complete. http://search. ebscohost. com/login.aspx?direct=true&db=bth&AN=1841 9841&site=bsi-live

—Marie Gould

INVESTMENT MANAGEMENT

ABSTRACT

This article focuses on investment management. It provides an overview of the history of investment management and the investment management industry. Active investment management, passive investment management practices, and management services in different investment environments such as corporations, endowments, and households, are discussed. Investment portfolios, pension funds, performance fees, and assets are described. The issues associated with the U.S. government's regulation of the investment management industry are also addressed.

OVERVIEW

Investment management, also called money management and asset management, refers to the process of investment analysis involving portfolio management, budget making, banking, tax planning, and investment risk assessment. Investment managers work for pension funds, corporations, governments, institutions, endowments, foundations, and high net worth individuals. Investment managers help grow and mange assets through multiple products and services including analysis, research, and risk management. Investment management is divided into two main types: Active investment management and passive investment management.

- Active investment management is an approach based on informed and independent investment decisions. Active investment management generally involves the frequent buying and selling of bonds. Active investment management has as its primary goal to outperform benchmark returns.
- Passive investment management, also referred to as indexing, involves investing in a wide range of assets classes and working to match the overall performance of the market. Passive investment management generally involves holding bonds to the point at which they mature.

Investment managers, both active and passive money managers, work to control and balance investment return, risk, and cost. Investment managers control return, risk, and cost by analyzing the following variables within a client's portfolio (Grinold, 2005):

- Exceptional return: Exceptional return refers to the residual return plus benchmark timing return.
- Benchmark return: Benchmark return refers to the standard value against which the performance of a security, index, or investor can be measured.
- Opportunity loss: Opportunity loss refers to the estimated lost resulting from not choosing the best option or solution.
- Transaction cost: Transaction cost refers to the cost resulting from buying or selling assets including commissions.
- Objective value: Objective value refers to the prevailing value established by the market.
- Information ratio: Information ratio refers to the expected exceptional return divided by the amount of risk assumed in pursuit of that exceptional return.

The following sections provide an overview of the history of investment management and the investment management industry. This overview will serve as the foundation for later discussion of investment management practices and services in corporations, endowments, and households. The issues associated with the U.S. government's regulation of the investment management industry are also addressed.

THE HISTORY OF INVESTMENT MANAGEMENT
The field of investment management began in the United States on a large scale following the Great Depression of the 1930s. Following the Great

Depression, the public and private sectors, in an effort to rebuild and stabilize the economy, began to actively manage investment portfolios through analysis, research, and risk management. The history of investment management during the twentieth century is characterized by shifting paradigms. The field of investment management has experienced paradigm shifts during the twentieth century regarding the role and purpose of organization and management. The organization and management paradigm in investment management has changed in the following ways over the last century (Ellis, 1992):

- **1940s:** Investment management in the 1940s was characterized by insurance plan dominated pension funds.
- **1950s:** Investment management in the 1950s was characterized by the growth of corporate pension funds. Pension funds refer to a category of funds that are collected and reserved to pay employees' pensions when they retire from active employment.
- **1960s:** Investment management in the 1960s was characterized by a growth in overall pension fund assets.
- **1970s:** Investment management in the 1970s was characterized by the multi-manager concept of pension fund investing in which plans divide the control of their funds among multiple investment managers. Pension plans and endowments began to prioritize the role of investment managers and compensate investment managers with high salaries.
- **1980s:** Investment management in the 1980s was characterized by an increasingly diversified asset and manager classification system. The categories of value manager, growth manager, and sector rotator emerged. Investment manager consultants became common. Investment products and options increased.
- **1990s:** Investment management in the 1990s was characterized by a growth in investment management fees. Performance fees, also referred to as investment management fees, became common practice. Performance fees are an amount paid to the investment manager of a hedge fund once positive performance has been achieved or reached. In addition, investment managers in the 1990s became ever-more specialized and classified according to an ever-expanding set of categories. As a result of the

changes in management categories that occurred in the 1990s, investment managers today may be immunized, dedicated, structured, or indexed. Managers are considered to be either value managers or growth managers. Managers can specialize in private placements or extended markets.

Ultimately, the changes in the field of investment management throughout the twentieth century were related to changes in the structure and operations of the market. The structure of the investment management industry has changed from concentrated to increasingly diversified or fragmented to capitalize on the increasingly efficient market (Ennis, 1997). In the twenty-first century, investment managers, who are often mobile and independent agents, are swiftly responsive to market changes.

The Investment Management Industry

The primary professional investment management association is the CFA Institute. The CFA Institute, which reports 90,000 members in 134 societies, is the association of investment professionals that awards the Chartered Financial Advisers (CFA) and the Certificate in Investment Performance Measurement (CIPM) designations and certificates. Corporations, such as Citigroup, Mellon Financial Corporation, Ashland Partners, State Street, ING, Morgan Stanley, Nicholas Applegate, SS & C Technologies, UBS, and the AIG Global Investment Group, seek out investment managers with CFA Institute certification. The Chartered Financial Advisers (CFA) certification program is a three-year program with three levels of exams. The Certificate in Investment Performance Measurement (CIPM) certification program is designed to train performance professionals to meet investment industry needs.

Development of the CFA Institute

The CFA Institute has its origins in the investment societies of the early twentieth century such as the Investment Analyst Society of Chicago, established in 1925 to promote investment education and professionalism, and the New York Society of Security Analysts (NYSSA) established in 1937. In 1947, the National Federation of Financial Analysts Societies (NFFAS) formed. In 1959, the NFFAS board formed the Institute of Chartered Financial Analysts (ICFA) to provide a certification of competence. In 1961, the

ICFA was formally incorporated and in 1963 the first investment manager certification examination was offered. In 2004, the ICFA changed its name to CFA Institute to better express its identity and strengthen brand recognition.

CFA Institute Code of Ethics

The CFA Institute promotes a code of ethics and standards of professional investment management conduct. The Code of Ethics and Standards of Professional Conduct includes a code of ethics, research objectivity standards, trade management guidelines, asset manager code, and soft dollar standards. The CFA Institute's Code of Ethics concerns ethical management behavior in the following areas: Professionalism; integrity of capital markets; duties to clients; duties to employers; investment analysis; recommendation, and action; conflict of interest; and responsibilities as a CFA institute member.

- **Professionalism:** Investment managers must posses a knowledge of the law; demonstrate independence and objectivity; and reject misrepresentation and misconduct.
- **Integrity of capital markets:** Investment managers with material nonpublic information should not use the information to affect the value of an investment. Investment managers must not engage in market manipulation to distort prices or inflate trading volume to mislead market participants.
- **Duties to clients:** Investment managers must demonstrate loyalty, prudence, care, fair dealing, suitability, performance presentation, and preservation of confidentiality with clients.
- **Duties to employers:** Investment managers must demonstrate loyalty and fair compensation arrangements with their employers.
- **Investment analysis, recommendations, and action:** Investment managers must demonstrate diligence and reasonable basis for making investment recommendations and taking investment actions.
- **Conflicts of interest:** Investment managers must disclose all conflicts of interest. Investment managers must give priority of transactions to transactions for clients and employers over transactions that would benefit managers or corporations.
- **Referral fees:** Investment managers must disclose any compensation or benefit received for the recommendation of financial products or services.

APPLICATIONS

INVESTMENT MANAGEMENT PRODUCTS & SERVICES

Investment management falls into three main groups or categories: Corporations (pension funds), endowment funds, and households. Investments are made with specific time horizons in mind: The long run, the trading horizon, the decision horizon, then planning horizon, and the planning sub-horizons.

- Trading horizons are the shortest time in which an investment manager can carry out or revise a transaction. The institution rather than individual investment managers and analysts establish the length of the trading horizon.
- Decision horizons are the period of time between deciding to revise a portfolio and executing the decision.
- Planning horizons are the period of time over which things matter to the decision maker. Planning horizons are generally multiple decades long.
- Planning sub-horizons are directly connected to targeted issues and concerns such as retirement. For example, when investment managers build the portfolio for retirement purposes, the length of time until retirement is called the planning sub-horizon.
- Long run horizons are a series of short periods linked to the faraway investment objective or goal.

Despite the shared forecast variables, optimal investment policy is not general to all investment environments and clients. Investment policy varies between corporations, endowments, and households.

PENSION FUND MANAGEMENT

Corporate investment management generally focuses on corporate pension fund management. Investment managers attempt to grow the pension surplus within their organizations. Pension surplus refers to the difference between assets and liabilities. The main pension options available to corporate employees are defined benefit pension plans and cash-balance pension plans. Employer-based retirement and workplace savings plans are a form of financial risk protection. Investment managers oversee and administer pensions, individual retirement accounts, 457 deferred compensation plans, 401 (k) plans, and 403(b) plans. Pensions are programs that provide employees with retirement income after they meet minimum age. Individual retirement accounts (IRAs) are accounts to which an individual can make annual contributions of earnings up to a pre-determined amount. A 457 deferred compensation plan is a supplemental retirement savings program that allows individuals to make contributions on a pre-tax basis. The 401(k) plan is a retirement investment plan that allows an employee to put a percentage of earned wages into a tax-deferred investment account. The 403(b) plan is a retirement investment plan, which is offered by non-profit organizations, that allows an employee to put a percentage of earned wages into a tax-deferred investment account. The Employee Retirement Income Security Act (ERISA), which is the federal legislation that governs the administration and design of employer pension, health and welfare plans, regulates corporate investment management practices, products, and services. According to the Employee Retirement Income Security Act, corporate investment managers have a fiduciary responsibility to manage employee pensions in the best financial interests of employees.

ENDOWMENT FUND MANAGEMENT

The investment management practices for endowments vary significantly from those used in corporations. Endowment fund management is more similar to individual or household investment management than corporate investment management. The investment manager of an endowment considers variables, such as anticipated gifts, bequests, shadow investments, and cost of operations, when making investment decisions. Investment decisions usually follow the board of director generated and approved investment guidelines. Endowment fund portfolios generally include a percentage allocated to equities, a percentage allocated to fixed-income investment products, and a percentage allocated to alternative investments including real estate or hedge funds. Investment managers monitor the portfolio in an ongoing basis to ensure that the portfolio matches established investment policy and the portfolio allocation guidelines. Endowments usually have an endowment spending policy in place to control annual spending and ensure that annual spending decisions are in compliance with endowment goals and objectives.

INVESTMENT MANAGEMENT

In households, investment management is undertaken by individuals who may or may not have financial training. Households plan for the financial burden of retirement and college tuition through investment choices throughout the family life cycle. Defined-benefit pension plans, which were once the ubiquitous retirement investment choice, are being replaced by defined contribution plans in which the employee must decide on the mix of investments. Defined benefit plans specify benefits as a fraction of final pay scale before retirement and require no management by the household. Household investors are often overwhelmed with investment choices. For example, there are over 9,000 different mutual funds available for purchase by individual household investment managers. Household investment managers must manage investment risk as they plan for targeted expenditures such as home purchase, retirement, or college tuition. There are three main approaches to risk control or risk management in household investment management: Hedging, diversification, and insuring (Merton, 2003).

ISSUES

U.S. GOVERNMENT REGULATION OF INVESTMENT MANAGEMENT

The U.S. Securities and Exchange Commission (SEC), the U.S. governmental body responsible for protecting investors, maintaining fair, orderly, and efficient markets, and facilitating capital formation, regulates investment management activities. The U.S. Securities and Exchange Commission includes a Division of Investment Management. The Division of Investment Management regulates investment companies (such as mutual funds, closed-end funds, unit investment trusts (UIT), exchange-traded funds, and interval funds), including variable insurance products, and federally registered investment advisers. The U.S. Securities and Exchange Commission defines investment companies as any issuer which is or holds itself out as being engaged primarily, or proposes to engage primarily, in the business of investing, reinvesting, or trading in securities; is engaged or proposes to engage in the business of issuing face-amount certificates of the installment type; or is engaged or proposes to engage in the business

of investing, reinvesting, owning, holding, or trading in securities, and owns or proposes to acquire investment securities having a value exceeding 40 percent of the value of such issuer's total assets on an unconsolidated basis.

CATEGORIES OF INVESTMENT COMPANIES

The U.S. Securities and Exchange Commission divides investment companies into three main categories: Face-amount certificate company; unit investment trust; and management company. A face-amount certificate company refers to an investment company that is engaged in the business of issuing face-amount certificates of the installment type. A unit investment trust, according to the Securities and Exchange Commission, refers to an investment company which is organized under a trust indenture, contract of custodianship or agency, or similar instrument; does not have a board of directors; and issues only redeemable securities, each of which represents an undivided interest in a unit of specified securities. Unit investment trusts do not include a voting trust. A management company refers to any investment company other than a face-amount certificate company or a unit investment trust.

There are two main laws that regulate investment management practices: The Investment Company Act of 1940 and the Investment Advisers Act of 1940.

- The Investment Company Act of 1940 considers the following actions by investment companies to adversely affect the national public interest and the interest of investors and, as a result, to be illegal: Investors acquire or surrender securities issued by investment companies without adequate information concerning the character of such securities and the circumstances of such companies and their investment management; investment companies are operated in the interest of affiliated persons rather than in the interest of all classes of such companies' security holders; investment companies issue securities containing inequitable or discriminatory provisions, or fail to protect the preferences and privileges of the holders of their outstanding securities; investment companies are managed by irresponsible persons; investment companies employ unsound or misleading methods or are not subjected to adequate independent scrutiny; investment companies are reorganized or become inactive without the consent of their security holders; and investment companies operate without adequate financial assets or reserves.

■ The Investment Advisers Act of 1940 considers the following actions of investment advisers to adversely affect the national public interest and the interest of investors and, as a result, to be illegal: Investment advisers distribute their advice or analyses to clients by the use of the mails and means and instrumentalities of interstate commerce. Investment advisers distribute their advice or analyses related to the purchase and sale of securities traded on national securities exchanges and in interstate over-the-counter markets in such volume as substantially to affect interstate commerce, national securities exchanges, the national banking system, and the national economy.

In addition to the regulation of the activities of investment companies and investment advisers, the U.S. Securities and Exchange Commission oversees the investment adviser federal registration process. The U.S. Securities and Exchange Commission requires investment advisers to be registered with the federal government. The registration process involves supplying the U.S. Securities and Exchange Commission with the following information: The name and form of organization under which the investment adviser engages or intends to engage in business; the education, the business affiliations for the past ten years, and the present business affiliations of such investment adviser; the nature of the business of such investment adviser, including the manner of giving advice and rendering analyses or reports; a balance sheet certified by an independent public accountant and other financial statements; the nature and scope of the authority of such investment adviser with respect to clients' funds and accounts; and the basis upon which such investment adviser is compensated.

Registered investment advisers and managers are required to have and submit to the U.S. Securities and Exchange Commission and clients written compliance programs to ensure that the investment managers do not violate the rights of their clients. Compliance programs must include written descriptions of the following issues: Portfolio management processes; the accuracy of disclosures made to investors, clients, and regulators; proprietary trading by investment mangers; safeguarding of client assets

from conversion or inappropriate use of the investment manager; the accurate creation of required records and their privacy and maintenance; safeguards for the privacy protection of client records and information; trading practices; marketing advisory services; and business continuity plans. Ultimately, the U.S. Securities and Exchange Commission considers investment advisers and managers to be fiduciaries or trust holders for their clients. As such, the U.S. Securities and Exchange Commission requires that investment managers and companies behave in an ethical manner toward their clients.

CONCLUSION

In the final analysis, the field of investment management is a multifaceted form of investment analysis involving investments, portfolio management, budget making, banking, tax planning, and investment risk assessment. The tools, practices, and services of investment management vary based on the investment environments and clients.

BIBLIOGRAPHY

Barry, C., & Starks, L. (1984). Investment management and risk sharing with multiple managers. *Journal of Finance, 39*(2), 477-491. Retrieved August 29, 2007, from EBSCO Online Database Business Source Premier. http://search. ebscohost. com/login.aspx?direct=true&db=buh&AN=465 3210&site=ehost-live

Benaroch, M. (2002). Managing information technology investment risk: A real options perspective. *Journal of Management Information Systems, 19*(2), 43-84. Retrieved August 29, 2007, from EBSCO Online Database Business Source Premier. http:// search.ebscohost.com/login.aspx?di rect=true&d b=buh&AN=7721239&site=ehost-live

Blake, D., Rossi, A. G., Timmermann, A., Tonks, I., & Wermers, R. (2013). Decentralized investment management: evidence from the pension fund industry. *Journal of Finance, 68*(3), 1133-1178. Retrieved November 15, 2013, from EBSCO Online Database Business Source Complete. http:// search.ebscohost.com/login.aspx?direct=t rue&d b=bth&AN=87671757&site=ehost-live

Demarzo, P. M., Fishman, M. J., He, Z., & Wang, N. (2012). Dynamic agency and the q theory of investment. *Journal of Finance, 67*(6), 2295-2340.

Retrieved November 15, 2013, from EBSCO Online Database Business Source Complete. http://search.ebscohost.com/login.aspx?direct=t rue&d b=bth&AN=83485970&site=ehost-live

Division of Investment Management. (2007). U.S. Securities and Exchange Commission. Retrieved August 29, 2007, from http://www.sec.gov/divisions/investment.shtml

Ellis, C. (1992). A new paradigm: The evolution of investment management. *Financial Analysts Journal, 48*(2), 16-18. Retrieved August 29, 2007, from EBSCO Online Database Business Source Premier. http://search.ebscohost.com/login.aspx?direct=t rue&db=buh&AN=6944498 &site=ehost-live

Ennis, R. (1997). The structure of the investment-management industry: Revisiting the new paradigm. *Financial Analysts Journal, 53*(4), 6-13. Retrieved August 29, 2007, from EBSCO Online Database Business Source Premier. http:// search.ebscohost.com/login.aspx?direct=true&db=buh&A N=9709242151&site=ehost-live

Fleming, P. (1996). Identifying investment management problems: Two perspectives. *Journal of Accountancy, 182*(4), 68-69. Retrieved August 29, 2007, from EBSCO Online Database Business Source Premier. http://search.ebscohost.com/login.aspx?direct=true&db=buh&AN=96101230 74&site=ehost-live

Gallagher, D. (2003). Investment manager characteristics, strategy, top management changes and fund performance. *Accounting & Finance, 43*(3), 283-309. Retrieved August 29, 2007, from EBSCO Online Database Business Source Premier. http://search.ebscohost.com/login.aspx?direct=tru e&db=buh&AN=11680067&site=ehost-live

Grinold, R. (2005). Implementation efficiency. *Financial Analysts Journal, 61*(5), 52-64. Retrieved August 29, 2007, from EBSCO Online Database Business Source Premier. http://search.ebscohost.com/login.aspx?direct=true&db=b uh&AN=18486605&site=ehost-live

Guldimann, T. (2000). How technology is reshaping finance and risks. *Business Economics, 35*(1), 41-52.

McConocha, D. & Tully, S. (1993). Household money management: Recognizing nontraditional coup. *The Journal of Consumer Affairs, 27*(2), 258-274.

Merton, R. (2003). Thoughts on the future: Theory and practice in investment management. *Financial Analysts Journal, 59*(1), 17-23. Retrieved

August 29, 2007, from EBSCO Online Database Business Source Premier. http:// search.ebscohost.com/login.aspx?direct=true&db=buh&A N=9629051&site=ehost-live

Phan, H. V., & Hegde, S. P. (2013). Corporate governance and risk taking in pension plans: evidence from defined benefit asset allocations. *Journal of Financial & Quantitative Analysis, 48*(3), 919-946. Retrieved November 15, 2013, from EBSCO Online Database Business Source Complete. http:// search.ebscohost.com/login.aspx?direct=t rue&d b=bth&AN=90575785&site=ehost-live

Seidner, A. (1994). Wise management of investments: The CFO's role. *HFM (Healthcare Financial Management), 48*(10), 26-31. Retrieved August 29, 2007, from EBSCO Online Database Business Source Premier. http://search. ebscohost.com/login.aspx?direct=true&db=buh&AN=941 1295285&site=ehost-live

Standards of practice policy group. (2007). The CFA Institute. Retrieved August 29, 2007, from http://www.cfainstitute. org

SUGGESTED READING

Davanzo, L., & Nesbitt, S. (1987). Performance fees for investment management. *Financial Analysts Journal, 43*(1), 14-20. Retrieved August 29, 2007, from EBSCO Online Database Business Source Premier. http://search. ebscohost.com/login.aspx?direct=true&db=buh&AN=693 6269&site=ehost-live

Halpern, P., Calkins, N., & Ruggels, T. (1996). Does the emperor wear clothes or not? The final word (or almost) on the parable of investment management. *Financial Analysts Journal, 52*(4), 9-15. Retrieved August 29, 2007, from EBSCO Online Database Business Source Premier. http://search. ebscohost.com/login.aspx?direct=true&db=b uh&AN=9702215231&site=ehost-live

Parwada, J., & Faff, R. (2005). Pension plan investment management mandates: An empirical analysis of manager selection. *Journal of Financial Services Research, 27*(1), 77-98. Retrieved August 29, 2007, from EBSCO Online Database Business Source Premier. http://search.ebscohost.com/login.aspx?direct=true&db=buh&AN=16731579 &site=ehost-live

—Simone I. Flynn

INVESTMENT VALUATION & ANALYSIS

ABSTRACT

This article focuses on the fundamental concepts involved in investment valuation and analysis. The basic process of investing and key investment terminology will be introduced, followed by a discussion of applications to different types of investments, such as stocks, bonds, and money markets –and their relative advantages and disadvantages, such as rates of return, safety, liquidity, and tax features. Tools for interpreting the rate of return values, and other issues for understanding the complexities of analyzing an investment program, such as risk, growth, value, and financial reporting, are also discussed, as is the need for careful diversification in any investment program.

OVERVIEW

Simply put, an investment is the use of money (capital) to create more money. Individuals and companies make investments to earn profit that can be spent, saved, or re-invested, depending on the investor's strategic goals. Investing decisions are made based on factors such as the amount of available investment capital, the duration of the investment period, the level of risk, and the desired rate of return (yield) on the investment. Investors typically refrain from the consumption (use) of the invested capital while it is creating more money.

INVESTMENT EARNINGS
Successful investments earn money in one or both of two ways.

APPRECIATION
The first way is through the appreciation (increased value) of an asset that has been purchased, such as a stock that is sold at a higher price than at which it was purchased. The difference between the purchase price and the sales price, minus brokerage commissions and taxes, is referred to as a capital gain. Thus, if 100 stocks are purchased for $10 a share and later sold for $15 a share, the value of each share has increased by $5-and the stock's owner has made a capital gain of $500. Investments may be held for days, weeks, months, or many years in order to make

desired gains. Unsuccessful investments may never earn profits and are considered capital losses.

INTEREST & DIVIDENDS
The second way investments earn money is through interest or dividends. Interest is money paid to a lender for the use of the lender's money over a specified period of time at a particular percentage rate. Investors who put money into savings accounts receive interest from the banks that use and hold their money. Dividends are portions of a company's profits that are paid to shareholders who own interests in the company. For example, if you own 100 shares of a company that pays $1.50 per share, every year you would receive a check for $150. If a stock or a fund pays no dividends, then an investor relies on its potential for growth, or appreciation, over a longer period of time.

Because so many investment options are available, and since investing money can be risky, it is important to understand the potential value of an investment. Investors therefore are concerned with valuation, or the process of determining the current worth of an asset. In general, valuations can be made on a variety of factors, such as how much money the company has, how it manages its money, how it plans to manage its money in the future, or how much the company's holdings are worth. The following sections of this article cover different types of investments and some of the factors involved in their valuation.

APPLICATIONS

VALUE IN DIFFERENT TYPES OF INVESTMENTS
The value of an investment to the investor is contingent upon a number of factors. An investment portfolio, or the collection of investments, should be sufficiently diversified to minimize risk and achieve the best possible return. Safety is one factor in determining if the investment has value to an investor; rate of return is another. Different types of investments meet these goals in different ways.

DEPOSITS
The safest type of investments-also typically the

lowest-performing type-is a deposit with an insured commercial bank. A savings account is a perfect example of a simple, but secure, investment, but one which makes comparatively little return. Another form of a deposit-a certificate of deposit (CD)-usually earns a slightly higher rate, but "locks" in the invested funds for a specified amount of time, such as three months, six months, a year, or longer. In the case of the savings account and the CD, the bank essentially borrows the investor's money and uses it to further its own investment activities. The primary advantage of this type of investment is that commercial banks insured by the Federal Deposit Insurance Commission (FDIC) guarantee depositors that their money is safe; if the bank folds, the Federal government covers the depositors' losses.

BONDS

Bonds represent another type of investment. Bonds are loans that investors make to companies or some level of government for use in a capital project, such as a new highway, new construction, or a new utility system. Bonds are given ratings-from AAA to C-by services such as Moody's and Standard's to denote their level of safety and are usually offered in denominations of $1,000. The bonds pay a specified rate of interest while being held, and upon completion of the funded project, the principal is returned to the investor. Bank deposits, as well as money market accounts, bonds, and Treasury bills produce what is known as fixed income, that is, the investor can expect to receive a certain amount of payback for the money he or she has loaned.

STOCKS

Stocks, on the other hand, produce taxable dividends, but they also allow an investor to "own" a portion (share) of the company and vote, in the case of common stock, in company decisions. This type of investment is considered equity. Historically, the stock market has outperformed most other types of investment strategies, but also contains the highest risk and requires the most astute monitoring and patience.

MUTUAL FUNDS

Another major type of investment is a mutual fund, which is a collection of stocks, bonds, and other securities that are purchased by a financial manager, who sells shares of the collective group of investments to individuals and companies. A wide variety of funds exist, including very conservative (secure) investments, or more speculative (riskier) investments. Mutual funds may offer opportunities to invest in large-cap companies (companies with high capital), or companies with less capital-midsized caps or small caps. Generally, the more capital a company has, the safer the investment may be, because they have greater assets to cover for losses if one should occur.

RATE OF RETURN (YIELD)

The value of an investment is often determined on the basis of how much money it will make over a period of time. For example, a stock offers a return, a rate that is represented by the difference of the purchase price and the sales price, plus any dividends it earns during the period of ownership. This figure is referred to as the holding's Rate of Return, or yield, which may be calculated as follows:

$$\frac{\text{Ending Price} - \text{Beginning Price} + \text{Dividend}}{\text{Beginning price}}$$

For example, an investor buys stock for $1,000, sells it later for $1,200, and earns $100 in dividends while holding it. At the time of the closing, the owner has $1,300 instead of the $1,000 with which the investment began. Using the above formula, the investment has achieved a .3 or 30 percent return rate. This rate might or might not be considered "good," depending on how long it took to return that rate, and what other more profitable uses the investor could have made with the money had it been used in another investment.

A yield must also be evaluated in terms of inflation. Rates of return can be calculated either as nominal (not adjusting for inflation) or real (adjusting for inflation). The value of the nominal rate is reduced by the amount of inflation that exists during the holding period-so if a fund yielded an 18 percent nominal rate and the inflation rate was five percent, the real rate of return would be thirteen percent. The yield must also be analyzed in terms of its tax consequences, as a portion of that return will be taxed as dividends or interest. Thus, the "whole picture" must be taken into account when placing value on the return of an investment.

ISSUES

RISK
Nearly every type of investment contains some element of risk, or the degree of uncertainty on the return of an asset-in other words, the likelihood that the investment will not lose money. Part of the valuation process is to determine how much risk an investor is willing to take, and how much chance there is that the investment will fail. Investors who are risk averse are reluctant to make investments that have high risk; investors who are "risk tolerant" are more comfortable making higher-risk investments. The Risk- Return Tradeoff (Kapoor, Blabay & Hughes, 2007) is a helpful concept for deciding if an investment is worth making: Is the potential benefit of the investment worth the chances of losing it?

Investment risk comes from many sources. Keown (2003) identifies seven sources of risk:
- Interest rates during the lifetime of the investment;
- Inflation rates;
- The company's risk in operating the business;
- The company's management of its debt;
- How much money the company can produce (liquidity);
- The performance of the overall market;
- Political and regulatory issues;
- The exchange rate of the currency, and;
- Call risk-or the possibility that a lender will "call in" its loan early.

Any of these sources, or perhaps all of them, influences the value of an investment that could fail because of events internal or external to the company.

GROWTH, VALUE, & INTRINSIC VALUE
Investments can be evaluated on the basis of their current market value but also in terms of their growth potential. For example, investors might choose growth stocks because they believe that over time, these stocks will develop steadily and substantially. Growth stocks may pay little or no dividends, as their growth objectives lead them to re-invest all of their earned capital; many technology companies are growth-oriented. Value investments are those that are can be purchased at a low price (hence, they are "undervalued"), may have relatively high rates of return, and are characterized by

low price-to-earnings ratios (P/E). In general, making such investments (which is called "value investing") is more beneficial than making growth investments (Chan & Lakonishok, 2004) and are long-term (Kwag & Lee, 2006). Finally, investments with intrinsic value are those about which there is an "underlying perception" of future worth or potential-but making this type of investment, which is usually speculative, is highly subjective and often risky.

THE VALUE OF TAX-SHELTERED INVESTMENTS
The value of tax-sheltered investments (tax-deferred or tax-free investments) cannot be overstated. A tax-deferred fund, such as many pension programs that are set up by employers, allows the investor to contribute money on a pre-tax basis; in other words, an individual's taxable income would be lessened by the amount of money contributed to such an fund; he or she would not actually pay taxes on the contribution until they reached a specified retirement age, thus allowing the money to grow over a period of years without being taxed each year. Depending on tax brackets, as much as $14,000 of a person's yearly salary can be set aside, pre-tax, for retirement. The cumulative effect of these contributions and the growth they incur over a period of years or decades can dictate the quality of life retirees will experience when they retire and at what age they can retire.

Other forms of tax-advantaged investments would include certain Federal, state, or municipal bonds, the proceeds from which normally are not taxable within the jurisdictions they are offered. For example, income from a state-issued bond would usually be exempt from that state's tax structure. Also, individual retirement accounts (IRAs) allow individuals to contribute to accounts that earn interest but allow them to avoid paying taxes on that income until they reach a specific retirement age, usually 59 1/2 years. Also, depending upon an investor's tax bracket, the contributions an individual makes per year to an IRA may be deductible from that year's income tax. Thus, significant value of an investment is usually found not by how much money it makes, but how much money it makes *efficiently*.

THE VALUE IN FINANCIAL REPORTING
Companies seeking investors-either directly through stock purchases or through financial management funds-are required by the Securities and Exchange Commission (SEC) to disclose key financial

information about themselves. This information is designed to help an investor ascertain the value of an investment by analyzing the firm's liquidity, financial leverage, efficiency, and profitability (Madura 2006). This data is made available, in print on company websites, through several forms, including:

- Annual Reports-documents which disclose a company's or fund's activities for a calendar year, including its strategic decisions, acquisitions, new investments, etc.
- Balance Sheets-documents that report a firm's financial condition as of a particular date.
- Income Statements-reports of revenues and expenses for a specified period and which summarize the profit or loss for that period.
- Cash Flow Statements-ledgers that show all money going in and out of an organization.

These documents testify to how a company manages its debt, its growth, its investor obligations, and its assets. Additionally, once investors become part of an organized investment program, the issuing organization provides quarterly reports which reflect how the investor's money, collectively with other investors' money, has been spent, how much it has grown, and what the net gain or loss has been. This information can be compared to general market data that can be accessed through Yahoo! Finance, Motley Fool.com, MSNmoney, the New York Stock Exchange web site, or other financial resources, so each investor can make his or her own evaluation of the investment's performance. Careful, regular monitoring of any investment is a necessity for ensuring the success of any investment program.

CONCLUSION

The value of any investment is relative-what is a highly valuable investment to one person or company is not necessarily valuable to another. Choosing investments is contingent upon what the goals of the investment are, such as risk, yield, duration, liquidity, and tax consequences (Nickels, McHugh & McHugh, 2008). Most financial planners believe that younger investors-people who have a longer period in which to make money and recover losses-should be more assertive in their investment activities. On the other hand, individuals or companies with high incomes might seek investments that pay tax-deferred or tax-free returns. Financial planners advise

diversification of portfolios to achieve the best value for investments.

BIBLIOGRAPHY

Bodie, Z., Kane, A., & Marcus, A. J. (2007). *Essentials of investments.* New York: McGraw-Hill Irwin.

Chan, L. K. C., & Lakonishok, J. (2004). Added-Value and growth investing: Review and update. *Financial Analysts Journal, 60*(1), 71-86. Retrieved September 25, 2007, from EBSCO Online Database Business Source Premier. http:// search.ebscohost.com/login.aspx?direct=true&db=buh&AN=12246106&site=bsi-live

Heughebaert, A., & Manigart, S. (2012). Firm valuation in venture capital financing rounds: the role of investor bargaining power. *Journal of Business Finance & Accounting, 39*(3/4), 500-530. Retrieved November 15, 2013, from EBSCO Online Database Business Source Complete. http://search.ebscohost.com/login.aspx?direct=t rue&db=bth&AN=74089137&site=ehost-live

Investopedia.com. (n.d.). Retrieved September 20, 2007 from: http://www.investopedia.com

Kapoor, J. R., Dlabay, L. R., & Hughes, R. J. (2007). *Personal finance,* (8th ed.). New York: McGraw-Hill.

Keown, A. J. (2003). *Personal finance: Turning money into wealth.* Upper Saddle River, NJ: Prentice Hall.

Kwag, S. W., & Lee, S. W. (2006). Value investing and the business cycle. *Journal of Financial Planning, 19*(1), 64-71. Retrieved September 25, 2007, from EBSCO Online Database Business Source Premier. http://search. ebscohost. com/login.aspx?direct=true&db=buh&AN=194 24117&site=bsi-live

Loughran, T., & Wellman, J. W. (2011). New evidence on the relation between the enterprise multiple and average stock returns. *Journal of Financial & Quantitative Analysis, 46*(6), 1629-1650. Retrieved November 15, 2013, from EBSCO Online Database Business Source Complete. http://search. ebscohost.com/login.aspx?direct=true&db=bt h&AN=71818602&site=ehost-live

Madura, J. (2006). *Personal finance,* (2nd ed.). Boston, MA: Pearson Education.

Money.cnn. (n.d.). Retrieved September 20, 2007 from: http:// money.cnn.

Nickels, W. G., McHugh, J. M., & McHugh, S. M. (2008). *Understanding business,* (8th ed.) New York: McGraw- Hill Irwin.

Thollot, S., & Huh, E. (2013). PE fund valuation: What CCOs need to know. *Compliance Reporter,* 61. Retrieved November 15, 2013, from EBSCO Online Database Business Source Complete. http://search.ebscohost.com/ login.aspx?direct=true&db=bth&AN=87507889&site=eh ost-live

SUGGESTED READING

Benninga, S. (2000). *Financial modeling,* (2nd ed.). Boston: Massachusetts Institute of Technology.

Damodaran on Valuation: *Security analysis for investment and corporate finance.* Hoboken, NJ: John Wiley & Sons.

Investing with insiders. (2007). *Dow Theory Forecasts, 63*(34), 1-2. Retrieved September 25, 2007, from EBSCO Online Database Business Source Premier. http://search.ebscohost.com/login.aspx?direct=true&db=buh&AN=2629089 8&site=bsi-live

Koller, T. (2006). *Valuation workbook: Step-by-step exercises and tests to help you master valuation.* Hoboken, NJ: John Wiley & Sons.

Private equity: How long can the perfect storm last? (2007). *Financial Executive, 23*(7), 6. Retrieved September 25, 2007, from EBSCO Online Database Business Source Premier. http://arch.ebscohost.com/login.aspx?direct=true&db=buh&AN=26471868&site=bsi-live

Wang, P. (2007). Why bad returns don't make a fund bad. *Money, 36*(10), 70-72. Retrieved September 25, 2007, from EBSCO Online Database Business Source Premier. http:// search.ebscohost.com/login.aspx?direct=true&db=buh&AN=26590522&site=bsi-live

–William J. Wardrope

LONG-TERM DEBT

ABSTRACT

This article will explain long-term debt. The overview provides an introduction to the most common types of long-term debt and long-term debt lenders. This article will also describe how investors and creditors can determine a company's long-term debt by using mathematical formulas and by examining a company's balance sheet. In addition, the reasons why creditors and investors pay close attention to a company's long-term debt obligations are explained, as are the reasons why companies choose to use long-term debt to pay for their business growth objectives. Also, explanations of corporate financial analyses in which long-term debt is an important issue, such as identifying profitable borrowing, reading balance sheets and comparing the financial positions of various companies based on their assets and debt obligations are included to help illustrate how long-term debt factors into common corporate finance considerations.

OVERVIEW

There are many ways that companies finance, or pay for, their costs of doing business. Successful businesses earn profits that are re-invested back into the company to pay for research and development or other expansion efforts to further grow the business. However, there are many instances in which a company's earnings are not sufficient to cover its costs and growth objectives. For instance, young companies or companies that are struggling to stay afloat financially may not generate enough profit to cover all of their internal costs as well as the costs of growing and expanding. Even strong, stable companies may need to make significant purchases — such as equipment, building space or even the acquisition of another company — to continue to grow and remain competitive, and these costs may exceed the amount of liquid assets a company has on hand. And even after years of successful growth, a company may face lean years where the market plateaus, consumers' interests change or a competitive product or service begins to siphon off its customers or clients.

In situations such as these, companies must look beyond their earnings to consider options that will create an inflow of capital to help it grow or survive during times of economic hardship. A common form of financing that companies use to generate the resources it needs for significant projects is long-term debt.

Long-term debt consists of money that a company will use for a longer period of time, generally one year or more, and that the company will repay over time. Long-term debt may consist of loans that a company borrows or it may consist of debt securities that a company issues. These two forms of debt are known as debt financing or equity financing. Debt financing consists of short-term debt and long-term debt. These two forms of debt serve two very different functions. Short-term debt is debt that a company will pay off within 12 months and is usually acquired to pay for temporary increased expenses, such as purchasing additional inventory for sale during the holiday season. On the other hand, long-term debt consists of loans and financial obligations that will last for over one year. For example, long-term debt may consist of the mortgage a company holds on its corporate buildings and property or various business loans that it has assumed. In addition, a company's debt obligations, such as bonds and notes that will not mature before one year, are other forms of long-term debt. Securities such as T-bills and commercial paper are generally not considered long-term debt because their maturity dates are typically shorter than one year.

If a company decides not to use debt financing to pay for its business objectives, it may decide to pursue equity financing. Equity financing occurs when a company offers shares of the company for sale. The benefit of this form of financing is that the most common types of shares, such as common stocks and preferred stocks, do not require dividend distributions to shareholders. Thus, the company experiences an influx of capital when shareholders purchase stock in the company and the company is not required to pay an annual dividend. Shareholders profit from their investment only if the company makes enough money to authorize a dividend distribution or through the capital appreciation of the shares. On the other hand, shareholders are purchasing ownership in a company when they buy shares, and thus a company that makes a public offering of its shares exchanges its autonomy for equity in that shareholders may receive the right to vote on important corporate matters and thus will have a say in how the company is run.

There are many advantages of long-term debt that companies can exploit if they select the best form of financing for their needs while keeping their overall levels of debt manageable. For instance, long-term debt can provide much needed working capital that can be used to pay for ventures that will create profit and increase its earnings. In addition, if debt can be borrowed at a lower interest rate than the earnings a company will generate from plants, equipment or other resources purchased with the borrowed funds, borrowing can actually be profitable for a company. Thus, while debt is frequently discussed with negative connotations, some types of long-term debt can actually be good for companies. The following sections provide a more in-depth explanation of the basic financial concepts involving long-term debt.

BASIC FINANCIAL CONCEPTS

LONG-TERM DEBT DEFINED

"Term" refers to the time period for which money is borrowed and the period over which the loan will be repaid. Thus, long-term debt consists of money that a company will borrow to use for a long period of time, generally longer than one year, and that the company will repay over time, also longer than 12 months. Long-term debt primarily consists of longer term loans that are taken to pay for assets that companies will use for a period of many years, such as land, buildings, machinery, equipment or technology. Thus, long-term debt arises when the planned repayment of the loan and the predicted valuable life of the assets purchased exceed one year. Most long-term loans have a repayment period of five to seven years, although they may even be extended to 30 years.

There are a number of reasons why companies decide to incur long-term debt. Some companies may prefer to borrow money to purchase a significant acquisition that will generate additional profits while the company repays the loan in lower monthly installments over a period of time. The other form of debt financing that a company may consider is to issue fixed-income debt securities, such as bonds, notes or commercial paper. Debt securities issued by the company are purchased by investors, and their maturity dates-or the date in which the company must repay the principal of the security-may be longer than the length of a typical term loan. Thus, issuing debt securities allows a company to raise more money and borrow the money for longer periods of time than loans typically allow. However, in addition to honoring the debt securities and any interest they accrue, companies must also pay the underwriting fees involved in issuing securities. Long-term loans, on the other hand, generally consist of funds that are borrowed from a private entity such as a commercial bank. The loans a company borrows from a bank may be used to just about any purpose, but they generally have shorter terms than debt securities and thus require repayment sooner than the maturity dates of their outstanding debt securities. However, while companies must pay interest on the loans, there are no underwriting fees associated with long-term loans. Thus, companies must weigh all of their financing options to choose the form of financing that best suits their growth objectives and financial position.

TYPES OF LONG-TERM DEBT

There are many different types of long-term debt that businesses may incur in order to finance their growth and operations. The most common types of long-term debt are term loans, bonds and debentures. Bonds are generally classified as either secured or unsecured forms of debt securities. Secured bonds are backed by a company's assets. For instance, mortgage bonds are a form of secured bonds that are back by real estate. Unsecured bonds, called debentures, are not backed by a specific asset but are issued based on the full faith and credit of the issuing company. In addition, the various types of long-term debt may be assigned a priority status, which refers to the rank of the lender in terms of gaining access to a company's assets in the event of insolvency. For instance, a company may have some forms of long-term debt that are considered senior, which means they have a higher priority than lower-ranked subordinated debt.

TERM LOANS

Although companies do use bonds and debentures as a long-term debt financing option, term loans are the form of long-term debt most frequently used by businesses to finance their expansion efforts. A term loan is a loan from a bank to a company that has an established maturity date—usually five to seven years after the start of the loan—in which the company will repay the loan in monthly installments accounting for both principal and interest. When the principal of a loan is repaid in equal payments over the life of the loan, this process is called loan amortization. When monthly payments of principal and interest

are made, the companies are considered to be "servicing" their debt. Most companies choose to repay a loan in equal installments over a period of time so that the principal plus the interest is repaid in full upon the final payment. However, sometimes a company will borrow a loan that is structured so that an amount of principal is still due at the end of the loan period. That ending balance is called a balloon payment. This type of long-term loan is used to allow a company to make lower monthly payments over the life of the loan.

BONDS

Bonds have many characteristics similar to those of a term loan, but they are debt obligations, or IOUs, that are issued by private and public companies and purchased by investors rather than funds that companies borrow from and repay to lenders such as commercial banks. Bonds are usually sold in units of $1,000 and firms use the money they raise from selling bonds for a multitude of purposes, such as building new facilities or purchasing new equipment. When a company issues bonds, it promises to repay the bondholder all of principal, or the amount of the debt obligation purchased by the investor, in the future on a specified maturity date. A bond may have maturity date that is set a few years in the future, or even further, such as 10 years down the road. Until the bond matures, the issuing company pays the bondholder a stated rate of interest, called a coupon, at specified intervals, which are typically every six months. Unlike other types of securities that companies can issue, such as stocks, bonds do not give holders an ownership interest in the issuing corporation.

DEBENTURES

Debentures are a bond whereby a company uses its full faith and credit as collateral rather than a specific, tangible asset. Creditors who purchase debentures must rely on the credit rating and creditworthiness of the issuing company in determining the risk of this form of long-term debt. Because the risks involved with purchasing debentures is higher than other forms of debt securities, debentures often pay higher rates of return. Owners of debentures are called unsecured creditors of a company.

Convertible bonds are a type of debenture that provide the bondholder with the right to convert the bonds into shares of common stock at a later specified date. These bonds are an attractive financing option for companies because they allow the company to issue debt securities at a more affordable interest rate than other types debentures because they are less risky. They are also attractive to investors because convertible bonds allow bondholders to receive interest payments during the life of the bond while retaining the ability to convert the bonds to shares of common stock if the price of shares of the company's common stock increase above a threshold level, called a strike price. Thus, convertible bonds are a form of debt security that are appealing to both companies and investors.

Junk bonds are another form of debenture that companies issue if they do not have a strong enough credit rating to issue investment grade bonds. Bonds are classified as either investment grade or junk bonds. Investment grade bonds are issued by companies with higher credit ratings and thus are considered low or medium-risk investments. Since the risk of these bonds is lower, so are their returns. Because companies with lower credit ratings are considered a riskier investment, the junk bonds these companies issue pay higher returns. Thus, some investors are willing to purchase junk bonds from companies that the investors believe are relatively stable in order to take advantage of the higher returns that these debt securities offer.

COMMON LONG-TERM DEBT LENDERS

The most common financial institutions that make long-term loans are commercial banks, credit unions or other financial companies. Within these financial institutions are lenders that specialize in certain types of long-term debt, including mortgage lenders, term loan lenders and equipment leasing lenders. Lenders are willing to let companies borrow long-term debt because the companies eventually pay the lenders back all of the money they borrowed plus interest. Thus, long-term debt is considered an asset to the lender and a liability to the borrowing company. Since there is some risk that the company will not be able to repay the loan or will even go bankrupt, lenders do face the possibility that they will not make money on every loan. However, lenders factor these costs, along with the creditworthiness of a company, into the interest rate that is set for the long-term loan. These lenders of long-term debt are described in more detail in the following sections.

MORTGAGE LENDERS

Mortgage lenders are generally large companies that can afford to lend funds to companies for the purchase of land and commercial properties. Mortgage lenders include banks, credit unions, financial companies and other institutional lenders. Mortgage lenders take proactive steps to try minimizing the risk of a company defaulting on a loan or the property losing value. Thus, mortgage lenders investigate the financial soundness, or creditworthiness, of the borrowing company before making a loan. To make this assessment, lenders examine company documents such as current financial statements, balance sheets and financial

projections that show how the building will allow the company to expand its operations to generate profits. In addition, the lender will require that the company requesting a loan provide a significant amount of paperwork to demonstrate the value of the building the company wishes to purchase, such as its location, condition and proposed use.

LONG-TERM LOAN LENDERS

Commercial banks and credit unions are the most common lenders of long-term loans. Like mortgage lenders, the financial institutions that make long-term loans also investigate the creditworthiness of any company that seeks to borrow a long-term loan. To make this determination, lenders of long-term loans evaluate the company's business plan, products and services, management team and financial statements. In addition, these creditors consider the collateral that a company has available to support the loan and the purpose for which the loan is intended. Most creditors also require that companies provide financial projections that give a detailed history of their production methods and operations and their position in the marketplace.

EQUIPMENT FINANCIERS

Equipment financiers, which include commercial banks, credit unions and equipment vendors themselves, lend companies money to purchase equipment that will enhance the company's production abilities to generate increased corporate earnings. Equipment financiers require evidence of a company's financial stability and growth projections that is similar to the documentation required by long-term creditors. One difference is that companies must generally submit business plans that include two sets of financial projections-one projection based on the company's use of its current equipment and a second set based on the company's use of the newly purchased equipment. In addition to these financial projections, equipment financiers often require that companies generate an estimation of the useful economic life of any equipment it is considering purchasing and the probable resale value of the equipment over the course of its useful life.

LONG-TERM DEBT FINANCING

CALCULATING LONG-TERM DEBT

Creditors and investors need to be able to quickly calculate a company's long-term debt so that they can make decisions about whether to invest in the company or extend credit to the company based on the company's financial stability. Too much long-term debt can signal that the company has experienced low earnings or sluggish growth. Too little long-term debt may indicate that the company's management does not have a solid financial plan to grow the company over time. Thus, long-term debt can be an important factor in evaluating the financial position of a company at any given point in time.

The way creditors and investors calculate long-term debt is by using a formula known as the debt-to-equity ratio. The debt-to-equity ratio measures the percentage of the company that is indebted, or "leveraged." This calculation compares the company's total liabilities (including short term and long-term obligations) with the proportion of the company that is equity owned by shareholders and owners. The debt-to-equity ratio divides the company's total debt by the amount of shareholders' equity. Shareholders' equity equals the amount of common stock owned by shareholders plus firm profits or losses. The resulting figure is also an indication of the amount of money that a company could safely borrow over long periods of time.

The formula used to calculate a company's debt-to-equity ratio is as follows.

$$\text{Debt-to-Equity Ratio} = \text{Total Liabilities}/\text{Shareholders Equity}$$

For instance, to determine the debt-to-equity ratio of Corporation A, assume that its total liabilities are $5,000 and its shareholder equity is $18,000. The calculation would be as follows:

$$\text{Corporation A debt-to-equity ratio} = \$5,000/\$18,000 = 0.27 \text{ or } 27\%$$

In evaluating a company's debt-to-equity ratio, the higher the percentage of the debt-to-equity ratio, the higher the company's debt obligations. While the levels of debt-to-equity that are generally regarded as acceptable by investors and creditors may fluctuate according to economic factors in the markets, generally debt-to-equity ratios of less than 40% are considered acceptable, while ratios of 40 to 50% may indicate that a company will encounter problems with liquidity where it is unable to meet its operational costs and debt obligations for a period of time. Also, many creditors and investors assume that a debt-to-equity ratio greater than one means a company has been primarily financing its assets through debt. On the other hand, a ratio of less than one means that a company has used equity for most of its financing. In general, the debt-to-equity ratio includes both short-term and long-term debt in figuring a company's "total liabilities." However, some creditors and investors use only interest-bearing long-term debt instead of total liabilities in calculating a company's debt-to-equity ratio to get a more precise measure of a company's financial stability.

HOW COMPANIES ACQUIRE LONG-TERM DEBT

Companies acquire long-term debt when debt lenders, generally called creditors, provide loans to the company for use in major acquisitions, product development, geographic expansion or other growth objectives. Thus, companies borrow money to pay for their business expansion efforts and creditors lend money to earn interest as the companies pay back the borrowed money over time plus any accrued interest.

While the explanation of how companies acquired debt is relatively simple, the process that companies and creditors undergo before a loan is actually extended can be relatively complex, especially if the loan is for a significant amount of money. This is because creditors assume some risk in lending funds to a company in that there is no guarantee that the additional funds will enable a company to generate sufficient earnings to repay the loan. Even if a company does grow initially after it borrows debt from a creditor, the company could experience a loss of sales or production capabilities that cripple its financial stability. Thus, creditors carefully examine the financial status of any company that applies for a loan before lending funds in an attempt to reduce the risk that the company will default on the loan.

To borrow long-term debt from a creditor, a company must first determine how much money it needs to borrow, how much money it can afford to borrow, the length of time it intends to borrow the money and any collateral or assets it could use to back a loan. Then, companies typically draft a written business plan that details its cash flow, financial projections and earnings expectations. Creditors examine these calculations to try to determine a company's ability to repay the loan over the term of the repayment schedule.

Once a company has created a solid business plan and identified how much money it will need to finance its growth objectives, the company generally approaches a number of creditors in an attempt to secure financing at the most affordable interest rate. The interest rate that is assigned to a term loan is generally a function of the creditworthiness of the borrower, the economic conditions in the market and the purpose for which the funds are being borrowed. The interest rate is important because it determines the amount of money that the company will have to repay in addition to the principal. Companies prefer lower interest rates while creditors make more money from higher interest rates. The creditor will generally set the interest rate at a percentage that is competitive and yet takes into consideration the financial stability of the company. Once the interest rate is set and the loan is taken out, the rate usually remains constant for the life of the loan. Companies may repay a loan before its term to get out of debt sooner, but creditors may charge a penalty for early repayment of a term loan because the creditor was still expecting to receive interest payments on the outstanding balance of the loan.

Once a creditor has investigated the stability of a company and is ready to extend a loan, the creditor may also attempt to limit its risk by securing the loan through acquring ownership interest in the asset that a company intends to purchase with the borrowed funds. With this ownership interest, creditors minimize their risk of total loss in the event of a company's bankruptcy and liquidation and the company is also able to pay a lower interest rate on loans secured by assets. Finally, creditors also generally require that

companies maintain sufficient levels of insurance to protect the assets that they purchase with borrowed funds. In sum, to acquire long-term debt, companies approach creditors with a business plan that details their financial fitness. A company desires long-term debt because it provides the funds needed to attain assets and resources that will allow the company to grow and expand. Creditors investigate the financial stability of companies, and then determine whether to extend financing and, if so, they will set the interest rate. To protect their risk exposure, creditors normally require that a long-term loan be secured by the new assets the funds are being used to purchase as well as by an insurance policy. Companies use the borrowed funds to purchase the resources necessary to grow in size and profitability.

IMPLICATIONS OF LONG-TERM DEBT

Long-term debt plays an important role in the overall financial stability of a company. Companies are willing to assume some long-term debt in order to pay for important acquisitions, such as buildings or equipment, that will in turn enable it to expand and become more profitable. On the other hand, if a company acquires too much long-term debt, the payments that it must make to service the debt principal and any interest that accrues can erode a company's cash reserves, and may even destabilize a company's financial position to the point of bankruptcy. Thus, determining a company's long-term debt helps creditors and investors assess whether a company is financially sound so that it can pay its bills while still earning profits, or whether its debts and other liabilities threaten to erode its stability and profitability.

Creditors and investors examine a company's balance sheet in order to calculate its debt-to-equity ratio. In addition to looking at a company's total assets, liabilities and shareholders' equity, investors and creditors also distinguish between a company's short or current long-term debt and its overall long-term debt obligations. Liabilities that are considered short or current long-term debt include those portions of the company's total long-term debt that it must pay in the next 12 months. The reason why investors and creditors examine the current portion of long-term debt on a balance sheet is to get an indication of how much money the company will spend in the current year toward servicing its long-term debt. Once this figure is determined, it can then be compared to the company's cash reserves as listed on its balance sheet in order to determine whether the company has enough cash and liquid assets to pay the current obligations on its long-term debt. A company whose current long-term debt is equal to or greater than its cash reserves has a higher risk of default, and creditors will carefully consider this in deciding whether to extend loans to the company and in determining the interest rates of the loans.

While there is no simple way for investors or creditors to quickly assess a company's overall debt obligations, looking at a balance sheet to calculate its debt-to-equity ratio can provide a reliable indication of a company's financial fitness. An even more valuable resource is to calculate a company's debt-to-equity ratios over time. In other words, if a creditor or investor is able to look at a company's balance sheets over the last five to ten years and calculate the company's debt-to-equity ratio for each year, these ratios will reveal whether the company's overall debt is increasing, decreasing or remaining steady. In general, a financially stable and healthy company should be paying down its debts every year, and so its debt-to-equity ratios should be tracking downward over time.

In addition, investors or creditors may pay particularly close attention to the strength of a company's balance sheet when the economy begins to tip into a recession or downward cycle. This is because a company's debt-to-equity ratio may provide some indication as to whether the company has a strong enough financial position to weather an economic downturn. The debt-to-equity ratio is important during the start of a recession because companies with higher levels of debt are at a higher risk of struggling — or becoming unable — to pay the interest obligations on their outstanding debt should the company experience a flat or declining level of income. Companies unable to pay their debts face bankruptcy and liquidation. Companies that struggle to pay their debts become increasingly less credit-worthy, and thus are less able to acquire any further financing that may be necessary to stay afloat.

APPLICATIONS

LONG-TERM DEBT IN CORPORATE FINANCE ANALYSES
Long-term debt plays an important role in several corporate finance analyses. For instance, considerations

about long-term debt commonly arise when companies are considering whether borrowing money-including long-term debt-can actually be profitable for it. Also, creditors and investors can read a company's balance sheet to determine the financial stability and debt structure of a company in making their lending and investment decisions. Finally, long-term debt is a consideration for anyone who wants to compare the financial strength of a number of companies. The following sections explain these factors in more detail.

WHEN BORROWING IS PROFITABLE
Although it seems counterintuitive, there are instances where it is profitable for a company to incur long-term debt. For instance, if a company can earn a higher rate of return by borrowing money and reinvesting it back into the company to earn higher dividends than the interest rate at which the money was borrowed, it is actually profitable for the company to borrow the money. This would be the case if, for example, a company borrowed a long-term loan at an 8% annual interest rate but used to money to purchase equipment that would speed up production times so that the company earns an annual return of 12%. In this instance, the company nets a 4% profit by borrowing the money (12% return — 8% cost of borrowing money = 4% net profit).

However, just because assuming more long-term debt would be profitable for a company on paper, too much debt can do more harm than good. Companies that are already carrying substantial levels of debt may threaten their overall financial stability by incurring more debt, even if it could be obtained at favorable interest rates. For companies that have historically carried little or no debt, assuming some debt at a low interest rate could enable them to make significant investments to boost earnings and profitability.

Another factor that creditors and investors can consider to determine whether borrowing would be profitable for a company is to determine the type of debt that the company is attempting to acquire. Generally, debt securities issued to public investors have longer maturities than the long-term loans that companies acquire from commercial banks and other financial institutions. However, both larger long-term loans with higher payments and long-term debt securities issued with high interest rates can erode a company's earnings.

Also, creditors and investors should determine

the purpose for the debt to determine whether it is profitable for a company to incur long-term debt. If the new debt is being assumed to repay old debts that the company can no longer maintain, creditors and investors should weigh the benefits of profitable borrowing against the strain excess debt can create on a company's viability. A company increasing its debt load should have a plan for repaying it. Thus, even if assuming long-term debt seems affordable, or even profitable, for a company, creditors and investors must also consider whether the company has a solid and reasonable plan to repay the debt in a timely fashion while maintaining its other corporate expenses.

READING A BALANCE SHEET

A balance sheet reveals a company's assets, liabilities and shareholders' equity, or the owners' net worth. The balance sheet, income statement and cash flow statement, comprise a company's financial statements. Assets are the resources a company has available to finance and manage its business, while liabilities and equity are two way that firms support these assets. A company's liabilities are the financial obligations that it owes to outside parties. Long-term liabilities are debts and other obligations that are not due until at least one year from the date of the balance sheet. Owners' equity, or shareholders' equity in publicly traded companies, is the amount of money that was initially invested into the company to fund its start-up costs plus any retained earnings of the company.

Reading a balance sheet is an important means by which creditors and investors can assess how much long-term debt a company owes and the extent of its debt relative to its assets and shareholders' equity. The amount of long-term debt on a company's balance sheet is important because it refers to money the company owes but will not pay off in the 12 months. Creditors and investors can get an even better sense of a company's financial stability by examining a company's balance sheets for several consecutive years. Companies whose long-term debt is decreasing over time while cash reserves are remaining stable or increasing are considered financially stable with an improving financial outlook. When a company's debt is increasing and cash reserves are decreasing, its financial health is considered unstable or even deteriorating.

Companies with too much long-term debt face decreasing earnings and the possibility of defaulting on interest payments or even facing bankruptcy. Fortunately, before creditors decide to lend a company money and investors decide to purchase a company's bonds, the overall financial health of a company can be determined by carefully reading a company's current balance sheet and even comparing the balance sheets of the past several years. With this information in hand, creditors and investors can make far more informed decisions about the creditworthiness of the company and the degree of their risk should they lend money or invest in the company.

COMPARING THE FINANCIAL POSITIONS OF VARIOUS COMPANIES

When creditors and investors are considering whether to extend credit or invest in a company, they may compare the financial position of one company against other companies in the same industry that are of approximately the same size and net worth. One way that creditors and investors can assess the relative financial positions of various companies is to compare their debt-to-equity ratios. For instance, if a company has long-term debt of $10 million and equity of $8 million, the debt-to-equity ratio is 1.25 (10/8 = 1.25). If another company has long-term debt of $10 million and only $1 million in equity, its debt-to-equity ratio is 10 (10/1 = 10). This company is in a dire financial position. If a third company has $10 million in long-term debt and $20 million in equity, its debt-to-equity ratio of 0.5 (20/10 = 0.5) is a good indication that the company is financially solid.

Thus, a low debt-to-equity ratio of 1 or lower means that a company has larger amounts of equity relative to its debt, which strengthens its financial soundness. However, a company with low levels of long-term debt may also be overlooking opportunities to make the investments necessary to help it grow in profitability. On the other hand, if a company has a high debt-to-equity ratio of 2 or greater, it has assumed such high levels of debt that its creditworthiness and financial stability are at risk.

Aside from looking at balance sheets and performing debt-to-equity calculations, investors and creditors can also assess the financial stability of various companies by comparing the credit ratings that they have been assigned by credit rating agencies, such as Moody's and Standard & Poor's. Investors and creditors can use these comparisons to determine whether a company is at risk of being downgraded in its credit rating because it is highly leveraged and carrying excessive levels of long-term debt.

Thus, there are resources and tools that are available to help creditors and investors make sound decisions based on the financial stability of companies. While debt-to-equity ratios have been rising for the past two decades, the fundamental assessment of a company's financial wellbeing based on its levels of long-term debt has remained constant. However, while the debt-to-equity ratio alone does not provide a final answer on the financial position of a company, it is a valuable tool that can give interested parties a good sense of a company's stability based on a relatively simple calculation.

CONCLUSION

Although debt is commonly considered to be negative and bad for businesses, moderate levels of debt can be an important part of financing a company's growth and development. When a company borrows money to make investments that create new opportunities, this can enable the business to grow in profitability. However, companies must be careful not to borrow too heavily. Companies that assume too much debt or that misuse the borrowed money can undermine their ability to grow, even to the point of insolvency. A company's management team must always remain alert to striking the proper balance between maintaining appropriate levels of assets and liabilities.

While long-term debt can be used to finance a company's growth objectives, companies may also assume long-term debt simply because the interest rates on borrowed funds are lower than their earnings, making it profitable for a company to borrow. However, even profitable borrowing can become excessive wherein a company has assumed too much debt to remain financially stable. The management for every company must strive to determine the point where debt levels shift from profitable to risky. There is no definitive point at which this happens for every company. The debt level that is appropriate for one company may be unhealthy for another company. Safe levels of debt are ultimately a function of a company's ability to repay the debts while still retaining

the capacity to grow toward its profitability objectives. When companies take on too much debt, their earnings may begin to drop. Investors and creditors will look closely at falling earnings to determine whether the decrease is due to the company's debt structure, or simply the result of external causes, such as a cooling market or rising interest rates.

Creditors and investors are able to make informed decisions about a company's financial stability, by calculating the company's debt-to-equity ratio. The debt-to-equity ratio measures how much of a company's total capital is made up of debt. Most financial experts recommend that a company's debt-to-equity ratio should remain somewhere between 0.5 and 1.5. At these levels, the company has enough capital to finance its growth objectives, while retaining sufficient supplies of cash and other assets to allow the company to pay its debt obligations, grow at a steady pace and still be able to survive periods of time during which its earnings drop or the market slows. Thus, while a company's overall liability must be carefully monitored by its management, prudent assumption of some long-term debt can help a company finance significant projects, resources or acquisitions that will enable it to grow and expand in ways that it simply could not by relying solely on its earnings. There may even be times when a company should borrow long-term debt because it is profitable to do so. However, excessive levels of long-term debt can certainly be categorized as too much of a good thing and can erode the viability of a company's financial health.

BIBLIOGRAPHY

Aivazian, V., Ying G. & Jiaping Q. (2005). Debt maturity structure and firm investment. *Financial Management (2000), 34*(4), 107-119. Retrieved April 30, 2007, from EBSCO Online Database Business Source Complete. http://search.ebscohost.com/login.aspx?direct=true&db=bth&AN=19323984&site=ehost-live

Butler, A., Grullon, G. & Weston, J. (2006). Can managers successfully time the maturity structure of their debt issues? *Journal of Finance, 61*(4), 1731-58. Retrieved April 30, 2007, from EBSCO Online Database Business Source Complete. http://search.ebscohost.com/login.aspx? direct=true&db=bth&AN=21796404&site=ehost-live

Custódio, C., Ferreira, M.A., & Laureano, L. (2013). Why are US firms using more short-term debt?.

Journal of Financial Economics, 108(1), 182-212. Retrieved October 31, 2013, from EBSCO Online Database Business Source Complete. http://search.ebscohost.com/login.aspx?direct=t rue&db=bth&AN=86665002&site=ehost-live

Eisinger, J. (2005). Hedge-fund activism wins plaudits, but the focus is really on firms' cash. *Wall Street Journal — Eastern Edition,246*(76), C1-C4. Retrieved April 30, 2007, from EBSCO Online Database Business Source Complete. http://search.ebscohost.com/login.aspx?direct=t rue&db=bth&AN=18518934&site=ehost-live

Fan, J.H., Titman, S., & Twite, G. (2012). An international comparison of capital structure and debt maturity choices. *Journal of Financial & Quantitative Analysis, 47*(1), 23-56. Retrieved October 31, 2013, from EBSCO Online Database Business Source Complete. http://search.ebsco host.com/login.aspx?direct=true&db=bt h&AN=74405986 &site=ehost-live

Finlay, S. (2007). Loan terms of endearment. *Ward's Dealer Business,41*(2), 74-75. Retrieved April 30, 2007, from EBSCO Online Database Business Source Complete. http://search.ebscohost.com/login.aspx?direct=true&db=bt h&AN=24040845&site=ehost-live

Foust, D., Grow, B., Cowan, C., Arndt, M. & Henry, D. (2006). Where's the beef? *Business Week*, 3979, 30-33. Retrieved April 30, 2007, from EBSCO Online Database Business Source Complete. http://search.ebscohost.com/ login.aspx?direct=true&d b=bth&AN=20339370&site=eh ost-live

Goyal, V.K., & Wang, W. (2013). Debt maturity and asymmetric information: Evidence from default risk changes. *Journal of Financial & Quantitative Analysis, 48*(3), 789- 817. Retrieved October 31, 2013, from EBSCO Online Database Business Source Complete. http://search.ebscohost.com/login.aspx?direct=true&db=bth&AN=90575787 &site=ehost-live

Huyghebaert, N. & Van de Gucht, L. (2007). The determinants of financial structure: New insights from business start-ups. *European Financial Management, 13*(1), 101-133. Retrieved April 30, 2007, from EBSCO Online Database Business Source Complete. http://search.ebscohost.com/login.aspx?direct=true&db=bth&AN=23615550&s ite=eh ost-live

Kyereboah-Coleman, A. (2007). The impact of capital structure on the performance of microfinance institutions. *Journal of Risk Finance (15265943),8*(1), 56-71. Retrieved April 30, 2007, from EBSCO Online Database Business Source Complete. http://search.ebscohost.com/login.aspx? direct=true&d b=bth&AN=24467022&site=ehost-live

Sender, H. (2006). High-risk debt still has allure for buyout deals. *Wall Street Journal: Eastern Edition,247*(137), C1-C5. Retrieved April 30, 2007, from EBSCO Online Database Business Source Complete. http://search.ebscohost.com/login.aspx?direct=true&db=bth&AN=21117213 &site=ehost-live

Suggested Reading

Port of Tacoma refinances long-term debt. (2006). In *Pacific Shipper, 81*(42), 6. Retrieved April 30, 2007, from EBSCO Online Database Business Source Complete. http://search. ebscohost.com/login.aspx?direct=true&db=bth&AN=2350 3179&site=ehost-live

Rastogi, A., Jain, P. & Yadav, S. (2006). Debt financing in India in public, private and foreign companies. *Vision (09722629), 10*(3), 45-58. Retrieved April 30, 2007, from EBSCO Online Database Business Source Complete. http://search.ebscohost.com/login.aspx?direct=true&db=bt h&AN=24186491&site=ehost-live

Schmukler, S. & Vesperoni, E. (2006). Financial globalization and debt maturity in emerging economies. *Journal of Development Economics, 79*(1), 183-207. Retrieved April 30, 2007, from EBSCO Online Database Business Source Complete. http://search.ebscohost.com/login.aspx?direct=t rue&d b=bth&AN=19061312&site=ehost-live

— Heather Newton

M

MANAGERIAL FINANCE

ABSTRACT

Managing the finances of a corporation can be complex and involved and requires capable and experienced financial leadership and management. Corporations seek to provide a return on investment to stockholders and need money to finance daily operations and long term plans. Managerial finance is made up of the investment decisions financial managers make. These can be decisions about dividend policy, capital spending, funding of long and short term projects and managing long and short term debt. Financial managers also have to balance their decisions with the risk involved. Financial managers use specific tools and techniques to make investment decisions and evaluate and assess the appropriate techniques based on company strategy and current economic conditions.

OVERVIEW

Finance looks at how businesses make, use and deploy financial resources. Managerial finance considers the challenges of the financial manager who must make decisions about the techniques used to manage company finances. The decisions that the financial manager makes affect the ability of the company to adequately use its cash and liquid assets, raise funds when needed and make investment moves that benefit stockholders.

Faulkender & Wang (2006, p 1957) note that investors and shareholders care about the amount of cash that a firm has because "corporate liquidity enables firms to make investments without having to access external capital markets." In this way, companies avoid transaction costs. Companies have an objective to produce a positive financial result to ensure the continuation of the company and to provide value to investors and stockholders. When a company is publicly owned, it is important that companies make decisions that are not simply in the interest of internal stakeholders but

that consider the objectives of external stakeholders such as stockholders and financial analysts. These external stakeholders are interested in predicting the profitability of a company for investment reasons.

FINANCIAL ANALYSIS

There are two techniques of financial analysis involved in security selection and valuation. These include fundamental analysis and technical analysis.

- Fundamental analysis involves researching industry information, financial statements and other factors to determine the true value of a firm.
- Technical analysis is tracking trends and patterns that might exist in stock price.

In order to make corporate investment decisions, financial managers must understand the time value of money, capital budgeting, capital structure and dividend policy. In addition, financial managers face the problem of dealing with and making decisions about risk and return. Risk is the chance that you will get a result other than the one you expected. Other topics financial managers consider include capital budgeting, raising capital, cash flow techniques, market efficiency and the capital asset pricing model (CAPM). One technique used by financial managers is that of discounted cash flow (DCF). French (2013) provides an overview of how the DCF model is used quarterly. This technique makes sure that companies examine the income produced by capital investments.

EFFICIENCY

Market efficiency can refer to economic efficiency or information efficiency.

- Economic efficiency has to do with how funds are allocated or directed and what the transaction cost is for these positions.
- Information efficiency refers to the availability of critical information related to investments and transactions.

Besley & Brigham (2001) note three types of information efficiency: Weak, semi-strong, and strong. Each refers to the relative strength of information related to price, price movement and how useful that information is in relation to the return on investment. The capital asset price model (CAPM) relates risk to return when considering the value of a stock. Morgenson & Harvey (2002) noted that CAPM is a model for the pricing of risky securities.

Time Value of Money

The time value of money is a statement of how one feels about money. It is the notion that a dollar today is worth more than the promise of a dollar in the future. Financial managers must observe how money reacts over time in order to decide the best use of money and what investments make sense. If a company has money tied up in investments, there is a cost that the company incurs because that money is not available to do something else. There are certain benefits of capitalizing on time. "Equity market timing" is "issuing shares at high prices and repurchasing at low prices" (Baker & Wurgler, 2002).

Capital Budgeting

Capital budgeting is the process of analyzing various investment alternatives in machinery and equipment and is used for planning long term acquisitions of capital assets. Although capital equipment may be useful for a company, the cost has to be balanced against the reward. For example, a manufacturing company may be in a position where old equipment is costing the company money because of high repair and maintenance costs and lost production. In addition, the older equipment might present a safety cost to employees and maintenance workers and may interfere with worker productivity because employees spend a lot of time dealing with equipment breakdowns. Similarly, a company may decide to invest in new equipment but it may be costly, there may be long lead times on the equipment and it may take a long time to get a return on the capital investment. Ghahremani, Aghaie, and Abedzadeh (2012) studied the effectiveness of various capital budgeting techniques over four decades and argue for the importance of adopting the real option approach to capital budgeting decisions.

Capital Structure

Capital structure refers to the framework a company uses to generate financing for assets. Companies may choose to use debt or equity financing or some combination of the two. When raising capital, a financial manager has many options. Companies can use internal money for projects or can turn to venture capital firms or banks. Loans can be obtained either as short term, working capital loans or long term loans.

Dividends

A dividend is money that is paid out of a company's profit to holders of stock. Dividend policy describes how a company will decide whether or not to pay dividends. Dividends are typically paid quarterly and can be paid out in cash or more stock to the stockholders. One of the measures of dividend policy used by financial managers is dividend yield. Dividend yield is a function of the annual dividend per share divided by the price per share (Morgenson & Harvey, 2002).

Cash Flow Analysis

An analysis of cash flow examines the in and outflows of cash and whether or not enough cash is available to meet company needs. Companies can breakeven, have a positive cash flow or net loss of cash. Projecting cash flow can prevent uncomfortable shortfalls which may result in borrowing or otherwise changing the company's financial position. However, excessive cash can uncover other signs of mismanagement. Financial managers may make changes in product prices or analyze where costs are coming from to identify the business units that generate the most in cost. Some companies find cash relief by improving their ability to collect on bills. That is why some companies employ collections agencies as an adjunct to their own accounts receivable personnel to collect stubborn, delinquent accounts. Other companies may look for ways to increase sales to bring in more cash. Financial managers also find ways to create cash reserve to prevent restrictions on company activities due to lack of cash flow.

Financial Markets

The financial markets in which the marketplace invests, buys and sells fall into the categories of markets for goods and services, financial assets, money balances, and resources (Schenk, 1997). The financial manager may deal with external parties in the course of investing or seeking financing. These institutions include banks, insurance companies and investment brokerages.

THE ROLE & DECISIONS OF THE FINANCIAL MANAGER

Financial managers are responsible for acquiring needed funds for the company and positioning these funds so that they will be invested in projects that will maximize the return on investment and the enhance the value of the company.

It may sound as if the job of a managerial finance professional is an easy one and that each professional only needs to know a few formulas. However, the job is quite complex; the professional has to consider the industry, economic conditions, internal size and structure as well as financial opportunities. Pagano and Stout (2004) looked at the weighted average of cost of capital for two large firms, Microsoft and General Electric. The authors found that using three different methods, they yielded three different results, meaning that financial managers must go beyond the equations and use a myriad of techniques, subjective and objective, to make corporate investment decisions. So while financial expertise is needed and required, other skills such as decision making and weighing alternatives are also important. The financial information possessed by the financial manager must be augmented with up to date market and industry information and with new tools for analyzing corporate investments.

Managerial finance has gone through a number of evolutions regarding its context (Besley & Brigham, 2001). During the 1940s and 50s, an emphasis was placed on liquidity while the 1950s and 60s saw a shift towards maximizing the value and analysis of alternatives. Risk management was the focus of the 1970s while the 1990s considered globalization, government regulations and increased use of technology. The focus of financial managers again evolved in the post 2007 recession economy (West, 2013). Financial managers are seen as the coordinators and directors of financial decisions and must receive coherent input from other parts of the business such as operations and marketing to adequately make decisions.

Some of the ways in which financial managers optimize a company's value is by efficient forecasting and planning, coordinating major investment and financing decisions, control of financial information

gathering and reporting and participating in financial markets (Besley & Brigham, 2001).

FINANCIAL INSTRUMENTS

Tangible and financial assets are the primary instruments that financial managers deal with and have to maximize. A tangible asset may have value to others and can be sold or borrowed against. Similarly, financial assets are financial instruments which promise the holder a cash flow distribution at some point in the future. The types of financial instruments that financial managers may work with include equity and debt instruments such as:

- Certificates of Deposit
- Treasury Bills
- Eurodollars
- Commercial Paper
- Common Stock
- Preferred Stock
- Corporate Bonds
- Term Loans
- Treasury notes and bonds.

One of the ways in which a corporation can use financial instruments it has issued is to buy tangible assets that are income-producing assets.

DEBT

Financial managers must analyze corporate activities related to short and long-term debt. Debt is when a loan is made to someone or some entity and has the features of principal value, face value, maturity value and par value. Principal value is also called principal amount or simply principle. It is equivalent to the amount being borrowed. Par, maturity or face value is the amount that will be paid on a financial security such as a bond when mature. A feature of debt that financial managers must consider is the fact that interest payments will be due in addition to principal payments. Certain types of debt result in turning over controlling interests in the company.

Some examples of short term debt are treasury bills, repurchase agreements, commercial paper and certificates of deposit. Examples of long-term debt include term loans, bonds (government treasury or municipal bonds, corporate bonds, mortgage bonds). Equity financing can take on the form of preferred or common stock. Preferred stock is preferred over common stock when dividends are distributed.

Some of the features of preferred stock that are different from common stock are the possible allowance for cumulative dividends or the conversion of preferred stock into common stock (Besley & Brigham, 2001).

Common stock allows stockholders to have a stake of ownership in a firm. These stockholders may also have a preemptive right to purchase additional shares sold by the company. Capital stock is a term that refers to all the stock issued by a company and includes common and preferred stock. A company's charter authorizes the number and value of shares of stock available (Morgenson & Harvey, 2002)

Financial managers may decide to participate in the financial markets through the use of derivatives. Derivatives are financial securities based on an underlying asset like a stock or bond. Derivatives are considered to be risky investments but have the potential for a high rate of return and can possibly balance out a portfolio.

VIEWPOINT

COMPARING OPTIONS FOR INVESTMENT & RAISING CAPITAL

Financial managers have many choices for investing a firm's money and must weigh those options in a way that maximizes value for the company. First, financial managers have to consider risk when choosing a financial security. One of the issues that may be important to a company is what tax implications will result from a particular type of security. In addition, the value and cost of an investment over time can impact whether or not the investment is selected for short or long term.

CHOOSING A FINANCIAL INSTRUMENT

The financial instrument that is best depends on your point of view. Financial managers will have to discover whether or not an investment is worthwhile from the issuer's or the investor's point of view (Besley & Brigham, 2001). Some characteristics of bonds include fixed interest payments and an interest expense that is deductible. However, they do not provide ownership and there may be some restrictions on dividends. Preferred stock may have disadvantages tax-wise by providing for higher after-tax costs because its dividends are not deductible. An advantage

of preferred stock is the guarantee of a fixed payment though payouts on these fixed payments are not guaranteed. Common stock also doesn't have an obligation for companies to pay dividends but stockholders may have voting rights and some control.

INTERNATIONAL MARKETS

International markets offer opportunity for investment as global financial investing increases and as returns on global securities grow. Some examples of global investing include American depository receipts (ADRs) which are stocks in foreign countries where the stock is held in trust by that country's banks. There are foreign debt instruments and Eurodebt (Eurobonds, eurocredits, euro-commercial paper) available for investing. Foreign equity products include eurostock or stock that is traded in other countries or Yankee stock which is stock issued for foreign companies and traded in the U.S. (Besley & Brigham, 2001).

FINANCIAL MARKETS

Financial markets are the network and system of institutions, individuals, financial instruments, policies and procedures that allow borrowers and investors to get together. Financial flow can occur when a company sells its stock directly to the purchaser or when there is indirect transfer of funds through banks or intermediaries. Financial managers can choose from money markets or capital markets when investing. Money markets are for financial instruments that are typically mature within one year or less. Capital markets are markets with instruments that have maturities of greater than one year.

PRELIMINARY ACTIONS

There are many decisions to make when trying to raise capital for a company. Financial managers have to initially decide on the optimal amount of money needed. The type of securities required to raise the level of capital needed must also be considered. Investment bankers must be consulted to assist in navigating the market. Before setting the offer price of securities, the costs related to the offer must be itemized. A rather complex selling process involves registration with the Securities and Exchange Commission and preparing a prospectus for investors. Banks agree to underwrite the newly issued securities. The company's investment banker assists in setting up a secondary market for the securities. The Securities and Exchange Commission (SEC) is a governmental agency that regulates any issuing or trading of stocks and bonds. The SEC wants to make sure companies are not committing fraud and that investors are being given an accurate picture of what they are investing in and how. The reason for this close regulation is to prevent insider trading and manipulation of the market.

THE COST OF MONEY

Financial managers always have to consider the cost of money. This can include interest rates on loans as well as equity to stockholders in terms of dividends and capital gains. When analyzing an opportunity, financial managers consider cost and whether or not the cost is reasonable based on what the company is allowed to invest in with money. Money can also be affected by the risk of investing in a depreciating asset that quickly loses value or inflation which makes things worth less over time. There are several categories of risk associated with cost of money decisions. These include the default risk premium which is the difference between interest rates on corporate bonds and U.S. treasury bonds. Inflation and liquidity premiums are premiums or add-ons to securities based on inflation or for securities that are not able to be made into liquid assets quickly. Interest rate risk affects investors with possible loss if the interest rates are fluctuating. Financial managers have to stay abreast of current financial information and cannot make decisions simply based on company strategy or company policy. External financial pressures can be exerted by Federal Reserve policy, changes in industries, the federal deficit or a dramatic change in business activity in the marketplace (Besley & Brigham, 2001).

INTERNAL MANAGERIAL FINANCE ACTIVITIES

While financial managers are well served to monitor financial news and updates, there are many activities that are central to managerial finance that take place within the confines of a company. Managerial finance often means the analysis of financial reports. Some of the reports issued by firms are consumed externally. These include the annual report which includes the basic financial statements such as the income statement, balance sheet, statement of retained earnings, cash flow statements and notes.

- An income statement is a summary of the revenues brought into the company and the expenses that were incurred by the company over the quarter or year.
- Balance sheets show the company's financial position as a snapshot of a period in time.
- The statement of cash flows shows the impact of the firm's activities such as operational cash flows, flows related to investing or financing over a certain period of time.

Knowing how much cash a company has is only part of the picture. It is important to see how the cash is used as well. Financial managers may perform ratio analysis to understand the company's liquidity position and may show how well a company manages its assets. Financial managers use ratio analysis to analyze how debt is being used and how much financing activity is taking place. Ratio analysis can also tell how profitable a company is and what the earnings are in relation to other companies in similar industries or of similar size. Although ratio analysis provides a lot of information, it can be misleading if the company has several different business units that operate in different or multiple industries. It can be complex to extract an accurate picture and extrapolate that to financial decision making.

Finally, financial managers are responsible for financial planning and control. The planning aspect involves projecting the sales and income based on the company's sales efforts and current production levels. In addition, financial managers must determine the resources needed to implement financial plans. Control is monitoring that takes place to make sure the companies activities are in line with plans and to make adjustments where needed. Monitoring and planning are assisted by automation and are ongoing processes that are subject to change based on internal or external forces.

BIBLIOGRAPHY

Baker, M. & Wurgler, J. (2002). Market timing and capital structure. *Journal of Finance, 57*(1), 1. Retrieved October 1, 2007, from EBSCO Online Database Business Source Complete. http://search.ebscohost.com/login.aspx?direct=true&db=bth&AN=5889290&site=ehost-live

Besley, S. & Brigham, E.F. (2001). *Principles of finance* (2nd ed.). Boston: Southwest College Publishing.

Faulkender, M. & Wang, R. (2006). Corporate financial policy and the value of cash. *Journal of Finance, 61*(4), 1957- 1990. Retrieved October 1, 2007, from EBSCO Online Database Business Source Complete. http://search.ebscohost.com/login.aspx?direct=true&db=bth&AN=21796398&site=ehost-live

French, N. (2013). The discounted cash flow model for property valuations: Quarterly cash flows. *Journal of Property Investment & Finance, 31*(2), 208-212. Retrieved on November 15, 2013, from EBSCO Online Database Business Source Complete. http://search.ebscohost.com/ login.aspx?direct=true&db=bth&AN=85804861&site=eh ost-live

Ghahremani, M., Aghaie, A., & Abedzadeh, M. (2012). Capital budgeting technique selection through four decades: With a great focus on real option. *International Journal of Business & Management, 7*(17), 98-119. Retrieved on November 15, 2013, from EBSCO Online Database Business Source Complete. http://search.ebscohost.com/login.aspx?direct=true&db=bth&AN=80037203&site=eh ost-live

Gordon, R. & Lee, Y. (2007) Interest rates, taxes and corporate financial policies. *National Tax Journal, 60*(1), 65-84. Retrieved October 1, 2007, from EBSCO Online Database Business Source Complete. http://search.ebscohost.com/login.aspx?direct=true&db=bth&AN=24699957&site=eh ost-live

Morgenson, G. & Harvey, C. R. (2002). *The New York Times Dictionary of Money Investing.* New York: Times Books.

Pagano, M.S. & Stout, D.E. (2004). Calculating a firm's cost of capital. *Management Accounting Quarterly, 12*(3), 243 — 256. Retrieved November 18, 2007, from EBSCO Online Database Business Source Complete. http://search.ebscohost.com/login.aspx?direct=true&db=buh&AN=14027648&site=ehost-live

Schenk, R. (1997). *Overview: financial markets.* Retrieved November 21, 2007 from http://ingrimayne.com/econ/ Financial/Overview8ma.html.

West, P. (2013). Thriving in the post-crisis economy: Managing a nexus of capabilities. *Strategic Direction, 29*(4), 3-6. Retrieved on November 15, 2013, from EBSCO Online Database Business Source Complete. http://search. ebscohost. com/login.aspx?direct=true&db=bth&AN=8665 5297&site=ehost-live

SUGGESTED READING

Czurak, D. (2007). City getting a bond aid. *Grand Rapids Business Journal, 25*(44), 3-7. Retrieved November 18, 2007, from EBSCO Online Database Business Source Complete. http://search.ebscohost.com/login.aspx?direct=t rue&db=buh&AN=27261837&site=ehost-live

Krishnan, C. N. V. (2007). Optimal wage contracts under asymmetric information and moral hazard when investment decisions are delegated. *Journal of Economics & Finance, 31*(3), 302-318. Retrieved November 18, 2007, from EBSCO Online Database Business Source Complete. http://search. ebscohost.com/login.aspx?direct=t rue&db=buh &AN=27439574&site=ehost-live

Mankin, E. (2007). Measuring innovation performance. *Research Technology Management, 50*(6), 5-7. Retrieved November 18, 2007, from EBSCO Online Database Business Source Complete. http:// search.ebscohost.com/ login.aspx?direct=true&d b=buh&AN=27377099&site=eh ost-live

Schoder, D. (2007). The flaw in customer lifetime value. *Harvard Business Review, 85*(12), 26. Retrieved November 18, 2007, from EBSCO Online Database Business Source Complete. http:// search.ebscohost.com/ login.aspx?direct=true&d b=buh&AN=27329791&site=eh ost-live

– Marlanda English

MONEY & BANKING

ABSTRACT

This article focuses on the influences of money and banking on a global economy. There is an introduction of internet banking as well as a discussion of how the Basel Committee on Banking Supervision provides an avenue for the banking industry to address banking supervisory issues across the world.

OVERVIEW

Financial relationships and the manner in which consumers handle their money have changed over the years. "It has become commonplace to argue that the rapid growth in securities transactions during the 1980s, domestically and internationally, is evidence that financial relationships matter less than they used to" (Calomiris & Ramirez, 1996, p. 44). Consumers do not have a need to develop a personal relationship with their bankers. They are comfortable managing their finances via non-traditional media. Calomiris and Ramirez (1996) found evidence that many believe innovation (i.e. new technological breakthroughs such as the use of computers in banking) has led consumers to seek out new ways to find information to resolve issues and manage problems.

Technology has also allowed regulators to relax the restrictions on bank scale and scope. As a result, banks have been able to enter non-traditional banking practices such as security underwriting, derivative sales, mutual fund control, and venture capital financing (Calomiris & Ramirez, 1996). Kaufman and Mote's (1990) work explored how the expansion of banking powers has allowed the relaxation of regulatory policy, which has minimized the use of legislative action in order to get results. These types of actions have assisted the growth of a universal banking system.

APPLICATION

E-BANKING

Technology has made it possible for financial institutions to offer electronic banking to their customers. In 2013, the *IUP Journal of Bank Management* reported

that 50 percent of banking transactions were electronic-based, and that this share was increasing "at an incredible rate." (Kaur, 2013) "Electronic banking, also known as electronic fund transfer (EFT), uses technology as a substitute for checks and other forms of paper transactions" (Fullenkamp & Nsouli, 2004, p. 94). Fullenkamp and Nsouli have defined it as "the use of electronic methods to deliver traditional banking services using any kind of payment media" (p. 7).

BENEFITS OF ELECTRONIC FUNDS TRANSFER
Customers find the service beneficial for several reasons:
- Automated Teller Machines (ATMs) — ATMs are electronic terminals that allow consumers to have access to their funds at any time. Financial institutions will provide their customers with a card which allows them to withdraw money from these machines.
- Direct Deposit — Many employers have mandated that employees have their payroll directly deposited into a checking or savings account. Once the funds reach the bank, the bank processes the transactions so that their customers will have access to the funds on the morning of their pay date.
- Pay-by-Phone Systems — A benefit to consumers is when their banks allow them to pay their bills by calling in the transactions and transferring funds between accounts.
- Personal Computer Banking — Given the use of technology, many consumers will base their banking selection on whether or not they can perform transactions online using their personal computers.
- Point-of Sale Transfers — Consumers may use their ATM cards in many stores to purchase retail items. This process is similar to using a credit card, but the funds come out of a checking account.
- Electronic Check Conversions — There are times when a consumer may write a check at a merchant's business and the transaction will become an electronic payment at the point of sale (HSBC — North America Military Financial Education Center, n.d.).

CONCERNS: ENSURING AGAINST FRAUD

With the rise of electronic banking's popularity, financial institutions and consumers must be cautious and protect information that is considered private and privileged. "Financial institutions are clearly responsible for compromised data in their possession that results in fraud, and account holders have typically been held responsible for guarding against the theft of their banking information as well as any fraud perpetrated as a result of compromised credentials" (Tubin, 2005, p. 3). In order to avoid a compromised situation, financial institutions must develop techniques that will assist in authenticating online banking users.

In the past, many customers used a password to gain access to their accounts. This approach is considered to be an example of single factor authentication. Although allowing users to select an "easy to remember" password can be convenient, it does not assist in the fight against emerging fraud. Unfortunately, there have been many online scams where criminals have tricked customers into providing their user name and password. Many banks have moved toward the practice of creating authentic user names and alphanumeric passwords to minimize the effects of these scams. In addition, there has been secondary criteria added to the log in process. "Adding a second factor, something you have or something you are, as a requirement for authentication increases security well beyond the traditional single-factor approach because it requires the criminal to gain possession of both authentication factors somehow to commit fraud" (Tubin, 2005, p. 10). This approach is called two-factor authentication. This process uses some type of hardware authentication token and the secret password. If the password is compromised, the hardware token will not work. If the hardware token is lost, the password is useless.

The journal *Credit Management* cites a decline in the incidence of fraud losses which it attributes to the increasing use of new industry technology such as fraud detection software, chip cards, and other chip and Personal Identification Number (PIN) technology. Other reasons cited are increased customer awareness, decreased online banking, and increased use of preventive software. (Card, 2011)

VIEWPOINT

BASEL COMMITTEE ON BANKING SUPERVISION

The Bank of International Settlements is responsible for promoting monetary and financial stability. This organization meets on a bimonthly basis to discuss monetary and financial matters. The organization is composed of four major committees, and they are: The Basel Committee on Banking Supervision, The Committee on the Global Financial System, and The Markets Committee.

BANKING SUPERVISION: A GLOBAL NECESSITY

As mentioned in the overview, there has been an increase in the relaxing of regulations in order to promote global banking. With this type of action, a need for supervision of banks around the world is critical. The Basel Committee on Banking Supervision offers an avenue for the banking industry to discuss banking supervisory matters. The overall objective of this entity is to increase knowledge and comprehension of key supervisory problems and increase the efficiency and value of banking supervision across the globe. In order to achieve this objective, the organization seeks to exchange information on national supervisory problems, methods and procedure and advance the common agreement worldwide (Bank for International Settlements, n.d.). The Committee's Secretariat is situated near the Bank for International Settlements in Basel, Switzerland, and the staff includes professional administrators who come from member corporations.

BASEL II AND BASEL III

Basel II, second of the Basel Accords, was introduced in response to the various financial crises of the 1990s. Adopted in 2006, Basel II quickly showed its limitations with the 2007 crisis that "strongly impacted the financial markets and the world economy generally." Within Basel III, a number of requirements aim at strengthening the resilience of the financial system (Marius, 2013), to be applied to the accord's three pillars: Minimum capital requirements, supervisory review and market discipline (Riskglossary.com). Basel III criteria entering into force between 2013 and 2018 constitute adjustments aimed to stabilize the world economy and long-term economic performance.

Based on the level of market risk allowed according to the 1996 Amendment, banks have choices when determining how they will evaluate their credit risk and market risk.

- Banks may select a standardized approach for their credit risk. Such a method acts as a foundation for a rating-based method or an advanced rating-based method.
- For operational risk, banks may choose a traditional indicator technique, a standardized approach or an internal measurement method.

BASEL SUBCOMMITTEES

The Committee reorganized in October, 2006, and was operated by four main subcommittees. These subcommittees were the Accord Implementation Group, The Policy Development Group, The Accounting Task Force, and the International Liaison Group (Bank for International Settlements, n.d.).

- The Accord Implementation Group (AIG) — The purpose of this group is to provide information and advance the consistency rates for the implementation of Basel III. Although the AIG offers an outlet with which members can communicate the details of their intentions to implement Basel III, the purpose of the subcommittee is not to require a uniform application of the corrected framework. There are three subgroups in this subcommittee and they share information and consult about the certain issues revolving around Basel III implementation.

The three subgroups are: The Validation Subgroup, the Operational Risk Subgroup, and the Trading Book Subgroup. The Validation Subgroup is charged with exploring problems having to do with the validation systems that help create the ratings and parameters that act as inputs for the internal ratings-based methods of evaluating credit risk. The Operational Risk Subgroup is responsible for addressing problems connected mostly to the banks' incorporation of advanced evaluation methods for operational risk. The final subgroup, Trading Book, develops standards that will provide a treatment for default risk in the trading book.

- The Accounting Task Force — The Accounting Task Force has been charged with ensuring that the international accounting and auditing

methods and techniques help to further sound risk management at financial institutions, encourage market regimen through clearness, and strengthen the immunity and well-being of the banking system. There are three working groups: The Conceptual Framework Issues Subgroup, The Financial Instruments Practices Subgroup, and the Audit Subgroup.

- The International Liaison Group — This subgroup compensates for the former Core Principles Liaison Group and is charged with focusing on the first incorporation and revisions of the 1997 Core Principles for Effective Banking Supervision. In addition, the subgroup offers a way for the Committee to communicate effectively with international supervisors.

CONCLUSION

Financial relationships and the manner in which consumers handle their money have changed over the years. Financial institutions continue to grow their electronic banking services offered to their customers. Although payment services, for example, are popular among consumers, financial institutions are obligated to provide documentation to their customers explaining their legal rights and responsibilities for their accounts. The documentation that the financial institution provides its customers lists the following information:

- The telephone number and address of the person to be notified if the consumer thinks an unauthorized transfer has been or may be made, a statement of the institution's "business days" (generally days the institution is open to the public for normal business), and the number of days a consumer has to report suspected unauthorized transfers.
- The type of transfers a consumer can make, fees for transfers, and any limits on the frequency and amount of transfers.
- A summary of the consumer's right to receive documentation of transfers, to stop payment on a preauthorized transfer, and the procedures to follow in order to stop payment.
- A notice describing the procedures the consumer must follow in order to report an error on a receipt for an EFT periodic statement, to request more information about a transfer listed on a statement

and how long the consumer has to file a report.

- A summary of the institution's liability to the consumer if it fails to make or stop certain transactions.
- Circumstances under which the institution will disclose information to third parties (Free Consumer Information, n.d., p. 2).

If an individual elects to use EFT services, the following tips may be helpful in keeping their personal information secure (HSBC — North America Military Financial Education Center, n.d.):

- Always know where one's ATM or debit card is located and file a report if the card is missing.
- Select a PIN number that is not associated with any personal information like addresses, telephone numbers, social security numbers or birth dates.
- Store and evaluate the receipts from all forms of EFT with the help of periodic statements.
- Know and trust merchants before providing bank account numbers and pre-authorized deficiencies in the account.

BIBLIOGRAPHY

Bank for International Settlements (n.d.). About the Basel Committee. Retrieved September 19, 2007, from http:// www.bis.org/bcbs/

Bank for International Settlements (n.d.). Monetary and financial stability. Retrieved September 19, 2007, from http:// www.bis.org/stability.htm

Calomiris, C., & Ramirez, Carlos (1996, February). Financing the American corporation: The changing menu of financial relationships. Retrieved on October 16, 2007, from http://ideas.repec.org/p/nbr/nberhi/0079.html

Card, F. (2011). Success against techno fraud. *Credit Management*, 22-23. Retrieved November 16, 2013, from EBSCO Online Database Business Source Complete. http://search.ebscohost.com/login.aspx?direct=true&db=bth&AN=69632664&site=ehost-live

Free Consumer Information (n.d.). Electronic banking basics. Retrieved October 16, 2007, from http://www.ifg-inc.com/ Consumer%5fReports/ElectBank.shtml

Fullenkamp, C., & Nsouli, S. (2004, February). Six puzzles in electronic money and banking.
Retrieved October 16, 2007, from www.imf.org/external/pubs/ft/wp/2004/ wp0419.pdf

HSBC — North America Military Financial Education Center (n.d.). Electronic banking. Retrieved October 16, 2007, from http://militaryfinance. umuc.edu/planning/ check%5felec%5fbank. html

Kaufman, G., & Mote, L. (1990, September/October). Glass- Steagall: Repeal by regulatory and judicial reinterpretation. *Banking Law Journal, 98*, 225-264.

Kaur, R. (2013). The impact of electronic banking on banking transactions: a cost-benefit analysis. *IUP Journal Of Bank Management, 12*(2), 62-71. Retrieved November 16, 2013, from EBSCO Online Database Business Source Complete. http://search.ebscohost.com/login.aspx?direct=t rue&db=bth&AN=88142168&site=ehost-live

Marius, M. M. (2013). The framework resulting from the Basel III regulations. *Annals of the University of Oradea, Economic Science Series, 22*(1), 1103-1112. Retrieved November 14, 2013, from EBSCO Online Database Business Source Complete. http://search.ebscohost.com/ login.aspx?direct=true&db=bth&AN=90545805&site=eh ost-live

Riskglossary.com (n.d.). Basel committee on banking supervision. Retrieved on September 19, 2007, from http://www. riskglossary.com/link/basle%5fcommittee.htm

Tubin, G. (2005, April). The sky is falling: The need for stronger consumer online banking authentication. Retrieved October 16, 2007, from http://64.233.169.104/search?q=ca che:FHJT8Xa2TlMJ:www-304.ibm.com/jct03004c/businesscenter/fileserve%3Fcontentid %3D82467+tubin%2Bba nking%2Bauthenticatio n&hl=en&ct=clnk&cd=1&gl=us

SUGGESTED READING

Dheer, S. (2006). Is a FedEx model of money movement in banking's future? *U.S. Banker, 116*(5), 72-72. Retrieved October 19, 2007, from EBSCO Online Database Business Source Complete. http://search.ebscohost.com/login.aspx? direct=true&db=bth&AN=20579718&site=ehost-live

Fest, G. (2006). Correspondent bankers: How much is enough? *Bank Technology News, 19*(3), 12-13.

Retrieved October 25, 2007, from EBSCO On-line Database Business Source Complete. http://search.ebscohost.com/login.aspx?direct=t rue&d b=bth&AN=20726282&site=ehost-live

Material world. (2007). *Economist, 385*(8551), 99. Retrieved October 25, 2007, from EBSCO Online

Database Business Source Complete. http://search.ebscohost.com/ login.aspx?direct=true&d b=bth&AN=27099167&site=eh ost-live

—Marie Gould

MONEY MARKETS

ABSTRACT

For businesses seeking to find asset security in between their investments, there are two general choices. The first is a long-term capital investment strategy, such as the acquisition of bonds. The second is more short-term investment strategy, one that provides shorter term financial return with more liquid assets available. It is to the latter of these concepts, money markets, which this paper focuses on with the aim of defining an important part of any strong economy.

OVERVIEW

Calvin Coolidge once said that the "chief business of the American people is business," adding that Americans are "profoundly concerned with producing, buying, selling, investing and prospering in the world" ("Coolidge," 1996). Indeed, the backbone of a strong capitalist economy like that of the United States is an extensive marketplace that offers its patrons the opportunity to maximize profits and minimize losses.

At the core of any business or commercial enterprise is financial solvency. A business relies on an ability to protect its assets by placing them in savings, hoping to see growth and expecting to avoid losses. This simple concept is in fact an extremely complex one; dependent on the preferences and decisions of the individual business owner. Some experience modest gains upon their savings but benefit from the protection by conservative investment strategies. Others seek a higher yield, while accepting the potential for sudden loss. Depending upon the specific case, long-term or short-term growth can be a focal point for a business and its funds.

For businesses seeking to find asset security in between their investments, there are two general choices. The first is a long-term investment strategy,

such as the acquisition of bonds. The second is a more short-term investment strategy, one that provides shorter term financial return with an availability of more liquid assets. It is to the latter of these concepts, money markets, that this paper focuses with the aim of defining an important part of any strong economy.

MONEY MARKETS — AN INTRODUCTION

A marketplace is an entity wherein items are bought or sold. In the stock market, for example, individuals invest in interests in publicly traded companies, seeking to profit from their positive performance and to avoid losses when the stocks they hold wane in value. Money markets are similar to the stock market concept, except for the fact that in a money market (as its name suggests), it is money that is traded rather than stocks.

The basic premise of a money market is that individuals invest monies into money market funds (which, like mutual funds, spread investment monies around to various market members in order to foster stability and maximum opportunity). The funds return, usually on a monthly basis, a portion of the earnings on the investor's money in the form of dividends. The targets of investment, known as "instruments," are typically government sponsored (Treasury issues, known as "T-Bills") accounts, bank-sponsored accounts (so-called "CDs, or Certificates of Deposit) or short-term corporate paper (Pritchard, 2009).

Money markets are constructed for the purpose of strengthening investments on short-term borrowing and lending relationships. A corporation, for example, might sell paper (unsecured obligation such as accounts receivable or inventory ("Commercial paper," 2009)) on the market to meet its financial needs. On the other hand, an investor who profited from another investment might deposit some of those funds into a CD as a safe way to earn more money on interest and dividends ("The money market," 2009).

Money market funds were first introduced to Wall Street in 1971, when investment entrepreneur Bruce R. Bent created the Reserve Fund. Bent's idea was not the first money market fund in history, however. Several years earlier, in 1968, John Oswin Schroy introduced the Conta Garantia to the Brazilian marketplace. 31 years after Conta Garantia was floated to investors in Rio de Janeiro and 28 years after Bruce Bent took the money market fund to a much grander scale, there are approximately 2,000 money market funds in operation worth $2.3 trillion in assets.

TYPES OF MONEY MARKET FUNDS

There are two basic types of money market funds in operation. The first of these money market funds are "retail" accounts. These funds are typically offered to high-net worth investors who tend to use the accounts in between investment actions. In other words, an investor may sell a given share or asset on the stock market, and take his or her liquid earnings from the sale and "park the cash" into a retail account, where it can further generate modest interest while the investor looks for another intermediate- or long-term investment opportunity. Such funds comprise about 40 percent of all money market assets, and are offered primarily by brokerage houses. Retail accounts also prove useful for people who are simply seeking a safe, risk-free investment for their liquid assets. The largest of the retail accounts is the Fidelity Cash Reserve, which boasts about $120 billion in assets and a seven-day yield rate of 3.4 percent (Kosnett, 2008).

The second form of money market fund is the "institutional" fund. This type of money market fund is offered to large corporations, government agencies and other sizable organizations. These entities collect free-floating cash within their programs and deposit them, in many instances on an automatic, nightly basis, into the institutional fund. Like retail accounts, they are offered largely by brokerage houses and are useful for the purposes of putting a good use to idle funds ("Money market funds," 2009).

RECENT SURGES IN MONEY MARKET USE

In both of these cases, money markets typically represent safe havens for liquid assets during particularly unsteady economic times. By 2008, money market mutual fund assets reached an all-time high, having increased by more than $19 billion to a total of $3.43

trillion, according to one watchdog group. In 2008 alone, the increase in money market assets was staggering — a 43 percent jump worth $1.1 trillion. The causes for this surge in money market participation were two-fold. First, signs of a deteriorating economic landscape led a much larger percentage of the population to install their liquid assets in less volatile markets. Second, the Federal Reserve was wary at the time to cut interest rates, which meant that entities paying back on loans within the money market did so at higher interest rates, thereby ensuring a stronger return for market investors ("Money fund asset gains," 2008).

In 2008, the money market again came to a critical use when Wall Street giant American International Group (AIG) was close to complete closure. The federal government, deciding that AIG's influence was too important to allow the company to collapse, lent nearly $85 billion to AIG through US Treasury securities, effectively giving the federal government almost 80 percent of equity holdings. A British bank, Libor, bolstered the loan (Karnitschnig, et al, 2008).

Money markets are considered relatively safe and secure institutions for investors. At a typical $1 per share, money market funds are short-term in nature (the maturity of such investments are between one day and one year), which helps prevent severe impacts should the companies involved encounter rough waters. Additionally, money market funds are liquid-based, which means an investor's money is easily accessed like that of a checking account. During times of stock market volatility, investors often pour their money into money accounts to help weather the storm.

In 2008, for example, two of The Vanguard Group's money market funds, the Vanguard Admiral Treasury Money Market Fund and the Vanguard Treasury Money Market, saw enormous surges in money market investment activity. While the stock markets saw increased unpredictability and assets began suffering as a result, these two money market funds saw extremely large growth over a one-year period — the former saw an increase of $5.4 billion and the latter saw $1.7 billion more — as investors poured their money into the typically safe, conservative funds (Sullivan, 2009).

Despite this relative safety; however, it is important to remember that with any investment, there are both benefits and risks to the investor. This paper next turns to an overview of the positive and negative aspects of money markets.

THE BENEFITS OF A MONEY MARKET

Money markets exist for the purposes of borrowing and lending. In light of this fact, any investment into a money market must be expected to provide conservative returns.

In an average or bull market (a period in which investment prices rise faster than their historical average), such a conservative return provides the investor with another avenue to experience a consistent return on profits already generated from other investments.

Under United States Securities and Exchange Commission rules, most money market funds must invest at least 95 percent of their assets in so-called "first-tier securities" (such as the aforementioned Treasury certificates and private bank notes). Such securities must have an exceptional credit rating (T. Rowe Price, 2009). This practice, coupled with the short-term nature of investments, money markets represent to the investor a relatively safe account.

TYPES OF MONEY MARKET INVESTMENTS

There are two types of money market investments — money market funds and money market deposit accounts. The latter of these, deposit accounts, have been federally insured, as they are bank accounts, since their introduction. However, the US Department of the Treasury announced in September of 2008 that it would establish a temporary guarantee program for money market funds as well (US Securities & Exchange Commission, 2009). During an increasingly unstable market period, then- President George W. Bush included a $50 billion earmark for the protection of the money market industry.

The Treasury Department's implementation of this one-year program underscores its position that money markets are invaluable components of the US economy. According to a statement issued after the program's introduction, "Maintaining confidence in the money market fund industry is critical to protecting the integrity and stability of the global financial system" (US Department of the Treasury, 2008).

GROWING ATTRACTIVENESS OF MONEY MARKETS

Since the introduction of money market funds in 1972, interest in such accounts has grown exponentially. This trend is due in no small part to inflation. In the 1970s, inflation created considerable widespread concern among leaders and consumers alike.

However, inflation during and after the 1980s sent interest rates skyward, particularly as expectations for the impact of inflation drove investment practices. Such increases led to significant returns on money market investments, particularly in T-bills. While interest rates have stabilized with industrialized economies gaining a better hold on inflation, the potential returns on money markets (especially in a down market) remains strong in the 21st century.

The attractiveness of money markets for investors has long been the conservative returns they offer the investor. In a down economy, however, money markets have also proven durable and, in fact, bolstered by the troubled economy. The economic crisis that began in 2008 provides an excellent illustration of this point.

MONEY MARKETS DURING ECONOMIC CRISIS

In December of 2008, the Federal Reserve reduced a key interest rate one percent to nearly zero in order to help stimulate some growth. Under such circumstances, one would anticipate that money markets would suffer, given the lower rates on return. However, the opposite was true — one-year CDs yielded an average of almost two percent, the same rate it showed seven months earlier. The key was the number of large-scale financial institutions, as well as an increasing number of bank holding companies, that took control of failing institutions. With commercial paper and Treasury issues dwindling, these institutions looked to deposit accounts for support, and in light of the demand, they remained willing to offer investors higher yield rates — sometimes three or even five percent (as was the case for Washington Mutual before it was seized by regulators).

Adding to the positive yield environment was the fact that smaller financial institutions are looking to compete with larger corporations. With lenders like the now defunct GMAC (which financed the now reorganized automaker General Motors) and Morgan Stanley offering three percent, smaller banks looked to offer higher returns as well in order to stay competitive (Kiviat, 2008). Put simply, as havok may be wreaked upon corporate viability, the money markets that are used to finance commercial enterprises provide ongoing viability for investors, even if the yield is conservative and the gain only of a short-term nature.

THE DOWNSIDE OF MONEY MARKETS

Of course, the fact that money market investment entails short-term deposits with conservative gains means that the investor is losing out on potentially large gains over a long period of time. Between 1925 and 1993, for example, the average return on a money market investment like T-bills averaged less than four percent. Investment in the S&P 500 market, meanwhile, saw a return average of nearly three times that figure, at 10.7 percent (Jones, 1995).

In a strong economy, money markets appear to yield less of a return on investment. Still, money markets have demonstrated a consistency in return, particularly in downward economic times. Then again, market tumult can even impact the money markets, as the recent 2008 implosion on Wall Street demonstrated.

On September 19, 2008, investment giant Lehman Brothers closed its doors, unable to cover its securities. Worried money market investors quickly and in great volume placed redemption orders, looking to recoup their investments before they experienced losses on them. The nation's largest money market fund, the Reserve Fund (which had invested in Lehman Brothers), was unable to purchase all of Lehman's holdings. To make this buyout happen, the Reserve Fund had to lower its share price below $1, which would inevitably cause losses to money market investors. As mentioned earlier in this paper, the Treasury stepped in to guarantee investments made before September, but those who invested after that guarantee was implemented were left to experience losses (Waggoner, 2009).

The case of Lehman Brothers underscores the point that the long-standing reputation of money markets as consistent moneymakers for the investor (albeit yielding small returns) is not impervious to the elements. In fact, money markets are subject to risk, especially when the firm or firms in which money market funds invest cannot cover their debts.

When the Lehman Brothers incident occurred, the high rate of redemption orders that were placed subsequently caused the Reserve Fund to lock, freezing out investors from their money for nearly six weeks. Between 400,000 and one million people were unable to access their funds, and a class action lawsuit was filed against the Reserve Fund to recoup the frozen funds. Investors expressed dismay at the company's actions, citing what they believed to be the

Reserve Fund's time-honored reputation for stability and reliability (Henriques, 2008).

SENIOR INVESTORS & MONEY MARKETS

The economic crisis that began in 2008 cast a shadow of doubt on the reliability of money markets during a recession. Still, a large percentage of investors continue to place their liquid assets in money market funds despite the risks involved in times of economic tumult. Among the most stalwart of investors in this arena have been those who live on limited incomes: Seniors.

A recent study of senior money market investors shows the risks and gains involved with such investments during an unstable market. About 37 percent of American retirees kept a sizable percentage of their liquid assets in money market funds. Despite such incidents as the Lehman Brothers collapse (and the Reserve Fund's decision to break the $1 tradition to offset the collapse), retired seniors' dedication to such liquid accounts was consistent despite losses. 65 percent of those who had half or less of their liquid assets invested in the money markets reported losses because of the economic downturn. Interestingly, 49 percent of those who had invested over half of their assets in the money markets experienced such losses. Additionally, while seniors tend to leave their assets invested in one type of fund regardless of the economic recession, the second-largest percentage of retirees (17 percent) who want to move their assets from one type of investment to another do so by moving them into money markets, where the returns are not stellar but consistent ("Despite financial crisis," 2009).

The issue surrounding those money market investors with limited incomes underscores an important point about the downside of such investment activity. In a money market, the interest rate is in general proportional to the amount of assets the investor deposits. Money markets therefore tend to give greater returns to those who can afford to invest more (Kennon, 2009). This fact is an important distinction from primary investments in CDs (although CDs are often one of the securities used in money markets), as CDs base interest on the maturity of the investment. The short-term nature of the money market investment, therefore, can bring greater returns to wealthy individuals and companies, while less affluent people and organizations see more modest returns.

In light of the positive and negative aspects of money markets and investments therein, it is a frequent question of investors to financial experts as to whether a money market fund is a wise choice. Then again, like any other market, an individual or corporate investment is a matter of preference. As shown here, money markets provide a safe investment as well as an invaluable mechanism for financial institutions and loan recipients to facilitate a stable transaction.

CONCLUSION

In the early 20th century, attorney Horace Rackham was tempted to invest in the new business owned by his client, Henry Ford. The President of the Michigan Savings Bank advised him against it, suggesting that Ford's brainchild, the automobile, was a mere fad destined to disappear. Rackham ignored the advice and invested $5,000 in Ford stock. Later, he sold the stock — for $12.5 million ("Ford stock," 2009).

Investments are a matter of preference for the investor. As this paper has demonstrated, money markets represent a useful vehicle for a great many investors (as well as the companies who take part in the market to obtain loan assistance). Money markets will not provide a yield that is even close to the figure Horace Rackham saw with his mature Ford stock — the short-term nature of money market investments, coupled with a typically conservative return, prevent such potentials.

Then again, money markets have long been considered reliable and relatively stable when compared to stock markets. This fact is particularly interesting for investors during economic downturns. As this paper has shown, the recession that began in 2008 sent investors into the money markets in great numbers; seeking even a modest return, but most importantly, desiring the ability to remove their funds at the first sign of trouble.

Money markets have their benefits and risks, especially during fiscal crises. In a 21st century filled with a myriad of diverse international markets, money markets are likely to continue to attract investors at every income level.

BIBLIOGRAPHY

Blanton, K. & Weisman, R. (2008, September 18). Money market funds battered. *Boston Globe*. Retrieved February 17, 2009, from http://www.boston. com/business/markets/ articles/2008/09/18/money%5fmarket%5ffunds%5fbatte red/.

Coolidge, C. (1996). *Columbia World of Quotations*. Retrieved February 10, 2009, from Bartleby.com. http://www.bartleby.com/66/46/14846.html

Commercial paper. (2009). Retrieved February 13, 2009, from Investorwords.com. http://www.investorwords.com/961/ commercial%5fpaper.html.

Money fund asset gains surpass $1 trillion over past 52 weeks. (2008, February 29). Retrieved February 18, 2009, from Crane Data News Archives: February 2008. http://www. cranedata.us/archives/news/2008/2/

Despite financial crisis, retirees leave income on the table. (2009). *Pension Benefits, 18*(2), 8. Retrieved February 17, 2009, from EBSCO Online Database Business Source Complete. http://search.ebscohost.com/login.aspx?direct=t rue&db=bth&AN=3 6400267&site=ehost-live

Enriques, D.B. (2008, October 28). Reserve Fund's investors still await their cash. *New York Times*. Retrieved February 17, 2009, from The New York Times Online. http://www. nytimes. com/2008/10/29/business/29fund.html

Flynn, K. (2013). Money fund protection incomplete. *Money, 42*(7), 18. Retrieved November 15, 2013, from EBSCO Online Database Business Source Complete. http://search. ebscohost. com/login.aspx?direct=true&db=bth&AN=889 07452&site=ehost-live

Ford stock. (2009). Retrieved February 18, 2009 from Anecdotage.com. http://www.anecdotage.com/index. php?aid=14827

Frozen-out banks will face changed world on return to money markets. (2013). *Euroweek, (1311)*, 31. Retrieved November 15, 2013, from EBSCO Online Database Business Source Complete. http:// search.ebscohost.com/ login.aspx?direct=true&d b=bth&AN=89014041&site=eh ost-live

Jones, A.N. (1995). The high price of safe investments. *Business Press, 7*(41), 12. Retrieved February 17, 2009, from EBSCO Online Database Regional Business News. http://search. ebscohost.com/login.aspx?direct=true&db=b wh&AN=9601292941&site=ehost-live

Karnitschning, M., Solomon, D., Pleven, L. & Hilsenrath, J.E. (2008, September 16). US to take over AIG in $85 billion bailout. *Wall Street Journal*.

Retrieved February 16, 2009, from http://online. wsj.com/article/SB122156561931242905. html

Kennon, J. (2009). In this market: Money market versus certificate of deposit. Retrieved February 16, 2009 from About.com. http://beginnersinvest.about.com/cs/banking/ a/062501a.htm

Kiviat, B. (2009, January 12). Savings are sexy again. *Time, 173*(1), 49. Retrieved February 17, 2009, from EBSCO Online Database Academic Search Complete. http:// search.ebscohost.com/login.aspx?direct=true&db=a9h&AN=35921435&site=ehost-live

Locke, L. G., Mitra, E., & Locke, V. (2013). Harnessing whales: The role of shadow price disclosure in money market mutual fund reform. *Journal of Business & Economics Research, 11*(4), 187-196. Retrieved November 15, 2013, from EBSCO Online Database Business Source Complete. http:// search.ebscohost.com/login.aspx?direct=t rue&d b=bth&AN=86858802&site=ehost-live

Money fund. (2009). Retrieved February 18, 2009 from Nationmaster.com. http://www.nation-master.com/encyclopedia/Money-fund

The money market: A look back. (2009). Retrieved February 10, 2009, from Investopedia.com. http://www.investopedia.com/articles/06/moneymarketlookback.asp

Money market funds offer safety and liquidity; but you'll sacrifice returns. (2009). Retrieved February 17, 2009, from About.com. http://bonds. about.com/od/bondfunds/a/moneymarket.htm

Pritchard, J. (2009). Money market funds — risks and benefits. Retrieved February 10, 2009, from About.com. http:// banking.about.com/od/ investments/a/moneymarketfund. htm.

Sullivan, T. (2009, February 9). Popularity is painful for Treasury money markets. Barrons. Retrieved February 16, 2009, from http://online.barrons. com/article/ SB123396546990458869.html.

T. Rowe Price. (2009). Benefits of money market funds. Retrieved February 16, 2009, from http:// individual.troweprice.com/public/Retail/ Mutual-Funds/Money-Market- Funds/Benefits

US Securities and Exchange Commission. (2008, October 7). Money market funds. Retrieved February 16, 2009, from http://www.sec.gov/answers/ mfmmkt.htm

US Treasury Department. (2008, September 19). Treasury announces guaranty program for money market funds. Retrieved February 16, 2009, from http://www.ustreas. gov/press/releases/hp1147. htm

Waggoner, J. (2009, January 30). What's in store for money funds? *USA Today,* 4b.

SUGGESTED READING

Low rates challenge money funds. (2009). *Consumer Reports Money Adviser, 6*(2), 10. Retrieved February 18, 2009, from EBSCO Online Database Business Source Complete. http://search.ebscohost.com/ login.aspx?direct=t rue&db=bth&AN=36302945& site=ehost-live

Money-fund assets grow. (2009). *Wall Street Journal — Eastern Edition, 253*(24), C9. Retrieved February 18, 2009, from EBSCO Online Database Academic Search Complete. http://search.ebscohost.com/ login.aspx?direct=t rue&db=a9h&AN=36415226& site=ehost-live

Nickerson, K. (2009, January 8). Yield work. *Money Marketing,* 18. Retrieved February 18, 2009, from EBSCO Online Database Business Source Complete. http://search. ebscohost.com/ login.aspx?direct=true&db=bth&AN=3618 0652&site=ehost-live

Platt, G. (2009). Shortage of dollars supports greenback. *Global Finance, 23*(1), 57-58. Retrieved February 18, 2009, from EBSCO Online Database Business Source Complete. http://search.ebscohost.com/login.aspx?direct=t rue&db=bth&AN=3 6406552&site=ehost-live

Waggoner, J. (2009, January 30). What's in store for money funds? *USA Today,* 4b.

— Michael P. Auerbach

O

ONLINE TRADING

ABSTRACT

This article concerns securities trading on the Internet or Online Trading. This method of trading evolved as technological advances changed the way in which investment products are bought and sold. With the advance of technology, securities trading in general became more automated. Moreover, as the Internet expanded, it became a marketplace for a variety of consumer goods which led to the creation of an electronic securities trading market. In the beginning, discount brokerage firms developed software that enabled customers to buy and sell securities online. Today, online trading continues to evolve as brokerage firms and other financial institutions are offering more traditional investment services while providing other financial services as well. This article is an overview of the evolution of online trading and includes a discussion of new trends in this ever-growing field of securities trading.

OVERVIEW

The Internet has become a convenient avenue for people to conduct a variety of consumer and financial transactions. The ability of customers and commercial enterprises to exchange information electronically allows for credit card and utility payments, the purchase of and payment for consumer products, bank account maintenance, as well as for conducting financial transactions — including the buying and selling of stocks, bonds, mutual funds, and other investments. These financial transactions are commonly referred to as online trading. In order to understand online trading, a brief history of the evolution of the Internet and technological advances in securities trading are worth considering.

The Internet is the worldwide system of computers that exchange information electronically. The system was originally developed by the United States Defense Department in the 1960s in order to create an information exchange system that would enable key government agencies and the military to route data around failed electrical circuits in the event of a nuclear attack. By the 1970s, colleges and universities started accessing this information-exchange system in order to share research data. While the Internet remains largely unregulated, there are various standards and conventions, such as the File Transfer Protocol (FTP) and the protocol commonly known as the World Wide Web, that govern the storage, retrieval, and exchange of information.

Websites became more popular throughout the 1990s as numerous commercial enterprises began to exchange information and to communicate electronically through email with the assistance of such pioneering Internet Service Providers (ISPs) as America Online, CompuServe and Yahoo. Today, there are a number of ways to access the Internet and there are a broad array of services available that provide access to free information, data, software, games, consumer products, and banking and investment services (Russ, 1996).

As the Internet evolved and the information age began to advance, changes were also occurring in the way in which financial transactions were being conducted. This can be seen, in part, by the creation of NASDAQ — the electronic stock exchange established in 1971 by the National Association of Securities Dealers (the NASD). NASDAQ stands for National Association of Securities Dealers Automated Quotations System, and it is the market where most growth company stocks such as technology stocks are traded. Shortly thereafter, in 1975, the U.S. Congress deregulated the stock brokerage industry and one major change was the elimination of the New York Stock Exchange's (NYSE) ability to set commission rates charged by its members. This led to the establishment of discount brokers, who took orders to buy and sell securities, but these companies did not offer investment advice or perform research. Since the administrative expenses were far less than those incurred by traditional brokers, this new breed of brokers was free to offer buy and sell services at a discount (Stefanadis, 2001).

In addition to limiting their services to placing buy and sell orders for less money, discount brokers attracted a more savvy group of investors. These investors were quite often people who were employed in the financial services sector or who had experience with investments and were looking to trade for their own accounts. They also had the time and ability to perform their own research as well as to conduct due diligence. In order to do so, an investor needs to have an understanding of the basic concepts of finance such as the time value of money, asset valuation, and risk management. Moreover, these investors need to be able to analyze financial statements of publicly traded companies in order to determine their net worth, profits, losses, and revenues, all of which are critical to asset valuation.

As the demand for services of discount brokers began to grow, these companies began to develop software programs and construct hardware platforms that enabled investors to actually conduct financial transactions in real time over the Internet. These investors came to be known as day traders. Day traders are investors who buy and sell stocks during the day with the goal being to make profits as the value of those stocks changes throughout the day (Landis, 2004).

In order to do so, day traders use money that is borrowed, and this is known as buying on margin. Buying on margin is not a new practice as financial service professionals, investment companies, and sophisticated investors have bought and sold stock on margin for quite some time. Moreover, buying on margin is a practice that is regulated by the New York Stock Exchange (the NYSE) in conjunction with rules established by the NASD. However, it is a risky practice and an inexperienced investor can suffer large financial losses. While there were pre-existing regulations in place governing margin transactions, in April 2001 the NYSE promulgated stricter guidelines for margin trading being conducted by day traders (SEC, 2005).

The advent of online trading by the discount brokerage firms led to the establishment of new business enterprises that specialized in conducting stock transactions on the Internet. Some of the early companies in this field were Charles Schwab Corp.,

Fidelity Investments, TD Waterhouse, E*Trade and Ameritrade (TD Waterhouse and Ameritrade eventually merged to form TD Ameritrade). Not only did these entities lead the way in developing a new form of securities trading and establishing a new type of business enterprise, they have also had an impact on the greater financial services market by branching into more traditional consumer finance services like check writing, electronic bill paying, and issuing credit cards and debit cards (Snel, 1999).

The NYSE and the NASD, as well as the U.S. Securities Exchange Commission (SEC) along with other state regulatory agencies, all regulate the securities industry as had been the case prior to the development of the Internet and the advent of Online Trading. Moreover, the early twenty-first century has been a period of increasing regulatory scrutiny of the financial services sector. Important developments in this regard have been the increased financial reporting requirements of the Sarbanes-Oxley Act of 2002 (SOX), the compliance requirements of the Patriot Act, the Dodd-Frank Wall Street Reform and Consumer Protection Act of 2010, and the Jumpstart Our Business Startups Act of 2012.

The Sarbanes-Oxley Act is a federal law that requires publicly traded companies to file yearly financial statements more promptly than in the past (prior to SOX, firms were required to provide annual financial statements 90 days after the end of fiscal year; the requirement is now 45 days). Publicly traded companies are also required to provide quarterly financial statements, and senior management is required to attest to the accuracy of these financial statements. The Patriot Act became Federal law in October 2001, shortly after the events of September 11th. The Act incorporates previous laws aimed at curtailing money laundering and bank fraud and its intent is to prevent the financing of terrorist activities by requiring financial institutions to verify customers' identities. This has had far reaching implications for investors and companies alike, especially as it relates to online trading. For investors who trade online or otherwise are involved in buying and selling securities, having quicker access to financial statements, and the increased scrutiny of those financial statements enables investors to have a better picture of the value of assets underlying potential investments. At the same time, the requirements of SOX and the Patriot Act have required companies to enhance their technology

NASDAQ Studio. *Via Wikipedia.org*

across the board in order to prepare and file financial statements more expediently, as well as to confirm the identities of customers (Hintze, 2005).

APPLICATIONS

The concept of buying stocks online might sound easy to some, but online trading, much like placing buy/sell orders with discount brokers, requires an investor to have an understanding of financial investing. Although online brokers have expanded their services over the years by offering research and analytical tools to customers, full service brokers still provide investment advice and long term financial planning. Accordingly, investing online requires an investor to consider a number of factors.

First, investors need to know what their investment objectives are. There are different types of investment strategies, such as investing for value, growth, or income. Investing for value requires investing in larger companies that have a proven track record of profitability, and investing in these entities usually

means holding the stock for a long period of time. Investing in a growth company entails investing in new businesses that are bringing new goods or services to the market that have growth potential. To invest for income means to invest in companies that pay dividends on its shares of stock. Moreover, investors need to determine what their long term and short-term investment goals are and to what extent they can assume the risk of losing their investment (Belkiaris, 2003).

Once these decisions have been made, an investor can choose an online broker. There are now a number of brokers who provide online trading services and many of the traditional stock brokerage outfits, mutual fund companies and banks offer online trading tools as well. Further, the range of services offered by these entities, and the administrative personnel available for providing research and analysis varies. A lot also depends on how much and how frequently an investor intends to trade online, and the fees they are willing to pay for securities transactions. This is important because brokerage

The New York Stock Exchange. *Via Wikipedia.org*

rates are typically based on the size and frequency of trades. Investors who trade more frequently get a discount. Price is not the only consideration, however, as investors also need to evaluate a website's functionality, whether research and technical assistance is provided, and whether stop-loss orders are provided. A stop-loss order is a customer order to a broker that sets the sell price of a stock below the current market price. This will protect profits or prevent losses if the stock drops.

After these determinations are made and an investor has registered for an online trading account with an online broker, he or she will be required to deposit and maintain a minimum balance in the account. Placing an order over the Internet requires an investor to know the stock symbol of the company as well as the exchange on which the company's shares are traded. An investor then needs to decide how many shares to buy and whether the purchase will be an at market order or an at limit order. An at-market order is an order to purchase the stock at the current market price, so the timing of placing the order is important since the value of stock fluctuates in real time over the course of a trading day. An at-limit order, on the other hand, is an order that sets the highest amount an investor is willing to pay for the stock.

After the order is placed and the trade has been settled, an investor will be provided with a transaction confirmation from the online broker. This confirmation is usually an email transmission, so it is a good idea for an online trader to print out the email and retain a copy in the event a problem arises with the transaction, as well as for tax purposes. Finally, shares that are traded online are registered electronically so online investors do not receive an actual paper stock certificate (Belkiaris, 2003).

There are risks that experienced investors must contend with as well. The first, of course, is the possibility of losing money. Depending on market conditions, stock prices can and do fluctuate during a trading day and by not placing an order correctly or at a price that is above the market rate, an online trader can lose his investment. There are also financial privacy and security issues to consider. This is an important consideration as the evolution of online trading has been followed by a rise in Internet securities fraud, and federal and state law enforcement authorities have conducted numerous cyber crime investigations. These investigations have uncovered illegal activities of computer hackers who raid online brokerage accounts, place unauthorized sales orders that online brokers process. The proceeds from the sale are subsequently wired to falsified accounts. In some cases, investors who were not actively monitoring their online trading accounts have lost all of their investments.

In most instances, hackers do not get access to investor accounts by breaking into the online brokers' systems. Instead, hackers are able to access accounts through home personal computers that do not have sufficient computer virus protection. In these cases, once a virus made its way onto an investor's personal computer, usually through an email transmission, the virus was able to access any financial information on the computer and automatically begin emptying out online accounts. In addition to not having sufficient virus protection, many investors have had account passwords that were relatively easy to crack or had not been changed for a long period of time. While the total losses from Internet securities fraud have been small relative to the total amount of assets now being traded online, investors, brokers and investigators are concerned about the effect cyber crime will have on the online trading industry (Borrus, 2005).

VIEWPOINTS

Despite the fact that online trading is not the best means of buying and selling shares of stock for some investors, and while there has been a rise in Internet securities fraud, online trading has been beneficial to many securities brokers and investors. Once investors established Internet connections with brokerage firms, executing trades has become much less expensive. Further, brokers have been encouraged to enhance their trading platforms and computer software and this has enabled these companies to automate the order placement process. In so doing, brokers are able to limit the amount of administrative personnel necessary to process these transactions and this has decreased the cost of doing business.

The Internet has become a powerful device for providing financial information and investors now have access to more information about asset valuations. Also, investors have a means of exchanging information with each other by virtue of the countless Internet chat rooms and discussion boards where investors post tips and detailed analyses of a broad array of investments. This information has enabled investors to become increasingly sophisticated; many can effectively execute transactions without the assistance of a professional broker (Stefanadis, 2001).

Trading financial instruments on the Internet is continuing to shape the financial services industry.

In order to compete more effectively with the large brokerage companies, many online brokers have begun branching out into other sectors of the financial and banking marketplace. For example, E*Trade, the Online broker that was originally located in Palo Alto, California has relocated its company headquarters to New York, and has established a mortgage bank as well. The company has moved beyond solely providing online trading services to provide its customers with mortgage loans, retirement planning, and other services.

This strategy is one that many other financial services firms are also employing. Essentially the goal is to provide customers with one-stop shopping for banking and investment products. There are, however, different schools of thought as to whether or not this trend will be beneficial to investors or to the financial services industry. Some companies contend that consumers will benefit from the aggregation of their financial accounts since it can enable them to access all of their financial information quickly and provide them with a means of transferring assets more expediently. However, there is no guarantee that investors will be comfortable with having all of their assets with one entity and all of their financial information stored in one location. Moreover, in light of the rise of cyber crime where hackers gain access to online accounts through home computers, investors do need to consider the risk involved with having their financial security breached.

The Internet age is continuing to evolve as rapid technological changes are also taking place in the telecommunications industry. The widespread use of smart phones and tablets gives people ready access to the Internet without even having to log on to a computer, and investors can track their investments and move money over these devices. With all changes in technology happening all the time, it is not clear how the new communications technology will change the way online trading will be conducted. At this point investors have benefited from the lower costs of conducting trades, having access to enhanced financial products, and mostly, from having more information at their disposal. (Stefanadis, 2001). The online trading industry continues to evolve to account for the rapid changes in technology. Market analyst Alexander Camargo said "Mobility and social media have come of age and are legitimate channels among online brokers. HTML5 and more advanced cloud-based trading platforms are just beginning to have an impact" (2013).

BIBLIOGRAPHY

Bekiaris, M. (2003, February). Online investing. *Money,* 36- 43. Retrieved January 24, 2007, from EBSCO Online Database Business Source Premier. http://search.ebscohost.com/login.aspx?direct=true&db=buh&AN=9159070 &site=ehost-live

Bergsman, S. (2004). Trading on its name. *Mortgage Banking, 64*(6) 28-34. Retrieved January 25, 2007, from EBSCO Online Database Business Source Premier. http://search. ebscohost. com/login.aspx?direct=true&db=buh&AN=125 37178&site=ehost-live

Borrus, A., McNamee, M., Grow, B. & Carter, A. (2005, November 14). Invasion of the stock hackers. *Business Week,* (3959), 38-40. Retrieved January 24, 2007, from EBSCO Online Database Business Source Premier. http:// search.ebscohost.com/login.aspx?direct=true&db=buh&AN=18752224&site=ehost-live

Camargo, A., & Fonseca, I. (2013, March 25). The race for self-directed investors: Developments in online trading among brokers and banks. *Celent.* Retrieved November 22, 2013 from http://www.celent.com/reports/race-self-directed-investors-developments-online-trading-among-brokers-and-banks

Hintse, J. (2005, Fall Supplement). Automation can overcome IPO compliance hurdles: For broker-dealers, tech savvy pays. *Traders Magazine,* 8-10. Retrieved January 24, 2007 from EBSCO Online Database Business Source Premier http://search.ebscohost.com/login.aspx?direct=true&db=buh&AN=28544322&site=ehost-live

Landis, D. & Anderson, J. (2004). Day trading take 2. *Kiplinger's Personal Finance, 58*(4) 56-59. Retrieved January 26, 2007, from EBSCO Online Database Business Source Premier. http://search.ebscohost.com/login.aspx?di rect=true&db=buh&AN=12406371&site=ehost-live

Ray, R. (1996). An introduction to finance on the Internet. *Financial Practice and Education, 6*(2) 95-101. Retrieved January 24, 2007, from EBSCO Online Database Business Source Premier. http:// search.ebscohost.com/login.aspx?di rect=true&d b=buh&AN=9708072802&site=ehost-live

Ody, E. (2011). The best of the online brokers. *Kiplinger's Personal Finance, 65*(2), 34–37. Retrieved November 22, 2013 from EBSCO online database, Business Source Complete. http://search.ebscohost.com/login.aspx?direct=t rue&db=bth&AN=5 7096151&site=ehost-live

Rossignoli, C., Zardini, A., & Cantoni, F. (2013). When customer behaviours change, should banks' approaches to online trading stay the same? *Journal of Internet Banking & Commerce, 18*(2), 1–16. Retrieved November 22, 2013 from EBSCO online database, Business Source Complete. http://search.ebscohost.com/login.aspx?direct=true&db=bt h&AN=91095272&site=ehost-live

Snel, R. (1999). Race to corner financial services market. *American Banker, 164*(232), 6A-9A. Retrieved January 26, 2007, from EBSCO Online Database Business Source Premier. http://search.ebscohost.com/login.aspx?direct=tru e&db=buh&AN=2623126&site=ehost-live

Stefanadis, C. (2001, Spring/Summer). Trading places. *Stern Business Spring Summer 2001.* Retrieved January 25, 2007, from Stern School of Business/ New York University http://www.stern.nyu.edu/ Sternbusiness/spring%5f2001/ brokers.html

U.S. Securities and Exchange Commission. (2005, October). Day trading: Your dollars at risk. Retrieved on January 26, 2007, from SEC website http://www.sec.gov/answers/ daytrading.htm

SUGGESTED READING

S., H. H. (2013). Online traders show loyalty. *Money (14446219), (159),* 75. Retrieved November 22, 2013 from EBSCO online database, Business Source Complete. http://search.ebscohost.com/login.aspx?direct=true&db=bt h&AN=89450159&site=ehost-live

Salcedo, Y. (2004). Getting educated the online way. *Futures: News, Analysis & Strategies for Futures, Options & Derivatives Traders, 33*(15) 61. Retrieved January 24, 2007, from EBSCO Online Database Business Source Premier. http://search.ebscohost.com/login.aspx?direct=tru e&db=buh&AN=15241655&site=ehost-live

Shakshuki, E. & Abu-Draz, S. (2005). Multi-agent system architecture to trading Systems. *Journal of Interconnection Networks, 6*(3) 283-302. Retrieved January 24, 2007, from EBSCO Online Database Business Source Premier. http://search.ebscohost.com/login.aspx?di rect=true&db=buh&AN= 18140737&site=ehost-live

Weisul, K. (1998). Online traders: Changing the face of IPOs. *Inter@ctive Week, 5*(46) 62-64. Retrieved January 25, 2007, from EBSCO Online Database Business Source Premier. http://search.ebscohost.com/login.aspx?direct=tru e&db=buh&AN=1347307&site=ehost-live

– Richa S. Tiwary

OPTIONS & FUTURES MARKETS

ABSTRACT

Investors have choices when choosing to invest in financial securities. The options and futures markets offer investments in securities based on the future. The investor's ability to guess what might happen in the future can pay off in profits to the investor. Options are used to reduce the portfolio risk from speculative investing. Futures are riskier than options but have the benefit of higher returns. In the end, the investor may decide to reduce the risk of futures and options by using managed accounts similar to mutual funds. The knowledge of the market and risk will ultimately determine the success of the investor in futures and options.

However, the ability of the investor to weather volatility, tolerate risk and invest for the long term is directly tied to whether or not success will be realized.

OVERVIEW

Futures and options are financial instruments that focus on the future. Options give an investor the right but not the obligation to purchase a financial instrument at some time in the future (Kansas, 2005). Futures are contracts between two parties that give the buyer the right and obligation to purchase a financial instrument at some time in the future. Options giving the right to buy are called "call" options.

Options giving the right to sell are called "put" options (Faerber, 2006). Futures can be any type of financial security including stocks, bonds, stock indexes, currencies, and commodities such as oil, coffee, orange juice, soybeans, gold, silver, pork bellies and corn. According to Ira Krulik, C.O.O. of New York Portfolio Clearing, "Options and futures and futures do walk hand in hand; most traders are trading these two interchangeably and simultaneously" (Timberlake, 2011).

FINANCIAL EXCHANGES

Options and futures are traded at financial exchanges. Options are traded at the Chicago Board Options Exchange (CBOE) using brokers and market makers (Faerber, p. 51, 54). Market makers are firms that buy and sell stocks for their own stock inventory while brokers are companies that sell stock on behalf of financial institutions and the general public. The CBOE is the largest options market in the world. The Philadelphia Exchange is a regional exchange that lists options. The Chicago Mercantile exchange lists futures and options while the New York Mercantile Exchange lists futures.

INVESTMENT VEHICLES

Groz (1999) reviewed five categories of investments including stocks, mutual funds, bonds, options and futures. All have different benefits and disadvantages.

- Options are used to reduce portfolio risk from speculative investing.
- Futures are riskier than options but have the benefit of higher returns. It is also possible for investors to reduce the risk of investing in futures by using managed accounts which are similar to mutual funds and balance out the risk of investing directly in futures. However, as with any managed account, the investor has to be certain that the fees associated with the account are warranted when compared to the long term returns of the account.

Groz (1999) likens options to bonds in that they have a specific, date-driven end point. For bonds, this ending point is a maturity date. For options, the ending point is expiration date. Godin (2001) stated that the seller is the party who determines the expiration date and the price at which the buyer can exercise their option called the strike price. The strike price is only valid, however, if the buyer exercises the option before the expiration date. From this example, it is easy to see how dependent options are on

time and how volatile options can be. An investor can make a decision that is based on the best knowledge they have available today. Yet, in an instant — as soon as the next day — the buyer may find that market conditions have changed dramatically. Godin (2001) found the "premium" or price of options to be dependent on the market demand, current stock price and the time that remains before the option expires.

OPTIONS: PROS & CONS

Options have benefits and drawbacks as an investment. Godin (2001) referred to options as the right to buy or sell stock at a certain price. Godin noted that many investors aren't really interested in buying or selling the stock their option is based on. Instead, they use the buying and selling of the options as the investment. The downside is option volatility or the propensity to go up and down rapidly. However, when used optimally for the investor's benefit, they can be used as a hedge against risk in the investor's portfolio.

MAKING MONEY

The way buyers make money on options depends on the decisions they make about time and selling the option. For example, a buyer purchases an option to buy called a call option. The option is purchased at a specific expiration date and strike price. If the price of that stock goes up, the buyer has some choices to make. The buyer can exercise their right to buy shares of the stock represented by the option. They can then sell the stock they purchased at the higher price since it has gone up in the market. So the goal of purchasing call options is that the stock price will rise higher than the strike price of your option. Sell options or put options work in a similar way but in a different market direction. You may purchase a put option on a stock that you expect to fall in price. If the price of the stock falls below your strike price before the option expiration date, you can exercise your right to sell shares at a higher price, thus making a profit.

RISK

Options offer no advantage to investors if the underlying investment, stock for example, is at the same price as the strike price because the investor can neither buy nor sell to make a profit. When an investor closes their option position, they are selling their options back to the open market in order to make a profit (Godin, 2001). Ultimately, Godin suggests that the ability to enjoy investing in options or any risky investment vehicle is directly related to how well the investor can tolerate risk and rapid changes in the market. If the investor is fearful of bear markets when prices are decreasing and often doing so rapidly, it is likely that the investor will choose to liquidate the falling investments at a loss. Similarly, Jones (2006) described a long-running bull market where prices are rising. Just as a bear market might instill fear in the investor, a bull market might instill false confidence. Knowing your own ability to tolerate risk and need to avert risk can be valuable in determining the appropriate investment strategy. Investments in stock are usually for the long term but risk averse and small investors often don't have the wherewithal or the ability to tolerate periods of downturn.

The basic question investors must ask themselves about options is how confident are they that a specific situation will occur in the future. Kansas (2005) notes that options are less risky than the actual stocks themselves because the most an individual might lose in a day of market activity is the initial investment made. However, Kansas also describes options investing as "complex and risky" requiring the investor to have education and knowledge of risk and somewhat intricate mathematical abilities. Kansas recommends options only for seasoned investors and suggests part time investors stay on the sidelines. The most volatile period for options based on stocks is the "triple witching" session once a quarter on the third Fridays of March, June, September and December when most stock options expire on the same day (Kansas, 2005). Volatile periods are also times to avoid for novice investors.

TYPES OF OPTIONS
Options are generally purchased with expiration dates of no more than a year away and often expire monthly. Other types of options include long term options, index options and futures options.
- Long term options, as the name implies, allow the investor to purchase options with expiration dates farther into the future.
- Index options are based on indexes such as the Standard and Poor's 500.
- Futures options are complex options based on futures where the option itself is not an obligation to buy, but the underlying futures contract does have the obligation.

STRATEGIES FOR BUYING OPTIONS
Groz (1999) explains that options contracts require a relationship between the buyer and the seller called a "zero-sum game" meaning that one person wins and the other person loses. If you profit, the other player experiences losses. However, even if a player experiences a loss, the transaction may provide value to the player by reducing risk, improving the relationship between assets and liabilities, creating a position in the market or other benefits. Groz suggests five strategies called "combination strategies" that investors can use for options:
- Buy stock and buy put: For situations when the underlying asset is declining in value and the investor wants to preserve a position in the market.
- Buy stock and sell call: When the investor wants to get income from the underlying asset.
- Buy stock, buy put, sell call: A combination of the above strategies to provide insurance to the investor against loss.
- Straddles and strangles: Strategies for getting profit from volatility with a straddle meaning to buy puts and calls at the same price and see which one works, strangles being to buy puts and calls at different prices.
- Calendar spread: To spread option positions out over time providing for options that expire in the near term and those that expire in the long term and balancing profits and losses.

It is clear that these strategies are not for the novice, as great losses could come just from trying to understand how to create these positions.

FUTURES: PROS & CONS

REDUCED RISK
Godin (2001) called futures contracts an agreement to take delivery of a specific type of commodity at a certain price sometime in the future. These contracts date back to the time when the economy was primarily agriculture-based and speculation was often based on corn, wheat and other agriculture commodities. Farmers wanted futures contracts to ensure that they would get a fair price for their commodities regardless of the conditions at the time of harvesting the product. For example, if there ended up being a glut of a certain commodity at the end of the season, the farmer might have to take lower prices

for commodities without having negotiated a futures contract. Farmers can also use these contracts to raise money now while delivering the product later. The investor may purchase the futures contract in hopes of selling the commodity at a higher price later. Early futures markets can be traced back to 18th century Japan where rice growers sold contracts to ensure certain prices. *Farmers Weekly* (2007) discussed how the grain market is unpredictable and how it is becoming increasingly necessary for farmers to limit the amount of risk for their own survival. Futures provide a vehicle for reducing agricultural risk.

FUTURES MARKETS

The biggest difference in futures and options is that futures are a "promise to actually make a transaction" (Morgenson & Harvey, 2002). Futures and options are part of a class of investment called derivatives because they derive their value from an underlying investment such as a stock, commodity or precious metal. Each futures exchange specializes in certain kinds of futures. For example, the Chicago Board of Trade specializes in corn and wheat while the New York Mercantile Exchange specializes in gold and silver. Investors can turn to online and print publications such as the *Wall Street Journal* to track the daily changes in the futures market.

Futures markets are essential to an economy where goods are produced, bought and sold. Futures allow someone to assume risk with the promise of some reward in the future. For example, manufacturers of food products who are dependent on certain commodities may want to reduce the fluctuation of their costs due to the regular consumption of a particular commodity. Market fluctuations in the price of the commodity may adversely affect the ability of the manufacturer to make a profit. In cases like these, it is suggested that manufacturers make purchases of commodities needed in the futures market and sell futures of their finished product (Groz, 1999). This strategy provides a means of balancing out natural fluctuations. Commodities were the only asset class where volumes grew solidly on a global basis throughout the recession in the early 2000's. (Lavelle, 2011)

REASONS FOR FUTURES INVESTMENT

Futures investing can be done by investors for speculation, insurance or both.

- Financial speculation is when investors venture into various financial transactions and financial instruments with the hope of receiving profits, dividends, interest and financial value from the speculative activity. Some call this speculation gambling. Speculation without forethought and knowledge can be thought of as gambling.
- The investment in futures may be done to protect the investor against various types of risk. Insurers increasingly manage asset risk with options, futures, and other derivatives (Fodor, Doran, Carson, & Kirch, 2013). Hedging strategies may involve futures because the investor is trying to protect a portfolio from market volatility. However, futures are no guarantee when an investor wants to hedge.

Cotter and Hanly (2006) measured five performance metrics across seven international markets and found mixed results from hedging strategies. It seems that the performance is hard to predict and can be based on whether or not the investment strategy is for short or long term hedging. An arbitrage strategy may emerge because the investor sees an opportunity with futures to make money because of price differences in different markets. Investors may see these investments as a strategy for increasing or protecting an investment, but when using these complex strategies for profit Faerber (2006) found futures to be among the riskier of investments.

Futures are different from stocks because they are bought on margin. Margin is the minimum amount of money an investor must have in their account to purchase or sell a futures contract. Futures seem like a feasible investment alternative because the margin requirements are smaller than those for stock purchases. Faerber (2006) describes the stock margin as 50% of the price while futures margins vary from 2 to 10%. According to Morgenson & Harvey (2002) margin allows the investor to borrow money from the broker to purchase securities. So a margin account is a combination of a loan and cash to purchase securities.

According to Groz (1999), futures contracts conclude in one of two ways. The ownership of the underlying asset is transferred or a cash settlement is made. Change of ownership is called an "actual delivery" while a cash transaction is called a "cash settled" contract. Futures based on stock indexes are usually settled with cash for convenience.

VIEWPOINT

FUTURES & OPTIONS TRADING STRATEGIES, ANALYSIS & OPPORTUNITIES

Although risky, there is growing interest in the futures and options markets. The Chicago Board Options Exchange (CBOE) is the largest options exchange and offers options on over 1200 publicly traded stocks. The CBOE has hundreds of millions of options contracts at any one time and had a net income of $18.7 million in the second quarter of 2007 (Clary). CBOE also lists long term options, index options and financial options called interest rate options.

Investing in options requires knowledge of how they work, analysis of the opportunities and the development of a personal options investing strategy. This means a lot of work and study and perhaps engaging the services of a professional options trading advisor. The advantages of options are that they require a small amount of initial investment, losses are limited and options can be used in a hedging strategy to avoid large losses from unfavorable changes in stock prices. Options investors can use options as a source of income by doing what Faerber (2006) calls "writing options." Writing options are simply selling call or put options and receiving income from the premiums the buyers pay.

Various strategies for profiting from options may seem more like "hocus-pocus" than science though much analysis is scientific and professionals use complex mathematical formulas and computer analysis programs. Some investors may not even understand the strategies used if guided by a professional. Denault, Gauthier, & Simonato (2006) described a lattice strategy that examines the correlation of options prices to the underlying stock price that minimizes bias due to option pricing. Bias is 'noise' or error in pricing estimates when basing option pricing on the underlying stock price. Denault et al also noted changes in strategy and performance based on whether the option was U.S. or foreign based. This example continues to illustrate the complexities of options investing. Tompkins (2006) discussed equally complex options investing strategies that benefit from the volatility of the European market. Various hypotheses and analysis exist about activity in

the foreign financial markets, and competing strategies have emerged as a result. However, the investor may become weary of all the analysis and want to simply make an investment decision and see results. The degree of patience the investor has can also affect the returns that are experienced.

ANALYSIS OF FUTURES MARKETS

Faerber (2006) discusses two ways of analyzing futures markets including fundamental analysis and technical analysis.

- Fundamental analysis is looking at factors that influence the "physical supply and demand" for commodities. This type of analysis looks at production and imports of the commodity. The price is influenced by current and projected supply and demand.
- Technical analysis is looking at historical movements in volume and price to determine projected volumes and price. Technical analysts look at data to isolate trends and possible investment opportunities.

FINANCIAL FUTURES CONTRACTS

Faerber suggests having a strategy before investing in futures so that when prices rise or fall, obvious action is dictated by a sound strategy. Opportunities in futures exist in what Faerber calls a "growing segment of the futures market" — financial futures contracts. These are futures contracts representing positions in financial securities. Interest-rate futures, interest indexes and foreign currencies are examples of financial futures contracts.

- Interest rate futures include treasury bonds, notes and bills as well as foreign government bonds.
- Currency futures contracts are based on future delivery of foreign currencies such as the Japanese yen, the Swiss franc or the Mexican peso.
- Stock index futures are based on the Dow Jones Industrial Average or the Standard and Poor's 500 index
- Global futures offer opportunities if investors can capitalize on trends. For example, Mohan (2007) noted that coffee is the largest trading commodity in the world primarily because of its emphasis in developing countries. Mohan projects average exports of coffee to be around $5 — 12 billion in the period between 1997 and 2005.

MANAGED FUTURES

Managed futures offer investment possibilities to investors who do not want to have daily responsibilities for managing their futures account. Prior to the 1980's futures investors primarily looked to futures investing for hedging purposes. Then, managed futures came into vogue. Managed futures investors employ third party financial experts to help the investor profit from fluctuations in price. Such financial experts are called Commodity Trading Advisors (CTAs). CTAs are useful for today's futures market which is increasingly diversified including global opportunities. The advantages of managed futures are increased chances of higher returns and the reduction of risk in an investment portfolio.

CONCLUSION

Futures and options are risky but offer rewards. They are complex but can be managed using various strategies and financial advice. The ultimate test of whether or not an investor can profit from options and futures rests with the discipline the investor has in the approach to the market, if the investor can weather volatility storms and the consistency of strategy and investing.

BIBLIOGRAPHY

Clary, I. (2007, July 30). As exchanges merge, Chicago options mart is in catbird seat. *Financial Week.* Retrieved October 31, 2007, from http://www.financialweek.com/apps/pbcs. dll/article?AID=/20070730/REG/70726014/1021/TOC

Cotter, J. & Hanly, J. (2006). Reevaluating hedging performance. *Journal of Futures Markets, 26*(7), 677-702. Retrieved September 30, 2007, from EBSCO Online Database Business Source Complete. http://search.ebscohost.com/login.aspx?direct=true&db=bth&AN=20854145&site=ehost-live

Denault, M., Gauthier, G. & J. Simonato. (2006). Improving lattice schemes through bias reduction. *Journal of Futures Markets, 26*(8), 757. Retrieved September 30, 2007, from EBSCO Online Database Business Source Complete. http://search.ebscohost.com/login.aspx?direct=true&db=bth&AN=21395447&site=ehost-live

Faerber, E. (2006). *All about investing: the easy way to get started.* New York: McGraw-Hill.

Fodor, A., Doran, J. S., Carson, J. M., & Kirch, D. P. (2013). On the demand for portfolio insurance. *Risk Management & Insurance Review, 16*(2), 167-193. Retrieved November 21, 2013, from EBSCO Online Database Business Source Complete. http://search.ebscohost.com/login.aspx?direct=true&db=bth&AN=91957828&site=ehost-live

Godin, S. (2001). *If you're clueless about the stock market and want to know more.* Chicago: Dearborn Trade Books.

Groz, M. M. (1999). *Forbes guide to the markets: becoming a savvy investor.* New York: John Wiley and Sons.

Jones, G. (2006). A time to sell? *Futures: News, Analysis & Strategies for Futures, Options & Derivatives Traders, 35*(9), 26. Retrieved September 30, 2007, from EBSCO Online Database Business Source Complete. http://search. ebscohost. com/login.aspx?direct=true&db=bth&AN=21558566&site=ehost-live

Kansas, D. (2005). *The Wall Street Journal: complete money & investing guidebook.* New York: Three Rivers Press.

Lavelle, Gavin. "Commodities will be bigger than anything else" - *FOi* Meets... Gavin Lavelle. (2011). *FOi: Future & Options Intelligence, (1610),* 5. Retrieved November 18, 2013, from EBSCO Online Database Business Source Complete. http://search.ebscohost.com/login.aspx?direct=true&db=bth&AN=59696931&site=ehost-live

Learn with us how to profit from risk. (2007). *Farmers Weekly, 146*(13), 3. Retrieved September 30, 2007, from EBSCO Online Database Academic Search Complete. http://search.ebscohost.com/login.aspx?direct=true&db=bth&AN=24823427&site=ehost-live

Mohan, S. (2007). Market-based price-risk management for coffee producers. *Development Policy Review, 25*(3), 333- 354. Retrieved September 30, 2007, from EBSCO Online Database Academic Search Complete. http://search.ebscohost.com/login.aspx?direct=true&db=a9h&AN=24977055&site=ehost-live

Morgenson, G. & Harvey, C. R. (2002). *The New York Times dictionary of money investing.* New York: Times Books.

Timberlake, J. (2011). NYPC eyes options for growth. *Wall Street Letter, 01-02.* Retrieved November 21, 2013, from EBSCO Online Database Business Source Complete. http://search.ebscohost.com/login.aspx?direct=true&db=bth&AN=65205732&site=ehost-live

Tompkins, R. (2006). Why smiles exist in foreign exchange options markets: Isolating components of the risk neutral process. *European Journal of Finance, 12*(6/7), 583-603. Retrieved September 30, 2007, from EBSCO Online Database Business Source Complete http://search.ebscohost.com/login.aspx?direct=true&db=bth&AN=22342966&site=ehost-live

SUGGESTED READING

Colon, S. (2006). Futures and options' interns get taste of the market. *Bond Buyer, 357*(32447), 6. Retrieved September 30, 2007, from EBSCO Online Database Business Source Complete. http://search.ebscohost.com/login.aspx?direct=true&db=bth&AN=22032593&site=bsi-live

McMahon, C. (2007). Options on futures: At the tipping point? *Futures: News, Analysis & Strategies for Futures, Options & Derivatives Traders, 36*(4), 54-56. Retrieved September 30, 2007, from EBSCO Online Database Business Source Complete. http://search.ebscohost.com/login.aspx?direct=true&db=bth&AN=24751952&site=bsi-live

Overview of derivatives. (2007, May 1). *Federal Reserve Bulletin,* A3. Retrieved September 30, 2007, from EBSCO Online Database Academic Search Complete. http://search.ebscohost.com/login.aspx?direct=true&db=a9h&AN=26023447&site=ehost-live

Profitable futures — helping farmers turn industry challenges into financial reward. (2007). *Farmers Weekly, 146*(26), 25. Retrieved September 30, 2007, from EBSCO Online Database Academic Search Complete. http://search.ebscohost.com/login.aspx?direct=true&db=a9h&AN=25912098&site=ehost-live

–Marlanda English

P

PORTFOLIO MANAGEMENT

ABSTRACT

There are many reasons for investing. Some investors do it for a living while others pursue it as a hobby. Some invest for a quick return while others look for long term benefit. All investors large and small engage in some type of portfolio management. Portfolio management is how an investor decides what to do with the collection of investments under the investor's control. The management of an investment portfolio is driven by the skill and knowledge of the investor, the opportunities available to that investor, the goals of the investor and the investor's response to economic activity and investment performance. There are a number of strategies an investor may use to manage a portfolio and a number of tasks to maximize portfolio management. All of this starts with goals and continues with investor education. Although many portfolio managers and investment advisors are available, the individual investor must exert control over how investments are managed. Adjustments to a portfolio may take place because of changing objectives or may depend on where the investor is in his or her life cycle. Risk also determines what moves an investor will make. Often, investors close to retirement will look to build portfolios and limit risk.

OVERVIEW

When we think of a portfolio we think of a folder or collection of related items. If you are an artist, you might have a portfolio or collection of your works of art. Many professionals in many fields create portfolios that represent who and what they are and what they can do. Professional portfolios can be useful for professionals whether they are teachers, graphic artists, speakers, managers, technology professionals and so on. A financial portfolio is the collection of financial investments and in essence the financial position or situation for an individual or a company. This means that you include liquid assets like cash as well as real estate, stocks and bonds, 401K plans and insurance. Your portfolio considerations also include credit liabilities and can impact your ability to acquire new investments.

Companies may also have cash or real estate or stock as investments. However, they may often have different goals than individuals. Instead of personal security, companies may have objectives based on the company stakeholders. Another difference between individuals and companies is that a company may be able to afford a team of specialists who analyze investment options and performance. Individuals may have a professional financial advisor or may simply do the best they can on their own. An investment company is one that will manage the funds of investors based on the investor's objectives for a fee to manage the funds.

ACTIVITIES INCLUDED IN PORTFOLIO MANAGEMENT

Managing your portfolio includes deciding what is in the portfolio, what to keep, what to acquire next and how to leverage what you have to get other investments. A simple portfolio decision for an individual might involve changing the asset allocation in a 401K plan, to move away from investment in international stocks to other investments, based on the performance of the investment and how much risk the investor is willing to allow. Joshi (2007) quoted a financial planner who felt that many people just follow what they see or hear instead of having a goal they can stick to and pursue relentlessly. Without a specific goal and strategy, individual investors may be frightened or wiped out by any crisis situation. A crisis may signal a need for a change in strategy but not necessarily a move away from objectives. Sticking to a goal requires patience and if you don't know why you are investing, it will be difficult to achieve your goals with the ups and downs in the marketplace.

Many investment plans offered to employees regularly provide information to the individual investor as to what the performance is of certain investments and may even include a 'sure thing' fund that may have a guaranteed performance level. These funds have a lower rate of return but typically less risk. Smaller, individual investors may prefer these funds because it is less likely that they will lose money on the investment. In addition, if someone is expecting to work for a period of years for one employer at a specific income-level, that individual can almost predict what amount of money the investment will grow to over time.

SMALL INVESTOR PITFALLS

There can be pitfalls related to the patience of the small investor. Joshi (p. 149 - 150) interviewed a financial consultant who noted that the small investor is often not looking at the investment for the long term such as a period of 5 — 10 — 20 years. Also, the small investor may have unrealistic expectations as to where the investment may grow over time. It is unlikely that a stock that has performed a certain way and yielded a certain percentage of income over the last 10 years will dramatically increase that income unless specific, unforeseen world changes occur. Dramatic changes also don't continue forever. The small investor may also want to use a strategy called diversification where the investments are balanced in such a way to limit the risk of the investors. If you invest too much in one thing, the entire investment is jeopardized if the single investment plummets. This can be disastrous to most average workers who spend an entire lifetime working to support themselves and their families in the hopes of living comfortably in old age. For example, the workers at Enron, who had money invested in Enron stock, saw their lives change dramatically after the collapse of the company. As the stock rose, employees nearing retirement could dream of possibly retiring early, paying off debts and investing in items they may have always wanted.

UNRELIABILITY OF PORTFOLIO MANAGEMENT

Portfolio management can be described as both art and science because while experience is helpful in determining what makes a good investment, there are incidents and situations that cannot be anticipated. War, natural disasters, inflation, new inventions, company failures, industry changes and rumors can all impact the value of an investment. What constituted a perfect investment at one point might be a terrible

investment at another time. For example, one part of the country may be an excellent investment for real estate. The land may be cheap and resold at a higher cost. The community may be a desirable one to live in. However, after the prices rise past a certain point, the investment may not make sense because the resale value may be lower. Improvements in the community such as highways and airports may cause additional congestion which may make it less desirable to live in and more difficult to sell.

OWNERSHIP & DECISION-MAKING

Portfolio management is a difficult task for the average individual investor because the investor may not possess a solid foundation of financial skill and education. Often financial advisors are simply people trying to make a living at advising others in the area of finance and may not possess a high level of skill in investing. The individual advisor doesn't necessarily have access to the best financial minds. Even with a financial advisor at your side, no matter how good, the buck stops at the desk of the investor.

In addition to seeking professional help, the investor must also become a student of finance and understand how investments work. This is a distasteful task for some and simply boring for others. The earlier in life that an individual learns about finance, managing money and investing, the more likely it is that the individual will take ownership in investing. Besides ownership and initiative, the investor must be able to make decisions. These decisions should be driven by a sound set of financial objectives. The investor should have some reason for investing and be able to ask the right questions to determine what outcomes are desired from investing.

INVESTMENT CONSIDERATIONS

Some life situations may drive an investor's desire to invest. If the individual has witnessed difficult situations in their families due to loss of employment, illness or other situation, they may be very motivated to plan for the care of their families and themselves in old age. Benzoni, Collin-Dufresne, & Goldstein (2007) explored the connection between the investor's age and the makeup of the investor's portfolio. Investors have to consider their age and the amount of time they have to invest because investing is a long term activity and assets only provide real return over the long haul. When individuals become parents they may have a desire to provide for the care and education of children and feel investing allows them to plan and take control of the future financially.

Cane (2007) found the complications in the job of the financial advisor when the investment portfolio objective included caring for a family member with a disability. This is especially true if the disabled member is a child since the parents may not live long enough to personally manage the financial affairs of a child. In these cases, the considerations may go beyond financial considerations and include caretakers who will manage the financial affairs of the disabled individual. A disabled child may not be able to handle finances and make decisions even at an adult age if the disability is a mental one. Similarly, the disabled child

may be unable to dispose of the affairs of the parents upon their death and may be unable to work to provide self support. Cane noted that trusts could be set up for a disabled person to provide income, supplemental needs trusts to provide for needs without counting as income and pooled supplemental trusts to provide for management of the trust portfolio even if it isn't big enough to interest a large manager. The key for disabled persons is to make sure that assets are not in their name. This action makes certain that the disabled person can still take advantage of services provided by the government for people with disabilities.

If someone is fortunate enough to have a good income, it may be desirable to invest a portion of that income in case the situation or economy changes. Some investments are rewards for people who spend most of their life working. Investments in a second or vacation home may provide investors with a goal to achieve or something that they can pay for and enjoy. A real estate investment may become a retirement home, be sold later for income, to pay for education or to upgrade a first home. High risk investments that allow high returns can provide a windfall for an investor to use for early retirement, travel or to spend on luxury items. Individuals who work on commission or receive bonus checks or overtime may look for ways to invest their extra earnings in order to avoid simply spending them.

FIVE RULES FOR INVESTING
Ownership and accountability means taking measured steps as it relates to managing your portfolio.

Joshi (2007) offered "five golden rules of investing" including:
- Don't trade — too difficult for the average investor if you don't do it all the time.
- When thinking stocks, think long term — that's where stocks perform best.
- Diversify to avoid short term crises.
- Invest regularly and see investing as a long term activity.
- Set goals to achieve lifelong goals.

BALANCING A PORTFOLIO
Mannes suggested that people don't look at their portfolios often enough to realize how much they may have changed. Mannes recommended the following guidelines to balance a portfolio and keep it from getting out of control:
- Decide when to rebalance
- You can do it on a regular schedule such as annually or quarterly or
- You can decide to do it when the investment moves away from your initial target for it.
- Pick a trigger point that tells you when to move things around.
- Limit actions with tax consequences such as selling.
- Simplify it by using the tools that fund managers provide for making these decisions.

Sometimes the biggest problem that the small investor may encounter is that there are so many decisions, so many ways to make them and so much information available. It may lead to financial information overload or paralysis.

ASSET ALLOCATION
There are many investments an investor can select. These assets fall into classes. An asset class is a category of assets and can include stocks, bonds, real estate and foreign securities (Morgenson & Harvey). Asset allocation is a way to protect the investor from unforeseen actions and to prepare for the future. Uncertainty is a fact of life and asset allocation is a result of strategy, not a guarantee. Asset allocation is based on the fact that the investor has many options when deciding where, how and how much money to invest in specific investments.

Blankson (2005, p. 1) considered doing a good job of asset allocation as a way to build wealth and security and to ensure protection from single, disastrous events. Blankson (p.2) believes the small investor is very likely to avoid asset allocation. This could be due to the simplicity of not having to decide. It could be much easier to put all of your money in one bank or have all of your investment in your home. Blankson advises against the simple route citing natural and financial disasters of previous years as proof that putting your money in one place is dangerous.

As people become more computer literate and software becomes more user friendly, investors can more easily track their own investments. Many online finance sites and investment companies also have online tools for their customers to use. Asset allocation involves more that simply tracking the assets. The investor must also compare allocation opportunities and determine which course of action is best based on the information available, the risk involved and the investment objectives. The small investor will almost always have real estate as a part of the investment portfolio. Since a place to live is a requirement for most people, many will dream of owning and pursue owning a home. For many investors, this may be the largest investment they will make in a lifetime.

Bogoslaw (2007) felt that middle aged investors should concentrate on diversification and balance as strategies for asset allocation. If the investor has held an investment for a period of time, it is likely that things have changed. Stocks that were a small part of a portfolio could have grown in terms of the percentage of the portfolio over time. Morningstar has an asset allocation software program that is used to analyze the portfolios of new customers. The analysis is to show customers where they might have thought they were diversifying their portfolios but really they were only selecting different fund names that financially are moving the same way. It is also suggested that the middle aged investor really know their portfolio. If an investor began investing twenty years ago and only glances at the monthly or quarterly account statements, he or she may not have a true picture of what the portfolio is, how it has changed and what allocation adjustments may be needed. Bogoslaw also reminds the middle aged and older investor that he or she is less likely to be able to withstand a major crisis or downturn as compared to earlier in a career. The closer you are to retirement the more you want to concentrate on maximizing the return on the portfolio and to have a portfolio with high equity.

Bogoslaw discussed life-cycle funds which are investments that automatically change based on the age and life-cycle of the investor. Allocation changes are made automatically for the investor based on how close to retirement the investor may be. Life-cycle funds are desirable because they take "emotion" out of investing by using a life-cycle specific formula for selecting investment allocation.

VIEWPOINT

SMALL INVESTOR KNOWLEDGE & CONTROL

The small investor can be impacted by investment decisions that they don't make. Many small investors simply choose to invest in large companies or the programs offered by their employers because they aren't sure what to do. The small investor doesn't really know how a company is run or the people who make the decisions. Because of human nature, people may try to gain an advantage in investing. This has shown up in the investment world through high level company executives exaggerating company performance or selling shares of stock when they know that company performance will be poor. Financial managers have been known to give insider information to their favorite clients.

Serafin (2007) noted that even after mutual fund scandals and efforts by regulators to force independence in financial management decision-making, financial managers are still engaging in activity that hurts the small investor, especially passing on exclusive information. Serafin identified failed attempts by the Security and Exchange Commission (SEC) to require that fund boards be made up of outsiders. These were struck down in 2005 and 2006 although some complied voluntarily. The SEC wanted 75% of fund management boards to be made up of outsiders. Serafin indicated that 80% of mutual fund boards have made an effort to adhere to the 75% outsider guideline. However, the presence of outsiders hasn't seemed to improve performance and only reduce the likelihood of conflicts of interest. Serafin suggested the small investor pay attention to the costs associated with managing funds and how high the turnover is of fund managers.

On the other hand, many people would not get involved in investing if there wasn't a company investment program to participate in at work or professional fund managers to take the burden out of making financial decisions. Most average investors don't have the knowledge and don't feel confident in acquiring that knowledge in the time they have outside of work, family obligations and personal interests. In addition, if the investment does poorly, the professional manager or someone else can take the blame. It takes time and energy to set up and manage company investment programs; however, this is good business and provides for the security of workers. Most programs allow workers to invest a generous amount of income and some companies match the investment put in by the employee. The programs are an attractive and low involvement way that people can learn about and participate in investing.

Storch (2007, p. 9.) reported on lawsuits against large companies (Boeing, Kraft and others) charging that the companies allowed their employees to be charged extra fees in 401K plans. The fees are important because they offset the return investors get. Over the long term, slight reductions in the percentage of return can add up and significantly reduce the portfolio value for the employee investor. Someone else investing in the same thing and having the same portfolio would make much more money if the fees incurred to manage the portfolio are smaller. The companies were sued because it was felt they had a responsibility to manage the cost of 401K programs and to reduce the possible cost employees would incur. The Department of Labor has responded by requiring additional disclosure from companies with 401K plans. With activity like this, what is the small investor supposed to do? There are expected expenses with managing a 401K plan. Some of these include variable annuity expenses if insurance makes up part of the investment portfolio. There are also the costs of trades if the portfolio contains stocks or bonds. Surrender charges are incurred if the company decides to switch retirement plans. Similarly, there are market value charges if the investor decides to leave a guaranteed income plan. Mutual funds have a special 12(b)1 fee that goes to the financial advisor. Banks and other entities can be paid fees for managing the shareholder accounts and records. While these fees may be viewed as a convenience fee, they still negatively impact the return on investment.

No investment is foolproof and all eggs shouldn't go in the same basket. So employees of companies that have 401K plans shouldn't be the only place employees place their investments even if the company

is large, established and has a long track record of success and loyalty to employees.

BIBLIOGRAPHY

Blankson, S. (2005). *Asset allocation: the key to financial security.* Upper Saddle River, NJ: Prentice-Hall, Inc.

Benzoni, L., Collin-Dufresne, P. & Goldstein, R. S. (2007). Portfolio choice over the life-cycle when the stock and labor markets are cointegrated. *Journal of Finance, 62*(5), 2123-2167. Retrieved September 16, 2007 from EBSCO Online Database Business Source Complete. http://search.ebscohost.com/login.aspx?direct=true&db=bth&AN=26438960&site=ehost-live

Bogoslaw, D. (2007, September 5). Do you have an age-appropriate portfolio? *Business Week Online,* 24. Retrieved September 16, 2007, from EBSCO Online Database Business Source Complete. http://search.ebscohost.com/login.aspx?direct=true&db=bth&AN=26484629&site=ehost-live

Cane, B. (2007). Caring ever after. *Bank Investment Consultant, 15*(9), 31-35. Retrieved September 16, 2007, from EBSCO Online Database Business Source Complete. http://search.ebscohost.com/login.aspx?direct=true&db=bth&AN=26448699&site=ehost-live

Joshi, R. (2007). Where to invest now? *Business Today, 16*(18), 149-152. Retrieved September 16, 2007, from EBSCO Online Database Business Source Complete. http://search.ebscohost.com/login.aspx?direct=true&db=bth&AN=26375310&site=ehost-live

Mannes, G. (2007, February 13). Get your portfolio in balance. *Money Magazine.* Retrieved September 16, 2007 from http://money.cnn.com/2007/02/13/magazines/moneymag/asset%5fallocation.moneymag/index.htm

Morgenson, G. & Harvey, C. R. (2002). *The New York Times dictionary of money investing.* New York, NY: Times Books.

Serafin, T. (2007). Who's in charge here? *Forbes, 180*(5), 162-164. Retrieved September 16, 2007, from EBSCO Online Database Business Source Complete. http://search.ebscohost.com/login.aspx?direct=true&db=bth&AN=26520028&site=ehost-live

SMITH, A. (2013). Smart Investors Keep It Simple. (cover story). Kiplinger's Personal Finance, 67(11), 36-37. Retrieved November 15, 2013, from EBSCO Online Database Business Source Complete. http://search.ebscohost.com/login.aspx?direct=true&db=bth&AN=90617035&site=ehost-live

Sosnoff, M. (2013). Fear and leverage on wall and broad. *Forbes, 192*(7), 1. Retrieved November 15, 2013, from EBSCO Online Database Business Source Complete. http://search.ebscohost.com/login.aspx?direct=true&db=bth&AN=91812091&site=ehost-live

Storch, K. (2007). True costs of 401(k) plans. *Employee Benefit Plan Review, 62*(3), 9-10. Retrieved September 16, 2007, from EBSCO Online Database Business Source Complete. http://search.ebscohost.com/login.aspx?direct=true&db=bth&AN=26375016&site=bsi-live

Teller, J., & Kock, A. (2013). An empirical investigation on how portfolio risk management influences project portfolio success. *International Journal of Project Management, 31*(6), 817-829. Retrieved November 15, 2013, from EBSCO Online Database Business Source Complete. http://search.ebscohost.com/login.aspx?direct=true&db=bth&AN=89114195&site=ehost-live

SUGGESTED READING

Clark, K. (2007). No amateur investing, please. *U.S. News & World Report, 143*(10), 70. Retrieved September 27, 2007, from EBSCO Online Database Business Source Complete. http://search.ebscohost.com/login.aspx?direct=true&db=bth&AN=26619670&site=bsi-live

Stock, H. J. (2007). Living the life. *Bank Investment Consultant, 15*(9), 23-25. Retrieved September 16, 2007, from EBSCO Online Database Business Source Complete. http://search.ebscohost.com/login.aspx?direct=true&db=bth&AN=26448697&site=ehost-live

Stock, H. J. (2007). The baby boomer explosion could blow up in advisors' faces. *Bank Investment Consultant, 15*(9), 11. Retrieved September 16, 2007, from EBSCO Online Database Business Source Complete. http://search.ebscohost.com/login.aspx?direct=true&db=bth&AN=26448695&site=ehost-live

Wang, P. (2007). Why bad returns don't make a bad fund. *Money, 36*(10), 70-72. Retrieved September 27, 2007, from EBSCO Online Database Business Source Complete. http://search.ebscohost.com/login.aspx?direct=true&db=bth&AN=26590522&site=bsi-live

— Marlanda English

PREFERRED STOCK

ABSTRACT

This article will explain the corporate security of preferred stock. The overview provides an introduction to the basic characteristics of preferred stock. These characteristics include the most common types of preferred stock, typical classifications of preferred stock and the rights of preferred stockholders. In addition, factors that a corporation's board of directors typically considers in determining whether to issue preferred stock are explained, including creating equity, minimizing corporate financial obligations and controlling a corporation's governance. In addition, issues that can affect the value of preferred stock, such as stock splits, stock repurchase programs and risk are explained to help illustrate the role that preferred stock can play in the growth and profitability of a company.

OVERVIEW

Stocks are among the most popular investment options for modern investors. Stocks are shares of a company that provide investors with partial ownership in a company. Thus, owning a stock is tantamount to being part owner of a company. Corporate ownership provides stockholders with many benefits. Shareholders gain the right to influence how a company is run through their voting power, and they have a right to benefit from company's profits if and when they are distributed in the form of dividends, as well as a claim on the company's assets in the event of liquidation. The more shares of a company an investor owns, the more influence the investor has regarding the way the company is run and thethe greater the investor's claim on the company's earnings and assets.

Thus, there are many reasons why investors purchase shares of stock, including shares of preferred stock.

There are also many reasons why companies issue stock. When a company issues stock, it is generally trying to generate corporate finances to subsidize specific growth objectives. Companies may choose from several types of stock to issue shares of stock that will best serve the corporation's needs. The two most common types of stock that corporation's issue are common stock and preferred stock. Common stock provides shareholders partial ownership in a company as well as certain rights. For instance, common shareholders are entitled to the right to vote on the board of directors and other important corporate matters such as stock splits or a merger. Common stock, however, has limited priority. This means that common shareholders only have access to a company's assets after a company's creditors and preferred shareholders have been paid. For instance, when a company is profitable, common stock shareholders receive dividend payments only after the distribution of dividends to all preferred shareholders. And in the event of a corporate liquidation, common stock shareholders receive only those assets left after all creditors, bondholders and preferred shareholders have received their full payment.

Preferred stock is generally considered a less risky investment in that it combines the ownership element of common stock with a more senior priority status for debt repayment. While an investment in preferred stock does not provide shareholders with a promise that they will receive a fixed rate of return on their shares or that their investment is protected and will be repaid in full (as bondholders and creditors enjoy), preferred shareholders have priority over common-stock shareholders, and thus are paid dividend distributions before any common-stock shareholders are paid. Venture capitalists invest primarily in preferred stock, and the U.S. Treasury, through the Troubled Assests Relief Program, acquired vast amounts of preferred stock as a mechanism for preserving corporate giants.

Thus, there are several differences between common stock and preferred stock. As a result, when a company issues both common stock and preferred stock, it creates two classes of owners with each group having different rights and privileges. In sum, with preferred shares, investors are usually guaranteed a fixed dividend while common-stock shareholders

receive variable dividends that are never guaranteed. Also, in the event of liquidation, preferred shareholders are paid before the common shareholders but after debt holders. Thus, preferred shareholders trade a more secure investment for fewer voting rights than common shareholders possess.

The following sections provide a more in-depth explanation of these concepts.

BASIC FINANCIAL CONCEPTS

TYPES OF PREFERRED STOCK
There are a number of different types of preferred stock. Corporations may issue these types of stock by themselves, or these characteristics may be combined to create more specialized forms of corporate securities. The following categories represent the most commonly issued forms of preferred stock.

- Cumulative: These shares give their owners the right to "accumulate" any dividend distributions that were due but not paid because of a corporation's financial shortfalls. If a company's earnings and profits begin to increase and the company decides to resume paying dividends, cumulative shareholders receive their missed payments in addition to their current dividend distribution before any common-stock dividends are distributed. For example, if Corporation A has 5,000 shares of $5 cumulative preferred stock outstanding but the board of directors did not declare a dividend in 2005 or 2006, these shares will have to be repaid in full in any future distributions before any common-stock dividends may be declared. Thus, if in 2007 the board of directors declares a dividend, cumulative preferred shareholders must be paid $75,000 (5,000 shares x $5 x 3 years) before any payment can be made to any common-stock shares.

- Non-Cumulative: Holders of non-cumulative preferred stock lose their dividend for any period in which the directors do not declare a distribution. In other words, dividend payments do not accumulate. However, non-cumulative preferred shares retain a preference that generally entitles them to a fixed amount of money before distributions can be paid to common-stock shares. However, this right is not absolute. A corporation's board of directors must first declare a dividend before the preferred non-cumulative shareholder has any right to receive a payment.

- Participating: Generally, preferred shares are entitled only to their stated preference, or the payment rights that are assigned to that type of share. However, preferred shares may be designated as "participating," in which case they have a right to participate in whatever the common-stock shares receive while still receiving their own preference. Thus, if, during a given year, common stock dividends are greater than those of preferred stock dividends, participating preferred shares entitle their shareholders to "participate" in these dividend increases so that the shareholders receive the share's own preference along with the higher dividend payments of common-stock shares.

- Convertible: These shares may be converted into shares of common stock at a set rate at the shareholder's option. The value of convertible shares tends to track the price of the common stock. When convertible stock is delivered in exchange for common stock, the parity price is the price at which the shares of common stock are equal in value to shares of preferred stock. Thus, if a preferred convertible stock is converted into two shares of common stock, the parity price of the common stock is one half the price of the preferred convertible stock. Convertible shares typically receive a conversion price when they are issued to allow for a simple conversion to a company's common stock at the given rate.

- Callable: These are shares that the corporation reserves the right to "call," i.e., to buy back at some price that is generally premium to the issued price. Thus, these shares must be sold back to the issuer at its request.

These features of preferred shares can be combined to create different forms of corporate preferred stock. For example, a corporation could issue a non-cumulative, participating preferred stock or a convertible, cumulative, participating preferred stock. A corporation's board of directors typically weighs the financial needs of the company against the characteristics and benefits of each form of preferred stock to determine which types of shares to issue.

CLASSES OF PREFERRED STOCK

In addition to various types of preferred stock, there are also different classes of preferred stock. The classes of preferred stock differ according to the precedence given to each class regarding the distribution of dividends and company assets at liquidation. When a company issues several classes of preferred shares, the classes are generally distinguished by being labeled as Class A or Class B preferred, with the Class A shares having precedence over shares of Class B for dividends and priority at liquidation. A company may issue classes of stock to indicate ownership in a specific division or subsidiary of the company or to indicate shares that sell at different market prices or that have differing dividend policies, voting rights or transfer restrictions.

RIGHTS OF PREFERRED STOCKHOLDERS

Like common stockholders, preferred stockholders have several rights as shareholders. First, preferred stockholders have the right of preference in dividend distributions. While a company does not have to pay dividends, if dividends are paid, preferred stockholders must receive full payment before any common stockholders receive dividends. In addition, if the preferred stock is cumulative, the accumulated dividends must also be paid along with the current dividends before common-stock dividends are paid.

Another right of preferred stockholders is that they have priority to the claims of common stockholders in the event of a corporate liquidation. This means that preferred shareholders may recover at least the par value, or the stated value, of their preferred shares before any common-stock shareholder may assert a claim to the liquidated assets. In addition, while preferred stockholders generally do not have the voting rights of common-stock shareholders, some preferred shares are issued with special voting preferences akin to the voting rights of common stock. These voting rights may enable preferred stockholders to vote to elect the board of directors or in specific rare circumstances, for example when new shares are being issued or when a taregt company's acquisition is being approved, just as common shareholders are routinely entitled to vote. Yet another right of preferred stockholders is that because preferred shares typically involve protective provisions that prevent new preferred shares with a senior claim to the corporation's assets from being issued, preferred shareholders do not have to face the prospect of a new stock being issued that would require its dividends be paid before any preferred shareholder is paid. Finally, preferred shares usually contain a call provision, which entitles the issuing corporation to repurchase the share when it chooses to do so. However, the corporation must usually repurchase the shares at a premium, thus protecting the investment of a preferred shareholder.

These basic rights represent the customary rights of preferred shareholders. However, preferred shares, like other securities, may be issued with a wide range of discretionary rights. Some corporation charters have provisions that authorize issuing preferred stock whose terms and conditions are not drafted in advance, and thus it can be decided by the board of directors when the shares are issued. These "blank check" preferred shares are frequently used as defense against takeovers in the event that another company attempts a hostile takeover of the corporation. To ward off such a potential takeover, the company may issue "blank check" preferred shares that have been assigned a very high liquidation value that must be paid in full if a change of corporate control occurs or that have specialized voting powers that enable shareholders to vote against the pending takeover attempt. Thus, potential investors who are considering investing in any company should carefully investigate all of the documents that the corporation files with the state regarding the terms of its formation. In addition, shareholders should stay abreast of any changes in the corporation's formation or governance by attending the annual meeting and examining any correspondence issued by the corporation about possible or impending corporation actions.

CORPORATE OBJECTIVES IN ISSUING PREFERRED STOCK

EQUITY CREATION
There are several reasons why corporations issue preferred stock. The main reason is to raise funds to finance its business operations. The three most common means by which corporations finance their growth objectives are by issuing common stock, issuing preferred stock or by borrowing loans and accumulating other forms of debt. These forms of equity creation represent different types of corporate financing. Corporations may generate funds

through two types of financing-equity financing or debt financing. Issuing securities such as common or preferred stock is a form of equity financing because it allows a company to collect funds from investors who buy shares without creating a corporate objective to repay the debt. This is because common and preferred shareholders generally are not guaranteed a profit or repayment at a fixed rate, but receive dividends only on the company's earnings and only if the board of directors approves a dividend distribution. On the other hand, generating corporate debt in the form of commercial-bank loans or issuing bonds is the most common form of debt financing.

Debt financing, unlike equity financing, does require that the corporation repay the debt plus any accrued interest. Thus, a corporation may choose equity financing to fund its growth by issuing preferred stock without incurring certain repayment obligations. However, the sale of preferred stock does not mean a corporation receives an influx of capital without incurring any ensuing obligations to shareholders. As explained above, preferred shareholders do have a right to preference in the event of any dividend distributions and a prior claim to the company's assets in the event of liquidation that must be paid before any common-stock shareholder is paid. In addition, corporations that pay timely dividends become an attractive investment for potential shareholders, thus creating an incentive for corporations to declare dividend distributions, which protects the investment of its shareholders.

MINIMIZE REPAYMENT OBLIGATIONS
As explained in the previous section, companies issue stocks, such as preferred stocks, instead of generating debt through commercial-bank loans or issuing bonds to minimize inflexible repayment obligations. Preferred shareholders have no general right to receive distributions. However, preferred stock is less risky than common stock because once a distribution is lawfully declared, preferred shareholders generally are treated as creditors of the corporation and their claim to the distribution takes priority to claims of any common-stock shareholders. Since preferred shares do not require periodic dividend distributions, if the company is in a tight financial spot, it can skip paying dividends to preferred stockholders while it could not skip a payment to a creditor or to bondholders. This is why companies may decide to issue preferred

stock during a period of financially difficulty. The sale of preferred shares generates corporate equity when the company needs an influx of funds without obligating it to a set repayment schedule that bonds and other forms of debt require. Thus, issuing preferred stock is a means of creating equity while minimizing corporation repayment obligations.

CONTROL CORPORATE GOVERNANCE

Not all companies may issue preferred stock to create equity. Only those companies organized as corporations may issue stock. This is because other types of companies, including sole proprietorships and limited partnerships, have a different ownership structure. Corporations are business entities that are owned by shareholders, while sole proprietorship or limited partnership structures are owned by either a sole proprietor or partners, respectively. The owners of the corporation become its owners by purchasing shares of the corporation's stock.

There are a number of reasons why a company may decide that becoming a corporation is the best course of action. The first reason is that incorporation affords a company the right to issue stock to create equity for its business objectives. Second, incorporation separates the company's identity, legal standing and assets from its owners. This means that, in general, the owners of a company cannot be personally sued or their assets taken if the company is sued for any corporate wrongdoing. This concept, known as limited liability, is a way for owners to protect their personal assets so that if the company is sued or faces bankruptcy, the owners will not face the potential loss of their personal assets.

However, once a corporation is formed, it may pursue its goals of creating equity by issuing stock either to a select group of individuals or to the general public. The corporation may issue a number of different types of securities, including common stock or preferred stock. A company may decide to issue preferred stock for several reasons. First, dividend payments to preferred shareholders may be suspended at the discretion of the board of directors in the event of a company's financial problems. Second, issuing preferred stock enables the current ownership of a corporation to retain some control over its corporate governance. Some companies may decide to limit the shares of stock the corporation will issue to the founders of the company or to its employees. These

companies are called "private" companies because their stock is held privately by a defined group of individuals, and thus is not able to be purchased by the public on any of the securities exchanges.

All corporations are initially formed as private entities, and this enables corporate founders to keep control over a company's initial growth and profits. However, private owners may later decide to raise funds to finance the company's growth by offering the public an opportunity to share in the ownership of the company by purchasing shares of its stock. This process changes a company from being a privately held corporation to being a publicly held company. The actual opportunity by which public investors are offered the opportunity to buy stock in a formerly private company is called an initial public offering.

Companies choose to undergo an initial public offering to expand operations, finance existing debt, build a new product or pay for a new project. When a company goes public, the company's founders can decide which type of stock to offer investors. Private companies often choose to issue preferred stock in the initial public offering in order to maintain some form of control over the corporation's governance. Since preferred stock does not generally carry the right to vote as common stock does, the issuance of preferred stock enables the company's founders to keep stockholders' economic interests in the company separate from the day to day business operations. Thus, a private company may choose to issue preferred stock in lieu of common stock so that its founders to not have to make concessions with the votes of shareholders as would be the case if common-stock shares were issued. Issuing preferred stock, therefore, allows a company to create equity while protecting its founders' interest in maintaining some form of control of its governance.

APPLICATIONS

FACTORS THAT AFFECT THE VALUE OF PREFERRED STOCK

STOCK SPLITS

A corporation whose stock is performing well may decide to divide its existing shares into multiple shares and distribute the additional, newly created shares to existing shareholders in proportion to the multiple of the split. For instance, a commonly used split is a two-for-one increase wherein each share is divided into two units, giving each stockholder an additional share for each share the investor currently holds. However, stocks can be split in other ways such as two-for-one, five-for-one, or any multiple that the company approves.

Many investors assume that a stock split automatically increases the value of the stock. However, this is not always the case. When a stock splits, the price per share also drops so that the value of the stock stays relatively stable. While the mechanics of the stock split may not have a significant effect on the value of a stock, the collective psyche of the investors in the market may impact the stock's value. This can happen if, for instance, a profitable company with high-priced shares splits its stock so that the price of its shares drops. When this happens, the stock

becomes more affordable and thus more attractive to the average investor, allowing more investors to purchase more shares of the company. This drives the value of the stock up so that investors have not only more stocks, but more stocks that have increased in value. In addition, a stock split is generally announced in the media, and this draws attention to the stocks as an investment opportunity and signals to investors the confidence of the company's management that the corporation will be profitable in the months and years ahead.

STOCK REPURCHASE PROGRAMS

A stock repurchase program, or also referred to as a buyback, occurs when a corporation repurchases or buys back shares of stocks that it previously issued. When a corporation repurchases its own stock, it takes those shares out of circulation and thus reduces the number of shares of corporate stock that are outstanding. The effect of a buyback is that each shareholder suddenly owns larger percentage of the company.

There are a number of reasons why companies might choose to repurchase stock. First, a corporation may be striving to raise its price to earnings ratio in that with fewer shares in the market, each share generates more earnings, and this boosts the earnings per share ration. In addition, a corporation may repurchase shares of its stock to offer the shares as an incentive to employees or management. Also, a corporation's management may announce a stock

repurchase program to signal that it believes the company's stock is undervalued and will increase in value because it is optimistic about the company's future. However, investors must research a stock repurchase program carefully because when a company's shareholders vote to authorize a buyback, the corporation is not obligated to follow through with the buyback. Some companies, then, may announce buyback plans to boost the perceived value of its stock without retaining any intention to actually repurchase shares of its stock. Thus, a stock repurchase program can either be a form of posturing by the company or it can be carefully conceived profit-making effort that is actually implemented by a corporation. In either case, stock repurchase programs can have an effect on the value of preferred stock.

RISK

Risk is an element of any investment that must be considered but that is hard to quantify. When a company sells stock, investors who purchase shares risk the possibility that the company may not make money in exchange for the ability to receive dividends if the company is profitable. Thus, companies sell stock to make money in the form of corporate financing and investors buy stock to make money in the form of dividends that enhance the net worth of their investment portfolios. But, with the possibility of making money comes its opportunity cost, or what the company and its investors must forge in order to have the ability to make money. When corporations sell their stock to raise capital, they must relinquish some of the corporation's earnings by paying dividend distributions and some control of the corporation's governance to shareholders who may be given the right to vote on corporate activities. When investors buy stock and become shareholders, they give up money they currently have in order to gain the possibility of participating in the distribution of a company's earnings and a say in how a company is run.

Preferred shares are similar to common stock in that they both symbolize an ownership unit of a company. Any investment in a company's stock comes with a certain amount of risk because shareholders are not guaranteed that a corporation will be profitable. However, preferred stock is considered to be a less risky investment than common stock because preferred shares are generally allocated larger dividend payments than common-stock shares and because the dividends of preferred shares are typically guaranteed by the corporation while common shares are not guaranteed dividend payments. Thus, if a company's profits fall, the company may pay dividends to preferred stockholders but not to common stockholders in order to save money. Also, in the event of liquidation, preferred stockholders have a higher priority in their claim to the company's assets than do common shareholders. In sum, preferred shares offer risks and benefits to both an issuing corporation and to investors, and both sides must carefully weigh the pros and cons of their financial goals in order to decide the best course of action to take.

CONCLUSION

Preferred stock is an attractive means to create equity for corporations and to create wealth and corporate ownership for investors. While preferred shares may not experience the price appreciation or voting rights of shares of common stock, preferred stock is considered a solid investment. This is because preferred stockholders have rights that offer some protection for their investment, such as the fact that preferred shares are generally guaranteed a regular dividend while shares of common stock are not. In addition, preferred stockholders have preference when a dividend payout is authorized so that preferred stockholders get paid before common stockholders, and preferred stockholders can take advantage of the prime distribution of a company's liquidated assets while common shareholders may not raise a claim to corporate assets until all preferred stockholders have received full compensation. On the other hand, while preferred stock signify ownership in a company as does common stock, owners of preferred stock generally do not get the voting rights in corporate matters that common shareholders receive. Overall, then, preferred stock offers basic rights that prompt investors to purchase such shares. And, many corporations issue preferred stock when making an initial public offering because of the security's favorable features.

When investors do decide to purchase shares of preferred stock, they must first make a determination as to what type and classification of shares to buy. In addition, investors must be mindful of certain factors that can affect the value of preferred stock, such as stock splits, stock repurchase programs and risk.

BIBLIOGRAPHY

Bildersee, J. (1973). Some aspects of the performance of non-convertible preferred stocks. *Journal of Finance, 28*(5), 1187-1201. Retrieved April 17, 2007, from EBSCO Business Source Complete. http://search.ebscohost.com/ login.aspx?direct=true&db=bth&AN=4653758&site=eh ost-live

Braham, L. (2007). Overlooked and underpriced. *Business Week,* (4027), 130. Retrieved April 17, 2007, from EBSCO Business Source Complete. http://search.ebscohost.com/ login.aspx?direct=true&db=bth&AN=24381071&site=eh ost-live

Bratton, W.W., & Wachter, M.L. (2013). A theory of preferred stock. *University of Pennsylvania Law Review, 161*(7), 1815-1906. Retrieved October 31, 2013, from EBSCO Online Database Business Source Complete. http://search. ebscohost. com/login.aspx?direct=true&db=bth&AN=889 50297&site=ehost-live

Brooks, L., Edwards, C. & Ferreira, E. (1984). Risk-return characteristics of convertible preferred stock: Comment. *Journal of Portfolio Management, 10*(2), 76-78. Retrieved April 17, 2007, from EBSCO Online Database Business Source Complete. http://search.ebscohost.com/login.aspx? direct=true&d b=bth&AN=15191654&site=ehost-live

Feldman, A. (2007). Putting founders first. *Inc., 29*(3), 29-31. Retrieved April 17, 2007, from EBSCO Online Database Business Source Complete. http://search.ebscohost.com/ login.aspx?direct=true&d b=bth&AN=24359765&site=eh ost-live

Kelly, D. & LeRoy, S. (2007). Liquidity and liquidation. *Economic Theory, 31*(3), 553-572. Retrieved April 17, 2007, from EBSCO Online Database Business Source Complete. http://search.ebsco-host.com/login.aspx?direct=t rue&db=bth&AN=2 4422813&site=ehost-live

Lehmann, R. (2007). Preferred prosperity. *Forbes, 179*(3), 106. Retrieved April 17, 2007, from EBSCO Online Database Business Source

Complete. http://search.ebscohost.com/ login.aspx?direct=true&db=bth&AN=23854967&site=ehost-live

Long-run operating performance of preferred stock issuers. (2011). *International Journal of Business & Finance Research (IJBFR), 5*(2), 61-73. Retrieved October 31, 2013, from EBSCO Online Database Business Source Complete. http://search.ebscohost.com/login.aspx?direct=true&db=bth&AN=54846096&site=ehost-live

Schonberger, J. (2011). Preferred stocks. *Kiplinger's Personal Finance, 65*(4), 36. Retrieved October 31, 2013, from EBSCO Online Database Business Source Complete. http://search.ebscohost.com/login.aspx?direct=true&db=bth&AN=59303389&site=ehost-live

Soldofsky, R. (1984). Reply. *Journal of Portfolio Management, 10*(2), 79-80. Retrieved April 17, 2007, from EBSCO Online Database Business Source Complete. http://search.ebscohost.com/login.aspx?direct=true&db=bth&AN=15191656&site=ehost-live

Vetter, D. & Wingender, J. (1996). The January effect in preferred stock investments. *Quarterly Journal of Business & Economics, 35*(1), 79. Retrieved April 17, 2007, from EBSCO Online Database Business Source Complete. http://search.ebscohost.com/login.aspx?direct=true&db=bth&AN=9511166009&site=ehost-live

SUGGESTED READING

Saperstein, R. (2006). Corporate cash management: Historical overview. *Financial Executive, 22*(9), 24-25. Retrieved April 17, 2007, from EBSCO Online Database Business Source Complete. http://search.ebscohost.com/login.aspx?direct=true&db=bth&AN=22989976&site=ehost-live

Soldofsky, R. (1981). The risk-return performance of convertibles. *Journal of Portfolio Management, 7*(2), 80-84. Retrieved April 17, 2007, from EBSCO Online Database Business Source Complete. http://search.ebscohost.com/ login.aspx?direct=true&db=bth&AN=15636206&site=ehost-live

Sprecher, C. (1971). A note on financing mergers with convertible preferred stock. *Journal of Finance, 26*(3), 683. Retrieved April 17, 2007, from EBSCO Online Database Business Source Complete. http://search.ebscohost.com/ login.aspx?direct=true&db=bth&AN=4656234&site=ehost-live

–Heather Newton

R

REAL ESTATE FINANCE

ABSTRACT

Real estate finance governs how investors pay for real property they acquire. Investors can use their own funds to acquire property but will often turn to financing companies to obtain mortgages. As with any type of investing, the investor should become educated about the process of acquiring real estate and how to understand the language of lenders. The process can be complicated but is assisted by engaging competent professionals to assist. Owning real estate is more like owning a business than other types of investments because there is the question of maintenance, repairs and tenant management which require much more of the investor's time and resources than other investments. Borrowers with special assets such as IRAs may have a unique avenue for financing while the cash poor, self employed and credit challenged may have to look to other alternatives to successfully invest in real estate.

OVERVIEW

Real estate finance is a popular topic among professionals and amateurs alike. Real estate is important because it is a primary investment vehicle in the U.S. economy. In addition, there are many complex financing vehicles that make it possible to construct various types of real estate deals. Whether you are a small investor, a first time investor, experienced, interested in residential or commercial property there is something for you in real estate finance. Real estate investment requires looking carefully at properties to acquire, and knowing how to finance these properties and the management of them once acquired. Galinnelli (2005) discusses the importance of deciding what type of ownership to obtain for holding title to real estate, such as individual ownership which provides no protection against personal liability or partnerships, or corporations and limited liability companies.

Real estate is also called real property. Real estate finance begins with a tangible property of some type such as land or buildings. Real estate property for the individual investor can mean owning a home, income property such as a multi-tenant apartment building or owning commercial space for rental to businesses. Vacation homes and condominiums are other examples of property an investor might consider.

The players involved are often real estate and financing professionals and the investor. Real estate professionals specialize in the process of identifying and acquiring property. Attorneys play the role of preparing and examining legal documents and aspects of ownership. Mortgage and loan officers assist in the financing of real estate deals. Accountants can help owners manage the day-to-day finances of investment properties.

Garton-Good (1999) described the primary players in mortgage financing as:
- Primary lenders;
- Secondary market;
- Private mortgage insurance market.

Primary lenders are traditional banks and companies that provide mortgage loans, however, these entities may sell loans before they are paid off and secondary market entities may purchase these loans. Some major players in the secondary market are Fannie Mae (Federal National Mortgage Association), Ginnie Mae (Government National Mortgage Association) and Freddie Mac (Federal Home Loan Mortgage Corporation). Private mortgage insurance insures 20% of a loan against the possibility of a borrower defaulting on a loan.

Anderson (2007) discussed the importance of trust in a real estate transaction relationship. Real estate investing can be a complex process; open, continuous communication is needed to make sure the needs of the investor are met and that a win-win situation is possible for the buyer and the seller. The success of dealing with the investor often depends on the investor's expectations and the possible uses the investor has for the property. If the investor is unclear on exactly what they want, they may continue to be dissatisfied with the investment throughout the process of acquisition. Being truthful from beginning to end can help the investor and the various players in the process of obtaining real estate to find common ground.

REAL ESTATE FINANCE PRODUCTS

There are several types of products that can be used to finance an investment in real estate. They include the buyers own cash or some sort of leveraging of other financing. Warr (2005) encourages investors to have a goal of creating "maximum leverage to make the most of their buying dollar. Benke & Folwer (2001) encouraged maximizing leverage which means any way that the borrower can delay "cash outflow."

MORTGAGES

If investors do not have or want to use their own cash for acquiring property, real estate is usually financed through a mortgage. A mortgage is "a loan secured by the collateral of some specified real estate property that obliges the borrower to make a predetermined series of payments" (Morgenson & Harvey, 2002). A conventional mortgage loan is one that comes from an institution such as a bank or insurance company. A nonconventional loan comes from an unconventional source like the property seller.

There are four basic parts to a loan: the principal amount that you borrow, the length or term of the loan, the annual interest rate, and the amount that you pay each payment period (Galinnelli, 2005). Mortgages can have a fixed interest rate or one that adjusts periodically. The adjustable rate mortgages (ARM) base the adjustment on some index such as the prime rate. There are combinations of these types of mortgages as well. There are mortgage products that allow the borrower to pay the interest only for a period of time as well as products that move from fixed to adjustable and vice versa. Galinnelli (2005) suggests that investors select products based on their own situation and the profit that can be anticipated from the property. In addition, investors should compare lenders in terms of interest rates, loan to value ratios and debt coverage ratios. Loan to value ratios

compare the selling price to the appraised value while debt coverage ratios which are a comparison of what the investors debt is and the impact of adding a mortgage loan.

REAL ESTATE INVESTMENT TRUSTS

Real estate investment trusts (REITs) are another investment opportunity. REITs are "trusts that invest directly in real estate or loans secured by real estate assets..." (Morgenson & Harvey, 2002). Bogoslaw (2007) indicated that the housing slump in the United States might frighten investors away from real estate investments. However, he pointed to international real estate investment trusts or mutual funds with international real estate as one method of avoiding problems. Europe, Western Europe and industrial Asia are seen as areas where expansion is planned and real estate investments may make sense. Bogoslaw noted that private REITs aren't publicly traded and have more stable cash flows because they are not influenced by the stock market. Investors can also look at using their IRAs for real estate investing as well as owning a vacation home or part of one with other investors.

WHY PEOPLE INVEST IN REAL ESTATE & CONSIDERATIONS FOR SUCCESSFUL INVESTING

People often invest in real estate because they see it as a financial benefit. If a person wants to transition from renting their own home to owning it, this can be a powerful financial reason for owning a home. Others may see owning property as a long term investment or business venture that can be taken on while the individual is still employed in some other occupation. Some see real estate as a way to grow a nest egg for the future and to have retirement income from tenants. However, many investors are unaware of the responsibilities and requirements of owning and managing real estate.

KNOWLEDGE REQUIREMENTS

Teger (2007) applauded investors who want to own real estate but likened owning real estate to owning a small business. Teger recommended having a plan just like a small business to avoid becoming overwhelmed with the great responsibility involved in owning and managing property. Understanding and planning for owning real estate means having a great understanding of the property, local market rates for rent and the length of time it may take to rent unoccupied space. Owners of real estate must know the impact of a vacancy on their overall profits. Galinnelli (2005) suggested that before even purchasing a property that investors compare the possible purchases based on the cash flow and long term profitability. Asking the right questions up front can avoid problems later.

LEASE AGREEMENTS

Leases are agreements between owners and tenants and spell out the responsibilities of each. Understanding the language and terms of the lease are important should any legal action or eviction be required. Owning the property is just the beginning, Teger felt that owners needed to be certain that lease agreements provided for sufficient increases to help the property owner make a profit. Management of tenants requires understanding each lease in detail. Owners have responsibilities to collect rent and tenants need to provide notice if they are moving. All of these details are contained in lease agreements.

CREATING A DESIRABLE PROPERTY

Besides tasks connected with managing tenants, there are other tasks related to the actual upkeep, repair and improvement of the property. While owners may spend a lot of time thinking about how to collect rent from tenants and whether or not those rents will provide a profit for the owner another consideration is making the property a desirable one to live in or work in, in the case of commercial property. As with any other tangible property, real estate buildings require repair and upkeep. The owner is responsible for those tasks and must complete repairs in a timely fashion or risk vacancies as tenants who are dissatisfied leave.

STRATEGIES FOR PROPERTY INVESTMENT

Migdal (2007) advised investors in real estate to prepare strategies in advance of purchasing. These strategies involve planning, looking at various purchase and financing scenarios and examining the possible profit from various real estate purchases. Teger (2007) suggested that owners think of themselves as business owners, write a business plan and have a good supporting team of professionals. These professionals include attorneys, accountants and relationships with skilled professionals to perform repairs.

Thinking of owning real estate as an investment only misses many of the key requirements in this type of business venture. Migdal (2007) agreed that the real estate market moves so quickly buyers have to rely on professionals well versed in all aspects of the real estate process and transaction.

Galinnelli (2005) agrees with Teger that a plan is necessary to be a successful investor in real estate. Investors should consider real estate a long term investment avoid the concept of flipping "properties for a quick profit." Bromiley (2007) calls flipping houses "buying, renovating and quickly selling for a profit." Bromiley advises: Know what you are getting into before buying and renovating a property, make sure you know what defects or problems the property may have and understand the types of permits required and work that needs to be done on the property.

STEPS TO CHOOSING A PROPERTY

There are three steps that an investor should take to identify the types of properties in which to invest (Galinnelli, 2005).

- The first step is to identify a price range based on the cash and financing available for the purchase and the amount of money that might be needed immediately for repairs and a cash reserve.
- The second step is to select a location for the property. Galinnelli cautioned novice investors from quickly hiring a management company for property. Novice investors need to understand the process of management and can only learn this by doing. In addition, management companies can be costly and eat away at profits. Investors need a base of knowledge in the area they are investing to determine where to get tenants, what the turnover rate is likely to be and how long they can expect before a vacancy is filled.
- The third step is to select the type of property. Many types of property are available for sale including single family homes, condominiums, multifamily properties with two to four units, multifamily properties above four units, commercial office, commercial retail, commercial industrial and other investments such as vacant land, hotels, and mobile home parks. Investors must consider the pros and cons of each of these types of property and understand their local market, if investing locally, for the type of property being considered.

Investors might look outside their local area to invest if prices are lower or there are other advantages but must weigh that against being physically away from the property. Galinnelli (2005) emphasized that investors should only choose properties within their skill levels.

Garton-Good (1999) suggested that real estate purchasers prepare for the purchase by reducing debt. The investor can increase the chances of getting a loan approved and getting favorable rates by paying off debt, paying down debt, refinancing high rate loans, consolidating loans and avoiding excessive credit card spending. Lenders can make suggestions for potential borrowers as to what actions might help the process of being approved for a loan. Once a loan has been approved, there are many categories of closing costs that the investor needs to understand and be prepared to pay. The smart buyer also knows that these fees can be negotiated and possibly reduced.

VIEWPOINT

OPTIONS FOR FINANCING OF REAL ESTATE

There will always be investors for real property and as a result, there will always be many different financing options for these investors. Selecting from among these alternatives is challenging and forces the investor to become educated on these options.

INDIVIDUAL RETIREMENT ACCOUNTS

Garton-Good (1999) noted that first time homebuyers can withdraw up to $10,000 penalty free from an IRA for a down payment or closing costs. Knight (2007) felt that opportunities exist for investors to use their IRAs (Individual Retirement Accounts) to purchase real estate. Knight said over $2.4 trillion in IRA rollovers is expected between 2003 and 2010 and high net worth individuals can use real estate to diversify their portfolios. Investors interested in this option would have to open a self-directed IRA meaning that the owner is making all the investment decisions. The self-directed account is managed by a custodian well versed in IRAs holding real estate investments. Self-directed IRAs are funded by 401K rollover, with money from an existing IRA or from a profit sharing plan.

Once a property is purchased, the IRA will be shown as the owner or owners if multiple people use their IRA or a loan can be made to the IRA. Knight noted the benefits of IRA financing of real estate include portfolio diversification and favorable tax benefits (Knight, 2007). When the IRA holder decides to retire and take benefits, a choice can be made to take all of the value of the real estate or to take a percentage of it. The remainder will still be owned by the IRA. Although there are benefits to this type of strategy, there are also drawbacks. For example, the investor can't sell a property he owns to his IRA. The investor cannot act as if he owns the property such as providing free repairs to the property owned by the IRA.

CASH BUYERS

Garton-Good (1999) noted the benefits of paying for real estate with cash. The cash buyer doesn't have to shop and learn about mortgages nor does this type of buyer have to worry about mortgage payments. The disadvantage of cash-buying is that the investor doesn't get to take advantage of the tax benefits of mortgages which includes deducting mortgage interest on income taxes. Another benefit of mortgages is that they usually require an appraisal, if the cash buyer skips this, they could overpay for a property. Buyers can also receive up to $11,000 per year without tax consequences to use as a down payment for a home (Garton- Good, 1999).

LOANS

Much of the success an investor has in getting financing has to do with creditworthiness. If a buyer of real estate has a poor credit score, is self employed or has other issues, the options open to this type of borrower may be limited. Having bad credit is one of the major reasons a mortgage is denied (Garton-Good, 1999). In the 1980's no documentation, low documentation (no doc/low/doc) loans became popular for the self-employed and other borrowers. Because of high default rates, those loans have become less available. No-doc/Low-doc loans usually require a higher down payment of 25% — 30%. A creative alternative for the self-employed is the 75/10/15 financing which involves two mortgage loans where the first mortgage is 75% of the purchase price. In this way, the borrower avoids private mortgage insurance (PMI) — required if an 80% or higher loan is taken, less documentation may be required and a more favorable interest rate may be obtained.

Another option for the self-employed might be to take a business loan instead of a personal mortgage loan (Garton-Good, 1999).

Individuals with poor credit can attempt to obtain subprime loans. However, with the increase of defaults on loans of this type, they will vary in supply. Subprime loans are loans available to the borrower with repetitive or extensive damaged credit and who are riskier and less likely to be picked up by the secondary mortgage market. There are three credit problems that would cause a borrower to seek a subprime loan: late payments of mortgages, late payments of credit cards, or a judgment or bankruptcy. The higher the amount that is provided as a down payment, the worse the individual's credit can be (Garton-Good, 1999).

While conventional fixed rate loans are the primary way investors finance mortgages, they can have disadvantages. For example, fixed rate conventional loans have fixed interest rates that remain the same even if interest rates go down. Some loan costs may also be higher than with other types of loans and creative financing may be limited. However, there are advantages to these same types of loans in that the interest rate is guaranteed not to go up and the lender may often choose not to resell this type of loan (Garton-Good, 1999).

Kosnett (2007) tapped into the trend of people wanting to invest in vacation homes in resort type areas. The attraction of these locales is beneficial if the investor wants to enjoy the property personally or if the property will be rented or sold. However, Kosnett cautions investors in vacation property to try to work with local lenders in order to have greater success.

REAL ESTATE INFORMATION

Investors can get information on real estate from real estate agents, for sale signs, newspaper ads, placing 'real estate wanted' ads, Internet searches and networking (Galinnelli, 2005). Migdal (2007) suggested maintaining relationships with asset and fund managers who know their markets and are likely to be aware of real estate opportunities that may be unadvertised.

Garton-Good (1999) saw the Internet as a powerful tool for doing real estate research online. Many banks and mortgage companies have their mortgage applications online and provide for the online transmission of important documents even with digital signatures. These changes provide convenience for the borrowers and can also speed up the process. Garton-Good recommended taking care to double check all information since there could be incorrect information online. This can be especially true if working with a lender not located in your local area but available online. There may be tantalizing offers but they may not pan out. Enlisting professionals such as an attorney is still a necessity when dealing with online financing organizations.

There are a several types of information that the real estate investor should keep in mind. These include mortgage trends and refinancing options. Investors must become avid consumers of real estate information to identify and follow mortgage trends and refinancing options. Garton-Good (1999) defined "housing bubble" as a period of rapid and high appreciation of property.

The housing bubble period may be a happy one for the investor as they see the property they've purchased appreciate in value rapidly. However, when the housing bubble bursts, the investor can't sell the property at the higher prices and may lose money when selling. If the investor has refinanced the property and taken cash out or otherwise obtained a loan against the higher value, there may be negative consequences if the property must be sold to pay the loans off. Refinancing offers are rampant and often attractive, but careful planning is needed when considering these options. Refinancing has to make financial sense and the timing has to be right to provide the investor with value. Investors should also be aware that credit is checked again during refinancing and credit problems or errors can block refinancing. Lenders may tout "no-cost" refinancing but the hidden costs may add up quickly (Garton-Good, 1999).

BIBLIOGRAPHY

Anderson, S. J. (2007). Real estate pros learn lessons from tough clients. *Mississippi Business Journal, 29*(31), 6.

Benke, W. & Fowler, J. M. (2001). *All about real estate investing: the easy way to get started.* New York: Mc Graw-Hill.

Bogoslaw, D. (2007, July 7). Real estate bets in shaky times. *Business Week Online,* 29. Retrieved September 16, 2007, from EBSCO Online Database

Business Source Complete. http://search.ebsco-host.com/login.aspx?direct=t rue&db=bth&AN=2 6003782&site=ehost-live

Bromiley, J. K. (2007). House flipping pitfalls could eat into profits. *Wenatchee Business Journal, 21*(8), C10.

Gallinelli, F. (2005). *Insider secrets to financing your real estate investments: what every real estate investor needs to know about finding & financing your next deal.* New York: McGraw-Hill.

Garton-Good, J. (1999). All about mortgages: insider tips to finance or refinance your home. Chicago: Dearborn Trade Publishing.

Jiawei, Z., Tony, T., & Joy, Z. (2013). Impact of home affordable refinance program on mortgage credit performance. *Real Estate Finance (Aspen Publishers Inc.), 30*(2), 47-53. Retrieved November 15, 2013, from EBSCO Online Database Business Source Complete. http://search.ebscohost.com/ login.aspx?direct=true&db=bth&AN=90069129 &site=ehost-live

Knight, J. (2007). Using an IRA to buy real estate. *Real Estate Finance (Aspen Publishers Inc.), 23*(6), 19-20. Retrieved September 16, 2007, from EBSCO On-line Database Business Source Complete. http:// search.ebscohost.com/ login.aspx?direct=true&d b=bth&AN=25752313&site=eh ost-live

Kosnett, J. R. (2007). Own your piece of paradise. *Kiplinger's Personal Finance, 61*(8), 42-45. Retrieved September 16, 2007, from EBSCO Online Data-base Business Source Complete. http://search. ebscohost.com/login.aspx?direct=t rue&db=bth& AN=25639434&site=ehost-live

Migdal, N. (2007). Faster than a speeding bullet. *Real Estate Finance (Aspen Publishers Inc.), 23*(6), 21-23. Retrieved September 16, 2007, from EBSCO On-line Database Business Source Complete. http:// search.ebscohost.com/ login.aspx?direct=true&d b=bth&AN=25752314&site=eh ost-live

Morgenson, G. & Harvey, C. R. (2002). *The New York Times Dictionary of Money Investing.* New York: Times Books.

Pattap, S. (2013). U.S. equity REITs and industrials — An exercise in contrasts. *Real Estate Finance & Investment,* 8. Retrieved November 15, 2013, from EBSCO Online Database Business Source Com-plete. http://search.ebscohost.com/login.aspx?di rect=true&db=bth&AN=88301306 &site=ehost-live

Sabatini, G. (2013). Sale-leaseback — Corporate real estate as a long-term source of financing. *Site Se-lection, 58*(3), 190- 196. Retrieved November 15, 2013, from EBSCO Online Database Business Source Complete. http://search.ebscohost.com/ login.aspx?direct=true&db=bth&AN=87813826 &site=ehost-live

Teger, L. (2007). Thinking about investment in real estate? Have a plan — first! *Hudson Valley Business Journal, 18*(22), 24.

Warr, G. D. (2005). *Make more money investing in mul-tiunits; a step-by-step guide to profiting from apartment buildings.* Chicago: Dearborn Trade Publishing.

SUGGESTED READING

Dahl, J. (2007). Great minds don't think alike. *Smart Money, 16*(8), 19. Retrieved September 16, 2007, from EBSCO Online Database Busi-ness Source Complete. http://search. ebscohost. com/login.aspx?direct=true&db=bth&AN=2576 3900&site=ehost-live

Kosnett, J. R. (2007). Own your piece of paradise. *Kiplinger's Personal Finance, 61*(8), 42-45. Retrieved September 16, 2007, from EBSCO Online Data-base Business Source Complete. http://search. ebscohost.com/login.aspx?direct=t rue&db=bth& AN=25639434&site=ehost-live

Taylor, M. (2004). A small world. *Mortgage Banking, 65*(1), 80-85. Retrieved September 16, 2007, from EBSCO Online Database Business Source Complete. http://search. ebscohost.com/ login.aspx?direct=true&db=bth&AN=1483 1469&site=ehost-live

– Marlanda English

REGULATORY ISSUES IN FINANCIAL SERVICES

ABSTRACT

This article will provide an overview of the regulatory issues in financial services. The article provides an introduction to financial services, which includes a history of the financial services industry, an explanation of the market share of the industry and descriptions of the major types of services offered by financial providers. In addition, this article also explains the most significant legislative regulations that have been enacted to govern the financial services industry, including a summary of the historical statutes that laid the framework for the modern finance and banking industries: The Sarbanes-Oxley Act of 2002, The Glass-Steagall Act, and The Gramm-Leach-Bliley Act. Further, the regulatory bodies that oversee the financial services industry are also described, including the Federal Reserve Board, the Securities and Exchange Commission, the Federal Deposit Insurance Corporation and the various self-regulatory organizations. Finally, the regulation of financial providers includes requirements for financial institutions to enter, expand or exit the market and to appropriately manage the risks inherent in the financial services industry; this article includes a brief description of each of these factors.

OVERVIEW

Financial services have been the focus of significant attention and legislation throughout the history of the United States. Even in the formation of the fledgling republic, many important legislative battles were waged over issues concerning the regulation of the financial industry. In the years following the Great Depression, the legislators of the New Deal created a regulatory framework that would govern the banking, securities and financial services industries. This shaped the nature and the practices of the financial services industry for over fifty years.

More recently, however, significant changes have taken place in the financial services industry. These changes have stemmed from technological advances, changing practices in financial services and new developments in governmental oversight. Their net effect has been to render obsolete many of the laws and regulations governing the industry, even as major statutes have been enacted in recent years that have transformed the financial services industry.

The following sections provide an overview of the financial services industry and introduce some of the most significant legislation that governs financial services providers today.

INTRODUCTION TO FINANCIAL SERVICES

Financial services refers to the duties and benefits related to money management and investment services that are provided by institutions within the finance industry, such as commercial banks, investment banks, insurance companies, credit card companies and stock brokerages. Financial services is the largest industry in the world in terms of earnings. In addition, the financial services industry is constantly changing as new technology and regulatory reforms have led to the transformation of financial institutions and significant developments in the services they provide.

The Gramm-Leach-Bliley Act of 1999 broke down some of the barriers that separated commercial and investment banking, and eliminated some of the restrictions that prevented full affiliation between securities firms and insurance underwriting activities. With the expansion of the services that financial institutions may now provide, many institutions that were formally considered banks, insurance companies or brokerage houses transformed their service offerings by introducing the provision of a full slate of financial services. For instance, companies that once exclusively dealt in insurance may now provide investment options such as certificates of deposit ("CDs") and investment brokerage accounts. Also, institutions that once offered only basic banking services now provide a full line of brokerage products, while companies that once focused only on brokerage accounts have expanded their offerings to include bank accounts and loans. The bill is considered controversial, particularly in light of the financial crisis that began in 2007.

The following sections provide a more detailed explanation of the history of financial services, the market share of financial services providers and the types of services typically offered by financial services institutions.

History of Financial Services
During the 1970s, the banking industry remained balkanized, in that most states restricted the ability of out-of-state banks to open branches in their states, and all states prevented out-of-state bank holding companies from buying their banks. Thus, rather than the large, nationally integrated banking system of today, there were thousands of banks throughout the United States, although most of them were small, local offices. Beginning in the 1970s, banking deregulation drastically changed the banking landscape. Banks could begin to open branches across state lines, and out-of-state bank holding companies could purchase banks anywhere. These changes accelerated during the 1980s, and were completed in the middle of the 1990s with federal legislation allowing banks to operate nationwide. While some regulatory constraints remain in that banks may not hold more than 10 percent of deposits nationally, the banking system in the United States has become increasingly open and integrated (Strahan, 2006).

In addition to changes in banking deregulation, legislative changes began to allow investment companies to provide consumers with basic banking services. Thus, although most Americans conducted routine checking and savings business at local banks, bank assets began to decline as consumers began to take advantage of new alternatives to conventional ways of banking, such as CDs and money market funds, which yielded higher interest. As a result of these changes, the mid-1980s saw a significant increase in the number of bank failures.

To stay competitive, banks found loopholes in the Glass-Steagall Banking Act of 1933, the reigning legislative regime that governed the banking industry and restricted the services that banks could provide, and began to offer services outside of traditional banking activities by creating mortgage and financing subsidiaries and developing conveniences such as debit cards and automatic teller machines (ATMs). By the mid-1990s, the banking and financial services industries were no longer clearly defined. Finally, a wave of mergers and acquisitions among financial institutions created powerhouse financial services companies that offer consumers an even greater range of services across a range of industries, including banking, insurance and investment management.

Although growth and profit continued in the 1980's, the financial services industry also experienced significant losses. On October 19, 1987, the New York Stock Exchange closed with the largest single-day drop in its history, losing 508.32 points, or almost one-fourth of its value. Another significant event in the financial services industry was the failure of hundreds of savings and loan (S&L) institutions in the mid-1980s. One reason for the S&L failures stemmed from the debt burden carried due to low-interest mortgages offered in the 1970s when inflation and interest was high. A government bailout costing billions of dollars was implemented to pay the insured depositors of failed institutions.

Finally, the financial services industry experienced significant losses in the wake of the attacks on New York City on September 11, 2001. The World Trade Center, which was destroyed in the attacks, had held many banks, insurance companies, brokerages and securities firms. Many of these companies lost personnel and important documents and records. The months following these events saw a further contraction in an already sluggish American economy. The events of 9/11 prompted the financial service industry to once again reevaluate its service offerings, and many of these institutions introduced more comprehensive electronic and virtual financial services, a trend that continues.

Market Share
As a result of the regulatory changes to the banking sector during the mid 1970s to 1990s, banks became larger and better diversified. For example, the share of assets held by banks rose dramatically, and banks became not only bigger but also more geographically diverse. For instance, throughout most of the 1970s, only 10 percent of the banking-system assets in most states were owned by organizations with operations outside the state. By the mid 1990s, this figure had risen to about 65 percent, as reform allowed bank holding companies to buy banks across the country (Strahan, 2006).

The changes in bank regulations not only altered the size and geographical scope of banks, but also increased their efficiency. Banking deregulation increased competition among banks and bank holding companies, and this competition drove financial institutions to improve their efficiency while offering higher quality customer service and lower priced bank services (Strahan, 2006).

Today, the financial services industry constitutes the largest group of companies in the world in terms of earnings, although other industries log greater numbers in terms of total revenue or numbers of employees. The financial services industry remains extremely competitive, as no single financial institution dominates the market share, but rather a number of top companies continue to jostle for market superiority. Despite this fragmentation, financial service companies remain some of the most profitable companies in the world, and the financial services industry continues to grow exponentially.

TYPES OF SERVICES OFFERED

Financial institutions now offer a wide range of financial services. The major types of financial services are deposits and transfers, savings and checking accounts, short-term borrowing, long-term borrowing, insurance, investment services and credit and debit cards. This range of services allows financial services institutions to compete and keep more of the business of their customers in-house, since consumers are able to obtain a wide range of services from the same institution. In addition, these institutions are able to lure customers from other institutions by offering better rates on the same host of services. The following sections will explain the types of services that are typically offered by financial services providers in more detail.

Deposits & Transfers

The transfer of funds with negotiable instruments, such as checks, is one of the most useful of financial services. Transfers by check provide parties with control over the amounts and timing of the transactions and with a record that can be used as evidence of payments or other transfers. Funds may also be deposited or transferred electronically, which is often less expensive than paper check transfers, in that electronic deposits and transfers are typically completed almost instantaneously. Finally, funds may also be deposited or transferred by telephone, through the use of an ATM or through a wire service.

Savings & Checking Accounts

Most banks offer checking and savings accounts for their customers. These accounts allow individuals to store their income and savings in accounts that are federally insured up to a certain dollar amount and provide convenient access to the funds through withdrawals and checking services. In addition, many of these accounts offer interest rates that, while generally minimal, allow consumers to incur some interest on the money they have deposited with the financial institution. In turn, financial institutions such as banks and credit unions pool these deposits to use as assets that enable them to extend loans and mortgages, and borrowers pay the financial institution a return on the money in the form of interest payments.

Short-Term Borrowing

Short-term borrowing consists of consumer loans that individuals may borrow or debt that is incurred by businesses through borrowing and lending in commercial paper. Consumer loans are smaller loans that individuals may borrow from banks, credit unions and finance companies. The amounts lent and repayment terms are tailored to the demands of the borrower and the concerns of the lender. These loans may be secured by an individual's assets or they may be unsecured if the financial history of an individual borrower is exceptionally strong. Because borrowers and lenders benefit from a reasonably close, personal relationship in that borrowers are typically customers of the financial institution, lenders are able to offer some flexibility in the amounts, repayment schedules and other terms of the loans.

Commercial paper functions essentially as an alternative to a bank line of credit. Once a business becomes large enough and maintains a high enough credit rating, then it may use commercial paper as a cheaper alternative to obtaining short-term funds using a bank line of credit. Commercial paper also permits borrowers and lenders to avoid the costs of certain federal regulations regarding borrowing and lending through banks and other financial institutions.

Long-Term Borrowing

Long-term borrowing is distinguishable from short-term borrowing with regards to the instruments that represent the indebtedness. Relatively few lenders provide individuals or businesses with debt maturing in more than four or five years that is not represented by a formal, often marketable, instrument. For individuals, these loans are generally secured with property, such as a mortgage. For businesses, the instruments usually are bonds that often are secured and that are not fully marketable unless they are registered with the Securities and Exchange Commission ("SEC").

Investment Services

Investment services provide people with the opportunity to contribute to a range of investment vehicles that are best suited for their needs according to the amount of money they wish to invest and length of time of the investment. In addition, many of these investment services are offered at very low transactions costs. These investments can be represented by a CD or money market mutual funds, which are very similar to savings accounts except that they represent a claim on specified market-valued assets. The investments are usually placed in a portfolio of assets and generally are insured through the federal government. Also, individuals may invest in U.S. Treasury bills or other more sophisticated options that involve shares listed on stock exchanges.

Insurance Services

Insurance brokers shop for insurance, such as corporate property and casualty insurance, for their customers. In addition, some financial institutions now offer some forms of insurance, such as annuities or life insurance. Insurance for individuals is

still generally underwritten by insurance companies and offered primarily through agents, insurance brokers and stock brokers. However, banking and investment corporations are increasingly offering a wide range of insurance options, including life insurance, retirement insurance, health insurance, and home and automobile policies.

Credit & Debit Cards

Throughout the 1990s, debit and credit cards became increasingly popular among American consumers. The ease of making purchases or transferring funds electronically made debit and credit cards replace cash as the purchasing method of choice. An ever-growing number of companies and associations began offering credit cards, and attempted to lure new customers by offering premiums and bonuses for the use of their cards. These offers included frequent-flyer miles, credits toward purchases from affiliated companies or a percentage of any money spent sent back to consumers in the form of cash or an account credit.

Since this time, the use of credit cards has expanded from infrequent large purchases to include such everyday purchases as groceries, fast food and gasoline. In addition, credit cards are being used by a broader cross-section of consumers. When credit cards were first offered, only individuals with solid credit and substantial incomes had access to them. Credit card companies began targeting students on many college and university campuses so that these young consumers would become the next generation of credit card users. Also, the wider range of credit and debit card options allowed even individuals with poor credit or a limited credit history to obtain these cards. In general, Americans charge more purchases with their credit cards than they spend in cash, and this disparity will undoubtedly continue to grow.

LEGISLATIVE REGULATION OF FINANCIAL SERVICES

The financial services industry in the United States has been regulated by federal laws and statutes almost since its inception. The U.S. Constitution grants Congress powers to collect taxes, borrow money, regulate commerce (with foreign nations and among the states) and coin money. In exercising these powers, Congress has enacted a regulatory framework that has undergone significant changes over time in response to trends in the finance and banking sectors. The following sections describe some of the major pieces of legislation that have been enacted over the years to regulate the financial services industry.

Early Legislation

The Securities Act of 1933 was the first Congressional law to impose regulation on the securities industry. Initial public offerings were required to be registered and disclosed to investors to protect them from fraud and misrepresentations. In 1934, The Securities Exchange Act created the Securities and Exchange Commission (SEC) and specified its licensing and other regulatory duties. This law also prohibits insider trading, the misuse of confidential information not available to the general public for personal gain.

The Investment Company Act of 1940 extended the SEC's regulatory authority to mutual fund and other investment companies. After the passage of this Act, these entities were required to comply with SEC rules in addition to any other industry regulations. Congress also passed the Investment Advisers

Act of 1940, which broadened the definition of an investment adviser to bring more of these activities under the purview of the SEC. This legislation was vital in that, as the investment management industry evolved, many investment professionals became investment advisers rather than brokers because the regulations governing advising were more lax. The new legislation offered investors greater protections from misleading, fraudulent or erroneous investment advice.

Sarbanes-Oxley Act

Known also as the Corporate Responsibility Act of 2002, the Sarbanes-Oxley Act was signed in the wake of Enron and other accounting and corporate governance scandals. It instituted radical reforms in four key areas: Corporate responsibility, criminal penalties, accounting regulation and consumer protections.

In terms of corporate responsibility, Sarbanes-Oxley requires the chief executive officer (CEO) and chief financial officer (CFO) of a corporation to certify financial reports and audits submitted by the corporation. In addition, CEOs and CFOs are required to forfeit profits and bonuses from earnings that have been restated because of securities fraud, and corporate executives are prohibited from selling company stock during blackout periods, when company employees may not modify their company retirement or investment plans. Finally, the Act requires financial employees to report company stock trades within two days and that companies must provide immediate disclosure of material changes in their financial condition.

Sarbanes-Oxley also introduced stricter criminal penalties for violations of the Act's provisions. For instance, the Act makes it a crime to destroy, alter or fabricate records in federal investigations or to defraud shareholders. These acts are punishable with a potential 20-year prison term. Sarbanes-Oxley also increases the penalties that CEOs and CFOs may face for falsifying statements or failing to certify financial reports. Finally, the Act requires that significant documents and emails related to corporate audits be preserved for five years and creates a 10-year felony for destroying such documents.

One major effect of Sarbanes-Oxley was its overhaul of corporate accounting regulations. The Act created the Public Company Accounting Oversight Board, where public companies must now be registered. Also, the Sarbanes-Oxley Act extends a statute of limitations on securities fraud to five years and liberalizes the ability of whistleblowers to sue for retaliatory actions by corporations.

Glass-Steagall Act

The Glass-Steagall Act was enacted in 1933 in the wake of the 1929 stock market crash and the Great Depression. The Act set up a regulatory firewall between commercial and investment bank activities and prohibited commercial banks from collaborating with full-service brokerage firms or participating in investment banking activities. Banks were given a year to decide on whether they would specialize in commercial or investment banking. Either way, the Act required that only 10 percent of the total income of commercial banks could stem from securities, although commercial banks could continue to underwrite government-issued bonds. Congress repealed the Glass-Steagall Act in 1999, with the passage of the Financial Services Modernization Act of 1999, also known as the Gramm-Leach-Bliley Act, which removed the regulations barring mergers among banking, securities and insurance businesses. Since then, the distinction between commercial banks and brokerage firms has blurred and many banks acquired brokerage firms and provide investment services.

Gramm-Leach-Bliley Act

In November 1999, Congress repealed the Glass-Steagall Act with the establishment of the Gramm-Leach-Bliley Act ("GLBA"), which eliminated the prohibitions against affiliations between commercial and investment banks. Thus, GLBA was designed to monitor mergers and affiliations, customer privacy protections and lending to lower-income communities. In addition, the GLBA allowed banking and other financial institutions to offer a broader range of services, including insurance underwriting and other investment activities. The GLBA permits the banking, insurance and securities industries to converge as long as appropriate safeguards are in place to protect the privacy of consumer financial data and guarantee the solvency of the institution.

In a significant step toward protecting sensitive financial information, the GLBA also limited the extent to which financial institutions could share clients' personal information, and requires that financial institutions routinely inform customers about their privacy policies and practices. The law also provided consumers with some control over how financial institutions use and share their personal information.

REGULATORY BODIES GOVERNING FINANCIAL SERVICES

The financial services industry is regulated by Congress, federal agencies and in some cases, even state agencies. The major federal agencies that regulate financial services are the Securities and Exchange Commission, Federal Deposit Insurance Corporation and the Federal Reserve Board. In addition, numerous self-regulatory organizations also provide internal policing for many of the sectors within the financial services industry. The following sections provide more detail about these regulatory bodies.

Federal Reserve Board

The Federal Reserve Board consists of the Board of Governors of the Federal Reserve System. The board is known for its role in influencing the U.S. money supply and economic policy, but it also has wide-ranging regulatory authority. The Federal Reserve Board regulates certain interest rates and bank mergers. The board also supervises the banking system by issuing regulations controlling the activities of bank holding companies and implements various federal statutes. The seven members of the Board of Governors are appointed by the president, subject to confirmation by the Senate.

The Securities & Exchange Commission

The Securities and Exchange Commission (SEC) is a government commission created by Congress to regulate the securities markets and protect investors. The SEC is authorized to promulgate regulations to promote full public disclosure and to protect the investing public against fraudulent and manipulative practices in the securities markets. The SEC is divided into four main divisions: Corporate Finance, Market Regulation, Investment Management and Enforcement.

The Division of Corporate Finance is responsible for overseeing the disclosure documents that public companies in the United States are required to file with the SEC. These documents include registration statements for public offerings, quarterly and annual filings, annual reports to shareholders, documents detailing mergers and acquisitions and proxy materials that are sent out to shareholders before annual meetings. Companies are required to provide "prudent and truthful" disclosure of material information, and these documents must be filed in a timely fashion.

The Division of Trading and Markets establishes and maintains markets by regulating the participants in the securities industry, such as the various brokerage and investment firms.

The Division of Investment Management preserves all rules that affect investment companies and their advisors.

Finally, the Division of Enforcement investigates violations and provides recommendations for further action if needed. This division has only civil enforcement authority, and thus cooperates with law enforcement agencies to bring about criminal charges.

Federal Deposit Insurance Corporation

The Federal Deposit Insurance Corporation (FDIC) is an independent U.S. federal executive agency designed to promote public confidence in the banking system. In addition, it provides insurance coverage for bank deposits up to $250,000. The FDIC was established in 1933, after bank customers could not withdraw the money they had deposited because of the failure of so many banks. To ensure that this will not happen again, the FDIC provides coverage for deposits in national banks, in state banks that are members of the Federal Reserve System and in other qualified state banks. The FDIC is managed by a five-member board of directors, and the directors are appointed by the president with the consent of the U.S. Senate.

Self-Regulatory Organizations

Self-regulatory organizations, or SROs, are bodies that assume some of the responsibility of policing their own industries. For instance, SROs have the responsibility of establishing rules to govern trading and other activities, setting qualifications for industry professionals, overseeing the conduct of their members and imposing discipline in instances of unethical or illegal behavior. The SEC oversees the SROs using authority granted to it by Congress.

APPLICATIONS

EFFECTS OF FINANCIAL SERVICES REGULATIONS

Efficient forms of regulation emphasize market discipline. The following sections will examine various aspects of the regulation of financial services.

REGULATION OF MARKET PARTICIPANTS

Most institutions that provide financial services, such as banks or credit unions, are required to get a charter from a state or federal agency before entering the market. At the federal level, the Office of the Comptroller of the Currency (OCC) grants national charters to commercial banks, the Federal Home Loan Bank Board (FHLBB) charters savings and loan associations and savings banks and the National Credit Union Association (NCUA) provides charters for credit unions.

Chartered depository institutions generally must also obtain deposit insurance from a federal agency. The deposits of commercial banks and most mutual savings banks are insured by the Federal Deposit Insurance Corporation ("FDIC") and the deposits of savings and loan associations and some mutual savings banks are insured by the Federal Savings and Loan Insurance Corporation (FSLIC). Credit union deposits are insured by the National Credit Union Share Insurance Fund (NCUSIF).

When financial services providers want to expand into new markets, they must first meet any relevant regulatory requirements. Expansion of commercial banks across state lines was once limited by rigorous federal and state restrictions on interstate banking. The McFadden Act, enacted in 1927, gave states the power to regulate bank branching, including branches owned by national banks. The McFadden Act specifically prohibited interstate branching by allowing national banks to branch only within the state in which it was situated. The Riegle-Neal Interstate Banking & Branching Efficiency Act of 1994 repealed most provisions of the McFadden Act, and permitted banks to acquire branch offices, or open new ones, in any state outside their home state after June 1, 1997. Although the Riegle-Neal Act specified that state law continued to control intrastate branching, or branching within a state's borders, most states passed laws enabling branch expansions within their territory soon after the Act was passed.

When financial services providers decide to exit the market, chartered financial institutions require the permission of their chartering agency to close branches or merge with another institution. In addition, the Federal Reserve, the FDIC, FSLIC or NCUSIF must approve the change.

INDUSTRY CONVERGENCE

Consolidation of all types of business activities became increasingly prominent beginning at the end of the twentieth century. In particular, consolidations were highest in the financial sector. Most of the merger and acquisition activity in the financial sector involved banking organizations. This convergence of companies offering financial services eradicated the traditional boundaries that once separated banks, brokerage firms and insurance companies and created a new type of financial services provider. The new financial services conglomerates aimed to provide customers with a range of options relating to all aspects of financial services that could be accessed from one company.

Consolidation of financial services providers has offered some benefits. For instance, financial consolidation generally has resulted in improvements in information technology, financial deregulation and increased shareholder pressure for financial performance. However, the convergence in the financial services industry also has had its drawbacks. Consolidation tends to reduce risk through diversification gains, but after consolidation, some firms have shifted toward riskier asset portfolios, and consolidation increases operating risks and managerial conflicts for those firms.

RISK MANAGEMENT

The loans made by chartered depository institutions are regulated to aid in controlling the risks of these investments for depositors and deposit insurance agencies. Legal lending limits have been set to establish the maximum amount a bank can lend to any one borrower. In addition, several federal and state laws govern the practices of lenders to ensure that loans are made fairly and yet with due consideration of a borrower's credit rating. For instance, regulations under the Reinvestment Act of 1977 forbid the alleged practice of redlining, or denying mortgage and home improvement loans on properties solely because they are old or located in older urban areas.

Also, the Truth-in-Lending Act requires disclosure of a standard interest rate and other terms on consumer loans and long-term leases of consumer goods. It also regulates the content of credit advertising and credit card distribution, terms and liabilities.

Some lending and collection practices of creditors also are constrained or prohibited by various laws. The Fair Credit Reporting Act regulates the content, accuracy and disclosure of credit and investigative reports furnished to creditors, employers and insurers in connection with consumer transactions. The Fair Debt Collections Practices Act prohibits abusive and coercive collection practices and requires bill collectors to provide debtors with certain information. In addition, states have enacted laws that similarly regulate credit practices that parallel federal laws, and in some cases are more severe. Because lenders must stay within statutory guidelines in terms of the debt-collection practices, they are more prone to carefully evaluate the creditworthiness of each borrower before extending a loan as an additional attempt to mitigate the risk of a borrower's default on the loan.

CONCLUSION

The financial services industry has changed dramatically over the last decades. The changes have been driven and prompted by shifts and developments in the regulatory framework that governs financial providers. Consolidations among financial services institutions have led to increased profits and an increased market share by the top providers. Larger national financial institutions have increasingly replaced smaller, regional entities, although many local banks and credit unions are still experiencing solid growth. These consolidations have, however, increased the range in services that financial providers may provide. In addition, the deconstruction of the prohibitions between the commercial banking and the investment banking and insurance industries, established by the Glass-Steagall Act and repealed by the Gramm-Leach-Bliley Act, have also enabled financial institutions to enhance the services they provide. While consolidations and legislative changes will continue to shape the financial services industry, financial institutions will also be affected by shifts in politics, demographics, economic cycles and emerging technology. Lawmakers, courts and business leaders undoubtedly will continue to strive to ensure that the financial services industry is poised to meet these new challenges.

BIBLIOGRAPHY

Adler, J. (2013). Big Bank Breakups and Tech Disruptions: Predicting the Future of Reform. *American Banker, 178*(34), 16. Retrieved December 4, 2014, from EBSCO Online Database Business Source Complete. http:// search.ebscohost.com/login. aspx?direct=true&db=bth &AN=85942463

Administrative law—agency design—Dodd-Frank Act creates the Consumer Financial Protection Bureau - Dodd- Frank Act, Pub. L. No. 111-203, 124 Stat. 1376 (2010) (to be codified in scattered sections of the U.S. Code). (2011). *Harvard Law Review, 124*(8), 2123-2130. Retrieved November 15, 2013, from EBSCO Online Database Business Source Complete. http://search.ebscohost.com/login.aspx?direct=true&db=bth&AN=61294566&site=eh ost-live

Batkins, S., & Brannon, I. (2013). The unknown costs of Dodd-Frank. *Regulation, 36*(3), 4-5. Retrieved November 15, 2013, from EBSCO Online Database Business Source Complete. http://search. ebscohost.com/login.aspx?direct=t rue&db=bth& AN=90581359&site=ehost-live

Blackwell, R. (2003). Treasury GSE plan draws flak from unlikely sources. *American Banker, 168*(72), 1-2. Retrieved June 18, 2007, from EBSCO Online Database Business Source Complete. http:// search.ebscohost.com/login.aspx?direct=true&db =bth&AN=10748216&site=eh ost-live

Brink, A.G., Jordan Lowe, D.D., & Victoravich, L.M. (2013). The effect of evidence strength and internal rewards on intentions to report fraud in the dodd-frank regulatory environment. *Auditing, 32*(3), 87-104. Retrieved November 15, 2013, from EBSCO Online Database Business Source Complete. http://search.ebscohost.com/login. aspx?direct=t rue&db=bth&AN=89428889&site=e host-live

Ceron, G. (2007). Spitzer panel to aid financial sector. *Wall Street Journal: Eastern Edition, 249*(125), A9.

Ferguson Jr., R. (2006). Thoughts on financial stability and central banking. *Vital Speeches of the Day, 72*(14/15), 428-432. Retrieved June 18, 2007, from EBSCO Online Database Business Source Complete. http://search.ebscohost.com/login.aspx?di rect=true&db=bth&AN=21723255 &site=ehost-live

Flohr, Annegret. (2014). *Self-regulation and Legalization: Making Global Rules for Banks and Corporations.* Basingstoke: Palgrave Macmillan.

Kaper, S. (2006). How financial services policy might shift if democrats win. *American Banker, 171*(213), 1-20. Retrieved June 18, 2007, from EBSCO Online Database Business Source Complete. http://search.ebscohost.com/ login.aspx?direct=true&db=bth&AN=23009555&site=eh ost-live

Roberts, E. (2007). Washington watch. *Credit Union Journal, 11*(14), 14. Retrieved June 18, 2007, from EBSCO Online Database Business Source Complete. http://search.ebscohost.com/ login.aspx?direct=true&db=bth&AN=24743769 &site=ehost-live

SEC, FSA hold talks. (2011). *Compliance Reporter,* 36. Retrieved November 15, 2013, from EBSCO Online Database Business Source Complete. http:// search.ebscohost.com/login.aspx?direct=true&d b=bth&AN=70209380 &site=ehost-live

Sloan, S. & Kaper, S. (2005). Washington people. *American Banker, 172*(53), 3. Retrieved June 18, 2007, from EBSCO Business Source Complete. http://search.ebscohost.com/ login.aspx?direct= true&db=bth&AN=24400976&site=eh ost-live

Spitzer panel to eye regulatory update. (2007). *American Banker, 172*(103), 20.

Strahan, P. (2006). Bank diversification, economic diversification? FRBSF Economic Letter. Retrieved March 31, 2010 from Federal Reserve Bank of San Francisco http://www. frbsf.org/publications/ economics/letter/2006/el2006-10. html

Wood, D. & Dugan, J. (2006, May 30). OCC preemption rules: OCC should further clarify the applicability of state consumer protection laws to national banks: GAO-06-387. *GAO Reports.* Retrieved June 18, 2007, from EBSCO Online Database Business Source Complete. http://search. ebscohost. com/login.aspx?direct=true&db=bth&AN=2101 7913&site=ehost-live

SUGGESTED READING

Biggs, John H., and Matthew P. Richardson. (2014). *Modernizing Insurance Regulation.* Hoboken, NJ: Wiley.

DeYoung, R. (2007). Safety, soundness, and the evolution of the U.S. banking industry. *Economic Review (07321813), 92*(1/2), 41-66. Retrieved June 18, 2007, from EBSCO Online Database Business Source Complete. http://search. ebscohost. com/login.aspx?direct=true&db=bth&AN=252 84424&site=ehost-live

Kaper, S (2006). Dems pledge light touch, but others not so sure. *American Banker, 171*(216), 1-3. Retrieved June 18, 2007, from EBSCO Online Database Business Source Complete. http://search. ebscohost.com/login.aspx?direct=t rue&db=bth& AN=23037732&site=ehost-live

Risks of Financial Institutions. (2005, Winter). *NBER Reporter,* 24. Retrieved June 18, 2007, from EBSCO Online Database Business Source Complete. http://search. ebscohost.com/ login.aspx?direct=true&db=bth&AN=200 01636&site=ehost-live

—*Heather Newton*

RISK & RATES OF RETURN

ABSTRACT

The relationship between risk and return in complicated, but in general, there is a direct tradeoff. Total risk is defined as variability in returns and can be separated into systematic and unsystematic risk. An investor can reduce unsystematic risk by maintaining a diversified portfolio. This article is devoted to exploring the components of risk and discussing techniques for reducing, measuring and pricing risk and return.

OVERVIEW

Risk consists of uncertainty and the possible exposure to a negative result. The stock market is fraught with risks as well as rewards. Why would a stock investor be willing to forgo a risk-free investment such as a savings account that reliably earns 1–2 percent interest for a security that could lose all its value? A smart investor understands the tradeoff and how to estimate the return required in order to compensate for risk.

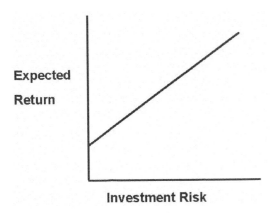

Expected Return Investment Risk

Most investors are risk averse and would prefer a low-risk alternative. However, there is a certain return where the investor is willing to take on additional risk. The riskier the investment, the higher the expected return must be. The following diagram illustrates the pattern of the risk-return trade-off.

There are five critical components to understanding risk and return:

- Defining risk;
- Measuring systematic risk and return;
- Measuring unsystematic risk and return;
- Reducing risk; and
- Pricing risk and return.

DEFINING RISK

Risk comes in many shapes and sizes. There are countless risks to consider when assessing an investment. The following are examples of some common risks:

- Legal risk is the possibility that a company will be subject to unexpected litigation.
- Industry risk includes such factors as changing technology, foreign competitors, etc.
- Operational risk is the potential for internal processes or systems to fail.
- Currency risk is an issue for companies that do business in other countries. They are subject to exchange rates that could unexpectedly fluctuate and affect profits.
- Liquidity risk is the chance that no one will buy a security that needs to be sold. This is different from the price per share dropping to zero. Generally publicly traded stocks have low liquidity risks. Shares of private companies or assets such as houses can have high liquidity risks.

The proceeding risks are just a few of the myriad risk factors that can affect a security. There are certain risks that are particularly important when discussing the risk of a fixed-income investment such as a bond. Interest rate risk, inflation risk, and credit risk can significantly affect the return on a bond:

- Interest rate risk is the possibility that interest rates will change before you sell a bond;
- Inflation risk refers to unexpected changes in inflation; and
- Credit risk is the potential that the issuer will default on its debt obligation. If a bond is defaulted, an investor can lose interest as well as principle.

As a rule, bond prices fall when interest rates and inflation rise. Bonds are acutely sensitive because they have coupon payments that are fixed into the future and do not adjust for changes in interest rates or inflation. Therefore, when interest rates and inflation rise, the present value of the bond is worth less than its purchase price. In general, short-term bonds carry a lower interest rate and less inflation risk. They have a lower risk premium because the duration of time is brief. Credit risk is another important factor when choosing a bond. Credit ratings, which can help assess risk, are published by companies such as Moody's and Standard and Poor's. Interest coverage ratios (EBIT/interest expense) can also provide insight into credit risk. If a company's earnings do not have enough cushion to cover interest expense, then there is a high risk of default.

Stock prices fluctuate for a variety of reasons, but here we will focus on placing risk into two very distinct categories. Understanding the differences between these two categories is the basis for financial evaluation of risk. Some stock price fluctuations are due to factors that affect many securities in the market. For example, an economic downturn can cause many companies to experience unexpected losses. These kinds of risks are very different from random factors that affect only one firm. For example, a union strike at an automotive firm would only affect that specific company. The financial community has defined two categories of risk: systematic or market risk, and unsystematic or firm-specific risk.

Systematic risk includes economic and market factors that affect almost every company in the market. This risk cannot be eliminated by diversification.

Interest rates and inflation are two kinds of risk that would fall into this category. Other examples of systematic risk include the country going to war or tax cuts approved by Congress.

Unsystematic risks are factors that only affect individual securities. Legal risk, industry risk, operational risk, currency risk, and liquidity risk fall into this category. Other examples of unsystematic risk include a fire in the main warehouse of a company, the CEO getting killed in an auto accident or a low-cost competitor entering the market. If you own only one stock, this kind of risk is very important. However, once you diversify your portfolio with several stocks, this unsystematic risk can be virtually eliminated. In financial markets, investors are only rewarded for bearing systematic risk, because this is the only kind of risk that cannot be eliminated through diversification.

REDUCING RISK

In 1952, Harry Markowitz introduced an investment strategy called "portfolio diversification." He demonstrated how an investor can reduce risk and the overall standard deviation, or spread, of returns by creating a portfolio of securities.

If two securities are positively correlated (i.e., move together when the market changes), there is no impact on risk. However, if two securities are negatively correlated (i.e., securities do not move together), the portfolio is considered diversified and risk is reduced. Gains from one security in the portfolio can offset losses from another, lessening the overall exposure to a negative return.

Portfolio diversification can only mitigate risk associated with unsystematic risk. As you increase the number of securities in your portfolio, unsystematic

risk can be virtually eliminated. However, you cannot diversify away systematic risk because, by definition, it affects all companies. Investors are only compensated for systematic risk because unsystematic risk is expected to be diversified away.

In portfolios of thirty-plus randomly selected stock, unsystematic risk is virtually eliminated.

MEASURING UNSYSTEMATIC RISK & RETURN

In order to measure risk, we must first understand rates of return. Suppose you invested $1,000 in a security and then sold it for $1,200. What was your rate of return? The past rate of return can be measure by the equation:

Amt. Received – Amt. Invested/Amt Invested = Rate of Return
$1,200 – $1,000/$1000 = 12%

Your next question might be what the return will be if you reinvest that money in a new security. To determine future expectations, we can calculate the expected value of a security. This is derived from the mean value of the probability distribution of possible returns. A probability distribution simply lists the potential returns and their associated probabilities. To calculate the expected return, we determine the weighted average of all the possible returns (Pr), where the weights are the probabilities (K) associated with each return and there are n possible outcomes.

$$\text{Expected return} = \sum_{i=1}^{n} Pr_i(K_i)$$

In practice, investors usually focus on three scenarios: a worst-case scenario, an expected-case scenario and a best-case scenario. Suppose a particular security A has a 10% chance of a –10% return (worst-case scenario), 75% chance of 5% return (expected-case scenario) and 15% chance of 15% return (best-case scenario). The expected return is:

$$0.1(-0.1) + 0.75(0.05) + 0.15(0.15) = 5\%$$

Expected return alone cannot tell us which stock to invest in. Two securities may have the same expected return, but one may have a very wide spread, or variability

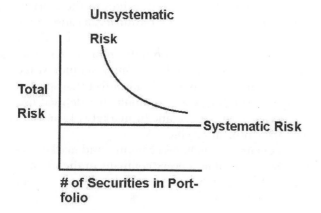

Unsystematic

Risk

Total

Risk

Systematic Risk

# of Securities in Portfolio

of returns. A wide spread indicates the possibility of some very negative returns and is therefore more risky. Take the following two examples. Both investment A and investment B have the same expected return, but A has a higher spread or standard deviation. Investors would generally prefer investment B.

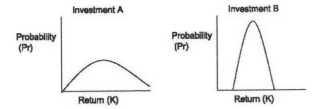

Standard deviation (s) is a tool that can help us evaluate the difference between investment A and investment B. The standard deviation measures the variability of the outcomes expressed in a probability distribution. Greater standard deviation means greater uncertainty and, therefore, greater risk. Standard deviation is expressed as the weighted probability average difference between an investment's possible returns and its expected return. Standard deviation is calculated using the formula:

$$\sigma_i = \left[\sum_{i=1}^{n} Pr_i (K_i - \bar{K})^2 \right]^{1/2}$$

Standard deviation is criticized because it scales in such a way that does not allow for direct comparison of more than one standard deviation. For example, take investment A with a 25% chance of a –5% return (worst-case scenario), 50% chance of 2% return (expected-case scenario), 25% chance of 9% return (best-case scenario), and an expected return of 2%. Compare this to investment B with a 25% chance of a –10% return (worst-case scenario), 50% chance of 4% return (expected-case scenario), 25% chance of 18% return (best-case scenario), and an expected return of 4%.

$$\sigma \text{ of A} = [(0.25*(-0.05-0.02)^2) + (0.5*(0.02-0.02)^2) + (0.25*(0.09-0.02)^2)]^{(1/2)} = 4.9\%$$

$$\sigma \text{ of B} = [(0.25*(-0.1-0.04)^2) + (0.5*(0.04-0.04)^2) + (0.25*(0.18-0.04)^2)]^{(1/2)} = 9.9\%$$

Is security B really two times more risky than security A? No, standard deviations cannot be used for this kind of direct comparison.

The coefficient of variation (CV) eliminates the scale problem by dividing standard deviation by expected return. Essentially, it gives us risk per unit of return.

$$CV = \frac{\sigma_i}{ER}$$

CV of security A = .049/.02 = 2.47

CV of security B = .099/.04 = 2.47

Using the CV method illustrates how the securities are actually equal in their riskiness.

Measuring unsystematic risk is important when you own just one security. However, since systematic risk can be virtually eliminated through diversification, we next need to focus on measuring systematic risk.

MEASURING SYSTEMATIC RISK & RETURN

Systematic risk remains even after diversification. To measure systematic risk, we look at how much a security moves when the market moves. This is called covariance. If a company's returns are more sensitive to changes in the market, then its risk is escalated. A company who moves in exact parallel is exactly as risky as the market. In the case that a company amplifies the markets returns, then the security is considered more risky. When a company moves in the same direction as the market, but not as much, it is less risky. Finally, a company that moves in the exact opposite direction of the market is called a hedge.

We use beta (or β) to measure this movement with the market. A beta is calculated by using a statistical tool called linear regression to measure how much the return on a security covaries with the market return. A beta of 1 indicates average risk. The S&P 500 tends to rise and fall with the same percentages of the market, and it has a beta close to 1. A beta greater than 1 indicates a security that has high sensitivity to market swings and is more volatile/risky. A security that is not very sensitive to market changes will have a beta under 1 and is considered less risky. A beta is a critical component in pricing risk in the capital asset pricing model, which will be described next.

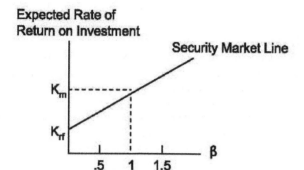

Expected Rate of
Return on Investment

PRICING RISK & RETURN

As stated previously, most investors are risk averse and expect to be compensated for taking on risk. We know that unsystematic risk can be mitigated through diversification, so we just need a model for pricing systematic risk. This is where the capital asset pricing model (CAPM) comes into play. CAPM is the most widely accepted model for pricing risk. This model assumes the securities markets are competitive and efficient. It also assumes that these markets are composed of rational, risk-averse investors whose goal is to maximize returns.

CAPM considers a linear relationship between required rate of return and risk. The required rate of return (K_j) is equal to the risk-free rate (K_{rf}) plus some risk premium:

$$K_j = K_{rf} + \text{Risk Premium}$$

It prices risk using a security market line (SML). Theoretically, every security should fall on the SML. If the security is above the line, that indicates that the security is underpriced. If the security falls below the line, it is overpriced.

The formula is expressed as:

$$K_j = K_{rf} + \underbrace{\beta_j (K_m + K_{rf})}_{\text{Risk Premium}}$$

K_j indicates the required rate of return for an investor. K_{rf} is the risk-free rate. A three-month treasury bond is a good approximation for K_{rf} because these bonds are backed by the United States government and have a β close to 0. Some researchers

in the financial community believe the duration of the risk-free security should match the duration of the cash flows. This logic would suggest using long-term treasury bonds. However, for our purposes, we will stick with a three-month treasure bond., β_j is the beta of the security. As discussed previously, the beta measures how sensitive the stock is to changes in the overall market. K_m is the return on market index. The S&P 500 index (β close to 1) is a good approximation of the market return.

Suppose a three-month treasury bond rate is 5%, the return on the S&P 500 index is 10%, and Company X has a beta of 1.5. According to CAPM, the required rate of return is

$$(0.05) + 1.5(0.1 - 0.05) = 12.5\%$$

There has been widespread criticism of CAPM. Many in the financial community believe additional risk factors should be taken into account. In addition, CAPM is based on expectations, and the beta is derived from historical financial data. A company's historical data might not reflect investors' expectations about future risk. Some researchers point to the dot-com bubble of the late 1990s as a period when investors lost sight of the risk-return tradeoff. Valuations were inflated, and the high-tech stocks of the late 1990s fell way below the SML. The market correction brought these overpriced securities back in line.

As a result of the doubts raised by CAPM, alternate theories have surfaced. Steven Ross's arbitrage pricing theory (ATP) is one that warrants discussion. The risk-free rate is the starting point for this model as well. However, ATP breaks systematic risk, or the risk premium part of the CAPM equation, into several factors. It assumes some securities will be more sensitive to certain factors than other securities. For example, interest rates will affect some firms more than others. A mortgage lending company would be more sensitive to interest rate changes than a health care company, for example. Factors can include inflation, industrial activity, and interest rate spreads, among others.

$$K_j = K_{rf} + b_1 (K_{\text{factor 1}} - K_{rf}) + b_2 (K_{\text{factor 2}} - K_{rf} + \ldots$$

where
K_j indicates the required rate of return

Krf is the risk-free rate

b1 is sensitivity to factor 1

Kfactor 1 is the return on factor 1

This model may provide a more thorough analysis of risk; however, it is much harder to apply. ATP requires several layers of complex statistics and requires investors to identify each factor to which the security is sensitive. ATP has more statistical noise

inherent in its model. CAPM appeals to many investors because it is simpler and more theoretically appealing. Both CAPM and ATP agree on the basic concepts that (a) investors require compensation for taking on additional risk and (b) are concerned with risk that cannot be eliminated through diversification.

CONCLUSION

The primary objective of investors is to capture the highest possible return on their investment. Ideally, investors will maximize their returns while minimizing risk. Portfolio diversification allows investors to minimize a portion of overall risk. This article has illustrated how investors are compensated with higher rates of return for taking on risk that cannot be eliminated through diversification. If investors are unwilling to accept risk, then they should expect a lower return. This risk-return trade-off has been translated into models for pricing risk.

In practice, each investor has a different threshold for risk. Investors tend to fall on a spectrum of risk aversion. On one side, there is the aggressive investor. The portfolio for an aggressive investor has a higher mix of equity securities (rather than debt securities) and looks to maximize growth returns (rather than investment income). The time horizon for these investments is generally long term (e.g., five or more years). The aggressive investor is not concerned with short-term volatility and tends to have a good understanding of the financial markets. On the other end of the spectrum is the conservative investor. The most conservative investments are those where the return is known prior to making an investment (e.g., savings accounts, bonds, other debt securities). These types of investments provide for some protection of principle with set income. The conservative investor forgoes higher returns for security.

Due to the shortcomings of the CAPM model as well as alternative pricing models, investors and financial managers should not rely on these theories alone to price risk. Nothing can replace the sound judgment and vigilance of an educated investor.

BIBLIOGRAPHY

Bodie, Z., & Merton, R. C. (1998). *Finance*. Upper Saddle River, NJ: Prentice-Hall.

Brealey, R. A., & Myers, S. C. (1996). *Principles of Corporate Finance*. New York, NY: McGraw-Hill.

Brigham, E. F., & Houston, J. F. (2003). *Fundamentals of Financial Management*. Cincinnati, OH: South-Western College Publishing.

Han, Y. (2011). On the relation between the market risk premium and market volatility. *Applied Financial Economics, 21*(22), 1711–1723. Retrieved November 19, 2013 from EBSCO online database Business Source Premier. http:// search. ebscohost.com/login.aspx?direct=true&db=buh &AN=64133726

Higgins, R. C. (1998). *Analysis for financial management*. Boston, MA: Irwin McGraw-Hill.

Jordan, B., Ross, S. A., & Westerfield, R. (2013). *Essentials of corporate finance* (8th ed.). New York, NY: McGraw-Hill.

Joshi, N. N., & Lambert, J. H. (2011). Diversification of infrastructure projects for emergent and unknown non-systematic risks. *Journal of Risk Research, 14*(6), 717–733. Retrieved November 19, 2013 from EBSCO online database Business Source Premier. http://search.ebscohost. com/login.aspx?direct=true&db=buh&AN=63884217

Keown, A. J., Martin, J. D., & Petty, J. W., & Scott, D. F. (1998). *Basic financial management*. Upper Saddle River, NJ: Prentice Hall.

The capital asset pricing model. (1998). *New England Economic Review*, 44–45. Retrieved April 1, 2007, from EBSCO Online Database Academic Search Premier. http://search.eb-scohost.com/login.aspx?direct=true&db=aph&AN=1293510&sit=ehost-live

Risk and return. (1991). *Economist, 318*(7692), 72–74. Retrieved April 1, 2007, from EBSCO Online Database Academic Search Premier. http://search.ebscohost.com/ login.aspx?direct=true&db=aph&AN=11715833&site=eh ost-live

Solomon, D., & Muntean, M. (2012). Assessment of financial risk in firm's profitability analysis. *Economy Transdisciplinarity Cognition, 15*(2), 58–67. Retrieved November 19, 2013 from EBSCO online database Business Source Premier. http://search.ebscohost.com/ login.aspx?direct=true&db=buh&AN=90542713

SUGGESTED READING

Cochrane. (1999). New facts in finance. *Economic Perspectives 23 (3)*, 36–59. Retrieved April 1, 2007, from EBSCO Online Database Academic Search Premier. http://search.ebscohost.com/login.aspx?direct=true&db=aph&AN=2267526&site=ehost-live

Daníelsson, J. (2011). *Financial risk forecasting: The theory and practice of forecasting market risk, with implementation in R and Matlab. Chichester, England: John Wiley. Retrieved November 19, 2013 from EBSCO online database eBook Academic Collection (EBSCOhost). http:// search.ebscohost.com/login.aspx?direct=true&db=e000xna&AN=391323&site=ehost-live*

Fama, E. F., & French, K. R. (2004). The capital asset pricing model: Theory and evidence. *Journal of Economic Perspectives, 18* (3), 25–46. Retrieved April 1, 2007, from EBSCO Online Database Business Source Complete. http://search.ebscohost.com/login.aspx?direct=true&db=bth&AN=14774675&site=ehost-live

Jagannathan, R., & McGrattan, E. R. (1995). The CAPM debate. *Quarterly Review, 19*(4), 2–18. Retrieved April 1, 2007, from EBSCO Online Database Academic Search Premier. http://search.ebscohost.com/login.aspx?direct=true&db=aph&AN=9602011014&site=ehost-live

Treynor, J. L. (1993). In defense of the CAPM. *Financial Analysts Journal, 49*(3), 11–13. Retrieved on April 1, 2007, from EBSCO Online Database Business Source Complete. http://search.ebscohost.com/login.aspx?direct=true&db=bth&AN=6936586&site=ehost-live

–Heather Wall Beckham

S

STOCK & BOND VALUES

ABSTRACT

This article explains the basic concepts that govern two of the most common financial instruments: stock and bonds. The first step in understanding stocks and bonds is to look at the underlying features of each security and how they can impact value. This article focuses on the discussion of common financial techniques for valuing stocks and bonds.

OVERVIEW

Stocks and bonds are two of the most common types of investments. Stocks are equity instruments whereas bonds are debt. A stock holder owns a portion of a company, but is not given a fixed return. A bond holder is considered a creditor of the company and is promised fixed interest payments, as well as a lump sum payment upon maturity. An investment portfolio is generally comprised of a mix of each of these securities. The value of both stocks and bonds can be determined by analyzing discounted cash flows. Although stock and bonds are each governed by the same overall market principles, these investments are very different with respect to risk and return. The mechanisms and processes for capturing value also vary between stocks and bonds.

This article will look at each security individually. We discuss bonds in detail, starting with basic bond characteristics. Subsequently, we will examine the mechanics for valuing and trading bonds, as well as factors that impact their value. We will then move our discussion to stocks. The media tends to focus on stocks more than bonds because the value of these securities can fluctuate significantly. There is a wealth of information available to the investor about any stock listed on a public exchange. We will use that information to understand how stocks capture value. In conclusion, we will explore the methods for combining stocks and bonds in a portfolio to maximize value and return for an investor.

BOND BASICS

A bond is a debt security. In this arrangement, the debtor agrees to make fixed payment of interest and principle over a specified time period to the holders of the bond. This kind of financial instrument usually pays a fixed interest rate (coupon) for a period of time and at the end of that duration (the maturity), it will pay the investor a predetermined lump sum (face value). The stream of cash flows for a bond investment is illustrated below, where there are n time periods until maturity, *PMT* is the coupon, and *FV* is the face value. A bond's interest rate is determined by general market interest rates at the time of issuance along with the credit risk and other features specific to that bond.

Bonds are traded using the full service of a discount brokerage house. There are several types of bonds that can be traded:

- Treasury Bonds — Lowest risk bonds because they are backed by the US government. The interest income is exempt from state taxes, but not federal.
- Mortgage Bonds or Government Agency Bonds — Bonds comprised of mortgage loans issued by the government agencies Ginnie Mae, Fannie Mae, and Freddie Mac. Interest is taxable and except for Ginnie Maes— these bonds are not backed by the U.S. government.
- Municipal Bonds — Bonds issued by state and local governments. Interest is often federal and state tax-exempt.
- Corporate Bonds — Bonds issued by companies.

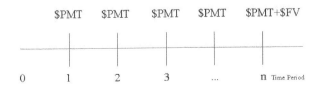

255

Interest is taxable and these bonds are more risky because the chance of default is much higher than for the government.

- Eurobonds — Bonds that are issued in one country's currency but then traded in a different country.
- Bond Funds — Mutual funds which compile different bonds together for the investor to purchase.
- Junk Bonds — High-risk bonds that are below investment grade as measured by credit agencies such as Moody's.

Bond Features

A bond contract lists the features of a bond, the coupon, par value, maturity, covenants, and repayment details. Bonds generally have fixed coupon payments and a fixed lifespan. However, a bond can possess certain features that can alter this arrangement. Special features of a bond can include the following:

- Convertible — The bond can be converted into a number of predetermined shares of stock at the bond holder's option or some cases, the company can retain the right to force conversion if the stock reaches a specified price level.
- Callable — The issuers of a bond can refund the bond by paying a predetermined fixed price, usually at a premium price, prior to maturity.
- Putable — The holder of a bond can sell the bond back to the company prior to maturity and receive full face value.
- Floating Interest Rate — With this feature, the coupon rate is not fixed. The rate is linked to an index (e.g., Treasury bill, LIBOR) and fluctuates with that market index.
- Interest Rate Cap or Floor — In order to limit extremes and risk in a floating interest rate bond, the cap and/ or floor feature can be employed. The cap sets forth a maximum interest rate that will be paid by the issuer. The floor sets forth a minimum interest rate that will be paid by the issuer.
- Sinking Fund — In this case, the issuer would have the option to pay off a portion of the face value over time, rather than at maturity. In other words, this gives the issuer the option to prepay the face value.
- Covenants — Restrictions that are put on the company by the bondholders to help limit risk and default exposure. Common covenants include restricting the types of investments the company can

make and limiting the dividends that can be paid out to stockholders.
- Zero Coupon — Bond where no coupon is paid. The only cash flow for this bond is the payment of face value at maturity.

We will come back to each of these features later in this article and examine how value is impacted by their inclusion.

Valuing Bonds

The initial price for a bond will be based on expected cash flows, discounted at an interest rate that is appropriate for the type of bond and the riskiness of the issuer. The expected cash flows of a simple bond are comprised of two parts. First, we look at the coupon (PMT) paid for n number of years until the bond matures with a discount rate of i. Interest rates used to discount cash flows are determined by general interest rates in the market, as well as by the term structure of the bond and the credit risk of the issuer. The second part of the equation is the face value (FV) discounted back to today's dollars.

$$PV = \sum_{t=1}^{n} \frac{PMT}{(1+i)^t} + \frac{FV}{(1+i)^n}$$

Take the example of Bond A, a 5-year bond with discount rate of 12%, annual coupon payments of $120, and a face value of $1000.

$$(120/(1.12)^1)+(120/(1.12)^2)$$
$$+(120/(1.12)^3)+(120/(1.12)^4)$$
$$+(120/((1.12)^5)+(1000/(1.12)^5) = \$1000$$

Financial calculators and software applications such as Excel have functions that can also quickly calculate the present value of a bond.

One of the most critical factors that impact a bond's value is interest rate fluctuations. As a rule, bond prices fall when interest rates and inflation rise. Bonds are acutely sensitive because they have coupon payments that are fixed into the future and do not adjust for changes in interest rates or inflation. Therefore, when interest rates and inflation rise, the present value of the bond is worth less than its purchase price.

To price the impact on interest rate fluctuations for a bond that is already on the market, we go back to our present value (PV) equation. To figure out whether a bond is selling at a discount or a premium we simply change the discount rate (i) to the going market rate and compare the PV to the FV. If interest rates fall and the coupon rate is greater than the discount rate then the bond will sell at a premium. This is called a premium bond. Take our previous example and suppose that the discount rate drops to 10%. The bond is worth $1075.82, a premium over the $1000 that was paid at issuance.

$$(120/(1.1)^1) + (120/(1.1)^2)$$
$$+ (120/(1.1)^3) + (120/(1.1)^4)$$
$$+ (120/(1.1)^5) + (1000/((1.1)^5) = \$1075.82$$

If interest rates rise and the coupon rate is less than the discount rate, then the bond will sell at a discount. This is called a discount bond. Let us go back to our example and see what happens when the discount rate rises to 14%. The bond is worth $931.34, a discount compared to the $1000 that was paid at issuance.

$$(120/(1.14)^1) + (120/(1.14)^2)$$
$$+ (120/(1.14)^3) + (120/(1.14)^4)$$
$$+ (120/((1.14)^5) + (1000/(1.14)^5) = \$931.34$$

Because bonds are bought and sold on public markets before their maturity, most investors are also interested in the annual rate of return they will receive if they hold a bond to maturity. Once a bond has been traded, its yield to maturity can be computed easily using a financial calculator or Excel. The bond's current return is based on the above equation for present value (PV). We are now just solving for i to get yield to maturity. You will enter the pieces of information you know and solve for the yield to maturity. For example, if Bond A only has 2 years left to maturity and is currently selling for $1200, what is its yield to maturity? On a financial calculator, you can solve for yield to maturity (i) by plugging in the following data:

The result gives us 6.51% yield to maturity. Note that PV must be given as a negative number when using excel or a financial calculator.

The closer to maturity, the closer the PV will be equal to the FV. At maturity, all bonds are equal to their face value. A premium bond will decrease over time until it reaches the face value at maturity and a discount bond will increase over time until it reaches the face value at maturity.

OTHER FACTORS THAT INFLUENCE BOND VALUES

The duration of the bond, or time until maturity, also influences the value of the bond. The longer the time to maturity, the more sensitive the bond is to changes in interest rates. These bonds have a higher risk premium. Therefore, the interest rate of a long-term bond is generally higher than a short-term bond.

Another rule of thumb is the higher the coupon, the lower the interest rate. Bonds with higher coupons have more cash flows in the earlier years and are less sensitive to interest rate risk. At one end of the spectrum is the zero coupon bond which has no coupon, only its face value at maturity. The present value of a zero coupon bond can vary significantly with fluctuations in interest rates because the payment is so far out into the future. This kind of bond will have a much higher interest rate than a simple bond.

The special features of a bond that were discussed earlier can also impact the value of the bond. If the feature benefits the holder of the bond, then the interest rate is lower. If the feature helps the issuer, then the interest rate increases. In the first column are features that generally provide the investor with upside and as a result, the investors will sacrifice some yield versus a simple bond without this feature. Features in the second column reduce upside potential for the investor, so the interest rates for these bonds would be higher.

n	i	PV	FV	PMT	Results
2	?	-$1,100	$1,100	$120	6.51%

BOND INTEREST RATE

Increases Upside Potential For Investors
Convertible
Putable
Callable
Sinking Fund (can be both)

Decreases Upside Potential For Investors
Sinking Fund
Interest Rate Floor
Interest Rate Cap

Since bondholders are creditors of a company, credit risk is another important component of a bond's value. Credit risk is the potential that the issuer will default on its debt obligation. The higher the issuer credit risk, the higher the interest rate. Although bonds generally have a lower risk than stocks, there is always a chance of losing your investment. If a bond is defaulted, an investor can lose interest as well as principle. Credit ratings, which can help asses risk, are published by companies such as Moody's and Standard and Poor's. These companies rate bonds based on the probability that the company will default. The two main categories are investment grade bonds and Junk Bonds. Investment grade bonds have a lower chance of default than Junk Bonds, which are highly speculative. n i PV FV PMT Results 2 ? -$1,100 $1,100 $120 6.51%

Credit Ratings		
	Investment Grade	Junk Bonds
Moody's	Aaa, Aa, A, Baa	Ba, B, Caa, C
S	AAA, AA, A, BBB	BB, B, CCC, D

Interest coverage ratios (EBIT/Interest Expense) can also provide insight into credit risk. If a company's earnings do not have enough cushion to cover interest expense, then there is a high risk of default.

When a company does default, there are two alternatives.

- Chapter 11 — a reorganization in which the company remains a going concern. This option stops creditors from closing the company down and seizing the assets. Management must make a case that it can successfully reorganize the business to generate more value than if the parts were sold off.
- Chapter 7 — a liquidation or sale of the assets of the company. In a liquidation event, unsecured creditors usually get nothing.

STOCK BASICS

When an investor purchases a share of common stock in a corporation, it gives that investor ownership in the company. As a common stockholder, an investor is entitled to voting rights as well as residual claims to future earnings and assets once all debts/obligations are satisfied. However, in the event of bankruptcy, common stockholders usually receive nothing. Voting rights are important because common shareholders use this right to elect a Board of Directors. One of the primary duties of the Board of Directors is to hire the management team and determine their compensation packages. Since shareholders are more content when they are making higher returns, the ultimate goal of management, if they want to keep their jobs, it to maximize share price or value of the stock.

Along with voting rights comes the claim to dividends. When a company makes a profit it can either reinvest the profits (retained earnings) or distribute it to stockholders (dividends). Dividends are usually cash distributions, but can also be additional stock. Many investors look at dividends as a measure of the health of the company. Changes in dividend policy can signal changes in the company's value. A company that forgoes dividends and reinvests in its business must choose investments that have a higher return than the discount rate. If not, the company could increase its earnings, but it would erode shareholder value. As a result, stock price would decline.

Preferred stock is a hybrid security that has some components of debt and some features of common stock. The preferred stockholder has claims on earnings and assets of the company that are senior to that of common stockholders. Usually there are no voting rights in this class of stock. Preferred stock generally provides for an annual fixed dividend payment that is to be paid in full, for past and present dividends, before common stockholders can begin to receive any dividends. However, failure to pay dividends cannot force a company into bankruptcy.

There are a number of public stock exchanges where an investor can buy and sell stocks. These exchanges facilitate the buying and selling of specific stocks listed on their exchanges. The New York Stock Exchange (NYSE) and NASDAQ are two of the most well-known US exchanges. The Tokyo Stock Exchange and London Stock Exchange are two of the largest stock exchanges outside the US. Investment banks market and issue new shares of a stock on these exchanges. New equity issued by firms that already have outstanding stock is called a seasoned offering. An initial public offering (IPO) involves firms that are not yet traded.

VALUING STOCKS

There are several accepted methods for valuing common stock. We will discuss three of the most widely used techniques.

- Present value of all future dividends
- Free Cash Flow method
- Multiples of comparable firms

DIVIDEND MODEL:

The first method we will discuss for valuing common stock is to determine the present value (PV) of all future dividends. What if a stock has no dividends? Is it worthless? No, it is not worthless because a firm always has the potential to start paying dividends and if the firm is sold in a takeover, the sale price can be considered a lump sum dividend at the end. The formula for this method is illustrated below with future dividend estimates (DIV) discounted back with the required rate of return (i) for an infinite number of periods.

$$PV = \sum_{t=1}^{\infty} \frac{DIV_t}{(1+i)^t}$$

Because this formula requires forecasting an infinite number of dividends into the future, it is not a realistic method. Therefore, a more practical application called the dividend growth model was developed. The dividend growth model makes some simplifying assumptions, but the basic premise of the theory remains intact. The dividend growth model assumes that dividend growth (g) is constant and that stock price is expected to appreciate at the same rate.

$$PV = \frac{DIV}{(i - g)}$$

Take the following example of Company A, which is expected to pay dividends of $5 this year and thereafter; the dividend is

expected to grow by 5%. If the required rate of return is 10%, the company's share price is $100.

$$5/(0.1-0.05) = \$100$$

The dividend growth model is criticized because

constant growth is a major assumption that does not apply to many companies. For this reason, we will now look at alternative methods for valuing stock.

FREE CASH FLOW MODEL:

The free cash flow valuation model is often preferred to the dividend growth model in cases where firms do not pay dividends or the dividends and growth are hard to forecast. The basic premise for the free cash flow model is to take the present value of the cash the firm could distribute after meeting all obligations. Free cash flow is the amount of cash available to investors (revenues less all costs and investments). To get the present value of the free cash flow, we forecast out each year's free cash flow (FCF) and then add a terminal value that assumes constant growth (g). We then discounted all those values back with the cost of capital (i).

$$PV_{FCF} = \sum_{t=1}^{t} \frac{FCF_t}{(1+i)^t} + \frac{\frac{FCF_{t+1}}{(i-g)}}{(1+i)^{t+1}} \} \text{ Terminal Value}$$

Let us take an example of Company B that has free cash flow of $100 for year 1, $200 year 2, then is expected to reach a constant free cash flow growth rate of 5%. Cost of capital is 10%. The present value of the cash flows is:

$$((100/(1+0.1)^1))+((200/(1+0.1)^2)) +((200*1.05)/(0.1-0.05))/(1+0.1\ 1)^3 = \$3412$$

If the company is being sold or closed, an alternative terminal value would be to determine what the sale price or liquidation value is during the final year and discount that number back instead of using the constant growth perpetuity.

$$PV_{FCF} = \sum_{t=1}^{t} \frac{FCF_t}{(1+i)^t} + \frac{FCF_{t+1}}{(1+i)^{t+1}} \} \text{ Terminal Value}$$

Coming back to valuing the common stock, we now take the present value of the free cash flow and subtract the value of debt and value of preferred stock.

Common Stock Value = $PV_{FCF} - V_d - V_{ps}$

In our example above, if debt is worth $400 and there is no preferred stock, the common stock value is $3412 — $400 = $3012. This is the value of the firm. We can take this number and divide by the amount of shares outstanding to come up with a price per share.

MULTIPLES:

Using multiples is one of the simplest ways to value a stock. The premise of this model is to find a company in a similar industry, with a similar risk profile and similar business model. The known critical statistics of the comparable company are then used to extrapolate value for the company in question. The most commonly used comparison is price per share compared to earnings per share. This is referred to as the P/E ratio.

P/E ratio = $\dfrac{\text{Price Per Share}}{\text{Earnings Per Share}}$

If a company's earnings per share are $20 with price per share of $40, then it has a P/E ratio of 2. If we apply that to a comparable company with earnings per share of $10M, then the price per share should be $20.

$$\frac{40}{20} = \frac{X}{10} \quad X = 20$$

There are other multiples that can also be applied. Price per Share/Cash Flow is a popular multiple because it takes into account all capital investments. In other industries, Price per Share/Revenue would be a good comparison. The appropriate multiple really depends on the company and industry specifics. For a web portal, it could be Price per Share/ Click-Throughs or for a cable system it could be Price per Share/Subscribers.

Critics of this method point out that no two companies are exactly alike and therefore cannot be used for direct comparison. This method is often used in conjunction with other methods as a check to make sure the stock price is reasonable.

VALUING PREFERRED STOCK

As noted earlier, preferred stock differs from common stock in several ways. It is really a hybrid, somewhere between a bond and a stock. Therefore, the valuation technique takes lessons from both stocks and bonds. To value preferred stock, we simply assume the fixed dividend payment (DIV) in perpetuity and then discount it back (i) to present day.

Preferred Stock Value = $\dfrac{DIV}{i}$

Take the following example: If Company C provides an annual dividend of $2.50 on its preferred stock and the discount rate is 10%, the value of the preferred stock is $25.

$$2.5/0.1 = \$25$$

CONCLUSION

Stocks and bonds are two of the most prevalent investment vehicles. Bonds have a certain amount of security because fixed payments are guaranteed unless the company goes into default. Stock returns are much more risky, but also have a higher rate of return. Certain information about a publicly traded stock is required to be disclosed to investors. Using historical data and the information the company provides, an investor can estimate the future cash streams that will come from the stock and analyze the risk associated with those cash streams. In the end, no investment comes without risk, so it is best to diversify your portfolio.

An investment portfolio can utilize bonds to offset the volatility of stocks. This kind of asset allocation can reduce overall risk. Each asset class (stocks and bonds) should also be diversified to guard against poor performance of any one investment. The optimal ratio of stocks to bonds varies for each investor. The portfolio for an aggressive investor has a higher mix of stocks and generally has a long-term time horizon (5+ years). On the other side of the spectrum is the conservative investor. This investor will hold a greater majority of bonds and is interested in the stable income that the coupons can provide. An investor close to retirement should consider this kind of conservative portfolio.

BIBLIOGRAPHY

Bodie, Z. & Merton, R. C. (1998). *Finance.* Upper Saddle River, New Jersey: Prentice-Hall.

Braham, L. & Gutner, T. (2003). Return of the P/E. *Business Week,* (3828), 83. Retrieved April 6, 2007, from EBSCO Online Database Academic Search Premier. http://search. ebscohost. com/login.aspx?direct=true&db=aph&AN=945 4528&site=ehost-live

Brealey, R. A., & Myers, S.C. (1996). *Principles of Corporate Finance.* New York: McGraw-Hill.

Brigham, E. F., & Houston, J. F. (2003). *Fundamentals of Financial Management.* Cincinnati, Ohio: South-Western College Publishing.

Callen, J. L., Khan, M., & Lu, H. (2013). Accounting quality, stock price delay, and future stock returns* Accounting quality, stock price delay, and future stock returns. *Contemporary Accounting Research, 30* (1), 269–295. Retrieved November 20, 2013 from EBSCO Online Database Business Source Complete. http://search.ebscohost.com/ login.aspx?direct=true&db=bth&AN=86170292 &site=ehost-live

Keown, A. J., Martin, J. D., Petty, J. W., & Scott, D. F. (1998). *Basic Financial Management.* New Jersey: Prentice Hall.

Kosnett, J. R. (2013). Dump your bonds? No way. *Kiplinger's Personal Finance, 67* (11), 46. Retrieved November 20, 2013 from EBSCO Online Database Business Source Complete. http://search.ebscohost.com/login.aspx?direct=t rue&db=bth&AN=9 0617040&site=ehost-live

Luehrman, T. A. (1997). What's it worth? A general manager's guide to valuation. *Harvard Business Review, 75*(3), 132 — 141. Retrieved April 6, 2007, from EBSCO Online Database Business Source Complete. http://search.ebscohost.com/ login.aspx?direct=true&db=bth&AN=97051962 07&site=bsi-live

Novotná, M. (2013). A multivariate analysis of financial and market-based variables for bond rating prediction. *Economic Computation & Economic Cybernetics Studies & Research, 47* (2), 67–83. Retrieved November 20, 2013 from EBSCO Online Database Business Source Complete. http://search.ebscohost.com/login.aspx?direct=t rue&db=bth&AN=8 9707073&site=ehost-live

SUGGESTED READING

Black, F. (1990). Why firms pay dividends. *Financial Analysts Journal 46*(3), 5. Retrieved April 6, 2007, from EBSCO Online Database Business Source Complete. http://search. ebscohost. com/login.aspx?direct=true&db=bth&AN=693 6554&site=ehost-live

Fabozzi, F. J., Kalotay, A. J., & Williams, G. O. (1993). A model for valuing bonds and embedded options. *Financial Analysts Journal, 49*(3), 35–46. Retrieved April 6, 2007, from EBSCO Online Database Business Source Complete. http:// search.ebscohost.com/login.aspx?direct=t rue&db=bth&AN=6936590&site=ehost-live

Feldman, A. (2013). The benefit of fearing disaster. *Fortune, 168* (5), 57. Retrieved November 20, 2013 from EBSCO Online Database Business Source Complete. http://search. ebscohost. com/login.aspx?direct=true&db=bth&AN=900 52563&site=ehost-live

Hodges, S. D. & Schaefer, S. M. (1977). A model for bond portfolio improvement. *Journal of Financial and Quantitative Analysis, 12*(2), 243–260. Retrieved April 6, 2007, from EBSCO Online Database Business Source Complete. http:// search.ebscohost.com/login.aspx?direct=t rue&db=bth&AN=4762255&site=ehost-live

P´stor, L. & Pietro, V. (2003). Stock valuation and learning about profitability. *Journal of Finance, 58* (5), 1749–1790. Retrieved April 6, 2007, from EBSCO Online Database Business Source Complete. http://search.ebscohost.com/ login.asp x?direct=true&db=bth&AN=10832847&site=eh ost-live

A penny in whose pocket? (2001). *Economist, 359*(8223), 71–72. Retrieved April 6, 2007, from EBSCO Online Database Academic Search Premier. http://search.ebscohost.com/login.aspx?direct=true&db=aph&AN=4487594 &site=ehost-live

Valuing stocks with the dividend discount model. (2001). *Dow Theory Forecasts, 57*(26), 7. Retrieved April 6, 2007, from EBSCO Online Database Business Source Complete. http://search.ebscohost.com/login.aspx?direct=true&db=bth&AN=5791938&site=ehost-live

–Heather Wall Beckham

STOCK INDEXES

ABSTRACT

This article discusses some of the major stock indexes in the US including their history and relevance to today's investors. Stock indexes, or stock market indexes, are lists of stocks and statistics that reflect the composite value. Broad-based indexes such as the Dow Jones Industrial Average or the S&P 500 in the US are representative of the performance of the entire market. For this reason, these indexes are closely watched as a reflection of how investors view the state of the economy. Specialized indexes allow investors to track portfolios for specific sectors of the overall market which are much more manageable. Specialized indexes track performance of stock portfolios that are grouped by common attributes such as market or size of company. This essay discusses some of the major broad-based indexes and current trends surrounding the use of traditional indexes. Stakeholder issues are discussed from the standpoint of what current stock indexes provide for managers, investors and policy makers. A new generation of stock indexes is emerging to meet additional stakeholder demands and these are discussed along with other emerging trends in the use and creation of stock indices.

OVERVIEW

There is no perfect stock index. Indexes are developed to gauge performance of groups of stocks. As the proliferation of stocks increases in our global economy, the greater the need to develop new indexes that help stakeholders to monitor performance of certain stock segments.

The Dow Jones Industrial Average (DJIA) index was started in 1896 by Charles Dow and indexed 11 stocks at its inception. Today, the DJIA tracks 30 stocks that are known as "blue-chip" stocks. The "blue-chip" companies that are indexed in the DJIA are considered industry leaders in a variety of segments including: Energy, banking communications, retail and entertainment.

METHODS FOR STOCK INDEXING

The Dow indexes its stocks using a price-weighted system. Price-weighted indexing means that the total prices of all stock are added together and divided by the number of stocks in the index. Market capitalization is the method of indexing used by many of the other major indexes such as the NASDAQ and S&P 500. Market capitalization takes into account total market value and not just price. Market capitalization is felt by many to be a better indicator of overall market performance. The other major criticism of the Dow is that because it only tracks 30 stocks (out of the thousands of stocks on the market), it isn't considered very representative of the market as a whole.

NASDAQ, STANDARD AND POOR'S 500 & WILSHIRE 5000

NASDAQ

The NASDAQ index was started in 1971 and is a market-weighted index that tracks a large number of technology stocks (sometimes referred to as "tech heavy"). The NASDAQ does track over 5000 technology related stocks and as such, is a good representation of stocks from the tech sector. However, the NASDAQ doesn't do as good a job of indicating the markets as a whole. Other drawbacks cited for the NASDAQ are that the index includes a number of small companies that tend to increase volatility in the market.

Standard and Poor's 500

Another major stock index is the Standard and Poor's 500 (S&P 500) which indexes "large cap" companies. These companies have market capitalization of over $10 billion as calculated by the companies number of shares multiplied by the stock price. It's important to remember that stock prices change over time and therefore the companies referenced in the index may also change. The "large cap" or "big movers" are indicative of company size (Wayman, 2007).

Wilshire 5000

The Wilshire 5000 is considered the "total market index"; it was started in 1974 by Wilshire Associates. The index came about due to the availability of computer technology that allowed for efficient indexing of large amounts of statistical data. The Wilshire has been called the "nation's broadest-based index" and is thought by many to be the most accurate reflection of the overall market. The index now includes stocks from 6700+ firms (essentially every public firm and is therefore highly representative of the overall market)-not the 5000 that are stated in the index name. The Wilshire is not often cited in the financial press because the index is considered by many to offer "too broad" a view of the US markets. The Wilshire is so diverse that it is not easy to tell which sectors are moving the market (ex: tech, industrial, small or large).

Major US Indices (Street Authority, 2007)

Dow Jones Industrial	S&P Mid Cap
Standard and Poor's	S&P Small Cap
Nasdaq Composite	Russell 3000
Nasdaq 100	Russell 2000
Wilshire 5000	Russell 1000

Dow Jones Industrial S&P Mid Cap Standard and Poor's S&P Small Cap Nasdaq Composite Russell 3000 Nasdaq 100 Russell 2000 Wilshire 5000 Russell 1000

The Dow Jones, NASDAQ, S&P 500 and Wilshire indexes are just a representative four out of the hundreds of stock indexes that are now available to benchmark stock performance. The first three

(DJIA, NASDAQ & S&P) are very visible, broad-based indexes and as such, are often cited for financial reporting purposes as good indicators of investor confidence in the US economy. Current literature indicates that stakeholders such as money managers, clients/investors and policy makers need to monitor other indexes to make sound decisions about stock market investments and to meet their respective objectives. There is no consensus from stakeholders about which index is best; all have benefits and drawbacks. Investors and fund managers are continuously on the lookout for new and better designed indexes that will help to monitor investment portfolios.

APPLICATIONS

EVALUATIONS OF STOCK INDEXES

By definition, a stock index is a representative sample or snapshot of stocks that is a subset of the larger universe of stocks. There are literally hundreds of stock indexes available for the individual investor or market fund manager to monitor on a daily basis. Yet, even with the proliferation of indexes, the big three (Dow Jones Industrial Average, S&P 500 and NASDAQ Composite) "rule the headlines" and serve as the major sources of stock market analysis for most investors and managers (Wayman, 2007). There is plenty of criticism in the industry and media about the shortcomings of the major US indices in their ability to provide real insight into many markets.

Pros of the Major US Indices

The DJIA, S&P and NASDAQ indexes are useful tools for tracking market trends and historical perspectives. Investors who look at how indexes react to economic trends over time will have a better understanding of why trends occur. These indexes can be useful tools for helping investors make better investment decisions.

Cons of the Major US Indices

The major US indexes are subject to calculation bias. Most indexes (with the exception of DJIA) are market-weighted indexes. This simply means that stocks of larger companies with larger market presence have a larger influence on the index. Large stocks influence the index much more than small companies (with smaller market share-market cap).

Many feel that if the index is weighted toward large company stocks, the index can't really describe the health of the overall index. This overweighing means that if the "big dog" is sick, the whole "market" gets the flu, regardless of the strength of the smaller stocks that are in the index (Wayman, 2007). A more equally weighted index would be more democratic and do a better job of capturing the impact of smaller stocks that may be rising but ignored due to scrutiny of larger companies.

Other Concerns

The stocks that are included on indexes are picked by committees who do their best to choose stocks that reflect the economy in a given year. Committees generally meet on a yearly basis to re-define the stocks to be included on the index. Because the stocks included in a given index change over time, one cannot assume that the index will reveal trading patterns of the same stocks over a long period of time. Another challenge for many is the knowledge that indexes are not as dynamic as the market itself. For this reason, some critics state that the indexes don't always reflect where growth will be in the market.

STOCK MARKET FLUCTUATIONS

Market "Crashes" & their Causes

Stock market indexes are often quoted in the media as barometers of the overall health and vitality of the economy. Many stakeholders, including policy makers and individual investors pay close attention to daily fluctuations reported by the market indexes. There have been a number of documented "crashes" in the last several decades, and investors and indexes almost always tend to react to them in similar ways. The following is a timeline of "market crashes" and the related event that caused the reaction (Marcial, 2007):

- 1973 Oil Embargo
- 1987 Double-Digit Interest Scare
- 1998 Russian Debt Default
- 2000 Dotcom Bust
- 9/2001 Terrorist Attacks in US
- 2/2007 Chinese Market Trouble
- 8/2007 Sub-Prime Mortgage Scare
- 5/2010 "Flash Crash" High Frequency Trades Triggered by Single Large Sell
- 8/2011 Downgrading of U.S Credit Rating and European Sovereign Debt Crisis

Domestic Issues Affecting Stock Indexes

Stock market indexes are highly susceptible to pivotal events as indicated by the above list. Credit trouble in the US in 2007 has been a dominant theme throughout the year and has caused speculation that similar ills could spread into the global economy. The now-famous sub-prime mortgage troubles in the US are the type of issue that puts stock markets on high alert. In the US, stock indexes are affected by a number of domestic issues including (Steverman, 2007):

- Earning news-from retailers and manufacturing companies
- General economic data (consumer spending, employment)
- Interest rates from Federal Reserve (how much consumers and businesses can expect to pay when borrowing money).

Affects of Interest Rates on Stock Indexes

In the US, the Federal Reserve Open Market Committee (FOMC) assesses the risk to credit markets and ultimately recommends changes in interest rates. In the case of a credit crunch, an interest rate cut would help to pump money into the financial system. Bond markets are very sensitive to interest rate changes and also acutely aware of current credit woes. While stock indexes monitor equity markets and therefore are not directly tied to credit issues, stock indexes react to trouble in other areas of the financial markets and the economy as a whole (Coy, 2007). In a world where financial capital, debt and markets are globally interconnected, trouble in one area of the financial markets can easily cause reactions or "over-reactions" in other markets.

Some have described the global asset markets as "effectively shockproof" and point out that "every major developed and emerging market stock index is up on the year" (Wolf, 2007). This claim has been made despite the news of the sub-prime mortgage woes in the US, tightening global money, international trade tensions and even threats of a nuclear armed Iran. If history were to repeat itself, these issues would spell major trouble for US and international stock markets. Instead, there's "lots of global liquidity" coming from cheap and easy to access credit. Low global interest rates are freeing up money to fuel markets and money is also coming from other sources including: Hedge funds, private equity and leveraged buy-outs.

ARGUMENTS FOR NEW INDEX DEVELOPMENT

The major US stock indices have evolved over time to index the stocks in companies from different market segments. Within the 10 major US stock indices, technology, blue-chip, large cap and small cap companies are all represented by their own indexes. As industries and markets expand and markets become more subject to global influences and events, there is a growing move toward developing more specialized indexes to meet stakeholder needs. Investors simply may not be getting the information that they need from the indexes as they exist today.

"Maybe it's time for a new stock index — one that will give a better picture than the current indexes do of how the average investor, or the average portfolio, is doing in the market at any point in time. That was the idea behind the first indexes. They were a shorthand way for investors to know roughly how their portfolios were doing" (Clowes, 2001).

There are many indexes to help track US stocks — most are capitalization weighted and therefore are not really able to provide investors with a true idea of how a given portfolio is doing at a particular time. As a reminder, capitalization weighted indexes are stock indexes where each stock affects the index in relation to its market value. Because an index is capitalization weighted, "overheated" sectors or industries dominate the index. This concept is best explained using the following example:

"This [historic] example [post dotcom bust] shows- the impact of the tech stock sector on the S&P 500. The technology sector accounts for just 7% of the gross domestic product, but 36% of the S&P 500. Partly as a result of that weighting, in 1999 the S&P showed a total return of 21%, but the median money manager in the PIPER universe was up only 18.2%. This is because most of the gain in the S&P 500 was accounted for by just a few of the stocks in the index. Only about half of the S&P 500 stocks were up or flat in 1999. The others were down" (Clowes, 2001).

Many investors view cap-weighted indexes as showing distorted results in the markets. As we will discuss later in this article, some stakeholders have begun to create their own stock indexes using alternate criteria in an effort to help assess their portfolio performance.

ISSUES

FLAWS IN MARKET CAPITALIZATION

"When John Bogle, founder of the Vanguard Group, introduced the first retail index fund in 1976, he sparked a revolution in investing: Throw out the fund manager, keep costs low, and weight the stocks in the portfolio by their current market value. Today, $3 trillion in pensions and mutual funds are indexed" (Wagoner, 2007, 1).

Today, indexing by market capitalization has become the punching bag for many. "Critics of the S&P 500 and other widely used barometers say the indexes are inherently flawed because they are dominated by a handful of companies and because they must, by their very nature, add more shares of stocks that are rising and trim positions in stocks that are failing. Therefore, as investors move money in and out, managers of index funds are forced to buy stocks when they are overpriced and sell them when they are undervalued. If they don't trade, their funds no longer replicate the index they promise to track" (Landis, 2006).

A good example of the above scenario can be illustrated by what happened to the S&P index from March 2000 to Jan 2001. The S&P stock index dropped 25% while the average stock price rose 20%. Critics say that there has to be an explanation for such an overall drop in the index causing investors to lose "big" while prices of most individual stocks were actually rising.

"Like most indexes, the S&P 500 holds stocks in proportion to their market value (share price times the number of shares outstanding). So its holdings of the biggest company, ExxonMobil, with a market value of $415 billion as of mid August, are roughly 729 times greater than its holdings of number 500, Gateway, a $569-million firm" (Landis, 2006, 6).

"To own a representative sample of the market — the purpose of indexing — you need more shares of larger companies and fewer shares of smaller ones. Often, this results in index-fund managers buying more shares of companies as their prices rise, even

265

if those shares are already expensive. At the same time, they must sell stocks that are out of favor even if they are well priced to buy. Rob Arnott, a California money manager and editor of Financial Analysts Journal tells investors the following about stocks in market-cap indexes. 'If you have money in a market weighted index, you can be absolutely assured that most of your money is in overvalued companies'" (Landis, 2006, 7).

Consider the following stats:

■ At the end of 1999, the 10 biggest companies in the S&P 500 were valued at $3.1 trillion and made up 25% of the index total.

■ In 2007, the 10 biggest companies in the S&P 500 were valued at $2.3 trillion and made up 20% of the index total.

Today, the S&P 500 is not as top heavy as it was during the dotcom boom, but the statistics from 1999 clearly show that "the stocks with the biggest run-ups have the biggest effect on the index" (Wagoner, 2007).

ALTERNATIVES TO MARKET-WEIGHT INDEXING

Jeremy Siegel, a professor at the University of Pennsylvania's Wharton School has proposed an alternative to market-weight indexing. His company, WisdomTree, has developed two dozen funds that are indexed according to a company's earnings or dividends, rather than traditional market capitalization. Seigel is quick to point out that investors are the ones who suffer when indexes are over-weighted with large cap stocks. Seigel recounted a scenario that involved the Vanguard Index Fund and its indexing of Yahoo Stock in 1999. According to Seigel, the Vanguard Index was "forced" to buy overpriced shares of Yahoo due to the hype and run-up. Seigel himself was aware that his fund was investing heavily in expensive shares of Yahoo, but wasn't certain that other investors were aware of the situation. In any case, Seigel was looking for a "way out" and came up with the idea of an alternative index that would not overweight stocks such as Yahoo in his portfolio.

Active management of stock portfolios requires fund managers to analyze, build and manage stock purchases. Index funds are passively managed collections of stocks that represent a particular sector or class of assets. Index fund performance can beat active management of a portfolio in many cases and saves money, but many investors employ a strategy of indexing and active management to manage stock portfolios. Even with hundreds of stock index alternatives available, however, investors are calling for more choices than the traditional stock indexes. Stakeholders want access to real-time stock data; and they also are looking for indexes that offer insights into more diverse market segments.

DIVIDEND-WEIGHTED INDEXES

Dividend weighted indexes have been proposed as an alternative to traditional capitalization-weighted indexes. Dividend weighted funds index according to company earnings and dividends. Dividend-weighted funds follow a value-oriented strategy.

VALUE-WEIGHTED INDEXES

Value indexes invest in undervalued stocks and are typically for more conservative investors. Value indexes are essentially the opposite of growth indexes. Growth stocks do better during a "bubble" when money pours out of value stocks and into growth stocks. At the bottom of the market, money moves out of growth indexes and back into value indexes.

FUNDAMENTAL INDEXES & INTELLIGENT INDEXES

Fundamental indexes are less vulnerable to market flux and hold stock in equal proportions. For example, one set of fundamental indexes weights holdings on sales, dividends, cash flow and book value. These measures help to place a firm's "footprint" in the economy-by using multiple statistics for indexing and weighting.

Intelligent indexes follow similar principals to the fundamentals indexes. They simply use different criteria to index a company's stock. One intelligent index claims to use 23 factors to construct its indexing algorithm. Factors include: Measures of value, price momentum, risk and timeliness — all factors are intended to highlight companies "with the greatest investment merit" (Landis, 2006).

EXCHANGE TRADED FUNDS

Exchange Traded Funds (ETFs) are much like mutual funds (baskets of stocks that are bought and sold). ETFs are actually based on indexes which make them exchange traded index funds. There are nearly 700 ETF in existence today and only 2-3% index broad market funds. Criticism of ETFs is loud, but investors love them and they are gaining in popularity. ETFs track an index but can be traded like a stock at any time of the day-unlike their close relative the mutual fund. Purists cite the profusion of ETFs as insanity and the next gimmick in the market. Criticism centers around the lack of inclusion of broad-market funds in ETFs, but investors love their flexibility and access to non-traditional sectors. ETFs can track well known indexes (one closely matches the S&P index) while others index countries, regions, or commodities such as oil, gold or silver.

PRIVATE PLACEMENT — AVOIDING STOCK INDEXES

Private exchanges are gaining popularity as alternatives to selling company shares in public offerings. Instead of selling in traditional indexes, shares are sold to large investors who trade on secondary markets. One famous example of such a private or hybrid marketplace was launched by Goldman Sachs with the release of an electronic market called GS TrUE (Goldman Sachs Tradable Unregistered Equity). Goldman Sachs sold 15% of its Oaktree Capital Management for $880 million to a collection of hedge funds. Other heavyweight firms such as Merrill Lynch and Morgan Stanley are also investigating similar offerings. Private equity sales are known as 144A securities and the NASDAQ is planning to get in on the action with the creation of a new electronic portal trading system that will serve as a clearinghouse for 144A securities. The NASDAQ exchange is a competitor of the private exchanges, but sees an opportunity to complement its tracking of public markets with the new private exchange information.

In the case of the sale of Oaktree shares, Goldman Sachs specifically did not want to have pressure to show steady growth in a period of time their business market was considered to be "volatile." Other advantages to private or hybrid exchanges is for private equity and venture capital firms which includes the ability to cash out "equity" from companies that are not in fully public markets. While private exchanges are not expected to see a lot of active trading (many investors hold onto shares) there are some distinct advantages to trading in the private exchanges. Some of the benefits include: Relative stability in the market, avoidance of class action litigation and Sarbanes-Oxley compliance and less pressure to make quarterly earnings numbers. The avoidance of regulatory hurdles that must be met by companies trading in public exchanges will only make private exchanges more popular as companies take advantage of leveraging their own equity.

CONCLUSION

There are literally hundreds of stock indexes available to help investors and fund mangers track portfolio performance. The major US stock indexes such as the Dow Jones Industrial Average, S&P 500 and NASDAQ are broad market indexes that provide insight into the performance of many sectors of the US economy, and some would argue; the health of the nation's economy as a whole. Stock indexes are subject to fluctuations from a number of different factors and as such are closely watched by stakeholders and policy makers. Indexes such as the Russell 1000 track small cap companies and other "under-reported" sectors that are ignored by the larger stock indexes. While the major US indices offer coverage for a number of market sectors, investors are demanding more flexibility in indexes. In today's digital world where data is king and complex computations can be calculated with ease, there is an abundant supply of data with which to create and weight stock indexes. One may expect that savvy investors will continually seek out ways to slice and dice stock index data in the ongoing effort to "time and trade" the market.

BIBLIOGRAPHY

Clowes, M. (2001). Time to update indexes. *Pensions & Investments, 29*(1), 10. Retrieved September 8, 2007, from EBSCO Online Database Business Source Premier. http:// search. ebscohost.com/login.aspx?direct=true&db=buh&AN=4025330&site=ehost-live

Coy, P. (2007, August 8). Sorry, Wall Street. *Business Week Online,* 13. Retrieved September 10, 2007, from EBSCO Online Database Academic Search Premier. http://search. ebscohost.com/login.aspx?direct=true&db=aph&AN=26137081&site=ehost-live

Gastineau, G. (2006) The best index for the thoughtful indexer. *Dow Jones Indexes.* Retrieved September 8, 2007, from http://www.djindexes.com/mdsidx/downloads/ articles/BestIndex%5fGastineau.pdf

Hail the hybrids. (2007). *Economist, 383*(8541), 86. Retrieved September 8, 2007, from EBSCO Online Database Academic Search Premier. http:// search.ebscohost.com/ login.aspx?direct=true&db=aph&AN=25422476&site=eh ost-live

He, L. T. (2013). Mean reversion of volatility around extreme stock returns: Evidence from U.S. stock indexes. *International Journal of Business & Finance Research (IJBFR)*, 7(4), 91-101. Retrieved November 15, 2013, from EBSCO Online Database Business Source Complete. http://search. ebscohost.com/login.aspx?direct=true&db=bth&AN=86260857&site=ehost-live

Landis, D. (2006). Reinventing the INDEX. *Kiplinger's Personal Finance, 60*(10), 44-47. Retrieved September 8, 2007, from EBSCO Online Database Academic Search Premier. http:// search.ebscohost.com/login.aspx?direct=true&db=aph&AN=22342500&site=ehost-live

Paudyn, B. (2013). Credit rating agencies and the sovereign debt crisis: Performing the politics of creditworthiness through risk and uncertainty. *Review of International Political Economy, 20*(4), 788-818. Retrieved November 15, 2013, from EBSCO Online Database Business Source Complete. http:// search.ebscohost.com/login.aspx?direct=t rue&db=bth&AN=89683208&site=ehost-live

Steverman, B. (2007, June 29). Stocks flat after fed holds steady. *Business Week Online*, 14. Retrieved September 8, 2007, from EBSCO Online Database Academic Search Premier. http:// search.ebscohost.com/login.aspx?direct=true&db=aph&AN=25760912&site=ehost-live

Stock indexes. (2007). *QuickMBA*. Retrieved September 10, 2007, from http://www.quickmba. com/finance/invest/indices.shtml

Tan, A. (2013). Europe's surprising rebound. *Kiplinger's Personal Finance, 67*(10), 44. Retrieved November 15, 2013, from EBSCO Online Database Business Source Complete. http://search.ebscohost.com/login.aspx?direct=t rue&db=bth&AN=90056901&site=ehost-live

Waggoner, J. (2007, April 16). Great minds don't think alike about index funds. *USA Today*, 4B.

Waid, R. (2005). The Dow Jones Wilshire U.S. style indexes. *Wilshire Associates, Inc.* Retrieved September 8, 2007, from http://www.djindexes.com/mdsidx/downloads/ DJW%5fstyle%5fwaid.pdf

Wayman, R. (2007) The ABCs of stock indexes. *Investopedia*. Retrieved September 10, 2007, from http://www.investopedia.com/articles/analyst/062502.asp

Wilshire 5000 index (2007) *Street Authority.com*. Retrieved September 10, 2007, from http://www.streetauthority.com/ terms/index/wilshire5000.asp

SUGGESTED READING

Dodds, L. (2007). Brics and cement: Building in new markets. *Global Investor*, (203), 69-70. Retrieved September 8, 2007, from EBSCO Online Database Business Source Premier. http://search.ebscohost.com/login.aspx?direct=true&db=buh&AN=25890584&site=ehost-live

Fortune, P. (1998, November/December).A primer on stock indexes. *New England Economic Review*, 25-40. Retrieved on September 8, 2007, from http://www.bos.frb. org/economic/neer/neer1998/neer698b.htm

Kosnett, J. (2007). Why stocks will keep going up. *Kiplinger's Personal Finance, 61*(7), 50-52. Retrieved September 10, 2007, from EBSCO Online Database Academic Search Premier. http://search.ebscohost.com/login.aspx?direct=true&db=aph&AN=25295468&site=ehost-live

Waggoner, J. (2007, August 3). How to find a fund that doesn't make your eye … *USA Today*, 8B.

–Carolyn Sprague

STRATEGIC FINANCIAL MANAGEMENT

ABSTRACT

This article focuses on how organizations such as nonprofits may create a financial system that allows them to manage their operations and maintain financial stability. The article provides recommendations on how to create and implement policies that will support a strong financial system as well as a process that auditors may use in order to audit the records.

OVERVIEW

In order for organization's to be successful, they must create a strategic plan that will position the firm for growth and competitiveness. The senior management team will need to analyze all data, including the financial records, to ensure that the organization can make a profit, remain competitive and be positioned for continued growth.

A social service organization (Making Ends Meet, n.d.) identified four important stages in the financial planning process. These stages are reviewing the past, forecasting the future, setting strategies and plans, and setting annual budgets. Each of these phases is of equal importance and some of the tasks at each phase include:

REVIEWING THE PAST:
- Monitor recent trends in demand and expenditure
- Monitor trends in funding streams
- Monitor and report on actual performance and outcomes, including end-of-year position and performance against specific performance indicators for similar organizations
- Collect comparative information about actual costs and cost drivers
- Review the results and evaluate the recommendations from any external inspection reports and management letters from external auditors (Strategic financial planning, n.d., "Stages of financial planning").

FORECASTING THE FUTURE:
- Evaluate the impact of national policies and strategies
- Identify and estimate levels of the various funding streams
- Review the impact of local policy initiatives and priorities
- Determine the future impact of known trends on demand and expenditure
- Identify the financial implications of demographic trends and other "drivers" of demand which are outside the control of the organization (Strategic financial planning, n.d., "Stages of financial planning").

SETTING STRATEGIES & PLANS:
- Take into account the corporate context for strategic planning
- Link financial planning with service, human resource and asset management planning

- Collect information on the knowledge and skill base required for effective budget management at all organizational levels
- Engage all key stakeholders in the strategic financial planning (Strategic financial planning, n.d., "Stages of financial planning").

SET ANNUAL BUDGETS:
- Come to consensus on what the budget process should be
- Ensure budgets are informed by financial plans
- Involve budget managers in budget setting
- Match commitments and expected changes in demand with resources available
- Respond to unexpected changes
- Review budget structures
- Engage with key stakeholders
- Ensure short term decisions in budget setting do not undermine longer-term priorities and strategies.

As the organization goes through the financial planning process, key decision makers should determine the types of policies that need to be in effect in order to be successful at each of the individual phases.

APPLICATION

FINANCIAL POLICIES
The board of directors is very important in the governance of non-profit — 501(c)(3) organizations. Individuals who accept these positions are committed to organizational oversight. Part of this responsibility includes making sure that the organization is fiscally sound. Loyalty, care and obedience are considered to be three basic functions of trustees and these three functions are the benchmark for financial policies created by the board of directors (National Center for Nonprofit Boards, 1996).

What does each of these functions symbolize?
- Loyalty implies that the board members will act in the best interest of the organization and avoid any actions or decisions that will appear to be a conflict of interest with the mission of the organization.
- Care refers to the promise that board members will review, critique, and respond to any reports that are related to the organization, especially as

it relates to management, programs and financial matters.

- Obedience ensures that the organization will adhere to all laws and regulations that affect the operation of the organization.

In order to successfully fulfill these obligations, the board of directors should ensure that they are able to:

- Make decisions that are in the best interest of the organization;
- Enforce guidelines that prohibit the use of assets to benefit professional staff or the board members;
- Assist in preventing conflicts of interest;
- Make sure there is a quorum at each meeting so that important decisions can be made; especially at meetings that will allow the organization to operate smoothly (National Center for Nonprofit Boards, 1996, p. 5).

Finances & Daily Activities

One of the most important decisions that a board can make concerns the daily operation of the organization. The board should have a clear understanding of the organization's financial status. Financial decisions and transactions are critical to the daily activities of the organization. Therefore, it is imperative that there are policies in place that will assist the staff members with performing daily activities. In order to achieve financial stability, the board must develop and implement a "system of financial accountability, a financial plan that reflects the organization's mission, a sound investment strategy, and adequate reserves" (National Center for Nonprofit Boards, 1996, p. 6).

Creating a Successful Financial Plan

Once the board has an understanding of the organization's financial position, it can create strategic policies to manage the organization's financial structure. The National Center for Nonprofit Boards (1996) recommended a five step process to creating a successful financial plan for 501(c)(3) organizations.

- **Step 1 — Establish the Structure** Since the magnitude of work would be too much for a single person, the responsibilities of an effective financial planning and oversight should be divided among all of the board members. The professional staff and other resources should be used

as necessary. Although the full board is ultimately held responsible for decision making, there are laws that support delegating the task of financial evaluation and assessment to committees. When establishing the financial structure, the board is responsible for:

- Making sure that the responsibilities for financial oversight are covered through the committee structure;
- Scrutinizing all financial considerations before they come to the floor for board vote; and
- Overseeing everything that the board does.
- **Step 2 — Define Responsibilities and Set Limits** The designation and clarification of financial responsibilities and limits are necessary so that an organization can avoid confusion and minimize conflict. By adhering to this rule, an organization should be able to successfully complete and submit Form 990 to the Internal Revenue Service. When the board defines responsibilities and sets limits, it should:
- Make clear assignments of financial responsibility;
- Be responsible for carefully reviewing financial reports submitted to governmental agencies, such as the Internal Revenue Service, to ensure that there are no problems; and
- Create guidelines that prohibit expenditures for certain purposes and outline limits in other areas. This information should be detailed in financial policy statements.
- **Step 3 — Understand and Use Available Tools** Since most board members are not seasoned financial experts, it is important for each board member to have access to the tools that will assist them with understanding the financial ramifications of an organization's actions. As a result, the board should:
- Structure financial policies that compliment and strengthen the strategic plan;
- Use the budget as a tool for setting financial policy;
- Review the organization's revenue sources to determine whether they are sustainable;
- Build and monitor the organization's reserve funds to safeguard against unexpected events;
- Use financial statements to evaluate whether actual expenditures match the goals of the budget and strategic plan; and
- Write a policy specifying acceptable uses for reserve funds; and

- Use the audit to check internal systems, and carefully review the audit before accepting it.
- **Step 4 — Use Internal Resources Strategically** When creating financial policies, the board should identify and appoint the key players as well as monitor the authority that is given to each person. Three of the key players tend to be the chief executive; the staff finance officer; and the treasurer. Board members are responsible for:
- Appointing and monitoring the chief executive and key staff;
- Ensuring that the staff members receive adequate training to upgrade their skills;
- Regulating the power given to each individual who has financial responsibilities;
- Implementing a policy that requires two signature authorizations for checks that exceed a predetermined amount;
- Regulating the chief executive's capability of accepting gifts or committing to investments without first gaining board authorization;
- Creating a "check and balance" with functions in order to prevent fraudulent activities; and
- Investigating how to get bonding insurance for the treasurer and key staff.
- **Step 5 — Effectively Use External Resources** The board may need the assistance of external resources, such as consultants, in order to operate efficiently. The board should:
- Choose a bank that is federally insured and not connected to the organization;
- Review insurance policies to determine if the organization provides adequate coverage;
- Develop an investment policy that clearly conveys the board's investment goals and their link to the organization's mission;
- Avoid unnecessary investment risks;
- Ensure that investments are structured to allow for immediate availability of cash; and
- Hire a qualified investment consultant and monitor results on a regular basis.

VIEWPOINT

STATISTICAL SAMPLING
The previous section described how 501(c)(3) organizations can set up their financial system in order to monitor key personnel and the processes that they have in place. A five step process was presented, and the third step indicated that there should be an audit to check internal systems. An organization may suggest that an internal or external auditor check their books. Auditors are continually seeking new tools to assist with the auditing function so that they do not have to rely on their judgment. "To meet their clients' needs in environment of heightened competition and runaway inflation, many auditors are turning to scientifically supported methods of planning, executing and evaluating audit procedures to obtain evidential matter. Statistical sampling is one such method" (Akresh & Zuber, 1981, p. 50). There are many ways that an accountant can set up a statistical sampling. Hitzig (2004) provided a model that worked on the premise that one could set up a statistical sampling by defining the population, frame and sampling unit.

- **The Population** The population is the combination of every account or transaction that the auditor desires to use in order to arrive at the conclusion. The first step in the process is to define the test objective. Once the test objective has been determined, the auditor should define the population. The steps are in this order so that the auditor can draw a sample based on the specific test objective.
- **The Frame** Once the testing has been completed, the auditor must attribute the results to the items versus the population since auditors tend not to choose a sample straight from the population itself. This representation is referred to as the frame. The frame allows the auditor to establish a foundation for further identification of items that should be incorporated into a sample.

In most cases, the accounting population is presented in a list format (i.e. payroll file, accounts receivable detail). This list (or frame) tends to streamline and simplify the sample selection process. However, the population's sample frame is not required to be a list. Sometimes, the geographical locations that floor plans or other population identifiers can reveal are used as frames. Also, there may be an occasion where the auditor has to create an appropriate frame when one is not available. Regardless of whether or not a list is used, the selection of a frame is usually centered on availability and usefulness. The frames that prove to be the most accessible are computer data files. If

271

these files are used, there is an opportunity to integrate them by applying computer-assisted auditing methods and data retrieval techniques.

There are some circumstances where the auditor has to be on alert to make sure that they do not encounter any problems with their samplings. Hitzig (2004) provided some examples such as:

- Over Specified Frames

In the event that there are frame units that fail to include population membership, the units are not applied to the end result that the auditor might be looking for.

- Underspecified or Incomplete Frames

As the auditor makes plans to collect a sample, he/she must ensure that each item seen in the population is simultaneously included in the frame. If the frame is not completed, then there is a probability of some significant members of the population not being accounted for in the sample. If this type of action were to occur, "there is a violation of AU 350's requirement for representativeness, which requires that every item in the population under examination must have a chance of being selected. If a frame is incomplete, there is an opportunity for biased estimates of the population value that is under examination. This statement is true especially if the auditor is not careful to distinguish between the size of the population and the size of the frame on which the selection of the sample was performed" (Hitzig, 2004, "Overspecified Frames").

- **The Sampling Unit** A population is comprised of basic units that are assembled to form the sampling unit. The sampling unit is determined by the auditor's choice of frame. The item that the auditor conducts the examination upon is referred to as the sampling unit, and the sampling unit is vouched or traced. The examination can be conducted by inspection, observation or confirmation.

Auditors tend to make the statistical sampling procedures flexible. If the collection and assessment processes are performed adequately, there is a high probability that there will not be any questions regarding validity due to technical issues. For example, if the total documented amount of the sampling units is equivalent to the total documented amount of the population being scrutinized, then the technical information is validated and accepted. Therefore, it is considered genuine.

How are sampling units selected? Auditors have different preferences. However, listed below are some common trends in the field.

- **Accounts.** Accounts are the preferred method of sampling unit, especially if dealing with consumer accounts (i.e. credit cards). Using this approach will allow the auditor to precisely confirm the net balance in any designated account. However, there may be problems if an auditor attempts to confirm account balances on commercial accounts. Therefore, commercial accounts tend to be controlled through vouchers payable systems.
- **Open invoices.** If an organization has a collection of open invoices that are ready to be accessed right away, then open invoices would be the preferred method. Since the open invoices only consist of debits to the accounts receivable, the auditor will need to administer a different test technique for crediting the accounts.

Since many organizations document their purchases in a vouchers payable method, they have found that it is simpler to validate separate invoices versus account balances. This selection of sampling units can also be associated with equal probability (i.e. basic random sampling) or with probability in relation to size (i.e. dollar-unit sampling).

- **Invoice line items.** Dollar-unit sampling allows an auditor to select a particular invoice line product as the indicated sampling unit. Such an approach is referred to as subsampling (Leslie, Teitlebaum, & Anderson, 1980). In this scenario, "a computer program identifies the invoice and the dollar within the invoice in which the selected line item is located. The auditor is responsible for manually identifying the line item by footing the invoice until the selected item is found. The auditor only has to vouch for that item, and every other selected line item in the sample. In dollar-unit sampling, the auditor projects the results associated with the selected line items by using the total book value of the frame as the representation of the frame size" (Hitzig, 2004, "Invoice line items").

CONCLUSION

In order for organization's to be successful, they must create a strategic plan that will position the firm for growth and competitiveness. The senior management team will need to analyze all data, including the financial records, to ensure that the organiza

tion can make a profit, remain competitive and be positioned for continued growth. As the organization goes through the process, key decision makers should determine the types of policies that need to be in effect in order to be successful at each of the individual phases.

The board of directors is very important in the governance of non-profit — 501(c)(3) organizations. Individuals who accept these positions are committed to organizational oversight. Part of this responsibility includes making sure that the organization is fiscally sound. Loyalty, care and obedience are considered to be three basic functions of trustees and these three functions are the benchmark for financial policies created by the board of directors (National Center for Nonprofit Boards, 1996).

An organization may suggest that an internal or external auditor check their books. Auditors are continually seeking new tools to assist with the auditing function so that they do not have to rely on their judgment. "To meet their clients' needs in environment of heightened competition and runaway inflation, many auditors are turning to scientifically supported methods of planning, executing and evaluating audit procedures to obtain evidential matter. Statistical sampling is one such method" (Akresh & Zuber, 1981, p. 50). There are many ways that an accountant can set up a statistical sampling.

BIBLIOGRAPHY

Akresh, A., & Zuber, G. (1981). Exploring statistical sampling. *Journal of Accountancy, 151*(2), 50-56. Retrieved August 25, 2007, from EBSCO Online Database Business Source Complete. http://search.ebscohost.com/login.aspx?direct=true&db=bth&AN=4585670&site=ehost-live

Bryce, H. (1996). *The nonprofit board's role in establishing financial policies.* Washington, DC: National Center for Nonprofit Boards.

Hitzig, N. (2004). Elements of sampling: The population, the frame, and the sampling unit. *CPA Journal, 74*(11), 30-33. Retrieved August 26, 2007, from EBSCO Online Database Business Source Complete. http://search.ebscohost.com/login.aspx?direct=true&db=bth&AN=15023175&site=ehost-live

Leslie, D., Teitlebaum, A., & Anderson, R. (1980). *Dollar unit sampling: A practical guide for auditors.* London: Pitman.

Mf Saltaji, I. (2013). Corporate governance relationship with strategic management. *Internal Auditing & Risk Management, 8*(2), 293-300. Retrieved November 15, 2013, from EBSCO Online Database Business Source Complete. http://search.ebscohost.com/login.aspx?direct=true&db=bth&AN=90542685&site=ehost-live

Robertson, C., Blevins, D., & Duffy, T. (2013). A five-year review, update, and assessment of ethics and governance in strategic management journal. *Journal of Business Ethics, 117*(1), 85-91. Retrieved November 15, 2013, from EBSCO Online Database Business Source Complete. http://search.ebscohost.com/login.aspx?direct=true&db=bth&AN=90521145&site=ehost-live

Strategic financial planning. (n.d.). *Making ends meet: A website for managing the money in social services.* Retrieved September 3, 2007, from http://www.joint-reviews.gov.uk/ money/Financialmgt/1-22.html

Wang, T., & Bansal, P. (2012). Social responsibility in new ventures: profiting from a long-term orientation. *Strategic Management Journal, 33*(10), 1135-1153.Retrieved November 15, 2013, from EBSCO Online Database Business Source Complete. http://search.ebscohost.com/ login.aspx?direct=true&db=bth&AN=78388200&site=eh ost-live

SUGGESTED READING

Agundu, P. (2005). Strategic management dynamics: Training imperatives for up-moving accounting and financial professionals in the banking industry. *Finance India, 19*(2), 525-533. Retrieved August 26, 2007, from EBSCO Online Database Business Source Complete. http://search.ebscohost.com/login.aspx?direct=true&db=bth&AN=18775463&site=ehost-live

Bromiley, P., & James-Wade, S. (2003). Putting rational blinders behind us: Behavioural understandings of finance and strategic management. *Long Range Planning, 36*(1), 37-49. Retrieved August 26, 2007, from EBSCO Online Database Business Source Complete. http://search.ebscohost.com/

login.aspx?direct=true&db=bth&AN=9340554
&site=ehost-live

Hyperion financial management, strategic finance, reports & analyzer. (2004). *DM Review, 14*(2), 75. Retrieved August 25, 2007, from EBSCO Online

Database Business Source Complete. http://search.ebscohost.com/login.aspx?direct=t rue&d b=bth&AN=12432153&site=ehost-live

—Marie Gould

SUB-PRIME LENDING

ABSTRACT

This article examines the growth of sub-prime lending over the last two decades. The difference between sub-prime loans and traditional prime loans is explained. The benefits of sub-prime loans for borrowers are reviewed along with the problems that sub-prime loans present for borrowers and for the overall economy. Abuses in the sub-prime loan industry, often referred to as predatory lending practices, are explained and efforts to remedy and prevent these abuses are examined. The nature of predatory lending and its impact on individuals, the economy, and society are explained. Major settlements with abusing lending companies over predatory practices are also reviewed.

OVERVIEW

Sub-prime lending is a relatively new and rapidly growing segment of the financial market that provides credit to borrowers who, for one of numerous reasons, would generally not be extended credit. Borrowers, for example, who fail credit history requirements in the standard (prime) mortgage market have greater access to credit in the sub-prime market. One of the major benefits of sub-prime lending is growth in the number of homeowners. Sub-prime lending is also high-cost borrowing for those seeking and accepting such credit. Sub-prime lending cost has two major aspects: Credit history and down payment requirements. This is in contrast to the prime market, where the borrower's cost is primarily driven by the down payment providing they have an adequate credit history (Chomsisengphet & Pennington-Cross, 2006).

Sub-prime lending is often viewed as having both promises and peril for the economy as well as the individual borrower. The plus side is that sub-prime lending provides an opportunity for homeownership to those who would be otherwise excluded from the market because of discrimination or the inability to qualify for a mortgage in the past. Because poor credit history is often associated with more delinquent payments and defaulted loans, the interest rates for sub-prime loans are generally considerably higher than for prime loans (Chomsisengphet & Pennington- Cross, 2006).

Two legislative reforms allowed lenders to deliver risk-adjusted pricing that made loans available to higher-risk mortgage borrowers. The Depository Institutions Deregulatory and Monetary Control Act in 1980 eliminated rate caps and made sub-prime lending more feasible for lenders. In addition, the Tax Reform Act of 1986 eliminated interest deductions on consumer and auto loans while still allowing interest deductions on mortgage debt. According to the Department of Housing and Urban Development (HUD), the number of sub-prime lenders tripled, growing from 70 to 210 between 1994 and 1997. Sub-prime, together with alternative A mortgages, virtually replaced agency (Fannie Mae and Freddie Mac) loans.

However, in the late 1990s, financial troubles hit many sub-prime lenders who were plagued by aggressive accounting policies with respect to property valuations. This forced restatements of financials, which for many essentially wiped out their net worth. As a result of the restatements, several sub-prime lenders filed for bankruptcy and went out of business (White, 2006).

The tradition in the mortgage market was to set minimum lending standards that take into consideration a borrower's income, payment history, and down payment with some input from the local underwriter about their knowledge of the borrower. This is a non-price credit rationing approach. The sub-prime lending market is based on several different pricing tiers and loan types, which to a large extent has helped to move the mortgage market closer to price rationing, or risk-based pricing. Overall, the ultimate success of the sub-prime market will determine to what extent the entire mortgage market incorporates risk-based prices for each borrower (Chomsisengphet & Pennington-Cross, 2006).

Sub-prime lending helps to bring people into the borrowing market who probably would not have other opportunities to obtain credit. But there have definitely been abuses, especially with lending practices for people living in minority neighborhoods where 50% or more of residents are minorities. These borrowers have 35% greater odds of being saddled with prepayment penalties on sub-prime mortgages than borrowers who live in predominantly white neighborhoods (Mink, 2005) (Karger, 2007). These trends exist despite that offering loans at preferable interest rates on the basis of gender or race is illegal in the United States (Tucker, 2007).

Because of a lack of alternatives, sub-prime borrowers were attracted to alternative mortgages that provide for equity growth, which in turn has a positive impact on their credit profile. When interest rates started to rise and housing price appreciation simultaneously slowed, many sub-prime borrowers could not refinance to gain more favorable terms. Many also were unable to maintain their mortgage payments when their loans were adjusted to the higher interest rate. They also could not sell their homes because of a slow down in home sales. In the past, delinquency and default rates were closely linked to local economic conditions. Both delinquency and default rates are rising today even in some locations that have low unemployment and strong economies ("Housing Boom & Bust," 2007).

Trends indicate that the default rate for sub-prime loans is about six times higher than for prime loans. Problems can be compounded because sub-prime borrowers encounter more difficulty in obtaining cheaper loans when interest rates fall. Thus, borrows are locked into high rate loans. This obstacle often results in "reduced access to financial markets, foreclosure, and loss of any equity and wealth achieved through mortgage payments and house price appreciation" (Chomsisengphet & Pennington- Cross, 2006).

APPLICATIONS

REGULATING THE SUB-PRIME MARKETPLACE

Over the last two decades, sub-prime lending programs offered by banks and other lenders have provided financial opportunities for borrowers who had impaired credit or no credit history. Sub-prime lending has supported home mortgages, automobiles, consumer credit, and credit cards. Many community banks have often offered sub-prime loans as part of an outreach program to help meet the requirements of the Community Reinvestment Act. As a result, many families were able to become homeowners because of the accessibility of credit through these programs. Such loans usually served a useful purpose and were distinguishable from sub-prime loans made on predatory terms(Bahin, 2007).

ABUSES

Some lending institutions or companies have been identified as having practices that are considered abusive to the borrowers who most often obtain sub-prime loans. Furthermore, the disclosure of expanded data required to be in compliance with the Home Mortgage Disclosure Act (which exposes pricing data for loans) has led "some groups to conclude that a number of lenders have violated fair lending laws." In addition, there have been "several high-profile cases filed alleging that lenders have violated the Fair Housing Laws and the Equal Credit Opportunity Act" (Bahin, 2007).

LEGAL ACTIONS

Observers have expected that various types of actions will occur over the next few years including:

- Congress will continue to pass legislation that prohibits existing and emerging predatory practices and otherwise regulates the activities in the mortgage industry.
- States will continue to enact laws that impose additional requirements for lenders.
- Federal banking agencies will focus more attention on compliance with laws and regulations on the part of lending organizations.
- More class action suits will be filed on the behalf of borrowers who believe that they have been discriminated against or misled by lenders (Bahin, 2007).

LEGAL SETTLEMENTS

The economic importance of the sub-prime market cannot be understated for the economy as a whole and for the individuals obtaining sub-prime loans. The effects of sub-prime lending are pervasive. The class actions suits that have already been filed (and others are probably still pending) involve a long list of sub-prime lenders and their aggressive lending practices (Koppel, 2007). Well over 20 sub-prime lenders have been closed down or sought buyers over the last few years. These include New Century Financial and General Electric (Stewart, 2007).

Many lenders have been accused of issuing sub-prime mortgages that prey upon the poor or uninformed consumer. The lenders have offered high-risk clients an opportunity at homeownership but with interest rates well above the going rate and above what many borrowers could actually pay (Ordower, 2007). Sub-prime loans that have gone bad have often devastated lenders and set back borrowers financially (Roney, 2007).

In 2006, Ameriquest Mortgage Company decided to settle a complex and multi-state investigation concerning allegedly deceptive consumer lending practices. The settlement was massive and included $295 million to repay borrowers who took out loans between January 1, 1999 and December 31, 2005. In addition, the company agreed to pay $30 million to cover the costs of the investigations.

In 2002, Household Finance Corporation's had nearly $500 million settlement with several states over similar allegations. Citigroup's had a $215 million and another $70 million settlement with the Federal Trade Commission and the Federal Reserve Board over lending practices.

OUTCOMES OF THE SETTLEMENTS

Settlements often required changes in how the lending process is managed and executed. These include several oral disclosures for first lien loans. These disclosures were above and beyond the existing Truth-in-Lending Act (TILA), Real Estate Settlement Procedures Act (RESPA), and other mandated written disclosures that are designed to disclose key loan terms. These include the repayment terms, interest rates, monthly payments, existence of a prepayment penalties, and escrowed amounts, among other points.

In addition, the Ameriquest settlement required the company to provide consumers with a single page

disclosure of the key loan terms within three days of obtaining loan pricing. This disclosure applied sub-prime loans as well as any other loan the company was making. Household was also required to issue the one page summary of key loan terms.

Another key aspect of these types of settlements is a requirement to provide borrowers with a new written summary disclosure if there is a material change in the terms of a loan. The new disclosure must be mailed in a timely manner before closing or otherwise delivered or made available to the consumer at least three days before closing of all loans. Such changes include an increase in interest rates, increase in discount points, increase in repayment terms, decrease in the loan amount greater than one percent, or an addition of a prepayment penalty. Ameriquest was required to use a pricing model for loans. The model is designed to offer the same interest rate and number of discount points to all potential borrowers having the same credit risk characteristics.

Ameriquest specifically faced other numerous restrictions in how it conducted business. The company was prohibited from soliciting borrowers with existing non-prime loans for refinancing within the first 24 months of the loan term unless the company received a request for a pay-off statement or is contacted by a borrower who inquires about refinancing. Ameriquest was also required to use loan closers for the closing of all non-prime loans that are independent of the branch office where the loan is originated and is not a relative of an employee processing the loan. At the closing of a loan, independent loan closers are required to have the borrower sign a statement certifying that:

- The borrower understands that the loan is being approved because of the dollar amount of income reported by the borrower.
- The dollar amount of income reported on the loan application by the borrower is accurate.
- That any false statements about the dollar amount of income of the borrower may subject the borrower to criminal penalties.

The Ameriquest settlement established a model program for dealing with the independence of the appraisal function. This was designed to ensure that the branch office had the absolute smallest role possible in the appraisal process. This was implemented by establishing a panel of qualified, approved appraisers for each state in which the company does business. To become a member of the panel, an appraiser must be in good standing with their state licensing authority. They must also have had their past audit work reviewed for quality and compliance if they had done appraisals for Ameriquest in the past (Mayk, 2007).

ISSUE

THE DYNAMICS & IMPACTS OF PREDATORY LENDING

The marketplace for and the availability of mortgage loans have changed considerably over the past several decades. According to the General Accounting Office (GAO), the biggest change has been the emergence of a market for sub-prime mortgage loans. Most mortgage lending still takes place in the prime market, which involves traditional lenders and borrowers with credit histories that classify them at a low risk of default. However, the sub-prime market serves borrowers who usually have poor credit histories or limited incomes, and who cannot meet the criteria for loans in the prime market.

Because of a lack of regulation in the past, there have been numerous abuses. Predatory lending, which is an umbrella term that is generally used to describe circumstances in which a lender takes unfair advantage of a borrower (including practices such as deception, fraud, or manipulation) to make a loan with terms that are disadvantageous and sometimes very detrimental to a borrower ("Consumer Protection," 2004).

ATTRIBUTES OF PREDATORY LENDING

Predatory lending is difficult to define because various types of loan attributes by themselves may or may not be abusive. However, depending on the context of the loan and the ability of the borrower to repay, terms such as prepayment penalties can be abusive in the context of some loans while not in other loans if they can benefit a borrower. While there is not a universally applied definition of predatory lending, loans based on predatory practices often have the following characteristics and lending practices:

- Excessive fees which generally exceed amounts that can be justified by the costs of the services provided or the credit and interest rate risks involved. Lenders often add these fees to the loan amounts rather than requiring payment up front, and thus the borrowers usually do not know the exact amount of the fees they are being charged.
- Excessive interest rates that are not legitimately based on the credit characteristics of borrowers or the loans themselves. However, in many cases, predatory lenders charge interest rates that far exceed what could possibly be justified by risk-based pricing calculation. In some cases, lenders have steered borrowers that have excellent credit records to higher-rate loans and succeeded in doing so because the borrower is not informed.
- Single-premium credit insurance, a loan feature that repays the lender should the borrower die or become disabled; often the lender adds the full premium for the policy to the total loan amount financed. This practice unnecessarily raises the amount of interest a borrower pays.
- Lending to borrows that do not have the ability to repay often involving loans that have monthly payments that equal or exceed a borrower's total monthly income.
- Flipping loans, a practice where lenders refinance a borrower's loan repeatedly in a short period of time without any benefit to a borrower; because of high fees, this often strips the equity the borrower has in the home being financed.
- Fraud or deceptive practices that predatory lenders may execute such as inflating property appraisals, manipulating or providing false information on loan applications or settlement documents. Such practices can also include bait and switch tactics that mislead potential borrowers about the terms of their loan.
- Excessive prepayment penalties for prepaying a loan that predatory lenders have used to help to trap a borrower into a high-cost loan.
- Predatory loans can contain balloon payments that a borrower is not likely to be able to afford, often resulting in foreclosure or refinancing with additional high costs and fees ("Consumer Protection," 2004).

CAUSES OF PREDATORY LENDING PRACTICES

The General Accounting Office's 2004 report showed that many economic and legal factors contributed to the growth of the sub-prime market and to predatory lending practices. There were "changes in tax laws that increased the tax advantages of home equity loans." There were also "rapidly increasing home prices that provided many consumers with substantial" growth in their home equity. Many loan companies entered into the sub-prime market that had previously made only prime loans. As credit scoring and automated underwriting became more prevalent, it was easier for lenders to price the risks associated with making loans to borrowers with poor credit histories. Sub-prime mortgage loans "grew from $34 billion in 1994 to more than $213 billion in 2002 and in 2002 represented 8.6 percent of all mortgage loans" ("Consumer Protection," 2004, p. 21).

It is rather widely accepted that the majority of predatory lending occurs in the sub-prime market, which has grown dramatically in recent years. There are several reasons why lenders may become predatory. Profit is always the key motive but many practices go far beyond the desire just to maintain the balance sheet. From a business perspective, lenders need to "charge higher interest rates and fees for sub-prime loans than they do for prime loans to compensate for increased risks and for higher servicing and origination costs. In many cases, risks and costs can justify the additional cost of the loan to the borrower, but in other cases such charges may not be justified. Because sub-prime loans involve a greater variety and complexity of risks, they are not the uniformly priced commodities that prime loans generally are. This lack of uniformity makes comparing the costs of sub-prime loans difficult," which can increase a potential borrower's vulnerability to abuse ("Consumer Protection," 2004, p. 21).

Although several advocacy groups take the position that sub-prime lending inherently involves abusive practices in a majority of loan situations, analysts generally contend that "only a small portion of sub-prime loans contain features that are considered abusive. In addition, according to officials at HUD and the Department of the Treasury, the emergence of a sub-prime mortgage market has enabled a whole class of credit-impaired borrowers to buy homes or access the equity in their homes. At the same time, however, federal officials and consumer advocates have expressed concerns that the overall growth in sub-prime lending and home equity lending in general has been accompanied by a corresponding increase in predatory lending. For example, lenders and brokers may use aggressive sales and marketing tactics to convince consumers who need cash to enter

into a home equity loan with highly disadvantageous terms" ("Consumer Protection," 2004, p. 21-22).

THE PROVISION OF SUB-PRIME LOANS

Companies that offer sub-prime loans are most often mortgage and consumer finance companies, but banks, thrifts, and other institutions also offer some sub-prime loans. Some lending companies originators focus primarily on making sub-prime loans, while most offer a variety of prime and sub-prime loans. According to the GAO, HUD identified 178 lenders who concentrated mostly on sub-prime mortgage lending in 2001, and "fifty-nine percent of these lenders were independent mortgage companies (mortgage bankers and finance companies), 20 percent were non-bank subsidiaries of financial or bank holding companies, while the rest were other types of financial institutions" ("Consumer Protection," 2004, p. 22). Only ten percent of the organizations offering sub-prime loans were federally regulated banks and thrifts. As of 2004, there is no set of comprehensive and reliable data available on the extent of predatory lending nationwide. There are several reasons for the lack of data:

- The lack of a standard definition of what constitutes predatory lending makes it inherently difficult to measure
- Any comprehensive data collection on predatory lending would require access to a representative sample of loans and to information that can only be extracted manually from the physical loan files.
- Because such records are not only widely dispersed but also generally proprietary, to date, comprehensive data have not been collected ("Consumer Protection," 2004, p. 23).

EVIDENCE OF PREDATORY LENDING

Data or no data, "policymakers, advocates, and some lending industry representatives have concluded, and expressed concerns, that predatory lending is a significant problem" ("Consumer Protection," 2004, p. 23). Although the extent of predatory lending cannot be readily or easily quantified, there are indicators that suggest that it may be prevalent. The GAO maintains that "primary among these indicators are legal settlements, foreclosure patterns, and anecdotal evidence. In the past several years, there have been major settlements resulting from government enforcement actions and private party lawsuits that accused lenders of predatory and abusive lending practices" ("Consumer Protection," 2004, p. 23).

Among the largest of these settlements have been the following:

- In 2002, Household International agreed to pay up to $484 million to homeowners across the nation to settle allegations by states that it used unfair and deceptive lending practices to make mortgage loans with excessive interest and charges.
- In 2002, Citigroup agreed to pay up to $240 million to resolve charges by FTC and private parties that Associates First Capital Corporation and Associates Corporation of North America (The Associates) systematically engaged in abusive lending practices.
- First Alliance Mortgage Company entered into a settlement in 2002 with FTC, six states, and private parties to compensate nearly 18,000 borrowers more than $60 million dollars ("Consumer Protection," 2004, p. 23-24).

Concerns about predatory lending in the sub-prime market were further fueled by foreclosure trends. Between January 1998 and September 1999, the foreclosure rate on sub-prime mortgages was "more than 10 times the foreclosure rate for prime loans." Although it could be expected that loans made to less creditworthy borrowers could result in a higher rate of foreclosure, the extent of this difference raised flags for the policy makers and analysts. Some analysts suggest that it is "at least partly the result of abusive lending" and particularly of loans made "without regard to the borrower's ability to repay" ("Consumer Protection," 2004, p. 24).

Overall, the rate of foreclosures of sub-prime mortgage loans "increased substantially since 1990, far exceeding the rate of increase" for sub-prime loans that were made to borrowers. A study conducted for HUD noted that while the increased rate in sub-prime foreclosures could be the result of abusive lending, it could also be the result of other factors, such as an increase in sub-prime loans that are made to borrowers with the least ability to repay ("Consumer Protection," 2004; Cutts & Van Order, 2005).

CONCLUSION

Sub-prime lending is a fairly new and quickly growing segment of the financial market that provides credit

to borrowers who, for one of numerous reasons, would generally not be extended credit. Borrowers, for example, who fail credit history requirements in the standard (prime) mortgage market have greater access to credit in the sub-prime market. One of the major benefits of sub-prime lending is the growth in the number of homeowners (Chomsisengphet & Pennington-Cross, 2006).

Sub-prime lending helps to bring people into the borrowing market who probably would not have other opportunities obtain credit. But there have defiantly been abuses, especially with lending practices for people living in minority neighborhoods where residents have 35% greater odds of being saddled with prepayment penalties on sub-prime mortgages than borrowers who live in predominantly white neighborhoods.

In the late 1990s, these lenders were plagued by aggressive accounting policies with respect to property valuations. This forced restatements of financials, which for many essentially wiped out their net worth. As a result of the restatements, several sub-prime lenders filed for bankruptcy and went out of business. Well over 20 sub-prime lenders have been closed down or have sought buyers over the last few years (White, 2006).

Because of a lack of regulation in the past and perhaps hope that the sub-prime market could improve the home sales market while providing more home ownership opportunities for lower income people, there have been numerous abuses. The GAO report describes predatory lending as "an umbrella term that is generally used to describe circumstances in which a lender takes unfair advantage of a borrower (often through deception, fraud, or manipulation) to make a loan with terms that are disadvantageous" and sometimes very detrimental to a borrower (p. 18).

Although several advocacy groups take the position that sub-prime lending inherently involves abusive practices in a majority of loan situations, analysts generally contend that only a small portion of sub-prime loans contain features that are considered abusive. Policymakers, advocates, and some lending industry representatives have concluded that and expressed concerns that predatory lending is a significant problem. Although the extent of predatory lending cannot be readily or easily quantified, there are indicators that suggest that it may be prevalent

("Consumer Protection," 2004).

BIBLIOGRAPHY

Bahin, C. (2007). More regulation of sub-prime lending. *Community Banker, 16*(9), 70-71. Retrieved January 5, 2008, from EBSCO Online Database Business Source Complete. http://search.ebscohost.com/login.aspx?direct= true&db=bth&AN=26467413&site=ehost-live

Chomsisengphet, S., & Pennington-Cross, A. (2006). The evolution of the sub-prime mortgage market. *Review (00149187), 88*(1), 31-56. Retrieved January 5, 2008, from EBSCO Online Database Academic Search Premier. http://search.ebscohost.com/login.aspx?direct=true&db=aph&AN=19628275&site=ehost-live

Consumer protection: Federal and state agencies face challenges in combating predatory lending. (2004, January). United States General Accounting Office (GAO). Washington, D.C. 20548. http://www.gao.gov/new.items/ d04280.pdf

Cutts, A., & Van Order, R. (2005). On the economics of sub-prime lending. *Journal of Real Estate Finance & Economics, 30*(2), 167-196. Retrieved January 5, 2008, from EBSCO Online Database Business Source Complete. http://search.ebscohost.com/login.aspx?direct= true&db=bth&AN=16184490&site=ehost-live

Garwal, S., Amromin, G., Ben-David, I., Chomsisengphet, S., & Evanoff, D. D. (2014). Predatory lending and the subprime crisis. *Journal of Financial Economics, 113*(1), 29–52. Retrieved November 21, 2014, from EBSCO Online Database Business Source Complete. doi:10.1016/j.jfineco.2014.02.008http://search.ebscohost. com/login.aspx?direct=true&db=bth&AN=96021914

Housing boom and bust. (2007). *Congressional Digest, 86*(10), 297-300. Retrieved January 5, 2008, from EBSCO Online Database Academic Search Premier. http://search.ebscohost. com/login.aspx?direct=true&db=aph&AN=28055333&site=ehost-live

Karger, H. (2007). The home ownership myth. *Dollars & Sense,* (270), 13-19. Retrieved January 5, 2008, from EBSCO Online Database Business Source Complete. http://search.ebscohost.com/login.aspx?direct=true&db=bth&AN=25293500&site=ehost-live

Koppel, M., & Wood, R. (2007). Sub-prime lending controversy fuels familiar tax issues. *Tax Adviser, 38*(12), 714-716. Retrieved January 5, 2008, from EBSCO Online Database Business Source Complete. http://search.ebscohost.com/login.aspx?direct=true&db=bth&AN=27714578&site=ehost-live

Makarov, I., & Plantin, G. (2013). Equilibrium Sub-prime Lending. *Journal of Finance, 68*(3), 849–79. Retrieved November 21, 2014, from EBSCO Online Database Business Source Complete. http://search.ebscohost.com/ login.aspx?direct=true&db=bth&AN=87671750

Mayk, J. (2007). Sub-prime lending lessons from the Ameriquest settlement. *Real Estate Finance (Aspen Publishers Inc.), 23*(5), 21-25. Retrieved January 5, 2008, from EBSCO Online Database Business Source Complete. http://search.ebscohost.com/login.aspx?direct= true&db=bth&AN=24474028&site=ehost-live

Mink, M. (2005). Predatory sub-prime mortgages drain wealth. *Credit Union Executive Newsletter, 31*(5), 2-3. Retrieved January 5, 2008, from EBSCO Online Database Business Source Complete. http://search.ebscohost.com/ login.aspx?direct=true&db=bth&AN=16422302&site= ehost-live

Ordower, G. (2007). The loan shark lobby. *Nation, 284*(14), 5-6. Retrieved January 5, 2008, from EBSCO Online Database Academic Search Premier. http://search.ebscohost.com/login. aspx?direct=true&db=aph&AN=24422932&site=ehost-live

Roney, M. (2007, March 12). Sub-prime lending's next act. *Business Week Online,* 8. Retrieved January 5, 2008, from EBCSO Online Database Academic Search Premier. http://search. ebscohost.com/login.aspx?direct=true&db=aph&AN=24370709&site=ehost-live

Stewart, J. (2007). The sub-prime mess. *Smart Money, 16*(6), 35-36. Retrieved January 5, 2008, from EBSCO Online Database Business Source Complete. http://search.ebscohost.com/login.aspx?direct=true&db=bth&AN=25147177&site=ehost-live

Tucker, P. (2007). Sub-prime lenders target women unfairly. *Futurist, 41*(3), 7-7. Retrieved January 5, 2008, from EBSCO Online Database Academic Search Premier. http://search. ebscohost.com/login.aspx?direct=true&db=

aph&AN=24550890&site=ehost-live

White, B. (2006). A short history of sub-prime. *Mortgage Banking, 66*(6), 17-19. Retrieved January 5, 2008, from EBSCO Online Database Business Source Complete. http://search.ebscohost.com/login.aspx?direct=true&db=bth&AN=20182495&site=ehost-live

SUGGESTED READING

Collins, B. (2007). Sub-prime defaults soar in 2006. *Mortgage Servicing News, 11*(3), 1-29. Retrieved January 5, 2008, from EBSCO Online Database Business Source Complete. http://search.ebscohost.com/login.aspx?direct=true&db=bth&AN=25116313&site=ehost-live

Coy, P. (2007, December 17). The sub-prime mess, now in plastic? *Business Week,* (4063), 032. Retrieved January 5, 2008, from EBSCO Online Database Academic Search Premier. http://search.ebscohost.com/login.aspx?direct=true&db=aph&AN=27794791&site=ehost-live

Dymi, A. (2007). Almost half of '06 mortgages to minorities were sub-prime. *National Mortgage News, 32*(4), 2-2. Retrieved January 5, 2008, from EBSCO Online Database Business Source Complete. http://search.ebscohost.com/login.aspx?direct=true&db=bth&AN=27102067&site=ehost-live

England, R. (2007). A cloud over the economy. *Mortgage Banking, 68*(2), 38-48. Retrieved January 5, 2008, from EBSCO Online Database Business Source Complete. http://search.ebscohost.com/login.aspx?direct=true&db=bth&AN=27494340&site=ehost-live

Filisko, G. (2007). Sub-prime lending fallout. *National Real Estate Investor, 49*(7), 93-96. Retrieved January 5, 2008, from EBSCO Online Database Business Source Complete. http://search.ebscohost.com/login.aspx?direct=true&db=bth&AN=25775514&site=ehost-live

Isaac, W. (2007). Worries about sub-prime lending are overblown. *American Banker, 172*(190), 2. Retrieved January 5, 2008, from EBSCO Online Database Business Source Complete. http://search.ebscohost.com/login.aspx?direct=true&db=bth&AN=26937657&site=ehost-live

Live now, pay later. (2007). *Economist,* 383(8523), 31. Retrieved January 5, 2008, from EBSCO Online Database Academic Search Premier. http://

search.ebscohost.com/login.aspx?direct=true&db=aph&AN=24617743&site=ehost-live

Mcgeer, B. (2007). Small bank looks for exit after a sub-prime disaster. *American Banker, 172*(81), 1-4. Retrieved January 5, 2008, from EBSCO Online Database Business Source Complete. http://search.ebscohost.com/login.aspx?direct=true&db=bth&AN=24886251&site=ehost-live

Oshinsky, J., Fleishman, B., Murray, J., & Fields, J. (2007). Insurance coverage for sub-prime lending losses, litigation, and investigations. *Real Estate Finance (Aspen Publishers Inc.), 24*(3), 15-17. Retrieved January 5, 2008, from EBSCO Online Database Business Source Complete. http://search.ebscohost.com/login.aspx?direct=true&db=bth&AN=27143044&site=ehost-live

Smith, M., & Hevener, C. (2014). Subprime lending over time: The role of race. *Journal of Economics & Finance, 38*(2), 321–44. Retrieved November 21, 2014, from EBSCO Online Database Business Source Complete. http://search.ebscohost.com/login.aspx?direct=true&db=bth&AN=94833915

Sub-prime lending. (2007). *National Mortgage News,* 32(10), 1-22. Retrieved January 5, 2008, from EBSCO Online Database Business Source Complete. http://search.ebscohost.com/login.aspx?direct=true&db=bth&AN=27769538&site=ehost-live

Swindell, B. (2007, June 14). Fed hears conflicting testimony on sub-prime market. *CongressDaily,* 4. Retrieved January 5, 2008, from EBSCO Online Database Academic Search Premier. http://search.ebscohost.com/login.aspx?direct=true&db=aph&AN=25421379&site=ehost-live

The gamble on sub-prime. (2006). *Broker Magazine, 8*(7), 34-40. Retrieved January 5, 2008, from EBSCO Online Database Business Source Complete. http://search.ebscohost.com/login.aspx?direct=true&db=bth&AN=21901540&site=ehost-live

White, B. (2007). Sub-prime lending market: Avoiding risk in a risky business. *Mortgage Banking, 67*(8), 19-22. Retrieved January 5, 2008, from EBSCO Online Database Business Source Complete. http://search.ebscohost.com/login.aspx?direct=true&db=bth&AN=25151954&site=ehost-live

–Michael Erbschloe

TRADING & MARKETS

ABSTRACT

This article focuses on how traders and funds have an effect on the financial market. The success of the financial market is important to everyone the world over. The article explores the role of a trader and reviews hedge funds and how their emergence has changed the market.

OVERVIEW

FINANCIAL MARKETS

The success of the financial market is important to everyone across the world. "We live in a world that is shaped by financial markets and we are profoundly affected by their operation. Our employment prospects, our financial security, our pensions, the stability of political systems and nature of the society we live in are all greatly influenced by the operations of these markets" (Fenton-O'Creevy, Nicholson, Soane, & Willman, 2005, p. 1-2). If the market is not healthy, there is potential for crises.

Financial markets could be defined in two ways. The term could refer to organizations that facilitate the trade of financial products or it can refer to the interaction between buyers and sellers to trade financial products. Many who study the field of economics tend to utilize both definitions, but finance scholars more often use the second definition. Economic markets can be both domestic and international.

Financial markets can be seen as an economics term because it highlights how individuals purchase and sell economic securities, merchandise and other products at low transaction prices that emulate effective markets. The overall objective of the process is to gather all of the sellers and put them in one place so that they can meet and interact with potential buyers. The goal is to create a process that will make it easy for the two groups to conduct business.

When looking at the concept of "financial markets" from a finance perspective, one could view financial markets as a way to facilitate the process of raising capital, transferring risk and conducting international trade. The overall objective is to provide an opportunity for those who want capital to interact with those who have capital. In most cases, a borrower will issue an acknowledgement to the lender agreeing to return the capital in full. These receipts are also known as securities and they are both purchasable and sellable. Lenders expect to be compensated for lending the money. Their compensation tends to be made through interests or dividends.

TYPES OF FINANCIAL MARKETS

There are different categories of financial markets, and some of them are:

- **Capital markets.** Capital markets are comprised of primary and secondary financial venues, and are considered a critical factor in American capitalism. Newer securities that were formed more recently are purchased and sold in the primary market and investors sell their securities in the secondary markets. Companies rely on these markets to raise funds for the purchase of equipment required to run the business; conduct research and development; and assist in securing other items needed for the operations of the company.
- **Stock markets** — In order to raise a large amount of cash at one time, public corporations will sell shares of ownership to investors. Investors gain profits when the corporations increase their earnings. Many view the Dow Jones Industrial Average as the stock market, but it is only one of many components. Two other components are the Dow Jones Transportation Average and the Dow Jones Utilities Average. Stocks are traded on world exchanges such as the New York Stock Exchange and NASDAQ.
- **Bond markets** — Bonds are the opposite of stocks. Usually, when stocks go up, bonds go down. The

differing forms that bonds come in include Treasury bonds, corporate bonds, and municipal bonds. The most significant results are usually from mortgage interest rates.

- **Commodity markets.** Commodity markets help the trading of raw or primary commodities run more smoothly. The commodities are traded on regulated commodities exchanges. According to Amadeo (n.d.), the most significant commodity to the American economy is oil, and the cost is decided upon by the commodity's prospective market. Futures "are a way to pay for something today that is delivered tomorrow, which helps to remove some of the volatility in the American economy. However, futures also increase the trader's leverage by allowing him to borrow the money to purchase the commodity. If the trader guesses wrong, it can have a huge impact on the stock market, and the American economy" (Amadeo, n.d., "What are commodities").

- **Money markets.** Money markets offer short-term debt financing and investment. The financial market is the international money market for briefer, more temporary borrowing. The market allows for temporary liquid funding for the international economic system. Borrowers tend to accept loans for shorter time periods that rarely extend beyond 13 months. Money markets trade by using paper as their financial instruments.

- **Derivatives markets.** Derivatives markets offer tools to facilitate the governance of and control over economic risks.

- **Futures markets** Allow for standardized forward contracts that trading products can use in the future.

- **Insurance markets.** Help to further and redistribute the variety of risks that might be dealt with.

- **Foreign exchange markets.** Help to make trading easier for foreign exchange.

- **Hedge fund markets.** In recent times, hedge funds have accelerated in popularity because of their assumed higher returns for high-end financiers. Because hedge funds invest most often and more heavily in future stocks, some investors believe that they have slowed the once steady evaporation of the stock market and, by extension, the American financial state. But in 1997, Long Term Capital Management, the then biggest hedge fund in the world, nearly diminished the U.S. economy entirely (Amadeo, n.d.).

APPLICATION

HEDGE FUNDS

Hedge funds have become popular over the last years due to their ability to take both short (sold) and long (bought) positions (Lubochinsky, Fitzgerald & McGinty, 2002). In other words, positions are "market neutral" but with leverage (Edwards, 1999). The funds are well received because they have the ability to utilize "active management skills to earn positive returns on capital regardless of the market direction" (Lubochinsky, Fitzgerald & McGinty, 2002, p. 33).

A hedge fund is a small group of investors who have formed a private club. Given the extent of the risks involved and the need to bypass regulation, most of the members of the small investor group are high-net-worth investors with over one million dollars in net worth or more than $200,000 in annual income. Therefore, many of the traditional mutual fund investors are not a part of this group. Some of the differences between hedge funds and mutual funds are that hedge funds.

- Can buy a wider variety of securities;
- Are restricted to fewer investors;
- Can try to produce a gain regardless of whether or not stock and bond markets are rising or falling;
- Have not been subjected to strict SEC regulations and disclosure requirements (one exception is the new "funds of funds");
- Tend to concentrate their portfolios in fewer investments;
- Have more leeway to "time" the market;
- Cannot advertise;
- Can limit the number of contributions and withdrawals;
- Have a compensation method based on incentive and management fees that are usually much higher than those for mutual funds; and
- Can invest in long, short and leveraged securities (Evans, Atkinson & Cho, 2005).

The "hedge fund" club will invest in a variety of securities, and they use diverse market philosophies and analytical techniques to develop models that will yield them the greatest return. The models tend to be sophisticated, quantitative and proprietary to the fund.

Most hedge funds have two distinct features. First, the funds need to be what is called absolute return funds. The goal is not to get too many returns over a short benchmark period. Earning the proper absolute returns for the risk at hand is the main goal of the process. The second feature is the funds' use of leverage. The level of leverage involved tends to vary. There are three main mechanisms that hedge funds can leverage into new asset positions. They are: Traditional margin loans have been extended by prime brokers to their clients, fixed income hedge funds make extensive use of repurchase agreements, and leverage can be obtained from the use of all types of derivative positions including future contracts, total return swaps, and options (Lobochinsky, Fitzgerald, & McGinty, 2002).

In addition, there are different types of hedge funds. According to Evans, Atkinson and Cho (2005) the following list is an example of the various types of hedge funds.

- **Relative value (or "arbitrage") funds.** The practice of combining longer security positions with shorter positions that will help to compensate for each other and gather returns that act independently from market movements.
- **Event-driven funds.** Long-term positions that revolve around certain types of business transactions like mergers, acquisitions, and tenders. Such forms of hedge funds often involve lengthy positions in a company's stock that acts as a leading mark for takeover.
- **Equity funds.** Occurs when any type of position is taken in security equities. In addition, focus is given to obtaining a fast and hearty turnaround from businesses that have the potential to increase their standing.
- **Global asset allocator (or "macro") funds.** This is the most diverse and complex global investment. It combines stocks, futures, forward contracts, options and commodities. This type of hedge fund may take a long position in a currency that is undervalued and an equal, short position in another currency that is overvalued.
- **Short-selling funds.** There is a trade with securities or currencies that are considered to be overpriced, but not owned by the hedge fund. The desired outcome is to be able to buy them back at lower prices in order to generate gains.

THE LONG TERM CAPITAL MANAGEMENT (LTCM) COLLAPSE

One of the most important events in hedge fund history involved Long Term Capital Management (LTCM). LTCM collapsed in August, 1998. The event almost caused a crisis in the world economy. What happened? LTCM was a hedge fund that was set up in 1994. Its purpose was to exploit arbitrage opportunities. The investment team included some of the more respected theorists and traders in each respective industry. John Meriwether, a well known trader from Salomon Brothers' arbitrage group, was the leader of the LTCM team.

In the first two years of trading, investors earned approximately 45% in returns. However, the return level dropped significantly in 1997. The fund was operating with funds of $4.7 billion, and loans brought the value of the funds to approximately $125 billion. The objective was to seek assets whose prices were closely related.

Unfortunately, there was a turn of events in the market on August 17, 1998. Russia defaulted on its public debt, and investors began to panic. The reaction caused a negative effect on the market and LTCM found it hard to reposition itself. As a result, LTCN received assistance from a group of fourteen major banks that had been organized by the US Federal Reserve. If the Federal Reserve had not stepped in, LTCM's defaults would have caused many banks around the world to collapse.

VIEWPOINT

TRADERS

"The role and importance of international financial markets and the traders who inhabit them have grown dramatically in the past few decades. The level of financial flows in these markets can rise to quite staggering levels" (Fenton-O'Creevy, Nicholson, Soane, & Willman, 2005, p. 2). Professional traders are highly visible, especially in the media. For example, there have been times when one can get a glimpse of a trading floor on the local news or there is a talk show host interviewing a senior trader to explain the trends and future of the market. In addition, professional traders tend to be in a position to exploit market imperfections and have access to priviledged information, critical mass, or proprietary knowledge and models.

TRADERS & THEIR STRATEGIES

Traders can be divided into three categories, which are trading on behalf of the customer, market making and propriety trading (Abolafia, 1996). Traders with the least amount of risk are the ones who act on behalf of the customer. At the other end of the spectrum are proprietary traders who take on the greatest risk. Regardless of the category, traders tend to utilize a set of strategies and approaches in order to make a profit. Four of the main strategies include:

- **Insider Strategy** — The trader achieves an advantage by exploiting priviledged access to information (Casserley, 1991). However, the trader must be cautious because some of techniques may be illegal. For example, information about company earnings and potential takeovers could be considered illegally obtained information. Insider strategies gives the trader an opportunity to anticipate market movements.
- **Technical Strategy** — Some traders attempt to exploit market imperfections by analyzing past price information. One form of technical strategy involves the use of patterns in price data in order to identify potential turning points in price trends. This is referred to as charting. Traders will attempt to identify trends early, buy into those trends and exit before the trend breaks. There are a number of traders who will use the technical strategy to compliment other techniques.
- **Fundamental Strategy** — Fundamental strategies focus on the relationship between the economic value of the underlying asset and the market price. Traders will use this strategy to seek expertise and information in order to obtain an accurate valuation of securities. There is an assumption that market values will converge to theoretical values.
- **Flow Strategy** — This strategy predicts prices as a function of demand and supply for securities in the market (Fenton-O'Creevy, Nicholson, Soane, and Willman, 2005).

Fenton-O'Creevy, Nicholson, Soane, & Willman (2005) argued that traders had to be comfortable with a certain level of risk. In their minds, most traders: Did not pause to think about the risks that they were taking, see risk as a price to pay in order to achieve what they want or need, have a psychological need to seek out risky ventures, and may have a conception of risk that tends to be irrational and distorted.

CONCLUSION

Financial markets could be defined in two ways. The term could refer to organizations that facilitate the trade of financial products or it can refer to the interaction between buyers and sellers to trade financial products. Many who study the field of economics tend to utilize both definitions, but finance scholars more often use the second definition. Economic markets can be both domestic and international.

Most hedge funds have two distinct features. First, the funds tend to be what is called absolute return funds. The goal is not to earn excess returns over a fixed benchmark. It is to earn the appropriate absolute returns for the risk that is involved. The second feature is the funds use of leverage. The level of leverage used by hedge funds tends to vary. There are three main mechanisms that hedge funds can leverage new asset positions. They are: Traditional margin loans extended by prime brokers to their clients, fixed income hedge funds make extensive use of repurchase agreements, with leverage obtained from the use of all types of derivative positions including future contracts, total return swaps, and options (Lobochinsky, Fitzgerald, & McGinty, 2002).

Evans, Atkinson, and Cho (2005) created a list of typical risks associated with hedge funds. Examples of such risk include:

- **Political risk.** When an investment is made in a foreign nation and under the laws and sovereignty of that nation, the risk is loss due to possible nationalization.
- **Transfer risk.** This occurs when a foreign government restricts the delivery of a foreign currency.
- **Settlement risk.** A dispute between the parties to a contract could prevent the fulfillment of the contract in accordance with its stated terms.
- **Credit risk.** This happens when the counter party to a contract does not perform due to insolvency.
- **Legal risk.** This occurs when the contract is declared unenforceable due to legal problems.
- **Market risk.** Market movements can cause losses.
- **Liquidity risk.** This occurs when a market dries up and it becomes impossible to liquidate a position.
- **Operations risk.** Clerical errors can cause risk (Evans, et. al., 2005).

Traders can be divided into three categories, which are trading on behalf of the customer, market making and propriety trading (Abolafia, 1996). Traders with the least amount of risk are the ones who act on behalf of the customer. At the other end of the spectrum are proprietary traders who take on the greatest risk. Regardless of the category, traders must utilize a set of strategies and approaches in order to make a profit.

BIBLIOGRAPHY

Abolafia, M. (1996). *Making markets: opportunism and restraint on Wall Street.* Cambridge, MA: Harvard University Press.

Amadeo, K. (n.d.) An introduction to the financial markets. Retrieved on July 31, 2007, from http://useconomy.about.com/od/themarkets/a/capital%5fmarkets.htm.

Casserley, D. (1991). *Facing up to the risks.* New York: John Wiley & Sons, Inc.

Edwards, F. (1999). Hedge funds and the collapse of long term capital management. *Journal of Economic Perspective, 13*(2), 189-210.

Evans, T., Atkinson, S., & Cho, C. (2005). Hedge fund investing. Retrieved September 10, 2007, from https://www.aicpa.org/PUBS/jofa/feb2005/evans.htm.

Fenton-O'Creevy, M., Nicholson, N., Soane, E., & Willman, P. (2005). *Traders: Risks, decisions, and management in financial markets.* Oxford: Oxford University Press.

Lubochinsky, C., Fitzgerald, M., & McGinty, L. (2002). The role of hedge funds in international financial markets. *Banca Monte dei Paschi di Siena SpA, 31*(1), 33-57.

SUGGESTED READING

Blumberg, D. (2007). Bond prices recover from Friday's fall. *Wall Street Journal — Eastern Edition, 250*(7), c9.

Dorr, D. (2007). Longevity trading: Bridging the gap between the insurance markets and the capital markets. *Journal of Structured Finance, 13*(2), 50-53.

Ewing, J. (2007, August 2). Deutsche bank calms jittery markets. *Business Week Online,* 20. Retrieved August 26, 2007, from EBSCO Online Database Business Source Complete. http://search.ebscohost.com/login.aspx?direct=t rue&db=bth&AN=2 6053448&site=ehost-live

—Marie Gould

TRADING COSTS

ABSTRACT

Trading costs are defined as the costs associated with trading securities. Trading costs are impacted by explicit costs, bid-ask spread, market impact and opportunity costs. Actively managed funds incur much higher costs than passively managed index funds or broad-based exchange funds. Over the life of an investment fund, the trading and management costs can have a significant negative impact on portfolio return. Many of the costs associated with trading are hidden from investors. Hidden costs include: Brokerage commissions, direct trading costs and soft dollars. Soft dollars, or in-kind business agreements, are exchanges between institutional investors and service providers. Soft dollars are under scrutiny by Congress and the Securities and Exchange Commission and will require greater disclosure to account for where soft dollars are actually being applied. Trading costs associated with mutual fund trading comprise a significant amount of money for investors over time and can adversely affect wealth creation for individual investors. Savvy investors will educate themselves about all the costs associated with their investment funds and look for better investment opportunities. Two such options exist in low-cost funds such as passively managed index funds and exchange-traded funds which incur significantly lower trading costs to investors over the life of their investments.

OVERVIEW

A recent study entitled "Scale Effects in Mutual Fund Performance: The Role of Trading Costs" by Gregory Kadlec, Roger Edelen and Richard Evens examines the effects that different trading costs have on mutual fund performance. The trio studied the performance of 1,706 funds from 1995-2005 in what may be the most comprehensive study to-date about the factors that affect mutual fund performance — specifically related to fund trading and costs. "Scale effects in trading, rather than other factors in fund management are the primary cause of diminishing returns to scale in the mutual fund industry" (Wasik, 2006).

The trading costs associated with mutual funds are significant to this discussion because of the significant numbers of individual investors that have money invested in these funds. About 50% of adults invest in mutual funds, according to 2006 estimates and the number is expected to grow. Mutual funds are popular with individuals because they offer professional portfolio management across a diverse number of funds and require a minimum investment to get started. Mutual funds are a ubiquitous investment choice for Americans and an investment option that most working persons are familiar with. Many of the trading costs associated with mutual funds are also associated with trading of stocks and other securities. This essay discusses common trading costs associated with trading stocks and those costs that are unique to mutual fund trading.

THE TWO TRADING COSTS

Trading costs can add up for investors in a number of ways, but there are really two distinct costs associated with trading. They are:

- Gross cost, or, the total cost to trade (brokerage commission, bid-ask, cost per trade-market forces).
- Net cost, or, the cost of fund performance caused by trading (portfolio turnover and scale effects).

Gross costs can be broken into a number of generally agreed upon categories. These include:

- Explicit Costs (brokerage commissions, fees and taxes).
- Market Maker Spread (also known as the bid-ask spread and is essentially the difference between the bid and ask prices that the fund specialist sets for a stock; the specialist keeps the difference as compensation for facilitating the "deal").
- Market Impact (the affect that high volume trades have on influencing the market. The impact can be temporary or permanent).
- Opportunity Cost (cost of a missed opportunity or next best choice when making a trading decision.

In trading, there is a price movement that occurs before the trade executes) (Trading Costs, 2007).

EXPENSE RATIOS

A mutual fund's expense ratio is the measure of what it costs an investment company to operate a mutual fund. This figure is readily available to the investor and includes operating expenses, management fees, administration fees and all asset based costs. Expense ratios do not include brokerage fees, trading fees or soft dollar costs. The Net Asset Value of a fund records all fund expenses but doesn't break out some of the hidden costs, making many trading costs invisible to the investor.

Fund operating expenses vary widely depending on the type of fund. The largest component of operating expense is the fee paid to a fund's investment manager/advisor. Other costs include record-keeping, custodial services, taxes, legal expenses, and accounting and auditing fees. Some funds have a marketing cost referred to as a 12b-1 fee, which would also be included in operating expenses. Curiously, a fund's trading activity (the buying and selling of portfolio securities) is not included in the calculation of the expense ratio (Investopedia, 2007).

Trading costs associated with mutual funds impact individual investors in obvious and non-obvious ways; specifically through the gross and net costs defined previously. Trading costs associated with buying and selling stocks and securities also have a great impact on retail and institutional investors. Trading costs can adversely affect the performance of funds for investors as will be shown in subsequent discussions. Non-obvious costs such as brokerage commissions and soft dollar costs can affect fund performance and add on significant costs for investors. Much scrutiny has been given to the need for increased disclosure and transparency in documenting trading costs for investors. This essay will outline legislative efforts that are underway to offer investors information regarding "hidden" trading costs. Alternatives to costly managed funds, such as index funds and exchange traded funds will also be discussed. Passively managed index funds and lower-cost exchange traded funds (ETFs) can increase fund performance and shareholder value through reduced trading costs for investors and significantly improve return on investment.

APPLICATIONS

BROKERAGE COSTS

Brokerage commissions have long been public, albeit buried in fund prospectuses and documents called Statements of Additional Information. Despite this, commissions account for only about 20% of the true costs of trading (Goldberg, 2007).

Broker commissions may only account for 20% of the true costs of trading, but there is still room for abuse in passing along the cost of inflated commissions to investors. Because broker commissions are not revealed in expense ratios, the costs are often hard to discern.

The following example illustrates how broker commissions can affect a fund's performance when other factors are equal. This example examines two funds (Fidelity Discovery and Mairs & Power Growth) that reported similar (strong) market returns and identical expense ratios in the same year.

"Both funds charged 0.7 percent for finding large-company stocks trading on the cheap. Those expense ratios, however, don't tell the whole story. All funds (even index funds) ring up brokerage costs when they buy and sell stocks — costs that aren't included in the expense ratio. Instead, they are plucked from a fund's assets — and they add up quickly" (Wherry, 2006). By flipping its portfolio 2.3 times in 2005, Fidelity Discovery racked up $65 in brokerage commissions for every $10,000 invested, nearly doubling the fund's published expenses. Meanwhile, Mairs & Power Growth, known for its long view, sat on its picks. Its tiny 3 percent turnover added just a penny in trading costs. (That same year, Mairs & Power Growth gained 4.4 percent, versus Discovery's 2.1 percent return — though the disparity isn't due solely to trading costs) (Wherry, 2006).

Broker commissions are directly related to portfolio turnover because brokerage costs get rung up every time stocks are bought and sold. Flipping a portfolio can rack up big commissions, but doesn't necessarily benefit the investor as is seen in the example above.

Mutual fund brokerage commissions and implicit trading costs vary significantly among various types and styles of domestic equity funds, and when summed they are not infrequently larger than a fund's regulatory expense ratio. This is true in the

current study for the Vanguard 500 Index Fund. The continuing bad news is that disclosure of brokerage commissions and implicit trading costs remains effectively hidden and completely hidden, respectively, from fund shareholders (Haslem, 2006).

PORTFOLIO TURNOVER

Portfolio turnover, as previously discussed, has a direct affect on brokerage commissions; every time a stock is bought or sold, trading costs add up. There's no evidence that portfolio turnover positively impacts a fund's performance, often because value is eaten up by higher trading costs and commission rates.

Studies have failed to find any long-term causal correlation between higher priced investment managers and more robust return on investments. Admittedly, as with most rules, exceptions do exist, and you may find a pricey manager who can demonstrably handle your plan investments with an excellence that warrants the extra cost. Over time, though, such exceptions are rare. If plan assets are invested in high-turnover funds, the upfront management fees may look fairly innocuous, but that may mask the fact that trading costs are capturing even more of your assets than the management fees themselves. Studies have shown high portfolio turnover rates can add significant additional amounts to the total cost of plan investments (Bowe, 2006). "Portfolio turnover [a hot topic these days] is a measure of how frequently a portfolio's securities are bought and sold. Turnover in a portfolio has a cost — the cost of buying and selling securities or other investments. A 100% rate, for instance, would signal that your fund manager, on average, doesn't hold any investment in the portfolio for more than a year" (Bowe, 2006).

SCALE EFFECTS ON MUTUAL FUND PERFORMANCE

The 2007 report titled "Scale Effects in Mutual Fund Peformance: The Role of Trading Costs" states that buying and selling stocks costs an averaged of 1.44% annually in fund trading costs that are passed along to investors. What kind of fund is traded and why the fund manger is buying or selling a stock also impacts the costs to investors. Trading does tend to boost performance when managers make informed decisions about trades and when executed, does add value to the fund. As much as 30% of all trading is executed due to investors moving in or out of funds. These trades are simply executed by a fund manager as a service to the investor, rather than a conscious, researched trade by the manager. Trading resulting from investors moving in and out of funds has been found to reduce fund performance by 1.4 % points per year. A similar scenario for trading has to do with fund managers rebalancing funds to stay within defined fund parameters. In both of these cases, trading is executed by a manger in an administrative capacity. Studies show that on average, every dollar spent on trading, costs investors 42 cents in fund performance. If one were to multiply the 1.44% spent annually on trading by 42 cents, the cost to fund performance is calculated at 0.60% of performance annually (Goldberg, 2007).

Large trades cost more to execute than small trades. A fund manager who wants to divest of a large number of stocks from a portfolio will sell blocks of stocks over time. Divesting of large numbers of stocks inevitably pushes the price of the stock down as a result of the increase of stock for sale (supply and demand). Delaying the sale over a period of time can also cost a fund (delays in selling can cost) which is also known as an opportunity cost. The report also points out numerous other factors that may affect trading costs.

SIZE OF COMPANY

Domestic stock funds spend an average of 1.44% annually on buying and selling stocks and every dollar spent on trading, costs investors 42 cents in fund performance (Goldberg, 2007).

Compare the trading costs in % listed below, and one can easily see how the size a company or the type of fund compares to the average of 1.44. To calculate the cost of performance to the fund one must multiply the % given by 0.42 cents.

The biggest predictor of total trading costs is the size of the companies in which a fund specializes. These percentages show the total annual trading cost passed on to investors. Trading cost for small cap companies are much higher than for large cap companies (Goldberg, 2007).

- Small cap companies = 2.85%
- Mid cap companies = 1.73%
- Large cap companies = 0.77%

TYPE OF FUND

Another predictor of total trading costs has to do with the type of fund in a portfolio. Value funds cost less in terms of trading cost than do growth funds (Goldberg, 2007). Value funds are considered to be undervalued in price, while growth stocks are expected to grow at an above average rate relative to the market. Compared to the annual fund average of 1.44%, both value and growth stocks are higher than the industry average, but value stocks cost the investor less in terms of fund performance and therefore are a better place to invest.

- Value funds = 1.21%
- Growth funds = 1.84%

SIZE OF FUND

Size of funds by asset has significant impact on the cost per trade. Larger funds with lots of assets suffered fund performance while fund performance improved for trades in small funds. These findings bolster the case for investing in funds with small asset bases to improve fund performance (Goldberg, 2007).

- Large funds. For every $1.00 spent on trading costs, large fund performance drops by 88 cents.
- Small fund. For very $1.00 spent on trading costs, small fund performance improved by 38 cents.

ISSUES

SOFT DOLLARS

Soft dollars are payments made by institutional investors (administrators of mutual funds and other money managers) to providers of services such as trading and research. The difference between soft dollars and hard dollars is that instead of paying the service providers with cash ("hard" dollars); the mutual fund will pay in-kind with brokerage business ("soft" dollars) (Wayman, 2004).

Soft dollars don't leave a paper trail the way that hard dollars (fee for services) do. Soft dollar costs, most often designated for research, are hidden in trading costs and passed along to investors. The disadvantage to investors, of course, is that they don't have a direct way of analyzing the soft dollar costs between differing funds. Since soft dollars mix up research with trading costs, there's increasing suspicion around the practice. It is not a question of who will pay for the research costs; investors will ultimately end up paying for all costs associated with fund maintenance.

Soft dollars have been around since 1975 when their use was made legal by the addition of section 28(e) to the Securities and Exchange Commission (SEC) Act of 1934. Since then, the use of soft dollars has increased greatly and also the questions surrounding what services are actually being provided in exchange for the soft dollars.

The lack of transparency surrounding the use of soft dollars has sparked a number of regulatory and legislative efforts since 2001. The timeline below outlines some of the efforts by Congress and the SEC to address various issues (Bresiger, 2007):

- 2003 House Financial Services Committee hearings.
- 2004 Sen. Fitzgerald's Mutual Fund Reform Act.
- 2005 Mutual Funds Integrity and Fee Transparency Act.
- 2006 SEC interpretive ruling.
- 2007 Chris Cox letter to Congress concerning Soft Money.

The SEC's 2007 statement of soft dollars was clear in determining that commission revenues or soft dollars could be used for research as long as documentation exists to insure that soft dollars don't go toward funding overhead. Commission sharing, popular in the UK, was also supported by the SEC. Commission sharing states that funds can direct a portion of feed to cover broker/dealer trading costs and the remainder to research from a different source as long as there was full disclosure in accounting for the particular costs.

In 2007, Chris Cox (chairman of the SEC) sent a letter to Congress outlining four concerns regarding soft money:

- Soft dollars may create conflicts of interest between money managers and clients.
- Soft dollars may contribute to higher brokerage costs.
- Soft dollars are difficult to administer.
- Soft dollars impede development of efficient markets.

Research services from third party research firms were estimated at $9.31 billion in 2004 and are expected to grow to nearly $12 billion by 2009. With increased pressure by the SEC and Congress for transparency in reporting where soft dollars are spent, independent research firms are well positioned to track and document research costs. Independent research firms focus on companies and funds generally ignored by large brokerage firms whose focus is generally on large cap stocks.

The use of soft dollars is pervasive by brokerage firms and fund managers and while its practice is legal, there is much concern about just how costly the practice is to investors. Investors aren't fully aware of the practice of soft dollar payments and many are unaware that they are unwittingly paying for the practice through their fund assets. Documented cases of abuse of soft dollar payments are common and as such, more accountability to asset owners (investors) will be forthcoming.

ETF & INDEX FUNDS TO LOWER COSTS
Much has been written about the costs that investors have had to shoulder due to inflated trading costs and unscrupulous practices by fund managers. There is some good news for investors who want to fight back and take control of their investment portfolios. Bright spots for investors include the capability to invest in low cost funds that offer significantly reduced trading costs.

Exchange Traded Funds (ETFs) follow index benchmarks like the S&P 500; they also track sectors like energy, financials and health care. Once the investment choice for institutional and retail clients, exchange traded funds are becoming a popular investment option for the individual investor. The ETF is similar to a mutual fund in that it allows an investor to own a fractional share in a portfolio. This ownership of a small piece of a security is similar to ownership in a traditional mutual fund. ETFs are traded on the stock exchange and the value fluctuates during the day. Mutual fund values are based on the value of the fund at market close. Benefits of ETFs include:

- Lower cost to purchase than mutual funds.
- Lower expenses.
- ETFs are an efficient taxable investment; the implications are similar to the sale of stock.

Much of the recent movement to ETFs in the qualified plan marketplace is the result of both the Department of Labor's and the general media's focus on retirement plan expenses. ETFs can typically provide lower costs in the institutional and individual marketplace; however, to achieve the cost savings from the ETF in a 401(k) plan, the provider must determine how to reduce trading commissions to make the low expense ratio become a benefit to participants that is not offset by trading costs (Robertson, 2005).

If the lower expenses proffered by ETF providers are true, the potential savings from ETF offerings in a 401(k) plan can be significant. ETF providers estimate that the savings from an all-ETF platform are as high as one percent of plan assets, depending on the cost ratio of the 401(k) platform. In other words, a plan with $1 million in plan assets could save $10,000 per year. For a participant over 30 years, that one-percent savings could be worth as much as an additional $200,000 or more for retirement (assuming growth at 8 percent per year, $12,000 per year contribution, and $50,000 balance) (Robertson, 2005).

The cost savings related to reducing the ratio expense for a given mutual fund cannot be overstated. The following example further illustrates the impact that mutual fund expenses can have on a stock market that is delivering modest returns.

"Over the next ten to twenty years, expense ratios and similar fees could be a huge millstone on wealth accumulation and wealth preservation. [For example] from the peak of March 2000 to the lows of early October 2002, it's estimated that falling stock prices wiped out over $7 trillion in market value. How long will the market take to "heal itself?" It could take a long time. A growing consensus holds that stocks just won't deliver the returns we grew accustomed to from 1984 to 1999. If history is a guide, real stock returns could average 2 to 4 percent a year over the next 10 to 20 years. If lower expectations for stock returns materialize, mutual fund fees and expenses will have an even greater adverse impact on wealth accumulation and especially on wealth preservation and income security at retirement. Let's say you'll want $40,000 income from your 401(k) assets without drawing down principal. If real investment return is 4 percent you'll need $40,000 divided by 0.04 or $1 million principal. But if you're paying 1 percent in fees your real return is 3 percent, so you'll need $40,000 divided by 0.03 or $1.333 million principal; and if 2 percent, $2 million. The arithmetic is brutal!" (Lemoine, 2003).

CONCLUSION

Trading costs can adversely affect the performance of an investment fund. High turnover of funds adds to brokerage fees and erodes investor assets by eating away at market gains. Individual investors are unaware of many hidden trading costs associated with the management and trading of mutual funds. Fund managers accept soft dollars in return for quid-pro-quo relationships between brokerage houses; while the practice of accepting soft dollars is legal, the SEC is siding with the investor in requiring more disclosure of where soft dollars are spent. There is a growing chorus of criticism regarding the secrecy and obfuscation surrounding trading cost to investors. There's vocal support for much more full and transparent disclosure for the following costs: Brokerage commissions, direct trading costs and soft dollars. Predictions are that funds administrators will work toward more successfully disclosing this information to investors in the future due to increased pressure. Finally, investors are moving away from actively managed funds and the high trading costs associated with them. Investors are including more passively managed funds in their portfolios. Index funds and ETFs are popular choices for investors and more companies are offering these lower cost options to investors along with their more traditional funds offerings. Investors are more aware than ever of the impact that trading costs are having on their individual wealth creation. Individual investors are calling for more accountability from fund administrators and are increasingly unwilling to absorb what they see as unnecessarily high trading costs.

BIBLIOGRAPHY

Anand, A., Irvine, P., Puckett, A., & Venkataraman, K. (2012). Performance of institutional trading desks: An analysis of persistence in trading costs. *Review of Financial Studies, 25*(2), 557-598. Retrieved November 15, 2013, from EBSCO Online Database Business Source Complete. http://search.ebscohost.com/login.aspx?direct=true&db=bth&AN=70438142&site=ehost-live

Bowe, S. (2006). Be aware and be fair: What fiduciaries need to know about plan expenses. *Benefits & Compensation Digest, 43*(1), 25-30. Retrieved September 28, 2007, from EBSCO Online Database Business Source Premier. http:// search.ebscohost.com/login.aspx?direct=true&db=buh&A

N=19450815&site=ehost-live

Bresiger, G. (2007). Soft-dollar bill on the horizon. *Traders Magazine, 20*(269), 22-24. Retrieved September 28, 2007, from EBSCO Online Database Business Source Premier. http://search. ebscohost.com/login.aspx?direct=true&db=b uh&AN=25939015&site=ehost-live

Damodaran, A. (n.d.). Trading costs and taxes. New York University. Retrieved September 28, 2007, from http:// pages.stern.nyu.edu/~adamodar/ pdfiles/invphiloh/tradingcosts.pdf

Edelen, R., Evans, R., & Kadlec, G. (2013). Shedding light on "invisible" costs: Trading costs and mutual fund performance. *Financial Analysts Journal, 69*(1), 33-44. Retrieved November 15, 2013, from EBSCO Online Database Business Source Complete. http://search.ebscohost.com/ login.aspx?direct=true&db=bth&AN=85390012 &site=ehost-live

Goldberg, S. (2007). Why trading costs so much. *Kiplingers. com* Retrieved September 28, 2007, from http://www.kiplinger.com/columns/value/archive/2007/va0717.htm

Glover, H. (2006). SEC rule boosts soft-dollar spending. *Money Management Executive, 14*(30), 1-15. Retrieved September 28, 2007, from EBSCO Online Database Business Source Premier. http:// search.ebscohost.com/ login.aspx?direct=true&d b=buh&AN=21878313&site=eh ost-live

Haslem, J. (2006). Assessing mutual fund expenses and transaction costs. *Journal of Investing, 15*(3), 52-56. Retrieved October 2, 2007, from EBSCO Online Database Business Source Premier. http:// search.ebscohost.com/login.aspx?di rect=true&d b=buh&AN=22462526&site=ehost-live

Lemoine, A. (2003). Advice — mutual-fund expenses. *The Investment FAQ.* Retrieved October 1, 2007, from http:// invest-faq.com/cbc/adv-mfund-expenses.html

Robertson, J. (2005). Lower costs or hidden problems: The legal concerns for ETFs in 401(k) plans. *Journal of Pension Benefits: Issues in Administration, 13*(1), 33-36. Retrieved September 28, 2007, from EBSCO Online Database Business Source Premier. http://search.ebscohost.com/login.aspx?direct=t rue&db=buh&AN=18419831 &site=ehost-live

The bid ask spread. (2000). *Investor Home.* Retrieved September 28, 2007, from http://www.investorhome.com/ daytrade/spread.htm

Trading costs. (n.d.). *QuickMBA.* Retrieved September 28, 2007, from http://www.quickmba. com/finance/invest/ tradecost/

Waskik, J. (2007). Soft-dollar, trading costs devour fund returns. *Bloomberg.* Retrieved September, 28, 2007, from http://www.bloomberg.com/apps/ news?pid=20601039&ref er=columnist%5fwasik& sid=aPUdYOylNPTE

Wayman, R. (2004). Soft dollars: The good, the bad and the ugly. *Research Stock.* Retrieved October 1, 2007, from http://www.researchstock.com/cgi-bin/rview. cgi?c=bulls&rsrc=RC-20040128-F

Wherry, R. (2006). Upfront fees, backdoor costs. *Smart Money, 15*(11), 28-28. Retrieved October 2, 2007, from EBSCO Online Database Business Source Complete. http://search.ebscohost.com/login.aspx?direct=true&db=bt h&AN=22756919&site=ehost-live

What are soft dollars and why should investors be aware of them? *Investopedia.* Retrieved September 29, 2007, from http://www.investopedia.com/ ask/answers/04/011404.asp

SUGGESTED READING

Hume, L. (2006). NASD fines American funds $5M. *Financial Planning, 36*(10), 32-32. Retrieved October 2, 2007, from EBSCO Online Database Business Source Premier. http:// search.ebscohost.com/login.aspx?direct=tru e&db=buh&AN=22895009&site=ehost-live

Robertson, J. (2005). Lower costs or hidden problems: The legal concerns for ETFs in 401(k) plans. *Journal of Pension Benefits: Issues in Administration, 13*(1), 33-36. Retrieved September 28, 2007, from EBSCO Online Database Business Source Premier. http://search.ebscohost.com/login.aspx?direct=t rue&db=buh&AN=18419831 &site=ehost-live

Soft dollar standards. (2004). *Centre for Financial Market Integrity.* Retrieved September 30, 2007, from http:// www.cfainstitute.org/centre/ethics/ softdollar/pdf/ SoftDollarStandards2004.pdf

—Carolyn Sprague

U

USE OF MANAGERIAL ECONOMICS IN FINANCE

ABSTRACT

This article focuses on how financial professionals utilize managerial economics in making decisions to resolve business problems. Managerial economics highlights how financial professionals make decisions regarding resource allocation, strategic, and tactical issues that relate to all types of firms from an economic perspective. Profits and wealth maximization are key factors in managerial economics. Profits are very crucial to a firm's bottom line, and wealth maximization is a long term operational goal. Market structures take into consideration: The number of firms in an industry, the relative size of the firms (industry concentration), demand conditions, ease of entry and exit, and technological and cost conditions.

OVERVIEW

Managerial economics highlights how financial professionals make decisions regarding resource allocation, strategic, and tactical issues that relate to all types of firms from an economic perspective. These professionals use a series of techniques in order to find the most efficient way to reach the best decisions for the firm. The major emphasis is to provide the analytical tools and managerial insights essential to the analyses and solutions of those problems that have significant economic consequences, both for the firm and for the world economy.

Managerial economics occurs when the fundamental principles of microeconomics is applied in the decision making process of business and managerial problems. It can be applied to problems in private, public and non-profit organizations. According to Skim and Siegel (1998), the basic steps in the decision making process are:

- **Recognize and define the problem.** Once a problem has been identified, an exact statement describing the problem should be prepared.
- **Select a goal.** Is it profit maximizing or cost minimizing?
- **Identify any constraints.** All possible constraints need to be identified.
- **Identify alternatives or define decision variables a firm is trying to solve for.**
- **Select the alternative consistent with the firm's objectives or determine the optimal solution** (i.e. profit-maximizing or cost-minimizing solution), p. 3.

Managerial economics connects the practical and theoretical aspects of economics. Many economists will utilize a variety of techniques from other business fields such as finance and operations management. Most business decisions can be analyzed with the techniques used in managerial economics. However, it is most often used in:

- **Risk Analysis** Assorted uncertainty models, decision guidelines, and risk quantification methods help to interpret how much risk is involved in a given arrangement of decision.
- **Production Analysis** Microeconomics methods help to assess the effectiveness of production, the best factor distribution, the costs involved, the frugality of scale and the company's estimated cost function.
- **Pricing Analysis** — Microeconomic methods facilitate the analysis of multiple pricing options that involve transfer costs, joint product costs, cost discrimination, cost elasticity approximations, and deciding upon the right pricing technique for the job.
- **Capital Budgeting** — Investment theory allows for the examination of a corporation's capital purchasing decision.

Managerial economics is "the systematic studies of how resources should be allocated in such a way to most efficiently achieve a managerial goal" (Shim & Siegel, 1998, p. 2).

PROFITS

Profits are very crucial to a firm's bottom line. When a firm is able to make a profit, there is an assumption that the company has done a good job of effectively and efficiently in controlling cost while producing a quality product or performing a quality service. However, there are different types of profits. Two types of profits are accounting profits and economic profits. Accounting profits are determined by the difference between the total revenue and the cost of producing products or services, and they appear on the firm's income statement. Economic profits are determined by the difference between total revenue and the total opportunity costs. The opportunity costs tend to be higher than accounting and book-keeping costs.

Profits tend to vary across industries, and there are a number of theories that attempt to provide an explanation as to why this occurs. Five of the most discussed theories in this area are:

- Risk-Bearing Theory. When the owners of a company make investments into the firm, they take on a certain amount of risk. In order to compensate them for their investment, the company will need to have an above average return on economic profits. An example would be a firm that has investors such as venture capitalists or angel investors.
- Dynamic Equilibrium Theory. Every firm should strive to have a normal rate of profit. However, each firm has the opportunity to earn returns above or below the normal level at any time.
- Monopoly Theory. There are times when one firm may have the opportunity to dominate in its industry and earn above normal rates of return over a long period of time. These firms tend to dominate the market as a result of economies of scale, control of essential natural resources, control of crucial patents and/or government restrictions. An example would be utility companies.
- Innovation Theory. A firm may earn above normal profits as a reward for its successful innovations, such as patents. An example would be a pharmaceutical organization such as Astra Zeneca.
- Managerial Efficiency Theory. A firm may be able to earn above average profits based on its strong leadership team. This type of organization gains profits as a result of being effective and efficient. An example would be General Electric under Jack Welch's leadership.

WEALTH MAXIMIZATION

Wealth maximization is a long term operational goal. Shareholders have a residual claim on the firm's net cash flows after expected contractual claims have been paid. All other stakeholders (i.e. employers, customers) have contractual expected returns. There tends to be a preference for wealth maximization because it takes into consideration (Shim & Siegel, 1998):

- Wealth for the long term
- Risk or uncertainty
- The timing of returns
- The stockholders' return.

Criterion for this goal suggests that a firm should review and assess the expected profits and or cash flows as well as the risks that are associated with them. When conducting this evaluation, there are three points to keep in mind. First, economic profits are not equivalent to accounting profits. Second, accounting profits are not the same as cash flows. Lastly, financial analysis must focus on maximization of the present value of cash flows to the owners of the firm when attempting to maximize shareholder wealth.

When making decisions, the financial management team has to anticipate certain factors and realize that they may not have control over some of them. Factors outside of their control tend to be ones that are a part of the economic environment.

- Factors under administrative command
- Products and services made available
- Production technology
- Marketing and distribution
- Investment plans of action
- Employment policies and compensation
- Ownership form
- Capital structure
- Successful capital management tactics
- Dividend policies
- Alliances, mergers, spinoffs
- Factors not under management control
- Level of economic activity
- Tax rates and regulations
- Competition
- Laws and government regulations
- Unionization of employees
- International business conditions and currency exchange rates

In order for wealth maximization to be at the optimal level, certain conditions need to be in place. The process has a good chance to be successful when:

- **Complete markets are secure.** Liquid markets are needed for the firm's inputs, products and by-products.
- **There is no asymmetric information.** Buyers and sellers have the same information and no information is hidden from either group.
- **All re-contracting costs are known.** Managers know or expect the exact impending input costs as a portion of the current worth of anticipated cash flows.

When one reviews the wealth maximization model, there are some basic assumptions made about how the financial management team should respond. Some recommendations include:

- Develop a dynamic long term vision/outlook.
- Anticipate and manage change.
- Secure strategic investment opportunities.
- Maximize the present value of expected cash flows to owners.

In order to account for timing, future cash flows must be discounted by an interest rate that represents the cost of the funds being used to finance the project. Financial analysts have found the time value of money to be an important factor when making decisions on projects. Present value is the value today of future cash flows, and the computation of present values (discounting) is the opposite of determining the compounded future value. The discounted cash flow (DCF) analysis is a tool that tends to be used to account for the timing of cash inflows and outflows.

The purpose of using the DCF analysis is to get an estimate of how much money can be gained by investing in a specific project. An adjustment for the time value of money is also taken into consideration. DCF analysis uses the weighted average cost of capital to discount future free cash flow projections in order to get the present value. Once the present value has been determined, it is used by financial analysts to determine whether or not a project is a potential investment. Good prospects are those projects in which the DCF analysis is higher than the current cost of the project investment. Currently, there are four different DCF methods utilized. The type of method utilized is determined based on the financing schedule of the firm. The four methods fall into two categories — equity approach and entity approach. The "flows to equity approach" falls under the equity approach. There are three methods under the entity approach, they are: The adjusted present value approach, weighted average cost of capital approach and the total cash flow approach.

However, there are some pitfalls with using the DCF analysis. Harman (2007) pointed out three potential problems with DCF.

- **Operating Cash Flow Projections** "The first and most important factor in calculating the DCF value of a stock is estimating the series of operating cash flow projections. There are a number of problems with earnings and cash flow forecasting that can generate problems with DCF analysis. The most prevalent is that the uncertainty with cash flow projection increases for each year in the forecast, and DCF models often use five or even 10 years' worth of estimates" (Harman, 2007, "Problems with DCF"). Analysts might be able to estimate what the operating cash flow will be for that year and the impending year. But, the projecting earnings and cash flow becomes more compromised as time progresses. Cash flow projections for a certain year will also weigh heavily on the recorded results from past years. Small, incorrect estimations during the first few years of a model can dramatically increase any differences in cash flow projections that are made down the road.
- **Capital Expenditure Projections** "Free cash flow projection involves projecting capital expenditures for each model year. The degree of uncertainty increases with each additional year in the model. Capital expenditures can be largely discretionary. In a down year, a firm may elect to reduce capital expenditure plans since they tend to be risky. While there are a number of techniques to calculate capital expenditures, such as using fixed asset turnover ratios or even a percentage of revenues method, small changes in model assumptions can widely affect the result of the DCF calculation" (Harman, 2007, "Problems with DCF").
- **Discount Rate and Growth Rate** "There are many ways to approach the discount rate in an equity DCF model. Analysts might use the Markowitzian $R = Rf + ? (Rm - Rf)$ or the weighted average cost of capital of the firm as the discount rate in the DCF model. Both approaches are quite theoretical and may not work well in real world investing appli-

cations" (Harman, 2007, "Problems with DCF"). Other methods involve choosing to use an "arbitrary standard hurdle rate" to estimate and assess each equity investment. Such a technique lets each investment be analyzed alongside the others. It is often hard to choose a particular estimating technique for discount rates that is both accurate and concise.

APPLICATION

MARKET STRUCTURES

Market structures take into consideration:

- The number of firms in an industry
- The relative size of the firms (industry concentration)
- Demand conditions
- Ease of entry and exit
- Technological and cost conditions.

The preferred structure is dependent on the type of industry. Therefore, the financial management team of each firm determines which of the above-mentioned factors will be a part of the decision making process.

The level of competition tends to be dependent on whether there are many (or a few) firms in the industry and if the firm's products are similar or different. Given this information, four basic approaches to market structure and the types of competition have been established.

- **Perfect(Pure) Competition** (Many sellers of a standardized product) Characteristics of perfect competition are: Large number of buyers and sellers
- Homogeneous product
- Complete knowledge
- Easy entry and exit from the market.

A firm using this approach tends to be small relative to the total market, and it will offer its product at the going market price. A firm in this format operates at an output level where price (or marginal revenue) is equal to the marginal cost and profit maximized. This format is more theoretical because there is no firm that operates at this level.

- **Monopolistic Competition** (Many sellers of a differentiated product)

Characteristics of monopolistic competition are: One firm, no close substitutes, no interdependence among firms, and substantial barriers to entry. In addition, there tends to be many buyers and sellers, there is product differentiation, easy entry and exit and independent decision making by individual firms. An example of a firm fitting this profile would be a small business selling differentiated, yet similar, products. These firms will utilize three basic strategies in order to obtain their principal goal of maximum profits: Price changes, variations in the products, and promotional activities.

- **Oligopoly** (Few sellers of either a standardized or a differentiated product)

Characteristics of an oligopoly are (1) few firms, (2) high degree of interdependence among firms; (3) product may be homogenous or differentiated, and (4) difficult entry and exit from market. The market fits this approach when there are a small number of firms supplying the dominant share of an industry's total output. Oligopolists are interdependent based on all levels of competition — price, output, promotional strategies, customer service policies, acquisitions and mergers, etc. Therefore, decision makers may have a hard time anticipating what rivals will do in reaction to their position, which makes the process complex. Two popular models are Cournot's duopoly model and kinked demand curve. An example would be the NCAA. This organization controls the revenues and costs of its member schools. It has the power to limit the number of games and times that a school can have its games televised. The NCAA retains control over costs through its restrictions on the compensation of student athletes.

- **Monopoly** (A single seller of a product for which there is no close substitute)

A monopoly occurs when one firm produces a highly differentiated product in a market with significant barriers to entry. It may be large or small, and it must be the only supplier. In addition, there are not any similar substitutes available. Since the monopoly is the only producer, it is known as the industry, while its demand curve is called the industry demand. An example would be an electric utility company in a specific geographic area.

What is the difference between the monopoly and pure approach? A profit-maximizing monopoly firm will produce less and charge a higher price than firms collectively in a purely competitive industry. However, both demand and cost may be different for a monopoly firm (i.e. a monopoly may be able to take advantage of economies of scale).

VIEWPOINT

CAPITAL BUDGETING

Many organizations charge the finance department with overseeing the financial stability of the firm. The chief financial officer (CFO) may lead a team of financial analysts to determine which projects deserve investment. "The economic theory of the firm suggests that to maximize its profit, a firm should operate at the point where the marginal cost of an additional unit of output just equals the marginal revenue derived from that output, and this may be equally applicable to the capital budgeting process" (Shim & Siegel, 1998, p. 279). Capital budgeting is an example of how a firm may conduct a cost-benefit analysis. There is a comparison between the cash inflows (benefits) and outflows (costs) in order to determine which is greater. Capital budgeting could be the result of purchasing assets that are new for the firm or getting rid of some of the current assets in order to be more efficient. The finance team will be charged with evaluating (1) which projects would be good investments, (2) which assets would add value to the current portfolio, and (3) how much the firm is willing to invest into each asset.

In order to answer questions about potential assets, there are a set of components to be considered in the capital budgeting process. The four components are: Initial investment outlay, net cash benefits (or savings) from the operations, terminal cash flow, and net present value (NPV) technique. "Capital budgeting is a financial analysis tool that applies quantitative analysis to support strong management decisions" (Bearing Point, n.d.).

Capital budgeting seeks to provide a simple way for the finance department to see the "big picture" of the benefits, costs and risks for a corporation planning to make short term and/or long term investments. Unfortunately, many of the leading methods have experienced problems, especially when a firm is using a standardized template. Examples of potential problems include:

The benefits, costs, and risks associated with an investment tend to be different based on the type of industry (i.e. technological versus agricultural).

A corporation may highlight the end results of the return on investment model and the assumptions that support the results versus a balanced analysis of benefits, costs, and risks.

If a firm does not account for the above-mentioned scenarios, there is a possibility of the results being skewed, which would make the data unusable. This type of error could hinder a project from getting approved. Therefore, it is critical for financial analysts to have a more effective and efficient technique to use. Bearing Point (n.d.) identified several leading practices that organizations are using in order to avoid reporting faulty information. The theme in all of the techniques is that capital budgeting is not the only factor considered. Other quantifiable factors are utilized in order to see the big picture.

Consider the nature of the request — The type of benefit obtained by the investment will determine the nature of the request. Therefore, it may be beneficial to classify the benefit types into categories such as strategic, quantifiable and intangible.

All benefits are not created equal — Benefits should be classified correctly in order to properly analyze them. There are two types of benefits — hard and soft. Hard benefits affect the profit and loss statement directly, but soft benefits do not have the same affect.

Quantify risk — Make sure that the risks are properly evaluated. In most cases, risks are neglected. Also, it would be a good idea to build a risk factor into whatever model is utilized.

Be realistic about benefit periods. Make sure that the expectations are realistic. In the past, corporations have created unrealistic goals for the benefits period by (1) anticipating benefits to come too early and (2) reusing models that reflect the depreciation period for the capital asset.

CONCLUSION

Managerial economics highlights how financial professionals make decisions regarding resource allocation, strategic, and tactical issues that relate to all types of firms from an economic perspective. Managerial economics occurs when the fundamental principles of microeconomics are applied to the decision making process of business and managerial problems. It can apply to problems in private, public and non-profit organizations. Managerial economics connects the practical and theoretical aspects of economics. Many economists will utilize a variety of techniques from other business fields such as finance and operations management.

Profits are very crucial to a firm's bottom line. There are two types of profits — accounting profits and economic profits. Profits tend to vary across industries, and there are a number of theories that attempt to provide an explanation as to why this occurs.

Wealth maximization is a long term operational goal. There tends to be a preference for wealth maximization because it takes into consideration (1) wealth for the long term, (2) risk or uncertainty, (3) the timing of returns, and (4) the stockholders' return (Shim & Siegel, 1998). "The economic theory of the firm suggests that to maximize its profit, a firm should operate at the point where the marginal cost of an additional unit of output just equals the marginal revenue derived from that output, and this may be equally applicable to the capital budgeting process" (Shim & Siegel, 1998, p. 279). Capital budgeting is an example of how a firm may conduct a cost-benefit analysis.

BIBLIOGRAPHY

Andreae, C.A. (1970). The study of finance as a management science. *Management International Review (MIR), 10*(1), 87-99. Retrieved November 15, 2013, from EBSCO Online Database Business Source Complete. http://search.ebscohost.com/login.aspx?direct=true&db=bth&AN=12253215&site=ehost-live

Bearing Point (n.d.). Improve your capital budget techniques. Retrieved July 9, 2007, from http://office.microsoft.com/ en-us/help/HA011553851033.aspx

Harman, B. (2007, July 9). Top three DCF analysis pitfalls. Retrieved July 28, 2007, from http://www. investopedia. com/articles/07/DCF%5fpitfalls. asp.

McGuigan, J., Moyer, C., & Harris, F. (2007). *Managerial economics: Applications, strategies, and tactics.* Southwestern Publishing.

Mintz, O., & Currim, I.S. (2013). What drives managerial use of marketing and financial metrics and does metric use affect performance of marketing-mix activities?. *Journal of Marketing, 77*(2), 17-40. Retrieved November 15, 2013, from EBSCO Online Database Business Source Complete. http://search.ebscohost.com/login.aspx?direct=t rue&db=bth&AN=85725800&site=ehost-live

Shim, J., & Siegel, J. (1998). *Managerial economics.* New York: Barron's Educational Series, Inc.

SUGGESTED READING

Block, W. (2001). Cyberslacking, business ethics and managerial economics. *Journal of Business Ethics, Part 1, 33*(3), 225-231. Retrieved July 25, 2007, from EBSCO Online Database Business Source Complete. http://search.ebscohost.com/login.aspx?direct=true&db=bth&AN=5440168&site=ehost-live

Cafferata, R. (1997). Nonprofit organizations privatization and the mixed economy: A managerial economics perspective. *Annals of Public & Cooperative Economics, 68*(4), 665-689. Retrieved July 25, 2007, from EBSCO Online Database Business Source Complete. http://search.ebscohost.com/login.aspx?direct=true&db=bth&AN=4491985&site=ehost-live

Guiffrida, A., & Nagi, R. (2006). Economics of managerial neglect in supply chain delivery performance. *Engineering Economist, 51*(1), 1-17. Retrieved July 25, 2007, from EBSCO Online Database Business Source Complete. http://search. ebscohost.com/login.aspx?direct=t rue&db=bth&AN=19906612&site=ehost-live

—Marie Gould

WARRANTS & CONVERTIBLES

ABSTRACT

This article begins with a brief history and an overview of financial investment vehicles, providing insight from the corporate as well as the investor's perspective. The reader is offered a detailed description of warrant certificates and convertible bonds, underscored with the benefits and disadvantages of each. The circumstances under which warrants or convertibles are issued by companies as a financial vehicle for investors, as opposed to common or other types of stocks or bonds is made apparent, offering valuable perspective to potential investors or issuers of these vehicles. The role of the Securities and Exchange Commission (SEC) in governance and oversight of companies' security offerings is not insubstantial and a brief high-level mention is delivered in this review.

OVERVIEW

HISTORICAL PERSPECTIVE ON INVESTING

In 1792, the first organized stock exchange was transacted in New York. Financial leaders at the time developed and agreed to a formal document of rules, regulations and fees for trading stocks and bonds; hence the launch of the stock market phenomenon. In simpler times, securities were auctioned off to the highest bidder, with the seller paying a commission on each stock sold. History holds lessons for the experienced, in terms of investments and risk, highlighted in the rapid growth in the stock market and in investors' frenetic drive to swift profits.

In addition to investors' entrepreneurial drive, interest in the common good has played a vital role in the world of stocks, bonds and investments. Soon after the United States became involved in World War II, it became paramount to enhance the efficiency and safety of existing rail transport systems. Success in the wartime endeavor hinged upon accessibility and mobility for people and resources. The railroad system at the time was woefully inadequate in terms of financing, which subsequently disadvantaged the rail's ability to meet demand.

The Interstate Commerce Act of 1887 was responsible for having created the Interstate Commerce Commission, which, under great influence from private farmers and others, prohibited the railroads from increasing rates sufficient to meet growing operating costs. Compounding the cash scarcity, the strict regulations most certainly prevented the rail from creating a positive financial margin with which to make needed capital investments in the company. Put simply, the railroads, a key element in our nation's transportation infrastructure, simply could not support growth or sustain operations without investors and their cash. The railroads ultimately were built with money from men who hoped to earn a large profit from their investment in operations and capital.

In context, today's large corporations with vast numbers of stockholders still rely on investors' interest to grow, much as the railroads offered a financial interest and a public service to the country during a critical time of conflict. The story of economics has always been influenced by enlarging corporations, in particular those representing importance to the public at large. Commodities, such as oil, wheat, corn and soybeans, are a modern day example of investments of great public import and guaranteed financial growth. The rail of yesterday, given its history, might well have been considered a primary commodity of its time.

APPLICATIONS

INVESTMENT VEHICLES

Companies can offer investors numerous venues in which to place their financial interests and test their financial expertise, no matter their level of experience.

Ford Motor Company headquarters in Dearborn, Michigan. *Via Wikipedia.org*

Corporations may finance part of their business by leveraging themselves with securities they promise to pay back, with interest, in addition to the principle. Variations on this model will be introduced later in this essay. The more debt the company incurs, naturally, the higher the organization's financial risk. A few examples of investment vehicles utilized by corporations and the government to support their financial needs include:

- Convertibles;
- Corporate, municipal, or treasury bonds;
- Common Stock;
- Commodities markets;
- Governmental, corporate and municipal bonds;
- Warrant certificates.

WARRANTS

Common stock warrants offer the investor the right to buy common stock at a specific price, in the future, within a set period of time. In some cases, warrants have no expiration date; these are known as perpetual warrants. If one were looking to identify warrants on the stock listing, he or she would look for the suffix "wt." An installment warrant is an option that offers a share on credit; with the installment vehicle, the investor pays for half the share now and for the rest later. The initial installment provides the owner half a stock. The premise behind installment warrants is that they represent a long term call option (opportunity to exercise a warrant when stock price exceeds the initial investment price, resulting in a net profit) for investors who are inclined to speculate that the price of stock will increase in the long term; the longer the life before the warrant's expiration, the higher its value and the safer the investor's money. The anticipation for the investor is that the company will see increased profits in its future years, thereby growing its dividends. The owner of the warrant can watch and speculate (within the context of the expiration date) until such time as the stock and dividends look attractive enough to 'exercise' or turn the warrant over to stock ownership.

It is evident that investors should educate themselves thoroughly in the warrant vehicle and the issuing company before making this somewhat speculative investment; this education includes attention to transaction costs which will impact profit and loss calculations. "ABN AMRO's (a global banking group) Aaron Stambulich notes that while installments offer a lower-risk form of leverage than other forms of equity lending, investors still need to spend the time acquiring the knowledge to use them properly,'" (Walker, 2007).

Shorter term warrants do exist; they represent a higher risk with a robust appeal of higher returns to the investor. Both long and short-term warrants are priced lower than the common stock purchase price, thereby creating leverage and risk to the corporation, similar to bond arrangements (bonds are in essence a loan with interest). Warrants, however, do not earn interest and usually have an expiration date which can vary depending on the model employed; the key point is that warrants become worthless at expiration date or when the cost of common stock drops to a very low rate. Warrants offer no dividends or voting rights to the warrant owner. "{Warrants} are derivatives — this means they derive their value from and give investors exposure to an underlying asset, such as a share, basket of shares, index, currency or commodity, at a fraction of the underlying asset's cost (Walker, 2007).

Valuation of the Warrant

The value of the warrant is the price of the company's common stock minus the warrant's option price. As a simple example, if the price of the warrant certificate is $15 and the common stock purchase price is $20, the warrant is worth $5. In contrast, if the warrant certificate price is $20 and the stock price is $15, the warrant holds no value. It will remain so unless the stock price, in this case, enjoys favorable appreciation to bring its value above the warrant price. The higher the common stock's price, obviously, the greater the warrant's value. If the common stock is volatile, all the better for the warrant owner, as this too increases the value of the warrant.

When a warrant certificate is exercised (turned over for stock ownership) the number of shares in the company increases and the stock price does decrease overall. If there are warrants outstanding, the owners of the stock are obligated to satisfy the call (exercising) from warrant holders. The money paid to purchase the warrant at the outset goes directly to the company as does the money paid when the owner exercises the warrant to purchase common stock. The new shares generated through an exercised warrant are accounted for in financial reports as *fully diluted earnings per share*, which represents what the earnings per share would be if all warrants were exercised and all outstanding convertible securities, were converted to stock. In essence, the denominator (total outstanding shares) increases, so the value of earnings per share dips lower.

Warrants are sometimes attached to bonds or preferred stock as a means to reduce the interest or the dividends that have to be paid to sell the securities. These particular warrants, issued in this bundled format can be separated and traded independently of the bond or stock and are termed detachable warrants.

Warrants as Stock Options

In today's highly competitive environment, companies struggle to attract a strong, talented workforce. Stock options, sometimes offered as an enticement to potential employees, are commonly issued by companies in the form of a warrant. Start-up companies will offer the stock option as an alternative or adjunct to salary, in order to minimize cash expenditures, while creating an attractive option for recruitment purposes. The disadvantage of warrant stock options, if exercised, is that it decreases the value of the existing shareholders' stock, as referenced earlier in this essay.

Public Accounting & the Securities and Exchange Commission (SEC)

When a warrant is exercised (converted to stock), although it means more funds for the company, the company's balance sheet has historically retained the debt.

"Issuers ordinarily expect to account for common stock and warrants as equity, and account for debt as liabilities" (Dyson, 2007). The Financial Accounting Standards Board (FASB) and the Securities and Exchange Commission (SEC) recognize that for issuers there may be inconsistency and misinterpretation on how warrants and convertibles are reported on the books. The SEC has required registrants {of the SEC} to restate their financial statements to reflect its current interpretation of the existing literature (Dyson, 2007). Companies' first step is to identify whether they fall under the scope of the FASB's SFAS 150 which lists the various features of securities placing the instrument as a liability as opposed to an asset. The author of *Freestanding Warrants and Embedded Conversion Options*, Robert A. Dyson, cautions as follows:

"In recent years the accounting for detachable warrants and convertible securities has grown more complex. The increased SEC interest and constantly evolving rules have created much risk for both preparers and auditors of financial statements. The incorrect application of EITF 00-19 has resulted in financial statement restatement reflecting the reclassification of equity instruments to liabilities and changes of fair value of those liabilities as charges to earnings" (Dyson, 2007).

It is not within the scope of this essay to provide financial accounting direction, rather to provide to the business reader highlights of important issues and an awareness of corporate obligations. Identifying regulatory applications and staying abreast of constantly changing directives and definitions is a key to the success of any executive whose business is involved with sales or investment in financial vehicles.

CONVERTIBLE SECURITIES

There are two types of convertible securities addressed in this essay: First is the convertible bond and the second is convertible preferred stock.

First, the convertible bond is, by definition, issued by a corporation, and not by the government. A convertible bond is nothing more than an arrangement whereby the bond can be converted into specific predetermined numbers of common stock in the company, should the bondholder exercise the option. A conversion price is identified so as to make the security attractive when the stock price increases substantially. The value of the bond is not an exact science, but represents the estimate of the value of common stock in the company at the time of its issuance, as if there were no conversion options. The conversion ratio dictates how many shares into which the convertible bond can be converted.

Preferred stock convertibles provide for conversion of the security to preferred stock, which is a favorable class of ownership in which the investors' dividends are paid out before common stock dividends are. Preferred stock owners generally do not have voting rights, unlike common stockholders. The preferred stock is attractive to some investors because it offers fixed dividends as well as appreciation in shares (e.g. equity) in the company.

Convertibles are more attractive to the issuing company than are other types of bonds, because the interest paid on the convertible is lower. A second attractive feature of the convertible bond to the issuing corporation is that it does not, like a warrant, issue new stocks to shareholders or dilute existing stock value. The formula used to transition preferred convertibles to common stock generally includes an anti-dilution provision, of particular import to owners. Similar to warrants, convertibles are attractive to investors who have reason or hope to believe that the company's ultimate stock value will go up. The investor, of course, should be well informed about the company into which he or she is investing money; the value of research, knowing the market and experience cannot be overstated. Companies issuing convertibles tend to be the more speculative ventures on the whole and should alert the investor to watch for risk as well as opportunity.

Advantages of Convertibles

Advantages of convertibles, to the investor, include their tendency not to dip as greatly in value in a Bear Market (a downturn and devaluation in the market) as do common stocks. Should the company go into default (inability to pay), convertibles can be transitioned safely to a bond or preferred stock. In purchasing convertible securities, the investor enjoys the safety of a bond yet is offered the opportunity for value appreciation. Another very attractive feature of convertibles is that they may be purchased through tax-deferred retirement accounts. This represents an opportunity which swings some investors readily to this option.

Disadvantages of Convertibles

Disadvantages of convertible securities include the expectation that they yield less than the common shares or a bond issued by the corporation. Investors should take heed that companies issuing convertibles are often those facing a financially challenging situation, and may be issuing convertible securities as a last chance option for garnering monies for financing. Another disadvantage of convertibles is that the issuing companies may also call the bond, forcing conversion to common stock at a convenient time for the issuer, which may not be a favorable time for the investor to convert. If the common stock price reaches a specified ratio, the issuer is permitted to force conversion before the end before the end of the normal protection period.

Case Study — Ford Motor Company
Ford Motor Company, facing substantial losses in its North American market, and facing near-term liquidity issues, announced plans in late 2006 to raise $18 million to restructure its operations, $3 million of which will be sold in the form of convertibles, which would be converted to Ford Common Stock. A company the size of Ford entering such a high yield market for the first time has raised some eyebrows. Shelley Lombard, senior high yield analyst for the New York company, *Gimme Credit,* states, "The fact that this issuer has not been in the high yield market before and that this company is a very troubled company is what makes this significant" (S., M., & S., G., 2006). Matt Eagan, a portfolio manager with the Boston-based company, Loomis and Sayles states, "Market demand is high and hedge funds will be hungry for Ford's bonds, particularly if they are convertible bonds. If they do end up issuing a convertible bond, we see that there's a lot of demand in that space" (S., M., & S., G., 2006). It is predicted that this unusual offering from Ford could be precedent-setting if successful in growing the companies' capital. Other large corporations will take notice and possibly follow suit.

Case Study — In the Throes of Financial Difficulty for Luminent
Luminent Mortgage Capital, Incorporated, has defaulted on a $90 million debt and is facing even more financial difficulties. Issuing of warrants as an investment vehicle, with the assistance of Arco Capital Corporation will occur in an effort to preserve the financial survival of the company. *American Banker* reports: "Arco Capital Corp. Ltd. of San Juan, Puerto Rico, has agreed to provide up to $125 million of financing to {Luminent Mortgage Capital Inc}, a San Francisco real estate investment trust (Hochstein, 2007). "In return", Luminent said Monday, "Arco has received warrants to buy a 49% voting stake and a 51% "economic interest" in the REIT at an exercise price of 18 cents a share. The warrants are good for

five years beginning Aug. 30" (Hochstein, 2007).

Luminent acknowledged "the possibility of sizeable dilution to existing ... stockholders" as a result of the issuance of warrants" (Hochstein, 2007). However, it also said the board's audit committee, "pursuant to an exception provided in the New York Stock Exchange's stockholder approval policy, expressly approved the decision not to seek stockholder approval for the issuance. The committee did so because delays in securing such approval "could, given the external climate, seriously further jeopardize the financial viability of Luminent" (Hochstein, 2007).

Case Study — Good News for Mirant Warrant Holders
"With the $45 billion buy out of TXU {a Dallas based energy company} looming in the smokestacks, chatter of a possible Mirant deal has intensified, bringing to light what is arguably the best play on the utility — its warrants. Should Mirant, an international electricity and producer and seller be acquired for $41 per share, as some analysts estimate, warrant holders will realize a 22% gain, while holders of common stocks will gain 10%. The warrants were purposely developed to protect their owners in case of a cash takeover," (Louria, 2007). For warrant holders, this is good news because specific features were built into the warrants which will very possibly create a windfall for them, contrary to usual happenings in cash takeovers. Until recently, protective features on warrants were not common; but in today's environment of rapid company buy-outs, investors are well-advised to be alert to the availability of such safeguards.

Case Study — Competition for a Warrant offered by Money Magazine
In a well-received competition just this year (2007), warrants were offered to the readers of *Money* who could most closely predict the price of commodities; oil in particular. The response was "A wave of Money readers {trying} to estimate the price of oil a couple of months ahead — a keen investor from Canberra is the winner," (Field, 2007). Commodities have become an attractive vehicle to investors because of the wide global demand for oil as well as growing international tensions with oil-rich countries; these tensions are likely to drive the cost of oil even further. Anyone driving a motorized automobile today is acutely aware of the impact of cost increases in oil. Warrants were offered as a desirable investment vehicle; the

response clearly supported the growing attraction of this option. "Part of the appeal of commodity warrants lies in the leverage they offer. Warrants require a far smaller investment than the underlying futures contracts, and the percentage returns can be very high. Investors in commodity warrants certainly don't have to wait long to know if they have made or lost money. For the record commodity warrants issued by CWA (Commodity Warrants Australia) have an average term of 92 days though the average time to maximum profit is just 16 days. CWA says, between August 2005 and February 2007 — a period during which demand for commodities has boomed — around 65% of CWA's commodity warrants generated a positive result, with the average return being 38.4% (Field, 2007).

CONCLUSION

Knowledge is power, and loaning, buying or selling in the financial market should be approached with much thoughtful preparation. Smaller investors may unwittingly put their trust in an advisor, thinking their investment is safer with what he or she thinks may be an expert in the field. Investment costs and financial risks should be of paramount import to the investor, who is closely monitoring the market for attractive opportunities which provide sufficient safety to meet the investor's comfort level.

Companies, accountable to shareholders or stockholders, rely on their historical performance and their projections for success in the future. Wise resource management, accountability and attention to the SEC guidelines, current and future, are the responsibility of the company attracting the investor. This essay

has given a broad overview only and has hopefully enlightened investors and issuers alike to the vast risks and opportunities available in the exciting work of financial markets.

BIBLIOGRAPHY

Dyson, R. (2007). Freestanding warrants and embedded conversion options. *CPA Journal, 77*(4), 40-49. Retrieved September 15, 2007, from EBSCO Online Database Business Source Premier. http://search.ebscohost.com/ login.aspx?direct=true&db=buh&AN=24729316&site=eh ost-live

Field, N. (2007). Warrants winners. *Money (14446219)*, (92), 94-95. Retrieved September 17, 2007, from EBSCO Online Database Business Source Premier. http://search. ebscohost. com/login.aspx?direct=true&db=buh&AN=258 90115&site=ehost-live

Kim, W., Kim, W., & Kim, H. (2013). Death spiral issues in emerging market: A control related perspective. *Pacific- Basin Finance Journal*, 2214-36. Retrieved November 15, 2013, from EBSCO Online Database Business Source Complete. http://search.ebscohost.com/login.aspx?direct=t rue&d b=bth&AN=85174023&site=ehost-live

Louria, A. (2007). Hoping for a warrant windfall. *Investment Dealers' Digest, 73*(9), 9-14. Retrieved September 16, 2007, from EBSCO Online Database Business Source Premier. http://search.ebscohost.com/login.aspx?direct=tru e&db=buh&AN=24341643&site=ehost-live

S., M., & S., G. (2006). Ford may jump start with new convertible bond. *High Yield Report, 17*(46), 1-8. Retrieved September 16, 2007, from EBSCO Online Database Business Source Premier. http://search.ebscohost.com/ login.aspx?direct=true&d b=buh&AN=23305561&site=eh ost-live

Schwienbacher, A. (2013). The entrepreneur's investor choice: The impact on later-stage firm development. *Journal of Business Venturing, 28*(4), 528-545. Retrieved November 15, 2013, from EBSCO Online Database Business Source Complete. http://search.ebscohost.com/login.aspx?direct=t rue&db=bth&AN=87734829&site=ehost-live

Walker, C. (2007). Get a lot for a little. *Money (14446219)*, (92), 86. Retrieved September 16, 2007, from EBSCO Online Database Business Source Premier. http://search. ebscohost. com/login.aspx?direct=true&db=buh&AN=258 90106&site=ehost-live

Wigan, D. (2013). Convertible bonds: Investors seek convertible cover from rate rises. *Euromoney, 43*(534), 38. Retrieved November 15, 2013, from EBSCO Online Database Business

Source Complete. http://search.ebscohost.com/login.aspx?direct=true&db=bth&AN=92025076&site=ehost-live

SUGGESTED READING

Daves, P., & Ehrhardt, M. (2007). Convertible securities, employee stock options and the cost of equity. *Financial*
Review, 42(2), 267-288. Retrieved September 16, 2007, from EBSCO Online Database Business Source Premier. http://search.ebscohost.com/login.aspx?direct=true&db=buh&AN=25276408&site=ehost-live

Koh, P. (2007). Convertibles' Atlantic drift. *Euromoney, 38*(454), 44-44. Retrieved September 16, 2007, from EBSCO Online Database Business Source Premier. http://search.ebscohost.com/login. aspx?direct=true&db=buh&AN=24291287&site=ehost-live

—Nancy Devenger

GLOSSARY

12b-1 Fee: An extra fee charged by some mutual funds to cover promotion, distributions, marketing expenses, and sometimes commissions to brokers. A genuine no-load fund does not have 12b-1 fees, although some funds calling themselves "no-load" do have 12b-1 fees (as do some load funds). 12b-1 fee information is disclosed in a fund's prospectus, is included in the stated expense ratio, and is usually less than 1%.

401 (k): A retirement plan that employees sponsor in order to receive tax benefits on retirement savings.

501(c)(3): The section of the Internal Revenue Code that grants tax exemption to nonprofit institutions such as religious, educational, charitable, and scientific organizations.

Abandonment Option: When the choice is made to abandon an investment instead of waiting for the investment to produce a return.

Absolute Priority: The practice of creditors' claims taking priority over shareholders' claims during liquidation or reorganization. Shareholders only receive compensation after debtors have received their full payment.

Accounting Information System: An organization's chronological list of debits and credits.

Accounting Methods: The rules for reporting income and expenses.

Accounting Profits: The difference between the total revenue and the cost of producing goods or services.

Accounts Payable: A financial account for paying debts owed to suppliers and others.

Accounts Receivable: The accounts for which payment is owed.

Agency Security: Relatively low-risk obligations that are issued by "agencies" or enterprises that the U.S. government supports.

Allocation: The systematic distribution of a limited quantity of resources.

Angel Investors: Angel or Angel Investor defines an individual who offers capital to startup businesses in need of added value. Angel investors often boost the companies' financial worth due to their connections and expertise in the field.

Annual Percentage Rate: The simple interest rate or percentage which invested money earns over a period of one year.

Annual Report: A corporation's annual statement of financial operations. Annual reports include a balance sheet, income statement, auditor's report, and a description of the company's operations.

Appreciation: The increased market value of an asset over time.

Arbitrage Pricing Theory (APT): An alternative to the capital asset pricing model that breaks risk into multiple factors. The risk premium is calculated for each factor that affects the company.

Arbitrage: Technology applied to business for processing data and transferring information.

Articles of Incorporation: A document that incorporators must file with the state to form a corporation and that sets out certain mandatory and optional information about the business and governance of the corporation.

Asset Allocation: How the assets in an investor's portfolio are allocated to different investments based on how much risk the investor can tolerate.

Asset: A resource having economic value that an individual, corporation or country owns or controls with the expectation that it will provide future benefit.

Asset Management: In financial services, the management of a client's investments by a bank.

Asset Valuation: The determination of the net market value of a company's assets on a per share basis.

Audit: A formal assessment of an organization's accounting records. Audits are traditionally performed by independent public accounting firms.

Audit Trail: A record of transactions in an information system that provides verification of the activity of the system.

Authorized Shares: Established in a company's charter, authorized shares refers to the maximize number of stock shares that a company can issue. Shareholders can vote to change this number.

Automated Teller Machines (ATMs): Electronic terminals that allow consumers to have access to their funds at any time.

Balance Sheet: A document showing a firm's assets, liabilities, and equity for a specified period of time.

Bank: Banks are commercial institutions licensed to receive deposits, and whose primary business is making and receiving payments as well as supplying short-term loans to individuals.

Bank of International Settlements: Extends its services to central banks around the world and other official financial corporations and countries. The bank does not serve individuals or private companies.

Banker's Acceptance: A short-term credit investment created by a non-financial firm and guaranteed by a bank. Acceptances are traded at a discount from face value on the secondary market. Banker's acceptances are very similar to Treasury-bills and are often used in money market funds.

Bankruptcy Risk: Sometimes called insolvency risk. The risk for companies associated with having liabilities that exceed assets. Also called negative net worth.

Basel Committee on Banking Supervision: An institution created by the central bank Governors of the Group of Ten nations. It was created in 1974 and meets regularly four times a year.

Bear Market: A financial situation where the market sees falling prices.

Behavioral Finance: A field of study that combines economics and psychology to analyze how and why investors make their financial decisions.

Benchmark Return: The standard value against which the performance of a security, index, or investor can be measured.

Beta: Measure of a security's market risk determined by how a security's returns vary with market conditions. Denoted by symbol β.

Bias: A personal preference or prejudice.

Bid-Ask Spread (aka Spread): Refers to the difference between the current bid and the current ask (in over-the-counter trading) or offered (in exchange trading) of a given security (Investor Words, 2007).

Board of Directors: Qualified individuals who are chosen by a company's shareholders to supervise and manage the company.

Bond Fund: A collection of bonds, managed by financial experts, who used "pooled" money from numerous investors to establish a diversified portfolio.

Bond Issue: The act of offering a large set of bonds for sale to the public; the main source of bonds available for individual purchase.

Bond Laddering: A financial strategy involving the purchase of different bonds which have different maturity dates.

Bond Markets: The market where many different kinds of bonds are available and utilized, either through exchange or through over-the-counter trades.

Bond: A certificate showing that an investor has loaned a company money to be paid back upon a specified maturity date.

Broad-Based Index: An index that reflects the movement of the whole market.

Broker: Assists in the buying and selling of financial securities by acting as a 'go-between' between buyer and seller to reduce search and information costs.

Brokerage Commissions: Refers to the fee charged by a broker or agent for his/her service in facilitating a transaction, such as the buying or selling securities.

Budgeting and Control: A budget is a detailed report of financial activity. Budgetary control is oversight and monitoring of a budget to make sure it remains in line with corporate objectives and standards.

Bull Market: A market where prices are increasing.

Business Strategy: The context for specific business decisions and operating strategies.

Business Units: Self sufficient groups within a form that create and distribute pre- and post-order supporting services for different products to consumers worldwide.

Buy Side: The side of Wall Street comprising the investing institutions such as mutual funds, pension funds and insurance firms that tend to buy large portions of securities for money-management purposes. The buy side is the opposite of the sell-side entities, which provide recommendations for upgrades, downgrades, target prices and opinions to the public market. Together, the buy side and sell side make up both sides of Wall Street.

Call: A contract that gives the holder the right to purchase a given stock at a specific price within a designated period of time.

Callable Bonds: Bonds that are redeemed by the issuer before their maturity date.

Capital Asset Pricing Model (CAPM): A model used in finance to determine a theoretically appropriate required rate of return (and thus the price if expected cash flows can be estimated) of an asset, if that asset is to be added to an already well-diversified portfolio, given that asset's non-diversifiable risk ("Capital asset pricing model," 2009).

Capital Budgeting: Capital budgeting involves deciding which long-term projects are worthy of investing in and undertaking. Choosing such potential projects usually involves making comparisons of anticipated discounted cash flows and the internal rates of return.

Capital Gain: The difference between the net cost of a security and the net sales price, if the cost is less than the price.

Capital Investment: Money a corporation uses to invest in a capital asset such as equipment or other long term asset such as land or buildings.

Capital Loss: The difference between the net cost of a security and the net sales price, if the cost is more than the price.

Capital Market: Where those raising finance can do so by selling financial investments to investors, e.g. bonds, shares.

Capital Structure: The total amount of a company's long-term debt, short-term debt, common equity, and preferred quity. Companies use money from this fund to finance all general operations and expansion using different sources.

Capital: Capital is the combination of all durable investment goods, which are usually added and calculated with units of money.

Cash Flow Statement: A document reporting the money going in and coming out of a firm.

Cash Management Forecasting: A prediction of the amount of money that will move through an organization.

Cash: Legal tender or coins that can be used in the exchange of goods, debt, or services. Sometimes also including the value of assets that can be converted into cash immediately, as reported by a company.

CD: Certificate of deposit — a bank-sponsored security.

Certificate of Deposit: A debt instrument issued by a bank that usually pays interest.

Chief Financial Officer (CFO): Person in an organization who directs the corporation's finances. CFOs are responsible for overseeing financial statements and reporting and for overseeing compliance issues.

Coefficient of Variation: Measures the relative spread of a security by dividing the standard deviation by the expected return.

Cognitive Science: The interdisciplinary study of perception, memory, judgment and reasoning.

Collective Bargaining: The process whereby workers organize collectively and bargain with employers regarding the workplace (employment, wages, and benefits).

Commercial Banks: A corporation that receives deposits, offers business loans, and other similar services. Though commercial banks give their services to individual citizens, they usually invest more of their efforts to lending money to and taking deposits from companies.

Commercial Paper: An unsecured, short-term debt instrument issued by a corporation, typically for the financing of accounts receivable, inventories and meeting short-term liabilities.

Commission: A set fee or percentage of the sale that is given to a sales representative for convincing a customer to make a purchase.

Commodities: A term for products of value, for which there is demand. The resources are produced in large quantities by many different producers; the items from each are considered comparable — some examples include oil, soybeans, and pork bellies)

Commodity Markets: A market where buyers and sellers of raw materials (eg. wool, sugar, coffee, wheat, metals, etc.) trade.

Common Stock: A share in the ownership of a company with voting rights and residual claims to earnings and assets once all senior claims are satisfied.

Compound Interest: Interest that is applied based on the principal per annum plus accrued interest from previous years.

Compounded Interest: Interest earned on principal plus already-accrued interest.

Control System: The method by which an organization properly compensates its employees; involves supervision, instruction, and appraisal.

Corporate Bond: A debt security issued by a corporation.

Corporate Credit Rating: Corporate credit ratings are assigned by credit rating agencies (for example Standard & Poor's) and are designated by letter groupings (for example AAA, B, or CC). These ratings serve as finance indicators to potential debt securities investors.

Corporate Debt: Short or long term debt issued as securities by corporations. Short term debt is issued as commercial paper. Long term debt is issued as bonds/notes.

Corporate Development: The activities that companies undertake to grow through inorganic means such as mergers and acquisitions, strategic alliances and joint ventures.

Corporate Finance: An area of finance that deals with operating a corporation, making financing decisions and making investment decisions for the corporation.

Corporation: A firm that is owned by stockholders and managed by professional administrators.

Correlation Coefficient: Measure of the extent that two variables move together.

Cost Analysis: The microeconomic strategies that evaluate and assess the effectiveness of production, the best factor allocation, and the economies of scale and cost function.

Cost Benefit Analysis: A systematic and formalized set of procedures for assessing whether to fund and implement a service, product, or program.

Cost of Debt: The current interest rate that a

company pays on its debt. This cost can be accounted for either before- or after-tax returns, but is usually measured after taxes since interest rates are tax deductible. The cost of debt is one part of the company's capital structure.

Cost of Equity: A firm's cost of equity refers to the financial amount demanded by the market in exchange for owning certain asset and being responsible for the risk of ownership.

Cost-Effectiveness: An orderly and measurable method for examining the costs of various ways of gaining the same stream of benefits or a specific goal.

Coupon Rate: The rate of interest applied in calculating the coupon payment amount.

Coupon: Interest rate on a bond that is paid at fixed intervals off its face value.

Credit Crunch: A shortage of available loans. This could raise interest rates, but it usually means that certain borrowers are unable to get loans due to credit rationing.

Credit Rating: A quantitative evaluation of the credit responsibility of individuals and corporations. It is calculated based on the history of borrowing and repayment as well as the current availability of assets and extent of liabilities.

Credit Risk: In the enterprise risk management model, this type of risk occurs when the other party cannot perform to the standards agreed upon under the contract because of their hesitancy or failure to make the payments on time.

Credit Supply Uncertainty: Degree to which credit supply is plentiful or lacking; has an impact on the size, length and terms of any bond issuance or refinancing authorization.Pag

Credit Union: A member-owned and operated financial cooperative whose profits are shared amongst the owners.

Criterion: A dependent or predicted measure that is used to judge the effectiveness of persons, organizations, treatments, or predictors. The ultimate criterion measures effectiveness after all the data are in. Intermediate criteria estimate this value earlier in the process. Immediate criteria estimate this value based on current values.

Cumulative: If a payment (interest or dividend) on a bond or share is missed in one period, those securities are given priority when the next payment is made. These arrears must be cleared up before shareholders received dividends.

Cure Period: A cure period is often outlined in a contract, offering a defaulting party to readjust the cause of a default. For instance, cure period if a certain amount of time allowed for the owner to find a solution to a problem that has occurred in the operation of a business.

Current Assets: An asset on the balance sheet that is expected to be used or sold within a year.

Current Liabilities: Debts that are due within a year.

Day Trader: Investors who buy and sell stocks during the day with the goal being to make products as a stock's value changes throughout the day.

Debenture Bond: A security issued on the basis on a company's financial reputation rather than on specified assets.

Debt: A relationship where a borrower receives funds from a lender and is obligated to pay back the lending amount plus interest.

Debt Financing: Debt financing occurs when a firm advancing its capital through the means of selling bonds to individuals or institutions who are willing to invest. In exchange for the money lent, the investors become creditors and expect to be repaid with interest on the debt that was incurred.

Debt Ratio: A ratio that signifies what fraction of debt a company has proportionate to its assets. The measurement provides an idea regarding the influence of the company as well as the future risks the company faces.

Debt Security: A security that represents a loan given to an issuer by an investor. In exchange for the loan the issuer makes a commitment to pay interest and completely repay the debt on a predetermined date. Page 5

Debt-to-Equity Ratio: A calculation of a company's financial influence measured by dividing its total liabilities by stockholders' equity. It signfies what fraction of equity and debt the company is using to support its assets.

Declaration Date: The date when company directors meet to determine the date and amount of the next dividend payment. After the payment has been approved it is referred to as a declared dividend.

Default Risk: Risk that a debt holder will not make timely payments of interest and principle as they come due. Firms such as Moody's and Standard and Poor's provide ratings to assess this risk.

Defined Benefit Pension Plan: A plan that agrees to pay a predetermined amount to each person who retires after a certain number of years of service.

Defined Contribution Plan: A pension plan where the contribution amount is set at a specific level while benefits vary depending on the return of investments. In some plans such as a 401(k), 403(b) and a 457, employees make voluntary contributions into a tax deferred account which may or may not be matched by employers.

Denominations: Face value of the debt instrument.

Depression: A severe and prolonged recession characterized by inefficient economic productivity, high unemployment and falling price levels.

Derivatives: "Derivatives are financial instruments that have no intrinsic value, but derive their value from something else. They hedge the risk of owning things that are subject to unexpected price fluctuations, e.g. foreign currencies, bushels of wheat, stocks and government bonds" (Davies, 2007, 2).

Discount Broker: A broker that takes orders to buy and sell stocks but does not offer investment advice or research.

Discount Rate: Rate that could be earned on an alternate investment (opportunity cost).

Discounted Cash Flow Analysis: A valuation method used to estimate the attractiveness of an investment opportunity.

Distribution Period: The distribution date refers to the time span between the declaration date and the record date, which is generally a few days.

Distribution: The payment of a dividend or capital gain.

Diversifiable Risk: Risk that can be mitigated through diversification. Also known as unsystematic risk.

Diversification: Investment strategy designed to reduce risk by acquiring several securities; also called "portfolio diversification."

Dividend: A taxable payment announced by a company's board of directors and distributed to its shareholder, often on a quarterly basis. Dividend payments are taken out of a company's earnings.

Dollar Unit Sampling: A method that incorporates a combined-attributes-and-variables method of inferring through the use of statistics. The technique is useful in sampling variables and attributes at the same time, but it is unique due to its establishment of sampling units as separate and solitary dollars instead of physical units like inventory items. The dollar unit sampling methods are usually carried out on the inventory items that contain the dollars chosen.

Earnings Per Share ("EPS"): The portion of a company's profit allocated to each outstanding share of common stock. EPS serves as an indicator of a company's profitability.

EBITA: Earnings before interest, taxes, depreciation, and amortization.

Economic Profits: The difference between the total revenue and the total opportunity costs.

Efficient Market Hypothesis: A theoretical framework

for understanding how securities are valued in the marketplace.

EITF-00-19: 'Emerging Issues Task Force '- formed in 1984 in response to the recommendations of the FASB's task force on timely financial reporting guidance; available for public viewing. (http://www.fasb.org/eitf/about%5feitf.shtml).

Electronic Banking: The use of electronic methods to deliver traditional banking services using any kind of payment media

Electronic Fund Transfers: The use of technology as an alternative for paper transactions like bank statements and checks.

Embedded Derivatives: (also called structured notes or hybrid instruments — a hybrid of different types of investments) Derivative contracts that exist as part of securities.

Empirical: Theories or evidence that are derived from, or based on, observation or experiment.

Employee Retirement Income Security Act: Federal legislation that governs the administration and design of employer pension, health and welfare plans.

Enterprise Risk Management: A basic shift in the method that company's use in assessing and approaching risk involved in investments. Aon's ERM methodology uses company's expertise in assessing and analyzing risk, recognizing causes for concern, and proactively create methods to agree and conform to preexisting regulations.

Equity: In general, ownership in any asset after all debts connected to the asset are paid off.

Equity Capital: Money invested in a business by owners, stockholders or others who share in profits.

Equity Financing: Financing based on the equity of a business.

Equity Market: (Stock Market) A system that allows for the trading of company shares. This type of a system allows investors to take advantage of a company's success through stock price increases.

Equity Premium Puzzle: The observation that returns on individual stocks over the past century are higher than returns on government bonds.

Exceptional Return: Residual return plus benchmark timing return.

Exchange Traded Fund: Funds that track indexes and can be traded like stocks at any time during the day. ETFs bundle securities within an index; they never track actively managed mutual funds. A broker is necessary to purchase an ETF and thus a com mission fee will be incurred; ETFs have lower transaction fees and operating costs overall making them a better cost investment than a traditional mutual fund.

Expected Return: Weighted average of possible returns of a security, where weights are probabilities associated with each return.

Expense Ratio: A measure of what it costs an investment company to operate a mutual fund. An expense ratio is determined through an annual calculation, where a fund's operating expenses are divided by the average dollar value of its assets under management. Operating expenses are taken out of a fund's assets and lower the return to a fund's investors.

Expropriation: The action of the state in taking or modifying the property rights of an individual in the exercise of its sovereignty.

FABS Statement 95: Requires that a statement of cash flows classify cash receipts and payments according to whether they stem from operating, investing, or financing activities and provides definitions of each category (FASB).Page 6

Face Value: Face amount of a bond that is paid at maturity. Also called Par Value.

Face-Amount Certificate Company: An investment company which is engaged or proposes to engage in the business of issuing face-amount certificates of the installment type, or which has been engaged in such business and has any such certificate outstanding.

FASB (Financial Accounting Standards Board): The designated United States (private sector) organization that establishes financial accounting and reporting standards

Federal Deposit Insurance Corporation: Government agency which guarantees depositor's bank accounts.

Federal Government: Form of government in which a group of states recognizes the sovereignty and leadership of a central authority while retaining certain powers of government.

Federal Reserve Board: The governing body of the Federal Reserve System, comprised of seven members of the Board of Governors who are appointed by the president and confirmed by the Senate. The board sets federal monetary policy and makes key economic decisions.

Fiduciaries: Parties that hold something of value in trust for an individual or group.

Fiduciary Responsibility: The responsibility that a board of directors or fund managers has in assuring that investment activities and decisions are appropriate and adequately documented.

File Transfer Protocol: An early protocol governing the exchange of information over the Internet.

Financial Accounting: Reporting of the financial position of an organization to external stakeholders.

Financial Institutions: A corporation that gathers funds from public organizations and individuals and puts them in other financial assets like deposits, bonds, and loans instead of tangible properties.

Financial Management: The method of controlling economic resources, such as accounting, economic reporting, budgeting, and gathering accounts receivable, managing risks, and insuring businesses.

Financial Market: A market for buyers and sellers of financial securities.

Financial Planning: The analysis of personal financial circumstances and the design of a program to meet financial needs and objectives.

Financial Policy: Description of the choices and criteria a corporation develops for the amount of debt the corporation can tolerate, how it will finance projects, how it will mitigate risk and maximize value of the company while yielding a return to stockholders.

Financial Securities: are economic investment instruments that provide a means for individuals, investment banks, mutual funds, or retirement funds to invest money in a company, an industry sector, or even a region of the country or the world.

Financial Statements: Financial statements are documents that note the status of a company's assets, expenses, revenues, and liabilities.

Financing Cash Flow: Measures the flow of cash between a firm and its owners and creditors. Negative numbers can mean the company is servicing debt but can also mean the company is making dividend payments and stock repurchases (Essentials of Cash Flow, 2005).

Financing: The act of providing funds for business activities, making purchases or investing. Financial institutions and banks are major players in financing since they provide capital to businesses, consumers and investors to help them realize their organizational goals.

First Tier Security: A security such as a Treasury Bill or CD, which has the highest credit rating and is therefore more viable than other securities.

Fiscal Policy: The federal government's budgetary decisions.

Fixed Costs: Costs that remain relatively constant over time such as rent, utilities, taxes and insurance.

Fixed Exchange Rate: Also known as a pegged exchange rate, a fixed exchange rate is when the government or central bank links the official exchange rate to another country's currency or the price of gold. A fixed exchange rate system is meant to keep a country's currency valued at a specific amount.

Fixed Income Securities: A debt instrument that presents holders with annual payments of interest in constant amounts over a fixed term.

Float: The amount of shares that are publicly owned and available to be traded. The float number is calculated by subtracting the number of restricted shares from the total number of outstanding shares. Also known as "free float."

Floating Exchange Rate: An exchange rate system where the currency value is established by the foreign-exchange market based on the supply and demand for that individual currency compared to other currencies in the market.

Forward Contract: A cash market transaction where the product is not delivered until after the contract has been set. The price is established on the first trade date despite the fact that the delivery will be made later..

Frame: When the auditor attributes the results of a testing to the items versus the population, he or she will come up with a list. This list allows that the auditor have a strong foundation with which to identify items that will then be part of a larger sample.

Free Cash Flow (FCF): Refers to cash that is available for distribution among all the security holders of a company. They include equity holders, debt holders, preferred stock holders, convertibles holders, and so on.

Fundamental Analysis: A method in which to evaluate a security by attempting to measure its intrinsic value by examining related economic, financial, and other qualitative and quantitative factors ("Fundamental analysis," 2009).

Futures Contract: A legal contract to buy or sell a commodity in the future.

Futures Markets: Focus on margins as they relate to the initial deposit of "good faith" that is made to an account with the intent to then engage in a futures contract. The margin is also known as good faith due to its help in debiting daily losses that may be incurred.

Futures: A term designating the standardized contracts covering the sale of commodities for future delivery on a futures exchange.

Generally Accepted Accounting Principals (GAAP or US-GAAP): The standard framework of guidelines for financial accounting. Includes standards, conventions, and rules. GAAP accommodates variation in accounting methods, further allowing the results of financial reporting to vary depending upon the purpose.

Government Securities: Securities issued by U.S. government agencies — also called agency securities. Although these securities have high credit ratings, they are not the same as Government Obligations such as Treasury securities and are not backed by the full faith and credit of the U.S. Government.

Government Security: A government debt obligation backed by the credit and taxing power of a country with very little risk of default. These include short-term Treasury bills, medium-term Treasury notes and long-term Treasury bonds.

Growth: Economic expansion as measured by any of a number of indicators such as increased revenue, staffing, and market share.

Growth Companies: Companies whose rate of growth considerably surpasses that of the typical in its category or the inclusive rate of financial gain.

Growth Stock: Shares in a company whose earnings are predicted to increase at an above-average rate in relation to the market. Also known as a "glamour stock." A growth stock does not usually pay dividends because the company prefers to reinvest earnings in new capital projects. Growth stocks include most technology companies.

Growth Stocks: Ownership of companies with strong earnings or earning potential.

Hedge Fund: A fund generally used by wealthy entities outside of the purview of many rules and regulations that govern mutual funds. Since these funds are largely unregulated they allow for aggressive investement strategies that are unattainable to cannot be utilized in mutual funds. Examples include selling short, leverage, program trading, swaps, arbitrage, and derivatives.

Hedge: A transaction that offsets an exposure to fluctuations in financial prices of some other contract or business risk. It may consist of cash instruments or derivatives.

Hedging: Hedging refers to the strategy of making an investment to reduce the potential risk of disadvantageous price movements in an asset. Investors rely on this strategy when they are uncertain about future market movements.

Heuristics: A performance enhancing technique that relies on experience and practical efforts.

Hierarchy of Needs: A theory of motivation developed by Abraham Maslow. According to Maslow, there are five levels of need: Physiological, safety, belongingness, esteem, and self-actualiza

High Yield Debt: A bond rated lower than investment grade when it is purchased. These bonds are riskier in situations of default or adverse credit but usually yield higher returns than higher quality bonds to entice investors.

Holder of Record: The name of the person who is the registered owner of a security.

Incentive: An inducement or reward that is used to motivate an employee to perform a desired action or behave in a manner that supports the organization's goals and objectives. A financial incentive is an incentive that is monetary or financial in nature, such as a pay raise, bonus, or stock options.

Income Statement: A report of a firm's revenues and expenses over a specified period of time.

Index Fund: An index tracker is a collective investment scheme (usually a mutual fund) that aims to replicate the movements of an index of a specific financial market, or a set of rules of ownership that are held constant, regardless of market conditions.

Individual Retirement Account: A type of savings that allows investors to receive tax deductions during the year of their contribution and to defer taxes until a certain age is reached.

Inflation: The rate at which the general level of prices for goods and services rises.

Information Ratio: The expected exceptional return divided by the amount of risk assumed in pursuit of that exceptional return.

Insolvency: The stage at which a business can no longer cover its debts because of the depletion of its assets.

Institutional Market Fund: Money market fund that is owned by a corporation, government agency or other large organization and into which unused liquid assets are automatically deposited.

Interest Rate: The price of borrowing money expressed in an annual percentage.

Interest: Cost of using money, conveyed as a rate per specific period of time, usually one year, which is known as an annual rate of interest.

Intermediary Business: A service business designed to facilitate transactions, to act as go-between, to provide critical linkage between monies and specific projects.

Internal Rate of Return (IRR): A capital budgeting method used by firms to decide whether they should make long-term investments. A project is a good investment proposition if its IRR is greater than the rate of return that could be earned by alternative investments (investing in other projects, buying bonds, even putting the money in a bank account).

International Capital Budgeting: When projects are located in host countries other than the home country of the multinational corporation.

International Financial Reporting Standards (IFRS): Known by its former term, International Accounting Standards (IAS), and as International GAAP, these accounting standards have been adopted by more than one hundred countries, excluding the United States.

Internet Service Provider: A company that provides a customer access to the Internet, also known as an ISP.

Internet: The world wide system of computers that exchange information electronically.

Intrinsic Value: The present value of a firm's expected future net cash flows less the rate of return.

Investment: The use of money to create more money.

Investment Bank: A financial institution that performs services such as underwriting, acting as an intermediary between an issuer of securities and the investing public, facilitating mergers and other corporate reorganizations, or acting as broker for institutional clients.

Investment Cash Flow: Lists all the cash used or provided by the purchase and sale of income-producing assets.

Investment Management: The process of investment analysis involving investments, portfolio management, budget making, banking, tax planning, and investment risk assessment.

Investment Objective: What the investor hopes to gain by investing.

Investment Risk: Loss of income when an investment matures and is re-invested at a lower rate of return.

Investment Vehicle: Broad term defining any method by which money can be invested

Investments: The gathering of a financial product with the assumption and hope that favorable returns will be present over time. Generally, investments refers to the expending of money in order to make a larger sum of money.

Investor Confidence: The attitude of investors regarding risk. Investor confidence in markets and companies is essential to raising the capital necessary to expand infrastructure and enter new markets.

Lease Agreement: The formal legal document entered into between a landlord and a tenant to reflect the terms of the negotiations between them; that is,

the lease terms have been negotiated and agreed on, and the agreement has been reduced to writing. It constitutes the entire agreement between the parties and sets for the their basic legal rights.

Leverage: In general, the amount of debt used to finance a firm's assets.

Leveraged Buyout: (LBO): When a company is taken over using borrowed money. The new company's assets are used as collateral for the borrowed finances.

Leveraged Recapitalization: A technique employed to avoid involuntary acquisition. Using this strategy, a company takes on a significant amount of debt in order to repurchase stocks through a buyback offer or dispenses a significant dividend between current shareholders. The company share price then increases significantly, which makes the company less appealing as a takeover target.

Liability: A company's legal debts or obligations that arise during the course of business operations.

Limit Order: An order that sets the highest amount an investor is willing to pay for the stock.

Limited Liability: The concept that the neither the owners of a corporation, called shareholders, nor the directors or officers are personally liable for the obligations of the corporation. Generally, corporate owners risk only their original investment.

Liquidate: The act of selling the entirety of company assets, paying outstanding debts, and distributing the remainder to shareholders before going out of business.

Liquidity: How easily a security can be bought and sold.

Liquidity Risk: In the enterprise risk management model, the concept involves funding and market liquidity.

Loan: A transfer of an asset from a person or entity to another person or entity with the expectation it will be repaid.

Loans: A private version of borrowing that involves very few parties.

Long-Term Investments: An account on the asset side of a company's balance sheet that represents the investments that a company intends to hold for more than a year, such as stocks, bonds, real estate and cash.

Major US Stock Indices: Shown in Figure 1: Dow Jones Industrial, Standard and Poor's, NASDAQ Composite, NASDAQ 100, Wilshire 5000, S&P Mid Cap, S&P Small Cap, Russell 3000, Russell 2000, Russell 1000.

Management Company: Any investment company other than a face-amount certificate company or a unit investment trust.

Managerial Accounting: Financial reporting that is aimed at helping managers to make decisions.

Managerial Economics: The branch of economics applied in managerial decision making.

Margin Call: A call to customers with brokerage accounts to require them to bring their account balance up to the required minimum.

Mark to Market: A daily debiting or crediting of a margin account based on the close of the daily trading session to avoid contract default.

Market Capitalization: Measure of the most recent stock price multiplied by number of oustanding shares (shares issued).

Market Order: An order to buy or sell a futures contract at whatever price is currently available.

Market Risk: In the enterprise risk management model, it refers to adverse movements in price or rates.

Matching Principle: Also known as the hedging principle or cash flow matching approach, refers to the process of balancing an organization's assets with its liabilities; allows cash outflows to match cash inflows.

Maturity Date: The date on which the principal amount of a note, draft, acceptance bond or other debt instrument becomes due and is repaid to the investor and interest payments stop.

Maturity: The date at which principal and last coupon payment are paid on a debt instrument.

Merit Pay: An increase in salary that is given to an employee based on the employee's individual performance. Merit pay can be given to an employee on a one time, lump sum basis in the form of a bonus for outstanding work. Merit pay raises given for consistent outstanding work, on the other hand, become part of the employee's salary and are given on a continuing basis.

Mezzanine Loan: Mezzanine loans can be compared to second mortgages, apart from the fact that a mezzanine loan is secured by company stock of the company owning the property rather than by the real estate property itself.

Modern Portfolio Theory: An idea that follows risk-averse investors and their ability to create portfolios to increase the anticipated returns hinging on the market risk level. The theory focuses on risk and the idea that it is an essential and significant piece of gaining higher returns.

Monetary Policies: Government policies that control, shape, or impact how a nation's money supply and exchange with other currencies is managed.

Money Market Deposit Account: Market sensitive bank account that has a minimum balance requirement ($1,000), limits checks to 3 per month, and the funds for these accounts are considered liquid.

Money Market Fund: Akin to a mutual fund, provides investors with a broad range of securities in order to maximize returns and stability within a money market. <BI.-Retail Market Fund:

Money Market Instruments: Forms of debt that mature in less than one year and are very liquid.

Money Markets: Money market securities are often considered a safe alternative to riskier ways of investing. They usually return a lower interest rate that aligns properly with the temporary cash storage and short-term future expectations.

Mortgage: A security instrument in which real

property is pledged as collateral for the payment of a mortgage note.

Mortgage Banker: A company or individual that originates mortgage loans and sells them to investors, while taking care of borrowers' loan payments, records, taxes and insurance.

Mortgage Servicing: The collection of monthly payments and penalties, record keeping, payment of insurance and taxes, and possible settlement of default involved with a mortgage loan.

Motivation: The needs and thought process that determine a person's behavior. Motivating factors do not necessarily remain constant, but may change with the individual's current circumstances.

Multinational Corporation (MNC): A company that invests its one facilities and other assets in a country other than its own.

Municipal Bonds: Securities issued by local governments such as states or cities.

Mutual Fund: An investment business that provides new shares and re-purchases current shares based on the requests of the shareholders. The company also utilizes its assets to invest in different and diverse contracts of other businesses.

NASD: The National Association of Securities Dealers, a non profit organization established to standardize securities exchange practices and to enforce fair and equitable rules of securities trading.

NASDAQ: The National Association of Securities Dealers Automated Quotations System, the first and largest electronic stock market.

National Futures Association: A self regulatory industry organization enacted by Congress in 1974.

Neoclassical Economic Theory: A school of economic thought, which began in the nineteenth century in response to perceived weaknesses in classical economics, that focuses on productivity growth, supply and demand, rational investors, and efficient markets.

Net Asset Value: In the context of mutual funds, the total value of the fund's portfolio less liabilities. The NAV is usually calculated on a daily basis.

Net Present Value (NPV) Technique: The method of calculating the value of an investment by adding the initial cost and the current value of anticipated cash flows.

Net Present Value: The difference between the present value of cash inflows and the present value of cash outflows. NPV is used in capital budgeting to analyze the profitability of an investment or project.

Net Worth: The total stockholders' equity or net assets; the amount by which a company's assets exceed its liabilities.

Neuro-economics: An area of study that combines neurology, economics, and psychology to analyze how people make economic choices.

New York Stock Exchange: The largest stock exchange in the world by dollar volume. Trades are conducted by buyers and sellers on the floor in auction format.

Non-diversifiable Risk: Risk that cannot be mitigated through diversification. Also called systematic risk.

Non-price Credit Rationing: A traditional approach to mortgage lending which was to set minimum lending standards taking into consideration a borrower's income, payment history, and down payment with some input from the local underwriter about their knowledge of the borrower.

Objective Value: Prevailing value established by the market.

Offer: A willingness to sell a futures contract at a specific price.

Office of Thrift Supervision: A bureau of the U.S. Treasury Department responsible for issuing and enforcing regulations governing the nation's savings and loan industry.

Online Trading: The buying and selling of stocks and

bonds over the Internet.

Open End Mutual Fund: A type of fund that allows investors to buy and sell shares directly. Share price is Net Asset Value (NAV).

Operating Business Plan: Dynamic document that highlights the strengths and weakness of the company and guides the company toward learning and increased efficiency.

Operating Cash Flow: Measures the cash used or provided by a company's normal operations.

Operational Risk: The level of risk and loss involved from poor internal processes, incompetent financiers or systems, or due to unreliable, external events.

Opportunity Costs: The cost of passing up the next best choice when making a decision. For example, if an asset such as capital is used for one purpose, the opportunity cost is the value of the next best purpose the asset could have been used for (Investor Words, 2007).

Opportunity Loss: The estimated loss resulting from not choosing the best option or solution.

Optimal Investment: Investment strategy that most accurately meets revenue-generating and corporate goals.

Option Contract: A contract where the buyer has the option but not the obligation to buy a futures contract at a specified time for a certain price.

Option: Contracts with a seller and a buyer that give the buyer the right, but not the obligation, to buy or sell the asset.

Outstanding Shares: Stock currently held by investors, including restricted shares owned by the company's officers and insiders, as well as those held by the public. Shares that have been repurchased by the company are not considered outstanding stock.

Over-the-Counter: Options are traded between private parties, an instrument is traded over-the-counter (OTC) if it trades under circumstances other than a formal exchange.

P/E Ratio: Price of a stock divided by its earnings per share. Also known as a multiple, it gives an investor an idea of how much they are paying for each dollar of earnings.

Par Value: A ratio expressing the price of a sold bond per $1,000 of its denomination.

Patriot Act: Federal law aimed at preventing the financing of terrorist activities by requiring financial organizations to verify the identity of their customers.

Pay for Performance: An incentive plan in which employees are rewarded financially for high performance and contributing to the organization's goals. Pay for performance plans are applicable to all levels within the organization.

Payable Date: The date set by the company directors on the declaration date on which dividends will be paid to shareholders.

Payment Date: The date on which a declared stock dividend is scheduled to be paid.

Pecking-order: Preferred order of financing options.

Pension Funds: A category of funds that are collected and reserved to pay employees' pensions when they retire from active employment.

Pension Surplus: The difference between assets and liabilities.

Performance Assessment: The process of evaluating an employee's work performance and providing feedback on how well s/ he is doing (typically against some standard of performance for that job).

Performance: The overall results of general activities of an organization or investment over a certain period of time.

Periodicity Principle: Occurring at regular intervals.

Perquisites ("perks"): Something given to the employee in return for work over and above regular pay or compensation. Perks may include such things as health insurance, a company car, or a private office.

Personal Computer Banking: A service offered by financial institutions where their customers are able to perform financial transactions via the internet.

Piecework: A pay system that is based on the number of items processed by an individual employee during a specified unit of time.

Ponzi Scheme: Pyramid scheme in which investor monies are transferred from one account to another in order to give the impression of a return on investment.

Population: The assortment of all files and accounts that the auditor wants to use in order to arrive at the conclusion.

Portfolio Management: The process of creating and implementing decisions regarding investment mix and related policies. Other responsibilities include corresponding investments to their objectives, allocating assets for people and businesses, and assessing the balance of risk versus performance.

Portfolio Turnover: The measure of how frequently fund assets are bought and sold; typically for a 12 month period. The measure can be calculated in the following way: (total of new securities purchased) or (total of securities sold) [which ever total is less] / NAV.

Portfolio: A collection of investments held by an individual or group.

Post-Modern Portfolio Theory: A theory which proposes how rationally thinking investors tend to utilize diversification to their advantage by including it in their portfolios. It also proposes how delicate and unstable assets should be appraised.

Predatory Lending Practices: Ways in which lenders abuse or exploit borrowers through predatory terms in loans.

Predatory Terms: Terms in a loan that are considered abusive or unfairly detrimental to the borrower.

Preferred Stock: A type of hybrid security that combines the ownership element of common stock with the senior priority status of debt. Preferred stock represents a form of ownership in a company but does not have the same voting rights as common stock. While common stock features variable dividends that are not guaranteed, preferred stockholders are generally guaranteed a fixed dividend. In the event of liquidation, preferred shareholders are paid off after debt holders but before common shareholders.

Present Value Analysis: The evaluation of the current value of impending payments that are discounted at the rate R, which is known as the current bank balance that is paying interest at the rate R that is necessary in order to accurately imitate the future payment values.

Present Value: Current value of a future stream of income payments; calculated by dividing future value by a term-specific compounded interest rate.

Pre-tax Basis: Condition in which money is set aside for investment before taxes are imposed on it, thereby reducing the tax liability.

Price Weighted Index: An index which includes constituents based on their price. In the case of a stock market index this suggests that stocks are included proportionately based on their stated prices.

Price-Earnings Ratio: The price of a stock divided by the per-share earnings of the stock.

Pricing Analysis: Microeconomic methods that are utilized in order to assess different pricing decisions.

Principal Shareholder: A shareholder who owns 10% or more of a company's outstanding shares.

Principal: In lending relationships, the amount of money originally lent to the consumer.

Private Banking: Personalized financial and banking services offered to a bank's wealthy, high net worth clients.

Private Equity Firms: Any type of non-public Ownership Equity security not listed on the public exchange. An investor who wants to sell private equity securities must find a buyer without the help of a public marketplace. There are three ways in which private equity firms usually obtain returns on their investments: An IPO, a sale or merger of the company they own, or a recapitalization.

Private Equity: Equity capital available to companies or investors, but not quoted on a stock market. The finances obtained through private equity can be used for a variety of company activities such as developing new products and processes, exanding available capital, making acquisitions, and strengthening a firm's balance sheet.

Private Placement: The opposite of a public offering, a private placement is a direct private offering in which only a limited number of sophisticated investors are included.

Probability Distribution: Listing of probabilities and their associated outcomes.

Production Analysis: Microeconomic methods that help to assess production effectiveness, the best factor allocation, the costs, the benefits of scale, and the estimation of the company's cost function.

Profit Maximization: A hypothesis that the goal of a firm is to maximize its profit.

Pro-rata Rights: The investor is given the right to maintain ownership in the company through future investment rounds.

Prospect Theory: A rubric for understanding how the framing of risk influences economic decision-making.

Psychology: The science that studies mental processes and behavior.

Public Company Accounting Oversight Board (PCAOB): A private sector, nonprofit, self-regulatory body overseeing the auditors of public companies. The PCAOB was created when Sarbanes-Oxley became law.

Purchase and Assumption Transaction: The financial arrangement through which the operations and holdings (assets and debts) of a floundering back are taken over by a healthy bank or lending institution.

Pure Risk: Where no gain occurs but where it is possible for no loss to occur.

Puts: An option that allows the holder to sell a given stock at a specific price within a designated period of time.

Rate of Return: Gain or loss of an investment over a specified time, expressed as a percentage over the initial investment cost.

Real Estate: A piece of land and all physical property related to it, including houses, fencing, landscaping, and all rights to the air above and the earth below the property.

Realtor: A designation given to members of real estate firms affiliated with the National Association of Realtors (NA), who are trained and license to assist clients in buying and selling real estate.

Recession: A short-term period of widespread economic decline.

Record Date: The date established by an issuer of a security for the purpose of determining the holders who are entitled to receive a dividend or distribution.

Regression Analysis: A statistical measure that attempts to determine the strength of the relationship between one dependent variable (usually denoted by Y) and a series of other changing variables (known as independent variables). The two basic types of regression are linear regression and multiple regression (Investopedia, 2007).

Regulatory Compliance: The management of a fund in accordance to all laws and regulations that govern the funds investment and distribution activities.

Reinforcement: An act, process, circumstance, or condition that increases the probability of a person repeating a response.

Remediation: In the context of Sarbanes-Oxley, remediation is the process by which companies identify errors and omissions in compliance processes and go about correcting the actions.

Research Services: The process of gathering information about a group of investments. Research supports investment decisions by fund managers, brokers and is often paid for by soft dollars.

Reserves: Resources accumulated above the amount necessary to cover operating expenses.

Retail Bank: Mass-market banks which have many local branches of larger commercial banks and offer typical banking services.

Retirement Plan: An approach supplied by an employer that allows its employees to invest in their retirement.

Return on Capital: The return on investment a company receives for selling an asset.

Risk Adjusted Discount Rate: The risk-free rate (essentially the return on shorter term U.S. Treasury securities) added to the risk premium that is gathered from an assessment of the risks involved in a certain investment project.

Risk Analysis: Assessing the extent of risk of a decision based on different uncertainty models, decision rules, and methods of risk quantification.

Risk Assessment: A technique used to measure two different quantities of risk: The size of the possible loss and the likelihood of the loss occurring.

Risk averse: An investor with a low tolerance for risk and who — with investment decisions — will choose to avoid risk more often than not. The risk averse investor can tolerate a lower return than high losses.

Risk Aversion: Natural human dislike of taking risks and tendency to avoid additional risk.

Risk Diversification: A management strategy in which the bank deliberately invests in a wide range of projects, each with different time lines, to help prevent massive financial problems should any one project collapse.Page 4 Bank Insolvency and Failure

Risk Management Association: A professional organization that is driven by members who try to further their members' abilities to find, recognize, evaluate and control the results of credit, operational, and market-based risks involving companies and their customers.

Risk Management: The ability to value assets over time in order to minimize the risk of loss of principal.

Risk Premium: Reflects systematic risk as measured by beta.

Risk: Degree of uncertainty of return on an asset.

Risk-based Pricing: Many of the loans in the sub-prime lending market are based on an analysis of the risks that each individual borrower presents with their credit history, the property they want financed, and their ability to pay, or for the lender to recover the loan amount in some manner.

Risk-Free Rate: Yield on risk-free investment. A three-month treasury bill can be used as an approximation.

Risk-Return Trade-off: Risk-averse investors require higher rates of return to induce them to invest in higher risk securities.

Rule 144A: A rule that increases the liquidity of the securities affected (private placement in this context). Organizations can trade these formerly restricted securities between themselves which removes the restrictions that were previously imposed to protect the public.

Sampling Unit: A unit that an aggregate is divided into in order for further sampling to commence. Each individual unit is selected separately, distinctively, and indivisibly.

Sarbanes-Oxley Act: Federal law requiring senior executives of publicly traded corporations to attest to the accuracy of annual financial statements and that requires internal policies and control procedures to ensure compliance with the act.

Savings Account: Essentially a loan a depositor makes to a financial institution.

Savings: An account that pays interest on a day-of-deposit to day-of-withdrawal basis.

Securities & Exchange Commission (SEC): The U.S. government agency that enforces the federal securities industry and the stock market.

Securities Exchange Commission (SEC): The Federal agency that regulates securities transactions.

Security Market Line (SML): Gives the expected rate of return of a security based on its risk.

Security: A debt instrument when backed by collateral to assure compliance with promises.

Security: Tradable instruments such as stocks and bonds that reflect an investor's ownership in, or debt obligations of, a company or government agency.

Self-Actualization: The need to live up to one's full and unique potential. Associated with self-actualization are such concepts as wholeness, perfection, or completion; a divestiture of "things" in preference to simplicity, aliveness, goodness, and beauty; and a search for meaning in life. In Maslow's hierarchy of needs, this is the ultimate level of motivator for behavior.

Sell Side: The retail brokers and research departments that sell securities and make recommendations for brokerage firms' customers. For example, a sell side analyst works for a brokerage firm and provides research to individual investors.

Share: A certificate that represents a single unit of possession in a business, mutual fund, or limited partnership.

Shareholder: Someone who owns stock shares in a corporation or mutual fund. In the case of corporations, shareholders have a right to declared dividends as well as voting rights in certain company situations.

Short-Term Investments: An account in the current assets section of a company's balance sheet that contains any investments that a company has made that will expire within one year. These accounts typically contain stocks and bonds that can be readily liquidated.

Simple Interest: Flat rate of interest applied to principal at the end of a year.

Small Business Administration: A governmental agency which makes loans to smaller companies.

Source Document: In finance, a document such as a purchase order, sales invoice or time card which provides original information on accounting transactions.

Speculative Risk: Risk where it is possible for a gain or loss to occur.

Spillover Effect: The consequential effects of the financial collapse of single business enterprise as it registers in other businesses or in similar businesses.

Stakeholder: One who has a share or an interest in an enterprise. Stakeholders in a company may include shareholders, directors, management, suppliers, government, employees, and the community.

Standard Deviation: Measure of the variability of outcomes expressed in a probability distribution. Denoted by symbol s.

Start-up: A corporate venture in its first level of growth.

Statistical Sampling: A technique of choosing a part of a population through calculating the mathematical probabilities involved. Such sampling helps to make more sound and scientific inferences having to do with the traits of the whole population.

Stock Certificate: Documentary proof of stock ownership.

Stock Index: Consists of a listing of market prices for a particular group of stocks, such as the S&P 500 and the NASDAQ Composite Index.

Stock Market: The business transacted at a stock exchange.

Stock: An item representing ownership rights (known as equity) in a corporation, and signifying a claim to a relative share in the corporation's assets and profits.

Stocks Option: An employee stock option is a call option (see "call' above) on the common stock of a company, representing a non-cash compensation for the employee, an incentive to participate in the company's success.

Stocks: A form of partial ownership or equity in the issuing entity.

Stop Loss: A customer order to a broker that sets the sell price of a stock below the current market price. This will protect profits or prevent losses if the stock drops.

Strategic Planning: A company's method of defining its personal strategy, plan, or decision making process regarding the allocation of its resources intended to help in pursuing a strategy, such as its capital and people.

Sub-investment Grade Loans: Also referred to as junk bonds, or high yield bonds, they are issued by companies carrying an uncertain credit rating. Any credit rating lower than "BBB" is considered to be an uncertain, or speculative, grade.

Sub-prime Lending: The practice of providing credit to borrowers who, for one of numerous reasons, would generally not be extended credit; could include borrowers for example, who do not meet credit history requirements within the prime mortgage market.

Sub-prime Market: That segment of the lending market that provides or specializes in making sub-prime loans.

Swap: A swap can be an agreement to swap interest rates, cash flow streams, or liabilities between two parties. The assets or liabilities being swapped must have equal value; swaps allow companies to reduce risk and/or realign contracts to better suit their investment needs.

Systematic Risk: Economic and market factors that affect most firms and that cannot be eliminated through diversification; also called "market risk."

Tax-sheltered Investments: Funds, such as IRAs, which allow the investor to defer or avoid taxes on returns.

T-Bill: A short term debt obligation by the U.S. government with a maturity date of usually less than one year, bought at less than par value.

Technical Analysis: A method in which to evaluate securities by relying on the assumption that market data (i.e. charts of price, volume, and open interest) may assist in predicting future (usually short-term) market trends ("Technical analysis," 2009).

Thrift Bank: A bank whose main purpose is to take deposits from consumers and offer home mortgages. Extended services such as corporate banking, brokering, or underwriting are not offered.

Time Value of Money: A dollar today is worth more than a dollar tomorrow or a dollar received later is worth less than one in hand today.

Time Value: Price put on the time an investor has to wait until an investment matures.

Traders: An individual or corporation that purchases and sells securities for the benefit of its own individualized account and not necessarily for the benefit of any potential clients.

Trading: The act of purchasing and selling securities, good, or commodities for the short-term in an attempt to earn fast profits.

Transaction Cost: Costs resulting from buying or selling assets including commissions.

Transfer Pricing: The estimated cost of products and services that a business provides to another part or department within the same corporation. The transfer pricing helps to measure each division's gain and loss as it stands separately from the company at large.

Transferability: The right of an owner of a corporation to freely transfer her shares to whomever she wants and whenever she wants. However, transferability of shares may be restricted by the collective agreement of corporate shareholders.

Treasury Bill : Government-sponsored security within a money market.

Treasury Bond: A marketable, fixed-interest U.S. government debt security with a maturity of more than 10 years. Treasury bonds make interest payments semi-annually and the income that holders receive is only taxed at the federal level.

Treasury Inflation-Protected Securities (TIPS): Government bonds that are adjusted for inflation.

Treasury Security: Debt obligations issued by the U.S. Government. They are backed in "full faith" by the government.

Trial Balance: Act of confirming that an organization's total debits equal the total credits; done by totaling both figures.

Underliers: The value(s) from which a derivative derives its value is called its underlier(s).

Underwriting: The process by which investment bankers raise investment capital from investors on behalf of corporations and governments that are issuing securities, both equity and debt. Also, the process of issuing insurance policies.

Unsystematic Risk: Risk associated with random events that affect specific securities. This risk can be virtually eliminated through diversification. Also called "firm-specific risk."

Valuation: The process of determining the current worth of an asset or company.

Value Investing: Purchasing stocks that are considered to be undervalued.

Value Stock: A stock that usually trades at a lower price proportionately to its fundamentals such as dividends, earnings, and sales, and is therefore deemed undervalued by a value investor.

Venture Capitalists: A term that defines an investor that gives capital to start-up companies or offers support to small corporations hoping to expand. Capitalists, however, lack any form of access to public funding.

Venture: Venture is often used to refer to a start-up or enterprise business.

Vertical Merger: The business act in which one firm acquires either a customer or a supplier.

Volatility: The degree of fluctuation a security has over a period of time.

Wealth Maximization: In an efficient market, it is the maximization of the current share price.

Working Capital Management: Working capital is current assets minus current liabilities without including short term debt. Working capital management is a plan that determines how a corporation is going to manage the working capital that is available. It may also include strategies for increasing and maximizing working capital.

Yield: The rate of return expected through or realized from a security or bond.

Zero Coupon Bonds: Securities that are purchased at a fraction of their face value, (par value) and pay no interest until they mature.

INDEX

Truth-in-Lending Act 4
Tversky, Amos 4
12b-1 Fee 5
2008 financial crisis 4
Tyco 5

U
United States 5
United States Congress 5

V
value-based management 5
venture capital 5
volatility 5

W
Wachovia Corp. 5
Wall Street 2, 5
Wal-Mart 5
Wells Fargo & Co. 5
Witter, Dean 5
WorldCom 5

X
Xerox 5